AFTER PIKETTY

AFTER PIKETTY

The Agenda for Economics and Inequality

Edited by

Heather Boushey

J. Bradford DeLong

Marshall Steinbaum

Harvard University Press

CAMBRIDGE, MASSACHUSETTS

LONDON, ENGLAND

First Harvard University Press paperback edition, 2019
First printing

Design by Dean Bornstein

Library of Congress Cataloging-in-Publication Data

Names: Boushey, Heather, 1970– editor. | DeLong, J. Bradford, editor. |
Steinbaum, Marshall, editor.
Title: After Piketty : the agenda for economics and inequality / edited by
Heather Boushey, J. Bradford DeLong, Marshall Steinbaum.
Description: Cambridge, Massachusetts : Harvard University Press, 2017. |
Includes bibliographical references and index.
Identifiers: LCCN 2016048076 | ISBN 9780674504776 (cloth : alk. paper) |
ISBN 9780674237889 (pbk.)
Subjects: LCSH: Piketty, Thomas, 1971– Capital au XXIe siècle. |
Capital—Social aspects. | Equality—Economic aspects. | Wealth.
Classification: LCC HB501 .A457 2017 | DDC 332/.041—dc23
LC record available at https://lccn.loc.gov/2016048076

As scholars, our work stands on the shoulders of those who've come before. It is in that spirit that we dedicate this volume to Anthony Atkinson (1944–2017), whose life's work to document and understand economic inequality inspired us—and we hope will continue to inspire generations of scholars to come—to ask fundamental questions about how the economy works and whom it works for.

Contents

CONTENTS

AFTER PIKETTY

Capital in the Twenty-First Century, *Three Years Later*

J. BRADFORD DELONG, HEATHER BOUSHEY,
AND MARSHALL STEINBAUM

Thomas Piketty's *Capital in the Twenty-First Century,* which we will abbreviate to *C21,* is a surprise best seller of astonishing dimensions.

Its enormous mass audience speaks to the urgency with which so many wish to hear about and participate in the political-economic conversation regarding this Second Gilded Age in which we in the Global North now find ourselves.[1] *C21*'s English-language translator, Art Goldhammer, reports in Chapter 1 that there are now 2.2 million copies of the book scattered around the globe in thirty different languages. Those 2.2 million copies will surely have an impact. They ought to shift the spirit of the age into another, different channel: post-Piketty, the public-intellectual debate over inequality, economic policy, and equitable growth ought to focus differently.

Yet there are counterbalancing sociopolitical forces at work. One way to look at Piketty's project is to note that, for him, the typical low-inequality industrialized economy looks, in many respects, like post–World War II Gaullist France during its Thirty Glorious Years of economic growth, while the typical high-inequality industrialized economy looks, in many respects, like the 1870–1914 Belle Époque version of France's Third Republic. The dominant current in the Third Republic was radically egalitarian (among the male native born) in its politics, radically opposed to ascribed authority—especially religious authority—in its ideology, and yet also radically tolerant of and extremely eager to protect and reinforce wealth. All those who had or who sought to acquire property—whether a shop to own, a vineyard, rentes, a factory, or broad estates—were brothers whose wealth needed to be protected from the envious and the alien of the socialist-leaning laboring classes.

Underlying Piketty's book is a belief that this same cultural-ideological-economic-political complex—that all those with any property at all need to band together to protect any threats to the possession or the profitability of such property—will come to dominate the twenty-first century political economy, in the North Atlantic at least. It will thus set in motion forces to keep the rate of profit high enough to drive the rise of the plutocracy Piketty sees in our future.

Two years ago we editors would have said, "maybe, but also maybe not." In the wake of the 2016 presidential election in the United States, however, Piketty's underlying belief looks stronger. While we will not repeat the cultural dominance of property of the 1870–1914 Belle Époque French Third Republic, we do look to be engaged in the process of echoing many of its main characteristics.

It is important to note that Donald Trump won the 2016 presidential election thanks to the electoral college and not because he got more votes. But he got a lot of votes, and he got them in some places that have historically voted Democratic but faced extreme economic dislocation in the recent past. Moreover, Hillary Clinton failed to achieve the margins among young voters and racial minorities that Barack Obama did, plagued as they are with historically low employment rates, despite the record-high student debt they were promised would lead to security in the labor market. And so Piketty's analytical political-economic case looks to us to have been greatly strengthened by Trump's presidential election victory.

Thus we believe our book is even more important now. And so we have assembled our authors and edited their papers to highlight what we, at least, believe economists should study *After Piketty* as they use the book to sharpen their focus on what is relevant and important.

Outside of Economics

In social science discussions outside of economics, we see Piketty's book making a definite splash. *C21* has achieved a major intellectual victory. It is shaping sociological, political science, and political-economic debate. Other social sciences definitely feel the impact of Piketty's arguments about the likelihood and effects of rising inequality.

What is that impact on historians, sociologists, political scientists, and others? We believe that the best summary sketch of the impact of *C21* on the social sciences outside of economics is, somewhat paradoxically, written by an economist: Paul Krugman. In Chapter 3 of this volume, Krugman notes that the last historical period of great inequality—the First Gilded Age—showed that such great inequality was perfectly compatible with what was then seen as radical (white, male) democracy, for "then as now great wealth purchased great influence—not just over policies, but over public discourse." As of this writing in December 2016, we see this in the prospective formation of an American cabinet richer than any before. It was not just that wealth provided a megaphone with which to amplify the voices of the wealthy both in the corridors of power and in the public sphere. In addition, wealth induced sociological patterns of emulation, including in what qualifies someone for high office and whose interest it's acceptable for senior officials to serve.

Krugman sees—accurately, we believe—the same links from economic inequality to politics and sociology operating today, and if anything, he sees them as operating more strongly today. It is as if political and sociological currents are responding not to what inequality is today but to what people perceive it likely to be a generation hence: "A curious aspect of the American scene is that the politics of inequality seem if anything to be running ahead of the reality. . . . At this point the U.S. economic elite owes its status mainly to wages rather than capital income. Nonetheless, conservative economic rhetoric already emphasizes and celebrates capital. . . . Sometimes it seems as if a substantial part of our political class is actively working to restore Piketty's patrimonial capitalism."

Krugman's conclusion is reinforced and underscored by the 2016 presidential election. It strikes us as remarkable that a candidate who knew so little and had no experience at governing could receive as many votes as he did based solely on his constructed persona of a straight-talker who would cater to the prejudices of regular guys, including championing their interests at the expense of professional elites and stopping minorities and immigrants from "cutting in line." Even as economists overwhelmingly rejected his candidacy, his supporters rejected the experts' (economics or otherwise) putative authority about what's good for the economy. Over the last four decades, in the name of promoting economic growth, the United States has sharply reduced effective tax rates on the rich, weakened organized labor and the bargaining power of workers more generally, and increased the educational attainment of the workforce by a substantial margin. These policies have produced an unequal, low-growth country and a voting public willing to embrace an angry proto-fascist populism. If Piketty's book was distastefully radical before, now it looks vitally necessary.

Sociologists, historians, political scientists, and others now seem to us to be healthily and productively wrestling with these questions. That part of the splash made by *C21* seems, to us at least, to be on track.

Inside of Economics

However, inside of economics the reaction seems to us to be less healthy. Piketty's appearances in economics seminars draw standing-room-only crowds. But the flow of scholarship within economics on the full panoply of issues he raises in *C21* has, to date at least, not been large. *C21* has not or has not yet had the impact that we—definite fans that we are—think it ought to have on economics research agendas and policy advocacy.

We believe that it ought to because we believe that *C21* is, as Robert Solow writes in Chapter 2, a very serious book. There is a great deal for economists to engage with. The Kaldor fact was that inequality—at least as driven by shifts in factor income shares—was by the mid-twentieth century no longer, and would never again be, an important changing economic observable. That Kaldor fact turns out not to be a fact—or, rather, to have been a transitory emergent historical pattern that has now dissolved. The Kuznets fact was that all or nearly all economies had been through or would go through an industrial age in which inequality rises and then a social-democratic mass-consumption age in which inequality falls and then stabilizes. It, too, turns out not to be a fact—once again merely transient historical contingency. Given that these two facts are not facts, Solow calls for economists—and economics—to take *C21* as seriously as Piketty deserves. Solow's call is a major part of our motivation for this book. The fact that economists, and economics as a discipline, do not appear to be responding optimally is the rest of our motivation.

Piketty's Claims

Therefore, our questions are these: How has Piketty moved the ball forward with respect to our understanding of the economy? What are the next steps for economic research to take, in light of what Piketty has done? In order to answer them, we need to first be clear on what the argument of *C21* is. As we see it, Piketty's best seller makes five central claims:

1. The post–World War II Social Democratic Age in the Global North (1945–1980, say) saw the industrial economies of the Global North as relatively egalitarian places (for native-born white men, at least). In those economies, relative income differences were moderated; long-standing racial gaps in wealth, income, and employment were narrowed; and political voice was widely distributed throughout the population. In those economies, the claims of wealth to drive political directions and shape economic structures were kept within bounds— although not neutralized.

2. That Social Democratic Age pattern was an unstable historical anomaly. Unlike many scholars, Piketty sees the rise of the social welfare state as the consequence of declining power of the plutocratic elite. He traces declining post-tax inequality to the wars and the introduction of progressive taxation, but not the social insurance, labor standards, and welfare infrastructures set up in the late nineteenth and early twentieth centuries. Because capital-destroying wars are an anomaly, the period of low inequality was as well.

3. That Social Democratic Age was preceded by the Belle Époque— so-called in Europe, and called the First Gilded Age in America. In that preceding epoch the claims of wealth, especially inherited wealth, to drive political directions and shape economic structures were dominant. In that age, differentials in relative income—and even more, in relative wealth—were at extreme values.

4. We are enmeshed in what appears to be an era of transition. While wealth concentration has just now returned to its early twentieth-century peak, Piketty shows that it remains the case that for the top 1 percent, the majority of income derives from earnings from labor, not capital.[2] On the other hand, inequality in capital income has been

rising rapidly since 2000, whereas inequality in labor income has stayed relatively constant since then.[3] It has not yet transpired that "the past devours the future," but we're getting there.[4]

5. Due to the powerful forces generated by the underlying dynamics of wealth, it is most likely that we are being driven to a Second Gilded Age, another Belle Époque, in which once again the claims of wealth, especially inherited wealth, to drive political directions and shape economic structures will be dominant, and in which differentials in relative income—and even more, in relative wealth—will once again be at extreme values, and in which the benefit of access to modern advances in health and education ceases to be universal, stalling, if not reversing, relative convergence in well-being across groups and individuals.

The Structure of Piketty's Argument

The central argument for these claims that Piketty makes can itself be hastily sketched in seven analytical steps:

1. A society's wealth-to-annual-income ratio will grow (or shrink) to a level equal to its net savings and accumulation rate divided by its growth rate.
2. Time and chance inevitably lead to the concentration of wealth in the hands of a relatively small group—call them "the rich." A society with a high wealth-to-annual-income ratio will be a society with an extremely unequal distribution of wealth.
3. A society with an extremely unequal distribution of wealth will also have an extremely unequal distribution of income, for the wealthy will manipulate political economy or other factors in such a way as to keep rates of profit at substantial levels and so avoid what John Maynard Keynes called "the euthanasia of the *rentier*."[5]
4. A society with an extremely unequal distribution of wealth and income will be one in which, over time, control over wealth falls to heirs and heiresses—an "heiristocracy."
5. A society in which wealth, especially inherited wealth, is economically salient will be one in which the rich will have a very high degree of economic, political, and sociocultural influence—and will be an unpleasant society in many ways.

6. The twentieth century (a) saw a uniquely high rate of economic growth due to the growth forces of the Second Industrial Revolution outlined by Robert Gordon, and due to successful convergence of the Global North to the economic prosperity frontier marked by the United States; (b) saw wars, revolutions, general chaos, and socializing and progressive tax-imposing political movements generate uniquely strong forces pushing down the rate of accumulation; but (c) gave way to a twenty-first century in which all of these forces are now ebbing, if they have not already completely ebbed away.[6]

7. Hence—although we are far from the limit yet—the logic of (1) through (5) is now at work. It is substantially more likely than not to work itself to completion. It will deliver a society unpleasant in a number of ways in a half-century or so.

In Piketty's view, we are now more than a full generation into this process of the passing away of North Atlantic social democracy. This process, however, has not yet come to an end. It will, he thinks, take another two generations or more for the logic he sees driving us on our current trajectory to work itself through to its completion. We haven't, in Piketty's view, seen anything yet, at least as far as the Global North's return to its default pattern of plutocracy is concerned.

The Poverty of (Much) Piketty Criticism

Even in this oversimplified thumbnail form, Piketty's argument is not simple. One would therefore expect that it would attract a large volume of substantive criticism. And, indeed, it has: there are many effective and thoughtful critiques of Piketty. To note a few examples:

- Matt Rognlie seeks to cast doubt on step (3), and has taken John Maynard Keynes's side of the debate over whether accumulation that leads to a rising wealth-to-annual-income ratio leads in fact to a rate of profit that falls faster than the wealth-to-annual-income ratio grows, thus creating a society with a high degree of wealth but a low degree of income inequality.[7]
- Tyler Cowen casts doubt on (2), (4), and (5): He argues that creative destruction will break up or at least limit the salience of cross-generational

dynastic accumulations. He further argues, echoing Friedrich von Hayek, that the "idle rich" are a valuable cultural resource precisely because they are not bound to the karmic wheel of earning, getting, and spending on necessities and conveniences, and so can take the long and / or heterodox view of things.[8]

- Daron Acemoglu and James Robinson point out that while Piketty "mentions policies and institutions . . . their role is ad hoc."[9]
- Still others hope for a new industrial revolution to create more low-hanging fruit and faster growth, accompanied by another wave of creative destruction, that will short-circuit (2), (4), (6), and (7).
- And there is the question of Piketty's neglect of human capital as an important form of property and a leveling factor in the modern age.

All in all, however, what has impressed us has been the limited substantive meat in the critiques of Piketty's overall chain of argument. The argument is complex and multi-stepped. All such arguments are vulnerable. Our coverage and reading of the critiques is far from complete: We try to survey the critiques of Piketty, but find ourselves reduced by the volume to simply surveying the surveys. And we see a remarkable number of arguments that seem to us to be largely substance-free. They come in the forms of amateur psychological diagnosis, red-baiting, misconstructions of Piketty's argument, miscalibrations of economic growth models, data errors, and more.

The nadir, perhaps, comes from the pen of Allan Meltzer of Carnegie-Mellon and of Stanford University's Hoover Institution. It accuses Thomas Piketty of being a Frenchmen, a former MIT professor, and a co-author with Emmanuel Saez at MIT, where the IMF's Olivier Blanchard was a professor. The latter is also French. France has, for many years, implemented destructive policies of income redistribution . . . , and so on.[10]

On the one hand, it is disappointing to see critiques that look not so much like academic analyses but more like things designed to reassure standard billionaires who are hoping to establish dynasties.

On the other hand, it is clear that the urge to set forth even low-substance critiques, plus the book's 2.2 million copies, is powerful evidence that *C21* has struck a very loud—if not resonant—chord. Many, many find that it is worth engaging. The question is: how?

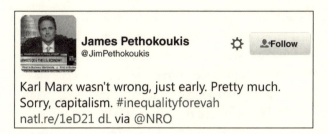

FIGURE 0-1: One man's tweeted summation of *C21*, short and not to the point.

We want to help drive a constructive engagement with Piketty's *Capital in the Twenty-First Century*. We want critique—sharp critique. But we want effective, useful critique that contributes to the advance of knowledge. We do not want things like Figure 0-1 that misrepresent Piketty's argument and in so doing subtract from rather than add to global knowledge. And we want to encourage work that will build on Piketty, and carry his data collection and his theoretical arguments further.

We believe that the essays we have collected here contribute to this task. To set the stage for them, we ask:

1. Is the argument of Thomas Piketty's *C21* right?
2. Should we care?
3. What are the implications?
4. What ought we do next?

Is Piketty Right?

Are the arguments in *C21* right? Or at least, if not definitely right, is Piketty's disturbing scenario plausible, something to worry about—and perhaps something to take action about in the hopes of turning the forecasts of *C21* into a self-denying prophecy?

Here the answer strongly appears to us to be: yes.

Piketty is right in maintaining that here in the Global North, as far back as we can look, ownership of private wealth—with its power to command resources, dictate where and how people would work, and shape politics—has always been highly concentrated. Piketty is right in maintaining that 150 years—six generations—ago, in the Belle Époque / First Gilded Age, the ratio of a typical Global North country's total private wealth to its total annual income was about six. Piketty is also right in maintaining that in the Age of Social Democracy some fifty years—two generations—ago, that capital / income ratio was about three. And Piketty is right to note that over the past two generations that wealth-to-annual-income ratio has been rising rapidly.

More debatable is whether the rise in wealth-to-annual-income ratios is driven by the forces Piketty highlights. And much more debatable is whether the rise in income inequality is being driven by a rise in wealth inequality that is itself a consequence of the rise in economy-wide wealth-to-annual-income ratios. These points are contestable, and are contested. But we would expect them to be contestable. There are lots of other influences on the distribution of income besides the forces Piketty places at center stage—some of which he writes about himself. And the forces that Piketty highlights have not yet had time since the end of the Age of Social Democracy to work themselves out.

Piketty's main argument is not about the causes of how things are now, but about what things will be like in fifty years and more. Notwithstanding that, there are plenty of indications available to us in the world today that substantial features of the last Gilded Age have recurred: a rising capital income share, a rising coincidence of labor income with capital income, a rising persistence of intergenerational fortunes impregnable from assault by the tax authorities.

Worthy of further debate is the relative autonomy from structural economic pressures possessed by institutions, politics, or social movements. Piketty's argument is based on a fairly deterministic theory of the future: the rich will manipulate the system to manage to maintain the rate of profit at 5 percent no matter how much wealth they accumulate. Piketty does give much more than lip service to the role of noneconomic forces. He encourages the reader to consider what the other social sciences might have to tell us. But in the end his argument is based on simple economic dynamics of wealth accumulation and inequality in the context of a healthy and relatively stable rate of profit.

Whatever institutional changes required to maintain this healthy rate of profit as wealth accumulates and so propel this vision forward are baked in.

However, institutions as they actually are might hamper his vision in a variety of ways. For example, as Heather Boushey points out in Chapter 15, an "heiristocracy" will almost certainly require a move away from gender equity—a trend that women and their allies may be prepared to fight against. Moreover, both David Grewal (Chapter 19) and Marshall Steinbaum (Chapter 18) argue that the history of inequality arises from the rise (in Grewal's case) and fall (in Steinbaum's) of what can be termed an "ideology of capitalism" and an associated body of law and policy. A "free market" independent of mercantilist or monarchical authority developed alongside the bourgeoisie of the eighteenth century and entered into a political alliance with the *ancien régime* in the nineteenth. Piketty argues that capitalism itself, rather than its ideology, is responsible for ever-widening inequality, and that it was the exogenous world wars of the twentieth century that briefly derailed it. But they also derailed its ideology, and that was not so exogenous. Piketty's argument is contestable and contested right now because the signal he focuses on is not yet emerging or has barely emerged from the noise.

But that is what we would expect to see if his argument is in fact correct.

However, that is also what we might well see if his argument is in fact badly off-base.

More secure is Piketty's claim that there might be substantial empirical problems with the pattern of the "euthanasia of the rentier," as expected by authors like Keynes, Rognlie, and others who assume that wealth is identical with productive capital in some neoclassical production function of income. Those authors expect that the logic of supply and demand will force large swings in societal wealth-to-annual-income ratios to be associated with large swings in the opposite direction in society-wide rates of profit. Profit rates will be high when capital is scarce relative to annual income, and low when capital is abundant. According to Keynes et al., these swings will be large enough that the rentiers' share of total income will remain roughly constant.

Thomas Piketty's response is, roughly, this: the Keynes-Rognlie argument sounds very good in neoclassical economic theory but fails in historical practice. Supply-and-demand tells us that when the economy's wealth-to-annual-income ratio varies, the rate of profit should vary in the opposite direction. But history tells us, to the contrary, that the annual rate of profit has plodded along at some 4 or 5 percent, largely independent of the relative scarcity or abundance of wealth. So much the worse for the logic of supply-and-demand.

Here we have an apparent historical fact: the relative invariance of the rate of profit with respect to what aggregate neoclassical production functions tell us should be its principal source of variation. But here Piketty does not put forward a theory:

- He might argue that physical capital, total wealth, rent-seeking political economy, and government-enforced monopoly rents work in an iron quadrilateral to maintain the rate of profit willy-nilly, no matter what the logic of production and the marginal-product theory of distribution say.

- He might argue that technology is such that physical capital does not face sharply decreasing marginal returns and so that the capital / income ratio and capital share move together and not inversely. He might argue that in the past what he calls "capital" was overwhelmingly agricultural capital in the form of land and in the future "capital" will overwhelmingly be information capital and that the neoclassical growth model was a valid first-order approximation only for the short interval that was the Age of Social Democracy.

- He might follow Suresh Naidu (Chapter 5), who argues that capital's share of national income, far from obeying the rules of marginal productivity pricing, is in fact determined by power, and the total stock of what Piketty and the neoclassicals call both wealth and capital is actually financialized claims on a forthcoming stream of revenue—the result, not of lengthy accumulation, so to speak, but of political control of the future.

But Piketty does not take any of these stands, or any other stand.

This seems to be a substantial hole in the book. It points out what is perhaps the most important and urgent research task opened up by Piketty. Is the apparent constancy of the rate of profit a robust reality? And if it is, what forces and factors maintain the constancy of the rate of profit?

Devesh Raval (Chapter 4) tries to advance the ball here. He reinforces the Rognlie-Keynes "euthanasia of the rentier" point that capital and labor are not substitutable enough to sustain Piketty's argument. If the story behind the constancy of the rate of profit isn't that marginal capital continues to be productive as it is accumulated, what is it? Is there a story? One possible story is provided by Laura Tyson and Michael Spence (Chapter 8), who see Piketty as very much barking up the wrong tree. Inequality is growing and will continue to grow. But its growth will not be driven by the factors in Piketty's growth models. It will be driven by the coming of the information age, and the shape of information-age technology, which for the first time does make human labor a substitute for rather than a complement to capital by greatly reducing the necessity of using human brains as routine cybernetic control mechanisms for basic matter manipulation and basic information processing.

Is Piketty's argument right? At the moment the answer is "perhaps." Not only does a great deal turn on the robustness of each of the links in his argument, but his argument is also conditional on the Global North's remaining on its current political-economic trajectory. So a lot turns on what we take the phrase "current political-economic trajectory" to mean. Under some interpretations of that phrase Piketty will surely be right. Under others he will surely be wrong. And we do need to distinguish which is which.

Should We Care?

Some—perhaps many—say that we should not care. One common thread of argument is that we simply should not care about inequality. In fact, according to this thread, inequality is, if anything, good: It is an engine of faster economic growth, by incentivizing human capital acquisition and engendering social mobility. It is not at all a problem for an economy, a society, or a country.

What is a problem, this thread of argument maintains, is poverty—especially dire poverty.

And, this thread continues, we are now much richer than our predecessors of six generations ago were. Back then, the Gilded Age or Belle Époque levels of inequality caused not just poverty but dire poverty. Hence, back then inequality was a serious problem. Now, however, because the Global North is so much richer, the amount of inequality that caused dire poverty then does not cause dire poverty today. In fact, it does not cause anything that we should call "poverty" at all—at least not if we take a historical perspective.

In the United States, policy-oriented organizations like Third Way argue that America's middle class is doing just fine. They point to the rise in real incomes—in no small part due to the added hours and earnings of women—as an indicator that Piketty's measures of the top 1 percent are just getting the story wrong. In the academy, many point to the great advances in medical care, sanitation, public education, literacy, disease eradication, and proliferation of leisure activities, to mention only a few, and claim that there is no prospect for reversing these gains in absolute well-being, regardless of what happens to the top 1 percent.

This is an old argument—250 years old, in fact. Adam Smith argued in his *Wealth of Nations* that your average working-class Briton lived in greater material comfort than an African king. In his *Theory of Moral Sentiments* Smith argued that the consumption of the rich was limited by the size of their stomachs, and thus that most of what they spent even on themselves was in fact a contribution to the leisure and comfort of their underlings.

However, this argument is probably wrong. Granting that economic growth above bare Malthusian subsistence up to Britain's eighteenth-century Augustan Age was impressive, and granting that economic growth since then has been magnificent, there are still powerful and important reasons to care, not just about what by historical standards is dire poverty and poverty, but about inequality and about what we call "poverty" today—even if the poor do have dishwashers, smartphones, and televisions.

First, anyone who has looked at the distribution of medical care in the United States and our abysmal health outcome statistics relative to other rich countries cannot help but see that inequality is a factor that leads enormous investments of resources to deliver little of ultimate value in the sense of human well-being and human satisfaction. The point generalizes beyond the health sector: an unequal economy is one that is lousy at turning productive potential into societal well-being. We could be doing better—and with a more equal distribution of income and wealth, we would be.

It's hard to prove that causality runs from inequality to health or other social welfare indicators, but a data point that illustrates the struggles facing parts of the United States left out of the new Gilded Age is found in the research of Anne Case and Angus Deaton. They show that the rise in mortality among middle-aged Americans from suicides and drug overdoses—both conditions that are associated with economic malaise—between 1999 and 2013 has been so large that it is similar to the rise in mortality caused by the

AIDS crisis through 2015.[11] Similar findings document that once-narrowing gaps in employment, health, and overall well-being have stopped closing, and in some cases have reopened.[12]

Second, as noted above, established wealth, especially inherited wealth, is by its nature hostile to the creative destruction that accompanies rapid economic growth. It is established wealth that is creatively destroyed. Plutocrats and their ideologues like to claim that too equal an income distribution destroys incentives to work and turns us into a "nation of takers." But a return to the inequality levels of the 1960s would not turn us into Maoist China. In the relevant range of levels of inequality, it appears to us significantly more likely that higher inequality will slow growth by depriving the nonrich of the resources to invest in themselves, their children, and their enterprises. It will further slow growth by focusing effort on helping the rich keep what they have at the cost of squelching the development of the new.

There is ample evidence across the United States that elites are engaged in what some call "opportunity hoarding."[13] We hear a lot about how the rich are able to garner human-sized airplane seats and now their own havens within cruise ships, but there are areas where their consumption limits the potential for others.[14] Elites are increasingly opting out of public schools, which deprives those schools of valuable parental engagement as well as income to the extent that these elites then fail to support levies for school financing. Such elite withdrawal leaves public schools open to political assault from forces hostile to the whole idea of universal free and equal high-quality public education.

Third, a society in which plutocrats deploy their resources to have not just a loud but an overwhelming voice will be a society in which government sets about to solve problems of concern to the plutocrats and not the people. And that is unlikely to be a good society.

This, too, pushes against a high-growth society. Plutocrats who are given the option of rent-seeking or trying to win in the competitive marketplace are likely to seek to close the door behind them. Case in point: as policymakers struggle to rein in the anticompetitive bent of newly powerful platform-based firms, we are seeing a win for those who arrive first—and peanuts for the rest. This kind of economy keeps prices high and stifles innovation, neither of which bodes well for economic dynamism.

Fourth, the predominance of wealth in the exercise of power extends far beyond the sphere of formal politics, well into the workplace, the home (even the bedroom), and civil society. Reliance on private wealth to finance higher education has already made that sector far more unequal, with very expensive mediocrity the lot of anyone unlucky enough not to gain access to its most restricted precincts (which explicitly favor the children of their alumni and implicitly those applicants similar to them), and with a greater degree of restriction on the curriculum and on the views of the personnel who teach it than would be obtained under a system that owes its existence to the continued support of the public.

Fifth, an unequal society is one in which employers can and do exploit their ability to pick winners and losers—and are driven to indignant outrage by the idea of a collective worker voice.

Labor economist David Weil (Chapter 9) sees increasing inequality in part both driving and being driven by a "fissuring of the workplace." In the past, large corporations would in a relatively efficient Coasian way serve as islands of central planning in the sea that was the market economy, employing workers at all levels: skilled professionals, midlevel administrators, and manual workers. Such a workplace is inevitably subject to strong egalitarian pressures: the presence of high-wage professionals pulls up everyone's calculus of what the firm can afford to pay its manual workers and what its manual workers deserve. But it has become profitable to break up that social construct if so doing can relax egalitarian sociological pressures, especially if nonenforcement of employment standards dating to the New Deal gives employers the option of exercising control without fulfilling their statutory responsibilities. We need to find out how strong are the forces Weil identifies, and whether they are a peculiar case or suggest that high inequality is likely to interfere with efficient inter- and intra-firm organization along a broad front.

Sixth, an unequal society is one in which *who* you know matters more to your ultimate well-being than *what* you know, and one thing we can tell by observing the behavior of the rich and their acolytes is that native ability to suck up to the rich is not equally distributed throughout the population. The rich prefer people who are like themselves—and a society in which the distribution of well-being is determined by "who the rich like" is unlikely to preserve the gains of racial and gender equality made during the Social Democratic era.

Moreover, Arthur Okun's argument in *Equality and Efficiency: The Big Trade-Off* that a good society is one that chooses a proper point on the equality-versus-efficiency frontier appears, in retrospect, to be in all likelihood substantially wrong if we try to apply it to our day.[15] More equality may well go along with greater efficiency.

So: Yes, we should care. And we do care.

What Are the Implications?

Suppose that Piketty has established that in a century from now, the Global North is highly likely to have a much higher wealth-to-annual-income ratio than today—and even that inherited wealth will be a much greater proportion of total wealth than it is today. Does this necessarily entail an unfavorable distribution of economic power and resources, an economy that falls short of its potential according to some utilitarian benchmark that takes account of declining marginal utility of wealth? Is it even the case that a society with a high wealth-to-income ratio must be grossly unequal?

Piketty says yes. On these issues he follows Marx, and Marx's insight that in a market economy with transferable wealth an egalitarian property distribution is unstable. From a starting point of equal division, time and chance will inevitably produce a large and extended upper tail with a size and length heavily and positively dependent on the magnitude of $r - g$, where r is not the safe interest rate but the average economy-wide rate of profit, and on the magnitude of the risk associated with capital returns. Thus, an economy with a high wealth-to-income ratio and a high share of national income made up of capital and other forms of wealth will be an unequal economy.

Piketty's argument is this:

> Many shocks . . . contribute to making the wealth distribution highly unequal. . . . There are demographic shocks . . . shocks to rates of return . . . shocks to labor market outcomes . . . differences in taste parameters that affect the level of saving. . . . A central property of this large class of models is that . . . the long-run magnitude of wealth inequality will tend to be magnified if the gap $r - g$ is higher. . . . A higher gap between r and g allows an economy to sustain a level of wealth inequality that is higher and more persistent over time . . . [converging] toward a distribution that has a Pareto shape for top wealth holders . . . [where] the inverted Pareto

coefficient (an indicator of top-end inequality) is a steeply rising function of the gap r − g. . . . See in particular Champernowne 1953; Stiglitz 1969; . . . Piketty and Zucman (2015, section 5.4). . . .

In this class of models, relatively small changes in r − g can generate very large changes in steady-state wealth inequality. . . . It is really the *interaction* between the r − g effect and the institutional and public policy responses—including progressive taxation of income, wealth, and inheritance; inflation; nationalizations, physical destruction, and expropriations; estate division rules; and so on—which in my view, determines the dynamics and the magnitude of wealth inequality.[16]

And, in Piketty's view, at least as expressed in the book, the interaction is likely to be unhelpful: greater wealth inequality will raise the demand for egalitarian policy responses, but it will also raise the ability of those with wealth to block such policy responses. The book portrays the forces favoring the formation of a dominant plutocracy as being so strong that they can be countered only by world wars and global revolutions—and even then, the correction is only temporary.

That is the view he expressed in *C21*. Since the publication of the book, though, Thomas Piketty has not played the role of a doomsayer who brings the message of inescapable rising inequality and encourages a passive response. Instead he has embraced the role of a celebrity public intellectual. And the message he has carried to all corners of the world is not the message expected from a passive chronicler of unavoidable destiny. If we look at what Piketty does—rather than what he writes—it is clear that he believes we can collectively make our own destiny, even if the circumstances are not what he, or we, would choose.

Branko Milanovic (Chapter 10) has a relevant critique here, not of Piketty-as-public-intellectual but of Piketty-as-author. In his view, these arguments of Piketty's (and before him, of Marx) are appropriate only for the institutional setup that Milanovic calls "new capitalism." There are other institutional setups possible in the future. Indeed, we have seen others in the past. In what we would tend to call advanced social democracy—for example, the post–World War II institutional order in which the state and society powerfully put their thumbs on the scales to equalize the distribution of claims to income that flow from "old property" and also to create "new property" in the form of citizen entitlements—there is no connection between the capital share and inequality in the distribution of income. And in what Milanovic calls "classical capitalism" (and Karl Marx would call "petit bourgeois society") the distribution is driven by the Ricardian triad of labor, capital, and land—and the dynamics are substantially different.

Almost two centuries ago Karl Marx dismissed the Milanovic-style critique as reflecting an irrational and unattainable longing for a "petty-bourgeois socialism" that could never be attained and that, if it did develop by accident, could never be maintained.

But that casual dismissal does not mean that Milanovic is wrong.

Piketty's world is particularly grim because it's predetermined. So long as the rate of profit is above the rate of growth, we're destined to move toward ever-increasing inequality. The only thing we can do is figure out how to tally up the massive wealth and tax it—if we can overcome the ability of wealth to protect itself by constraining political options.

As Gareth Jones points out in Chapter 12, this is a tall order, in no small part because capital has stepped outside the purview of the nation-state. The rise of wealth from industrialization occurred alongside the coalescence of the nation-state in Europe and elsewhere. The state was a means of promoting the accumulation of capital. Capital today aims often to avoid the confines of place or citizenship, choosing instead to wander the globe in pursuit of not only profits but unfettered access to those profits—as we've seen with Gabriel Zucman's pioneering research on tax havens and with such other improvements in our ability to survey the global wealth landscape as the release of the Panama Papers.

What Ought We Do Next?

For all these reasons, we judge that *C21* is a serious book warning us of likely—but not inevitable—distressing consequences of certain aspects of the future historical path that the world economy appears to have embarked on roughly thirty years ago. That raises some natural questions: Do we need to buy insurance? And what kinds of insurance ought we to buy? However, as Abraham Lincoln said in his "House Divided" speech in Springfield, Illinois, on June 16, 1858, such questions are in a sense premature: We need "first [to] know where we are, and whither we are tending," for only after knowing that "could [we] then better judge what to do, and how to do it."

The next move must be, as John Maynard Keynes liked to say, "with the head." And we have organized this book to set out our view of the agenda with respect to what we need to better understand.

When readers face a book as sprawling as this one is, they badly need help orienting themselves. We have tried to help. In Part I, three authors—Art Goldhammer (Chapter 1), Bob Solow (Chapter 2), and Paul Krugman (Chapter 3)—set out their different perspectives on *C21*-as-phenomenon and on *C21*-as argument-with-implications.

What is this thing "capital" that *C21* is about? Piketty offers definitions. But as is so often the case when a single concept is at the core of a striking and contestable argument, whether the concept can bear the argumentative load attached to it, and indeed what the concept really means, become contestable, uncertain, and worth examination. Part II thus examines the concept of "capital" from five different viewpoints.

Devesh Raval (Chapter 4) points out that Piketty presents his argument in economic-theoretic terms as a derivation from the historical fact that at the aggregate level capital and labor are highly elastic in substitution. Yet there is a great deal of research, much of it by Raval himself, strongly suggesting that at the micro level that is simply not the case—and here the aggregate should be a weighted average of the micro elasticities and the elasticity of demand for output. He highlights a puzzle at the center of any reading of *C21*: Is it at its core an argument that at the margin, capital continues to be productive as it is accumulated? And if that is not the case, what is left of the argument?

Suresh Naidu (Chapter 5) provides a possible response to Raval's puzzle, contrasting a "domesticated" Piketty, working within the machinery of an aggregate neoclassical economic production function, and a "wild" Piketty who breaks free. Naidu's answer is that what remains is a political-economic argument about how the wealthy in a Gilded Age structure property in such a way as to protect and increase the salience of the rents they extract.

The other three papers in Part II find flaws in Piketty's deployment of and use of the concept "capital." First, a great deal of the argument of *C21* is that the twentieth century was exceptional—that as far as the dynamics of wealth inequality are concerned, the twenty-first century is much more likely to be like the nineteenth and eighteenth centuries. Daina Ramey Berry (Chapter 6) critiques the image of those earlier centuries that Piketty draws in *C21*. In her reading of history, slavery was a much more salient institution in the "primitive accumulation" and extraction of wealth than Piketty allows for, both in terms of the depth and breadth of direct exploitation that it allowed and in how potential competition from slavemasters and their lash-driven shackled workers eroded the bargaining power of even free labor. If the factors she adduces are salient, that suggests that it might be much harder to sustain a Second Gilded Age in a free-labor twenty-first century than it was to create a First Gilded Age in the eighteenth and nineteenth centuries. Or does it? As Branko Milanovic might point out, barriers to international migration are a form of labor unfreedom, and one that becomes more salient the wider the gulf between the Global North and the Global South.

Second, a great deal of the argument of *C21* assumes that the only truly real forms of wealth are government-created rent and debt amortization flows, physical assets (land, buildings, machines), and control of the organizations that deploy such physical and financial assets. High wages, in Piketty's view, are more a chance and transitory outcome of favorable supply and demand conditions than a true, durable source of wealth and thus not a factor in driving the evolution of inequality. Eric Nielsen (Chapter 7) rejects this view, and sketches out the immense potential damage that would be done to Piketty's argument should human capital be a twenty-first century form of wealth on equal footing with other forms.

And third, Mike Spence and Laura Tyson (Chapter 8) argue that although in the past, land and industrial capital were salient factors in the dynamics of the evolution of wealth and its distribution, that will not be true in the future and is not even true now. Rather, they argue, one needs to hybridize *C21* with an argument like that of *The Second Machine Age* by Brynjolfsson and McAfee to create a framework for the inequality debate that we should be having today in order to understand our likely future.

Chapter 9 provides an intellectual bridge between the examination of "capital" and our survey of dimensions of inequality. Here David Weil—at the time of this writing an administrator of the Wages and Hours Division of the U.S. Department of Labor—points out the importance of the "fissured workplace." In place of the older model of large corporations employing workers of all skill levels and all job types, now jobs increasingly are outsourced to other corporations and other locations. Workers who would once have been employees, and thus entitled to de jure and de facto privileges associated with membership in a corporate business enterprise considered as a sociological community, are now excluded. The result is a race to the bottom—with a force that was not operating in the nineteenth century tending to raise inequality in the twenty-first, no matter what the other economic factors affecting the capital / labor split.

After examining the concept of "capital" and the functions it needs to perform in the argument of *C21*, in Part III we turn to authors who examine various dimensions of the inequality that an unequal distribution of capital can create. Branko Milanovic (Chapter 10) notes that the links between property ownership and control, on the one hand, and real on-the-ground inequality, on the other, depend critically on how the political system manages its political-economic institutions. Christoph Lakner (Chapter 11) criticizes Piketty's *C21* for telling the story of inequality as a comparative story of inequality within nation-states, thus missing the elephant in the room—which is that since the start of the Industrial Revolution, the evolution of equality across nation-states has been more decisive as a determinant of global inequality. Gareth Jones (Chapter 12) critiques the absence of "space" from *C21*, in which geography serves only as a "container for data" rather than a context for inequality and exploitation to play out. How geography enables and propagates inequality in a globalized world is, in his view, a salient factor completely omitted from *C21*. Emmanuel Saez (Chapter 13) points out how very much we do not know about inequality—and how badly, if we are to understand where we are and whither we are tending, we need to disaggregate our systems of National Income Accounts to include distributional measures, devote more resources to measuring wealth inequality, and understand the effects of regulation and taxation on inequality.

Mariacristina De Nardi, Giulio Fella, and Fang Yang (Chapter 14) point out that a high capital-to-annual-income ratio and a large capital share in income do not directly translate one-for-one into a determinant degree of higher inequality, and they examine the links and the slippage there. Heather Boushey (Chapter 15) examines the potential feminist-economics effects of the creation of what we might dub an "heiresstocracy": historically, gender relations become especially fraught and difficult, even for women one would adjudge to have considerable social power, when one's status and standing seriously depend on who one's parents and in-laws are.

Mark Zandi (Chapter 16) and Salvatore Morelli (Chapter 17) take us in a different direction. They begin the very important task of trying to assess how economic stability at the level of managing the business cycle and encouraging growth changes in an environment of rising inequality. Their conclusions are not quite the old academic standard, "more research is needed." They both see serious risks—but risks that can, perhaps, be managed or compensated for.

Part IV presents a different set of challenges to Piketty's argument. These four papers take big institutional-intellectual-history perspectives. Marshall Steinbaum (Chapter 18) makes the case that the post–World War II social democratic era of relatively low inequality was the result of the genocidal political and military catastrophes of the first half of the twentieth century and of the role played by those catastrophes in discrediting the pre–World War I First Gilded Age's unequal capitalist political-economic order. David Grewal (Chapter 19) sees the coming of the First—and the Second—Gilded Age as largely baked in the cake with the legal-political philosophical shift in the seventeenth and eighteenth centuries, which turned absolute dominion over property from an edge case to the canonical way in which Western societies thought about the control of concrete and abstract things and the responsibilities of "owners."

Ellora Derenoncourt (Chapter 20) wishes that Piketty had done more to address the deep institutional-historical origins of high degrees of wealth inequality, and fills in the gap by deploying Daron Acemoglu, James Robinson, and Simon Johnson's dichotomy between "extractive" and "inclusive" institutions—with a twist, for institutions that are "inclusive" and "developmental" for "citizens" may well be "extractive" and "exclusive" for "subjects." Elisabeth Jacobs (Chapter 21) tries to puzzle through how politics can be both everywhere and nowhere in Piketty's story. *C21* contains an argument that asserts both that there are fundamental laws of economics and that there are historically contingent and institutionally prescribed processes that shape growth and distribution without describing how the two dynamics interact in reality.

We want to highlight this last point, for it points to a contradiction that seems to us to be at the heart of *C21*'s dual nature as work of scholarship and as a global intellectual phenomenon. On the one hand, Piketty's central thesis is that our reversion to the economic and political patterns of the

Gilded Age is to be expected as normal for a capitalist society. On the other hand, Piketty himself as a celebrity public intellectual is not behaving like a passive chronicler of unavoidable destiny. He is acting as if he believes that the forces he describes in his book can be resisted—that we collectively make our own destiny, even if the circumstances under which we make it are not those of our choosing.

And then Thomas Piketty (Chapter 22) tells us what he thinks of our arguments, critiques, extensions, and explorations.

[1]

RECEPTION

ONE

The Piketty Phenomenon

ARTHUR GOLDHAMMER

Most books written by economists barely sell a few thousand copies. Piketty's *Capital in the Twenty-First Century*—all 700+ pages—sold more than two million worldwide in more than thirty languages. Excitement over the book began even before it was translated beyond the original French. In Washington, DC, local booksellers couldn't keep the book in stock. In this chapter, translator Art Goldhammer examines this "Piketty phenomenon." He asks: What made *C21* an international bestseller? Why was there such an appetite for the book, and was that enthusiasm sustained as the reviews came out? Was it the seriousness of the book's economic ideas, its accessible prose, or the Zeitgeist into which it was released? Goldhammer traces the Piketty phenomenon and provides insights into why it happened and what it all means.

The English edition of Thomas Piketty's *Capital in the Twenty-First Century*, which I translated from the French, appeared in the spring of 2014. Within a few months of publication, it had sold more than 400,000 copies—rare for any book, rarer still for a work by an academic economist comprising nearly 700 pages dense with statistical tables and graphs, not to mention an online technical appendix with references to dozens of academic papers and voluminous data.[1] A year later, global sales in more than thirty countries had climbed to an astonishing 2.1 million (see Table 1-1).

The book was reviewed not just in scholarly journals but in mass-circulation newspapers and magazines. Its author appeared on radio and television around the world—not just on public affairs and news programming, but also on widely viewed entertainment vehicles such as *The Colbert Report* in the United States.[2] He was invited to meet with U.S. Treasury secretary Jack Lew and presidential advisor Gene Sperling, and made a joint

TABLE I-I.

Sales of Capital in the Twenty-First Century *by country and language*
(source: Éditions du Seuil via Thomas Piketty, private communication to author)

Language	Number printed (as of December 2015)
French	274,910
English	650,000
German	108,270
Greek	7,357
Italian	71,353
Hungarian	1,850
Portuguese	155,367
Castilian	101,500
Korean	88,000
Japanese	163,000
Swedish	8,000
Turkish	33,000
Chinese simplified	282,500
Chinese complex	44,000
Polish	16,460
Serbian	1,750
Russian	7,000
Dutch	50,981
Croat	3,000
Norwegian	12,000
Danish	7,000
Catalan	10,000
Czech	5,500
Slovenian	4,380
Slovakian	1,905
Bosnian	1,000
Total	2,110,083

Other languages (sales figures unavailable): Romanian, Thai, Tamil, Hindi, Mongol, Bengali, Latvian, Arabic, Finnish, Macedonian, Vietnamese, Ukrainian public appearance with U.S. senator Elizabeth Warren. Piketty began to be spoken of as "the rock star" of economics, and *Bloomberg Businessweek* depicted him as such in a parody cover similar to that of a teen fan magazine.[3] Bookstores displayed mounds of the hardcover volume alongside other best-sellers. T-shirts bearing the formula $r > g$ popped up on college campuses and on the shirts of the Harvard University Press intramural softball team.[4] A session of the American Economic Association annual meeting in 2015 was devoted to the work, which drew laudatory reviews from two Nobel Prize winners. The *Financial Times* tried and failed to refute his findings.[5] He was offered and refused the French Legion of Honor, and his book was named "business book of the year" for 2014 by the very same *Financial Times* that had tried to discredit him a few months earlier.[6] For all of these reasons and more, *Capital in the Twenty-First Century* qualifies as a publishing phenomenon—indeed, more broadly, as a public phenomenon that calls for analysis.

That said, the analysis that follows will probably disappoint readers searching for explanations. In many ways the "Piketty phenomenon" defies explanation. Although I will mention a number of factors that appear to be correlated with the reception of the book, some of these existed for many years during which other works on inequality appeared without provoking such a massive public response. Correlation is not causation. Why the various influences we will discuss converged on *this* book and *this* author at *this* moment will, in the end, remain a mystery. If it were possible to predict why such phenomena occur, publishing would be a royal road to riches. A final caveat is that the analysis is pertinent exclusively to the United States. Undoubtedly, the attention the book attracted in the United States influenced its reception elsewhere, even in its native France, but to precisely what extent it is impossible to say.

The analysis will proceed in five parts. First, I will discuss anticipations of the book's reception and show that even the most optimistic forecasts failed to predict the extent of the Piketty phenomenon. Second, I will consider how the political and social context created by the Great Recession of 2007–2009 may have influenced the response to the work. Third, I will survey the major early critiques of the work, insofar as they may have influenced its reception. Fourth, I will consider academic responses to the work from outside the discipline of economics. And finally, I will assess the political response to *Capital in the Twenty-First Century* (hereafter abbreviated *C21*) and briefly discuss Piketty's conception of the relation between democracy and capitalism.

Anticipations and Projections

Prior to the book's publication, no one predicted the Piketty phenomenon. Ian Malcolm, the Harvard University Press editor who acquired the book, expected it might sell "as many as 200,000 over two or three years."[7] He based this estimate on his previous experience at Princeton University Press, where a colleague had published what he calls a "comparable" book: *This Time Is Different,* by Carmen Reinhart and Kenneth Rogoff. But that work, which deals with the history of financial crises, is comparable only in the sense that its authors were also academic economists who studied a time span longer than is customary in economics. It was reasonable, however, to conclude that the success of that volume demonstrated the existence of a substantial audience anxious about the state of the advanced industrial economies after the Great Recession of 2007–2009.

Nevertheless, the head of Harvard University Press, William Sisler, was less optimistic than the acquiring editor. He notes that HUP chose the work as the lead book in its 2014 catalog because "we did think it would make some noise, maybe 10,000–20,000 copies if we were lucky."[8] Sales of that order would indeed have been noteworthy for an academic book, where press runs in the hundreds of thousands (as opposed to the hundreds) are exceedingly rare. As it turned out, however, both the veteran publisher and the experienced editor underestimated the book's potential—the former by two orders of magnitude and the latter by one. The translator was no more prescient: He failed to ask for royalties, which with academic books seldom end "in the money."

Hence it is fair to say that no one anticipated the work's phenomenal reception, despite glowing recommendations and Piketty's already substantial reputation in both France and the United States. Piketty's work came to the attention of the press via Roger Guesnerie, a distinguished economist at the prestigious Collège de France. The book had the backing of its French publisher, Pierre Rosanvallon, also a distinguished professor at the Collège, whose work Ian Malcolm had previously published (and I had translated). One reviewer canvassed by the press praised the book as "the most important work of French social science of the past ten years."[9] Note the characterization of the work as "social science" rather than simply "economics" or "economic history." This was perhaps an additional plus for Harvard: Here was an opportunity to establish a beachhead in economics while adding an important title likely to appeal to one of the press's core constituencies. Taking the book on therefore made sense in terms of publishing strategy, although it was not without risk. Because the manuscript was not complete at the time the contract was signed, it was difficult to evaluate how great that risk would be. The finished book turned out to be almost twice as long as envisioned, thus increasing the cost of translation and potentially discouraging readers likely to be daunted by the sheer size of the volume.

Piketty had previously published nothing that would have augured success beyond a limited audience of academic economists and economic historians. Although his papers on income inequality, coauthored with Emmanuel Saez, were widely known—as I will discuss more fully in a moment—his major previous book was a long, dense, and specialized work on high incomes in France, published in 2001 and never translated into English.[10] Besides that, there was a short primer, *The Economics of Inequality* (also published in English only after *C21*), which contained none of the empirical data that would distinguish the author's mature work.

Translations of French scholarly work are often not commissioned until the work has been published in France and demonstrated its value through reviews in scholarly journals. This "test marketing" to some extent reduces the risks associated with any translation. But *C21* did not appear in France until after the translation was done. In fact, the French edition came out just weeks after I put the finishing touches on the English manuscript. I arrived for a visit in France just after publication and found, displayed in all the news kiosks, a magazine cover declaring that Thomas Piketty was *"un marxiste de sous-préfecture,"* a (ridiculously derogatory) characterization that did not augur well for the book's American reception. Nevertheless, it was also clear that this was a book that was being talked about, creating a stir.

Indeed, despite that caricatural review, the book sold briskly in the months after its appearance in France. It is sometimes said that the French edition did not do well until the translation became a best seller in the

United States, after which it enjoyed a second coming in France thanks to media accounts of Piketty's celebrity abroad. This is untrue. The book enjoyed solid sales in France from the beginning, in the tens of thousands of copies—a notable success and, given the smaller size of the French market, not at all disproportionate with its American reception. It did, however, enjoy a second surge in France in the wake of the American consecration.

Foreign sales are no guarantee of success in the American market, however. My several translations of the works of Piketty's patron Pierre Rosanvallon, a major public figure in France whose books sell there in large numbers, have not done nearly as well in the U.S. market, for example. This is perhaps because Rosanvallon's work depends on a certain familiarity with French history. His books may not "travel" as well as a work of economic history very deliberately conceived in comparative terms and aimed at a global audience—a book whose principal findings can be conveyed in a striking set of graphs and condensed to an hour's lecture. Indeed, some waspish commentators have wondered aloud how many of the book's American buyers actually read it to the end—or even beyond the beginning: The *Wall Street Journal,* relying on data collected through the Amazon Kindle e-reader, suggested that *C21* stood even lower on the "Hawking index" (a measure of the proportion of a work's pages actually read by purchasers) than the works of the celebrated physicist for whom the index was named.[11]

In any case, there were reasons to worry that the book's respectable initial performance in France might not be repeatable in the United States. In his native country Thomas Piketty already enjoyed a significant public presence, not just as an author of influential economic studies but also as a political actor. Before the 2012 French presidential elections, for example, the online news outlet *Mediapart* organized a debate about tax policy between Piketty and Socialist candidate François Hollande, who eventually became president.[12] At home, Piketty was therefore a public intellectual, but of course his prominence and identification with the social democratic left also guaranteed a hostile reception from partisan detractors on the right, exemplified by the previously cited comment dismissing him as a provincial Marxist. Because controversy sells, such antagonism might be considered a plus from a publishing standpoint. And it was safe to assume that a book arguing that inequality of both wealth and income had increased dramatically in the United States and the United Kingdom in the wake of Ronald Reagan and Margaret Thatcher would find vocal detractors among the numerous admirers of their neoliberal policies. Indeed, one of the more surprising aspects of the book's reception is that initially the most hostile reviews came from the left rather than the right, where the reaction was at first rather muted. I will come back to this point, but first I want to consider the public and political context in which the book appeared, which undoubtedly had a great deal to do with its reception.

The Political and Social Context

A plausible conjecture is that the book succeeded because it arrived at a propitious moment. The Great Recession of 2007–2009 had shattered confidence in the unregulated free market and even more in the ability of economists to understand the forces that account for the recurrent crises of the capitalist system. In 2008 Olivier Blanchard, a leading MIT economist who later became chief economist of the International Monetary Fund, felt confident in writing that "the state of macro is good."[13] Two years later he was writing about the need to rethink macro policy in a period of postcrisis recrimination and confusion.[14] Paul Krugman's presidential address to the Eastern Economic Association arraigned the profession for its failure to grasp the nature or even the possibility of a crisis of the sort that occurred in 2008.[15] Although the return of Keynes was briefly heralded in the months following the collapse of Lehman Brothers, it soon became clear that resistance to deficit spending remained strong in the political sphere and among the voting public. The armed truce between New Keynesian and New Classical macroeconomics to which Blanchard had pointed in his 2008 article collapsed with the crisis, leaving public and politicians in a quandary.

Among mainstream economists it therefore became respectable again to speak of the systemic inequities of capitalism—a theme that had become quasi-taboo in the period of neoliberal ascendancy (1980–2008), when talk of inequality was sometimes contemptuously dismissed as fomenting "class warfare" and the existence of inequality was justified as an incentive to intensified effort, innovation, and growth. Central banks responded to the worst recession since World War II by lowering interest rates, which helped to restore the value of portfolios of financial assets decimated by the crisis, yet unemployment remained stubbornly high. Banks and insurance companies benefited from public bailouts said to be necessary to prevent systemic collapse, while homeowners whose equity in their homes abruptly turned negative were left to fend for themselves. To many, it seemed that recovery was restricted to the rich, while the burdens of calamity continued to be borne by the less fortunate, who lost jobs and homes and struggled to make ends meet in straitened circumstances.

Inequality was not totally ignored in those years, however. As mentioned, Piketty was known in the United States prior to *C21* primarily as the coauthor of a series of papers he and his collaborator Emmanuel Saez published beginning in 2003 on growing income inequality in the United States.[16] This work attracted considerable attention. In particular, the authors' emphasis on the increasing disparity between the upper centile of the income distribution and the rest had achieved a sort of iconic status. The social movement known as Occupy Wall Street, which burst onto the scene in 2011, dramatized this contrast by adopting "We are the 99 percent!" as its slogan. It would be difficult to prove, however, that this slogan was directly inspired by the work of Piketty and Saez. The issue of income and wealth disparities had been raised regularly in the United States after 1980 and even before—indeed, all the way back to the inception of the republic. The increase in the ratio of CEO compensation to average worker compensation was a frequently cited statistic long before Piketty published.

Did *C21*'s expansive 250-year overview of income and wealth distribution under capitalism have any important effect on the way inequality was discussed politically? An economic cataclysm of the magnitude of the Great Recession occurs (one hopes) no more than once in a lifetime. In the wake of such an event, it is perhaps natural to want to look back at a longer arc of history in order to take stock of what is happening. But while such a turn to history may come naturally to scholars, there is reason to be skeptical that voters and pundits will react this way. Political polemicists seldom look, as Piketty does, at the long run. Voters are more likely to be moved by appeals to living memory than by comparisons to a Gilded Age most have never heard of. "Are you better off now than you were four years ago?" is a more standard political framing of "historical" time and quite possibly more effective than even the most compelling arguments about the long-term dynamics of the capitalist system.

In the months prior to the publication of *C21,* however, President Obama, seeking to articulate the themes that would define his second term, identified growing inequality in the United States as a crucial issue for the coming decade.[17] Despite slow improvement in the postrecession economy, including decreasing unemployment, concern about systemic inequities did not dissipate. In a review of *C21,* former Treasury secretary and prominent Harvard economist Larry Summers, referring to the recently renewed interest of the political class in the issue of inequality, singled out the public's persistently morose mood as the key to Piketty's warm reception: The book's success "should not be surprising," Summers wrote with retrospective certitude. "At a moment when our politics seem to be defined by a surly middle class and the President has made inequality his central economic issue, how could a book documenting the pervasive and increasing concentration of wealth and income among the top 1, .1, and .01 percent of households not attract great attention?"[18]

President Obama was not the only politician to seize on the issue of inequality in the months before the publication of *C21.* U.S. senator Elizabeth Warren also delivered a major speech on the subject, singling out growing income inequality in the United States, the subject of much of Piketty's work prior to *C21.*[19] Bill de Blasio, a progressive Democrat who won the mayoral race in New York City in 2013, had made income inequality a central theme of his candidacy.[20] It was not inequality per se that the crisis brought to the fore but rather a festering sense of injustice whose roots can be traced back to the mid-1980s, the very moment when, according to Piketty, wealth and income inequality began to increase. The Great Recession hurt both the very wealthy and the middle and lower classes, but the portfolios of the wealthy recovered quickly, whereas people who lost their homes lost them for good. It was this apparent *unfairness* that fueled political anger more than inequality as such.

The burgeoning interest in inequality was not limited to politicians but extended to the political class more generally. The Economic Policy Institute, a progressive think tank, had been pressing the issue of wage stagnation for many years (but focusing on the median wage earner rather than on the top centiles of the income distribution stressed by Piketty and Saez). In the fall of 2014, some months after the publication of *C21,* EPI's president Larry Mishel congratulated Federal Reserve chair Janet Yellen on her acknowledgment of the grave implications of growing inequality for the U.S. economy: "She deserves our applause for speaking some truths about social mobility and income inequality that are frequently overlooked.... There was no mincing of words."[21] He quoted Yellen at length: "It is no secret that the past few decades of widening inequality can be summed up as significant income and wealth gains for those at the very top and stagnant living standards for the majority. I think it is appropriate to ask whether this trend is compatible with values rooted in our nation's history, among them the high value Americans have traditionally placed on equality of opportunity."

Yellen's words hint at a concern that reaches beyond the numbers and charts—a concern that no doubt plagued the minds of noneconomists as well as the chair of the Federal Reserve. Her mention of deeply rooted American values suggests profound anxiety about a possible connection between increased inequality and reduced social mobility. In 2012 Alan Krueger, chair of the Council of Economic Advisers, gave a speech in which he called attention to an apparent inverse relationship between inequality (as measured by the Gini coefficient) and social mobility: the greater the inequality, the lower the social mobility. This relationship was soon dubbed "the Great Gatsby curve" and widely publicized.[22]

In short, the political context in early 2014 was favorable to a book that would describe how wealth and income distributions had changed and explain a phenomenon about which both ordinary citizens and political leaders had begun to express anxiety and perplexity. Democracy is imperiled if a substantial segment of the population comes to feel that it is condemned to permanent underclass status, barred from upward social mobility. The opportunity for advancement through education has traditionally been a touchstone of American democracy.

Of course, the perception that social mobility has decreased in recent years may not be accurate. The joint work of Raj Chetty with Piketty's collaborator Emmanuel Saez and others suggests that popular perceptions in this regard may be overstated. The perception nevertheless exists, possibly because increased income inequality magnifies the consequences of social stasis.[23] Indeed, worries about social mobility—especially *downward* mobility—are a source of particular anxiety among elements of precisely that group whose relatively high standing in the income distribution can be attributed to its educational success and to the expanded opportunities for educated workers that opened up in the postwar decades. Piketty calls this group "the patrimonial middle class," which consists of the upper one or two deciles of the income distribution. Many in this group enjoy substantially higher relative incomes than their parents, and possess and will pass on to their children substantially greater wealth. I would hazard a guess— difficult to support in the absence of statistical evidence but nevertheless plausible—that the lion's share of readers of Piketty's book belong to this group.

One other crucial point about the state of public opinion in the United States at the time the book appeared: In the minds of many Americans, the Supreme Court's decision in the *Citizens United* case opened the floodgates to the influence of money in politics. The potential power of concentrated wealth to distort the democratic political process is one of Piketty's underlying themes, although it remains somewhat underdeveloped in the book. Piketty implies that such influence is responsible for the transformation of the United States from a regime of steeply progressive income and estate taxes to one of low marginal tax rates on even the highest incomes. This transformation then creates incentives for top managers to seek larger and larger compensation packages and enables them to accumulate the excess income in the form of transmissible assets, thus allowing "the past to devour the future," as Piketty puts it in one of his most memorable lines. Yet if, as I surmise, the readership of Piketty's book is drawn largely from the ranks of the patrimonial middle class, there is something somewhat paradoxical about this theme, because the data show that members of this group have been net beneficiaries of the increasing concentration of wealth post-1980.

The apparent paradox disappears, though, if we assume that Piketty's readers in that group are drawn from the liberal-to-progressive end of the political spectrum, that is, from the professional elements of the patrimonial middle class, who owe their status largely to educational attainment and who tend to hold liberal-to-progressive political and social values.

To be sure, the fairness of the American educational system has often been questioned. The role of elite universities as gatekeepers for the top elites in many professions is one problematic aspect of education in the United States, given that high tuitions and legacy admission preferences tend to narrow access and transform elites into self-reproducing castes.[24]

During the three decades after World War II, which Piketty singles out as a period of reduced inequality, efforts were made to broaden access to elite higher education through the use of standardized tests such as the Scholastic Aptitude Test.[25] But as inequality began to rise again after 1980, the efficacy of such remedies was diminished by the structure of the American educational system. Public schools financed by local property taxes tend to funnel educational resources into wealthier communities. Paid test-preparation courses and private coaches, to say nothing of increased reliance on private schooling by the educated upper middle class, have to some extent neutralized the steps taken to level the educational playing field after World War II, partly in response to the country's need for scientists, engineers, and other professionals with advanced degrees.

What particularly concerns members of the professional group is the increasingly visible role of extremely wealthy and extremely conservative donors in financing the right wing of the Republican Party—an effort so successful that what was once a wing has now all but devoured the party itself.

One can thus hypothesize that the more liberal / professional component of the patrimonial middle class suffers from a form of the "status anxiety" that Richard Hofstadter diagnosed in other parts of the social spectrum and in earlier eras of American history. Many patrimonial liberals owe their affluence to educational and employment opportunities that opened up in the prosperous postwar decades—opportunities they fear will not be available to their children despite the advantages that their relative wealth affords them. They particularly resent the apparent destruction of the liberal consensus—what Arthur Schlesinger called "the vital center" of American political life—by a right-wing populism financed by what Theda Skocpol and Vanessa Williamson have called "roving billionaires" and fueled by an anti-elitist, anti-intellectual animus and resentment of the shift in values stemming from the cultural revolution of the 1960s, which had an especially pronounced influence in the circles frequented by these urban professionals in their youth.[26] Hence, this group—affluent "patrimonial" liberals—might be expected to feel especially anxious about the apparently enhanced political clout of very wealthy individual donors antagonistic to their own influence on the culture, and consequently particularly receptive to Piketty's message.

Of course, Piketty's work also found a substantial readership among younger readers, especially in universities. One sign of this was the rapid emergence of "Piketty reading groups" on college campuses across the country. What motivated them was a sense that we are living in a critical moment, a social and economic turning point whose causes and implications remain obscure. What Piketty promised was insight into the predicament of the present. In a sense, what Piketty offers, rather paradoxically in view of his bleak prediction of continuing high levels of inequality, is *reassurance:* The second Gilded Age, he suggests, in many ways resembles the first, and it should therefore be possible to tame it using similar instruments, which he summarizes hopefully under the head of "democratic control of capitalism." He may be right that "this time is *not* different." Then again, he may be wrong. But both the status anxiety of the older generation and the existential anxiety of the young facing an uncertain future undoubtedly contributed to the readiness of so many to wade into the unfamiliar waters of economic history and historical econometrics.

The Critical Reception

Reviews alone cannot account for a success as phenomenal as Piketty's, but there is little doubt that good press helped to launch the book in the American market. Attention was focused on *C21* even before it was widely available. One of the first accounts of the book to appear in English was by World Bank economist and inequality expert Branko Milanovic, who reviewed the French edition of the work. Milanovic noted that Piketty went far beyond his earlier work on distributive issues to provide "a general theory of capitalism": "Piketty's unstated objective is nothing less than the unification of the theory of economic growth with the theories of functional and personal income distribution."[27] The *Economist* took note of the book's imminent appearance, declared that it would be an epoch-making work, and promised a forum in its pages once the book was out.[28] In January of 2014, several months before publication, *New York Times* writer Thomas Edsall heralded the book's coming, noting that in France it had been described as "a theoretical and political bulldozer" and asserting that it defied both "left and right orthodoxy."[29] He also noted Piketty's claim that rising inequality had nothing to do with market imperfections but was instead a consequence of free markets working exactly as proponents claimed they should. In addition, Edsall quoted Milanovic's assertion that the work was "one of the watershed books in economic thinking."

In response to the extensive attention the book was receiving prior to publication, Harvard University Press decided to advance the official publication date by one month. Most important of all in stimulating initial interest was the repeated discussion of the book by Nobel Prize–winning economist Paul Krugman, first in his blog and regular *Times* column, then in a major review in the *New York Review of Books* and in a public appearance with another Nobel economist, Joseph Stiglitz, and Piketty himself at the City University of New York. Krugman could barely contain his enthusiasm: "This analysis isn't just important, it's beautiful," he wrote on April 16, 2014. "My admiration is only reinforced by my sheer, green-eyed professional jealousy. What a book!" In his most extensive comment on the book, Krugman called the work "extremely important," adding that because of it, "we'll never talk about wealth and inequality the same way we used to."[30] Given Krugman's influence as an economist and prominence as a public intellectual, it would be difficult to overstate his contribution to the book's success.

Meanwhile, yet another Nobel economist, Robert Solow, whose growth theory influenced Piketty's analysis, reviewed the book for the *New Republic* and hailed the younger economist's "new and powerful contribution to an old topic." Solow also singled out a key feature of Piketty's analysis that, as we will see in a moment, holds particular interest for scholars from other disciplines—namely, that "it is likely that the role of inherited wealth in society will increase relative to that of recently earned and therefore merit-based income."[31]

The early publicity also led to numerous invitations for the author to speak at influential public policy forums. In a whirlwind publicity tour in mid-April 2014, just after copies of the book reached stores, Piketty spoke to a joint session of the Economic Policy Institute and the Washington Center for Equitable Growth, to the Urban Institute, and to a gathering at the International Monetary Fund in Washington. As mentioned earlier, he also met with Treasury Secretary Jack Lew. From there he went to New York, where he spoke to the United Nations, the Council on Foreign Relations, and a large audience at CUNY, where he appeared with Krugman, Stiglitz, and

Milanovic. All of these events drew considerable press coverage, which brought the book to the attention of a far larger audience than would ordinarily be aware of a work of this genre.

After New York, Piketty flew to Boston, where he spoke to the Macroeconomics Seminar at MIT (attended by about five times as many people as usually attend that forum, despite a total absence of publicity of the event), followed by an appearance at the Kennedy School of Government at Harvard, where he addressed a standing-room-only crowd to which he was introduced by former Harvard president and Treasury secretary Larry Summers. Later he appeared with Senator Elizabeth Warren in a public meeting at Faneuil Hall. Throughout this period, newspapers continued to report on the astounding sales of Piketty's new book while portraying the handsome young economist as the "rock star" of a profession more commonly regarded as a "dismal science" whose practitioners rarely attract adulatory crowds. Bookstores reported shortages, as the press found itself unprepared to meet the initial early demand. Indeed, the book sold faster than any other work published by Harvard University Press in its 102-year history—so fast that the publisher had to turn to printers in India and England to meet the unexpected demand.[32]

It would be easy to multiply examples of laudatory reviews and enthusiastic public reactions to the author. It would be a mistake, however, to regard the reception of the book as uniformly positive. Perhaps the biggest surprise among the early reactions was that the most vociferous detractors came not from the mainstream but from the left-wing heterodox camp, which might have been expected to find heartening Piketty's strictures against the mainstream's "childish passion for mathematics" and his insistence on "putting the distributional question back at the heart of economic analysis."[33] Dean Baker of the Center for Economic and Policy Research, while agreeing with Piketty that inequality had increased, insisted to the *New York Times* that the principal reason for this was "rent-seeking" by protected actors such as lawyers, doctors, financiers, and owners of intellectual property, thus undercutting Piketty's far more radical claim that inequality is a natural and predictable consequence of the operation of perfect competition in free and unfettered markets. For Baker, "a big part" of Piketty's appeal was "that it allows people to say capitalism is awful but there is nothing that we can do about it."[34]

One of the most negative reviews of Piketty came from a fellow inequality researcher, James Galbraith, who upbraided the Frenchman for preferring his own definition of capital to Marx's or Joan Robinson's, resulting, he claimed, in "terrible confusion."[35] Yet even Galbraith conceded that Piketty calls attention to a significant shift in the dynamics of wealth accumulation—namely, an "inheritance flow" as high as 15 percent of national income in some countries today. Inadvertently, he, like Solow, thus singled out one reason Piketty's work has proved attractive to scholars in other fields, such as history and sociology. It is to this aspect of the Piketty phenomenon that I turn next.

The Reception beyond Economics

One gauge of the Piketty phenomenon is the interest his work aroused among academics in disciplines outside economics. In the spring of 2012, Piketty lectured at Harvard's Center for European Studies. His talk was essentially an outline of the still-unwritten *Capital in the Twenty-First Century*. The talk attracted an audience of perhaps a hundred or so students and scholars, mainly political scientists and sociologists. Three years later, in the spring of 2015 and nearly a year after the publication of *C21*, Piketty returned to Harvard, this time at the behest of Sven Beckert, a historian engaged in "the history of capitalism," a subfield that has recently come to prominence.[36] The largest hall in the university, which holds some 1,500 people, was not enough to accommodate all the students, faculty, and members of the general public who wanted to hear Piketty speak. Many had to be turned away.

The contrast between these two events illustrates the book's effect on Piketty's reputation within the academy. Publication transformed him from an influential economist whose work on inequality brought him to the attention of a handful of researchers outside economics, in fields such as sociology and political science where questions of distributive justice had long enjoyed greater salience than within economics itself, into a public figure whose pronouncements were eagerly awaited by the educated public at large. Piketty's calls in his text for closer collaboration between economists and social scientists held an obvious appeal to a scholar like Beckert, who is attempting to reorient the direction of his own discipline at a time when economics enrollments are up and history enrollments are down.[37]

Galbraith's review, though negative, nevertheless called attention to an aspect of Piketty's work that clearly holds particular appeal for historians like Beckert who are seeking to situate the history of capitalism in the *longue durée* of modernity: an inheritance flow that, in Galbraith's words, is "astonishingly high for a factor that gets no attention at all in newspapers or textbooks."

In the wake of the financial collapse of 2008, many scholars focused on the apparent fragility of capitalist economies, on the vulnerability of the indebted and the volatility of wealth. Yet Piketty's work reminds us that capitalism, since its inception, has been remarkably resilient despite the regular recurrence of calamity.[38] His data show that, over long periods during which the composition of capital undergoes profound changes, the return on capital nevertheless varies within a fairly narrow range. Wealth accumulated in boom times may be dented by recession but is seldom completely wiped out, and even when the creative destruction emphasized by Joseph Schumpeter hollows out the value of one category of assets, adroit capitalists (or their heirs) can adjust their portfolios to take advantage of new growth strategies. Across generations, heirs respond to the emergence of new opportunities, availing themselves of resources accumulated by their forebears to maintain their dominance.

Piketty's data on inheritance flows thus strengthen the notion that patterns of class domination tend to persist over lengthy periods—a notion that had fallen into neglect with the ascendancy of neoliberal ideology in the final decades of the twentieth century. Robert Lucas, whom Paul Krugman calls "the most influential macroeconomist of his generation," declared in 2004, for instance, that "of the tendencies that are harmful to sound economics, the most seductive, and in my opinion the most poisonous, is to focus on questions of distribution."[39] By making it once again respectable to raise distributional questions and to question the redistributive efficacy of competition alone, Piketty earned the gratitude of historians aware from their own work that economists like Lucas were entirely too sanguine in their belief that the normal operation of the market sufficed to ensure that wealth and its concomitant power did not settle all too comfortably into the hands of a restricted and (to a degree) self-reproducing class of capitalists. "Poisonous" ideas may after all turn out to be true.

The *Annales,* the flagship journal of French historians, devoted an entire special issue to Piketty's work and its relation to the social sciences, "which is by no means self-evident," the editors declared in their introduction.[40] In his book Piketty rather disarmingly states that one of his reasons for returning to France from the United States, where he taught briefly at MIT, was that economics as a discipline had not achieved the hegemony there that it enjoyed in the United States. French economists, he argues, therefore took a more modest approach to social reality, eschewing the imperious and imperial ambitions of their American colleagues and engaging in more comradely investigations with their brothers and sisters in the other social sciences.

His historian colleagues seem rather less confident of the modesty of their economic colleagues' ambitions. Nicolas Delalande, for example, while praising the ambition of Piketty's work, which for him recalls the scope of nineteenth-century works on political economy, questions whether Piketty has taken full account of historical work that bears on central issues raised in his book, such as the advent of progressive taxation. He notes that progressive taxes were debated well before World War I, which Piketty takes as a turning point, and indeed were adopted in a number of countries, including Prussia, Sweden, and the United Kingdom.[41] The ultimate significance of Piketty's work will largely depend on the way in which his broad interpretation of capitalism as a global system is extended, nuanced, and perhaps challenged by the more fine-grained analyses to which Delalande calls attention.

In another contribution to the *Annales* volume, the sociologist Alexis Spire proposed "taking seriously [Piketty's] invitation . . . to treat the book not as a treatise in economics but as a contribution to the social sciences more generally."[42] He cites approvingly Piketty's definition of economics as "a subdiscipline of the social sciences, alongside history, sociology, anthropology, and political science."[43] Spire's discussion demonstrates, however, that he and other sociologists did not await the publication of *C21* to discover the importance of inequality in structuring advanced industrial societies. Indeed, Spire expresses mild surprise at the absence from Piketty's book of much discussion of "the dynamics of social movements and their ability to impose institutional and regulatory changes."[44]

Piketty's call for closer cooperation among the social sciences thus gained him a hearing among noneconomists, but it remains to be seen whether and how it will be translated into institutional and disciplinary realities. Economists and historians bring very different training and skills to bear on their subjects. If Piketty's wish is to become a reality, it must be backed by organization and resources and mutual engagement to transcending disciplinary boundaries. The risk of an immense publishing success is that the substance of the book's arguments will disappear behind ritual references to its influence, which is assumed to be enormous merely because of the magnitude of its presumed readership. There is a danger—exemplified, perhaps, by the T-shirts and baseball uniforms emblazoned with the formula $r > g$—that Piketty will become what the historian Nancy Partner calls an "iconic intellectual." Iconic status, she writes, quoting the sociologist Dominik Bartmanski, bestows "emblem value," establishing "a social theory as a brand."[45] Iconic status makes it worthwhile for scholars in other disciplines to cite, or at least gesture toward, the work of an author in support of arguments they would have made in any case, whether that author had written it or not. The sociology of inequality is a field that was flourishing well before C21 was published. Some sociologists have privately expressed suspicion that inequality was yet another realm over which economists were seeking to extend their ever-expanding hegemony. Any nascent resentment among sociologists was diminished, however, by reports that publishers, encouraged by the huge success of Piketty's book, had begun offering unprecedentedly large advances to colleagues working in the suddenly fashionable field of inequality studies.[46]

Inequality and Democracy

I have discussed the political context in which Piketty's book was received, but what can be said about its political *consequences?* As Zhou Enlai did *not* say about the French Revolution, "It's too soon to tell."[47] Although President Obama, as noted earlier, did at one point say that inequality would be the crucial political issue of coming decades, he took no specific steps to combat it, perhaps because public response to his speech was tepid at best. Various Democrats in the United States have supported increases in the minimum wage, and specific legislation to that end has been passed in some localities, such as Seattle, yet hostility to trade unions, whose role in reducing inequality in the middle of the twentieth century is clear, remains high.

Piketty's own preferred remedy for the disease he diagnosed is a global tax on capital, but even he admits that this is a utopian proposal with little prospect of concrete action in the near future. Galbraith, who thinks little enough of the book's contribution to the empirical study of inequality, thinks even less of its contribution to political analysis: "If the proposal is utopian, which is a synonym for futile, then why make it? Why spend an entire chapter on it—unless perhaps to incite the naive?"[48]

A less-jaundiced appraisal would take into account the fact that Piketty's interest in taxation derives from the fact that taxes are an instrument not only for raising revenue but also for generating information. Unsurprisingly for a dedicated empiricist, Piketty believes that in order to exert control over the economy, political actors and citizens need accurate data. For him, the tax code is a potent tool for encouraging the production of such information. But the tax authorities are not the only source of useful data. Piketty also advocates legislation to compel banks and other financial corporations to share information about depositors' assets with public authorities. And progress has been made on this front in recent years, so in this respect Piketty's proposal is neither utopian nor naive.[49]

It is true, nevertheless, that Piketty invests great hope in the power of information to galvanize broad political participation and thus reinvigorate democracy: "Information must support democratic institutions; it is not an end in itself. If democracy is someday to regain control of capitalism, it must start by recognizing that the concrete institutions in which democracy and capitalism are embodied need to be reinvented again and again."[50] Here he invokes the work of the political philosopher Jacques Rancière but neglects that of numerous historians and political scientists who have shown that if democratic institutions can exert "control" over capitalism, to use a word that Piketty favors, those same institutions can also be exploited by the owners of capital to enhance the efficiency of the system. Regulation can rein in excesses while at the same time enforcing sectoral discipline in ways that increase returns to scale and thus encourage the concentration of capital that Piketty deplores. When it comes to the regulation of the economy, the logic of collective action often favors small groups of actors with well-defined interests and the means to make those interests heard by decision makers. Information fuels technocratic management as well as democracy, and arguments over its interpretation may dampen the enthusiasm and emotion on which social movements thrive. None of this undermines Piketty's advocacy of the liberating potential of information, but his case would be more persuasive if he offered a fuller account of how he expects the kind of information he hopes to collect to be used when interests conflict.

Conclusion

Capital in the Twenty-First Century, a work of vast scope and ambition, transformed Thomas Piketty from respected economist into iconic intellectual. It is a truism that every author loses control of a work once it becomes public property. This is even truer of iconic works. The significance of *C21* no longer depends exclusively or even primarily on arguments constructed by Thomas Piketty. It has become a floating signifier to which readers and nonreaders alike are free to attach their own interpretations. This is not necessarily the happiest fate that can befall an author. He is in a sense subsumed by a social phenomenon that will forever condition responses to his subsequent thinking. It is not an easy thing to capture the world's attention as Piketty did; it may be even more difficult to escape global notoriety in order to regain the serenity essential to self-renewal.

TWO

Thomas Piketty Is Right

ROBERT M. SOLOW

Income inequality in the United States and elsewhere has been worsening since the 1970s. The most striking aspect has been the widening gap between the rich and the rest. This ominous anti-democratic trend has finally found its way into public consciousness and political rhetoric. A rational and effective policy for dealing with it—if there is to be one—will have to rest on an understanding of the causes of increasing inequality. The discussion so far has turned up a number of causal factors: the erosion of the real minimum wage; the decay of labor unions and collective bargaining; globalization and intensified competition from low-wage workers in poor countries; technological changes and shifts in demand that eliminate mid-level jobs and leave the labor market polarized between the highly educated and skilled at the top and the mass of poorly educated and unskilled at the bottom.

Each of these candidate causes seems to capture a bit of the truth. But even taken together they do not seem to provide a thoroughly satisfactory picture. They have at least two deficiencies. First, they do not speak to the really dramatic issue: the tendency for the very top incomes—the "1 percent"—to pull away from the rest of society. Second, they seem a little adventitious, accidental; whereas a forty-year trend common to the advanced economies of the United States, Europe, and Japan would be more likely to rest on some deeper forces within modern industrial capitalism. Now along comes Thomas Piketty, a forty-two-year-old French economist, to fill those gaps and then some. I had a friend, a distinguished algebraist, whose preferred adjective of praise was "serious." "Z is a serious mathematician," he would say, or "Now that is a serious painting." Well, this is a serious book.

It is also a long book: 577 pages of closely printed text and seventy-seven pages of notes. (I call down a painful pox on publishers who put the footnotes at the end of the book instead of the bottom of the page where they belong, thus making sure that readers like me will skip many of them.) There is also an extensive "technical appendix" available online that contains tables of data, mathematical arguments, references to the literature, and links to class notes for Piketty's (evidently excellent) lecture course in Paris. The English translation by Arthur Goldhammer reads very well.

Piketty's strategy is to start with a panoramic reading of the data across space and time, and then work out from there. He and a group of associates, most notably Emmanuel Saez, another young French economist, a professor at Berkeley, and Anthony B. Atkinson of Oxford, the pioneer and gray eminence of modern inequality studies, have labored hard to compile an enormous database that is still being extended and refined. It provides the empirical foundation for Piketty's argument.

It all begins with the time path of total—private and public—wealth (or capital) in France, the United Kingdom, and the United States, going back to whenever data first become available and running up to the present. Germany, Japan, and Sweden, and less frequently other countries, are included in the database when satisfactory statistics exist. If you are wondering why a book about inequality should begin by measuring total wealth, just wait.

Since comparisons over vast stretches of time and space are the essence, there is a problem about finding comparable units in which to measure total wealth or capital in, say, France in 1850 as well as in the United States in 1950. Piketty solves this problem by dividing wealth measured in local currency of the time by national income, also measured in local currency of the time. The wealth-income ratio then has the dimension "years." The comparison just mentioned says in fact that total wealth in France in 1850 amounted to about seven years worth of income, but only about four years for the United States in 1950. This visualization of national wealth or capital as relative to national income is basic to the whole enterprise. Reference to the capital-output or capital-income ratio is commonplace in economics. Get used to it.

There is a small ambiguity here. Piketty uses "wealth" and "capital" as interchangeable terms. We know how to calculate the wealth of a person or an institution: you add up the value of all its assets and subtract the total of debts. (The values are market prices or, in their absence, some approximation.) The result is net worth or wealth. In English at least, this is often called a person's or institution's capital. But "capital" has another, not quite equivalent, meaning: it is a "factor of production," an essential input into the production process, in the form of factories, machinery, computers, office buildings, or houses (that produce "housing services"). This meaning can diverge from "wealth." Trivially, there are assets that have value and are part of wealth but do not produce anything: works of art, hoards of precious metals, and so forth. (Paintings hanging in a living room could be said to produce "aesthetic services," but those are not generally counted in national income.) More significantly, stock market values, the financial counterpart of corporate productive capital, can fluctuate violently, more violently than national income. In a recession, the wealth-income ratio may fall noticeably, although the stock of productive capital, and even its expected future earning power, may have changed very little or not at all. But as long as we stick to longer-run trends, as Piketty generally does, this difficulty can safely be disregarded.

The data then exhibit a clear pattern. In France and Great Britain, national capital stood fairly steadily at about seven times national income from 1700 to 1910, then fell sharply from 1910 to 1950, presumably as a result of wars and depression, reaching a low of 2.5 in Britain and a bit less than 3 in France. The capital-income ratio then began to climb in both countries, and reached slightly more than 5 in Britain and slightly less than 6 in France by 2010. The trajectory in the United States was slightly different: it started at just above 3 in 1770, climbed to 5 in 1910, fell slightly in 1920, recovered to a high between 5 and 5.5 in 1930, fell to below 4 in 1950, and was back to 4.5 in 2010.

The wealth-income ratio in the United States has always been lower than in Europe. The main reason in the early years was that land values bulked less in the wide open spaces of North America. There was of course much more land, but it was very cheap. Into the twentieth century and onward, however, the lower capital-income ratio in the United States probably reflects the higher level of productivity: a given amount of capital could support a larger production of output than in Europe. It is no surprise that the two world wars caused much less destruction and dissipation of capital in the United States than in Britain and France. The important observation for Piketty's argument is that, in all three countries, and elsewhere as well, the wealth-income ratio has been increasing since 1950, and is almost back to nineteenth-century levels. He projects this increase to continue into the current century, with weighty consequences that will be discussed as we go on.

≡ΙΙ≡

In fact he predicts, without much confidence and without kidding himself, that the world capital-income ratio will rise from just under 4.5 in 2010 to just over 6.5 by the end of this century. That would bring the whole world back to where a few rich countries of Europe were in the nineteenth century. Where does this guess come from? Or, more generally, what determines an economy's long-run capital-income ratio anyway? This is a question that has been studied by economists for some seventy-five years. They have converged on a standard answer that Piketty adopts as a long-run economic "law." In rough outline it goes like this.

Imagine an economy with a national income of 100, growing at 2 percent a year (perhaps with occasional hiccups, to be ignored). Suppose it regularly saves and invests (that is, adds to its capital) 10 percent of national income. So, in the year in which its income reaches 100 it adds 10 to its stock of capital. We want to know if the capital-income ratio can stay unchanged for next year, that is to say, can stabilize for the long run. For that to happen, the numerator of the capital-income ratio must grow at the same 2 percent rate as the denominator. We have already said that it grows by 10; for that to be 2 percent of capital, capital must have been 500, no more, no less. We have found a consistent story: this year national income is 100, capital is 500, and the ratio is 5. Next year national income is 102, capital is 510, the ratio is still 5, and this process can repeat itself automatically as long as the growth rate stays at 2 percent a year and the saving/investment rate is 10 percent of national income. Something more dramatic is true: if capital and labor combine to produce national output according to the good old law of diminishing returns, then wherever this economy starts, it will be driven by its own internal logic to this unique self-reproducing capital-income ratio.

Careful attention to this example will show that it amounts to a general statement: if the economy is growing at g percent per year, and if it saves s percent of its national income each year, the self-reproducing capital-income ratio is s/g ($10/2$ in the example). Piketty suggests that global growth of output will slow in the coming century from 3 percent to 1.5 percent annually. (This is the sum of the growth rates of population and productivity, both of which he expects to diminish.) He puts the world saving/investment rate at about 10 percent. So he expects the capital-income ratio to climb eventually to something near 7 (or 10/1.5). This is a big deal, as will emerge. He is quite aware that the underlying assumptions could turn out to be wrong; no one can see a century ahead. But it could plausibly go this way.

≡ΙΙ≡

The key thing about wealth in a capitalist economy is that it reproduces itself and usually earns a positive net return. That is the next thing to be investigated. Piketty develops estimates of the "pure" rate of return (after minor adjustments) in Britain going back to 1770 and in France going back to 1820, but not for the United States. He concludes: "[T]he pure return on capital has oscillated around a central value of 4–5 percent a year, or more generally in an interval from 3–6 percent a year. There has been no pronounced long-term trend either upward or downward.... It is possible, however, that the pure return on capital has decreased slightly over the very long run." It would be interesting to have comparable figures for the United States.

Now if you multiply the rate of return on capital by the capital-income ratio, you get the share of capital in the national income. For example, if the rate of return is 5 percent a year and the stock of capital is six years worth of national income, income from capital will be 30 percent of national income, and so income from work will be the remaining 70 percent. At last, after all this preparation, we are beginning to talk about inequality, and in two distinct senses. First, we have arrived at the functional distribution of income—the split between income from work and income from wealth. Second, it is always the case that wealth is more highly concentrated among the rich than income from labor (although recent American history looks rather odd in this respect); and this being so, the larger the share of income from wealth, the more unequal the distribution of income among persons is likely to be. It is this inequality across persons that matters most for good or ill in a society.

This is often not well understood, and may be worth a brief digression. The labor share of national income is arithmetically the same thing as the real wage divided by the productivity of labor. Would you rather live in a society in which the real wage was rising rapidly but the labor share was falling (because productivity was increasing even faster), or one in which the real wage was stagnating, along with productivity, so the labor share was unchanging? The first is surely better on narrowly economic grounds: you eat your wage, not your share of national income. But there could be political and social advantages to the second option. If a small class of owners of wealth—and it is small—comes to collect a growing share of the national income, it is likely to dominate the society in other ways as well. This dichotomy need not arise, but it is good to be clear.

Suppose we accept Piketty's educated guess that the capital-income ratio will increase over the next century before stabilizing at a high value somewhere around 7. Does it follow that the capital share of income will also get bigger? Not necessarily: remember that we have to multiply the capital-income ratio by the rate of return, and that same law of diminishing returns suggests that the rate of return on capital will fall. As production becomes more and more capital-intensive, it gets harder and harder to find profitable uses for additional capital, or easy ways to substitute capital for labor. Whether the capital share falls or rises depends on whether the rate of return has to fall proportionally more or less than the capital-income ratio rises.

There has been a lot of research around this question within economics, but no definitely conclusive answer has emerged. This suggests that the ultimate effect on the capital share, whichever way it goes, will be small. Piketty opts for an increase in the capital share, and I am inclined to agree with him. Productivity growth has been running ahead of real wage growth in the American economy for the last few decades, with no sign of a reversal, so the capital share has risen and the labor share fallen. Perhaps the capital share will go from about 30 percent to about 35 percent, with whatever challenge to democratic culture and politics that entails.

≣∥≣

There is a stronger implication of this line of argument, and with it we come to the heart of Piketty's case. So far as I know, no one before him has made this connection. Remember what has been established so far. Both history and theory suggest that there is a slow tendency in an industrial capitalist economy for the capital-income ratio to stabilize, and with it the rate of return on capital. This tendency can be disturbed by severe depressions, wars, and social and technological disruptions, but it reasserts itself in tranquil conditions. Over the long span of history surveyed by Piketty, the rate of return on capital is usually larger than the underlying rate of growth. The only substantial exceptional sub-period is between 1910 and 1950. Piketty ascribes this rarity to the disruption and high taxation caused by the two great wars and the depression that came between them.

There is no logical necessity for the rate of return to exceed the growth rate: a society or the individuals in it can decide to save and to invest so much that they (and the law of diminishing returns) drive the rate of return below the long-term growth rate, whatever that happens to be. It is known that this possible state of affairs is socially perverse in the sense that letting the stock of capital diminish until the rate of return falls back to equality with the growth rate would allow for a permanently higher level of consumption per person, and thus for a better social state. But there is no invisible hand to steer a market economy away from this perversity. Yet it has been avoided, probably because historical growth rates have been low and capital has been scarce. We can take it as normal that the rate of return on capital exceeds the underlying growth rate.

But now we can turn our attention to what is happening within the economy. Suppose it has reached a "steady state" when the capital-income ratio has stabilized. Those whose income comes entirely from work can expect their wages and incomes to be rising about as fast as productivity is increasing through technological progress. That is a little less than the overall growth rate, which also includes the rate of population increase. Now imagine someone whose income comes entirely from accumulated wealth. He or she earns r percent a year. (I am ignoring taxes, but not for long.) If she is very wealthy, she is likely to consume only a small fraction of her income. The rest is saved and accumulated, and her wealth will increase by almost r percent each year, and so will her income. If you leave $100 in a bank account paying 3 percent interest, your balance will increase by 3 percent each year.

This is Piketty's main point, and his new and powerful contribution to an old topic: as long as the rate of return exceeds the rate of growth, the income and wealth of the rich will grow faster than the typical income from work. (There seems to be no offsetting tendency for the aggregate share of capital to shrink; the tendency may be slightly in the opposite direction.) This interpretation of the observed trend toward increasing inequality, and especially the phenomenon of the 1 percent, is not rooted in any failure of economic institutions; it rests primarily on the ability of the economy to absorb increasing amounts of capital without a substantial fall in the rate of return. This may be good news for the economy as a whole, but it is not good news for equity within the economy.

We need a name for this process for future reference. I will call it the "rich-get-richer dynamic." The mechanism is a little more complicated than Piketty's book lets on. There is some saving from labor income, and thus some accumulation of capital in the hands of wage and salary earners. The return on this wealth has to be taken into account. Still, given the small initial wealth and the relatively low saving rate below the top group, as well as the fact that small savings earn a relatively low rate of return, calculation shows that this mechanism is not capable of offsetting the forecast of widening inequality.

There is yet another, also rather dark, implication of this account of underlying trends. If already existing agglomerations of wealth tend to grow faster than incomes from work, it is likely that the role of inherited wealth in society will increase relative to that of recently earned and therefore more merit-based fortunes. Needless to say, the fact that the aggregate of wage incomes grows only at a relatively slow rate does not exclude the possibility that outstandingly successful innovators, managers, entrepreneurs, entertainers, and others can accumulate large amounts of wealth in a lifetime and join the ranks of the rentiers. But a slower rate of growth certainly makes such success stories less likely. There will be more to say about this. Yet the arithmetic suggests that the concentration of wealth and its ability to grow will favor an increasing weight of inheritance as compared with talent.

Piketty likes to describe the distribution of income and wealth concretely, and not in terms of summary statistics. He looks at the proportions of the total claimed by the top 1 percent (sometimes also the top tenth of the 1 percent), the top 10 percent, the next 40 percent, and the bottom half. (He labels the 40 percent between the top decile and the median as the "middle class." There is an element of oxymoron in a middle class that lies entirely above the median; but I suppose this usage is no worse than the American habit of describing everyone between the clearly rich and the abjectly poor as being in the middle class.)

The data are complicated and not easily comparable across time and space, but here is the flavor of Piketty's summary picture. Capital is indeed very unequally distributed. Currently in the United States, the top 10 percent own about 70 percent of all the capital, half of that belonging to the top 1 percent; the next 40 percent—who compose the "middle class"—own about a quarter of the total (much of that in the form of housing), and the remaining half of the population owns next to nothing, about 5 percent of total wealth. Even that amount of middle-class property ownership is a new phenomenon in history. The typical European country is a little more egalitarian: the top 1 percent own 25 percent of the total capital, and the middle class 35 percent. (A century ago the European middle class owned essentially no wealth at all.) If the ownership of wealth in fact becomes even more concentrated during the rest of the twenty-first century, the outlook is pretty bleak unless you have a taste for oligarchy.

Income from wealth is probably even more concentrated than wealth itself because, as Piketty notes, large blocks of wealth tend to earn a higher return than small ones. Some of this advantage comes from economies of scale, but more may come from the fact that very big investors have access to a wider range of investment opportunities than smaller investors. Income from work is naturally less concentrated than income from wealth. In Piketty's stylized picture of the United States today, the top 1 percent earns about 12 percent of all labor income, the next 9 percent earn 23 percent, the middle class gets about 40 percent, and the bottom half about a quarter of income from work. Europe is not very different: the top 10 percent collect somewhat less and the other two groups a little more.

＝Ⅱ＝

You get the picture: modern capitalism is an unequal society, and the rich-get-richer dynamic strongly suggests that it will get more so. But there is one more loose end to tie up, already hinted at, and it has to do with the advent of very high wage incomes. First, here are some facts about the composition of top incomes. About 60 percent of the income of the top 1 percent in the United States today is labor income. Only when you get to the top tenth of 1 percent does income from capital start to predominate. The income of the top hundredth of 1 percent is 70 percent from capital. The story for France is not very different, though the proportion of labor income is a bit higher at every level. Evidently there are some very high wage incomes, as if you didn't know.

This is a fairly recent development. In the 1960s, the top 1 percent of wage earners collected a little more than 5 percent of all wage incomes. This fraction has risen pretty steadily until nowadays, when the top 1 percent of wage earners receive 10–12 percent of all wages. This time the story is rather different in France. There the share of total wages going to the top percentile was steady at 6 percent until very recently, when it climbed to 7 percent. The recent surge of extreme inequality at the top of the wage distribution may be primarily an American development. Piketty, who with Emmanuel Saez has made a careful study of high-income tax returns in the United States, attributes this to the rise of what he calls "supermanagers." The very highest income class consists to a substantial extent of top executives of large corporations, with very rich compensation packages. (A disproportionate number of these, but by no means all of them, come from the financial services industry.) With or without stock options, these large pay packages get converted to wealth and future income from wealth. But the fact remains that much of the increased income (and wealth) inequality in the United States is driven by the rise of these supermanagers.

There is not much understanding of this phenomenon, and this book has little to add. Piketty is of course aware that executive pay at the very top is usually determined in a cozy way by boards of directors and compensation committees made up of people very like the executives they are paying. There is certainly an element of the Lake Wobegon illusion: every board wants to believe that "its" high executives are better than the median and deserve to be paid more than the median.

It is of course possible that "supermanagers" really are supermanagers, and their very high pay merely reflects their very large contributions to corporate profits. It is even possible that their increased dominance since the 1960s has an identifiable cause along that line. This explanation would be harder to maintain if the phenomenon turns out to be uniquely American. It does not occur in France or, on casual observation, in Germany or Japan. Can their top executives lack a certain gene? If so, it would be a fruitful field for transplants.

Another possibility, tempting but still rather vague, is that top management compensation, at least some of it, does not really belong in the category of labor income, but represents instead a sort of adjunct to capital, and should be treated in part as a way of sharing in income from capital. There is a puzzle here whose solution would shed some light on the recent increase in inequality at the top of the pyramid in the United States. The puzzle may not be soluble because the variety of circumstances and outcomes is just too large.

≡ǁ≡

In any case, it is pretty clear that the class of supermanagers belongs socially and politically with the rentiers, not with the larger body of salaried and independent professionals and middle managers. So Piketty's foreboding vision of the twenty-first century remains to be dealt with: slower growth of population and productivity, a rate of return on capital distinctly higher than the growth rate, the wealth-income ratio rising back to nineteenth-century heights, probably a somewhat higher capital share in national income, an increasing dominance of inherited wealth over earned wealth, and a still wider gap between the top incomes and all the others. Maybe a little skepticism is in order. For instance, the historically fairly stable long-run rate of return has been the balanced outcome of a tension between diminishing returns and technological progress; perhaps a slower rate of growth in the future will pull the rate of return down drastically. Perhaps. But suppose that Piketty is on the whole right. What, if anything, is to be done?

Piketty's strong preference is for an annual progressive tax on wealth, worldwide if possible, to exclude flight to phony tax havens. He recognizes that a global tax is a hopeless goal, but he thinks that it is possible to enforce a regional wealth tax in an area the size of Europe or the United States. An example of the sort of rate schedule that he has in mind is 0 percent on fortunes below one million euros, 1 percent on fortunes between one and five million euros, and 2 percent above five million euros. (A euro is currently worth about $1.37.) Remember that this is an annual tax, not a onetime levy. He estimates that such a tax applied in the European Union would generate revenue equal to about 2 percent of GDP, to be used or distributed according to some agreed formula. He seems to prefer, as would I, a slightly more progressive rate schedule. Of course the administration of such a tax would require a high degree of transparency and complete reporting on the part of financial institutions and other corporations. The book discusses in some detail how this might work in the European context. As with any tax, there would no doubt be a continuing struggle to close loopholes and prevent evasion, but that is par for the course.

Annual revenue of 2 percent of GDP is neither trivial nor enormous. But revenue is not the central purpose of Piketty's proposal. Its point is that it is the difference between the growth rate and the after-tax return on capital that figures in the rich-get-richer dynamic of increasing inequality. A tax on capital with a rate structure like the one suggested would diminish the gap between the rate of return and the growth rate by perhaps 1.5 percent and would weaken that mechanism perceptibly.

This proposal makes technical sense because it is a natural antidote to the dynamics of inequality that he has uncovered. Keep in mind that the rich-get-richer process is a property of the system as it operates on already accumulated wealth. It does not work through individual incentives to innovate or even to save. Blunting it would not necessarily blunt them. Of course a lower after-tax return on capital might make the accumulation of large fortunes somewhat less attractive, though even that is not at all clear. In any case, it would be a tolerable consequence.

Piketty writes as if a tax on wealth might sometime soon have political viability in Europe, where there is already some experience with capital levies. I have no opinion about that. On this side of the Atlantic, there would seem to be no serious prospect of such an outcome. We are politically unable to preserve even an estate tax with real bite. If we could, that would be a reasonable place to start, not to mention a more steeply progressive income tax that did not favor income from capital as the current system does. But the built-in tendency for the top to outpace everyone else will not yield to minor patches. Wouldn't it be interesting if the United States were to become the land of the free, the home of the brave, and the last refuge of increasing inequality at the top (and perhaps also at the bottom)? Would that work for you?

THREE

Why We're in a New Gilded Age

PAUL KRUGMAN

Thomas Piketty, professor at the Paris School of Economics, isn't a household name, although that may change with the English-language publication of his magnificent, sweeping meditation on inequality, *Capital in the Twenty-First Century.* Yet his influence runs deep. It has become a commonplace to say that we are living in a second Gilded Age—or, as Piketty likes to put it, a second Belle Époque—defined by the incredible rise of the "one percent." But it has only become a commonplace thanks to Piketty's work. In particular, he and a few colleagues (notably Anthony Atkinson at Oxford and Emmanuel Saez at Berkeley) have pioneered statistical techniques that make it possible to track the concentration of income and wealth deep into the past—back to the early twentieth century for America and Britain, and all the way to the late eighteenth century for France.

The result has been a revolution in our understanding of long-term trends in inequality. Before this revolution, most discussions of economic disparity more or less ignored the very rich. Some economists (not to mention politicians) tried to shout down any mention of inequality at all: "Of the tendencies that are harmful to sound economics, the most seductive, and in my opinion the most poisonous, is to focus on questions of distribution," declared Robert Lucas Jr. of the University of Chicago, the most influential macroeconomist of his generation, in 2004. But even those willing to discuss inequality generally focused on the gap between the poor or the working class and the merely well-off, not the truly rich—on college graduates whose wage gains outpaced those of less-educated workers, or on the comparative good fortune of the top fifth of the population compared with the bottom four fifths, not on the rapidly rising incomes of executives and bankers.

It therefore came as a revelation when Piketty and his colleagues showed that incomes of the now famous "one percent," and of even narrower groups, are actually the big story in rising inequality. And this discovery came with a second revelation: talk of a second Gilded Age, which might have seemed like hyperbole, was nothing of the kind. In America in particular the share of national income going to the top one percent has followed a great U-shaped arc. Before World War I the one percent received around a fifth of total income in both Britain and the United States. By 1950 that share had been cut by more than half. But since 1980 the one percent has seen its income share surge again—and in the United States it's back to what it was a century ago.

Still, today's economic elite is very different from that of the nineteenth century, isn't it? Back then, great wealth tended to be inherited; aren't today's economic elite people who earned their position? Well, Piketty tells us that this isn't as true as you think, and that in any case this state of affairs may prove no more durable than the middle-class society that flourished for a generation after World War II. The big idea of *Capital in the Twenty-First Century* is that we haven't just gone back to nineteenth-century levels of income inequality, we're also on a path back to "patrimonial capitalism," in which the commanding heights of the economy are controlled not by talented individuals but by family dynasties.

It's a remarkable claim—and precisely because it's so remarkable, it needs to be examined carefully and critically. Before I get into that, however, let me say right away that Piketty has written a truly superb book. It's a work that melds grand historical sweep—when was the last time you heard an economist invoke Jane Austen and Balzac?—with painstaking data analysis. And even though Piketty mocks the economics profession for its "childish passion for mathematics," underlying his discussion is a tour de force of economic modeling, an approach that integrates the analysis of economic growth with that of the distribution of income and wealth. This is a book that will change both the way we think about society and the way we do economics.

I.

What do we know about economic inequality, and about when do we know it? Until the Piketty revolution swept through the field, most of what we knew about income and wealth inequality came from surveys, in which randomly chosen households are asked to fill in a questionnaire, and their answers are tallied up to produce a statistical portrait of the whole. The international gold standard for such surveys is the annual survey conducted once a year by the Census Bureau. The Federal Reserve also conducts a triennial survey of the distribution of wealth.

These two surveys are an essential guide to the changing shape of American society. Among other things, they have long pointed to a dramatic shift in the process of U.S. economic growth, one that started around 1980. Before then, families at all levels saw their incomes grow more or less in tandem with the growth of the economy as a whole. After 1980, however, the lion's share of gains went to the top end of the income distribution, with families in the bottom half lagging far behind.

Historically, other countries haven't been equally good at keeping track of who gets what; but this situation has improved over time, in large part thanks to the efforts of the Luxembourg Income Study (with which I will soon be affiliated). And the growing availability of survey data that can be compared across nations has led to further important insights. In particular, we now know both that the United States has a much more unequal distribution of income than other advanced countries and that much of this difference in outcomes can be attributed directly to government action. European nations in general have highly unequal incomes from market activity, just like the United States, although possibly not to the same extent. But they do far more redistribution through taxes and transfers than America does, leading to much less inequality in disposable incomes.

Yet for all their usefulness, survey data have important limitations. They tend to undercount or miss entirely the income that accrues to the handful of individuals at the very top of the income scale. They also have limited historical depth. Even U.S. survey data only take us to 1947.

Enter Piketty and his colleagues, who have turned to an entirely different source of information: tax records. This isn't a new idea. Indeed, early analyses of income distribution relied on tax data because they had little else to go on. Piketty et al. have, however, found ways to merge tax data with other sources to produce information that crucially complements survey evidence. In particular, tax data tell us a great deal about the elite. And tax-based estimates can reach much further into the past: the United States has had an income tax since 1913, Britain since 1909. France, thanks to elaborate

TABLE 3-1.

Income shares

	Low Inequality (Scandinavia 1970s / 1980s)	Medium Inequality (Europe 2010)	High Inequality (Europe 1910, U.S. 2010)
Top 1%	7%	10%	20%
Next 9%	18%	25%	30%
Next 40%	45%	40%	30%
Bottom 50%	30%	25%	20%

estate tax collection and record-keeping, has wealth data reaching back to the late eighteenth century.

Exploiting these data isn't simple. But by using all the tricks of the trade, plus some educated guesswork, Piketty is able to produce a summary of the fall and rise of extreme inequality over the course of the past century. It looks like Table 3-1. . . .

As I said, describing our current era as a new Gilded Age or Belle Époque isn't hyperbole; it's the simple truth. But how did this happen?

2.

Piketty throws down the intellectual gauntlet right away, with his book's very title: *Capital in the Twenty-First Century.* Are economists still allowed to talk like that?

It's not just the obvious allusion to Marx that makes this title so startling. By invoking capital right from the beginning, Piketty breaks ranks with most modern discussions of inequality, and hearkens back to an older tradition.

The general presumption of most inequality researchers has been that earned income, usually salaries, is where all the action is, and that income from capital is neither important nor interesting. Piketty shows, however, that even today income from capital, not earnings, predominates at the top of the income distribution. He also shows that in the past—during Europe's Belle Époque and, to a lesser extent, America's Gilded Age—unequal ownership of assets, not unequal pay, was the prime driver of income disparities. And he argues that we're on our way back to that kind of society. Nor is this casual speculation on his part. For all that *Capital in the Twenty-First Century* is a work of principled empiricism, it is very much driven by a theoretical frame that attempts to unify discussion of economic growth and the distribution of both income and wealth. Basically, Piketty sees economic history as the story of a race between capital accumulation and other factors driving growth, mainly population growth and technological progress.

To be sure, this is a race that can have no permanent victor: over the very long run, the stock of capital and total income must grow at roughly the same rate. But one side or the other can pull ahead for decades at a time. On the eve of World War I, Europe had accumulated capital worth six or seven times national income. Over the next four decades, however, a combination of physical destruction and the diversion of savings into war efforts cut that ratio in half. Capital accumulation resumed after World War II, but this was a period of spectacular economic growth—the *Trente Glorieuses,* or "Glorious Thirty" years; so the ratio of capital to income remained low. Since the 1970s, however, slowing growth has meant a rising capital ratio, so capital and wealth have been trending steadily back toward Belle Époque levels. And this accumulation of capital, says Piketty, will eventually recreate Belle Époque–style inequality unless opposed by progressive taxation.

Why? It's all about r versus g—the rate of return on capital versus the rate of economic growth.

Just about all economic models tell us that if g falls—which it has since 1970, a decline that is likely to continue due to slower growth in the working-age population and slower technological progress—r will fall too. But Piketty asserts that r will fall less than g. This doesn't have to be true. However, if it's sufficiently easy to replace workers with machines—if, to use the technical jargon, the elasticity of substitution between capital and labor is greater than one—slow growth, and the resulting rise in the ratio of capital to income, will indeed widen the gap between r and g. And Piketty argues that this is what the historical record shows will happen.

If he's right, one immediate consequence will be a redistribution of income away from labor and toward holders of capital. The conventional wisdom has long been that we needn't worry about that happening, that the shares of capital and labor respectively in total income are highly stable over time. Over the very long run, however, this hasn't been true. In Britain, for example, capital's share of income—whether in the form of corporate profits, dividends, rents, or sales of property, for example—fell from around 40 percent before World War I to barely 20 percent circa 1970, and has since bounced roughly halfway back. The historical arc is less clear-cut in the United States, but here, too, there is a redistribution in favor of capital underway. Notably, corporate profits have soared since the financial crisis began, while wages—including the wages of the highly educated—have stagnated.

A rising share of capital, in turn, directly increases inequality, because ownership of capital is always much more unequally distributed than labor income. But the effects don't stop there, because when the rate of return on capital greatly exceeds the rate of economic growth, "the past tends to devour the future": society inexorably tends toward dominance by inherited wealth.

Consider how this worked in Belle Époque Europe. At the time, owners of capital could expect to earn 4–5 percent on their investments, with minimal taxation; meanwhile economic growth was only around one percent. So wealthy individuals could easily reinvest enough of their income to ensure that their wealth and hence their incomes were growing faster than the economy, reinforcing their economic dominance, even while skimming enough off to live lives of great luxury.

And what happened when these wealthy individuals died? They passed their wealth on—again, with minimal taxation—to their heirs. Money passed on to the next generation accounted for 20 to 25 percent of annual income; the great bulk of wealth, around 90 percent, was inherited rather than saved out of earned income. And this inherited wealth was concentrated in the hands of a very small minority: in 1910 the richest one percent controlled 60 percent of the wealth in France; in Britain, 70 percent.

No wonder, then, that nineteenth-century novelists were obsessed with inheritance. Piketty discusses at length the lecture that the scoundrel Vautrin gives to Rastignac in Balzac's *Père Goriot,* whose gist is that a most successful career could not possibly deliver more than a fraction of the wealth Rastignac could acquire at a stroke by marrying a rich man's daughter. And it turns out that Vautrin was right: being in the top one percent of nineteenth-century heirs and simply living off your inherited wealth gave you around

AFTER-TAX RATE OF RETURN VS. GROWTH RATE
AT THE WORLD LEVEL, FROM ANTIQUITY UNTIL 2100

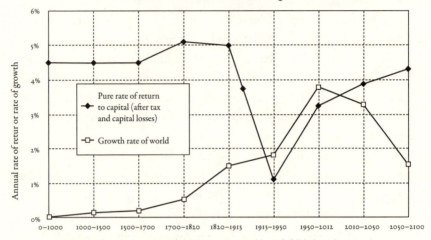

The rate of return to capital (after tax and capital losses) fell below the growth rate
during the twentieth century, and may again surpass it in the twenty-first century

FIGURE 3-1: After-tax rate of return vs. growth rate at the world level, from antiquity
until 2100.

Sources and series: See piketty.pse.ens.fr/capital21c.

two and a half times the standard of living you could achieve by clawing
your way into the top one percent of paid workers.

You might be tempted to say that modern society is nothing like that.
In fact, however, both capital income and inherited wealth, though less
important than they were in the Belle Époque, are still powerful drivers of
inequality—and their importance is growing. In France, Piketty shows, the
inherited share of total wealth dropped sharply during the era of wars and
postwar fast growth; circa 1970 it was less than 50 percent. But it's now back
up to 70 percent, and rising. Correspondingly, there has been a fall and then
a rise in the importance of inheritance in conferring elite status: the living
standard of the top one percent of heirs fell below that of the top one
percent of earners between 1910 and 1950, but began rising again after 1970.
It's not all the way back to Rastignac levels, but once again it's generally
more valuable to have the right parents (or to marry into having the right
in-laws) than to have the right job.

And this may only be the beginning. Figure 3-1 shows Piketty's estimates
of global *r* and *g* over the long haul, suggesting that the era of equalization

now lies behind us, and that the conditions are now ripe for the reestablishment of patrimonial capitalism.

Given this picture, why does inherited wealth play as small a part in today's public discourse as it does? Piketty suggests that the very size of inherited fortunes in a way makes them invisible: "Wealth is so concentrated that a large segment of society is virtually unaware of its existence, so that some people imagine that it belongs to surreal or mysterious entities." This is a very good point. But it's surely not the whole explanation. For the fact is that the most conspicuous example of soaring inequality in today's world—the rise of the very rich one percent in the Anglo-Saxon world, especially the United States—doesn't have all that much to do with capital accumulation, at least so far. It has more to do with remarkably high compensation and incomes.

3.

Capital in the Twenty-First Century is, as I hope I've made clear, an awesome work. At a time when the concentration of wealth and income in the hands of a few has resurfaced as a central political issue, Piketty doesn't just offer invaluable documentation of what is happening, with unmatched historical depth. He also offers what amounts to a unified field theory of inequality, one that integrates economic growth, the distribution of income between capital and labor, and the distribution of wealth and income among individuals into a single frame.

And yet there is one thing that slightly detracts from the achievement—a sort of intellectual sleight of hand, albeit one that doesn't actually involve any deception or malfeasance on Piketty's part. Still, here it is: the main reason there has been a hankering for a book like this is the rise, not just of the one percent, but specifically of the American one percent. Yet that rise, it turns out, has happened for reasons that lie beyond the scope of Piketty's grand thesis.

Piketty is, of course, too good and too honest an economist to try to gloss over inconvenient facts. "US inequality in 2010," he declares, "is quantitatively as extreme as in old Europe in the first decade of the twentieth century, but the structure of that inequality is rather clearly different." Indeed, what we have seen in America and are starting to see elsewhere is something "radically new"—the rise of "supersalaries."

Capital still matters; at the very highest reaches of society, income from capital still exceeds income from wages, salaries, and bonuses. Piketty estimates that the increased inequality of capital income accounts for about a third of the overall rise in U.S. inequality. But wage income at the top has also surged. Real wages for most U.S. workers have increased little if at all since the early 1970s, but wages for the top one percent of earners have risen 165 percent, and wages for the top 0.1 percent have risen 362 percent. If Rastignac were alive today, Vautrin might concede that he could in fact do as well by becoming a hedge fund manager as he could by marrying wealth.

What explains this dramatic rise in earnings inequality, with the lion's share of the gains going to people at the very top? Some U.S. economists suggest that it's driven by changes in technology. In a famous 1981 paper titled "The Economics of Superstars," the Chicago economist Sherwin Rosen argued that modern communications technology, by extending the reach of talented individuals, was creating winner-take-all markets in which a handful of exceptional individuals reap huge rewards, even if they're only modestly better at what they do than far less well paid rivals.

Piketty is unconvinced. As he notes, conservative economists love to talk about the high pay of performers of one kind or another, such as movie and sports stars, as a way of suggesting that high incomes really are deserved. But such people actually make up only a tiny fraction of the earnings elite. What one finds instead is mainly executives of one sort or another—people whose performance is, in fact, quite hard to assess or give a monetary value to.

Who determines what a corporate CEO is worth? Well, there's normally a compensation committee, appointed by the CEO himself. In effect, Piketty argues, high-level executives set their own pay, constrained by social norms rather than any sort of market discipline. And he attributes skyrocketing pay at the top to an erosion of these norms. In effect, he attributes soaring wage incomes at the top to social and political rather than strictly economic forces.

Now, to be fair, he then advances a possible economic analysis of changing norms, arguing that falling tax rates for the rich have in effect emboldened the earnings elite. When a top manager could expect to keep only a small fraction of the income he might get by flouting social norms and extracting a very large salary, he might have decided that the opprobrium wasn't worth it. Cut his marginal tax rate drastically, and he may behave differently. And as more and more of the supersalaried flout the norms, the norms themselves will change.

There's a lot to be said for this diagnosis, but it clearly lacks the rigor and universality of Piketty's analysis of the distribution of and returns to wealth. Also, I don't think *Capital in the Twenty-First Century* adequately answers the most telling criticism of the executive power hypothesis: the concentration of very high incomes in finance, where performance actually can, after a fashion, be evaluated. I didn't mention hedge fund managers idly: such people are paid based on their ability to attract clients and achieve investment returns. You can question the social value of modern finance, but the Gordon Gekkos out there are clearly good at something, and their rise can't be attributed solely to power relations, although I guess you could argue that willingness to engage in morally dubious wheeling and dealing, like willingness to flout pay norms, is encouraged by low marginal tax rates.

Overall, I'm more or less persuaded by Piketty's explanation of the surge in wage inequality, though his failure to include deregulation is a significant disappointment. But as I said, his analysis here lacks the rigor of his capital analysis, not to mention its sheer, exhilarating intellectual elegance.

Yet we shouldn't overreact to this. Even if the surge in U.S. inequality to date has been driven mainly by wage income, capital has nonetheless been significant too. And in any case, the story looking forward is likely to be quite different. The current generation of the very rich in America may consist largely of executives rather than rentiers, people who live off accumulated capital, but these executives have heirs. And America two decades from now could be a rentier-dominated society even more unequal than Belle Époque Europe.

But this doesn't have to happen.

4.

At times, Piketty almost seems to offer a deterministic view of history, in which everything flows from the rates of population growth and technological progress. In reality, however, *Capital in the Twenty-First Century* makes it clear that public policy can make an enormous difference, that even if the underlying economic conditions point toward extreme inequality, what Piketty calls "a drift toward oligarchy" can be halted and even reversed if the body politic so chooses.

The key point is that when we make the crucial comparison between the rate of return on wealth and the rate of economic growth, what matters is the *after-tax* return on wealth. So progressive taxation—in particular taxation of wealth and inheritance—can be a powerful force limiting inequality. Indeed, Piketty concludes his masterwork with a plea for just such a form of taxation. Unfortunately, the history covered in his own book does not encourage optimism.

It's true that during much of the twentieth century strongly progressive taxation did indeed help reduce the concentration of income and wealth, and you might imagine that high taxation at the top is the natural political outcome when democracy confronts high inequality. Piketty, however, rejects this conclusion; the triumph of progressive taxation during the twentieth century, he contends, was "an ephemeral product of chaos." Absent the wars and upheavals of Europe's modern Thirty Years' War, he suggests, nothing of the kind would have happened.

As evidence, he offers the example of France's Third Republic. The Republic's official ideology was highly egalitarian. Yet wealth and income were nearly as concentrated, economic privilege almost as dominated by inheritance, as they were in the aristocratic constitutional monarchy across the English Channel. And public policy did almost nothing to oppose the economic domination by rentiers: estate taxes, in particular, were almost laughably low.

Why didn't the universally enfranchised citizens of France vote in politicians who would take on the rentier class? Well, then as now great wealth purchased great influence—not just over policies, but over public discourse. Upton Sinclair famously declared that "it is difficult to get a man to understand something when his salary depends on his not understanding it." Piketty, looking at his own nation's history, arrives at a similar observation: "The experience of France in the Belle Époque proves, if proof were needed, that no hypocrisy is too great when economic and financial elites are obliged to defend their interest."

The same phenomenon is visible today. In fact, a curious aspect of the American scene is that the politics of inequality seem if anything to be running ahead of the reality. As we've seen, at this point the U.S. economic elite owes its status mainly to wages rather than capital income. Nonetheless, conservative economic rhetoric already emphasizes and celebrates capital rather than labor—"job creators," not workers.

In 2012 Eric Cantor, the House majority leader, chose to mark Labor Day—Labor Day!—with a tweet honoring business owners:

> Today, we celebrate those who have taken a risk, worked hard, built a business and earned their own success.

Perhaps chastened by the reaction, he reportedly felt the need to remind his colleagues at a subsequent GOP retreat that most people don't own their own businesses—but this in itself shows how thoroughly the party identifies itself with capital to the virtual exclusion of labor.

Nor is this orientation toward capital just rhetorical. Tax burdens on high-income Americans have fallen across the board since the 1970s, but the biggest reductions have come on capital income—including a sharp fall in corporate taxes, which indirectly benefits stockholders—and inheritance. Sometimes it seems as if a substantial part of our political class is actively working to restore Piketty's patrimonial capitalism. And if you look at the sources of political donations, many of which come from wealthy families, this possibility is a lot less outlandish than it might seem.

Piketty ends *Capital in the Twenty-First Century* with a call to arms—a call, in particular, for wealth taxes, global if possible, to restrain the growing power of inherited wealth. It's easy to be cynical about the prospects for anything of the kind. But surely Piketty's masterly diagnosis of where we are and where we're heading makes such a thing considerably more likely. So *Capital in the Twenty-First Century* is an extremely important book on all fronts. Piketty has transformed our economic discourse; we'll never talk about wealth and inequality the same way we used to.

[II]

CONCEPTIONS
OF CAPITAL

FOUR

What's Wrong with Capital in the Twenty-First Century's *Model?*

DEVESH RAVAL

Economist Devesh Raval has done important original research estimating the elasticity of substitution between capital and labor—the economic concept that plays a key role in *C21*'s theoretical model, underlying the famous assertion that inequality will continue to rise because r > g. Raval's research (along with others') shows that capital and labor are not substitutable enough to sustain Piketty's argument. Here, Raval reviews the theoretical apparatus Piketty offers, the state of economic research on the subject, and the puzzle this leaves at the center of *C21*: If the story of rising inequality isn't that marginal capital continues to be productive as it is accumulated, what is it?

The lasting contribution of Thomas Piketty's *Capital in the Twenty-First Century* is to demonstrate the importance of better measurement in economics. Focusing on inequality, Piketty broadens the set of facts available in multiple dimensions. He develops new national accounts statistics to examine a much longer historical time period than economists typically study, and uses administrative micro data to create new measures of inequality, such as the top 1 percent's share of national income. Piketty's facts bear on questions typically asked by macroeconomists (on capital's share of income) and by microeconomists (on inequality in labor income). For example, Piketty demonstrates that the capital share exhibits a long cycle over the past century, and that the income of top earners has increased much faster than that of the rest of society.

But the animating force behind the predictions in *Capital in the Twenty-First Century*—that inequality will explode and that owners of capital will take an increasingly large share of national income—is its economic model. This model harkens back to Marx's *Das Kapital,* and motivates the main policy prescription of a global wealth tax. Does it hold up to critical scrutiny?

I begin by presenting the economic model of *Capital in the Twenty-First Century.* Piketty's model predicts that a decline in economic growth will raise the capital share so long as the elasticity of substitution between capital and labor is greater than one. Therefore, I examine Piketty's estimation strategy for this elasticity in relation to the broader evidence on capital-labor substitution, and explain why most of the estimates of the elasticity are much lower than Piketty's estimate. I conclude by suggesting two other reasons for a rising capital share—labor-saving technological progress and exposure to international trade—and discuss the empirical evidence supporting them.

Model

In *Capital in the Twenty-First Century,* Piketty uses the standard neoclassical growth model of Solow and Swan to examine the evolution of the capital / output ratio—his Second Law of Capitalism—and the capital share—his First Law of Capitalism.[1] In particular, Piketty is interested in how a decline in economic growth, perhaps due to demographic change, would affect the capital share. Changes in the capital share affect the level of inequality in society, because, as Piketty documents, capital ownership is heavily concentrated in a few hands.

Second Law

Piketty's Second Law governs the steady-state value for the capital / output ratio, which Piketty denotes as β. In each period, savings S_t equals investment I_t. Piketty assumes that net savings is a constant s fraction of net output Y_t, so $S_t = sY_t$. In other parts of his book Piketty examines the implications of savings rates and rates of return to capital that vary across capital owners. These are, however, not part of his explicit model, and I will not cover them here.

On a balanced growth path, capital K_t and output Y_t grow at a constant rate g over time, so the investment-to-capital ratio is constant and equal to the growth rate. After rearranging terms, these assumptions imply:

$$\frac{sY}{K} = g \tag{1}$$

$$\beta = \frac{K}{Y} = \frac{s}{g} \tag{2}$$

In other words, the capital / output ratio β is constant over time and equal to the savings rate s divided by the growth rate g over the balanced growth path. Piketty uses this relationship to predict that if the growth rate falls, the capital / output ratio will rise. For example, with a savings rate of 12 percent, a fall in the growth rate from 3 percent to 1 percent would increase capital from 4 to 12 times net output.[2]

First Law

Piketty's First Law is simply an accounting identity; the capital share of income, which Piketty denotes as α, is the rental rate of capital r times the capital / output ratio β:

$$\alpha = \frac{rK}{Y} = r\beta \tag{3}$$

If factor markets are competitive, capital's rental price will be equal to its marginal product. To calculate the marginal product, I assume, for simplicity, a CES production function:[3]

$$Y = \left[a\left(A^K K\right)^{\frac{\sigma-1}{\sigma}} + \left(1-a\right)\left(A^L L\right)^{\frac{\sigma-1}{\sigma}} \right]^{\frac{\sigma}{\sigma-1}} \tag{4}$$

L is labor. Productivity can augment both capital—A^K—and labor—A^L. A larger A^K is thus akin to more capital, and a larger A^L to more labor.

The substitution elasticity σ is the elasticity of the aggregate capital / labor ratio K/L to a change in relative factor prices w/r:

$$\sigma = \frac{d \ln K/L}{d \ln w/r} \tag{5}$$

The marginal product of capital, and thus the rental price r, is:

$$r = \frac{dY}{dK} = a \left(\left(A^K \right)^{1-\sigma} \beta \right)^{-\frac{1}{\sigma}} \tag{6}$$

After substituting in how the rental price responds to changes in β and the Second Law, the First Law becomes:

$$\alpha = a \left(A^K \beta \right)^{\frac{\sigma-1}{\sigma}} = a \left(A^K \frac{S}{g} \right)^{\frac{\sigma-1}{\sigma}} \tag{7}$$

Piketty envisions a scenario in which population growth slows but technology, including A^K, remains the same. In that case, β will rise and the rental price r will fall. Predictions about the capital share then depend upon the degree of capital-labor substitution. When capital is more substitutable with labor, more use can be made of the extra capital, and so the fall in the rental price is smaller. If, as Piketty assumes, the elasticity of substitution σ is above one, the fall in g will also increase the capital share α.

Piketty's Estimation Strategy

Piketty's prediction that falling economic growth will raise the capital share depends upon how well capital can substitute with labor. To identify the capital-labor substitution elasticity, Piketty uses the relationship between the capital share α and the capital / output ratio β encapsulated in equation (7). Piketty documents that, over a long historical time period, both α and β exhibit a U shape, declining from 1910 to 1950 and rising from 1980 to 2010. Piketty then identifies the elasticity through the co-movement of these series, assuming that the movement in β causes the movement in α. He states: "Given the variations of the capital share observed during the 20th century, and the observed increase in rich countries during the period 1970–2010, we can conclude that this variation can be adequately explained with an elasticity of substitution slightly higher than 1 (1.3–1.6)."[4]

Figure 4-1 displays the growth rate in the capital / output ratio β and capital share α for the four countries for which Piketty develops a long-time series of observations—France, Germany, the United Kingdom, and the United States. The light grey bars indicate the capital / output ratio, and the black bars the capital share; the growth rate of each variable is depicted for both 1910 to 1950 (1929 to 1950 for the United States), and 1980 to 2010. For all four countries, both series decrease in the early period and increase in the later period. The decline in β is much greater than α in the early period, whereas for the later period α grows faster than β for the United States, slower for France, and about the same for the United Kingdom and Germany.

A more formal approach to estimation using Piketty's identification strategy would be to regress α on β, as in equation (7). I do so using data from all four countries in Figure 4-1 over the same time period, using data points for 1910 (1929 for the United States), 1950, 1980, and 2010. The estimated value of the elasticity is 1.34, within the range that Piketty reports.

The estimation strategy above requires data on the capital / output ratio β. Piketty measures capital in β by using the total value of wealth. Thus, he measures capital at its market value, so changes in the valuation of capital will affect Piketty's measure of β, as Rowthorn and Rognlie point out.[5] But changes in the valuation of capital should affect production only if they reflect changes in the quantity of effective capital. Piketty's estimating equation, equation (7), contains the product of the capital used in production and capital-augmenting technology A^K as the correct measure of effective capital.

Many of the economic shocks Piketty describes would affect the market value of capital without necessarily changing the amount of capital used in production. Take, for example, an increase in the probability that a factory is nationalized in the future. Because the market value of the capital in the factory depends upon its future income stream, the market value of the

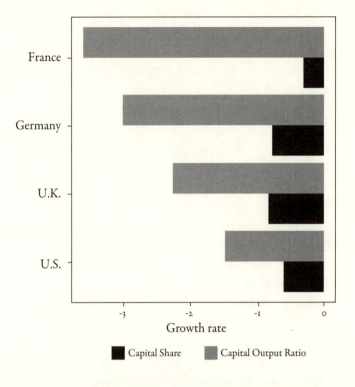

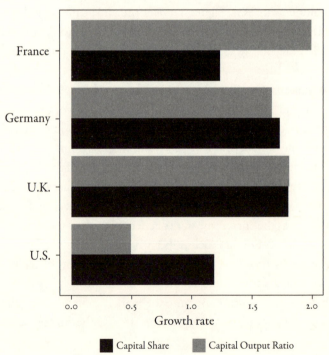

capital would decline. But nothing has changed in production: The factory continues to have the same amount of capital in production and the same production process.

The empirical analog to removing valuation effects is to remove capital gains from measures of β. In other words, the alternative is to measure capital at its book value. While measuring capital at book value removes valuation effects from β, it also removes intangible capital such as patents and brand value.

On a book-value basis, β does not exhibit the U-shape movement over time that the capital share does. Figure 4-2 displays the growth rate in β for the same four countries as above; the light grey bars include capital gains, and the black bars exclude capital gains. Including capital gains, we see a clear U in all four countries; β decreases from 1910 to 1950 and increases from 1980 to 2010. Excluding capital gains, no country exhibits the U shape. β increases for all of the European countries from 1910 to 1950, and decreases only for the United States. From 1980 to 2010, β falls for the Anglo-Saxon countries.

Both Rognlie and Bonnet et al. emphasize the role of housing capital, and rising housing prices, in the recent increases in β.[6] Bonnet et al. argue that a rent measure more closely approximates the actual increase in housing capital. They find that, under a rent-based measure, the capital / output ratio is stable or only slightly increasing for France, the United Kingdom, and the United States, unlike the price-based measure that Piketty uses. The rent-based measure does increase for Germany. Again, movements in β are very different after removing valuation effects. Policy changes that increase housing prices—for example, regulations that make it difficult to build new houses—may not improve housing services.

FIGURE 4-1: Growth rate in the capital / output ratio and capital share. (A) 1910 to 1950 (1929 to 1950 for the United States). (B) 1980 to 2010.

Note: Estimates based upon data provided by Thomas Piketty and Gabriel Zucman, "Capital Is Back: Wealth-Income Ratios in Rich Countries 1700–2010," *Quarterly Journal of Economics* 129, no. 3 (2014): 1255–1310, and are in percent change per year. The U.S. changes in the early period are based upon the 1929–1950 period rather than the 1910–1950 period, as capital share data is not available for 1910 for the United States.

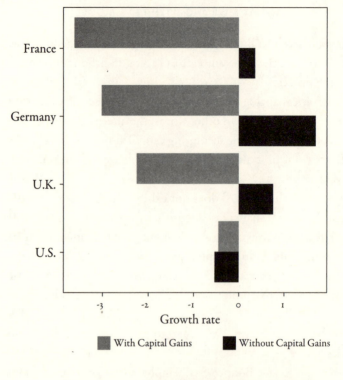

France

Germany

U.K.

U.S.

Growth rate

■ With Capital Gains   ■ Without Capital Gains

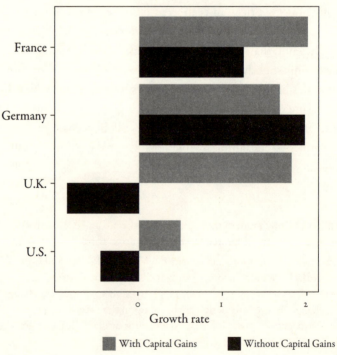

France

Germany

U.K.

U.S.

Growth rate

■ With Capital Gains   ■ Without Capital Gains

Capital-Labor Substitution

Piketty's estimates of σ are much higher than the typical estimate in the existing literature on capital-labor substitution. To compare to the literature, I convert Piketty's estimates to an elasticity based on a production function gross of depreciation. On a gross basis, Piketty's estimates range between 1.7 and 2.1.[7] Figure 4-3 depicts estimates found in the literature, based on forty-four estimates compiled in literature surveys by Chirinko and Leon-Ledesma, McAdam, and Willman as well as several papers written after these surveys.[8] Piketty's estimate is in grey. The median estimate in the literature is 0.54, only a few estimates are above one, and almost all are below Piketty's estimates.

Of course, the estimates in the literature vary across several factors, including the time period and country examined, the assumptions made on technical progress, the level of aggregation, and the econometric technique employed. Why does Piketty get estimates that are so different from estimates in the existing literature? And how should one go about estimating the capital-labor substitution elasticity? In other words, what conclusion should one draw about the validity of Piketty's estimate?

Identification

To answer these questions, we first turn to the topic of *identification*. An econometric parameter is identified if the data is consistent with only a single value for the parameter.

The identification strategy that Piketty uses—the historical co-movement of α and β—does not identify the elasticity without further assumptions on technology. Diamond, McFadden, and Rodriguez prove that, for any value of the elasticity, some path of movements in technology—productivities A^K and A^L—can rationalize the movements in α and β.[9] Intuitively, change in the capital share can come from relative factor supplies or relative factor demands. Identification requires assumptions about which is moving, such as

FIGURE 4-2: Growth rate in the capital/output ratio, with and without capital gains. (A) 1910 to 1950 (1929 to 1950 for the United States). (B) 1980 to 2010.

Note: Estimates, based upon data provided by Piketty and Zucman, "Capital Is Back," are in percent change per year.

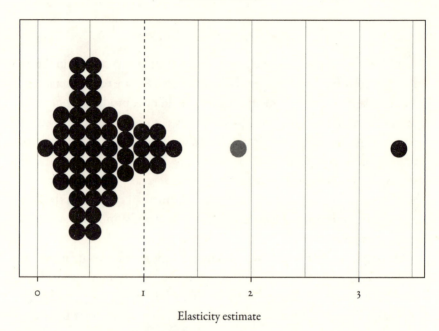

Elasticity estimate

FIGURE 4-3: Elasticity estimates in the literature. Piketty's estimate is in grey. The median estimate in the literature is 0.54.

Note: This plot depicts elasticity estimates based on surveys in the literature by Chirinko and Leon-Ledesma, McAdam, and Willman, as well as a number of papers written after those surveys: Oberfield and Raval; Raval; Karabarbounis and Neiman; Herrendorf, Herrington, and Valentinyi; Alvarez-Cuadrado, Long, and Poschke; Leon-Ledesma, McAdam, and Willman; Chen; and Lawrence (Ezra Oberfield and Devesh Raval, "Micro Data and Macro Technology," NBER Working Paper No. 20452 (September 2014); Devesh Raval, "The Micro Elasticity of Substitution and Non-Neutral Technology," http://www.devesh-raval.com/MicroElasticity.pdf; Loukas Karabarbounis and Brent Neiman, "The Global Decline of the Labor Share," *Quarterly Journal of Economics* 129, no. 1 [2014]: 61–103; Berthold Herrendorf, Christopher Herrington, and Akos Valentinyi, "Sectoral Technology and Structural Transformation," *American Economic Journal: Macroeconomics* 7 no. 4 (2015): 104–133; Francisco Alvarez-Cuadrado, Ngo Van Long, and Markus Poschke, *Capital-Labor Substitution, Structural Change and the Labor Income Share,* technical report [Munich: CESifo, 2014]; Miguel A Leon-Ledesma, Peter McAdam, and Alpo Willman, "Production Technology Estimates and Balanced Growth," *Oxford Bulletin of Economics and Statistics* 77, no. 1 [2015]: 40–65; Xi Chen, "Biased Technical Change, Scale, and Factor Substitution in US Manufacturing Industries," *Macroeconomic Dynamics* [2016]; Robert Z. Lawrence, "Recent Declines in Labor's Share in US Income: A Preliminary Neoclassical Account," NBER Working Paper No. 21296). The grey dot is the median of the estimates reported by Piketty. The vertical dashed line indicates an elasticity of one.

restrictions on how technology evolves or exogenous movements in factor prices or quantities.

The implicit assumption behind Piketty's identification strategy is that A^K, capital-augmenting productivity, is either constant over time or not correlated with changes in β. It is not obvious how to check whether these assumptions are true. A constant A^K is consistent with a long-run balanced growth path, although as Acemoglu shows, there may be considerable movements in A^K in the medium run.[10] Econometric approaches that allow for movements in A^K typically find that A^K is not constant. For example, Antras estimates an average fall in A^K of 1.3 to 1.6 percentage points per year over the postwar period.[11] A correlation between A^K and β due to their medium- or long-run trends could lead to substantial bias in any estimate of the elasticity.

Macro Estimates

The key issue with any estimate of the elasticity is how to confront the identification problem highlighted by Diamond, McFadden, and Rodriguez; that is, what to assume about movements in technology. Most estimates of the capital-labor elasticity are, like Piketty's, based upon the aggregate time series, but examine how changes in factor prices affect factor costs. Take, for example, the equation for the capital-cost-to-labor-cost ratio, derived from equation (5) after substituting in expressions for marginal products:

$$\ln \frac{rK}{wL} = \sigma \ln \frac{a}{1-a} + (\sigma-1)\ln \frac{w}{r} + (\sigma-1)\ln \frac{A^L}{A^K} \tag{8}$$

In this equation, one has to make assumptions on the change in $\frac{A^L}{A^K}$, which I will call the bias of technical change. Relative factor prices $\frac{w}{r}$ would identify the elasticity if they were not confounded with biased technical change. One possibility is to assume that $\frac{A^L}{A^K}$ is constant over time, so that all technical change is neutral and there is no biased technical change; this is Piketty's implicit assumption. In that case, movements in relative factor prices $\frac{w}{r}$ identify the elasticity. Another assumption is that $\frac{A^L}{A^K}$ is exponentially growing over time. In that case, equation (8) above contains a time trend, and variation in relative factor prices *away from their long-run trend* identifies the elasticity. A third possibility is that the rate of biased technical change itself varies over time.

Below I show how estimates of the elasticity change by estimating equation (8) under three different assumptions on biased technical change: allowing only neutral technical change, allowing for a constant rate of biased technical change through a time trend, and allowing for the rate of biased technical change to vary over time through a Box–Cox transformation as in Klump, McAdam, and Willman.[12] I use data on U.S. manufacturing from 1970 to 2010.

The left-hand plot in Figure 4-4 contains these estimates and their 95 percent confidence intervals. With no control for biased technical change, the estimate of the elasticity is precisely estimated at 1.9 and within the range of Piketty's estimates. After allowing for biased technical change, however, the estimate of the elasticity falls to 0.56 for a constant rate of bias and 0.69 for a time-varying rate of bias. These estimates are much more imprecise than the case without biased technical change. The estimated confidence intervals in both the constant and the time-varying bias cases include an elasticity of one; the confidence interval in the constant bias case ranges from 0.05 to 1.07. Intuitively, with biased technical change there is less identifying variation in factor price changes.

The right-hand plot in Figure 4-4 displays the rate of biased technical change, in percentage points per year, under each assumption. The regression model with a constant rate of biased technical change estimates a rate of biased technical change of 2.3 percent per year. Under the time-varying Box–Cox model, the rate of biased technical change increases from almost zero in 1970 to over 3.5 percent per year in 2010.

The above analysis on U.S. manufacturing data showed that elasticity estimates fall below one once the econometric specification includes some controls for biased technical change. Similarly, the recent literature allowing for biased technical change has, in general, estimated elasticities below one. For example, Antras estimates an elasticity of one using the U.S. aggregate

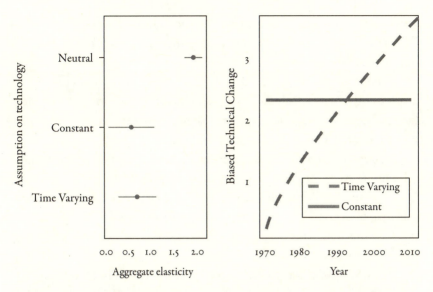

FIGURE 4-4: Elasticity and bias estimates from aggregate data. *(Left)* Aggregate elasticity estimates. *(Right)* Rate of biased technical change (in percentage points).

Note: The left side of the figure shows how estimates of elasticity vary when different assumptions are made about technical change. The right side of the figure displays the annual rates of technical change assumed under the constant (2.3 percent) and time-varying (0 rising to 3.5 percent) assumptions. The left plot displays the point estimate and 95 percent confidence interval for the aggregate elasticity of substitution from regressions based on equation (8). Specifications differ in assumptions on the bias of technical change. Technical change is respectively assumed to have no trend, follow a linear time trend, or follow a Box–Cox transformation of the time trend. The right plot displays the bias of technical change in percentage points, from either a linear or a Box–Cox specification of the time trend.

time series assuming that technological change is neutral, but significantly below one (between 0.6 and 0.9) after allowing exponential growth in A^K and A^L.[13]

Econometric approaches to estimating the aggregate elasticity still have to confront two major issues. First, there may not be enough identifying variation in the aggregate time series to estimate the elasticity after controlling for biased technical change. Leon-Ledesma, McAdam, and Willman perform a Monte Carlo analysis to examine this issue.[14] They find that, while it is difficult to obtain the true elasticity using aggregate time-series data, a "systems" approach that simultaneously estimates equations for the production function and its marginal products (as in Klump, McAdam, and Willman) performs better than just using information on factor marginal products as in equation (8).

Second, as we saw above, controlling for biased technical change may mean using more high-frequency movements in factor prices. If changing factors entails adjustment costs, then these approaches may end up estimating a more short-run elasticity. For the questions in *Capital in the Twenty-First Century,* a long-run elasticity is the appropriate elasticity. One solution is to isolate long-run variation in factor prices; for example, Chirinko and Mallick examine long-run variation in rental prices of capital using panel data on U.S. industries.[15] Their estimates of the long-run elasticity are much higher than those for the short-run elasticity, but still range from 0.40 to 0.65.

The major exception in the recent literature to the finding of an elasticity of substitution below one is Karabarbounis and Neiman.[16] They estimate an aggregate elasticity of 1.25 using cross-country variation in the growth rate of capital prices. The main advantage of their approach is that cross-country variation may help get at the long-run elasticity. However, their baseline strategy requires the change in A^K to be the same across countries or uncorrelated with rental price changes. Thus, they are subject to an identification problem with changing technology, similar to that in the earlier literature that assumed no biased technical change. In addition, as Mutreja, Ravikumar, and Sposi show, most countries import almost all of their capital goods, therefore much of the variation across countries over time may be due to differences in trade liberalization across countries.[17] However, changes in trade patterns and trade barriers can affect the capital share for multiple reasons other than capital prices, as I will discuss later, which would bias any estimates of the elasticity.

Micro Estimates

As we have seen, it is difficult to separate movements in factor prices from technology in aggregate data without placing strong a priori restrictions on technical change. An alternative approach is to use micro data on firms or manufacturing plants, for which there is arguably more plausibly exogenous, and long-run, variation in factor prices for identification.

A couple of recent studies have used micro data to estimate the long-run micro elasticity. Chirinko, Fazzari, and Meyer identify the elasticity using differences in the long-run movements in the rental price of capital across U.S. public firms.[18] They control for non-neutral technical change at the industry level, so their identifying assumption is that firm-level differences in rental prices have to be independent of firm-level changes in A^K. They estimate the elasticity to be 0.40, as do Barnes, Price, and Barriel using U.K. firm-level panel data with a similar approach.[19]

I have identified the elasticity using differences in wages across U.S. locations; for these estimates, local differences in wages have to be independent of firm A^L.[20] Because differences in wages across locations are highly persistent, this type of variation should help uncover the long-run elasticity. Using both ordinary least squares (OLS) and instruments for wages from local demand shocks, I obtain estimates of the elasticity close to 0.5.[21]

To understand movements in the aggregate capital share, the macro elasticity of substitution is required, not the micro elasticity. These elasticities can be very different, as Houthakker famously demonstrated, because the macro elasticity will incorporate substitution across producers as well as within them.[22] As Piketty and Zucman note, "the aggregate elasticity of substitution σ should really be interpreted as resulting from both supply forces (producers shift between technologies with different capital intensities) and demand forces (consumers shift between goods and services with different capital intensities)."[23]

Oberfield and Raval develop an aggregation framework, based on earlier work by Sato, that models these demand and supply forces in order to estimate the macro elasticity using micro data.[24] For simplicity, take a baseline case of an economy with one industry in which firms maximize profits in a monopolistically competitive environment and face competitive factor markets.[25] In that case, Oberfield and Raval show, the macro elasticity of substitution between labor and capital, σ^{Macro}, is a convex combination of the micro elasticity of substitution between labor and capital, σ^{Micro}, and the micro elasticity of demand, ε.

$$\sigma^{Macro} = (1-\phi)\sigma^{Micro} + \phi\varepsilon \qquad (9)$$

In response to a change in factor prices, the change in factor shares for the economy as a whole includes both substitution within individual plants and reallocation across them. The first term on the right-hand side in equation (9) is a substitution effect that captures how plants change their input mixes, and so depends upon the micro elasticity σ^{Micro}. With a rise in the wage, plants will tend to use less labor. The second term is a reallocation effect that captures how the size of plants changes with the change in input prices. When wages rise, plants that use capital more intensively gain a relative cost advantage. Consumers respond to the subsequent changes in relative prices by shifting consumption toward the capital-intensive goods. This reallocation effect is larger when demand is more elastic, because customers respond more to changing relative prices.

The weight between them, φ, is proportional to the cost-weighted variance of capital shares and lies between zero and one. When each plant produces at the same capital intensity, φ is zero and there is no reallocation across plants. Each plant's marginal cost responds to input price changes symmetrically, so relative output prices are unchanged. In contrast, if some plants produce using only capital while all others produce using only labor, all input substitution is across plants and φ is one. When there is little variation in capital intensities, within-plant substitution is more important than reallocation.

This aggregation approach allows one to use micro estimates of the elasticity of substitution to obtain the aggregate elasticity. Oberfield and Raval do so for the U.S. manufacturing sector. They estimate the plant-level elasticities of capital-labor substitution and demand from micro data, and compute the weight φ from the cross section of manufacturing plants. Because these elasticities are taken from the cross section, they make no assumption on movements in technology over time. They estimate a macro elasticity of 0.7, modestly higher than a micro elasticity of about 0.5, but well below Piketty's range.

For the United States, the differences in capital intensities across manufacturing plants are not large enough to mean a large difference between the micro and macro elasticities. The low micro elasticities estimated in the literature then imply macro elasticities below one. They do, however, find much larger differences in capital intensities for developing countries, where the prior literature documents major variation in capital intensity. Using the same demand and supply elasticities as for the United States, the greater heterogeneity in capital intensities in India implies an elasticity of 1.1.

Capital-Labor Substitution in the Twenty-First Century

The evidence presented in the preceding two sections points to an elasticity below one. One of the claims that Piketty makes, however, is that the elasticity of substitution has been rising over time. For example, as Piketty shows, most of capital was in land until the Industrial Revolution; Piketty argues that the elasticity between land and labor is less than the elasticity between modern capital and labor. What if new technologies, such as robots, raise the elasticity of substitution to the levels estimated by Piketty?

Klump and De La Grandville examine this question within the Solow growth model.[26] They prove that an economy with a higher capital-labor elasticity of substitution, with everything else initially equal, will have a higher capital share, per capita income, and per capita income growth. Thus, a higher elasticity of substitution means a richer, although more unequal, society.

With a high enough elasticity of substitution, an economy can have long-run growth without technical progress. De La Grandville show that, provided σ is high enough (and above one), there is a threshold savings rate above which capital and output grow forever.[27] The threshold savings rate increases in the population growth rate and decreases in the elasticity σ. The intuition here is that with a high enough elasticity, the marginal product of capital remains large even with a large capital stock, and so capital continues to grow faster than the rate of population growth so long as the economy saves enough of its output.

Even at the upper end of Piketty's estimates of the elasticity, the savings rate must be substantially higher, and population growth rate lower, in order for the perpetual growth scenario to hold. However, if Piketty's feared scenario comes to pass—a high elasticity of substitution and a low population growth rate—the Solow growth model implies that the economy would experience unbounded growth!

Capital Taxation

Piketty's main policy proposal to counteract increasing inequality from capital is a progressive capital tax. The desirability of this proposal, however, depends on the validity of Piketty's elasticity estimates. Given an elasticity below one, an increase in capital taxes would actually increase the capital share. In contrast, a reduction in the capital tax would work to reduce the capital share, and thus the level of inequality, through a rise in β.

The traditional argument in favor of capital taxation has been the opposite of Piketty's, arguing that the welfare cost of capital taxation is low because elasticities of substitution are low. Taxation has a welfare cost because people change their behavior in order to avoid the tax. For capital taxation, this is because people substitute away from capital. Chamley finds that the welfare cost of capital taxation is increasing in the elasticity; the welfare cost is reduced by roughly two-thirds when the elasticity is 0.6 rather than 2.[28] Thus, the welfare cost of capital taxation is much lower given the estimates in the preceding sections than under Piketty's estimates.

Alternative Explanations for the Rise in the Capital Share

If Piketty's explanation is incorrect, why has the capital share risen? Will the capital share continue to rise? In this section I examine two potential explanations, globalization and labor-saving technical change.

Globalization

The most prominent alternative explanation for the fall in the labor share is the increasing exposure of developed countries to global trade. I focus on the United States because that is the country most of the literature has examined. U.S. imports tripled as a share of GDP from 1970 to 2010, from about 5 percent of GDP in 1970 to about 16 percent in 2010. Trade with China has grown particularly rapidly, from about 1 percent of overall imports of goods to the United States in 1985 to 19 percent in 2010.[29] This massive increase in trade from China was due to rapid economic growth in China, as well as China's accession to the World Trade Organization (WTO) in December 2001.

The labor share could fall with increased trade if labor-intensive U.S. production shifts to labor-abundant countries. Elsby, Hobijn, and Sahin indeed find that the payroll share falls in industries that are more exposed to imports.[30] They find that industries with an extra percentage point increase in import exposure from 1993 to 2010 have, on average, a 0.87 percentage point fall in the payroll share.[31] For example, for manufacturing as a whole, their estimates imply that increased import exposure from China over this period reduced the payroll share by about 8 percentage points. The realized increase in imports can explain about 85 percent of the 1993–2010 fall in the aggregate payroll share.

This fall in the labor share could be due to decreases in employment, decreases in wages, or falls in both employment and wages. Acemoglu et al. find that exposure to Chinese trade led to U.S. job losses of 2.0 to 2.4 million over the 2000s.[32] Autor, Dorn, and Hanson examine how increasing exposure to Chinese imports affects different local labor markets across the United States; some U.S. labor markets are heavily exposed to manufacturing industries that experience a large rise in Chinese imports.[33] In these markets, they find that the rise in Chinese imports affects both employment and wages.[34] For a $1,000 rise in Chinese exports per worker in a ten-year period, manufacturing employment in the local labor market falls by 0.60 percentage points (or 4.2 percent), and employment to population falls by 0.77 percentage points. Wages fall by 0.75 percent for a $1,000 rise in Chinese exports per worker. For the local labor market, with the 90th percentile increase in Chinese imports per worker, the increased import exposure from China from 2000 to 2007 would have reduced both employment and wages by about 3.25 percentage points.

The authors then examine these changes separately for manufacturing and nonmanufacturing sectors; they find economically substantial and statistically significant falls in employment, but not wages for the manufacturing sector, and the reverse pattern for the nonmanufacturing sector. In addition, Chetverikov, Larsen, and Palmer find that low-wage earners bear the brunt of the trade-induced fall in wages.[35] Thus, increasing import competition likely affects the labor share through changes in both employment and in wages, with different impacts for different types of workers.

Manufacturing employment could fall through a number of channels; labor-intensive manufacturing producers could exit, could grow more slowly, or could produce products that require more capital-intensive production. Bernard, Jensen, and Schott find evidence for all of these channels, examining industry-level variation in the share of imports from low-wage countries such as China.[36] U.S. manufacturing plants in industries with greater increases in the share of low-wage-country imports are more likely to exit and have lower employment growth—although these effects are smaller for the more capital-intensive plants in the industry. They are also more likely to switch to producing products that are more capital intensive and thus face less import competition.

Increased import competition could also affect how firms operate by reducing the bargaining power of labor or by forcing firms to increase productivity in order to compete. Schmitz and Dunne, Klimek, and Schmitz examine how incumbent producers in the iron ore mining and cement industries, respectively, responded to a sudden increase in import competition by changing their work practices.[37] In both industries, union contracts specified that different types of repair work could be performed only by specific employees. In the cement industry, union contracts prohibited firing workers due to new equipment or new production methods, provided strict seniority rights, and prevented subcontracting tasks to outside companies. By restricting substitution away from labor or specific types of labor, such as senior employees or repair workers, these requirements likely increased employment and the labor share. After a massive surge in import competition, these requirements were mostly eliminated, and productivity and the capital-to-labor ratio rose.

Bloom, Draca, and Van Reenen find that Chinese import competition increased a number of measures of innovation—total-factor productivity (TFP), patents, and information technology (IT) investment—for producers, and led to reallocation within the industry to producers that had high levels of innovation initially.[38] This innovation could reduce the labor share if it resulted in labor-saving technology; the authors do find that employment falls with exposure to Chinese import competition, although less so for the higher innovation firms. It is unclear, however, whether the improvements in innovation were linked to the decline in employment.

Labor Saving Technical Change

Economists studying technical progress have found that the adoption of "General Purpose Technologies," such as steam power and electricity, has had wide-ranging impacts throughout the economy.[39] The latest such General Purpose Technology has been enabled by the massive improvement in computing power and information technology in recent decades. Can the IT revolution lead to "technological unemployment" and explain the rise in the capital share?

Autor, Levy, and Murmane provide a framework for understanding how new automation technologies affect production.[40] They find that new automation technologies substitute with what they term "routine" labor—labor employed in explicit, codifiable tasks—and complement labor engaged in "abstract" tasks such as high-level problem solving, creativity, and persuasion. Other "manual" tasks, such as janitorial work or food preparation, are much less affected by the new technologies. Autor, Levy, and Murmane show that new automation technologies lead to job polarization, as middle-skill routine tasks are automated away and high-skill abstract and low-skill manual tasks grow in demand.[41]

While this type of job polarization clearly affects the wages and employment of different types of workers, it is far less clear how it affects the overall labor share. First, within an industry, a fall in the share of income going to routine-task employees could be counterbalanced by a rise in the income share of abstract labor complementary with the new automation technologies. Second, the change in the overall labor share will depend upon how much demand for the industry rises as its price falls, how well workers can change their skills to match changing labor demand, and how well the economy reallocates such workers to other opportunities.

Take, for example, the introduction of the automated teller machine (ATM). As its name suggests, the ATM could perform the same functions as a bank teller. But as Bessen documents, employment actually increased with the introduction of ATMs, both because the number of bank branches rose as the cost of a branch fell, and because bank branches began to use tellers as "relationship managers" rather than merely clerks.[42] Basker, Foster, and Klimek examine the switch of gas stations from full service to self-service. In this case, customers are substituting their own labor for the gas station attendant's labor.[43] While Basker, Foster, and Klimek find that employment and payroll fall at gas stations that adopt self-service, with the cost savings passed on to consumers in the form of lower gas prices, employment in the gas station industry rises because of workers employed in new convenience stores attached to gasoline stations.

Autor, Dorn, and Hanson explicitly compare the effect of automation and trade by examining the effects of both forces on local labor markets.[44] They find that automation technologies increase the polarization of occupational employment, but do not reduce net employment. The authors do find, however, that exposure to Chinese trade does lead to reduced employment.

Beaudry, Green, and Sand examine the polarization hypothesis for the 2000s, the period with the largest decline in the labor share, and find that employment and wages decline for abstract labor.[45] Their model has abstract task labor used to produce knowledge capital. An improvement in technology in the 1990s leads businesses to temporarily hire abstract labor to build knowledge capital, but after that they need only enough abstract labor to maintain the knowledge stock already built. Thus, employment and wages of abstract labor fall in the 2000s. The Great Recession makes it is difficult to disentangle business cycle effects from structural changes in labor market changes during the second half of the 2000s, but Beaudry, Green, and Sand provide evidence that technological forces may be responsible for the falling labor share.

Future Changes in the Labor Share

Globalization seems unlikely to cause further large declines in the labor share. Barriers to trade are already fairly low. China was in a unique position over the previous three decades—large, growing rapidly, and transitioning from complete autarky. In addition, the United States has already shed much of the labor-intensive manufacturing employment that would be adversely affected by foreign competition.

If labor-saving technical progress is to blame for the recent fall in the labor share, will the fall in the labor share continue forever? Answering this question requires a model of the production of technical innovations. The degree and direction of technical progress likely depends on the profit from that technical progress. In a world in which the labor share has declined considerably, and so labor is cheap, there is little incentive to develop labor-saving inventions. This is what Acemoglu finds when σ is less than one and innovations are in A^L; the scarcity of labor encourages labor-saving innovation.[46] This type of model can help explain why the relatively labor-scarce United States grew faster than Britain over the nineteenth century (known as the Habakkuk hypothesis), or why Europe, not labor-abundant China, experienced the Industrial Revolution.

Acemoglu develops a model that endogenizes technical progress in which factor shares remain stable in the long run.[47] In his model, improvements in

A^K and A^L are the result of efforts by a profit-maximizing R&D sector. While all technical progress is labor augmenting under the balanced growth path, both A^K and A^L can increase along the transition path. The returns to improving A^K and A^L depend upon the capital share; when the capital share is high compared to its long-run equilibrium, there are large returns to developing A^K. The resulting improvements in A^K lower the capital share. In equilibrium, technical progress serves to stabilize factor shares, and so a Piketty-type apocalyptic scenario for labor does not occur.

Conclusion

In *Capital in the Twenty-First Century,* Piketty employs a growth model to explain how a falling rate of economic growth would affect the capital share. Under his model, a lower growth rate would increase the capital / output ratio; this rise in the capital / output ratio would also increase the capital share if the capital-labor substitution elasticity is above one. Piketty then estimates this elasticity to be substantially above one by using the historical co-movement of the capital / output ratio and capital share.

Piketty's identification strategy requires a major assumption on technology—that capital-augmenting technology A^K has been constant or uncorrelated with movements in the capital / output ratio over time. Estimates using the aggregate time series that relax this assumption, and so allow biased technical change, generally obtain estimates lower than one and much lower than those in Piketty. Estimates of the micro elasticity of substitution are also substantially below one; an aggregation framework that uses these estimates to estimate the macro elasticity also implies an elasticity less than one. Thus, Piketty's explanation for the declining labor share is unlikely to be correct.

Two alternative explanations for the decline in the labor share are globalization and labor-saving technological progress. A substantial body of evidence, including differences across industries and local labor markets, indicates that the rise of trade with China lowered the U.S. labor share. A number of mechanisms are likely at work. Labor-intensive producers may exit, shrink, change the products they sell, or change their work practices.

The current evidence on technological progress indicates that the development of automation technologies has polarized labor by reducing demand for routine labor that is substitutable with new technologies and increasing demand for abstract labor that is complementary with the new technologies. However, there is limited evidence that automation reduced the overall labor share. With endogenous technical progress, a decline in the labor share may eventually reverse with shifts in technology. More research is needed in order to understand how technology can affect the labor share.

FIVE

A Political Economy Take on W/Y

SURESH NAIDU

Drawing on a distinction between a "domesticated" and "wild" Piketty, economist Suresh Naidu takes on the challenge of modeling rising inequality as arising from the dynamics of wealth. But unlike Piketty, Naidu does not rely on the machinery of neoclassical production. Instead he takes seriously the market's valuation of the capital stock as reflecting beliefs about the future claims that the owners of capital are empowered to make on national production, as well as the rate at which the financial sector discounts those claims. That implicates the political sphere more than does Piketty's neoclassical model, and hence a set of policy instruments for controlling the capital share and the financial sector's take that go beyond Piketty's global wealth tax.

Forking Paths in Understanding Inequality

Piketty's Near-Success

In her "Open Letter from a Keynesian to a Marxist," Joan Robinson writes: "Ricardo was followed by two able and well-trained pupils—Marx and Marshall. Meanwhile English history had gone right round the corner, and landlords were not any longer the question. Now it was capitalists. Marx turned Ricardo's argument round this way: Capitalists are very much like landlords. And Marshall turned it round the other way: Landlords are very much like capitalists."[1] In his big red book, Piketty tries, like Henry George and a long stream of economists of the left before him, to perform the Marxian maneuver of turning what he sees as an upside-down argument right-side-up. Piketty argues that modern capital is very much like land—a source of rent. It is supplied inelastically, commands a share of output despite having little in the way of opportunity cost sacrificed in its provision, and in its influence and skewed distribution returns us to a financialized neo-feudal Gilded Age. Thus, an economy dominated by modern capital winds up as a *rentier* economy: an economy of robber barons, credentialed aristocrats, social conflict over distribution, and government captured by the rich.

But Piketty cannot quite manage to pull his maneuver off. He winds up trapped by the Marshallian apparatus he has built. In it, capital—wealth—is treated more as a stock of accumulated savings rather than a claim on future output, and so it looks less like Ricardo's land owned by parasites and more like, well, neoclassical-economic capital, the profit from which is the proper and socially useful reward for thrift.

As Piketty's book shows, capital—wealth—takes many forms, which run from real estate to financial assets, such as corporate shares and loans, and even to slaves. Wealth is most accurately conceptualized as a claim on future resources. It results from purchases of durable property rights over assets, such as machines, houses, patents, or oilfields, that are either productive (in which case people bid to use them) or extractive (in which case people pay to keep legal process from being used against them). The salience of wealth matters, and depends on how much of the economic pie it lays claim to. If the economy has produced a lot of output relative to capital, then it can cover the claims owed to holders of wealth with little effort. But if economy-wide output is relatively low, it will take much more of society's resources to cover the obligations owed to wealth holders. Piketty's book suggests that as global income growth (g) slows, society will need to fetter capital with taxes at the global level—or else see a new class of owner-*rentiers* gobble down more and more of the social pie.

The book is a template for good popular economics: historical and substantively important insights disciplined by original, carefully constructed data and an analytical framework inspired, but not fettered, by the mathematical models of the field.

This is not normal economics.

But unlike much economic writing on the left, economists would recognize it as economics (for better or worse).

In the text, if not in the models, the book also brings politics to the forefront of the analysis. The big movements in the series Piketty documents are driven by politics and policies. But the politics are exogenous to the model. They are not an endogenous part of the framework. Thus, Piketty has to delicately sail his way between the Scylla that is the "market fundamentals" of supply and demand for capital and labor, and the Charybdis that is the independent role of politics and policies.

Domesticated Piketty

Piketty's book has two interwoven arguments.

The first, the "domesticated Piketty" is a very standard model. It has stochastic and heterogeneous saving rates and uninsurable and undiversifiable rates of return on asset positions. It has competitive markets. It has a production function with a capital-labor elasticity of substitution that is greater than 1. It has a social welfare function that is egalitarian-meritocratic. This domesticated Piketty is an economist's delight. It combines a positive, quantifiable model of the economy with testable predictions in the context of a well-defined social objective function. It derives an optimal policy prescription. It is articulated in papers with coauthors. It yields a formula for the optimal wealth tax as a policy outcome.

It is, however, institution-and-politics free, and makes Piketty's project look like an (impressive) extension within a standard macro public finance framework.

This is the reading of Piketty that Krugman celebrates, and that Acemoglu and Robinson,[2] among others, pillory in going after "general laws of capitalism." I appreciate the grandeur of the modeling effort. However, I worry that this domesticated Piketty is an ill-suited model for the purposes for which Piketty seeks to use it. Piketty seeks to study the historical variation in wealth inequality. He seeks to place in their proper perspective the institutional changes that explain empirical variation in the economy's wealth-to-annual-income ratio (W / Y) and thus of wealth inequality. These include: the role of financial markets, market structure in general, and intrafirm bargaining over revenue. But the model of domesticated Piketty has, for these three at least, relatively little light to shed.

Wild Piketty

But there are shoots of something else breaking through: a "wild Piketty."

The wild Piketty suggests a different perspective. It sees the economy through a lens in which capital is the alchemy of today's income transmuted into secure claims on future income that are then bought and sold on asset markets. In this view, institutions of corporate governance, financial firms, labor market institutions, and political influence do most of the work in determining both W / Y and the distribution of wealth. This wild Piketty argument is hinted at in various places in the book, interviews, and sundry papers. It is a view of capital as an institutionally defined set of property rights that are then transacted on asset markets. This is where the ideas in Piketty's book tangential from the perspective of the domesticated Piketty model—the ideas about corporate governance and Tobin's Q, the speculations about foreign investment and weak property rights in Africa, the musings on whether slaves are net wealth or not—become the main story. In this view, capital is a set of property rights entitling bearers to politically protected rights of control, exclusion, transfer, and derived cash flow. Like all property rights, its delineation and defense require actions of state power, legal standardization, and juridical legitimacy. In the last instance, capital includes the ability to call on the government to secure the promised flow of income against potential violators, be they burglars, fugitive slaves, copyright violators, sit-down strikers, or delinquent tenants.

The political economy view would help us to write chapters in Piketty's book that are missing from the text but that are essential to fill in gaps in the wild Piketty argument—chapters on finance, market power, and endogenous policy making. We can understand the institutions and property rights that allow capital to accumulate as endogenous to the political system, and as the result the balance of political power across social groups.

Prominent among these institutions is the organization of the financial sector. Wealth is a price-weighted sum of otherwise incommensurate assets, and those prices are determined in financial markets, which aggregate flighty expectations about the future into prices today. Extensive, if not efficient, financial intermediation comes along with a high wealth / income ratio. The assets are themselves used to organize production with workers to produce goods and services sold to consumers, and the income flow accruing to owners of those assets depends on the wages paid to those workers and the prices charged to those consumers. The functioning of product and labor markets, and the institutions that regulate competition, prices, wages and employment, will determine the share of income commanded by holders of wealth. Finally, protecting the future flows of income accruing to the assets requires deploying the state in a variety of ways, not just via the tax system. This induces feedback loops where inequality in income today molds a political system that preserves that inequality tomorrow.

Finally, the political economy view lets us see more clearly what is normatively problematic about wealth inequality. Piketty writes in various places that wealth inequality and a society of rentiers is undemocratic, but the links are unspecified. Why should extreme inequality of wealth necessarily imply inequality of political power? But when wealth is understood as police-backed paper claims over resources, rather than the resources themselves, the undemocratic nature of wealth inequality becomes much clearer.

Alternative Ways of Looking at the Determinants of W / Y

$$W/Y = s/g$$

Piketty's basic model revolves around the dynamic accumulation of wealth, where:

$W_{t+1} = sY_t + W_t$, with s the savings rate, Y income, and W wealth. Thus, dividing both sides by: ,

$Y_{t+1} = (1+g)Y_t$, where g is the rate of GDP growth, and looking at the steady state, we get:

$$W/Y = s/g$$

This formula stresses average household (and corporate) savings rates and economic growth rates. It makes the wealth-to-GDP ratio look like a consequence of household and corporate savings decisions (net of depreciation) relative to the rate of innovation, human capital accumulation, and demographic growth. But while these forces are undoubtedly important, they are also quite mechanical. They seem at first glance invariant across institutional arrangements. This formula is as applicable in a planned economy as in a capitalist one. It obscures the peculiarly capitalist institutions that make private wealth possible.

W / Y and the Relative Incomes of the Rich

The capital share of income α is given by

$\alpha = \dfrac{rs}{g}$, where r is the profit rate. Thus the value of the economy's

wealth-to-annual-income ratio W / Y would matter little, in terms of the inequality of income flows, if r were to fall roughly along with g. But if g falls while r stays relatively constant, then the wealth-to-annual-income ratio and the wealthholders' share of total income both increase. The idea of steady upward pressure acting to raise the capital share is a generalization of an idea in Marx stated clearest in *Wage Labor and Capital*. Piketty takes the argument laid out there, jettisons the metaphysical flotsam of Marxian value theory, and focuses on just income and wealth—empirical magnitudes measurable over long streams of history, recorded as they are in tax, census, and probate records. However, the end point of the argument is similar: over the long run, most of the output will wind up owned by capitalists. The difference is in the mechanism: Piketty has a model with constant profit rate and falling growth in productivity improvements, rather than a constant wage and growth in productivity. Both are consistent with an ever-larger share of income going to capital over time.

What Marx is missing, according to Piketty, is the offsetting force of economic growth. New innovations, population growth, and more economic activity independently increase output and labor income. These are technological and organizational improvements, particularly in the production of wage goods, that may lower the value of labor power but increase the labor share.

I think it is a bit more subtle than that. Piketty fixes the rate of profit at higher than the rate of growth. Marx, justified by his theory of the constant existence of the reserve army of unemployment, fixes wages at a "historical and moral" level of subsistence. Thus, in Marx's framework, all productivity gains go to capital until and unless the "historical and moral" level of subsistence increases. In the competitive model favored by Piketty, productivity gains are transmitted to workers through labor market competition as firms compete to hire workers and thus increase workers' wages. Thus, Piketty needs overall productivity to grow by less than the rate of profit in order to secure an increasing share for capital. But in any case, the empirical prediction is the same: the share of output going to capital increases over time.

Either growth is constant but wages are fixed by institutions and the reserve army of labor, as in Marx. Or profit rates are fixed, and the productivity growth rates that would increase labor income in a competitive labor market are falling, as in Piketty. Capital demand is elastic and capital supply is inelastic in Piketty. Labor demand is inelastic and labor supply is elastic in Marx. In both cases, the surplus goes to owners of capital.

These forces making for economic growth, Piketty argues, have led generations of economists to dismiss as empirically false the basic tension in capitalism pointed out by Marx. Surely the rising standard of living experienced by workers all over the industrialized world put the lie to Marx's model of immiserating growth? The broad prosperity of the postwar era made many people sanguine about the market distribution of income, for they did not grasp the extent to which it was the product of unusual economic and political circumstances. In Piketty's argument, the period between World War I and the 1970s was one vast historical accident—in which massive wars, welfare states, and taxation policies restrained the rate of return on capital so that the growth rate was, for a brief window, below the profit rate. Piketty has documented the return to capitalist normal since the 1970s. And he has evolved his new ideas about the basic dynamics of capitalism in light of that history.

Structural Causes of $r > g$

But why is *the* structural tendency for the rate of profit to exceed the rate of growth $(r > g)$?

Piketty does not say.

He asserts it as a historical fact.

It could be that foreign investment allows capitalists of the core to constantly find investments abroad that keep the rate of return high, even at the expense of sovereignty and political stability in those countries. It could be because patterns of demand and production in the economy are such that we are very good at substituting capital for labor, and so increases in capital do not diminish the rate of return very much. We could also be very good at turning wealth into political influence and organizational power, keeping rates of return high and implying a much higher aggregate elasticity of substitution than models that restrict attention to demand and technology alone. It could be forces on the supply side of capital—the determinants of the savings rate. It could be because humans are less long-lived than capital, so we save for ourselves and ignore the impacts of our saving on the future capital stock. It could be because capitalists are prudent savers and innovative risk-takers, embodiments of bourgeois virtue, and *r* is the compensation required to induce them to undertake investments.

None of these satisfy Piketty. Particularly unsatisfactory are explanations derived from one pillar of optimal growth theory, the "intertemporal Euler equation," which holds that savings are only a means to one's own future consumption, either one's own in future years or one's psychic consumption today as one contemplates the rich and famous lifestyles of one's far-future descendants. Instead, a better way to think about savings is through models where accumulation and estates are ends in and of themselves. Piketty (with Saez) has been exploring this in academic papers. "Accumulate, Accumulate, that is Moses and his prophets" is a memorable line from Marx. But if it is an accurate description of the capitalist drive to invest and save, then it might be that the forces that drive the wealthy to accumulate are not just the realization of future consumption, but instead the inertia of corporate finance, an insatiable drive for economic security, sociological notions of identity or psychological fantasies of future empires or other structural imperatives.

Profit as a Kind of Rent

For example, the canonical text on corporate finance at midcentury, by Arthur Dewing, noted that "motives [that] have led men to expand business enterprises on the whole are not economic but rather psychological . . . the precious legacy of man's 'predator barbarism.'" These motives includes bequest motives—and so an important force behind accumulation is the desire to pass on wealth to children, regardless of their deservingness. But this might also be fruitfully thought of as personality changes: long life spans (particularly for the rich) make the normative line between bequests and future consumption blurry: couldn't somebody argue that your future self in seventy-five years is as much a different person from you as your child is?

When you start thinking of savings this way, the case for taxing capital becomes a lot clearer. If the supply of capital is more like real estate and less like footloose cash, basic economics suggests that we can tax it heavily. It won't disappear if you try to expropriate a part of it. You might even be doing some social good by doing so. If people are saving to pass inheritances on to their kids, then the opportunity cost of estate taxation is not old-age consumption but instead a trust fund contribution.

This also means that some classic (if fragile) theoretical results that say that optimal capital taxation should be o don't hold up anymore. Piketty suggests a fruitful research agenda here: Once freed from the consumption Euler equation, what theory of private-sector savings do we need to best understand inequality and growth? And the question about how to tax capital becomes less about the trade-off between savings and consumption, and more about how to implement global taxes to keep capitalists from taking their money offshore. Capital supply might be inelastic to the whole world, but it remains elastic for any individual country.

$$W/Y = \alpha/r$$

All this is fine, but it focuses us on the supply and demand for aggregate savings. It thus presumes that is the best way to account for wealth. However, it is clear from the data that there are very important contributions to determining W / Y made by capital gains and valuation effects. Most dynamic models suggest that these are merely transitory effects or temporary bubbles. But perhaps some of the valuation effects are fundamental. If so, how do we understand them?

One way is to take the "money view," beginning with the flows of income to various claimants as fundamental. In this view the primitives are the bargaining power of owners, α, the resulting amount of income that flows to the owners, αY, and the price of property rights to firms, which is set in financial markets as the discount or profit rate r. For simplicity, let us suppose that bargaining power of all owners is the same α, and that the capitalization rate $r\text{-}finance$ is equal for all firms, where I use $r\text{-}finance$ instead of r to distinguish the discounting rate applied to assets from the rate of return to savings. In a perfect financial market they would be the same. In an imperfect financial market with intermediation, however, the rate of return offered by the financial sector is $r\text{-}finance = r + \rho$, where r is the rate of return for savers and ρ is the user cost of financial services.

With the capital share of income and the financial rate of return as primitives, aggregate wealth to GDP becomes:

$$\frac{W}{Y} = \frac{\alpha}{r} = \frac{\alpha}{r^{finance} - \rho}$$

Just like s/g, this is just an accounting identity. It does, however, invite a different interpretation of private wealth. Wealth becomes not just an accumulated stock of past savings bottled into useful capital goods. It becomes, instead, a forward-looking claim on future resources. Rather than the sum of past savings crystallized into physical objects or social facts, what catches notice in this view is that wealth is the capitalized future incomes that flow to owners of property.

Class Struggle, Bargaining Power, Class Confidence, and Rates of Capitalization

Wealthholders' Market Position and Bargaining Power

$W/Y = \alpha/r$ shows that wealth can just as easily be seen as the ratio of two other forces than the savings rate s and the economy's growth rate g. α and r manage to provide as good an accounting decomposition of the data as the savings-to-growth ratio decomposition. The first term, α, is the share of income appropriated by owners of property. This could increase because capital is more productive, or because institutional changes have allowed owners of capital to grab more from firms—particularly the firms that produce the most revenue. This term determines, or perhaps reflects, how much income goes, as a flow, to the bearers of the property right. It reflects the distribution of bargaining power across the economy. The second term is *r-finance* $-\rho$, the rate of return that the financial sector imputes to assets such as firms, minus the share that the financial sector gets for intermediation. The second term reflects how financial markets aggregate social expectations to price the resulting property right, yielding an implicit rate of return. The value of wealth relative to income thus depends on a "Marx" term, α, and a "Keynes" term *r-finance* $-\rho$.

Concretely, widening the space of financial transactions allows more money to be pledged from the future to the present, bidding up the price of property rights today, and thus lowering the implicit discount rate *r-finance*$-\rho$,. While *r-finance* may be constant, determined by real rates of return across assets, as well as the fact that "John Bull can stand many things, but he cannot stand below 2 percent," the extent of financial capitalization, and the implicit share captured by finance ρ, may vary.

α captures as well any pure rents that capitalists are entitled to. Intellectual-property-intensive sectors, such as pharma, tech, and entertainment, and other sectors such as finance and energy are all sectors in which the value of capital is quite high. The tilt of the economy toward these sectors could be a component of the increase in W / Y. As is global real estate, which capital-izes the increased value of agglomerations, policies, and institutions.

However, complementary changes in α could come about because of changes in product markets, corporate governance, and wage-setting insti-tutions. α will be high in markets with low competition, where firms can extract high profits from consumers and workers. As we have learned from industrial organization, a large number of firms does not necessarily mean the market is competitive, particularly when the goods being sold are het-erogeneous and information frictions are high. In models of job search, the split of income between owners and workers is determined by the conditions of the labor market: the rate at which workers get job offers relative to the rate at which jobs are terminated. In efficiency wage models, it is determined by the efficacy of monitoring technology and the tightness of the labor market. In models with unions it depends on the unions' strike threat. But all of these have a common story: the income from ownership is revenue minus wages, so things that lower labor's share of income increase capital's.

Wealthholders' Bargaining Power over Time

Figure 5-1 shows the pattern of wealth inequality together with a measure of labor's bargaining power. We have a U in strike rates, an imperfect proxy for labor's bargaining power, tracking the inverted U in W / Y. Although not a great proxy for bargaining power of workers, it is somewhat better than union density, as strikes historically preceded the formation of the National Labor Relations Board (NLRB), and it is arguably the credible threat of the strike that is the source of labor's power in the United States, rather than density per se. If we take this as a force for reducing α, we can see that W / Y moves together with this measure of bargaining power.

Beyond intrafirm bargaining between workers and employers, there is also product-market power. In a world of generic increasing returns, high fixed costs, and low marginal costs, monopolies will be pervasive. This pro-vides a straightforward mechanism by which α increases, as monopolies

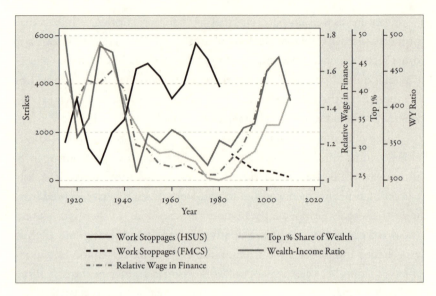

FIGURE 5-1: Using relative wages in finance as the measure of wealth inequality and work stoppages as a proxy for labor's bargaining power, we see that periods of low labor bargaining power coincide with periods of high inequality.

Source: Time-series plots showing strikes from the HSUS and the FMCS (left axis) and wealth / income ratio from Piketty (2014), top 1% share of wealth from Zucman (2016), and the relative financial wage premium from Phillippon and Reshef (2012).

transfer resources from consumers to owners of property. Indeed, one explanation for the lowered measured productivity growth in the past fifteen years is an increased role for market power, as increasing productivity does not translate into as much increased output (monopolists' restrict output), and so measured total-factor productivity (TFP) is lower even as capital's share is increasing. This view of the rise in wealth inequality makes the process less obvious and less inevitable than a view that sees wealth inequality as the quotient s / g of a growth rate bound to fall and a savings rate that had been depressed by midcentury political upheavals.

The rise in corporate concentration over the past fifteen years plays a role as well. Regulatory and technological changes have facilitated this, as has their interaction. The increasing economic importance of intellectual property law and an increasingly weak antitrust doctrine, facilitated by the law-and-economics movement, have made collusion and cartelization easier than the past.

In addition, there is very suggestive evidence that finance, in particular via large institutional investors, has a role in effectively facilitating cartelization. The airlines have become poster children for cartelization via finance, where a few institutional investors hold close to majority shares of United, Delta, Southwest, and others. Recent research shows that when additional airline shares are acquired by Blackrock, airline fares jump by 3 to 10 percent.[3] Interestingly, the major Gulf airlines, Etihad and Gulf Air, have strict foreign ownership restrictions, and so this has led to the U.S. airlines accusing them of anticompetitive practices. That monarchical Gulf Cooperation Council (GCC) parastatals are an important competitive force keeping down plane fares is amusingly absurd on one level, but generalized retrustification of the U.S. economy should make us dust off the old copies of Hilferding, Hobson, and Lenin that suggested that international conflict among national monopolies was a natural outgrowth of capitalism.

Corporate Control and Unfreedom

We can capture another one of the political dimensions of capital with incomplete contracts. Contracts between financiers, entrepreneurs, and workers (among others) can never be completely specified. Instead, large domains of the economic transaction are left to the discretion of one side of the market. A CEO like Steve Jobs complained about the power exercised by Apple's shareholders in the late 1980s as surely as Jobs's workers complained about the tyrannical power wielded by Jobs himself. As Ronald Coase argued, this distribution of power is not outside the market, but part of the transaction. Workers do what they are told because they can be kicked out of the firm, and CEOs are disciplined by boards of shareholders. As in the theory of the firm, capital often includes the right to exclude others when bargaining over jointly produced output, which raises the flow of income appropriable by owners.

These control rights will influence a commonly used measure of firm investment, Tobin's Q, the ratio of stock valuation to asset valuation. But Piketty points out that this measure as commonly used does not account for control; average stock prices reflect just the return on investment, but investors also care about having veto points over firm decision making. So in Germany and Japan, where nonshareholders have substantial say over corporate decision making (the stakeholder model), the Q is lower than in the United States and the United Kingdom. Piketty points out that German shares are "underpriced" because shareholders there do not have the same level of political power as shareholders in the United States and the U.K., because they have to share power with workers' councils and other stakeholders. The same thing is true of unions in the United States, where strong union victories in NLRB elections once reduced stock prices, yet it is very unlikely they changed the replacement value of the company's underlying assets.

Piketty spends a brief moment discussing how to interpret wealth in the form of enslaved people, which is instructive as to the difference between human capital and wealth. Under slavery, property rights to labor earnings gave an enormous share of output to owners of property. One estimate is that slaves were paid 48 percent of their marginal product, incorporating all the additional control rights conferred upon owners of slave property. However, Piketty points out that it is not clear whether slave wealth should be considered net wealth, as it could be thought of, somewhat bloodlessly, as a liability for slaves that is capitalized as an asset for slave owners. But in the end he agrees that this is wealth, because it is a market traded, institutionally protected stream of income. It is not the actual machine or building (or person), but instead the property right to the resulting income flow and the forum for trading it, that constitutes the true "capital." The Thirteenth Amendment imposes severe limits on what is enforceable in the labor contract, so that capitalizations of human capital do not (yet) occur in modern capitalism, and so it is worth distinguishing between human capital and wealth, as Piketty does. Of course, the enslaved people themselves are productive, generating output, and propping up the value of other assets. For example, following the Civil War, land values collapsed in slave areas, even relative to adjacent nonslave counties along the Ohio River, as slaves withdrew their labor and planters lost the productivity of the gang system. But the tradable property right to a flow of human labor can be productive beyond its immediate use in production: slaves were deployed as collateral for the business ventures of their owners and guaranteed extensive credit networks in the antebellum Atlantic economy.

Class Confidence and Capitalization Rates

The other component of the $W/Y = \alpha/r$ equation is $r = r\text{-}finance - \rho$. This term captures the fact that capital is not just a claim on today's output, but a claim on tomorrow's. Because of its durability, the other dimension setting the wealth-to-income ratio is the valuation of the future income stream accruing from the asset. This capitalization ratio $1/r$ is determined by the financial system, by corporate governance and creditor monitoring, by the demand and supply for future income, and of course by monetary policy—a point to which I return below.

How markets arbitrage property rights to future streams of income, and the extent to which expectations move money from the future to the present, is crucial to this view of W / Y. But these factors tend to get ignored when the steady-state formula is simply s / g. Indeed, the fundamental role of social expectations in determining the aggregate wealth-to-income role gets highlighted in this view. If wealth is effectively a title to an expected future income flow, then how markets aggregate expectations will have a role in determining the discount rate applied to those titles. Indeed, one role for institutions (such as the state's willingness to defend property rights) is to anchor these expectations, and ideas from Keynes and Minsky become important not just for the fluctuations in the business cycle but for the stock of wealth in society. The aggregated market expectations expressed in r may be why W / Y is a good indicator of crisis: it contains the miner's canary for hypertrophied optimism about the future

The financial wage premium shown in Figure 5-1 also closely tracks W / Y. This measures ρ, the flow of revenue accruing to financial services. As can be seen, it closely tracks financial deregulation, as well as W / Y. Holding the overall rate of return on firms fixed at $r\text{-}finance$, as the degree of financial rent seeking increases and the amount claimed by the financial sector ρ, increases, W / Y increases as well.

Focusing on, α/r also reveals features of the dispersion of wealth, rather than just its level. Consider that the variance of log wealth will be: $var(\log w) = var(\log \alpha Y) + var(\log r) - 2Cov(\log \alpha Y, \log r)$. Thus, the dispersion in rates of return as well as the dispersion in capital income will both increase inequality in wealth.

Importantly, wealth inequality decreases with the covariance term: when people with large shares of capital income also have low discount rates, given to them by either government privileges or financial services, wealth inequality increases. Financial institutions and markets may also increase the ability of the rich to take advantage of rents and dispersion in returns more broadly, creating political demand for arbitrary regulation and opportunities for arbitrage. Consider the recent evidence from Jason Furman and Peter Orszag, who argue that the rising importance of rents plays a role in increasing inequality.[4] They argue that artificially scarce housing stock in productive cities (where the scarcity is caused by both regulation and poor transportation infrastructure), or firms with strong patent rights, increasing returns, and facing thin labor markets are increasing α, the amount of income going to owners of property. But they also argue that the dispersion in firm equity returns and return on invested capital is increasing, which they interpret as evidence of rents (and one could add increasing spatial income segregation as another dimension). If the income going to owners of given firms / real estate is becoming increasingly dispersed, the returns to financial services that deliver high-yield portfolios goes up. Rich individuals might find it worthwhile to pay fees in order to increase the covariance of their share portfolio with the companies and locations that generate the most income for their owners, exacerbating wealth inequality.

Rentiers and Supermanagers

Seeing capital this way also blurs the line between supermanagers and rentiers. Supermanagers happen to have labor market contracts (in the form of bonuses and deferred pay as well as stocks and options) that entitle them to stupendous income when the firm is doing well. Far from a return on human capital, it distinctly reflects information constraints and legal norms (such as the granting of fixed numbers of options). It is not clear that this is "labor" income as much as it is a form of capital that requires you to run meetings and wear a power suit. We might do well to consider a continuum of "capital-like" contracts organizing a value chain, ranging from fixed wages for workers at the bottom to full residual claimants on risk for shareholders, with CEOs in the middle.

If CEO pay were capitalized like capital income, this would obviously exacerbate the wealth / income ratio enormously. This means that CEOs with these contracts will have high ownership shares in their firms, and

CEOs of large successful companies will also be extremely wealthy. The high covariance of CEO pay with profits of firms makes it look more like capital income than labor income, and so it is unclear that CEO pay net of base pay should be counted as labor income for economic purposes, despite the fact it comes on a W-2. On top of this, capital gains tax breaks increase the incentive to shift compensation packages toward capital income. These institutional forces of wealth accumulation are obscured when wealth is understood solely as savings + capital gains, and the wealth / income ratio is expressed solely as savings rates over growth rates. While I would not dispute the usage of that accounting framework for some purposes, the, α-r-$finance$-ρ. view is more illuminating of institutions of corporate governance, finance, labor and product markets, and overall changes in economic organization than the mechanical and institution-free s/g.

The Politics of Institutional Construction as the Fundamental Determinant of W / Y

If, as argued above, wealth is determined by the underlying rules of the game, then it increases the role of politics as a determinant of W / Y.

For "domesticated Piketty," politics enters only at the determination of the tax rate, redistributing after the market has done its marginal pricing work, and so reduces s in:

$$W/Y = s/g$$

But the institutional, money, political-economy view provides clues to help us explain why wealthholders fight so hard to translate newly earned wealth into political prerogatives and influence: they understand that continued accumulation depends on maintaining the promised flow of income, a task that requires durable policy commitments—that is, institutions. If both α and ρ are fixed by institutions themselves endogenous to the distribution of political power, then politics is intimately tied to the preservation and defense of wealth. The market structures and regulations that ensure a steady return to property titles, as well as maintenance of thick, liquid, and ideally low-tax markets in those titles are not guaranteed, but instead must be maintained via government administration and the legal system.

A Broader Set of Public-Policy Tools for Managing the Wealth Distribution

If you are interested in cutting down privately owned wealth relative to income, the basic levers are these:

- Lowering the share of income paid out to property titles.
- Regulating the financial markets that price those titles.

These include the typical roster of left-egalitarian policies: robust antitrust commitment, eliminating barriers to entry and mobility, a more aggressive private-sector labor movement, demanding more from shareholders at the bargaining table, weakened intellectual property rights, central bank policy, and public sources of investment (such as housing) and employment. But besides the bargaining power channel, regulating W / Y also means putting constraints on the ability to pledge money from the future via financial contracts—for example, by raising capital requirements and restricting the space of financial innovations—as well as potentially reforms of stock market microstructure or a financial transactions tax. Indeed Kuznets himself writes about the myriad options: "One group of factors counteracting the cumulative effect of concentration of savings upon upper-income shares is legislative interference and "political" decisions. These may be aimed at limiting the accumulation of property directly through inheritance taxes and other explicit capital levies. They may produce similar effects indirectly, e.g., by government-permitted or -induced inflation which reduces the economic value of accumulated wealth stored in fixed-price securities or other properties not fully responsive to price changes; or by legal restriction of the yield on accumulated property, as happened recently in the form of rent controls or of artificially low long-term interest rates maintained by the government to protect the market for its own bonds."[5] Contrast this panoply of options to the narrow focus in Piketty's oeuvre on taxation. Piketty's big policy idea is taxing capital directly and globally. The most compelling argument for this is that most of the return to capital is not paid out, but instead accumulated and added to the stock, and so taxing the stock directly is one way to get at the bulk of capital income. So, consistent with the measurement framework above, the share of income accruing to capitalists is in fact not observed. This is different, importantly, from dividend or capital gains taxation. It is a progressive tax on total wealth, not just the amount paid out to the holders of wealth or upon the sale of an asset. Indeed, the wealth tax immediately lowers the post-tax α, as it reduces the claim on income held by the owners of wealth. But the most important implication is that implementing the tax would require sharing bank information across borders, which would disable tax havens and produce reliable information on global wealth holdings. The idea is clearly Foucauldian: taxes produce the public subject of wealth and make it knowable, legible, and governable. The data alone, as the recent Panama Papers illustrate, can be used to improve the tax regime as well as document the distribution of wealth for public debate.

Piketty also discusses various fiscal systems, pointing out that on the expenditure side, universal public goods do more than targeted transfers in terms of equalizing income. Piketty argues that in Europe, at least, the state transfers roughly 25 to 35 percent of income in the form of entitlements and replacement incomes, and so there is unlikely to be a big increase in the economic size of the state, anything comparable to the increase in the mid-twentieth century. I think this is basically true, and the innovations in the welfare state will not come in the form of expenditures of higher percentages of GDP.

Piketty's Aversion to Macroeconomic Policy as a Tool of Wealth-Distribution Management

Importantly, Piketty takes a stand *against* two fiscal instruments: public debt and inflation. He argues that the public debt is largely a way to transfer from taxpayers to (wealthy) bondholders, and that inflation will not affect the vast bulk of wealth, which is held in real assets. I think there are those who would argue that this aversion to the public debt is a result of Piketty being supply-side focused and ignoring the more "Keynesian" determinants of wealth that the ρ parameter might make salient. Along with this, one thing that Piketty ignores is monetary policy in general. If monetary policy can affect real growth, it can also affect real inequality, and it is a force that, $\alpha\text{-}r$ emphasizes but $s\text{-}g$ does not.

For example, Kopczuk shows that much of the post-2000 increase in 0.1 percent share in wealth is driven by fixed income securities, which get capitalized at a high rate when Fed interest rates are low.[6] Monetary policy might have a role in explaining wealth holdings.

The Other Side of Political Economy:
The Influence of Wealth on Politics

Given the rich institutional menu of policies available for managing the distribution of income and making the wealth of the rich more salient, why don't we get redistributive policies?

The view spelled out by Piketty in his the book makes wealth inequality a problem for the social planner, not a problem of democracy. W/Y is an automatic result of s/g. The government needs to boost g and impose the proper taxes to shape s. While there is some gesture toward how political systems can change inequality, there is little in *Capital in the Twenty-First Century* about how inequality changes the political system. This is a gaping missing chapter in Piketty. Let me, very briefly, try to fill it—to illuminate the various mechanisms by which inequality in the economic domain also distorts government policy.

New Tools the Super-Rich Can Use to Manage Politics

In some ways, the commercialized politics of the twenty-first century offers entirely new tools for superwealth to manage the political system:

We have "markets in everything." The wealthy can purchase educational reform, the charity of their choice, think tanks, legislative language, political influence, and endless public broadcast of their ideas. Campaign contributions are a good place to start, with there being evidence that political donations (a) are a normal good,[7] and (b) have, at the top, a wealth elasticity close to 1.[8] This suggests that as the wealth distribution becomes more skewed, the campaign contribution distribution will also become more skewed. Indeed, Lee Drutman documents an increasing share of traceable individual campaign contributions (close to 25 percent) coming from the "1 percent of the 1 percent," which is around 30,000 people.[9] But from Brazil to Brussels, and from Washington to Beijing, money and promises of money grease the wheels of politics, sometimes detected, sometimes eliciting a brief round of outrage, sometimes not. It is difficult to celebrate "markets in everything" and not expect generalized corruption as the result. When speech and broadcast media are themselves allocated on markets, and the means to contest elections are allocated via the cash nexus, it is a short step to policy being set by the median dollar.

But we should not overstate this channel. Is it that all of the expenditures cancel each other out? Billionaires might be wasting their money, raising the wages of political consultants and the revenue of advertising companies in the process as in a classic Tullock contest. Parties, interest groups, and candidates burn resources to beat each other. Thus, any advantage by one side raises the returns to investments on the other side. But this cannot be all that is going on. The need for campaign finance shapes who politicians listen to. Recent work in political science, for example, convincingly finds that perceived contributors are much more likely to get a meeting with the politician or a senior chief of staff.[10] The marginal return to campaign contributions is quite high.

In a contest model, the increase in the supply of campaign finance being higher (because of higher inequality, for instance) can increase the marginal return for both sides of the contest. There is also the fact that the technology for turning money into sophisticated, data-driven, get-out-the-vote operations and policy influence has gotten better, increasing the "demand" for campaign contributions. Partly this is an aspect of changes in party organization, whereby party leadership has exercised more control, and so general funds wielded by party leaders have become more important. But we should not rule out technological and organizational changes in political finance. One example is the "leadership PACs," which are PACs created by members of Congress to fund other members, effectively creating a portfolio of campaigns for an eager donor to contribute to.

Old Tools the Super-Rich Can Use to Manage Politics

In other ways, however, the tools for superwealth to manage the political system are of long standing. Besides purchasing voice, the wealthy can also wield the threat of exit. A classic political tool is the capital strike, as Piketty points out in his brief discussion of the Mitterand government. Because property owners can transmute their assets into hidden, invisible obligations abroad, the disciplining effect of capital flight is an important one for any small open economy. Tax havens, as recent news and Gabriel Zucman's work have pointed out,[11] make this threat even more salient, and a paper by Ellman and Wantchekon[12] showed how the anticipation of capital flight could alone alter the outcome of elections. An older Marxism burned time and energy, for example, in the famous Poulantzas-Miliband exchange in

New Left Review,[13] debating exactly how capital owners controlled the formally democratic state. Did they do so by filling its administrative posts with their allies? Did they do so by threatening it with a capital strike? Miliband argued that the state was captured by the rich by virtue of the class background of the bulk of government leaders—and his children's unwillingness to publicly plump for egalitarian full-employment policies when they led the British Labour Party would seem to suggest that he was on to something. Poulantzas countered by saying it wouldn't matter if they were all loyal partisans of labor; the fact that the state needed private investment to keep the economy going was enough of a constraint to keep the state operating in the interest of capital owners—a position that underpins the arguments of the many, many who call for the summoning of the "Confidence Fairy." Indeed, capital flight likely stymied much of the redistribution that would have accompanied democratization in, for example, South Africa.

The rise of housing wealth is uniquely interesting, as housing and land are intrinsically tied to particular policies and local politics. The stock of housing wealth capitalizes not just amenities and agglomerations, but also local politics.[14] Because it is the perception of security that matters for the promises of future income enshrined in assets, laws and policies to alter those perceptions become political demands. Tough-on-crime policies and land-use regulations may have been devices demanded by NIMBY *petit rentiers* to prop up the value of houses and commercial real estate. In the decentralized policy world of the United States, housing markets severely constrain the level of redistribution that is feasible. For example, there is effectively no public school system in the United States: there is a private school system and the housing market. Similarly, at the world level, real estate allows the global rich to park their money (and their families) in countries with secure property rights and pleasant amenities. The accumulation of housing wealth may be a reflection of political arbitrage both within and between countries.

One domain worth examining further is how wealth inequality not only affects the mechanics of elections and lobbying, but also changes the space of policy ideas and political ideology. Perhaps this is because technical expertise on policy making is often scarce in government, thus the market for regulatory human capital allows hoarding of expertise by the private sector. Regulators with enough knowledge to effectively regulate are also those who are in high demand as employees and consultants by those that would be regulated. This leads to the well-known revolving-door problem. Financial regulation, with its daunting complexity, may be particularly susceptible to this. But indeed, it may be that the complexity is instrumental for the politics: raise the cognitive barrier to entry into the debate, and watch the political determinants of p be set completely behind the scenes by well-funded and well-informed insiders.

As another example, the lack of in-house policy-making resources allows for business-funded entities like ALEC that draft model legislation. Alex Hertel-Fernandez in recent work[15] shows that in states where legislators spend less of their time on policy-making activities and government is less professionalized, the chance of ALEC legislation being enacted is higher. Similarly, think tanks like Heritage, Hoover, and AEI have been able to parlay donations into rafts of policy on topics ranging from taxes to school reform to foreign policy.

A corollary of this is the influence wealth inequality has on scholarship, particularly in economics and finance. Top-tier economists regularly are solicited for consultations and high-paid talks with banks. The embrace of industrial organization by the private sector may be partially born out of a need to harness the tools of market design, but it is also a way to compromise experts who could credibly deliver pro-antitrust testimony in European or American regulatory hearings or judicial trials. The rise of business schools and financial economics owes a lot to the rise of wealth in the economy, in demand for both accreditation and supply of endowment money. Universities depend more on private than on public money, and the interests of the rich come to set the intellectual agenda here, too. Fourcade and her coauthors show a large rise in finance citations in economics.[16] They, further, write that:

> As the academic field of economics shifted toward business schools—
> and away from government—economists faced a new set of practical,
> intellectual, and political entanglements: higher levels of compensation,
> new connections and consulting opportunities, and often different
> politics as well (Jelveh, Kogut, and Naidu 2014). In the 1980s, suspicion
> of government action grew markedly within the field, and economists
> arguably supplied part of the intellectual rationale for the deregulatory
> movement in public policy and for the expanded use of price and market

mechanisms in education, transportation, healthcare, the environment, and elsewhere (Blyth 2002). Financial economists argued forcefully that the purpose of corporations was to maximize shareholder value, and provided a scientific justification for the management practices favored by a new generation of corporate raiders: leveraged buy-outs, mergers and acquisitions, and compensating corporate executives with stock options. In a recent indictment of the pervasiveness of the capture of economists by business interests, Zingales (2013) found that, when none of their authors worked in a business school, economics articles were significantly "less likely to be positive on the level of executive compensation, and significantly more likely to be negative."[17]

Spheres of Wealth-Dictated Injustice

Finally, there are the less tangible, but no less noxious, effects of wealth inequality on the allocation of pretty much everything.

When we have a full set of markets, Arrow-Debreu style, rich people (those with a more valuable endowment) receive a higher weight in the implicit social welfare function implemented by the market.[18] Indeed, one of the pernicious things about the combination of fantastic wealth inequality and extensive "markets in everything" is that the arbitrary whims of the 0.1 percent can change entire social priorities and the options the rest of us face. This is clearly true in market allocations, so that product spaces and pricing structures target the parts of the demand curve where rich people sit.

It is also potentially even more challenging when considering philanthropy and private provision of public goods. We might get technocratic do-gooders like Bill Gates. We might get a portfolio of politicians and think tanks backed by Sheldon Adelson or George Soros (or the Kochs and the Sandlers). But regardless of the merits of the work any of these mega-donors do, the fact that massive wealth inequality allows society's priorities to be engineered to the tastes of a few is profoundly undemocratic—even if it is better than the rich simply hoarding their wealth. Donors call the shots with respect to development policy, research priorities, and social reform initiatives. Their whimsy dictates the allocation of billions. Yale cultivates its loyal and well-heeled alumni to feed its endowment while low-cost, high-quality public universities are starved of funds by cash-strapped legis-latures. The world of extensive markets and enormous inequality allows much more of the allocation of resources to be influenced by the wealthy. The twenty-first-century capitalist keeps his social power, his bond with so-ciety, with his private wealth manager.

This private power, exercised via competitive markets for incomplete contracts in land, labor, and credit markets, can also undermine basic egali-tarian norms. A democratic republic should pass philosopher Phillip Pettit's "eyeball" and "sore loser" tests. The first test of an egalitarian society is whether individual citizens can afford look each other in the eye. The second test is that individuals do not feel like the system is rigged against them. Policies should have a presumptive bias toward creating a society that can pass these two tests.

Wealth inequality and at-will contracts for labor create a society that fails this first test. In such societies, we have more low-wage employees who have to laugh at the jokes of their bosses. We have more women workers who have to tolerate the unwanted advances of middle managers under the threat of layoff or foregone promotion. An economic democracy minimizes the threat that economic opportunities and everyday well-being can be drasti-cally altered by the idiosyncratic tastes of relatively few others. The everyday encounter most people have with accumulated wealth is not through prices in the market for shoes, or the society pages. It is, instead, through the indigni-ties, control, and threats inflicted by their employers, landlords, and bankers.

Feudal lords were wealthy, but the absence of certain types of markets made their social power less than a simple function of the value of the land over which they claimed to exercise *seisin*. Loyal men-at-arms and properly trained and mounted vassals were an independent basis of status. They were not simply purchasable.

Little of this cavalier privilege exists in modern capitalism. There is an important nasty complementarity between a "fully incentivized" world and massive inequality in income and wealth. When every action can have pecu-niary rewards attached to it, and every source of well-being can be priced at exactly a person's willingness to pay, the social power commanded by the rich is magnified in a way that is difficult to see when comparing a dollar in 1920 with a dollar today. The increased use of markets not only generates economic inequality, but also allows that economic inequality to generate political inequality, which may have been previously protected from market forces in some separate Walzerian sphere of distributional justice.

The old Hayekian line was that only large accumulations of private property could enable freedom. In the absence of private wealth, who could afford to undertake politics that might cross the will of those who controlled the levers of the all-mighty state? The still earlier Tocquevilleian line was that the liberties—plural—of the different estates were essential blockages to both absolutist tyranny and the potential tyranny of some future aristocracy of manufactures united in its own material interest and unchecked by any reciprocal ties of obligation to those to whom it does not swear to provide good lordship in exchange for vassalage but only pays a wage. Perhaps we are approaching Hayek's dream and finding that it is Tocqueville's nightmare.

Conclusion

We can now spell out the full political-economy equilibrium:

The "money view" lets us see the determinants of the wealth / income ratio as being more about bargaining, monopoly, and finance than about savings and growth rates. The "money view" leads us to examine noncompetitive, nonaggregative theories of distribution. It brings institutions into the forefront in explaining the capital-labor split of income, and the capitalization of expected future capital income into wealth at the current rate of profit. We no longer even attempt to deduce the distribution of wealth from the timeless principles of competitive markets and the twin Eulers: Euler's theorem applied to CRS production functions and an Euler equation for consumption. We wind up, instead, having to investigate the details of the economy—its idiosyncratic rules, market structures, and norms that govern distribution.

As a payoff from this point of view, we get to reinterpret and refine the Kuznets curve predictions.

Regulations, policies, norms, and "institutions" determine the capital share parameter α and the rate of profit r, which in turn determine the level of W / Y. The distribution and level of wealth can then generate political influences that alter those same regulations, norms, and policies. We can imagine multiple path-dependent Kuznets trajectories. They all begin with some technologically induced initial inequality of wealth (possibly including human capital). That level then reproduces itself by generating a set of institutions and policies that amplifies and secures the returns to wealth holding. This trajectory can lead to a "Kuznets plateau", which it would take a substantial shock to disrupt.

But there can be other trajectories.

In those other trajectories, the initial inequality does not alter institutions in a way that allows inequality to reproduce itself. In these latter trajectories, Kuznets transitions would be short and shallow—more Schumpeter's transitory winners than Pareto's permanent oligarchs.

Given the arc of increasing inequality in the West, we may well be headed for the first, long and painful, variant of the Kuznets transition.

SIX

The Ubiquitous Nature of Slave Capital

DAINA RAMEY BERRY

Historian Daina Ramey Berry takes on *Capital in the Twenty-First Century*'s characterization of slaves and slavery as a just another part of the capital stock, one that disappeared at emancipation and was quickly replaced by other varieties. Instead, Berry argues that slavery perfused the entire economy, not just plantation agriculture. She shows that slaves were owned by corporations and municipalities, that they constructed public infrastructure and constituted the patrimony of large nonprofit institutions. Further, as tradable property they sustained the financial system that in turn allowed capitalism to take shape atop the foundation it laid. Altogether, Berry argues, we cannot understand Capital in the nineteenth, twentieth, or twenty-first century without properly accounting for slavery, which *Capital in the Twenty-First Century* fails to do.

In the spring and summer of 1848, the Southern Railroad Company purchased eighty-two enslaved laborers from slaveholders in Virginia to complete a transportation route supporting trade between the Upper and Lower South (Figure 6-1). From May through July, the company spent $46,398 on enslaved men (n = 66, or 80.5 percent) and women (n = 16, or 19.5 percent). Juliet E. Washington, a slaveholder from Richmond, Virginia, sold twenty-six-year-old Phil to the company for $600 on May 15 after guaranteeing that there were no other claims against him and that he was "sound and healthy." Aside from his value and age, Washington noted Phil's color as "black or brown" and indicated that he was about "5 feet 3½ inches high" with a scar on "his right hand between his thumb and forefinger." Another slave named Scipio joined Phil that day, when his enslaver sold him for the same price, although he was slightly younger—twenty-two years old—with "no marks" and 5 feet 2½ inches high. Enslaved women including Nancy, Adaline, Lucy

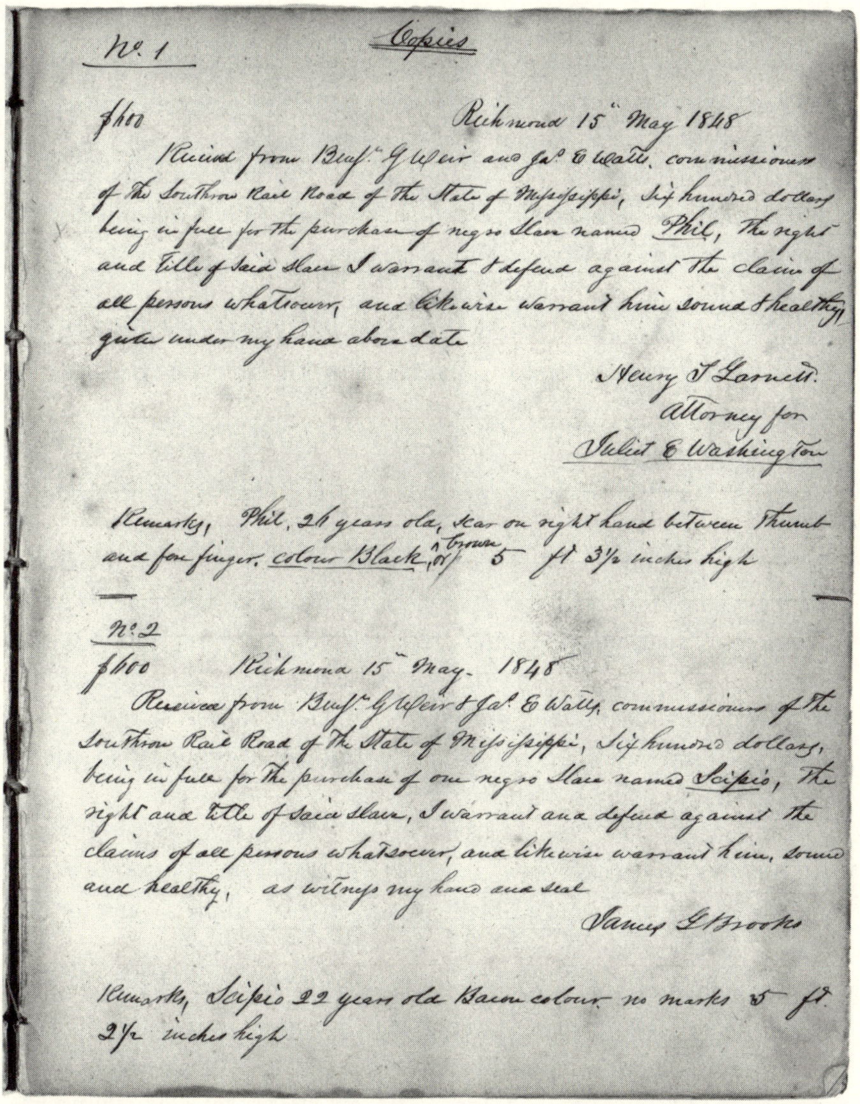

No. 1 Copies

$600 Richmond 15th May 1848

Received from Benjn. G Weir and Jas. E Watts, commissioners of the Southern Rail Road of the State of Mississippi, Six hundred dollars being in full for the purchase of negro Slave named Phil, the right and title of said Slave I warrant & defend against the claims of all persons whatsoever, and likewise warrant him sound & healthy, given under my hand above date

Henry T Garnett
Attorney for
Juliet E Washington

Remarks, Phil, 21 years old, scar on right hand between thumb and fore finger. colour Black, or brown 5 ft 3½ inches high

No. 2

$600 Richmond 15th May 1848

Received from Benjn. G Weir & Jas. E Watts, commissioners of the Southern Rail Road of the State of Mississippi, Six hundred dollars, being in full for the purchase of one negro Slave named Scipio, the right and title of said slave, I warrant and defend against the claims of all persons whatsoever, and likewise warrant him, sound and healthy, as witness my hand and seal

James G Brooks

Remarks, Scipio 22 years old Bacon colour no marks 5 ft 2½ inches high

FIGURE 6-1: One page from the ledger demonstrates purchases of enslaved people like Phil and Scipio to work on the railroad.

Source: Southern Railroad Ledger, Purchases for 1848, Natchez Trace Slaves and Slavery Collection, #2E775, Dolph Briscoe Center for American History, University of Texas at Austin.

Ann, Jane, and Eliza were also sold to the Southern Railroad Company. Some of the enslaved were sold in pairs, such as sisters Carolina and Harriett, and Juliet Ann and Henry, who were mother and son.[1] For three months, slaveholders in Virginia sold select enslaved people to the company to clear, grade, lay tracks, cook, clean, and serve the burgeoning railroad industry. Such labor transactions continued during the Civil War and after as freedpeople continued to search for wage-earning work.[2]

Why does it matter that U.S. railroad companies owned enslaved people? More importantly, what does this have to do with Thomas Piketty's *Capital in the Twenty-First Century*? The answers to these questions are grounded in definitions.

Defining Capital

Piketty's definition of capital is both inclusive and exclusive. Although he identifies three forms—real property, financial, and professional—he also mentions human and slave capital without defining the latter. This inclusive definition of capital "defined as the sum total of nonhuman assets that can be owned and exchanged on some market" literally omits enslaved people. Piketty sets them aside and tells the reader that human property is a special case that will be addressed later in the book.

This promised discussion of slavery is relegated to seven pages of Piketty's opus. In his opinion, slave capital was a component of private capital, and thus does not warrant a full discussion. He also fails to account for the public use of enslaved labor.

Through a series of questions he brings the reader to a specific set of definitions that address "forms" of capital as well as how capital "changed over time."[3] The first form, human capital—defined as "an individual's labor power, skills, training and abilities"—Piketty clearly states he "always excludes" from his book with the exception of a brief discussion in the subsection, "New World and Old World: The Importance of Slavery."[4] Piketty's second form of capital, real property, encompasses residential real estate and land. The next two forms, financial capital and professional capital, include "plants, infrastructure, machinery, patents, etc." and are "used by firms and government agencies."[5] Given these definitions, Piketty writes slavery or slave capital *out* of this narrative. However, his cursory attention to the institution as a whole, and enslaved people in particular, points to a significant gap in his argument. Enslaved people produced the financial capital that circulated in transnational markets through firms and governmental agencies that utilized their labor.

Piketty's book is the quintessential study of capitalism this millennium. It is dense, yet written in accessible language. His primary thesis can be streamlined into one brief sentence: Invested capital will grow faster than income, resulting in the rich getting richer. Exploring the history of income inequality in Britain, France, and the United States, he identifies important changes over time, which in most cases he attributes to wars, technological advances, property, investments, and so on. The book's online technical appendix offers more sophisticated analyses for the trained economist, political scientist, or interlocutor interested in tables, graphs, and more complex interpretations of this material. Delivering the news that the top 1 percent are on an upward trajectory that will continue to increase the gap between them and the 99 percent, there is still hope for those who follow the Occupy Wall Street movement because Piketty offers a redistribution plan to narrow the gap between the wealthy elite, the middle class, and the poor.

≡ll≡

This chapter focuses on enslaved people as literal human capital who infiltrated the very spaces from which Piketty excludes them. Emphasizing the last two categories of professional and financial capital through an exploration of government and private firms, I argue that Piketty grossly underestimates foundational aspects of the world economy. Simply put, he has written a book on the economy using definitions of capital that remove slavery from the equation and ignores the fact that slave trading and slave labor were at the foundations of Western economies from the fifteenth through nineteenth centuries. Most major European countries participated in the buying and selling of human chattel. The colonial and antebellum 1 percent became rich by exploiting enslaved people's labor—a dynamic of capital accumulation very different from the anodyne one Piketty models, in which passive saving and accumulation simply grow faster than earned income from labor. We have too much evidence from private and public companies that were built and sustained *because of* enslaved labor to tell the history of capital without it. First, however, we must begin with a working definition of slave capital.

As a scholar of slavery, my instinct is to define slave capital as the total value (in dollars) that any given enslaver (large or small) commodified in the bodies of slaves. This could be reflected in the amount of money inventoried in appraisals of estates, assessed through probate upon the death of an enslaver, levied annually in tax returns, calculated periodically in mortgages, deeded occasionally in gifts, insured strategically in policies, or determined posthumously in autopsies. Through these forms of enumerative documentation, values were determined based on a host of variables (including age, sex, skill, health, and temperament). Each individual enslaved person had a value that could be calculated and totaled to determine enslavers' net worth in human chattel. Likewise, slave capital is also represented in the profit enslavers made *from* the goods enslaved people produced, minus the amount of money it cost to care for them.

Slave capital = value in bodies + productive output of bodies
− cost (to sustain them)

In New World plantation societies, enslaved labor and enslaved people shaped the public and private wealth of a relatively elite population. Some of these elite families have been identified and exposed by contemporary movements and legislation to disclose public and private corporations' links to slavery. In the summer of 2015, University College London in conjunction with the BBC aired a two-part documentary titled "Britain's Forgotten Slave-Owners" and launched an open-source website, "Legacies of British Slave-Ownership," which traces the £20 million compensation policy offered to British slave owners to offset the loss of their slave capital in the wake of emancipation.[6] Such exposure comes in the wake of ongoing efforts led by Caribbean Community, formally known as the Caribbean Community and Common Market (CARICOM), who seek former slaveholding European nations to "engage Caribbean governments in reparatory dialogue" that addresses "the living legacies of these crimes."[7] An investigation into the long-term economic aftermath of slave capital has also occurred on smaller, or more individual scales. Some states and city governments in the United States have begun to grapple with slavery-era insurance policies that carry fiscal weight today. For example, the California State Legislature is-sued SB 2199, "Slavery Era Insurance Policies," in 2000 requiring companies to disclose records in their archives that relate to slave policies. Docu-menting this history according to the law provides "the first evidence of ill-gotten profits from slavery, which profits in part from capitalized insurers whose successors remain in existence today."[8] It is precisely these efforts, which expose disparities in wealth or that trace the economic effects of slave ownership on public and private finance, that function to inspire policies that might change them.

However, when an elite group of policyholders benefit from and control historical and existing policies, it is difficult to force them to make changes. Piketty projects that the top 1 percent will continue to increase their wealth with little motivation to redistribute. This was also true in the history of slavery, which has a traceable effect on individual and institutional wealth. Understanding this documented history provides an opportunity for policy changes that address inequality.

Historians argue that by the middle of the nineteenth century, "less than 25 percent of white southerners owned enslaved people."[9] They were the elite members of society, many of whom were political leaders, judges, doc-tors, and lawyers—individuals who influenced legislation and maintained their positions of power. In terms of disparities and historical legacies, this structure created generational wealth that has greatly plagued nations in-volved in the slave trade. If Piketty is correct in stating that "the return on all forms of capital is five percent per year" and that the value of slave capital in the United States from 1770 to 1810 represented 1.5 years of national in-come, then his estimates have been grossly undercounted because his defini-tions neglect all forms of slave capital housed in institutions and firms alike.[10] Human capital in the form of enslaved laborers contributed to the wealth of public and private businesses, including the Southern Railroad and Baltimore Life Insurance Company; public and private universities in-cluding the University of North Carolina and Dartmouth College; and state and municipal governments. This means that Piketty's assertion that he "always excludes human capital" is incorrect. In fact, he (in)directly *in-cludes* human capital through calculations of public wealth generated from businesses (insurance companies), industries (railroad), patents (cotton gin), and municipal governments (levees, canals, and bridges). The omission of slave capital generated on plantations and in private hands strikes me as problematic as well, but rather than discuss slave capital on plantations, I will directly addresses Piketty's omission by exploring the value of slave capital in industrial and municipal settings. Enslaved people were considered chattel, a movable form of real property. This means that they were simultaneously person and product, or as historian Walter Johnson notes, "a person with a price."[11] Slave capital represented wealth generated from enslaved people, yet human capital according to Piketty did not necessarily refer to human chattels.[12] For Piketty, slave capital and human capital are not always interchangeable. Understanding this phenomenon is one of the challenges of history, but it is an even greater challenge for those interested in the economics of slavery.

Historiography

Since the turn of the twentieth century, scholars interested in the intersection of slavery and economy have approached the topic in a variety of ways. Some focused solely on economic profitability, enslaved productivity, or technological advancement, whereas others were more concerned with regional crop specialization, temporal market changes, or slave-trading patterns. This brief list by no means covers all of the topical interests of scholars writing about slave economy, but it suggests the range of analytical approaches taken by historians focused on the economics of slavery.

W. E. B. Du Bois was one of the first to initiate conversation about slavery and economic development. Published in 1896 during what must be described as a low point in African American history, Du Bois's *Suppression of the African Slave Trade to the United States of America* was very much an economic history. African Americans in the 1890s suffered from vigilante justice in the form of widespread lynching and extreme discrimination. Du Bois, the first African American to receive a PhD in history at Harvard University, researched and wrote about the suppression of the slave trade, a topic he believed was "so intimately connected to . . . the system of American slavery, and the whole colonial policy" that one could not ignore it.[13] Relying upon a host of sources, including "national, state, and colonial statutes, Congressional documents, reports of societies, personal narratives," Du Bois was confident in his findings but humbly acknowledged that sources bearing the "economic side of the study have been difficult to find."[14] He did find, however, that by 1700 the trade in human chattel had become an "unquestioned axiom in British practical economics."[15] Focusing on the United States' shift from a group of colonies to a full-fledged nation, Du Bois identified a historical moment when debates about the trade could have led to an abolition of it along with the abolition of slavery. However, he concluded, American colonists "preferred to enrich themselves on its profits."[16]

Nearly two decades later, historian U. B. Phillips published the first book on slavery in the United States. Riddled with language reflective of the early twentieth century, a time of troubling race relations, rife with lynchings, segregation, and eugenics, Phillips clearly stated that "slaves were both persons and property, and as chattels they were investments."[17] In the pages that followed, he offered an economic analysis of slavery and slaveholding in the United States through the use of plantation records, account books, diaries, census data, and a host of other resources. He explored topics such as plantation management, slave prices, insurance, and enslaved laborers in the railroad industry. Phillips also criticized economists for virtually ignoring the subject of slavery—a criticism that is not true today, but one that some might direct at Piketty.

As scholars became more interested in slave economy, the conversation shifted to capitalism and slavery. In 1944, Caribbean historian Eric Williams published a study that remains a key text for understanding the intersection between slavery and capitalism. Like Du Bois, Williams highlighted the connection between the transatlantic slave trade, slavery, the rise of British capitalism, and emancipation, but he focused on the Caribbean.[18] He used British records to trace the history of slavery, arguing that "most writers of this period have ignored" the enslaved.[19] Rather than erasing them from this history, Williams devoted his final chapter to them. In it, he discussed British West Indian reforms to punishment, mobility, religious instruction, and labor regulation. It was this foundational work that created the burgeoning field of slavery and capitalism studies that reverberates in historical discussions today.

Few studies to date have garnered the same degree of discussion and criticism as Robert Fogel and Stanley Engerman's *Time on the Cross*. Writing nearly thirty years after Williams, in 1974, the two economists boldly introduced cliometrics to examine the quantitative aspects of slavery. Relying on mathematical and statistical formulas, this new methodological approach became popular after advances in computer processing occurred in the mid-late 1940s. Following the lead of Harvard scholars Alfred Conrad and John Meyer, Fogel and Engerman sought to reinterpret the history of slavery by making ten key controversial interventions.[20] They argued that enslavers made sound decisions about a "highly profitable" business; that slavery thrived on the eve of the Civil War; that field hands were hard workers; that slave breeding and family separation were exaggerated; and that enslaved laborers were similar to industrial workers in other parts of the world. They also posited that enslaved people were hardly whipped and were well cared for by their enslavers. They discussed rates of return on investments (slaves) and calculated prices and regional speculation. The use of tables and graphs created effective visual representations of their work while simultaneously provoking spirited debate that continues today. The data sets compiled in their research are still in circulation, and indeed, are cited by Piketty in his cursory discussion of slavery.

Like earlier scholars, Fogel and Engerman recognized that "slaves were involved in virtually every aspect of southern economic life."[21] Their work inaugurated a new field. Some would argue that the public outcry that greeted their work produced, among other things, the large numbers of students who flocked to work with them at the University of Rochester and later (Fogel) the University of Chicago. Thanks to their important work, the field of economic history as it pertained to slavery over the last forty years witnessed hundreds of publications on health and height data, breeding, birth weights, the domestic slave trade, crop specialization, and industrial slavery.[22]

The next major shift in this field is the recent (re)emergence of slavery and capitalism studies. For the past few years, historians have been writing about the impact of slavery on the American economy. For some this shift meant a turn to the study of cotton and the expansion of slavery in the lower Mississippi Valley. Walter Johnson of Harvard University is at the helm of these latest conversations. In *River of Dark Dreams* (2013), he makes a compelling argument inclusive of slavery and enslaved people that "the history of slavery, capitalism, and imperialism in the nineteenth-century Mississippi Valley" evolved from Thomas Jefferson's vision of an "empire for liberty."[23]

Rather than looking at the increasing sectionalism between the North and South, he found that Mississippi Valley slaveholders understood that "slavery was fundamental to the economic future of the South"; therefore, in the 1850s they supported the invasions in Cuba and Nicaragua and pushed for the re-opening of the slave trade on the eve of the Civil War. Their vision was much more global than previous scholars recognized, making the earlier scholarship of Du Bois and Williams even more relevant.

Johnson received his PhD from Princeton in the mid-1990s when slavery studies proliferated into micro-studies of regions and the lived experiences of people. Always an advocate of meticulous archival research, Johnson uses published slave narratives along with political speeches, rebellions, legislation, popular culture, and personal correspondence to tell the story of "slave racial capitalism" in the cotton kingdom.

A handful of scholars interested in related topics, including the expansion of slavery into the lower Mississippi Valley, the history of cotton in the world economy, and the nuances of the domestic traffic in slaves, have also published works related to imperialism, slavery, and capitalism in recent years. They include Joshua Rothman, Edward Baptist, Sven Beckert, and Calvin Shermerhorn, among others.[24] The trend to look beyond U.S. borders is most clearly and impressively executed by Beckert's global history of cotton in Asia, China, the Soviet Union, India, the United States, and Europe, which received the Bancroft Prize from the American Historical Association and was a finalist for the Pulitzer. This work came in the aftermath of a 2011 conference convened by Beckert and Seth Rockman titled "Slavery's Capitalism," hosted by Brown and Harvard Universities. All of these scholars attended the conference and many of us have essays in the forthcoming edited collection under the same title.

Baptist's work, *The Half Has Never Been Told,* struck a chord for its bold language, use of slave narratives, and indictment of a system that he argues used violence to make human chattel more productive. In a negative review published by *The Economist,* an anonymous reviewer criticized him for not writing "an objective history of slavery" because "almost all the blacks in his book are victims, almost all the whites villains."[25] The review alone, and the fact that the author published it anonymously, led many to question the ethics of such a well-respected news magazine. After widespread criticism and a scathing response from Baptist, the editor issued an apology.[26]

But why were so many outraged by this book? How did it differ from the others? First, Baptist made bold claims based on the voices of the enslaved. He argued that "forced migration and torture" were the weapons used to increase the productivity of the enslaved on "labor camps" (a term he used instead of "plantations"), not technological improvements in plantation machinery and crop variety.[27] He relied on the Works Progress Administration's collection of interviews with former slaves, which some discredit due to the method of their collection. These interviews were conducted in the 1930s mainly by white interviewers, and critics suggest they are full of judgment, questionable recollections, and laden with difficult-to-read dialect. But those who use them (myself included) recognize the value of sources from the perspective of the enslaved, however important it is to contextualize them. This is not a new controversy and it is not one that can be drawn upon racial lines. This half of the story, the perspective of the enslaved in their own words, from their testimonies, has not been told as much as the history of slavery has been told from enslavers' vantage point through correspondence, accounts, and inventories—documents rarely questioned and almost always taken at face value.

Aside from the use of slave narratives, Baptist forces readers to look at enslaved bodies. The book is organized around body parts: feet, heads, right hand, left hand, tongues, breath, seed, blood, backs, and arms. He covers a vast history with narrative prose that economists critiqued in a roundtable of reviews sponsored by the *Journal of Economic History*. Their criticisms are much more specific than the one introduced earlier, and many take issue with his interpretation of the increase in cotton-picking rate per slave. Alan Olmstead argues that Baptist has a "hostile attitude toward economics and economists." Another participant claims that he was not transparent with his data. Overall, the general feeling among the four reviewers is that the book falls short of its goals. Just like the controversy surrounding Fogel and Engerman's controversial study in the 1970s, Baptist's work will continue to generate conversation about slavery and the growth of American capitalism.

Economists have been writing about the economics of slavery since the late 1950s. Their detailed work relying on a handful of data sets allows them to analyze specific aspects of labor, production, markets, and pricing. Many of these scholars write about slave prices following in the footsteps of

Phillips. They develop price indices and predict values over time and space. All of their work is on prime-age men.[28]

Despite the new works by historians and the vast literature by economists, women are missing or overly victimized in studies of slave economy and capitalism. This is a significant omission / pattern, given that colonial law defined slavery through the bodies of women, meaning that the progeny of enslaved women inherited their status. Africanists and a few economists noted demographic changes in the number of women imported and one scholar recognized changes in prices around the closing of the transatlantic slave trade, but women's role and experiences with capitalism and commodification warrant further attention. Piketty only alludes to women in a parenthetical phrase about natural increase. Johnson and Baptist examine their victimization, but none of the scholars above address women's role in a market economy as hucksters (market women), tavern owners, slaveholders, diviners, healers, laundresses, and madams. We know enslaved women suffered sexual exploitation as outlined in their narratives and the work of historians such as Deborah Gray White, Darlene Clark Hine, Brenda E. Stevenson, Wilma King, and Thelma Jennings. However, from the moment of capture, enslaved women were also active participants in slave markets as commodified goods and as actors inserting their humanity. We know from the work of Stephanie Smallwood, Marcus Rediker, and Sowande' Mustakeem that female captives aboard slave ships led and participated in uprisings, gave birth, manipulated members of the crew, negotiated time above deck, and took their own lives as acts of defiance against their enslavement.[29]

Jennifer L. Morgan's forthcoming work, *Accounting for the Women in Slavery: Race and Numeracy in the Early English Atlantic,* promises to show not only that women were present but that their experiences and knowledge contributed to the history of slavery and capitalism. Starting on the shores of West Africa, Morgan traces women actors in this history and does not relegate them to victimhood. From trading to ship experiences during the Middle Passage, Morgan rewrites the history of the slave trade in a way that will change scholars' views of gender and economy in the New World.

My work, *The Price for Their Pound of Flesh: The Value of the Enslaved, from Womb to the Grave, in the Building of a Nation,* addresses gendered aspects of slave capital across the United States and from birth to death. Like

Morgan and Smallwood, I recognize the particularities of the commodification women experienced as the sole provider of "additional sources of labor." I, like Baptist, advocate for the use of slave narratives along with the records of enslavers. However, the discussion that follows, namely my thoughts about Piketty, focuses solely on public forms of capital—a shift away from the mono-crop economies of cotton that have been the focuses of recent scholarship.

Until recently it seemed like an imaginary disciplinary wall stood between historians and economists, and from where I sit, we have not done a very good job of talking to one another. We often had divergent conclusions about the methodology and rationale for economic growth over time. However, in the last twenty years or so, economists and historians have shared the dais in conference panels hosted by their respective fields. We have attended annual meetings of one another's disciplines and have responded to one another's work in journals and books. Tracing the early history of slave economy to the increase in slavery and capitalism studies today, it is clear that we are in a new era of cross-disciplinary discussions; these conversations are long overdue.

Slavery in Professional and Financial Capital

Enslaved women and men frequently were found working in urban spaces throughout the South, including Baltimore; Charleston, South Carolina; Mobile, Alabama; Natchez, Mississippi; and New Orleans.[30] They labored in shipyards, brick factories, and butcher shops, and traded goods at city markets (Figure 6-2). Women served as laundry workers and hostesses at taverns, and maintained interior spaces in government, medical, and university buildings along with enslaved male "janitors." Enslaved laborers also "graded, paved, and cleaned streets, built bridges, collected garbage, dug canals and sewers," serving as the backbone of municipal works.[31] Colonial and antebellum newspapers provide ample evidence of enslaved people's work in urban spaces. Women appear in ads requesting their labor as wet nurses, laundresses, seamstresses, and brick makers.

Using the definition of slave capital outlined above, Piketty failed to recognize that human capital permeated professional and financial settings, especially in city- and state-sponsored public works projects. We know that,

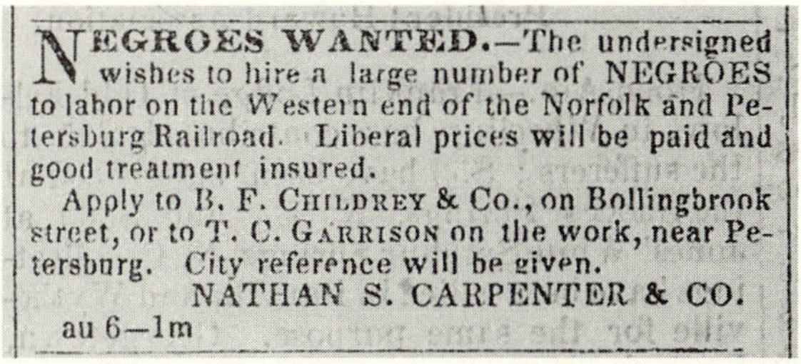

NEGROES WANTED.—The undersigned
wishes to hire a large number of NEGROES
to labor on the Western end of the Norfolk and Petersburg Railroad. Liberal prices will be paid and
good treatment insured.
    Apply to B. F. CHILDREY & Co., on Bollingbrook
street, or to T. C. GARRISON on the work, near Petersburg. City reference will be given.
                NATHAN S. CARPENTER & CO.
    au 6—1m

FIGURE 6-2: Advertisements for railroad work and other forms of labor appear in antebellum newspapers such as this advertisement which boasted about good wages and sound treatment.

Source: Petersburg *Daily Express,* September 3, 1855, page 3.

just like the eighty-two laborers purchased by the Southern Railroad in the spring and summer of 1848, enslaved people worked in factories, shipyards, cemeteries, and other public spaces much earlier. Their labor contributed to a range of public improvements, especially bridges, levees, canals, and a host of industrial enterprises.

On March 19, 1815, Judge Andrews of Concordia Parish, Louisiana, or-dered the city to require "all able bodies Negroes in ... the levee district" to assist in "completing the banks as soon as possible" in order to address the "rapid rise in the river" (Figure 6-3).[32] It appears that enslaved people worked to build and reinforce the levee. Sending them to aid in a crisis suggests that they had experience with this kind of work. It also indicates that it was not uncommon for "able bodied Negroes" to work for municipal governments. That blacks worked on this effort confirms that financial and professional capital included human chattel, individuals Piketty did not include in his calculations. Yet these are the very forms of capital he incorporates but ne-glects to acknowledge.

Some municipal governments also included slave capital. The city of Sa-vannah used enslaved people in a number of departments. As early as the summer of 1790, for example, the Savannah City Council recorded that "all male Slaves between the ages of 16 & 60 years, in or belonging to the City" were required "to work on & clear the streets ... from weeds & other in-cumbrances [sic]."[33] The city marshal and constables served as makeshift overseers supervising this group of laborers. Twenty years later, the records indicate that there were fifty-one African-born men, "healthy and athletic,"

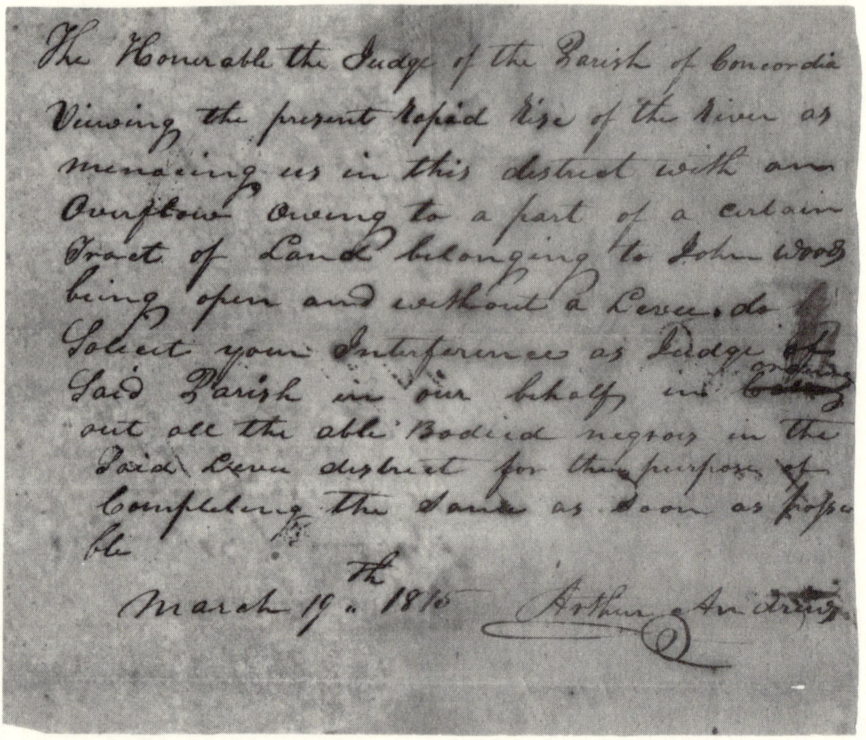

FIGURE 6-3: Court order for levee work in Concordia Parish, Louisiana, 1815.

Source: Natchez Trace Slaves and Slavery Collection, MS #2E77, Dolph Briscoe Center for American History, University of Texas at Austin.

whom the mayor required to work under the management of a Mr. William Richardson. It is likely that these individuals were illegally traded African captives, given the time period (August 1820). Even though it was illegal to participate in the transatlantic slave after 1808, we have ample evidence suggesting that an illegal market continued until the early years of the Civil War.[34] Apparently Mr. Richardson assured the mayor that he intended to use "these Africans" to "level the fortifications," which would save the city treasury nearly $4,000. The cost benefit outweighed the risks of using legal or illegal African captives, and the council allowed for provisional approval as long as the mayor "superintend the work."[35] Practices such as these confirm that slave capital frequently benefited government agencies in cities such as Savannah (Figure 6-4) even though they banned slavery for nearly the first twenty years of settlement.

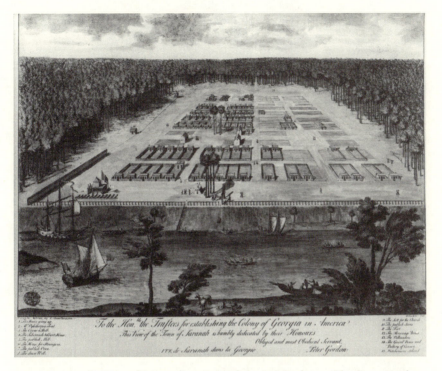

FIGURE 6-4: "A View of Savannah as it stood the 29 March 1734," by Peter Gordon. Source: Courtesy of the Georgia Historical Society, MS—1361—MP—001.

In addition to their contribution to public capital, enslaved people were also purchased by city governments. In February 1831 an alderman received permission on behalf of the Savannah Street and Lane Committee to authorize the "purchase of two able bodied Negro[es] for the use of the City." They were to work on roads and bridges near the "west end of the City." Anyone who had doubts about this practice of buying enslaved men for city use could rest assured in the financial justifications provided. It was in "the Interest of the City" that "every economy should be used and all means" explored.[36] Eleven years later, the practice continued. This time the city agreed "to purchase a sufficient number of able bodied Negroes" as long as they did not pay any more than $250 "for each Negro." One wonders the reason for the price cap, especially given that the value of enslaved men at that time would be significantly more than $250, particularly if the city wanted men in their prime years, fifteen to thirty years old.[37]

Using enslaved labor for municipalities was cost effective. Some cities, such as New Orleans, rented enslaved people from enslavers for a modest daily fee ranging from 25 to 50 cents. Many incarcerated slaves were put to use during imprisonment. Such practices worked so well that Crescent City paid over $30,000 annually for this type of labor.[38] Enslaved mechanics worked in "secondary manufacturing industries including cotton gin factories, shoe factories, tanneries, bakeries, and printing presses for city newspapers." One New Orleans brick-making factory owned one hundred enslaved persons, and a similar plant in Biloxi Bay had "116 male and 37 female slaves" who produced "ten million bricks annually."[39] These figures suggest that the output of publicly held slave capital outweighed the cost, and that government officials maintained good records to ensure worthy profit yields.

In the 1850s, lawmakers in Adams County, Mississippi, required enslaved women and men to conduct road duty. The Ashford family, for example, sent twelve to sixty-four men and women each summer between 1850 and 1856 to work on the road (Figure 6-5). J. P. Ashford signed an oath guaranteeing that all "eligible" bonds people contributed: "I solemnly swear to the best of my belief and judgment the foregoing list is a true and correct list of the names and number of slaves owned and possessed by me on the estate of J. P. Ashford liable to Road duty according to law in Adams County Mississippi."[40] On May 6, 1850, Ashford sent a slightly imbalanced group of men and women (twenty-nine females and thirty-five males). It is possible that some were husband and wife or perhaps mother-and-son or father-and-daughter combinations, as evidenced in surnames such as Mary and John Jackson and John, Bob, and Mary Smith. Over the course of six years, many of the same people labored for the county, but each year the numbers fluctuated and sometimes drastically decreased. In the summers of 1855 and 1856, only twelve of the Ashfords' slaves worked on the roads, and within this dozen there were, respectively, four and three women. Martha, Phillis, Ellen, and Louise started their work on June 13, and all but Martha returned a year later on July 18. These labor patterns indicate a routine cycle of slavery in public works. They also suggest a divergence from the plantation labor typically associated with slave capital. Temporary work for a local government by the enslaved is further evidence that human capital contributed to several economies.

A list of the names and numbers of slaves liable to Road Duty in the County of Adams May 4th 1850.

A. K. Farrar

1	Sam	32	Bill	63	Tom
2	Jemima	33	Angeline	64	Dorothy
3	Toot	34	Stephen	65	Sam
4	Emily	35	Mary	66	Moses
5	Clinton	36	Edmund	67	Hagar
6	Phillis	37	Mary	68	Rachel
7	Spencer	38	Henry	69	Henry
8	Creecy	39	Chloe	70	Candis
9	Adeline	40	Lewis	71	Winny
10	Winchester	41	Ann	72	Adam
11	Hannah	42	Celia	73	Susannah
12	Henry	43	Peter	74	Eliza
13	Delia	44	Martha	75	Stephen
14	Hannibal	45	Stephen	76	Joe
15	Maria	46	Milly	77	Orrin
16	William	47	Ann	78	Walker
17	George	48	Clinton	79	Willis
18	Jack	49	Levi	80	Martha
19	Hannah	50	Celia	81	Sylvia
20	Louisa	51	Nelson	82	William
21	Levin	52	Peter	83	Lydiann
22	Judah	53	Sylvia	84	Reuben
23	Rebecca	54	Jerry	85	Isabella
24	David	55	Lucy	86	Mary
25	Lydia	56	Marinda	87	Dan Boone
26	Angeline	57	Emily	88	Lucy
27	Kit	58	Frank	89	Henry Atkins
28	Sophia	59	Malenda	90	Mary Taylor
29	Arthur	60	Jim	91	Sam
30	Fanny	61	Wilson	92	Mat
31	William	62	Lucinda	93	Albert

FIGURE 6-5: One page from the ledger listing enslaved people assigned to road duty in Mississippi.

Source: Slave and Slavery Records MSS #2E777, Natchez Trace Collection, Dolph Briscoe Center for American History, University of Texas at Austin.

As I noted above, rather than purchasing enslaved people, municipalities also hired (another term for rented) them. Slave hiring represented a cost-effective use of bound labor for contracted periods of time.[41] In August 1842 the Savannah Streets and Lanes Council hired "eleven Negroes," of which the city owned three, "at the rate of one Hundred twenty five dollars per annum." But they requested permission to sell one of the city-owned slaves because he had "been behaving so badly for the last two weeks" that they were afraid he would run away. They put him in jail and recommended that the City Council "sell this boy as soon as the sum can be obtained which was paid for him." These public officials were clearly concerned with the fiscal impact of this case and assured council members they would not proceed until the equivalent funds could be returned to the budget in exchange for the recalcitrant laborer. Five days later, the city marshal reported "the sale of the Negro man London the property of the Corporation, he was sold on Tuesday last for $252.50."[42] We have no way to confirm if London was the individual addressed in the previous record, but the timing of this notation makes it seem plausible.

Enslaved (and free) blacks had to wear badges identifying their legal work in the city of Savannah as "butchers, carpenters, bricklayers, coopers, and porters." By the middle of the nineteenth century, other towns and cities worked with health officials to create "scavengers" to keep urban spaces clean and prevent the spread of disease. Some of this work involved chimney sweeping, sewage removal, trash duty, and disinfecting public buildings and office spaces. Scavengers are equivalent to modern-day sanitation workers; they drove carts throughout the city to pick up trash. In 1830 and 1831, for example, the city of Savannah paid for the services of Chance, Monday, Bob, and Ben. These men did the "dirty work" of keeping the city clean and disease free.

Slave capital also contributed to universities and medical colleges throughout the North and South. Several universities owned enslaved people and/or profited from the transatlantic slave trade, including public universities such as the University of North Carolina and the University of Georgia, as well as private schools such as the University of Virginia, Dartmouth College, Harvard University, and Brown University. "American academies," according to historian Craig Wilder, were "rooted in the slave economies of the colonial world."[43] Enslaved workers were valued enough that in November 1829, when James liberated himself from the University of North Caro-

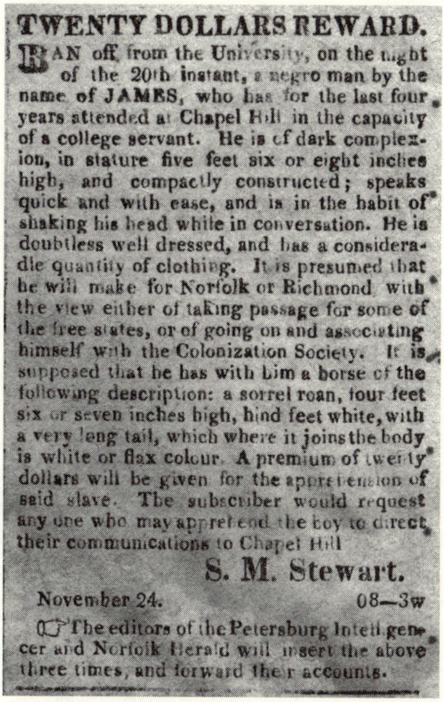

TWENTY DOLLARS REWARD.

RAN off from the University, on the night of the 20th instant, a negro man by the name of JAMES, who has for the last four years attended at Chapel Hill in the capacity of a college servant. He is of dark complexion, in stature five feet six or eight inches high, and compactly constructed; speaks quick and with ease, and is in the habit of shaking his head while in conversation. He is doubtless well dressed, and has a considerable quantity of clothing. It is presumed that he will make for Norfolk or Richmond with the view either of taking passage for some of the free states, or of going on and associating himself with the Colonization Society. It is supposed that he has with him a horse of the following description: a sorrel roan, four feet six or seven inches high, hind feet white, with a very long tail, which where it joins the body is white or flax colour. A premium of twenty dollars will be given for the apprehension of said slave. The subscriber would request any one who may apprehend the boy to direct their communications to Chapel Hill

S. M. Stewart.

November 24.   08—3w

☞ The editors of the Petersburg Intelligencer and Norfolk Herald will insert the above three times, and forward their accounts.

FIGURE 6-6: Rewards runaways like James appeared in antebellum newspapers and confirm the fiscal value of slave capital.

Source: Hillsborough Reorder, Hillsborough, NC, 29 November 1829, Courtesy of the University of North Carolina at Chapel Hill Image Collection Collection #P0004, North Carolina Collection Photographic Archives, The Wilson Library, University of North Carolina at Chapel Hill.

lina at Chapel Hill, the institution placed an ad in a local paper for his return (Figure 6-6). James allegedly "ran off from the university" after having served as the college servant for four years. The ad described him as five-foot-six or five-foot-eight tall, dark complexion, with the ability to speak "with ease." Perhaps because of his privileged status as a "college servant," James was "doubtless well dressed, and has a considerable quantity of clothing" in his possession. When he left, he took a horse with him to aid in his self-liberation.[44]

Wilson Caldwell also worked at the University of North Carolina at Chapel Hill. He served the university president along with his mother. His father was the body servant of Governor Tod Caldwell of North Carolina. The photograph in Figure 6-7 provides an excellent visual representation of

FIGURE 6-7: Image of Wilson Caldwell (1841–1898), enslaved at UNC Chapel Hill owned by the university president.

Source: Courtesy of the University of North Carolina at Chapel Hill Image Collection #P0002, North Carolina Collection Photographic Archives, The Wilson Library, University of North Carolina at Chapel Hill.

the type of clothing this university servant wore, perhaps articles similar to what James may have taken when he liberated himself.

Dressed formally, Wallace is pictured with a vest, tie, sport coat, and top hat. It appears that he probably owned a watch, as evidenced by the midwaist chain, items not typically owned by enslaved people on plantations. Wallace and enslaved women like Kitty, owned by a member of the Emory University

Board, have only recently become a part of the larger history of slavery and capitalism in the aftermath of national symposia on this subject.[45]

Rather than emphasize plantation slavery, I look at slavery in public spaces because it falls under the definitions of financial and professional capital Piketty describes. This evidence indicates the many ways that Piketty's account overlooks or miscalculates capital and slavery in the United States. The temporal structure of his argument stands as another limitation. Many of his examples come from 1770–1810, in what he loosely glosses as the United States. However, the American colonies did not become the United States until after the American Revolution in 1783. This periodization encompasses war years, the transition from the colonies to the states, the closing of the transatlantic slave trade (1808), and the eve of the War of 1812—all major turning points in American economic history that suggest a nation in flux and rich with all forms of inequalities.

Slavery and the American Presidency

Perhaps no topic better exemplifies the ambiguous discussion of slave capital than the histories of enslaved people owned by American presidents, and it is useful here to say a few words about slavery and the American presidency. After all, Piketty begins his discussion with Thomas Jefferson. Twelve of the first eighteen U.S. presidents owned enslaved people. Piketty is correct in singling out Jefferson,o noting that he "owned more than just land ... he also owed more than six hundred slaves"; however, he misses an opportunity to calculate the value of wealth represented by Jefferson's human capital. And if he is not interested in human capital, then why introduce Jefferson into this discussion? Below is a list of the twelve presidents and their slaveholdings:[46]

George Washington, 1st president, Virginia (250–300)
Thomas Jefferson, 3rd, Virginia (200)
James Madison, 4th, Virginia (more than 100)
James Monroe, 5th, Virginia (about 75)
Andrew Jackson, 7th, South Carolina / Tennessee (fewer than 200)
Martin Van Buren, 8th, New York (1)
William Henry Harrison, 9th, Virginia (11)
John Tyler, 10th, Virginia (about 70)
James K. Polk, 11th, North Carolina (about 25)

Zachary Taylor, 12th, Virginia (fewer than 150)
Andrew Johnson, 17th, North Carolina (8)
Ulysses S. Grant, 18th, Ohio (5)

Piketty uses Jefferson's slaveholding to transition into a discussion of the importance of slave capital. He also credits Jefferson for abolishing the slave trade in 1808. It is not entirely clear whether or not Du Bois would agree with this assessment. In his discussion, Piketty covers all of American slavery in a few paragraphs, saying in summary that "the slave economy was growing rapidly when the Civil War broke out in 1861, leading ultimately to the abolition of slavery in 1865."[47] Despite such a cursory discussion, he pulls together statistics from three data sets to create his figures 4.10 and 4.11.[48]

Again, Piketty misses an opportunity to address the slave capital of American presidents. What does it mean that the founding fathers owned enslaved people? How can a nation built on "life, liberty, and the pursuit of happiness" enslave and profit from a community of laborers? This historical irony contributes to the current state of economic disparity. Human capital is a form of free labor, and the history of countries, corporations, and municipalities in the West generated their wealth through slave labor.

Wealth building from the institution of slavery was not just a southern phenomenon. The North was just as culpable. Slave-trading firms, investors, and agents lived in the North and benefited from products produced in the South. Enslaved people's clothing and shoes were manufactured in northern factories while New England merchants owned the vessels on which enslaved people were brought to this country. These same vessels carried slave-produced goods to markets all over the world.[49]

When the evidence suggested above is included, it seems that "1.5 times the national income" would be a much larger number and clearly statistically significant and important enough not to "exclude." How would Piketty's claims differ with the inclusion of slavery at all levels of analysis, from public records to privately owned individuals who served at the helm of our government, namely American presidents? We have a variety of extant documents to write the history of slavery; there is no need to draw conclusions about slave prices from Quentin Tarantino's *Django Unchained!* Evidence from large enslavers is just one example of more appropriate parallels.

Conclusion

Enslaved people contributed to capital in public entities throughout the New World. In the United States they contributed with the building of levees and roads in the Deep South and their labor in shipyards, factories, and medical schools in the North. As human capital, their bodies and the products produced by them contributed to a national, local, and global economy. They were not paid for their work, and municipalities capitalized on their labor, saving unprecedented amounts of money. Piketty missed an important opportunity to contribute to ongoing conversations about the wealth generated from slave capital. Such dialogues are part of many contemporary conversations, including those led by historians such as Sir Hilary Beckles and Mary Frances Berry as well as MacArthur fellow and columnist Ta-Nehisi Coates, whose award-wining essay begins in the post-slavery era.[50] Piketty overlooked the very presence of slave capital that penetrated into the real property he explored. His facile attempt to acknowledge slavery consists of few cursory examples. It seems appropriate to end with a word of caution from Du Bois: "The riddle of the Sphinx may be postponed, it may be evasively answered now; sometime it must be fully answered."[51]

SEVEN

Human Capital and Wealth before and after Capital in the Twenty-First Century

ERIC R. NIELSEN

Economist Eric Nielsen takes aim at one of the core assumptions of Piketty's book: that what economists call "human capital" is not capital and not part of the story of rising inequality or social calcification. In fact, Nielsen argues, human capital ought to be counted as capital in the way Piketty tabulates the value of machines, factories, and farmland. Furthermore, Nielsen contends that the human capital research tradition within economics is necessary in order to explain rising inequality to date and in the future, something Piketty explicitly rejects. Nielsen summarizes a large body of recent research, looking at the importance of human capital over time and specifically the intergenerational wealth transmission and social mobility. He concludes that proper consideration of human capital would yield very different policy implications than the ones Piketty offers.

Thomas Piketty's *Capital in the Twenty-First Century* presents new, meticulously collected data relevant for understanding the division of national income between capital and labor, the degree of inequality in capital ownership, and the evolution of inequality in labor and capital income. Based on these remarkable and fascinating historical data, Piketty develops an analytic framework in which capitalism may, under some conditions, produce a runaway concentration of wealth in the hands of a few heirs. The book argues that advanced economies such as the United States and France may be heading to an extremely inegalitarian future dominated by inherited wealth.

While it is clear that income inequality has increased markedly within wealthy, developed countries, the cause of the increase is still an open question. Income inequality can increase through some combination of rising inequality in labor income, rising inequality in capital income, an increase in the share of national income accruing to capital (since capital is unequally held), and an increase in the covariance between capital and labor income. Piketty emphasizes capital-based explanations throughout *C21,* while his theory of labor income is quite speculative and unorthodox. In particular, Piketty explicitly rejects human capital theory—the dominant paradigm economists use to understand labor income and inequality at the individual level.

Labor income inequality has also increased dramatically over the past several decades, and labor earnings remain the dominant source of income for most households outside of the very top of the income distribution. Mainstream microeconomic research has tended to explain patterns in earnings inequality using human capital theory, in which the supply and demand for different types of skills drive earnings differences. The basic idea of human capital theory is that the stock of durable skills and attributes a person possesses acts like a stock of capital. Wages are then conceptualized as a "return" on the stock of human capital, so that human capital both explains differences in wages and operates as a store of wealth, much like physical capital. Human capital has proven to be an enormously useful conceptual framework for understanding a wide array of economic phenomena, including labor earnings and inequality, educational choices, marital sorting, fertility, parental investments in children, and intergenerational correlations in economic outcomes.

Capital in the Twenty-First Century explicitly dismisses human capital as useful for understanding inequality. The book defines "capital" and "wealth" equivalently as the market value of tradeable goods. This definition rules out human capital as a source of wealth *a priori,* because human capital cannot be fully bought or sold in a society that prohibits slavery. I argue in this chapter that the omission of human capital is a serious weakness for both the data and the theory presented by Piketty. Human capital is an important source of wealth for each generation and plays an important role in the transmission of economic advantage across generations. *C21* therefore presents only a partial, though still novel and important, picture of inequality and its evolution over time.

By focusing exclusively on capital bequests from parents to children, Piketty errs both by assuming too much about the bequest motives of the wealthy and by overlooking the significant wealth passed from parents to children in the form of human capital. Furthermore, the literature on intergenerational mobility, though unsettled, does not support Piketty's fears that high income and wealth inequality will lead to lower mobility and less equality of opportunity. I also argue, however, that "opportunity" and "mobility" are not well-defined terms in *C21,* and in economics more broadly, and that future work on mobility needs to incorporate insights from the rich literature on the technology of human capital production in children in order to meaningfully discuss these concepts.

The rest of this chapter proceeds as follows. I first discuss in detail the differences and similarities between human capital and physical capital, setting the stage for the second section, which shows that Piketty's arguments against counting human capital as wealth ultimately fail. The third section discusses the relationship between human capital, parental bequests, and intergenerational mobility, as dynastic inheritance is a key mechanism driving wealth concentration in *C21.* I then turn to some of Piketty's "noncompetitive" explanations for labor income inequality. Regardless of whether his particular claims ultimately carry the day, I argue that economics would do well to differentiate between varieties of human capital and sources of labor income that have very different social consequences. More human capital is not necessarily good if that human capital is paid to do something socially destructive. I conclude by discussing a policy that is easy to justify on both egalitarian and non-egalitarian grounds, unlike the wealth tax in *Capital in the Twenty-First Century*—early childhood education. Investing in the human capital of young children may have very large social returns while simultaneously decreasing the wealth gap between children born to high-income and low-income families.

A quick note on nomenclature: I will refer to Piketty's concept of capital / wealth as "capital" throughout this chapter. I will use "wealth" as a more general term describing both Piketty's concept (in which wealth and capital are equivalent) and human capital (which I will show is form of wealth as well).

What Is Human Capital?

Human capital is the dominant framework used by economists for making sense of individual inequality in income, wealth, health, and a host of other economic outcomes. The central idea in human capital theory is that individuals possess an array of skills and attributes that earn a return in the labor market. Skills are durable, context-dependent, and responsive to investment, which happen to be some of the key properties of traditional, physical capital. Human capital theory takes this analogy seriously by conceptualizing a person's embodied skills as a stock of "human" capital. Differences in wage rates and other outcomes are then explained by differences in human capital. A given worker's earnings can increase either because her stock of human capital increases (through education or on-the-job learning) or because the skills she already possesses become more valuable in the labor market, perhaps due to technological changes.

The term "human capital" can be confusing, as it suggests a false equivalence between labor income and capital income. Although I will stick with the standard terminology in this chapter, one could substitute the phrase "embodied, durable skills" in place of "human capital" without any loss in meaning. To be clear: Human capital is a distinct concept from physical capital, and the differences between the two can be very important depending on the context. It is worth going through these differences in some detail now, as I will argue later that none of these differences are relevant for Piketty's argument in his book.

A first key difference is that human capital cannot be fully bought or sold, unlike physical capital. This has the important implication that human capital cannot be used as collateral to obtain access to credit. Homeowners can take out loans backed by the value of their homes, but students taking out loans to finance college cannot promise to cede control of their human capital to creditors should the students fail to repay. Moreover, because only the rental rate, and not the price, of human capital is observed, valuing the wealth embodied in human capital is difficult.[1]

A second key difference is that human capital is inextricably tied to the particular person possessing it and cannot be used without its owner supplying labor. Workers' preferences, and not simply the productive capacity of their human capital, are therefore important determinants of how their human capital is used and compensated. A tractor does not care if it is made to work in a harsh environment, but a worker will. Among other things, this implies that income earned by human capital is less valuable in welfare terms than income coming from physical capital, as long as there is some disutility of supplying labor to the market. Of course, just the opposite may be true as well—the nonpecuniary benefits of some jobs may compensate workers for relatively low pay.

General Arguments against Human Capital

Before discussing the implications of the data and theory for microeconomic research on inequality presented in *Capital in the Twenty-First Century,* it is worth evaluating the book's main arguments against including human capital in its analysis. These arguments all fail to hit their mark. Human capital is an important source of wealth and is critical for understanding inequality, both in the cross-section and intergenerationally. Piketty is wrong to exclude it.

Piketty equates wealth with capital, which he defines as all and only those things that can be bought and sold. This definition immediately disqualifies human capital as wealth, yet nowhere does Piketty give a clear explanation of why the nonsalability of human capital is relevant to his overall argument.[2] The important features of capital in *C21* are that it is durable, produces a return without additional effort, and can be passed on to heirs. These features of physical capital do not depend on its salability and are clearly shared by human capital. Skills are durable, though they may fade over time or become obsolete. The possessor of a skill receives the wage bump associated with that skill for each additional hour of work with no additional effort. Although such a worker must suffer the disutility of supplying labor to receive the associated human capital premium, the key point is that this disutility need not increase as a worker's human capital stock increases. Indeed, high-wage jobs may well be less unpleasant to perform than low-wage jobs. Finally, skills are passed down from parents to children, both through inheritance and through deliberate parental investments.

Human capital is therefore a source of wealth by any reasonable criterion. The more human capital one has, the greater one's opportunities to command economic resources. As a simple example, consider two young men: the inheritor of a trust fund worth a half a million dollars and a penniless but very talented athlete with expected lifetime earnings of hundreds of millions of dollars. It is obvious that the wealthier of these two men is the athlete, yet Piketty's definition implies just the opposite.

As discussed in the previous section, there are some interesting subtleties in comparing income from human capital and income from physical capital, because the former necessarily involves supplying (potentially unpleasant) labor. The impossibility of using human capital as collateral likewise lowers its value relative to physical capital. Nonetheless, it will always be true that between two otherwise identical people, the person with more human capital is wealthier in the Piketty-relevant sense. The nontradability of human capital and the complications introduced by labor supply simply mean that measuring human capital wealth is difficult, not that human capital is not wealth.

A second broad argument in *C21* is that explanations based on human capital are naive and incomplete because they cannot fully explain individual-level inequality.[3] It is true that human capital differences can explain only some of the observed individual variation in economic outcomes. Yet this is not really a criticism, because human capital theory has never claimed to be capable of explaining all aspects of inequality. No economic theory, Piketty's included, has ever fit the data perfectly. Human capital can explain many systematic differences in outcomes across individuals, and economists are continually engaged in trying to understand what human capital does not explain and why. In this regard, human capital is no different from other economic theories.

Capital in the Twenty-First Century also argues that human-capital-based explanations of wage-earnings inequality are empty or tautological because they just relabel labor income as the return on the stock of human capital.[4] Microeconomists often use observed differences in outcomes as prima facie evidence of human capital differences in formulating new research hypotheses because such an approach has proven useful in the past. But economists do not simply infer underlying human capital differences from observed outcome differences, which actually would be tautological. Rather, human capital is posited to have an estimatable relationship to an observable, non-wage characteristic such as years of schooling, which then implies a testable relationship between the observable correlate of human capital and economic outcomes. Such a model could easily fail to explain differences in economic outcomes. It is a contingent empirical fact, not a tautology, that people who score highly on IQ tests earn more, on average, than those who score poorly.

Finally, Piketty argues that human capital is not substantially more important now than in the past because labor's share of national income has increased only modestly over the past century or so, with capital still receiving a sizable share of national income. Piketty correctly observes that economic theory does not imply that this share will rise further, even if technology develops in a way that is favorable to labor. This argument misses the point, however, because human capital's share of income is not the same as labor's share of income. The evidence that human capital has become more important in recent decades is that people invest more in skills and earn more per hour as a result of such investments. Human capital could rise in importance in the relevant sense even in a world with an increasing share of national income going to capital.[5]

There is actually fairly strong evidence that the relative importance of human capital in determining labor income has increased in recent decades. Katz and Murphy, for example, show that the wage premium earned by educated, skilled workers increased dramatically, even as the supply of such workers expanded.[6] This pattern suggests that the types of skills that require investment and education have become more valuable over time, although this explanation may work less well for the most recent changes in earnings inequality.

Another crude way to see the increasing importance of human capital is to divide labor's share of income into two components: income accruing to education and labor market experience (human capital) and income accruing to "raw" labor, which is what an uneducated, inexperienced, able-bodied adult could earn. A simple accounting exercise for U.S. data shows that raw labor's share of national income has declined steadily since the middle of the twentieth century while human capital's share of income has risen.[7]

Parental Bequests and Intergenerational Mobility before and after Piketty

Inheritance and mobility are closely related to the fundamental social good of equality of opportunity. It strikes most people as deeply unfair that some people, by virtue of their birth, are condemned to live in poverty while others inherit great wealth. Inheritance and birth-given advantages are ethically suspect, and inequality generated by such sources stands in tension with the ideals of equality and fairness. In contrast, inequality generated by differences in work effort, productivity, and ability are substantially less controversial and strike many as justified. Because such very different mechanisms could give rise to the same distribution of income and wealth, it is crucial to disentangle the factors creating inequality in determining whether egalitarian policies are warranted.

An extensive literature in economics seeks to understand the relationship between parental resources and children's resources as adults. Some of this research focuses on the direct effects of parental resources and investments on childhood outcomes, that is, on the technology of human capital production. Other research studies intergenerational mobility, or the degree to which relative economic standing in a society is passed on from one generation to the next. Piketty's discussion more closely follows this second literature, which I argue suffers from a lack of compelling and interpretable estimates. This critique applies to Piketty as well; his book fails to incorporate important insights from the research in human capital production into its account of the intergenerational transmission of wealth.

C21's discussion of mobility focuses almost exclusively on capital, whereas prior research has mostly studied mobility in education and labor income, both of which are more closely linked to human capital. Although both approaches are interesting in their own right, they must be considered jointly in order to fully understand the intergenerational transmission of economic advantage. Labor income and education inequality correspond to differences in wealth that are not captured by capital-based measures. At the same time, capital inheritance is potentially a very important channel of wealth transmission, especially for the most well-off, and one that is missed completely by measures of income and educational mobility.

Capital in the Twenty-First Century *and Inheritance Flows:*
An Interesting Start

In Piketty's book, the fact that capital returns are usually greater than the economic growth rate ensures that capital wealth grows relative to the overall size of the economy. If this accumulated capital is passed down intact from one generation to the next, a very small number of lucky heirs may end up controlling a large share of a country's capital. *C21* argues that this concentration of inherited capital will, in turn, lower mobility because the incomes available to those that inherit capital will dominate the potential income available through labor. Inheritance and marriage, rather than productive work, will become the primary paths to economic success and security.

To support this hypothesis, *Capital in the Twenty-First Century* presents historical data on inheritance flows, which are national-level variables showing the relative importance of inherited capital in an economy. A country will have large inheritance flows when the stock of capital is large, when the mortality rate is high, and when those who die own substantially more capital than those still living. Piketty documents that inheritance flows in France were quite high in the past, decreased substantially during the middle part of the twentieth century, and have since begun to increase again. This resurgence is driven largely by increases in the capital / income ratio and the ratio of the average capital of the dead to the average capital of the living. Similar patterns seem to hold elsewhere in Europe, while the resurgence in inherited capital seems to be more muted in the United States. Rising inheritance flows are a major piece of evidence in *C21* that inherited wealth is increasingly important and may come to dominate our future.

Unfortunately, inheritance flows do not track capital bequests from parents to their children. Inheritance flows will be high so long as the average capital held by those who die is high, regardless of how their estates are divided among their descendants and other entities. *C21* implicitly assumes that parents leave bequests almost exclusively to their children, but if the wealthy instead leave sizable fractions of their estates to charitable foundations and the like, the importance of aggregate inheritance flows in explaining intergenerational wealth mobility becomes much less clear. In addition, if the share of their wealth that parents leave to their children shifts over time, the inheritance flow time series may be quite different from the time series of capital inherited directly from parents. A separate question is what role fertility may play in mitigating or exacerbating the dynastic accumulation of wealth. Higher fertility will tend to dissipate large fortunes more quickly, as inheritances must be split among more heirs. *C21* itself notes the importance of fertility but does not make clear how sensitive its conclusions are to different plausible assumptions about the relationship between fertility and wealth.

Relatively little is known about why and to whom the wealthy leave bequests, because economists do not have a good understanding of why wealthy people save at such high rates. Standard savings motives, such as the desire to smooth consumption over time or self-insure against risks, do a decent job of explaining the savings behavior of normal people, but they work much less well for the very rich. The wealthy can already protect themselves against bad luck, and so they should save less (in percentage terms) than the nonwealthy. In fact, just the opposite is the case—the wealthy both save at much higher rates and run down their wealth in retirement more slowly than the nonwealthy. Warren Buffett, the famously frugal billionaire octogenarian, should be rapidly blowing through his great fortune, yet he has a savings rate approaching 100 percent.[8]

Rationalizing the high savings rates of the wealthy requires adding some additional forces to the standard list of saving motives. One approach with quite a bit of explanatory power is to simply suppose that some people have strong preferences for leaving bequests.[9] Surprisingly, it turns out that differences in the strength of the bequest motive across households are not easily explained by differences in their observable characteristics. One might suppose, for example, that the bequest motive is driven by a desire to leave wealth to one's children, yet the data suggest that the presence of descendants is far from the only important factor in predicting who will die with a sizable estate.[10] Many childless people die with large estates, and some people with descendants pass on relatively little. There is even some empirical evidence that inheritance has become less important in generating large fortunes over the same time period that income inequality began to increase dramatically in the United States.[11] There is substantial reason to doubt Piketty's strong predictions about the future of inheritance.

Better understanding the savings-and-bequest behavior of high-income households should be a priority for economic research going forward. If the rise in labor income inequality solidifies into greater capital inequality, then the differential bequest behavior of wealthy versus nonwealthy households may become an increasingly important force that increases wealth and income inequality. Whether capital bequests do, in fact, become more important depends on how much and to whom wealthy households give, yet it is precisely the behavior of these households that we know very little about. In order to make progress in understanding savings and bequest behavior at the top of the income and wealth distributions, economists must collect national-level data that specifically tracks how estates are allocated among descendants and other organizations. With better data, economists should be able to formulate and test more-realistic models that explain differences in the bequest motive across households.

Human Capital and Intergenerational Mobility

Capital in the Twenty-First Century does not consider human capital as a mechanism by which parents can pass on wealth to their children. Yet economists have learned that human capital is, in fact, transmitted across generations, both mechanically via inheritance as well as through deliberate parental investments. Parental bequests of human capital form a separate and important wealth transmission channel in addition to the capital bequest channel emphasized by Piketty.

In theory, parental bequests of human capital may either increase or decrease mobility. Parents from all socioeconomic backgrounds invest heavily in the human capital of their children, whereas only very wealthy parents typically leave capital bequests. Many different kinds of activities and expenditures may be viewed as parental investments in human capital. For instance, parents spend time helping their children with homework and spend money paying a premium in the housing market to live in a safe neighborhood with access to good public schools. Data on capital bequests significantly understate the size of the real bequests left by families at the lower end of the socioeconomic spectrum and may significantly overstate the overall degree of inequality in parental bequests. Standard bequest measures leave out all of the time, effort, and money that parents of all backgrounds spend improving the skills of their children as well as the value of human capital that is passed automatically from parents to children through genetic inheritance and automatic, unchosen features of the child's lived environment. Parental human capital investments may increase mobility, as the true gradient between parental resources and bequests to children may be less steep than capital inheritance-based measures would indicate. On the other hand, wealthy parents invest substantially more time and money in their children than parents with fewer resources, and this gap has increased in recent decades.[12]

Unequal parental investment expenditures by income class should be a force pushing down mobility, yet there is relatively scant evidence that parental income has a large causal effect on childhood outcomes once all of the factors that tend to be codetermined with parental income, such as parental education, age, marital status, neighborhood quality, and other socioeconomic factors, are accounted for. The fundamental empirical problem in teasing out the effect of parental income is that it is strongly correlated with most other variables that could plausibly affect childhood outcomes. Isolating the effect of parental income from all of these other factors is difficult, and most estimates of the direct effect of parental income are quite small.[13] It is likewise unclear how strongly parental expenditures affect childhood outcomes. One case in point: Researchers have not established a clear relationship between changes in parental resources and expenditures and changes in measured childhood academic achievement.[14] The methodological obstacles that need to be overcome in this type of empirical work are simply very large.

The most technically advanced and convincing papers studying human capital acquisition in children likewise do not generally find a large independent role for parental income. These studies instead suggest that a child's early environment, including the prenatal environment, is hugely important for the development of human capital.[15] These papers find support for the idea that certain skills have "critical periods" after which investments are much less effective. Further, they find that the ability to acquire new skills depends on past investments, so that skills beget skills in a virtuous cycle.[16] Rather than parental income per se, what seems to be important for the development of human capital is that children have healthy mothers and stable, nurturing home and school environments, especially during their early years. Low-income parents may have a hard time satisfying these desiderata with the limited means available to them, but billionaires are not likely to have a large advantage over upper middle-class parents—the inputs are simply not that expensive.

In short, the empirical evidence we have on the direct production of childhood human capital does not suggest that rapidly rising capital and income inequality will automatically lead to substantially greater human capital inequality in subsequent generations.

Piketty's analysis is more tightly linked to the empirical literature on intergenerational mobility, but this literature likewise does not paint a clear or consistent picture of how strongly parental advantages are passed down to children. Mobility estimates for income, the most-studied outcome in this literature, differ quite dramatically depending on the country, time period, and empirical method used. Some early empirical work suggested that parental advantages fade out almost completely within one or two generations, while more recent estimates tend to imply that advantages persist meaningfully for five or more generations (although recent work is not unanimous on this point). This lack of consensus is not surprising. Estimating income mobility is quite challenging empirically. The main difficulty is that income is hard to measure accurately, both because it tends to be quite volatile from year to year and because different types of jobs have distinct career progressions in earnings.[17] Data linking multiple years of earnings across multiple generations are quite rare so the empirical literature on mobility has had to rely on clever statistical approaches to deal with these measurement problems.

The research estimating intergenerational mobility for outcomes other than income is similarly unsettled. There is little consensus about what is driving the intergenerational correlations in education, which appear to vary substantially across time and geography. The various papers that try to tease out the importance of genetic inheritances versus other factors in these correlations often disagree. Consumption plays a central role in economic models of well-being, yet there is very little evidence on intergenerational mobility in consumption, largely because of data constraints. Similarly, there is comparatively little evidence on mobility in capital wealth because high-quality data on capital holdings linked across generations is scarce. (This is exactly the problem articulated in the previous section). Interestingly, the available evidence suggests that a substantial share of the intergenerational correlation in capital wealth is realized well before bequests come into play.

Moreover, what papers there are do not generally find that parental income has a strong independent effect on mobility.[18]

The dramatic increase in capital and income inequality highlighted in *C21* has led to some concern that mobility may be declining. This fear is intuitively plausible: if wealth can be used to secure various advantages for children, then an increase in wealth inequality might be expected to decrease mobility. In fact, there is little evidence that income mobility has decreased in recent years, and indeed there is fairly strong evidence that mobility has remained largely unchanged over many decades.[19] The apparent insensitivity of income mobility to changes in inequality might seem surprising, but in fact it is consistent with the generally small estimated effects of parental income on school completion and other measures of human capital. Of course, depending on savings-and-bequest behavior, consumption and wealth mobility may look substantially different from income mobility, especially for those households at the top of the wealth distribution. Nonetheless, there is little positive evidence supporting the concerns about mobility and opportunity articulated by Piketty. As I will argue in the next section, however, mobility estimates are themselves difficult to interpret in a meaningful way, because very different processes may give rise to the same observed level of mobility. The relative constancy of income mobility over time may mask important changes in the relationship between parental resources and outcomes in the next generation.

What Is Next for Mobility Research?

Although it is quite challenging to parse out the relative importance of the various determinants of human capital (genetics, school quality, and parental investments, among other factors), it is nonetheless clear that collectively these factors are very important determinants of intergenerational mobility. Parental income, by contrast, might not have a strong causal effect on children's outcomes. Nor is there good evidence that economic mobility has declined in recent decades as income inequality has increased. Piketty may be correct that wealth mobility will fall in the years to come, provided that his implicit model of savings-and-bequest behavior for the newly wealthy is correct. But there is little support for the argument that rising wealth and income inequality will harm labor income and educational mobility. At the same time, the data and analysis in *C21* and the discussion in this chapter suggest a number of new directions for microeconomic research on inequality. In this section I will outline several areas where future research may prove fruitful.

The standard approach to understanding inequality in microeconomic data does not distinguish between activities that increase aggregate wealth and those that decrease it nor does it differentiate between sources of inherited human capital that would strike most observers as fair and those that seem ethically dubious. Turning the discussion of inequality toward these kinds of distinctions is a major contribution of *Capital in the Twenty-First Century*. Piketty asks some trenchant questions that microeconomists would do well to take to heart. Indeed, he recognizes that "the key issue is the justification of inequalities rather than their magnitude as such." Not all markets are competitive and not all competitive uses of human capital are good.

As an example, consider the question of the high and rising share of income earned by senior corporate managers. Piketty attributes this increase to managers bargaining harder over their pay, since lower top tax rates make such negotiations more worthwhile. Others have attributed this rapid increase to "superstar" effects, whereby small differences in managerial skill (human capital) can be compensated very differently—even in a competitive and efficient labor market. For the sake of argument, suppose that the superstar explanation fits the data better, so that high executive earnings reflect competitive market-based measures of managerial productivity. Even in this case, an increase in top income shares might be objectionable if firms are themselves engaged in destructive activities. In a well-functioning market, firm profits are a signal that the firm's services are highly valued relative to the cost of providing them, and so rewarding executives for expanding profits makes sense both for the firm and for society as a whole. But if a firm instead makes profits by successfully insulating itself from competition or by breaking laws that protect the public, then rewarding its executives will simply have the effect of incentivizing socially destructive behavior. Human-capital-based explanations of earnings inequality are ill-equipped to differentiate between these two possibilities.

The problem, in short, is that crime sometimes does pay.

As another example, consider the inheritance of human capital in classical intergenerational models, such as in the canonical model of Becker and Tomes.[20] In these models, a child's total human capital is a function of two components: the human capital that is inherited automatically from the parent and the additional human capital that is generated by parental and societal investments. This framing of the question may fool one into thinking that the inherited component of human capital has some genetic / natural basis. Becker and Tomes, however, are quite clear that the inherited endowment represents anything that the parents do not have to explicitly expend resources to impart. In other words, endowments are just those components of human capital investment that are not responsive to prices. Inherited endowments may therefore include social networks, cultural attitudes, and much else.

Standard intergenerational models therefore elide distinctions that are ethically and economically relevant. That the scion of a well-connected family can earn a high income as a result of his father's Rolodex seems quite unfair. Moreover, this type of advantage may reduce overall wealth to the extent that such nepotism results in a misallocation of talent across the economy. In contrast, if someone inherits high intelligence, either genetically or through the home environment, it seems neither unfair nor undesirable to many that this person should earn a high income.

This distinction matters not just for how we feel about the inequalities we observe but also for what types of policies may be effective at reducing inequality. If the wealthy use their resources and connections to rig the game in favor of their own children, then policies that explicitly make it harder for them to succeed may be a sensible and effective remedy. If, instead, the wealthy ensure success for their children by passing on intelligence, good health, and norms about behavior, then the natural solution is not to discourage this type of wealth transmission at the top but to encourage and subsidize it at the bottom. In this second case, policies aimed at improving school quality, early home environments, and even prenatal health and nutrition are clearly superior to policies aimed at reducing human capital transmission and accumulation among the wealthy. (Indeed, in the next section I will discuss the potentially huge gains to increasing public investment in early childhood education.) Similarly, if star managers earn huge pay packages by rent-seeking, then the most obvious remedy would be to reduce the returns to rent-seeking by changing the regulation of industry. As always, policy should strive, where possible, to create rules and institutions that align public and private interests.

The literature on intergenerational mobility is hampered by a lack of testable theory. A number of papers develop models linking intergenerational mobility to economic fundamentals such as genetics, environment, and public and private human capital investments. By and large, these theories imply that most factors affect mobility in the manner that one would expect. For instance, progressive investment in human capital by the state can offset parental inequality in human capital investments and thereby increase mobility.[21] Ideally, one could take these theories to data to test the relative importance of various factors in determining intergenerational mobility.

Unfortunately, empirical tests of these models also rely on strong assumptions that are not well motivated by economic theory. A number of papers, for example, compare the outcomes of adopted versus biological children in order to tease out the relative importance of genetics and home environment. These papers typically assume, without any biological or economic justification, that genes and environment do not interact.[22] Because skills and investments seem to interact in a complicated, recursive fashion, there is no conceptually clean way to separate out the contributions of "nature" and "nurture." Moreover, the standard equity/efficiency trade-off, which states that there is a tension between investing to equalize outcomes across individuals and investing to equalize marginal returns across individuals, might really operate only at some ages and for some types of skills. Early, intensive investments in particularly deprived youth may promote both equity and efficiency whereas investments in such youth later in childhood may be quite inefficient.

Without a much richer and more detailed understanding of how human capital is created and how it is rewarded in the labor market, it is not possible to define "mobility" and "opportunity" meaningfully. Is it good if the intergenerational correlation in earnings declines? The answer to this question depends on how strong a correlation we would expect in an ideal world. For instance, suppose our gold standard is a world without inefficiencies in human capital investment (that is, a world in which the marginal return to society as a whole of human capital investment is equalized across all people). In this case, the expected intergenerational correlation in income would be greater than zero because some traits are partially determined by genetics, but beyond this it is very hard to say anything concrete. The answer also depends on how human capital is rewarded by the labor market. If the intergenerational association in earnings increases, is this because high-income parents have gotten better at rigging the game in favor of their children? or because traits that are more strongly inherited have become differentially more valuable? It is very difficult to define the relevant counterfactuals to answer these questions, but without such counterfactuals, empirical mobility estimates are not informative.

The complexity of the economic forces that generate cross-sectional and intergenerational inequality mean that almost any set of explanations can be fit to the data. Without substantially richer data and models, selecting among these various possibilities is essentially impossible. I believe a promising way forward would be to incorporate some of the methodological advances pioneered by Heckman and many coauthors on the technology of human capital formation. These models are dynamic and flexible; they allow for many different kinds of skills, inherited endowments, and interactions among endowments, parental investments, and social investments.

Understanding how human capital is created is a necessary first step in reliably interpreting intergenerational correlations in economic outcomes. Additionally, interpreting such correlations also requites that we understand what types of skills are valued in the labor market, how these market valuations have changed over time, and how these skills promote or detract from social welfare.

Early Childhood Education: A Win for Egalitarians and Non-Egalitarians Alike?

Piketty's proposal to combat rising inequality, a global wealth tax, seems designed to appeal only to those who believe that equality is an intrinsic good. Standard economic theories suggest that taxing wealth will lower the long-run stock of wealth, which will in turn lower wages. A possible effect of Piketty's plan, therefore, would be the immiseration of everyone to achieve a reduction in inequality, and indeed, some supporters of Piketty have openly embraced this trade-off. Even though it is possible that a wealth tax would in fact increase incomes (perhaps through a reduction in counter-productive rent-seeking), the general tone and argument in *Capital in the Twenty-First Century* strongly suggest that Piketty would favor giving up some other goods in order to decrease income and wealth inequality. The view that equality is intrinsically desirable is by no means universal among policy makers, social scientists, and political philosophers, and *C21* is ill-positioned to appeal to those who value equality solely for instrumental reasons.[23]

C21's focus on a contentious and divisive policy program is frustrating because there are a number of feasible policies that would be easy to support on both egalitarian and non-egalitarian grounds. Such policies are less reliant on a particular, contested political philosophy and are therefore more likely to gain widespread democratic acceptance. In this section I will briefly outline one such policy stemming from the literature already discussed on the technology of human capital creation: early childhood education. The potential benefits to early childhood education are huge, and, if implemented properly, may increase both the equity and the efficiency of the economy.

The possibility that early childhood investments could improve the long-term outcomes of children was shown in a number of interventions in the United States in the 1960s and 1970s. These programs featured intensive, high-quality support for children from mostly low-income and minority backgrounds. Follow-up studies years after the initial treatments have generally found very large effects on a wide array of adult outcomes, including school completion, income, criminality, and health. Although these programs were quite expensive, the magnitude of the improvements they generated were so large that they more than justified their costs.[24] These programs show that huge improvements are possible if disadvantaged children are given the right investments at the right times.

National-level programs, such as Head Start in the United States, seem to generate smaller and more mixed effects. Many students in these programs, for example, experience initial gains in test scores which then fade out over time. The estimated effects on outcomes such as school completion, earnings, and criminality appear to be more persistent but are still typically smaller in magnitude than the effects found in the early, intense interventions discussed above. The lower effectiveness of these larger-scale programs is not surprising, as they tend to be cheaper and lower-quality— children spend less time in these programs and the quality of the inputs they receive are likely lower. Yet even these much larger and much less expensive programs seem to yield sizable benefits, and these gains could be magnified even further by reallocating resources within a program to activities with the highest demonstrated rate of return.[25]

The key point here is that even if policy should prove unable to fully replicate the tremendous success of the most effective (and expensive) programs, the potential for still-large gains at a relatively low cost more than justifies continued research and investment in programs targeting young children. Moreover, the largest benefits seem to accrue to the most deprived children, suggesting that early childhood education may promote both equity and efficiency in a way that other reforms, such as subsidizing college attainment, may not. Early childhood education is an easy policy to support from almost any normative viewpoint. Finally, early childhood education has the considerable advantage that expanding current programs, or introducing new programs, is well within the aegis of current national governments, unlike a global wealth tax.

Conclusion

Capital in the Twenty-First Century presents intriguing historical data and advances a bold thesis on the causes and consequences of inequality. Yet the data and analysis suffer from the omission of human capital. Physical and human capital are both important sources of wealth, and no general account of inequality and its evolution is complete without considering them jointly. While including human capital will certainly alter the basic contours of *C21*'s thesis, the data and analysis in the book also suggest a number of paths forward for the microeconomic study of inequality.

The rise of top income shares calls out for better data and better models of the savings-and-bequest behavior of high-wealth households. The arguments using rent-seeking as an explanation for rising inequality suggest that we need to better understand how human capital and rent-seeking interact, and that we need to think more critically about what kinds of factors drive the neutrally named "endowments" in intergenerational human capital models and empirical work. Finally, the apparent stability of relative (income) mobility in a period of rising income inequality highlights the need for better data and richer models in the analysis of economic mobility that would render standard estimates economically interpretable.

EIGHT

Exploring the Effects of Technology on Income and Wealth Inequality

LAURA TYSON AND MICHAEL SPENCE

Economists Laura Tyson and Michael Spence argue that the real driving force behind rising inequality, especially in the decades to come, is to be found in technological change and globalization that displaces workers from routine tasks that can increasingly be performed by programmable machines. Thus, they see the book *The Second Machine Age*, by Brynjolfsson and McAfee, as being equal to *Capital in the Twenty-First Century* as a contribution to the inequality debate. In the coming decades, they argue, an increasing share of jobs will be vulnerable to replacement by intelligent machines and this is likely to drive earnings inequality between those whose work becomes more productive in the Second Machine Age and those whose work is no longer necessary.

Introduction

Growing income and wealth inequality—particularly the dramatic rise of the share of the top 1 percent in the United States and the other developed countries—has sparked a heated debate about the causes of inequality and about appropriate policy responses. Is inequality an inherent feature of capitalist systems? Did the period of less pronounced inequality after World War II herald the beginning of a new era of more inclusive capitalism? Or was it a transitory deviation from the long-run status quo, much more likely to be another Belle Époque or Gilded Age—a path back to a modern form of "patrimonial capitalism" in the developed countries? What can policy makers do to mitigate inequality and its attendant social and political costs without undermining innovation and growth? In this environment of debate about inequality and the nature of capitalism, Thomas Piketty's book, with its rich historical data, clarity of exposition, and penetrating economic analysis, quickly became a best seller and deservedly so.

With passion and rigor, Piketty explores what he believes to be the major forces behind increasing income and wealth inequality in developed capitalist economies during the last half century. Although we agree with much of his analysis, we believe that it suffers from a serious shortcoming: It pays inadequate attention to technological change and technology-enabled globalization as drivers of inequality during the last several decades. We believe that these factors are as significant for understanding inequality in the recent past and in the future as the factors that are central to Piketty's analysis. Bluntly, we believe that Erik Brynjolfsson and Andrew McAfee's book *The Second Machine Age* is as important a book as Thomas Piketty's *Capital in the Twenty-First Century* for understanding trends in the distribution of income and wealth during the last several decades and for predicting trends over the next several decades.[1]

In this chapter we focus on the role of technology in Piketty's work—both in his theory of wealth inequality and in his analysis of income inequality, particularly in the United States. We believe that both technology and globalization, the latter enabled by technology, have had a major impact on capital's share of national income—a key variable in Piketty's theory of wealth inequality—and on the growing inequality in labor incomes and overall incomes in the United States during the last thirty years. In contrast to Piketty, we think that these strong structural forces have played a significant role in the explosion of income even for the top 1 percent, although we agree with him that changing social norms, compensation practices, and tax policy, have also contributed to this result.

Technology is a major driver of productivity and economic growth—it creates prosperity. But the computer / digital revolution is also a major driver of inequality in a variety of ways: It favors more skilled over less skilled workers; it increases the return to capital owners over labor; it enables or "turbo-charges" globalization, reducing employment and constraining wage growth for middle-income workers, particularly in manufacturing and tradable services; it increases the income advantages of superstars and the super lucky; and it generates rents in highly imperfect markets.

Even engineers and scientists working on machine intelligence are surprised by the rapid advances in the ability of machines to substitute for human workers in a wide range of blue-collar and white-collar tasks across the income distribution.

These advances are due to a number of factors. In robotics, progress in sensor technology allows machines to detect and respond to their environment, thus expanding the scope of activities they can perform. Additive manufacturing also displaces labor, while reducing waste in materials, lowering the costs of customization, and allowing for production on demand (as opposed to on forecasted demand). But perhaps the most surprising strides have been in artificial intelligence (AI). Machines can now use learning algorithms and high-speed-network access to massive databases in order to acquire the ability to perform complex tasks without the benefit of algorithms that tell them precisely what to do.

In their book, Brynjolfsson and McAfee document the progress in artificial intelligence that is enabling computers connected to high-speed networks and huge databases to exceed what they were capable of only a few years ago. The leaps in machine intelligence, along with the connection of human beings around the world in a common digital network, will enable the development of new technologies, goods, and services.

The authors are optimistic about the "bounty," or economy-wide productivity benefits, of "brilliant" machines. But they warn that the distribution or "spread" of these benefits will be uneven, and will evolve over an extended period of time.

As smart machines become more powerful and pervasive, they will challenge a fundamental feature of market systems: In such systems, most people gain their income by selling their labor. So what happens when the labor of a large share of the working-age population, regardless of their education, is rendered technologically redundant or no longer commands an income adequate to provide a minimally decent or socially acceptable standard of living?

Trying to anticipate where the comparative advantage of human labor will lie fifteen years from now, let alone in fifty years, is a hazardous exercise. But we must try to detect the trends and project the consequences for changes in the structure of economies, the nature of labor markets, and the distribution of income and wealth. We will need policies that anticipate these changes and ease the dislocations resulting from them. In particular, we will need policies to modify the distributional consequences of the operation of these powerful technological drivers as they are translated into market outcomes.

In our discussion of Piketty's work, we focus on the role of technological change in explaining recent trends and predicting future trends in wealth and income inequality in the United States. We are convinced that it is essential to understand the ongoing digital revolution and the rise of intelligent machines to predict future trends and to develop policies to address their economic, social, and political costs.

Piketty and Technology

Technology's Roles in Piketty's Analysis of Wealth Inequality

Throughout his book and in his subsequent writings, Piketty emphasizes that his work is primarily about the history of the distributions of wealth and income, not about simple deterministic theories of what drives them over time. Indeed, much of his book focuses on how institutions, norms, power, and policy choices affect inequality. Despite Piketty's warnings, however, much of the commentary on and criticism of his work by economists has focused on his simple yet incomplete theory of the forces behind wealth inequality in capitalism.

Building on the traditions of Kaldor, Kuznets, and Solow, Piketty's theory rests on a standard production function in which output depends on capital, labor, and technology. Relying on his rich and unique data set spanning more than three centuries from the Industrial Revolution to the present, he makes two major assumptions. First, the rate of return on capital (r) normally exceeds the rate of growth (g) in capitalist economies. Second, the ownership of capital and hence the distribution of capital income are highly concentrated. Under these conditions, capital's share of overall income rises with economic growth, resulting in increasing wealth and income inequality. The assumption that capital owners save a much higher share of their income than labor does—an assumption also supported by centuries of data—amplifies these trends over time.

Technology appears in Piketty's theory in several ways. Technology is embedded in his two-factor production function. When technology is unchanging, increases in capital, like increases in labor, have diminishing returns. Over time, however, technological progress increases the output that can be produced from given quantities of inputs. The relative stability of the return on capital over many centuries, even while the stock of capital increased, reflects the fact that the positive effects of technological progress on capital's return offset the negative effects of diminishing returns. Technology drives growth through productivity improvements, and the balance between diminishing returns on capital and technological progress results in a fairly stable return on capital that exceeds the overall growth rate.

Capital's share of income—a major determinant of wealth inequality—depends on both the rate of return on capital and the ratio between capital and output, a ratio that is embedded in technology. In the standard production function Piketty uses, a rising capital share of income is consistent with a rising capital output ratio only if the elasticity of substitution of capital for labor is greater than one—that is, only if it is relatively easy to substitute capital for labor in response to changes in their relative prices. Piketty believes that the historical evidence satisfies this condition, and he even speculates that the capital–labor elasticity of substitution will be higher in the twenty-first century as a result of technological progress that will make it easier for capital to do the tasks historically done by labor. Slower growth, due to demographic changes and perhaps to slowing productivity as well, combined with capital-augmenting and labor-saving technological developments suggests to Piketty that the gap between r and g could get even larger in the twenty-first century, fueling greater inequality.

As many economists have noted, however, the empirical evidence indicates that historically the elasticity of substitution of capital for labor has been significantly less than one. If that's the case, Piketty's theory cannot adequately explain the rise in capital's share of income and the drop in labor's share of income throughout industries and countries since 1980. According to recent studies, other factors like capital-augmenting and skill-biased technological progress, offshoring—itself enabled by computer and digital technologies—and the changing composition of the industrial base are significant drivers of these global developments.[2] At most, the decrease in the relative price of capital, itself often attributed to advances in computing and IT power, explains about half of the decline in labor's share of income.

Overall, the heated debate among economists about the elasticity of substitution between capital and labor confirms that technological progress plays a key role in the evolution of capital and labor shares of national income. These shares in turn are major determinants of wealth and income inequality. Moreover, as technology has become more capital-augmenting and skill-biased, its influence on inequality has strengthened.

Piketty's standard production function includes only one form of capital. Brynjolfsson and McAfee distinguish between "digital capital" and physical capital and argue that the returns to the former are different from and higher than the returns to the latter. The rising share of profit is caused in part by rapid increases in the incomes of those who own claims on the returns to digital capital. These returns tend to follow a power-law distribution, with relatively small numbers garnering an outsized share of the returns. This is consistent with known properties of the economics of networks, especially platforms that become the dominant economic and social "marketplaces" and gain considerable market power and the associated rents (returns in excess of those in competitive market conditions) in the digital arena.

For our purposes, we note that the measurement of digital capital is challenging and thus far limited in scope. In addition, the returns to digital capital are difficult to separate both from the returns to the human capital of its creators and from the returns to the human capital of workers whose skills are complementary to it. Indeed, it is quite likely that a significant share of the income recorded as labor income—wages and salaries for the top 1 percent—is actually income generated by digital capital shared with certain kinds of complementary human capital, including innovators, entrepreneurs, venture capitalists, and top executives.

It is worth noting that embedded in these power-law distributions of returns to digital capital are very high returns to a few enterprises. A large fraction of these "outliers" are platforms providing digital marketplaces in information, facilitating transactions in goods and services, and enabling a peer-to-peer sharing economy for millions of individuals around the globe. Successful platforms generate outsized returns for two reasons. One is the well-known network effect that occurs when the value of a platform rises as the number of its users increases. The other is less well known. Most markets are characterized by two-sided informational gaps. Buyers and sellers are missing key information about the counterparties. This phenomenon is sometimes referred to as the "trust issue." Platforms become the locales of repeated transactions that generate information that in turn fosters the growth of future transactions. Using large and growing databases on buyers and sellers, platforms are able to provide increasingly sophisticated two-way evaluation systems to close informational and trust gaps that are standard market impediments, especially for small buyers and sellers who do not have established reputations. The two-way evaluation systems also change incentives and behavior in a positive way. Airbnb and Uber are good examples—both platforms link individual buyers and sellers and allow them to evaluate one another ex post. The combination of the network effect and the application of "big data" to reduce informational gaps and asymmetries gives successful platforms tremendous market power, and generates substantial outsized returns or rents to their owners—usually a combination of founders, venture investors, and employees.

While digital-capital-intensive companies can and do generate high concentrations of income and wealth, they also provide a range of digitally based services that are widely available at very low cost. Data on the consumer surplus generated by such services is hard to come by, but there is every reason to believe that the ratio of consumer surplus to either the revenue or the cost of provision of these services is abnormally high. This means that the distribution of "benefits" from such services may be much more equal than the distribution of wealth for the owners of the digital capital that provide such services.

Access to the benefits of digital platforms is increasingly global. Mobile Internet penetration was over 50 percent worldwide as of 2015, and is projected to increase to 65 percent by 2020. Surveys of consumers, particularly young consumers, by Boston Consulting Group and others suggest not only that the value of Internet services exceeds the costs by huge amounts, but also that consumers would be willing to give up as much as 15 to 20 percent of income to keep these services.[3]

To summarize, digital-capital-intensive companies are generating large concentrations of wealth. They are also delivering services with broad-based benefits at very low cost, a much more egalitarian part of the overall distribution picture. Digital capital might be making the distribution of wealth and income more unequal even as it makes the distribution of utility more equal.

Technology's Roles in Piketty's Analysis of Income Inequality

Piketty's theory of wealth inequality focuses on the evolution and distribution of capital income and its share in national income. Capital income accounts for only about 30 percent of national income, however, and growing inequality in labor income is the major cause of growing income inequality in the United States and other developed countries.

Piketty states clearly that the factors driving wealth inequality and income inequality are different, and that the relationship between r and g, which he believes is an important force behind changes in wealth inequality, is not a useful tool for understanding changes in labor income inequality.[4] So how does he explain the growing inequality in labor income, and what is the role of technology in his explanation?

Like many economists, Piketty believes that the race between technology and education has been a major driver of labor income inequality, at least for the bottom 99 percent of the wage distribution, over the last thirty years in the United States and other developed countries. Research by Goldin and Katz, which Piketty cites, and related research by David Autor and others on skill-biased technological change provide convincing empirical evidence for this view.[5] As a result of the dramatic decline in the cost of computing power, computer-enabled machines have transformed the composition of jobs and the distribution of labor earnings. These machines have substituted for workers in a growing number and range of jobs (both blue- and white-collar or manual and cognitive) that involve routine, codifiable tasks, while amplifying the productivity and increasing the demand for workers in two kinds of jobs: those that are intensive in abstract tasks, requiring problem-solving skills, adaptability, and creativity; and those that are intensive in manual and service tasks that require human labor.

The result has been polarization of the labor market: the simultaneous growth of high-education, high-wage jobs at one end of the occupational spectrum and low-education, low-wage jobs at the other end, both at the expense of middle-wage, middle-education jobs. A large body of evidence confirms employment polarization at the level of industries, localities, and national labor markets over the last twenty to thirty years.[6]

Recent studies find that polarization of the U.S. labor market continued during the recovery from the 2007–2008 recession.[7] According to recent research by McKinsey Global Institute, between 2000 and 2014 the United States economy created 8 million net new full-time-equivalent positions; two-thirds of those were in low-skill work while 2.5 million net production and transactions jobs were eliminated as routine tasks were automated on assembly lines though robots and in offices through software.[8]

For the last several decades, the education of the workforce has failed to keep pace with the skill requirements of technology in the United States and several developed economies. As a result, the earnings premium for education has risen sharply, and this has contributed significantly to the growth of inequality in labor earnings. In the United States, for example, about two-thirds of the considerable rise of labor income dispersion between 1980 and 2005 is the result of the increased premium associated with schooling in general and with postsecondary education in particular.[9] The premium for a college education began to widen dramatically in the 1980s. The growth in the supply of college graduates began to slow just as the technology-fueled demand for those with the skills associated with a college education began to increase—clear evidence of the race between education and technology. Over the last three decades, the earnings gap between college- and high-school-educated workers in the United States has more than doubled.

Although Piketty believes that the institutional rules of the labor market—such as the minimum wage, collective bargaining, and CEO compensation norms—influence the level and distribution of labor income over time, he also acknowledges that the race between education and technology has been the main explanation for growing labor income inequality, at least for the bottom 99 percent. His analysis rests on a standard marginal productivity approach in which wages depend on the supply and demand for skills, shaped by skill-biased and capital-augmenting technical change and by inequality in the access to education. Consistent with this view, he states that the "best way to reduce inequalities in income with respect to labor as well as to increase the average productivity of the labor force and the overall growth in the economy is to invest in education." This is the same conclusion espoused by most economists who have analyzed the causes and the remedies for growing labor income inequality in the United States during the last thirty years. But will access to education be a remedy in the future if digitization and smart machines displace even highly educated workers, limiting their employment opportunities and depressing their wages? Piketty does not address this question, a question that is central to those concerned about how workers will fare in the age of intelligent machines and robots.

Instead he focuses on what he says is "the most striking failure" of the education / technology explanation of labor income inequality: "its inability to adequately explain the explosion of very high incomes from labor in the United States," compared to other countries that are subject to the same structural and technological forces. In Piketty's view this is a major gap in the technology / education theory because the increase in the share of labor income going to the top 1 percent explains about two-thirds of the dramatic increase in their share of national income over the last thirty years, with the remainder explained by income from capital.

But if the education / technology theory and the marginal productivity approach on which it rests cannot explain why the wages of the top 1 percent have soared in some developed countries, particularly the United States, but not in others, what is the explanation? Why has pay exploded in the United States and to a lesser extent in the United Kingdom, Canada, and Australia for the top executives in both the financial and the nonfinancial sectors—a group that Piketty calls "supermanagers"—who make up the majority of those in the top 1 percent and top 0.1 percent of the income distribution? Piketty says the answers are institutional practices in such areas as managerial compensation and corporate governance, social norms, and tax policy.

One of the many virtues of Piketty's work is that it covers a wide range of countries and economies, permitting comparisons and therefore providing leverage in assessing different explanatory factors in generating income inequality. Although all of the developed countries display the same trend of rising income inequality during the last thirty years, there are considerable differences among them. These differences show up not only in the shares of the top 1 percent and top 0.1 percent, but also in other measures of income inequality. For example, the ratio of the average income of the top 20 percent to the bottom 20 percent in the United States is about 8.4, whereas the same ratio in Germany is 4.3, roughly half. And the United States has one of the most unequal wage distributions of the developed countries as a result of both relatively low wages at the bottom and extremely high wages at the top.[10] All of these developed countries have open economies and are exposed to the same global market forces and technological changes, so it is hard to see how these common features could explain large national differences in income inequality. It is therefore more than plausible that other institutional and policy factors, such as union bargaining power, tax policy, social norms, and governance structures, have played significant roles in different distributional outcomes.

Piketty makes a compelling case for the effects of such factors in the United States. He argues that although the education / technology race has been a major factor behind growing inequality in the bottom 99 percent of the U.S. wage distribution, it cannot explain the "discontinuities" in wage growth between the top 1 percent and the bottom 99 percent or within the top 1 percent itself. The pay of the top 10 percent has grown much more rapidly than the pay of the average or median worker but not nearly as rapidly as the pay of the top 1 percent; and the pay of the "supermanagers" or top executives who make up 60 to 70 percent of the top 0.1 percent has soared compared to those in the 99th percentile. Other indicators of wage inequality, such as the ratio between the wages of college- and high-school-educated workers and the ratios of wages at the 90th decile of the wage distribution to wages at the 50th and the 10th deciles, have also increased, but not nearly as much as the ratios between the pay of the top 1 percent and top 0.1 percent and the pay of the "bottom" 99 percent and the pay of the median or average worker.[11]

Piketty points out that these sharp discontinuities in pay growth at the very top of the income hierarchy cannot be explained by discontinuities in years of education, the selectivity of educational institutions, or years of professional experience. Perhaps these executives have unique unmeasured skills that have been enhanced by technology, causing their productivity and hence their pay to soar, but Piketty doesn't think so.

He asserts that their pay has little to do with their individual marginal productivity because it is impossible to attribute a firm's performance, as measured by such traditional indicators as sales or profits growth, to the decisions of its executives. In his view, the most convincing explanations for the dramatic growth of "supermanager" incomes in the United States are the practices that determine their compensation, practices controlled by the executives themselves and by compensation committees, most of whose members are themselves executives of other large corporations and earn comparable salaries. Piketty describes decisions made in this way as "largely arbitrary," reflecting both the hierarchical relationships and relative bargaining power of the individuals involved and the prevailing social norms and beliefs about the contribution of top executives to firm performance.

In publicly listed corporations, these decisions in principle are subject to the oversight of boards of directors who represent shareholders, but Piketty believes that corporate governance checks and balances on top executive pay are ambiguous and weak. As proof of the gaps in corporate governance and the absence of a productivity justification for the pay of top executives in the United States, he cites evidence that their pay depends on variables like sales and profits that in turn depend in part on external macroeconomic conditions over which they have little influence.

Finally, Piketty notes that large decreases in top marginal income tax rates in the United States, the United Kingdom, and other English-speaking developed countries after 1980 strengthened the incentives of top executives to seek large pay increases, triggering the takeoff of top executive pay in these countries at around the same time. One interpretation of the evidence is that the reduction in marginal tax rates increased executive effort, resulting in increased executive pay. This is the standard taxable-income elasticity argument—people work harder when their marginal income tax rate declines—applied to top executives. This is not Piketty's interpretation. Instead, he posits that tax cuts strengthened the incentive for successful rent-seeking behavior by top executives to redistribute business income from shareholders, workers, and other stakeholders to themselves.

The dramatic growth of CEO compensation in the United States after 1994 also shows evidence of the effects of another tax change, which allowed businesses to deduct top executive pay in excess of $1 million only if it was linked to performance.[12] In keeping with the prevailing view in the United States that executives represent shareholders and that shareholders are motivated by financial returns, companies elected to measure performance primarily by indicators of profitability such as earnings per share or total shareholder return. (A recent survey of changing CEO compensation practices in the United States highlights the role of changes in tax policy, including the 1994 change, as drivers of trends in CEO compensation over the last century).[13]

Although there is clear evidence that executive compensation has increased significantly both absolutely and relative to the pay of the bottom 99 percent, there is considerable debate about why this has happened. Some observers, such as Joseph Stiglitz, Paul Krugman, Robert Reich, Lawrence Mishel, and Lucian Bebchuk, share Piketty's view that high and rising executive pay reflects flawed corporate governance practices and changing social norms that allow successful rent-seeking behavior by executives.

Others, like Kevin Murphy and Steven Kaplan, argue that executive pay trends reflect efficient compensation necessary to align the incentives of executives with those of shareholders. From the perspective of shareholders, rewarding top executives on stock performance solves the "agency" problem and explains why there is a strong relationship between executive compensation and stock value, particularly in large firms. In this interpretation, it is the dramatic increase in company value—in part due to technological change and globalization that have reduced labor costs and increased market size—that explains the dramatic increase in executive pay.

A recent paper by Brynjolfsson, Kim, and Saint-Jacques also links the rise in CEO pay to technological change, in a different way. Based on data for more than 2,500 publicly traded companies over fifteen years and controlling for a variety of factors, including company size, market capitalization, median wages, and sector, they find that the "information technology intensity" of a company—as measured by the ratio of its IT capital stock to its total capital stock—"strongly predicts" the compensation of its top executives over time and explains differences in CEO pay across industries. Indeed, the authors find that IT intensity is generally the most significant variable explaining CEO pay in their sample. The authors hypothesize that information technology enhances the "marginal productivity" of top executives by improving their ability to monitor and enforce a company's strategic decisions—thereby increasing the "effective size" and market value of the companies they lead. In an "efficient market" for executive talent, this higher marginal productivity results in higher levels of executive compensation.[14]

The Brynjolfsson-Kim-Saint-Jacques analysis focuses on the effects of digital capital in the form of network-based information and communication technology systems on the ability of top managers to monitor and drive company performance. It seems highly plausible that by providing immediate access to and analysis of current data across the entire enterprise, such systems increase the span of control of top managers and CEOs. The result of these systems is disintermediation: a reduction in the vertical layers of middle managers engaged in supervision and an increase in the efficiency and quality of management oversight. These disintermediation effects are well documented in banking, retail, and in automated information systems within companies—even in the need for secretarial and administrative support in academia. The gains or rents from more effective management oversight and reduced middle management requirements enabled by IT go somewhere—in the Brynjolfsson-Kim-Saint-Jacques analysis they show up in CEO compensation. But why is that the case? More research is necessary to determine whether and in what contexts these disintermediation and efficiency gains go to consumers (in the form of lower prices or improvements in the quality of goods and services), to CEOs and upper management, to workers, or to shareholders.

The productivity-enhancing effects of IT are also a factor behind the dramatic rise in the pay of top professionals in the financial services industry in the United States and their growing share in the top 1 percent and top 0.1 percent. IT has enabled the financial innovations that have driven the explosion in the size of the financial services industry—innovations like credit default swaps, collateralized debt obligations, and high-speed trading, to name a few. These innovations have had a dramatic effect on the productivity of the financial services sector, as measured by indicators like transactions processed, volume of trades, and the introduction of new products and services. Such indicators do not evaluate whether the productivity and outputs of the financial sector have been a source of value-added for the overall economy. But the executives and traders in this sector are rewarded on the basis of such indicators. They are also rewarded on the basis of financial market asset prices over which they have little direct control and that depend on general macroeconomic conditions including central bank policy. As noted earlier, Piketty argues that the compensation of top executives should not depend on such "external" market conditions.

Finally it is important to note that much of Piketty's discussion focuses on compensation practices and corporate governance rules that are applicable to large U.S. corporations, not to S-corporations and partnerships—including private equity, hedge funds, and venture capital funds—where a large and growing percentage of business income is earned and where a significant share of the "supermanagers" in the top 1 percent and 0.1 percent earn their income. IT technology may be a significant factor behind the rise of these incomes both in the financial services sector and in the legal and other professional services firms that serve it.

Technology, Winner-Take-All Effects, and Rents: Gaps in Piketty's Analysis

In his analysis of the factors affecting the pay of supermanagers, Piketty does not discuss the possible winner-take-all or superstar effects of technology. According to the winner-take-all theory, technology raises the compensation of "best performers" relative to the compensation of others by enabling the best in any field to sell their skills to a wider market over time, displacing the demand for those who are less than best. Winner-take-all effects depend on both economies of scale in production (the very best in a field can reach large numbers of consumers) and economies of scale in consumption (a large share of these consumers prefer the very best to the next best alternatives). Digital communications and platform and social networking technologies generate both types of scale economies. Globalization, enabled by technology, strengthens the resulting winner-take-all effects.

Most often the superstar framework is applied to those in the arts, entertainment, and athletics—who accounted for less than 2 percent of taxpayers in the top 1 percent and about 3 percent in the top 0.1 percent in the United States in 2005. But the framework is more generally applicable to any individuals who earn the reputation for being among the "best" in their professions, including law, medicine, real estate, management consulting, and academic research. Together these professions accounted for more than 35 percent of the top 1 percent and about 25 percent of the top 0.1 percent in the United States in 2005.[15] The corporate governance rules that are the focus of Piketty's analysis of executive pay do not apply to these professions, although changing market conditions, social norms, and marginal income tax rates do. A recent study applies the superstar theory to "superstar CEOs" who gain global reputations for strong performance of their companies under their leadership.[16]

Presumably superstar incomes result in part from the fact that superstars are selling something (call it a service) that is, or is perceived to be, differentiated, even highly differentiated. What the exact nature of the differentiation is and how it is acquired depend on the category and defy easy answers. Sports stars come up through some kind of competitive system that defines and provides measures of "best performance." In the case of entertainers, the differentiation of established stars is clear, but both the process by which stars are discovered and whether that process is somewhat random are less clear. For established CEO stars, there are accessible performance data for companies, though the process of becoming a superstar manager probably would not pass a "controlled experiment" test, and there is an element of randomness or luck in the process.[17]

A related question is why the "rents" associated with superstar compensation do not get bid away. Or perhaps better, why are they not bid away faster than what we observe? In some cases, it could be that there is just a limited supply of certain kinds of unusual talent. That would be the standard argument in a world of complete and symmetric information. But one suspects that is not the whole story, and that there are time-dependent entry barriers, and parallel information diffusion processes, associated with the process of differentiation. Perhaps IT will lower some of these barriers over time, by lowering the costs of the superstar discovery process. But these issues take us well beyond the current corpus of economic theory.

The superstar theory of top incomes is closely related to the textbook concept of economic rent—payments over and above the minimum needed to bring a factor of production into productive use. As a result of globalization and digital technology, winners in winner-take-all conditions can earn considerable economic rent. This is another channel through which technology and globalization foster the growth of top incomes and exacerbate income inequality. Piketty overlooks this channel.

Technology also plays a role in rent defined as a return to a factor of production in excess of what would occur under "perfectly competitive" market conditions. Piketty eschews this definition of rent, defining it instead as the income earned by capital regardless of the form of that income. He asserts that his theory of the income earned by capital has "absolutely nothing to do" with imperfect competition. Our approach is different and reflects our view that technology and globalization often create market imperfections that generate considerable rent. The distribution of this rent between the owners of capital and labor and among various types of labor depends on policies, institutional practices, and norms.

We think it is best to think about the return to capital as a residual or as having a component that is a residual. There is a risk-adjusted cost of capital that suppliers of financial capital require ex ante in order to put funds into an enterprise. In theory in a perfectly competitive world, the labor market would set the wages and salaries for different types of workers, the owners of capital would get the required risk-adjusted return, the government would get its share through taxes, and the rest of the benefits of technological change would flow to consumers via the effect of competition on output prices. But these conditions are rarely realized.

Technological change generates rents in many ways. Market power from economies of scale and scope and first-mover advantages when entry barriers are high generate rents. Schumpeterian competition generates market power and rents that flow to innovators and entrepreneurs who may also be substantial owners of capital. These rents may prove transitory in the long run, but they are often more than sufficient to compensate innovators for their investment of time, effort, and the considerable risks taken. The network and first-mover effects of digital technologies and the intellectual property protection they receive can produce very large rents over long periods of time. Such effects help to explain the fact that the returns to digital capital and its owners exemplify a highly concentrated power-law distribution. It is also very difficult to separate these returns from the returns to the creators of that capital and from the returns to those whose skills are enhanced by it. And in an attempt to solve the "agency" problem of company governance, capital owners are likely to share the rents on their digital capital with top executives and top talent.

A growing body of research indicates that at least in the United States, rents from market power fed by strong patent and intellectual property protection, and by brand names for first-movers are substantial and flow primarily to upper level management and owners of capital, including digital capital, and to complementary human capital.[18] Often the income of super-managers is recorded as labor income, but it is really a combination of capital income and rent emanating from imperfectly competitive markets. In his excellent review of Piketty's book, Nobel laureate Robert Solow suggests that a large share of what is recorded as labor income for the top 1 percent in the United States is really capital income, with capital defined to include intangible assets.[19] We agree and we posit that a significant fraction of this capital income reflects the returns to technology.

In the next section we focus on technology and technology-enabled globalization because we believe that these forces are likely to become even more important drivers of income inequality in the future. To better understand the interaction between technology and income, we distinguish between different types of labor and capital. There is labor that is complementary to technology, and labor for which technology is a substitute. These distinctions between types of capital and types of labor will become even more important in the future with even greater digitization and the spread of intelligent robots and artificial intelligence.

Technology, Globalization, and Distribution

The trends in the distribution of income and wealth in developed economies during the last thirty years are, we believe, related to the rather dramatic shifts in the structure and composition of both their economies and their labor markets, caused by a combination of powerful technological and global market forces. The former forces are closely associated with an expanding set of digital and digitally capital-intensive technologies that are labor-saving and skill-biased; the latter with the globalization of supply chains made possible by these technologies and by the arrival of emerging economies, particularly China, as major participants in an increasingly interconnected and competitive global economy. These two forces are separate but related and reinforcing. Network-based information technology and management innovation have expanded the tools for managing complex global supply chains by enabling companies to source, monitor, and coordinate production processes at disparate locations quickly and cheaply. This has made pools of labor and human capital around the globe more accessible, and this in turn has increased competitive pressures on companies and their workers in the developed countries.

A key organizing principle for the spread of global supply chains has been labor arbitrage—reducing production costs by outsourcing or offshoring work to locations with low-cost labor. Both technology and greater openness to trade and capital flows in emerging market economies have enabled the expansion of complex supply chains and increased the downward pressure on wages in the United States and the other developed countries from lower-cost labor in these economies.

These structural shifts and transitions are not captured in the macro models of growth that are the foundation for Piketty's work. But they seem to us essential elements in deepening our understanding of the trends in income and wealth inequality during the last thirty years, and they are likely to continue to be important determinants in the future.

Piketty's macro models do not distinguish between types of labor, but to understand the forces driving wage inequality it is essential to do so. The effects of labor-saving and skill-biased technological change are apparent in trends in the composition of jobs. Labor economists distinguish jobs along two dimensions: manual and cognitive and routine and nonroutine. The distinction between cognitive and manual jobs is straightforward, characterized by differences in the extent of mental and physical tasks. If the tasks involved can be summarized as a set of specific activities accomplished by following well-defined instructions and procedures, a job is classified as routine. There are both routine manual (largely blue-collar) jobs and routine cognitive (largely white-collar) jobs. Both types of routine jobs tend to be middle-skill jobs. Nonroutine cognitive jobs tend to be high-skill jobs and nonroutine manual jobs tend to be low-skilled ones.[20]

Labor-saving and skill-biased technological change substitutes for labor in routine blue- and white-collar jobs that are "codifiable" and can be performed by machines.[21] In contrast, nonroutine cognitive jobs involve "abstract tasks" that are not "codifiable" and hence cannot be done by machines—at least at the present time. Skill-biased technological change complements the skills and increases the demand for workers in such jobs.

As noted earlier, in the United States and other developed countries the displacement of routine jobs by skill-biased and labor-saving technologies has resulted in labor market polarization—the simultaneous growth of high-skill, high-wage, nonroutine occupations, and low-skill, low-wage, nonroutine occupations at the expense of middle-wage, middle-skill, routine occupations. This polarization result is well documented in the empirical literature at the level of industries, localities, and national labor markets. In the United States, the share of middle-income occupations declined from about 60 percent in 1979 to 46 percent in 2012.[22] Similar trends are apparent in the other developed countries.

Consistent with the polarization thesis, U.S. employment expanded rapidly in both nonroutine manual and nonroutine cognitive categories between 1967 and 2000 while routine employment declined and then stagnated in the 1990s. After 2000, routine employment plummeted, nonroutine manual employment continued to grow, and nonroutine cognitive employment stagnated.[23]

Macroeconomic forces—two recessions, slow recoveries, and weak aggregate demand—are important factors behind weak gains in employment and wages, extending through the top of the skill distribution, since 2000. China's rise as a global exporter following its entrance to the WTO in 2001 also contributed to weak growth in labor demand and wages, particularly for middle-income, middle-skill jobs in U.S. manufacturing. The effects of weak macro demand and global competition are starkly apparent in the dramatic decline in routine employment after 2001.[24]

But it also seems likely that technology played a role in the slowing growth of nonroutine cognitive occupations during the last decade. As machines have grown in their ability to perform abstract nonroutine tasks, the elasticity of substitution of capital for even highly skilled and educated workers has probably increased. According to recent work at McKinsey Global Institute, 45 percent of the tasks that people are currently paid to perform can already be technically automated by adapting currently available technology. Even the highest-skill and highest-paid occupations in the economy, including doctors, lawyers, CEOs, and financial market executives, contain a significant share of activity that can already be automated. For the reasons we note below, we believe that as machines become ever more intelligent, this trend is likely to gather momentum in the future. According to McKinsey, nearly 11 million jobs across the skill distribution could be displaced by automation during the next decade—almost twice the historical rate of displacement.[25]

The technology-driven polarization of employment in the labor market has been a potent force behind the pattern of wage growth for different jobs and skills. Overall, those whose skills have been complemented or enhanced by technology have consistently enjoyed the largest wage gains, even during periods when overall wage growth has been slow. During the past thirty years, the real earnings gap between the median college-educated worker and the median high-school-educated worker among U.S. males working full-time in year-round jobs has nearly doubled. During the same period, wages have risen much faster at the top of the wage distribution than at the bottom while the median wage has stagnated. Between 1980 and 2013, the annual wage for the top 1 percent grew by 138 percent while the annual wage for the bottom 90 percent grew by only 15 percent.[26] During the same period, the real earnings of males with a high school or lower education level declined significantly, falling by 22 percent among high school dropouts and 11 percent among high school graduates, while the earnings inequality ratio, measured as the ratio of full-time earnings of males at the 90th percentile to males at the 10th percentile, climbed by more than 100 percentage points.[27]

Skill-biased and labor-saving technological change that substitutes computer-intensive machinery for workers performing blue-collar and white-collar routine tasks has been a major contributor to the stagnation of real wages for the median worker and the large drop in real earnings for non-college-educated workers in the United States. The decline in the penetration and bargaining power of unions has also contributed: the fraction of private-sector workers who belong to trade unions fell from about 24 percent in 1973 to less than 7 percent in 2016. There is a significant wage premium for union workers, one that is more pronounced for less skilled workers and that spills over and benefits nonunion workers.[28] A recent study by the IMF found that the decline in unionization has been strongly associated with a rise in the income share of the top 10 percent in the United States and other developed countries.[29] The study also found that reductions in the real value of the minimum wage are another powerful source of increasing wage and income inequality. In the United States the real minimum wage in 2015 was 24 percent below its peak value in 1968.[30]

In addition to polarizing technological change, declining unionization, and an eroding minimum wage, technology-enabled globalization and its effects on the economy's industrial structure have also been potent forces behind rising income inequality.[31] By structure we mean the size and growth of industries and sectors, viewed in terms of value added and employment. Through this lens we are able to see more precisely the impact of the integration of technology and global supply chains on the composition of output, employment, and productivity in the U.S. economy.

Because we are dealing with open economies, it is important to distinguish between sectors or subsectors that are trade-exposed and subject to external competition and those that are not. We will refer to those that are trade-exposed as tradable and the others as nontradable. The tradable part of an economy is the collection of sectors (or in some cases parts of sectors) producing goods and services that can be produced in one or several countries and consumed elsewhere. Examples would be most manufactured goods, and services like consulting, much of finance, designing products like computers, various aspects of marketing, remote management of IT systems, and software development. In contrast to tradable goods and services, nontradable goods and services are produced in the country in which they are consumed. The nontradable sector includes government, education, construction, hotels, restaurants, food service, traditional retail, domestic logistics, a whole host of repair and maintenance functions, hospitals, nursing homes, and a variety of local services.

Over time the tradable sector has been expanding, largely as a result of enabling technological developments in transportation, communications, and digitization, exposing a growing fraction of the United States and other developed countries to external competition while providing greater access to external demand.

The tradable sector is roughly 35 to 40 percent of the total economy in the developed countries and somewhat smaller when measured in employment. As Figures 8-1 and 8-2 show, in the United States, the nontradable sector is very large, accounting for roughly two-thirds of value added. Its share of employment is even larger, currently over 70 percent and climbing steadily toward 80 percent.

The similarity in the shares of the tradable and nontradable sectors across the developed countries reflects the similarity in the composition of final demand among them. By definition, the nontradable sector on the supply side has to match domestic demand. Thus, if the domestic demand for nontradable goods and services across developed economies is similar, then the size and composition of the supply side of the nontradable sector will be similar. The data confirm this.

The tradable demand sides of the developed economies are also similar, so the size of the tradable sector adjusted for the size of trade surpluses or deficits is similar. There are, however, significant differences among these countries in the composition of the tradable supply side. For example, small countries are more highly specialized on the tradable side for reasons of efficiency and competitiveness. They tend to export more of the output of the tradable sector and conversely import a larger fraction of tradable goods

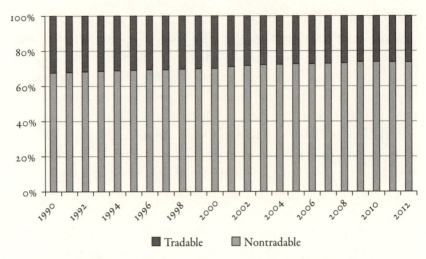

FIGURE 8-1: U.S. nontradable / tradeable value-added split (% of total) 1990–2012.

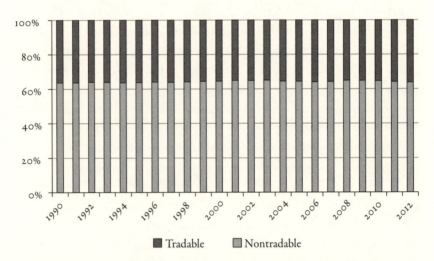

FIGURE 8-2: U.S. nontradable / tradable employment split (% of total) 1990–2012.

and services to satisfy their domestic demand. A larger economy like the United States is somewhat less specialized on the tradable side and consumes more of its tradable output domestically. By conventional measures it is less trade-exposed.

Even this can be a bit misleading in the area of manufacturing. It is better to think in terms of supply chains, which in the tradable sector are increasingly

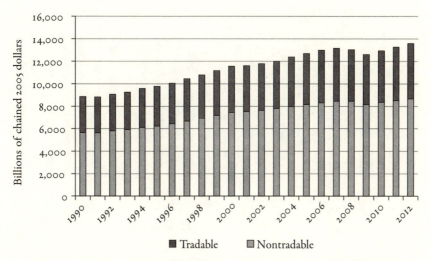

FIGURE 8-3: U.S. nontradable / tradable value added 1990–2012 (billions of chained 2005 dollars).

global. Supply chains have components. What moves across national borders in the global economy (or more precisely, the tradable part of the global economy) are components of supply chains, not whole industries or sectors. Global supply chains increasingly do not fit the model "Produced in country A and consumed in country B." Even a large economy like the United States, when examined from this point of view, will have a wider range of tradable industries than a small economy that is more specialized. Manufacturing value added is substantial in the U.S. economy, but a large and growing share of manufacturing value added is created in the high value-added service components of manufacturing supply chains. The result is a large divergence in the patterns of value added and employment within the tradable sector.

Figure 8-3 shows that in the U.S. economy in the two decades prior to the 2008 crisis, the tradable and nontradable sectors grew in value added at similar rates. The tradable sector, though smaller, actually grew a bit faster, but not dramatically so.

But as Figures 8-4 and 8-5 show, the picture is dramatically different when one looks at employment. Net incremental job creation in the tradable sector in the United States was negligible. Virtually all of the growth in employment—about 98 percent—occurred in the nontradable sector.

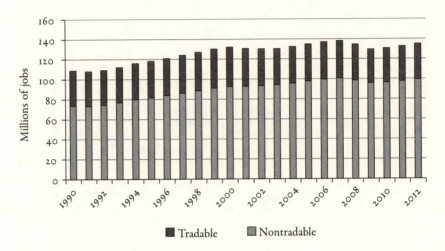

FIGURE 8-4: U.S. nontradable / tradable employment 1990–2012 (in millions).

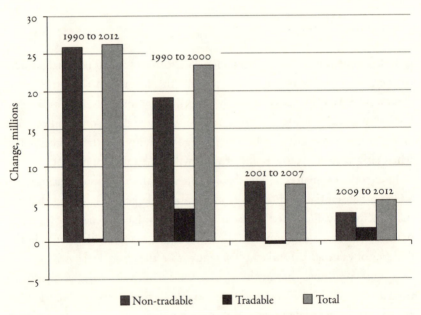

FIGURE 8-5: Change in employment 1990–2012 (in millions).

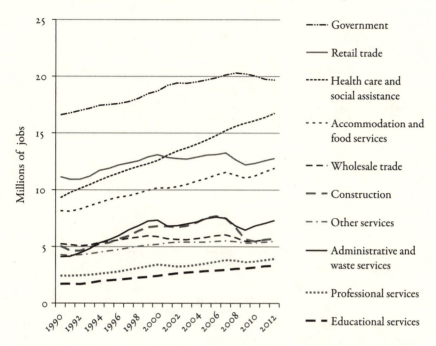

FIGURE 8-6: Nontradable employment, top ten sectors, 1990–2010 (in millions).

As can be seen in Figure 8-6, health care and government account for 37 percent of the growth in U.S. employment in the nontradable sector during this period. Adding in hospitality (hotels, restaurants, food service), retail, and construction raises this figure to over 60 percent.

Productivity is measured by value added per person employed (VAP) (or sometimes per hour of work). Aggregate productivity growth in the United States has been adversely affected by low productivity growth in the nontradable sector combined with its high and rising share of employment.[32]

Manufacturing accounts for roughly half the value added in the tradable sector, with services picking up the rest. Within the tradable sector, the employment declines during the last two decades occurred mainly in manufacturing industries, with a clear inflection point around 2001 when China entered the World Trade Organization, whereas the employment gains occurred in tradable service industries, many of which provide service components in the supply chains of the tradable manufacturing industries.[33] Overall, the employment gains and losses in the tradable sector netted out close to zero.

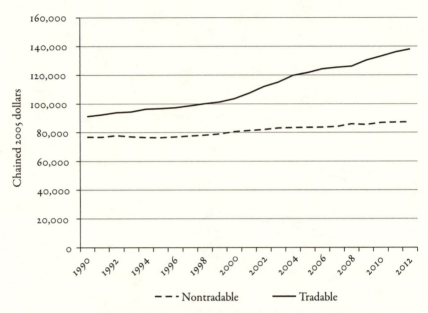

FIGURE 8-7: Real value added per job nontradable and tradable sectors, 1990–2010 (weighted averages in chained 2005 dollars).

But value added per person behaved very differently in the tradable and nontradable sectors. As Figure 8-7 shows, the growth of VAP in the nontradable sector (where all the incremental employment occurred) over the entire period was slow, whereas VAP in the tradable sector rose much more quickly, with a clear upward inflection point around 2000. In 1990, value added per person in the tradable and nontradable sectors was similar, about 10 percent higher on the tradable side. By 2008, VAP was 50 percent higher in the tradable sector than in the nontradable sector.

Total value added, not just value added per person employed, rose in most manufacturing industries quite rapidly throughout the period. It is not true that these industries declined in size or failed to grow, even as their employment declined. Manufacturing value added did not decline, but manufacturing employment did as routine jobs were replaced by technology and as portions of the manufacturing value-added chain associated with low- or mid-level value added moved offshore. Although total domestic value added in manufacturing would have been reduced by offshoring itself, it continued to grow as technology substituted for labor and as the domestic service components of manufacturing's global supply chain—high-value-added services like design, branding, marketing, and logistics—more than compensated for the reduction in domestic value added in manufacturing production as a result of offshoring.

For both the service and the nonservice components of manufacturing's supply chain that remained in the United States, the shift to skill-biased, digital technologies reduced employment but increased labor productivity and output. These technology-driven changes in jobs and employment were reinforced by the technology-enabled movement of lower-value-added jobs and components of the supply chain to China and other developing economies.

Though difficult to document with available data, it is likely that the movement of employment from the tradable to the nontradable sector pre-cipitated the movement of individuals from middle-skill, middle-income jobs in manufacturing to lower-skill, lower income, and less productive ser-vice jobs in the nontradable sector.

Labor-saving and skill-biased digital technologies affect both the trad-able and the nontradable sectors. One might then wonder how the U.S. economy managed to create almost 27 million jobs in the nontradable sector in the nineteen years up to the 2008 crisis. Part of the answer was unsustainable demand growth based on leverage. But as already noted and as reflected in Figure 8-6 major contributors to the expansion of employ-ment were large, labor-intensive, low-wage, nontradable industries: health care, government, hotels and restaurants, and retail. Some of these indus-tries, like the relatively high-wage construction industry and the govern-ment sector, were undoubtedly on expansion paths that could not persist indefinitely. Finally, the ability to generate large incremental employment in the nontradable service sectors was undoubtedly augmented by the down-ward pressure on wages caused by the large shift of labor out of the tradable sector into the nontradable one.

What does all of this have to do with growing income inequality? A great deal, we think. Value added per person turns into income for someone: workers, owners of capital, or the government. And value added per person is higher and has grown faster in the tradable sector of the economy where net employment has stagnated than in the nontradable sector where em-ployment has increased both absolutely and as a share of total employment.

There is no evidence that the government's share of the economy's total value added has increased. At the same time, we know from the data that capital's share in national income rose gradually in the 1990s and sharply after 2000 while labor's share fell to levels not seen since the 1950s. These trends were especially pronounced in the tradable sector, especially in traditional manufacturing production and IT.[34]

Basically, the evidence shows that the tradable sector shifted away from manufacturing production jobs to higher-value-added services, including the service components of manufacturing supply chains. These changes in the structure of the tradable sector triggered a precipitous drop in manufacturing employment, contributing directly both to the loss of middle-income jobs and to an increase in the demand for workers with the education and skills required to deliver higher-value-added services.

The observed rising wage premium to education is also consistent with these trends: the shift toward digitally capital-intensive nonroutine white- and blue-collar tasks where education is complementary to skill-biased technological change, and the change in the composition of the tradable sector toward higher-value-added services.

The shift of employment to the nontradable sector reinforced a supply / demand balance for labor that favored employers and disadvantaged workers. Combined with low and falling real minimum wages and small and declining levels of unionization, the power of labor in the low and middle wage and skill ranges to resist these technological and globalization pressures was limited. The shift of jobs from unionized manufacturing production in the tradable sector to nonunionized services in both the tradable and the nontradable sectors further eroded union coverage and union power.

Overall, as a result of these structural forces, the benefits or rents generated by globalization and technology went disproportionately to owners of capital, including high-end human capital. The uneven distribution of the benefits showed up in the well-documented widening gap between the growth of labor productivity and the growth of median and average real wages.[35]

In the tradable sectors, both technology and globalization were and still are both labor-saving in lower- to middle-skill routine jobs, and skill-augmenting in higher value-added nonroutine cognitive jobs. The upper end of the education and wage spectrum has therefore fared much better. Overall, for the most part, nonroutine jobs have been retained in both the tradable and the nontradable sectors.

The technological and global forces and resulting sectoral shifts identified here do not operate in exactly the same way in all developed countries, but their impacts on industrial structure, labor market composition, and income inequality are similar. Yet it is hard to argue that these forces provide an adequate explanation of trends at the very top of the income distribution where, as Piketty notes, cross-country differences are significant and the United States is something of an outlier. Governance structures and compensation norms, unions, minimum wages and other labor market institutions, taxes, and policies that support noncompetitive markets, generate significant rents, and foster rent-seeking behavior are factors behind these differences and are matters of legitimate policy concern. These are not competing explanations but instead are complementary ones that capture the multiple factors behind the increasing inequality of income and wealth that has bedeviled the United States and the other developed countries for the last thirty years.

Digital Technology and Globalization Going Forward

Brynjolfsson and McAfee document several accelerating trends in the power of digital technologies that are likely to affect the composition of jobs and employment, the returns to various kinds of human capital, and the distribution of income in the future.[36]

Robotics are advancing the frontier of what machines can do, including tasks that require a sophisticated situational awareness and an ability to react that seems to require relatively complex judgments. Advances in sensor technology are in part responsible.

Much of what intelligent digital machines can now do would have been thought beyond their capacity even relatively recently. The effect is to expand the scope of tasks and work susceptible to substitution of machines for labor. Put another way, the subset of jobs that could be classified as routine (both manual, cognitive, and mixtures somewhere in between) is expanding rapidly. For example, machines can now assemble some electronics products, combining newly developed capabilities in dexterity and "vision."

A second area of startling advancement is artificial intelligence, or AI. The questions are what machines with digital "brains" can learn to do and how quickly they can learn. Until a few years ago, experts thought that machines could be programmed to do a range of tasks (even complex intellectual tasks) through software that would tell the machines how to perform these tasks. Put another way, scientists and programmers would figure out how humans perform certain functions, then codify these processes and embed them in computer code that would enable machines to replicate what humans do.

In this paradigm, machines can do tasks and perform work in areas where we know the rules and processes and can embed them in software. In short, machines can do routine jobs that are codifiable, sometimes much faster and more accurately than the humans they replace.

But there are limits to this, because we don't know how humans do many things: recognize a chair, understand a sentence spoken with an accent, understand and translate between languages. Attempts to solve these kinds of challenges by developing new or more complex rules and logic, embedded in software, did not produce the hoped-for results. Indeed, some years ago it appeared that AI was hitting a series of dead ends.

Scientists and technologists then turned to what they term "brute force" and machine learning. Networks make huge databases, including images, recordings, films, and other things, accessible. The networks are getting faster, the storage capacity larger and quicker to access. Machines can learn by accessing and sorting through unimaginably large piles of information and data. This approach seems to be working more quickly than anticipated. It is referred to as machine learning, and much of it is learning by example, or more accurately, from lots of examples. An important part of machine learning is pattern recognition. This is in part enabled by the reach and sheer power and speed of networks and their component parts, including massive databases.

The result is that machines are now beginning to learn to do things that humans collectively know how to do but don't know how to codify completely. The advances in machine capabilities have surprised even experienced technologists and scientists in the field of AI.

The concepts of "routine" and "codifiable" help us understand the shifts in labor markets, economic structure, and some of the distributional effects in the past thirty years. Advances in AI suggest that the relation between person and machine may go well beyond "codifiable" and more toward "learnable" tasks, with consequences that are very hard to predict. The early accelerating trends suggest that intelligent machines may soon be able to do relatively complex nonroutine cognitive tasks.

A related development is the growth of "big data" or, more precisely, big data analytics. "Big data" simply refers to massive databases that are produced as a by-product of the functioning of existing digital processes and platforms. Think of the data that is accumulated in Google, or Facebook, or Amazon, or even Airbnb. Big data analytics encompasses processing power and the ability to do pattern recognition in reasonable time at low cost. For our purposes, big data may be in part a substitute for certain human functions, but it is more likely to be a complement to functions involving human analysis and judgment.

A third technology that deserves mention is 3D printing or additive manufacturing. It is what it sounds like: a three-dimensional inkjet printer using a wide range of "inks" ranging from plastics to titanium. What a 3D printer makes is a function of a data file that describes the object. 3-D printing is a technology that has gotten attention because it is customizable in the extreme and generates very little waste. Its costs are declining dramatically. The range of materials that can be used in "printing" is expanding. For supply chains and those who manage them, additive manufacturing is a technology that permits production to actual demand rather than to forecasted demand. This has enormous potential implications for the length, efficiency, and location of supply chains and retail channels. 3D printing is highly mobile and of course, related to our discussion here, it is digital-capital-intensive, skill-biased, and labor-saving.

Robotics and 3D printing appear to be expanding the scope of the intrusion of digital technologies into labor-intensive activities and sectors. That has implications for human capital investment and other policies in the developed countries. It also has implications for the "growth" model of early stage developing countries in which labor-intensive sectors have historically been a source of comparative advantage in manufacturing sectors, an important engine of growth for a period of time. If digital technologies surpass labor-intensive ones in terms of cost and quality in assembly and process-oriented manufacturing, this path to development will narrow and eventually close.

During the last half century successful early stage developing countries, particularly those not "blessed" with natural resource wealth, relied on connectivity to the global economy and comparative advantage in labor-intensive manufacturing to jump-start growth and transition to middle-income status. New digital and AI technologies, robotics, and 3D printing could bypass the labor-intensive technologies in cost and quality, pretty much independent of the cost of labor, and in the relatively near future. This won't happen in every industry at the same rate. But there is evidence that this trend is already started and moving quickly.

This raises questions about growth models for late arrivals in the development process. Where will their potential areas of comparative advantage lie, and what investment patterns in fixed assets, infrastructure, and human capital will be required to achieve it?

For most of the last several decades, the organizing logic of the global economy was that economic activity (think of it as components of global supply chains) moved toward valuable, attractively priced pools of labor, because labor was less mobile than capital and knowledge. But now digital-capital-intensive technologies are substituting for humans in the routine labor-intensive parts of manufacturing supply chains, where large numbers of people are employed around the world. As this happens and digital technologies make manufacturing mobile with little or no cost penalty, physical manufacturing activity will move toward market demand rather than toward labor, because there are efficiencies to be gained from proximity to the market.

Indeed, there is already evidence that as a result of technology-driven changes in global supply chains, many developing countries are running out of industrialization opportunities sooner and at much lower levels of development than early industrializers.[37] A recent study found that developing countries have a much higher share of jobs at risk from automation than developed countries, as technological breakthroughs erode the traditional labor-cost advantages of developing countries in tradable sectors and encourage the reshoring of tradable activities to the developed countries.[38] As a result of rapidly advancing technologies, the old patterns of globalization may have run their course, though one wouldn't know this from listening to the political dialogue, especially the protectionist and isolationist dialogue in the developed countries. The policy challenge now is how to adapt to new labor-saving and skill-biased technologies that can substitute for both routine and nonroutine labor in both developing and advanced countries alike. Whether we adapt well or badly depends on correctly identifying the challenge and developing the appropriate policy responses.

Technology, Inequality, and Policy Responses

Skill-biased and labor-saving technological change and technology-enabled globalization have been powerful forces behind growing wealth and income inequality in the United States and other developed countries during the last thirty years, and they are likely to become even more important in the future. Technology is following an unexpectedly fast trajectory to displace human labor and to do so in skill-biased and unequal ways. Inequality in market-based wealth and incomes is likely to increase over the next several decades, not because of features inherent in the capitalist system, but because of the effects of the digital revolution on the number and composition of jobs, the returns to knowledge and intangible capital, rents from imperfect competition, first-mover advantages, market power in networked systems, and the wages and livelihoods of workers who perform tasks and have jobs that can be better performed by machines at lower cost.

To conclude, however, that the "impersonal forces" of technological change will be major drivers of market-based inequality does not mean that public policy has no role to play in distributing the gains from technological progress more equitably. Sadly, many policies in the United States and some other developed countries have exacerbated rather than ameliorated the inequality propelled by these forces during the last several decades. Throughout his book Piketty explores how different policy choices and the different social values they reflect help explain why similar technological trends have been associated with different levels of inequality among the developed countries.

Even in a period of unparalleled technological change, societies can pursue the level of equality they desire using a variety of policy levers to foster a more equal distribution of disposable (after-tax and transfer) income than the distribution produced by market forces alone. Indeed, there are well-documented differences among developed countries in the extent to which tax and transfer policies have been effectively used to reduce the inequality of disposable income compared to the inequality of market income. The challenge is to craft policies that both promote technological progress—attempts to block it in Luddite fashion are doomed to fail—and distribute its "bounty" or benefits more equitably in accordance with social norms.

Numerous articles and books have been written about policy responses to contain income and wealth inequality. Because our remit in this chapter is technology and its effects on inequality, we will not provide detailed policy recommendations. Instead we briefly consider three areas of policy that are addressed in Piketty's book and in the book by Brynjolfsson and McAfee: education, progressive income taxation, and social benefits and income support programs.

Education

One area of policy on which Piketty, Brynjolfsson and McAfee, and most economists who study inequality agree is education. Piketty acknowledges that the race between education and skills has been the major factor behind increasing inequality in labor incomes, which in turn has been the major factor behind growing overall income inequality, even for the top 1 percent. He also notes that income inequality is less pronounced in the Nordic countries in part because of their high-quality, egalitarian, and inclusive educational systems. In contrast, in the United States, growing income inequality has resulted in growing inequality in educational opportunities and attainment levels by income levels.[39]

At least for the foreseeable future, the policies that are most effective at reducing inequality over the long run, while raising overall prosperity, will continue to be those that foster the skills of successive generations through making education and training opportunities widely available to all, regardless of income.

There is widespread agreement among experts that such policies must begin with early childhood education and extend through postsecondary education, lifetime learning, and retooling opportunities that enhance the flexibility of workers to move from job to job. But there is considerable disagreement about the kinds of education and skills—the cognitive and noncognitive capacities—that will be required in the future. The disagreement reflects uncertainty about how technology will change the composition of jobs and required skills and the pace at which it will do so. With the startling advances in digital technology, it is hard to predict what the demand side of labor markets will look like in ten or fifteen years.

Few question the need for more education in STEM fields (science, technology, education, and mathematics). Digital technologies will continue to complement the demand for workers in these fields, and increasing their supply will moderate the skill premium and reduce inequality. Perhaps in the coming decades, as David Autor predicts, continued technological change will support a significant number of middle-skill jobs that combine "specific vocational skills with foundational middle-skill levels of literacy, numeracy, adaptability, problem-solving and common sense."[40]

In this optimistic view, many middle-skill jobs will remain, combining routine technical tasks that can be performed with the help of smart machines and a set of nonroutine tasks in which humans continue to hold a comparative advantage over such machines. Medical support jobs are an example. Many such jobs require two years of postsecondary vocational training and in some cases a four-year college degree. This is also true for numerous skilled trade and repair occupations and clerical jobs. In this scenario, human capital investment should be at the center of a long-term strategy to boost the supply of human skills for which smart machines are complements and reduce the supply of human skills for which they are substitutes.

Historical experience indicates that as technology has increased human productivity, the result has been net job creation, not net job destruction. In the past, with a lag and with painful adjustment costs for dislocated workers whose jobs have disappeared, technological progress has fostered growth in demand for new goods and services, and this has increased demand for labor and more than offset the labor-substituting effects of such progress. The future outlook, however, is uncertain: perhaps as Brynjolfsson and McAfee believe there will be growing demand for jobs in areas like health and security despite rapid gains in labor-saving technologies, But there is reason for concern that the future will be different from historical experience. According to recent studies, half of all jobs in developed countries—and even more in emerging economies—are potential victims to displacement by labor-saving technology in the next few decades. And the pace of change is faster than expected. As Martin Ford observes in his recent award-winning book, robots, machine algorithms, and other forms of automation are already consuming a sizable share of jobs at the middle and low rungs of the skills pyramid and are poised to consume a growing share of skilled tasks and occupations, even those held by individuals with college and advanced degrees.[41]

Taxation

A progressive income tax system with high rates on top incomes heads the list of policy proposals for combatting income inequality. Most developed countries, including the United States, already have such a system—indeed, as Piketty observes, the creation of a progressive income tax system was a major innovation in taxation in the twentieth century and has played a key role in moderating income inequality. Current policy debates center around whether the marginal tax rate on top incomes should be increased and by how much. Both Piketty and Brynjolfsson-McAfee recommend a sizable hike in the top U.S. rate, albeit for somewhat different reasons. Brynjolfsson and McAfee posit that the market conditions fostered by digital technologies— network effects, increasing returns, and winner-take-all-effects—result in power-law distributions of the returns to the owners of digital capital and to labor whose talents are complemented by it. They also posit that economic rents are a "big part" of the very high and concentrated earnings of both capital and labor in these conditions. Consequently, they do not anticipate that higher marginal tax rates on these earnings in the United States, at least compared to current rates that are low by historical standards, would reduce the incentives of high earners to supply capital and labor to the detriment of growth.

Piketty posits that the optimal income tax rate—for the top 1 percent in the United States and other developed countries—is "probably above 80 percent," and asserts that such a rate would not only not reduce economic growth but would distribute the fruits of growth more widely while reducing the risk of a continued drift toward oligarchy and another Gilded Age. In his view, the capital and labor incomes captured by top earners are not the result of technology-driven power distributions of such incomes and the rents they encompass in imperfect market conditions. Rather, in his analysis, increases in capital income that flow primarily to the top earners are an inexorable feature of capitalist systems in which the rate of return on capital exceeds the growth rate. And the labor incomes of top earners are the result of social norms, corporate governance practices, the eroding power of unions, and political lobbying by these earners to influence policy to serve their interests.

We believe that the institutional forces identified by Piketty, and associated rent-seeking behavior in all its various forms, have contributed to growing income inequality. But we believe that the technological forces and associated market imperfections identified by Brynjolfsson and McAfee have also played an important role. Although more research is needed to assess and quantify the relative importance of these institutional and technological factors, both the Piketty and the Brynjolfsson-McAfee explanations provide a strong rationale for increasing the marginal income tax rate for top earners to combat income inequality.

Social Benefits and Income Support

In addition to progressive income tax systems and in lieu of direct income transfers from the rich to the poor, the developed countries provide social transfer and insurance programs to reduce inequality in disposable incomes and to provide access to critical social services like health, education, and retirement to their citizens, independent of their market incomes. Even in the United States, where such programs are significantly less generous and less redistributive than those in continental Europe, particularly the Scandinavian countries, the distribution of post-tax and transfer income is much more equal than the distribution of market income.

Piketty acknowledges the importance of what he calls "social state" programs for addressing income inequality in capitalist economies and suggests reforms to reorganize, modernize, and consolidate them. Brynjolfsson and McAfee share Piketty's support for such programs but are concerned that these are largely financed through taxes on labor. This concern is justified. The better machines become at substituting for human labor, the bigger the negative effects of such taxes on employment and worker incomes. They recommend consideration of both a carbon tax and a value-added tax in lieu of taxes on labor to finance social benefits in the future. Piketty also proposes a new progressive global tax on capital to contain wealth inequality. Some of the revenues raised by this new tax could substitute for taxes on labor to fund social benefits.

Today's labor markets are undergoing dramatic changes as digital platforms transform how they operate and revolutionize the nature of work. In many ways described by Brynjolfsson and McAfee these changes hold the potential to improve labor market efficiency and increase flexible employment opportunities. But the increasing digitization of the labor market and the rise of the "gig," or on-demand, economy has an important drawback: it is replacing traditional employer-employee relationships that have been the primary channel through which social benefits and protections have been provided to citizens in the United States and other developed economies. As more and more workers find themselves in nonstandard employment relationships, the traditional systems of financing and delivering social benefits will have to be modified.[42]

As smart machines become more powerful and pervasive, they will pose a rising challenge to a defining feature of a market economy—the fact that most people in such an economy gain their income by selling their labor. What happens if and when smart machines substitute for the labor of a large share of the working-age population, rendering them unable to earn an income that provides a decent standard of living, regardless of their education and skills? Brynjolfsson and McAfee raise this question and call for evaluation of "out-of-the-box" solutions, including a negative income tax or a basic income to provide a guaranteed minimum standard of living to citizens regardless of their employment status and the compensation they receive for their labor.

Ultimately, whether the benefits of technological change are distributed broadly or accrue to a small percentage of the world's population will depend not on the design of smart machines but on the design of smart policies appropriate for the new machine age.

NINE

Income Inequality, Wage Determination, and the Fissured Workplace

DAVID WEIL

Economist David Weil, who served as administrator of the Wages and Hours Division of the U.S. Department of Labor, writes here about the concept he dubbed the "fissured workplace," meaning the increasing stratification of the labor market outside the walls of individual firms. Instead of the old model of large corporations employing workers at all levels—skilled professionals, mid-level administrators, and manual workers, under a single roof, as was the case in the past—increasingly jobs are outsourced by function, and workers who would once have been employees, and thus entitled to de jure and de facto privileges, are now forced into a race to the bottom. This chapter analyses the extent of and motivation for that phenomenon and its implications for observed patterns of inequality and for future research into the labor market's functioning, concluding that it's time for economists to return to the old-fashioned concept of wage determination as a sui generis phenomenon worthy of study. All of that matters for C21 because it complicates the picture of future inequality as arising from a straightforward capital-labor split.

The post–World War II era was a remarkable period in reducing earnings inequality during a prolonged economic expansion. Wages and benefits of the workforce employed inside the walls of major businesses like General Motors, Hilton, GE, and Westinghouse moved in roughly the same direction as rising productivity. From 1947 to 1979, productivity increased by 119 percent while average hourly wages increased by 72 percent and average hour compensation (wages plus benefits) by 100 percent.[1] In the auto industry, that exemplar of the postwar era, expansion of consumer demand led to rising profits and executive compensation increases, and the pay for workers on auto assembly lines also rose. But so did the pay for janitors, maintenance personnel, clerical workers, and lawn care attendants also employed by automakers.

Those parallel movements began to change in the 1970s. Productivity growth over the three decades beginning in the late 1970s continued to rise, growing some 80 percent. Yet over the same period, average hourly wages increased a meager 7 percent and average hourly compensation by only 8 percent. Growing inequality has appropriately become a central concern for academic study and policy makers and of course a central reason for the intense interest in Thomas Piketty's *Capital in the Twenty-First Century.*

There is an enormous theoretical and empirical literature that attempts to explain the dramatic changes in how the gains of economic expansion have been shared in the United States and other industrialized nations. This body of literature probes the causes driving the decreasing share of national income going to the labor share and toward capital. It examines increases in inequality arising from observable characteristics of workers (the returns to work) as well as changes in the composition of firms. Studies of have dived deeply into the impact of skill-biased technology change, the impacts of globalization, and the secular decline of unions, among other sources driving inequality.[2]

This chapter sets out an alternative lens with which to undertake the analysis of inequality. I will argue that an important driver of that change over the last three decades has been an evolution of business organization that has fundamentally altered the employment relationship and, in turn, the way that wages are set for workers in a growing range of industries. My focus here is on the particular evolution of wage setting through the changing definitions of the boundaries of employment occasioned by what I have called the "fissured workplace."

As activities have been shed by lead businesses in many industries in the economy to other business entities, wage setting has been altered in fundamental ways. The motivations for a range of changed business practices related to the shedding of employment—for example, outsourcing, subcontracting, and misclassification of workers as independent contractors—are often misconstrued either solely as tactics instituted to dodge legal obligations or as a set of necessary adjustments made by modern, flexible business organizations. Both stories fail to explain the sources of a more fundamental realignment of employment now common in many sectors of the economy.

The consequence of this shift has been that in more and more labor markets, wage-setting processes that once led to a greater sharing of rents in both union and nonunion workplaces are now driven toward the marginal productivity of labor for workers whose jobs have been shed from leading businesses. While lead businesses—the firms that continue to directly employ workers who provide the goods and services in the economy recognized by consumers—remain highly profitable and may continue to provide generous pay for their workforce, the workers whose jobs have been shed to other subordinate businesses face far more competitive market conditions. Lower margins in these subordinate markets—which often are further "fissured" to other networks—create conditions for wage setting more consistent with competitive labor market models, where wages move toward marginal productivity.

The fissured workplace hypothesis explains how wage-setting norms are altered when workers are shed from lead employers to external businesses, effectively changing a wage-setting problem into a pricing problem. It also provides a story regarding not only the growing level of inequality in earnings, but why that inequality might be particularly associated with growing diversion in earning *among* rather than *within* firms. As a result, I argue that future research must refocus on the age-old question of wage determination (a phrase from an earlier era of labor economics) and its impacts on the labor share of income.

The Fissured Workplace Hypothesis

When we walk into a well-known hotel chain, we assume that the people who greet us at the front desk, or the people who clean our rooms each day, or deliver our room service, are employees of that hotel (as their uniforms and name badges imply). This, however, is not our twenty-first-century workplace. Many hotel workers are employed by separate management, janitorial, catering, and staffing companies. In some cases workers are jointly employed by the hotel and the businesses but often they may not even know for whom they work.

In my book *The Fissured Workplace,* I argue that capital markets drove the fissured workplace evolution.[3] In the last few decades, major companies faced, and they continue to face, pressure to improve their financial performance for private and public investors. They responded by focusing their businesses on core competencies—that is, what provides greatest value to their consumers and investors. A natural complement of this approach was to "shed" activities not essential to the core competency of the organization. Typically, this started with activities like payroll, publications, accounting, and human resource functions. It spread to outsourcing activities like janitorial and maintenance of facilities and security. But then the shedding went deeper—in many cases, into employment activities that would be regarded as core to the company.

As a result, the employment relationship "fissured" apart. And as in geology, once fissures start, they deepen: once an activity like janitorial services or housekeeping was shed, the secondary businesses doing that work deepened the fissures even further, often shifting those activities to still other businesses. The farther down in the fissures one goes, the slimmer the profit margins, and the greater the incentives to cut corners. Labor costs are often the first place employers look to reduce expenses to remain competitive, even at the cost of compliance. Typically, the farther away the laborer is from the ultimate beneficiary of that labor, the greater the chance for violation or exploitation. Violations tend to be greatest where margins are slimmest.

But lead businesses must still monitor and police the behavior of the subordinate firms that provide key activities so that they do not undermine core competencies like brand identities or new product development. Fissuring is therefore accomplished through a variety of business structures that allow them to do so: subcontracting arrangements and staffing agency contracts that are built on explicit and often detailed outcome standards and franchising, licensing, and third-party management systems with similarly extensive performance requirements.[4] Although a portion of the fissured workplace arises from an effort to thwart workplace policies, the above account indicates why it is mistaken to view that as the sole driving force, particularly at its source in lead business organizations. But whether the fissured workplace is associated with legitimate or illegitimate practices, employment relationships become more tenuous, responsibility for compliance with laws is shifted to other businesses and made murky, and the workforce becomes vulnerable to violations of even the most basic protections of our laws.

Drivers of Wage Determination

In virtually any market situation, businesses face incentives to lower costs. The more intense the competition, the greater is that pressure. Although the changes in capital markets sharpened that pressure, it would be folly to forget its ongoing presence in markets. It is therefore axiomatic that businesses will seek methods to reduce labor costs. Unit labor costs are driven by two factors: the price of labor (also known as wages and benefits) and the amount of output produced per each unit of labor input (also known as productivity). To the extent that shifting employment to other firms through practices like outsourcing reduces labor costs without compromising product or service integrity, one would expect a movement in that direction.

Many discussions of elements of fissuring—the increasing use of contracting and outsourcing and contingent work arrangements—focus on motivations driven by reducing labor costs. One important example is the long-term effort by businesses to avoid unionization. Unions raise wages, increase benefits, reduce management authority to unilaterally dismiss workers, and increase scrutiny of compliance with workplace regulations. The National Labor Relations Act precludes employers from simply closing down workplaces solely because of the presence of unions, or threatening to do so if a union is elected. But shedding employment can provide more subtle ways to shift away from a highly unionized workforce or move work to forms of employment that are both legally and strategically difficult for unions to organize, at least historically.

A second explanation is the desire to shift to other parties a wide range of required social insurance benefits like unemployment insurance and workers' compensation premiums as well as private benefits like insurance and retirement. Socially required and privately provided benefits make the cost to employers of hiring workers far greater than wages or salaries. Wages and salaries comprise 69.4 percent of employer costs per hours worked in the United States for all workers. An additional 7.8 percent of employer costs are related to federally required benefits (Social Security, Medicare, and Federal Unemployment Insurance) as well as state benefits (unemployment insurance and workers' compensation). Privately provided benefits for insurance (health, life, disability) and retirement average an additional 13.5 percent.[5]

To the extent that institutions like staffing agencies or smaller companies doing subcontracted work for a lead business comply with the law, required social payments should be captured in the price those subordinate labor providers charge. There is abundant evidence of extensive noncompliance in subcontracting chains, staffing agencies, and other businesses in fissured workplace networks arising from misclassification of workers as well as pay practices like piece rates that lead to violations of minimum wage and overtime.

Even given payment of legally required benefits, businesses in fissured structures may provide fewer—or no—benefits in the area of insurance or retirement, lowering the costs to the lead businesses that may draw on them. For example, the federal laws regulating employee benefits require that if a benefit like health care is offered to one worker, it must be offered to all workers. By shifting out employment to another business (such as a temporary agency that does not provide its workforce with health benefits), the company can lower the de facto cost of hiring additional workers.

A third incentive for shedding employment arises from the desire to minimize liability. With employment comes responsibility for outcomes like workplace injuries, illnesses, and fatalities as well as for discrimination, harassment, and unjust dismissal. If shedding employment shifts liabilities to other parties, it lowers expected costs to lead businesses.

All of the above explanations can reduce labor costs and the risks associated with employment. But attributing the dramatic rise in shedding employment solely to them does not adequately explain how lead businesses balance the benefits of lower costs from shedding employment against the benefits of continuing to use workers from inside their company, and why the fissured workplace has spread and deepened. There is something more subtle afoot. It requires thinking about wage determination in large companies.

Monopsony Power, and Wage Determination

The most autocratic and unfettered employer spontaneously adopts Standard Rates for classes of workmen, just as the large shopkeeper fixes his prices, not according to the haggling capacity of particular customers, but by a definite percentage on cost.

—Sidney and Beatrice Webb[6]

The large employers that dominated business in much of the twentieth century were in a different position than employers in traditional labor market models. The extreme case occurs in a company town where a single employer essentially provides the only jobs in the labor market. As the sole purchaser of labor, such an employer (or monopsonist) effectively faces the entire labor supply, and must pay higher wages if it wishes to increase the number of people employed.[7] For a unitary employer paying the same wage rate to workers for a similar job, the cost of an additional hired worker reflects not only the wage for that worker but also the incremental costs for all employees who have already been hired for that job, because the company pays all workers at the same wage as that paid to the last worker hired. As a result, the employer hires fewer workers and pays a lower wage than would occur in a competitive labor market with multiple employers.

Company towns are rare, but an employer need not rule over a coal town to wield some level of monopsony power. A common source of employer power in a labor market arises from information problems. A labor market works by matching workers' job preferences with employers' demand for workers. That makes information a critical lubricant in the operation of a labor market. Pure labor market models (which assume that markets function like a freewheeling bourse) assume that such information costs are minimal. Employer suitors quickly find their employee mates.

But information is not costless, nor is it held equally by all the parties in a labor market. In practice, a worker's search for a job is limited by time, knowledge, and geographic preferences. Large employers have more robust information because of their size, sophistication, and economies of scale in acquiring it. Workers, however, face "search frictions" in the labor market because of limited information on employment options as well as family, social, and other geographic ties that restrict their willingness to move.

Information asymmetries and search frictions create some degree of monopsony power, meaning that large employers set wages rather than simply accepting the going rate in the labor market. This gives them greater latitude in establishing compensation policies, although the employer's policies still must reflect the supply of workers and their contribution to the production of the firm.[8]

Some level of monopsony control and discretion in setting wages underlies the compensation and human resource policies set by major companies across the economy. As the social scientists Beatrice and Sidney Webb pointed out at the turn of the twentieth century, large employers that dominated the economy and the labor market required unified personnel and pay policies and internal labor markets for a variety of reasons: to take advantage of administrative efficiencies, to create consistency in corporate policies, and to reduce exposure to violations of laws.

Like the Webbs, early American labor economists conceived of wage setting within the firm as the outcome of a match-specific negotiation, but they focused attention on the roles played by limited outside options faced by workers and their impact on relative bargaining power. Richard Ely and his academic disciples in the "Institutionalist" school of labor economics highlighted the role that unionization and collective action play in setting wages, or more specifically, they argued that in the absence of unions, employers held a superior bargaining position, given the inelastic demand for labor arising from the barriers to mobility faced by workers as well as the pressing need to feed their families.[9]

A later generation of Institutional economists, like Sumner Slichter, John T. Dunlop, James Healy, and others studying collective bargaining in the post–World War II era, found similar managerial behavior in the major companies setting wage and price policies in critical sectors of the economy.[10] Setting wage policies via complex internal labor market systems with consistent wages across groups of workers arose not only in unionized settings. Fred Foulkes, for example, carefully documented similar wage- and salary-setting practices in relation to large, nonunion enterprises.[11]

The contemporary literature seeks to square the general existence of elaborate internal labor markets and findings like wage premiums in large firms with the operation of competitive labor markets. One view argues that these phenomena are not incompatible with the functioning of competitive labor markets, but simply reflect the complexity of labor as an input in production—an input whose productivity changes over the course of employment.[12] Another set of theories explains internal labor markets in terms of "implicit contract" theory, where risk-neutral employers strike agreements with risk-averse workers that smooth wages over time, accommodating both parties in the process. These arrangements have some of the characteristics of internal labor markets but arise from underlying supply and demand features. A third view explains internal labor markets as the methods by which firms overcome the day-to-day holdup problems, given that the employment contract between workers and employers is inherently incomplete—that is, it cannot adequately commit to language the complicated and changing nature of what the employer wishes the worker to do. As a result, a combination of explicit and implicit contract devices arises to prevent either party from cheating the other.[13]

None of these explanations, however, recognizes a basic aspect of the workplace: it brings together large groups of people, and people by nature are deeply social beings. Workers operating under one roof communicate and quickly discover a lot about their coworkers. This includes whether the person sitting in the next cubicle is being paid more for doing the same job. Paying individuals who do similar jobs different wages could have deleterious consequences on productivity, increase turnover, or even inspire a union-organizing drive. Unified personnel policies and simplified compensation structures for workers with varying levels of productivity play a fundamental role in reducing friction among workers.

Fairness and Wage Determination

Fairness matters. In contrast to assumptions of traditional economics that individuals maximize gains solely for themselves, a large empirical literature from psychology, decision science, and more recently behavioral economics reveals that people care not only about their own gains but also about those of others. In fact, people frequently gauge the magnitude of their own benefits relative to those of others. And they are often willing to sacrifice some of their own gains because of equally important beliefs about fairness.

The "ultimatum game" is one of the best demonstrations of the importance of fairness in human interactions and has been extensively tested experimentally and in the field. The game is simple: two people are told there is a pot of money (say $10) to be split between them. One player gets the right to decide how to split it. The second player can accept or reject the first player's decision. If the second player rejects it, no one receives anything. If people were completely self-interested, the expected result would be clear: the first player would keep almost everything and leave a few crumbs (coins) for the second player. Since the second player is still better off with a little (for example, $.50) than before the game started, he or she should accept any nonzero offer.

But that is not how the game turns out. The typical person in the second player position will reject lowball offers (looking across studies, offers below 20 percent of the pot of money are usually rejected)—even at the expense of walking away with nothing. Equally important, first players seem to understand this in advance, because they typically offer the second player 40 to 50 percent of the pot.[14] The results, which have been replicated many times in many different forms, attest to the importance of fairness, because they are based on one-round (non-repeat) games where the incentives are high for the proposer to take as much as possible and for the responder to accept any offer. When ultimatum games are played in multiple-round scenarios, the incentives to share that pot only become higher.

Fairness perceptions affect all kinds of real-world interactions and relationships. Relationships are an intrinsic part of the workplace, and fairness perceptions are therefore basic to how decisions are made within it. The factors driving wage setting arise not just from an employer's consideration of the additional output a worker might provide if given a higher wage, but on the worker's perceptions of the fairness of that wage. For example, Daniel Kahneman, one of the pioneers of behavioral economics, showed that people's perception of the fairness of a wage cut depends on why they feel it was done: cuts driven by increases in unemployment (and therefore more people looking for work) are viewed as unfair; a company that cuts wages because it is on the brink of bankruptcy is judged more favorably. Like the proposer in the ultimatum game, managers seem to understand this and seldom cut nominal wages in practice.

Similarly, fairness considerations about compensation depend not only on how much I think I deserve to be paid on an absolute basis (given my experience, education, skills), but also on what I am paid relative to others. Who are relevant comparison groups? It depends on where I am when making the appraisal. If I am looking for a job, my assessment is based on what I see in the labor market—as predicted by traditional economic theory. My sources of information may be incomplete, but I will be looking at comparable jobs in my search. The acceptability of a wage offer will bounce up and down with the overall conditions in the labor market.

Once I am inside an organization, however, the wage level that becomes relevant to me focuses on other workers in my company. Just as, in experiments, how two people split their joint gains matters as much (or more) than their absolute gains, once inside an employer's organization, I care more about what the person in the next cubicle is being paid than about what someone across the street doing the same type of work is being paid by a different employer.[15] "Referent wages" are important not only in terms of others doing work similar to mine, but also for those I perceive as at higher and lower levels of the organization.[16]

Large employers adopted the wage and internal labor markets used in previous decades because of two kinds of fairness notions as they apply to wages. Horizontal equity regards how people think about different pay rates for similar work. Vertical equity regards how they think about different pay rates for different types of work.

Large employers historically fudged horizontal compensation problems by creating consistent pay for people in comparable positions in a company, even if their performance varied. The vast majority of businesses (78 percent) interviewed in Truman Bewley's study of compensation policies cited "internal harmony and morale" as the main reason internal pay equity was important.[17] Labor market studies show that wages within firms vary far less than one would expect given the existence of considerable differences in productivity across workers. Firms move toward a single-wage policy for workers of similarly observable skill / ability because of the negative consequences arising from having multiple rates for workers who otherwise seem similar.

Workers' contentment with their wages also is affected by vertical fairness notions and norms. In particular, experimental and empirical evidence points to the fact that people look "up" in judging their pay, asking, What is my pay relative to the jobs at the next rung in my organization?[18] If the pay of the group just above me is too high—or if the gap widens over time—I may be less and less happy with the pay I receive, regardless of its absolute level.

In a large organization, vertical equity issues like these can be particularly vexing. Unionized workplaces in traditional manufacturing solved this problem through collectively bargained deals that linked these grades—often providing for upward ratcheting of the whole wage system (leaving relative wages intact) over time. The collectively bargained contract creates a transparent set of expectations of what is fair (in part because it reflects the preferences of the workforce, at least as represented by the union's negotiating committee). Large nonunion workplaces also must accommodate the demands of vertical equity in setting compensation policies, even though unfettered by collective bargaining. Higher wages in part reflect an effort to avoid unionization, but also an effort to avoid the kind of internal frictions described above. Studies of wage determination found that executives in large nonunion enterprises frequently justified formal internal pay structures on the basis of equity.[19]

Why Lead Businesses Shed Workers

Taking horizontal and vertical equity concerns together leads to a prediction that large firms might end up paying more for jobs at different levels of the organization to solve these problems than would occur on the outside. This aspect of wage determination explains the large-employer wage premium prevalent in the latter half of the twentieth century. Much of the literature seeks to explain firm size effects on the basis of underlying productivity differentials and related matching behaviors between workers and employers.[20] The fissured workplace hypothesis puts wage determination behavior by firms as central to the analytic problem. In the post–World War II era, lead businesses exercising some level of market power but facing the need to accommodate fairness perceptions among their workforce were led to select policies that resulted in wage premiums for a cross section of workers in larger firms. Over the last few decades, however, firms have become less constrained by those fairness perceptions in wage determination by changing the boundaries of employment through shedding activities to other business entities.

The basic monopsony model assumes that an employer will set a single wage rate for workers of a particular type (that is, skill or occupation) rather than follow what is called in a monopoly situation a price discrimination policy (that is, charging different prices to different consumers). The need to set a single wage for the workplace has the effect of pushing up the cost to the employer of hiring more workers of a given type, since the additional cost of one more worker requires paying him or her more, as well as more for all who are already employed at that type of work.[21]

In principle, an employer with monopsony power could compensate workers according to their individual contribution to production (or "marginal product," the additional output per worker) if it pursued a varied wage policy. But this goes against the fairness grain and, as we have seen, has never been a common form of compensation. Wage discrimination (à la price discrimination) is rarely seen in large firms despite the benefits it could confer. As long as workers are under one roof, the problems presented by horizontal and vertical equity remain.

But what if the large employer could wage discriminate by changing the boundaries of the firm itself? What if, instead of facing a wage determination problem for a large and varied workforce, it creates a situation of setting prices for work to be done by other parties external to the enterprise? If multiple businesses compete vigorously with one another to obtain that firm's business, each small firm would offer its workers wages to perform work for the lead firm. Under this setup, the large employer (or now former employer) receives a price for the contractors' services or production rather than being required to directly set and pay wages to the individual workers who actually undertake the work.

As such, the larger employer creates competition for work among different purveyors and pays them based on its assessment of their contribution. Less-efficient producers could be paid less than more-efficient producers. In this way, the lead organization faces a schedule of *prices for services* rather than *wages for labor,* leaving the task of compensation to the individual providers of the service or product. In effect, the lead firm devolves its employment activity to a network of smaller providers. In so doing, it creates a mechanism—a competitive market for services that in the past were handled internally through direct employment—in the form of a network of service providers.

By shifting employment to subordinate organizations external to the enterprise that operate in competitive markets, the lead firm creates a mechanism whereby workers will receive a wage close to the additional value they create. At the same time, this avoids the problem of having workers with very different wages operating under one roof. The lead firm captures the difference between the individual additional productivity of each worker and what would be the prevailing single wage rate if it set one.

As a result, two workers on the same project may effectively end up being paid very different wages, closer to something reflecting their individual marginal productivity than would be the case if they were in the direct employ of the parent organization. Such a mechanism would benefit the employer over the case where it set a single wage rate for workers with similar job titles but variation in productivity, or in cases where an employer's wage policy affects the market as a whole. A related argument for shifting work outward arises from the problems created by vertical equity expectations in internal labor markets. Even if workers have differing skill levels and job assignments, vertical equity norms in firms may lead large employers to pay lower-skill workers higher wages because of the presence of higher-paid workers whose compensation becomes a referent wage within the internal labor market.[22] Shifting those lower-skilled jobs outward can solve this problem.

Setting Wages by Setting Prices

Imagine that a hotel directly hired all of its workers—from landscapers, to maids, to valets, to front desk personnel. Horizontal equity would require comparable pay for those in a grade—and maybe even across the properties in a metropolitan area (particularly if the workforce moved among properties). Vertical equity would require considering the pay of maids and valets in setting the pay of landscapers and considering the wages of managers in setting the pay of desk personnel. The hotel would be required to create and administer a comprehensive pay and human resources policy.

But what if the hotel focuses its attention on its reputation (its core competency) and no longer sees the actual administration of hotels as central to its business strategy? This would allow it to cut loose the messy process of hotel operations to other organizations—particularly organizations that might bid against one another for the right to undertake that activity. Now the hotel could transform the production of hotel services into a market, with different entities competing for pieces of the business. Each provider would offer its services—which once would have been undertaken directly by the hotel itself—for a price.

As a result, the hotel would create competition for work among different purveyors and pay them a price based on its assessment of their contribution. Less-efficient producers could be paid less than more-efficient producers. In this way, the company faces a schedule of *prices for services* (for example, management of its workforce) rather than *wages for labor,* leaving the complex task of compensation to the individual providers of the service or product. In effect, the lead enterprise devolves its employment activity to a network of smaller providers. In so doing, it creates a mechanism—a competitive market for services that in the past were handled internally through direct employment—in the form of a network of service providers.

By shifting employment to smaller organizations operating in competitive markets, a large employer creates a mechanism to pay workers closer to the additional value they create but avoids the problem of having workers with very different wages operating under one roof. In so doing, the employer captures the difference between the individual additional productivity of each worker and what would be the prevailing single wage rate if it set one.[23]

Businesses at the top of supply chains split off employment so that they can focus their attention on more profitable activities connected to the revenue side of their income statement, leaving the manufacture of products or the provision of service to be fissured off. This has important implications for how the profitability of those companies is shared between different parties. Recall that in the former, integrated model of large employers, firms ended up sharing part of their gains with the workforce in the form of higher pay to deal with internal perceptions of fairness. That meant less to share with consumers in the form of lower prices and with investors in the form of higher returns.

With fissuring, the fairness problems are less acute and wages can be pushed downward. That means more gains to be passed on to consumers as lower prices or better returns for investors. In those fissured structures where a firm's core competency has attracted a particularly devoted customer base through branding or the ongoing introduction of cool new products, the reduced wage costs will flow particularly toward investors.[24] Shifting work outward allows redistribution of gains upward.

Increased Inequality and the Fissured Workplace Hypothesis

The fissured workplace hypothesis would suggest a distinctive source of earnings inequality. First, the fissured workplace hypothesis predicts that the earnings of workers undertaking the same work inside of companies have lower earnings when that work is shifted to contractors / firms outside of those companies. Empirical evidence on specific occupations that are shifted from "inside" to "outside" of a business confirm this prediction.

Janitors and security guards were in the vanguard of fissuring. By 2000 about 45 percent of janitors worked under contracting arrangements, and more than 70 percent of guards were employed as contractors.[25] As predicted by the above logic, shifting janitors and security guards from inside to outside the walls of lead businesses has indeed significantly impacted pay for workers in those occupations.[26] A study by Samuel Berlinski found that janitors who worked as contractors earned 15 percent less than those working in-house, and contracted security guards earned 17 percent less than comparable in-house guards.[27] Similarly, Arandajit Dube and Ethan Kaplan similarly found impacts of contracting, with a "wage penalty" for working as a contractor of 4 to 7 percent for janitors and 8 to 24 percent for security guards.[28]

More recently, Deborah Goldschmidt and Johannes Schmieder provide compelling evidence of similar effects on wage structures in Germany. They show significant growth in domestic service outsourcing of a variety of activities beginning in the 1990s. Using a carefully constructed sample allowing them to compare wages of food service, cleaning, security, and logistic workers, they examine the impact of moving the same jobs from "inside" to "outside" businesses engaged in domestic outsourcing. Their results using an events-study framework, show reductions in wages ranging from 10 to 15 percent of those jobs outsourced relative to those that were not. What is more, because of the ability to match workers who have experienced outsourcing to control for unobservable human capital characteristics, they argue that the reductions arise from the loss of wage premiums earned by workers when they move from inside to outside the outsourcing firm.[29]

The fissured workplace hypothesis, however, has broader implications about the drivers of increased earnings dispersion and income inequality over time. Increasing earnings inequality can arise from growing inequality within firms (more and more dispersion of earnings of the workers "inside" the walls) versus growing inequality between firms (more dispersion in earnings "outside" the walls of a given firm). The fissured workplace hypothesis would predict growing inequality from the latter effects (that is increased variation of earnings across firms). Lead businesses would continue to extract rents arising from their core competency. For the fairness reasons discussed above, they would continue to share some of those gains with the workers who remained "inside their four walls." At the same time, other firms who competed to provide the activities shed by lead businesses would have lower rents (for the traditional reasons predicted in competitive labor markets) and therefore less to share with their workforce. At the bottom of fissured workplaces, where firms compete to provide more homogeneous products and services for lead businesses, in more competitive markets with lower barriers to entry, one would find businesses with lower profitability, paying wages closer to marginal productivity.

The fissured workplace hypothesis heuristically describes manufacturing processes that have undergone significant outsourcing where the companies at the end of those supply chains (for example, companies like Apple that develop, brand, and market digital devices) are some of the most profitable in the economy while the earnings of suppliers who undertake specific steps of the manufacturing process farther down in the supply chain have far lower rates of return.

The fissured workplace hypothesis is therefore consistent with recent evidence on growing earnings dispersion in sectors that are increasingly reliant on franchising as a form of business organization. Branding products to consumers is a critical core competency in industries like eating and drinking and hospitality, and studies that compare wages earned by workers in branded companies find that those workers earn, on average, more than workers who work in similar, nonbranded companies in the same sector.[30] Franchising allows a company to split out the gains of developing and marketing the brand from the delivery of the actual product, with the franchisor capturing a significant portion of the rents of owning the brand, with the residual value going to the business entities purchasing use of that brand (the franchisees).[31] In the 1980s many branded chains in the fast-food and hotel industries sold off a high percentage of fast-food outlets and hotel properties to franchisees. This changed wage structures among the establishments within the sector, to a higher percentage of firms (franchisees) having a lower wage structure than the units that continued to be held by the franchisor. This would result in increased overall dispersion of earnings in the sector where franchising became more common, driven by growing divergence of earnings across franchisees and franchisors.[32]

A number of recent studies that have expressly focused on the sources of earnings inequality provide compelling evidence consistent with the fissured workplace hypothesis. Research by Erling Barth, Alex Bryson, James Davis, and Richard Freeman finds that the vast majority of increases in the dispersion of earnings between 1992 and 2007 arise from increases in the variance of earning between rather than within firms. In their matched data set, the authors find that about 80 percent of increased earnings inequality for those workers who stayed with the same establishment from one year to the next arose from growing divergence in the earnings of different establishments, as opposed to arising from growing divergences in the pay structure of the firms where they remained.[33]

Arguing that their results show that almost none of the growing dispersion of earnings arises from a widening gap between CEO pay and that of the workforce, Jae Song and colleagues find that virtually all of the earnings dispersion between 1978 and 2012 for firms with fewer than 10,000 workers arose from increased variation between rather than within firms. In their sample, the large wage gap between CEOs / high-level executives and average workers employed by the firm increased by only a small amount over the study period. Very large firms (those with more than 10,000 workers) are more affected by growing inequality within their ranks, as I will discuss below.[34]

David Card, Jörg Heining, and Patrick Kline found evidence of both "within" and "between" factors driving the growing inequality of wages in Germany. In their study, the authors found that inequality was roughly equally explained by increases in the heterogeneity of workers (within firm), increases in the heterogeneity of firms (between firm), and increases in the matching of workers and firms.[35]

These findings suggest that workers have experienced relatively less change in the inequality of their coworkers that *remain with them at their firms* than earlier accounts suggest. Instead, growing dispersion of earnings can be thought of as a "big bang" leading firms to rush away from one another, with lead businesses and their set of workers moving upward and subordinate firms and their associated distribution of earnings moving downward. This is consistent with the fissured workplace hypothesis, in that the distribution no longer includes workers whose activities and jobs have been shed to other employers external to the firm.

The fissured hypothesis, however, does not preclude increasing dispersion within firms as well, if there have been changes in fairness norms of behavior within those firms. For example, CEOs of lead businesses with valuable core competencies may extract more rents and propel themselves to ever higher levels of compensation—what Piketty aptly calls the "Takeoff of the Super-managers." Anecdotal evidence of the compensation practices of highly profitable enterprises in the finance and digital sectors certainly comport with this view. The CEOs in firms in the subordinate fissured universes may be less able to extract such rents, although evidence still shows they earn many, many times the earnings of average workers. This further heightens the overall extent of inequality, albeit from changing norms, capture of corporate governance, and other factors driving the excessive growth of executive compensation

In sum, recent studies offer compelling evidence consistent with the fissured workplace hypothesis. The fissured workplace has led to a separation of activities between lead businesses and subordinate networks of other enterprises who support them. This has enabled lead businesses in the economy to solve the pay problem suggested by the Webbs by transforming their wage determination woes into a conventional pricing problem. For those workers whose jobs no longer benefit from the penumbral effects of fairness in wage setting, the impacts have been significant.

Frontiers of Research: Wage Determination, the Fissured Workplace, and Inequality

The main problem with the theory of marginal productivity is quite simply it fails to explain the diversity of wage distributions we observe in different countries at different times. In order to understand the dynamics of wage inequality, we must introduce other factors, such as the institutions and rules that govern the operation of the labor market in each society.

—Piketty, *Capital,* 308

The generation of scholars who shaped the study of U.S. labor markets in the aftermath of World War II—John Dunlop, Frederick Meyers, Clark Kerr, and Lloyd Reynolds, to name the most prominent—were deeply influenced by their own experiences in wage determination, because many played the role of mediators and arbitrators in the emerging world of collective bargaining, serving on government panels (including the National War Labor Board) charged with wage and price controls, and engaging in dispute resolution in major industries such as coal, steel, and construction. Their scholarship reflected a preoccupation with the institutions that shaped wages, benefits, and workplace conditions.[36]

A new generation of labor economists in the 1960s, building on the wedding of the neoclassical economic framework with a mathematical approach to framing problems pioneered by Paul Samuelson, displaced the institutional approach, beginning in the 1960s, by turning the study of wage and workplace outcomes into a framework driven by the supply and demand for labor as a factor of production.[37] Scholars in this area like Gary Becker, H. Gregg Lewis, Jacob Mincer, and Sherwin Rosen approached the study of workplace outcomes, rooted in theoretical models and girded by mathematics, by drawing on the relative wealth of data available for studying labor markets and aided by the falling costs of analysis with the development of computers and early statistics software. The role of institutions in setting wages was gradually viewed as incidental to the ultimate labor market outcomes with both growing sophistication of statistical tools to analyze data and of mathematical models to shape theory.[38] Subsequent generations of leading economists like David Card, Richard Freeman,

Daniel Hamermesh, Larry Katz, and Alan Krueger in the 1980s and 1990s reintroduced institutional considerations into modern labor economics. Yet attention to wage-setting processes per se has remained a legacy of an earlier era.

As Thomas Piketty's quote makes clear, examining the structure of inequality provides a challenge for scholars to place institutions and wage-setting process into sharper and more central focus once again. This is particularly critical in understanding the changing nature of how rents are shared between labor and capital in the setting of wages. Here I briefly outline four broad groups of research questions that the fissured workplace hypothesis, and the broader questions of inequality posed by Piketty's *Capital*, place on the table:

1. We need to expand our understanding of how fairness norms play out in different types of firms / sectors of the economy. For example, how does the ratio of CEO to average employee pay differ between the firms who are rapidly moving upward in the distribution of firms from those mired in the middle or bottom portions of the distribution? Do we see widening of pay differentials in those firms at the top, which can square the views of Piketty and others on the impacts of super-managers with the previously cited findings of Barth, Bryson, Davis, and Freeman and Song et. al.? For example, Song et al. estimate that the faster income growth of the top 0.2 percent of earners at firms with more than 10,000 employees relative to average workers in their firms could be indicative of the dual effects of a big bang in the interfirm distribution of earnings combined with the impacts of a secondary big bang of the intrafirm distribution of earnings of that subset of select companies.

   Studying norms of wage setting as discussed in the prior section requires a broader set of methodological tools. Although fairness notions and behavioral motivations have entered the economics mainstream, a broader analytic lens is important. As Piketty notes, "The problem is now to explain where these social norms come from and how they evolve, which is obviously a question for sociology, psychology, cultural and political history, and the study of beliefs and perceptions at least as much as for economics per se."[39]

2. Similarly, what is the role of social norms in the way that wages are set at the lower levels of fissured industries (including at the geographic level)? How much does wage setting for those firms that have been shed comport with traditional predictions of economic theory, given their more competitive nature, versus still being affected by normative pressures on the employer as well as in the labor markets where workers are drawn? For example, there is a growing empirical literature on the impact of social networks on expectations of pay.[40] How do social networks affect the pay practices of low-wage firms? How do wages and related outcomes propagate in local / regional labor markets and how are they impacted by key referent wages (such as statutory minimum wages or socially defined wage referents like the "Fight for $15")? Answers to these questions have both academic implications regarding the functioning of labor markets as well as policy implications for where labor standards problems might be found and how policy tools can be used to affect them.

3. In a related vein, decisions to fissure activities have been gradually moving upward to higher and higher skilled jobs, including human resource planning, law, engineering, and journalism. How is wage setting evolving in these areas where workers positioned "inside" lead businesses historically had some bargaining power because skill provided them outside options arising from their human capital? How does the creation of more permeable labor markets for these workers because of fissuring change the structure of wages and wage determination for them?

4. If the fissured workplace hypothesis is promising, we need to build clearer models of it and undertake deeper research on its mechanisms. Richard Freeman has written "The economics of fissuring is a difficult problem. . . . [T]he basic market model predicts that competition will reduce establishment-based variation of earnings among comparable workers. Either our models misrepresent how a relatively unfettered labor market works in reality or we are missing important market forces in applying the model. From either perspective, the evidence of fissuring creates a puzzle to labor economics and social science more broadly. We need a new fissured market model that goes beyond

standard analysis, new measures of wage determinants in the existing framework, or some judicious mixture of the two."[41]

The empirical work discussed in the prior section demonstrates that economists are diving into the core question of what is driving growing inequality in the United States and economies around the world.[42] There is clearly a need for further work on the contribution of the factors discussed here as well as contending theories about the evidence. In this regard, I would echo what Freeman notes above as well as Piketty, who writes: "The problem of inequality is a problem for the social sciences in general, not for just one of its disciplines."[43]

I have the unique opportunity to think about the questions of income inequality as an academic who has studied this question for many years, and more recently as the head of the federal agency most responsible for the enforcement of basic labor standards. My experience in both roles make me emphatically feel that there are few more fundamental questions that we must explore given the consequences of growing inequality on a democratic political economy.

[III]

DIMENSIONS OF INEQUALITY

TEN

Increasing Capital Income Share and Its Effect on Personal Income Inequality

BRANKO MILANOVIC

We tend to assume that those with high incomes from capital are also those who are the richest overall; that is, that the association between being capital-rich and overall-income-rich is very close. This is implicit in Piketty's analysis. He argues that as the share of capital in national income rises, interpersonal inequality will also rise. In our first chapter addressing the dimensions of inequality, economist Branko Milanovic asks under what conditions this is likely to be true.

Milanovic imagines three kinds of societies: socialist, where there is an equal per capita distribution of capital assets; classical capitalist, where workers draw their entire income from labor and capitalists derive their entire income from capital; and "new" capitalist, where everyone receives income from both labor and capital. He uses these archetypes to examine what happens to the inequality—as measured by the Gini coefficient of interpersonal income inequality—if Piketty's α—the share of capital in net income—rises. Unsurprisingly, he finds that the institutional setup matters. The way the rising share of capital income gets transmitted into greater interpersonal inequality varies between different social systems as a function of the underlying asset distribution. In new capitalism, a rising share of capital income almost directly translates into a higher Gini, while in classical capitalism, this is true once the share of capitalists becomes sufficiently high. In a socialist world, however, a rising capital share does not imply rising interpersonal Gini.

Methodological Contributions of Piketty's *Capital*

When discussing *Capital in the Twenty-First Century,* we need to distinguish between its analytics and methodology, its recommendations, and its forecasts. One can agree with the analytics without agreeing with the recommendations, or the reverse. The methodology introduced by *Capital*—because it seems to fit quite well the likely evolution of the rich world in the decades to come, and more importantly because it provides a novel way to look at economic phenomena—is probably the most significant contribution of the book. It will affect not only how we think of income distribution and capitalism in the future but also how we think about economic history, from ancient Rome to prerevolutionary France.

The most important methodological contribution of Piketty's book is his attempt to unify the fields of economic growth, functional income distribution, and personal income distribution.[1] In the standard Walrasian system, the three are formally related—but in actual work in economics they were generally treated separately, or some were even simply left out. Functional income distribution was studied much more by Marxist economists. Neoclassical economists tended to assume that capital and labor shares were broadly fixed. This view changed only fairly recently, and we are now witnessing an upsurge of interest in the topic.[2] Piketty's emphasis on the rising share of capital income contributed to this efflorescence.

Personal income distribution tended to be studied almost as divorced from the rest of economics, because in a Walrasian world, agents come to the market with the already-given endowments of capital and labor. Because the original distribution of these endowments is not the subject of economics (narrowly defined), personal income distribution was assumed to be whatever the market generates. But in *Capital,* the movements in the capital / income ratio—driven by "the fundamental inequality" or "central contradiction of capitalism," namely r > g (return on capital greater than the growth rate of overall income)—lead to the rising share of capital income in net product. This, in turn, leads to a greater interpersonal inequality.

This chapter concentrates on the last point, which is usually implicitly taken for granted: A greater share of capital is associated, it is thought almost implicitly, with a rising interpersonal inequality. This view is understandable because during most of economic history, people with high capital income were also people with high overall income. Therefore, a greater share of net product going to capitalists came to be associated with greater interpersonal inequality.

In a recent paper investigating the association between higher capital shares and income inequality over the long run (going back in some cases to the mid-nineteenth century), Erik Bengtsson and Daniel Waldenström find, in a country fixed-effect setting, that the correlation has typically been positive and fairly strong. For the entire sample of fifteen advanced economies, they find that, on average, each percentage-point increase in the capital share was associated with a 0.89-point increase in the (log of) top 1 percent income share. When other controls are introduced, the size of the coefficient is reduced, but it remains positive and statistically significant.[3] Margaret Jacobson and Filippo Occhino similarly find that for the United States, a 1 percent increase in the capital share tended to increase Gini by between 0.15 percent and 0.33 percent.[4]

Maura Francese and Carlos Mulas-Granados use more recent 1970s–2010 Luxembourg Income Study microdata from forty-three countries, and decompose the overall change in disposable income Gini into its accounting components: concentration coefficients of labor and capital, labor and capital shares, and changes in taxation and social transfers.[5] Unlike Bengtsson and Waldenström, they find a negligible impact of higher capital share, and conclude that most of the increase in disposable income Gini was driven by the rising concentration of wages. They complement the decomposition analysis by a regression on a sample of ninety-three countries, for the 1970s–2013 period, of capital (labor) share on Gini. Once controls are introduced, labor (capital) share is insignificant.[6]

So the link between greater capital share and increased interpersonal inequality is not as simple and unambiguous as it seems. Even when there exists a positive relationship between the two, the strength of that relationship varies.

The chapter is organized as follows. In the next section I discuss in general the link between the rising share of capital in net income (Piketty's α) and the Gini coefficient of interpersonal income inequality. Next I look at this relationship in three ideal-typical societies: socialist, classical capitalist, and "new" capitalist. (The terms are defined there.) In the penultimate section

I present the empirical analysis of the relationship using 138 harmonized household surveys from seventeen advanced economies. In the last section I discuss policy implications.

It may be useful, even before we embark on the study of the relationship between α and Gini, to indicate why this is important. The increase in capital share is not, by itself, an inequality "problem"; that is, it does not necessarily lead to an increase in interpersonal inequality. For example, when the underlying distribution of capital is egalitarian, an increase in α may cause a decrease in interpersonal inequality or leave it unchanged. Hence, even for the proponents of strong egalitarianism, the increase in capital share cannot be a problem as such. It becomes a "problem" only because in most real-world situations, the underlying distribution of capital assets is extremely skewed. The realization of this fact leads me, in the prescriptive part, to argue in favor of equalization of ownership of assets among individuals. This provides a realistic agenda for fighting inequality and is especially relevant for the rich societies where a rising wealth / income ratio implies that, unless the return on capital decreases sufficiently, a greater share of national net product will be received by asset-holders. Thus, we have a choice among acquiescing in the rising interpersonal inequality, trying to reduce it through taxation, or working on the deconcentration of asset ownership.

Focusing on the distribution of assets is, in my opinion, a more promising policy than Piketty's emphasis on taxation of capital. But regardless of whether one tool is better than the other, they are two complementary ways to address rising inequality in the ever more affluent societies (that is, in societies with a rising K / Y ratio).

Going from Functional to Personal Income Distribution

The main link between the functional and the personal income distribution is provided by the relationship $r > g$. But in order to lead to a rising interpersonal inequality, it needs to satisfy the three following requirements.[7]

First, r must be overwhelmingly used for investment and not for consumption. Clearly, if all of r was simply consumed by capitalists, the K / Y ratio in the next cycle would remain unchanged, and dynamically there would be no increase in either $\beta = K / Y$ or in the share of total income derived by capital (α). This is the point on which Debraj Ray in his critique of

Capital has strongly insisted.[8] Yew-Kwang Ng makes the same point.[9] It is indeed a formally correct argument, but misses the entire point of what capitalism and capitalists are. If capitalists were interested solely in consumption, in spending most of their income on what Adam Smith nicely termed "baubles and trinkets," the process would play out as Ray imagines. But capitalists are precisely capitalists because they do not consume all surplus and are interested in expanding the scope of their operations, and thus in investing all or most of r. The assumption of the saving rate out of r being close to 1 is not only well founded in the precedents from theoretical economics (in modern times, from Kalecki, Solow, and Kaldor, and obviously all the way back to Ricardo and Marx) but is equally well founded in the empirical behavior of the rich, and in what are the central features of capitalism as a system.[10]

But the rising β and even a rising α do not ensure by themselves transmission into greater interpersonal inequality. For this to happen, concentration of capital income has to be very high. Working with only two factor incomes, those of labor and capital, for the overall inequality of personal income to go up, the requirement is that the more unequally distributed source has to grow relative to the less unequally distributed source. With capital income this condition is relatively easily satisfied, because in all known cases the concentration of capital income is greater than the concentration of labor income. In the United States, for example, Gini of income from capital (calculated across household per capita incomes) is in excess of 80, while similarly calculated Gini of labor income is around 40. The situation is identical in other countries. This is simply a reflection of the well-known heavy concentration of capital assets and of the fact that about a third of Americans have zero net capital assets, and hence draw no income from ownership.

The third requirement is that the association between capital-rich and overall income-rich people be high. A simple high concentration of a given income source will not guarantee that that source contributes to inequality. Unemployment benefits have a Gini that is generally in excess of 90 (because most people receive no unemployment benefits during any given year), but because recipients of unemployment benefits are generally income-poor, an increase in the share of unemployment benefits in total income reduces income inequality. Technically, the third requirement is (in the case of the Gini coefficient with which we work here) expressed in the form of a high correlation between rankings according to capital income and rankings according to total income. Put simply, this requirement means that people who receive large capital incomes should also be rich. Empirically, this requirement is easily satisfied in most countries.

We tend to see the transmission from a rising capital income share into an increasing interpersonal inequality as a foregone conclusion, precisely because we tend to take as given:

1. High saving out of capital income
2. High concentration of assets
3. High correlation between one's drawing a large capital income and being rich.

But this is not always so, or at least the strength of that transmission is variable. We move to a more formal derivation of the relationship.

We know that total income Gini can be decomposed into inequalities contributed by each income source, in our case capital (c) and labor (l) as in (1):

$$G = s_l R_l G_l + s_c R_c G_c \tag{1}$$

where s_i = share of a given income (i-th) source, R_i = correlation ratio between the source and total income, G_i = Gini coefficient of an income source, and G = overall income Gini. R_i in turn is equal to the ratio of two correlation coefficients (ρ's), namely, between income source and recipients' ranks r (from the poorest to the richest) according to total income, and between income source and recipients' ranks according to income source itself. For capital income, the correlation ratio can be written:

$$R_c = \frac{covar(r(y),c)}{covar(r(c),c)} = \frac{\rho(r(y),c)\sigma_{r(y)}\sigma_c}{\rho(r(c),c)\sigma_{r(c)}\sigma_c} = \frac{\rho(r(y),c)}{\rho(r(c),c)} \tag{2}$$

Notice that if people's ranks according to total income and income from capital coincide, $R_c = 1$. In all other cases, $\rho(r(y),c) < \rho(r(c),c)$ and $R_c < 1$. For unemployment benefits mentioned above, $R_i < 0$.

For the rising share of capital income (s_c)[11] to increase overall income Gini, we need therefore to have two "transmission" tools: Gini coefficient of capital income (G_c) and R_c, positive and high.[12]

The rest of the chapter will deal with these two "transmission" tools. Equation (2) gives the definition of R_c, which I also call "elasticity of transmission" between the change in capital share and change in personal income inequality. The definition of G_c is a standard one, with the Gini coefficient calculated across the entire distribution but with individuals ranked by their amount of capital income (rather than by total income as we normally do in calculations of overall income Gini). Note that every Gini point increase in the concentration of capital income will be translated into $R_c s_c$ Gini point increase in total income Gini. Similarly, as the share of capital in total income increases by a percentage point, Gini will go up by $R_c G_c - R_l G_l$.

Transmission of Higher Capital Income Share into Personal Inequality: Three Social Systems

It is useful to consider three ideal-typical social systems and to observe how they "transmit" an increased share of income from capital into personal income distribution.

SOCIALISM We assume that in socialism, returns from capital are distributed equally per capita. This could happen in two ways: All capital can be state-owned and the returns from it can be distributed equally among members of a community, or every member can have the same amount of (privately owned) capital on which she or he receives the same return.[13] A variant of that is a "social dividend" proposed by James Meade in the 1970s and 1980s and more recently the "minimum inheritance" idea proposed by Tony Atkinson.[14] They differ, however, from our ideal-typical socialism in that, under the latter, all capital income is distributed equally per capita whereas in Meade and Atkinson's schemes only a part of national income from capital is thus distributed.

Now, $r > g$ will not be "transmitted" into greater interpersonal inequality because $G_c = 0$. In such a society, we can write income of an individual i (y_i) as $y_i = l_i + \bar{c}$ where labor income (or more realistically, log of labor income) l is distributed normally with the mean $\bar{l}$ and standard deviation $\sigma_l l : N(\bar{l}, \sigma_l)$ and income from capital is a constant $\bar{c}$. R_c will be equal to zero because the correlation between the ranks according to total income and amounts of capital income will be 0 and the numerator of (2), $\rho(r(y), c)$, will be equal to zero.

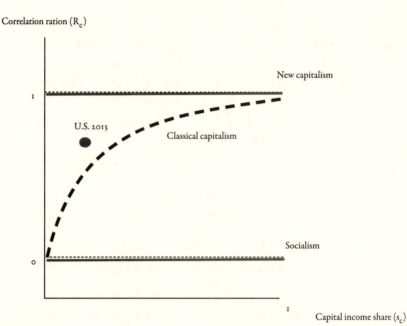

FIGURE 10-1: Transmission of rising capital share into interpersonal inequality.

Note: Three ideal-typical social systems and how they "transmit" an increased share of income from capital into personal income distribution.

The same result obtains if we distribute capital randomly across individuals, regardless of their labor income. In that case, G_c will be positive, and individual income becomes $y_i = l_i + c_i$ where now both labor income (or log of labor income) and capital income are normally distributed with $l : N\left(\bar{l}, \sigma_l\right)$ and $c : N\left(\bar{c}, \sigma_c\right)$ but are basically uncorrelated. The "transmission" will again fail because there would be no clear association between being a capitalist and having a higher overall income. R_c may be positive or negative (it will just depend on how the lottery of capital incomes gets correlated with the distribution of labor incomes) but it would be very small in the absolute amount.[15]

In any case, the transmission from greater share of capital to interpersonal income distribution will be weak: nil or quasi nil across any value of s_c. This is shown in Figure 10-1 by the line denoted "socialism," which we draw to be almost undistinguishable from $R_c = 0$ for all values of s_c. Basically—and this is key—we have full independence of personal income distribution

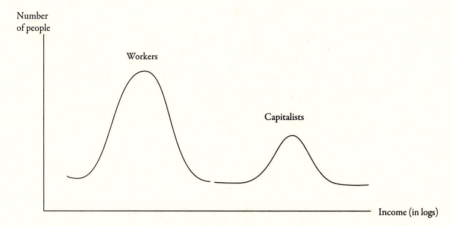

FIGURE 10-2: Social structure of classical capitalism (simplified).

Note: Capitalism's social structure can be depicted as two social groups differing in their size and income levels.

from the rising share of capital in net output. The former is "insulated" from the latter.

CLASSICAL CAPITALISM In classical capitalism, ownership of capital and labor is totally separated, in the sense that workers draw their entire income from labor and have no income from the ownership of assets, while the situation for the capitalists is the reverse. Moreover, we shall assume that all workers are poorer than all capitalists. This is an important simplifying assumption because it gives us, as shown in Figure 10-2, two social groups that are nonoverlapping by income level. When the groups are nonoverlapping, Gini is exactly decomposable across the recipients (see equation 3), and this simplifies the relationship between Gini calculated across income sources and Gini calculated across the recipients.

In general, Gini calculated across recipients belonging to groups i $(1,2,\ldots r)$ is equal to

$$G = \frac{1}{\mu} \sum_{i=1}^{r} \sum_{j>i}^{r} \left(\bar{y}_j - \bar{y}_i \right) p_i p_j + \sum_{i=1}^{r} p_i s_i G_i + L$$

where μ = overall mean income, $\bar{y}_i$ = mean income of i-th group, p_i = population share of i-th group, s_i = share of i-th group in total income, and L = the overlap term that is generally calculated as a residual and is positive when there are recipients from the mean-poorer group who are richer than (overlap with) some recipients of a mean-richer group. Because in our case all workers are poorer than all capitalists, L disappears and the expression for the Gini simplifies:

$$G = \frac{1}{\mu}\left(\bar{y}_k - \bar{y}_w\right)p_k p_w + p_k s_k G_k + p_w s_w G_w$$
$$= s_k p_w - s_w p_k + p_k s_k G_k + p_w s_w G_w = s_k\left(p_w + p_k G_k\right) + s_w\left(-p_k + p_w G_w\right) \tag{3}$$

where we use subscripts w for workers, and k for capitalists.

Overall inequality, whether calculated across income sources or across recipients, must be the same, so (3) must be equal to (1), and thus

$$s_c\left(p_w + p_k G_c\right) + s_l\left(-p_k + p_w G_l\right) = s_l R_l G_l + s_c R_c G_c$$
$$s_c\left(p_w + p_k G_c - R_c G_c\right) + s_l\left(-p_k + p_w G_l - R_l G_l\right) = 0 \tag{4}$$

where we make use of the fact that the share of labor income (s_l) is exactly the same as the share of income received by workers (s_w), and the share of capital income is equal to the share of income received by capitalists, $s_c = s_k$. Similarly, $G_k = G_c$ and $G_l = G_w$. Annex 1 shows further manipulations of the relationship. At the end we obtain a positive and concave relationship between s_c and R_c (as shown in Figure 10-1 by the curve denoted "classical capitalism"). The transmission from an increased capital share into a higher interpersonal inequality increases in s_c but does so at the diminishing rate. It asymptotically tends toward 1 when s_c approaches unity.

Some intuition will help explain the result. Suppose that classical capitalism is such that there is only an infinitesimally small number of capitalists (at the extreme, just one person) and that all other individuals are workers, so that both s_k and s_c are low.[16] By assuming a sole capitalist, we also assume that she or he is the richest person in the community (but not so extravagantly rich to drive s_c very high). The correlation coefficient in the numerator of R_c, cov($r(y)$, c), will be low because ranks according to total income, running from 1 to 100, will not be correlated with the amount of income from capital. We shall have two vectors, that of ranks [1 2 3 . . . . . . n] and that of capital income [0 0 0 0 . . . K] where K = total capital income (received by one person only). Now, the denominator of R_c will be obtained from a correlation between a vector where the ranks for all recipients but the top will be the same (because they all have the same, nil, amount of income from capital)—that is, between a vector such as $\left[\dfrac{n}{2}\dfrac{n}{2}\dfrac{n}{2}....n\right]$, and $[0\ 0\ 0 ... K]$. Such a correlation will be much higher (actually, equal to 1) and the ratio between the two correlation coefficients will thus be low. We can illustrate it with a numerical example. Let $n = 100$ and K any random number but which we selected to be 100. The correlation in the numerator is 0.17, that of the denominator 1. Hence $R_c = cov(r(y), c) = 0.17$.

Consider now the other extreme, where classical capitalist society is composed mostly of capitalists and an infinitesimally small number of workers, so that s_c approaches unity. It is clear that a person's rank according to capital income will entirely (or almost entirely) coincide with his or her rank according to total income, and $cov(r(y), c) \approx cov(r(c), c)$ and thus $R_c \approx 1$. In other words, there would be practically no difference between total and capital income because at the limit they are the same. This makes the two correlation coefficients almost the same and their ratio $R_c \approx 1$.

NEW CAPITALISM We assume that new capitalism differs from the classical capitalism in that all individuals receive income from both capital and labor. Thus, instead of the two sharply delineated groups, workers with income $(l_i, 0)$ and capitalists with income $(0, c_i)$, we have for all individuals positive labor and capital incomes (l_i, c_i). We assume further that the amounts of both labor and capital income received increase monotonically as we move toward (total-income-) richer individuals. A poor person's income would be, for example, $(2,1)$, a middle-income person's would be $(7,3)$, and a rich person's income $(24,53)$.

Monotonic increases of labor, capital, and total income (such that if $y_j > y_i$ then we must have $l_j > l_i$ and $k_j > k_i$) ensure that the ranks according to capital, labor, and total income are the same. Thus, $R_c = R_l = 1$. This is why in Figure 10-1 we draw the "transmission" function for new capitalism at $R_c = 1$ throughout.

Two elaborations of this situation, however, are possible. We can have a situation illustrated in Figure 10-3 by the *labor income* and *capital income2*

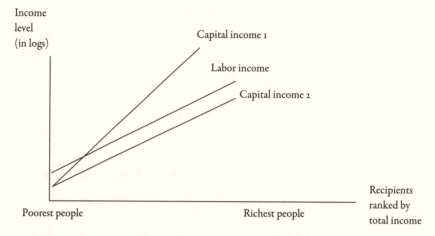

FIGURE 10-3: Labor and capital income across recipients in new capitalism (simplified).

Note: Two possibilities exist. Either the proportions of labor and capital income stay constant throughout the distribution or the share of capital income increases with total income.

lines, for example: The proportions of labor and capital income stay constant throughout the distribution—that is, both amounts of capital and labor increase by the same percentage as we move from poorer to richer recipients. A person's income can be written as $y_i = \varsigma_i\left(\bar{l}+\bar{c}\right)$ where ς_i increases in i, indicating that everybody receives a specific portion of both overall labor and capital income. In other words, as we move up along the income distribution, we move from income that can be written as (2,1) to (10,5) to (200,100) and so on, where every individual receives twice as much labor income as capital income, but the absolute amounts of both differ. Obviously, richer people receive more of both. In that case (let's call it "new capitalism 2"), Ginis of labor and capital will be the same and the Gini coefficient of total income can be written as

$$G = s_l\bar{G} + s_c\bar{G} = \bar{G} \tag{5}$$

When r > g and the share of capital income goes up, overall inequality is unaffected. Thus, in the "new capitalism 2" where everybody (poor and rich alike) has the same composition of total income (for example, everybody's total income is composed of 70 percent labor income and 30 percent capital income), a rising share of capital income does not get transmitted into an increased interpersonal inequality. Note that this happens because the rising capital share leaves Gini of capital income unchanged (and Gini of capital income is the same as Gini of labor income). In socialism, this happens because $G_c = 0$.

A more realistic version of the new capitalism (named "new capitalism 1") is the one where the proportion of capital income increases as a person becomes (total-income-) richer. This can be written (in a continuous case) as

$$\frac{d\left(\frac{c}{l}\right)}{dy} > 0 \text{ with } \frac{dc}{dy} > 0 \text{ and } \frac{dl}{dy} > 0 \text{ ensuring that absolute incomes from both}$$

capital and labor are higher for richer individuals.[17] The relationship $\mathrm{cov}(r(y),c) = \mathrm{cov}\,(r(c),c)$ then still holds, because the rankings according to total income and the rankings according to capital income coincide and thus $R_c = 1$, but now an increase in the capital share pushes the overall Gini up. This happens because capital income (depicted by the *capital income1* line in Figure 10-3) has a greater Gini than labor income and as the share of a more unequally distributed source increases, so does the overall Gini. The actual increase in Gini will be $G_c - G_l$.

New capitalism represents a strong departure from the model of classical capitalism.[18] Every individual receives both labor and capital income, and in principle (if their shares were the same across the distribution), we could obtain the same outcome as in socialism, namely full orthogonality of personal income distribution from the rising share of capital income. This seems unlikely, however, as rich countries today are in effect closer to "new capitalism 1," where the share of capital income is greater for the rich households.

Under "new capitalism 1," the transmission from increased capital share into greater interpersonal inequality may be as strong as in classical capitalism. Suppose that $s_c = 0.3$ and that it increases to 0.35. Under classical capitalism with R_c (say) around 0.6, these 5 additional percentage points of net income received by capitalists will increase the overall Gini by about 3 points. Under the "new capitalism 1," the increase will be

$(G_c - G_l)$ times 5. The $G_c - G_l$ gap is empirically about 0.3 –0.5 (0.8 –0.9 minus 0.4 –0.5), so the Gini increase may be 1.5 –2.5 points. The new capitalism may be just marginally more successful than classical capitalism in checking the spillover from the rising capital share into a greater interpersonal inequality.

Transmission of Higher Capital Income Share into Personal Inequality: Empirical Results

How does the transmission of higher capital income into personal inequality, summed up in the elasticity parameter, look empirically in the advanced capitalist economies? I use a sample of 138 standardized household surveys produced by the Luxembourg Income Study, or LIS, covering seventeen capitalist economies over the 1969–2013 period, and calculate all the relevant statistics (Gini coefficients, concentration coefficients, correlation ratios for capital and labor income). The number of surveys by country ranges from twelve for Canada and eleven for the United States to five for Switzerland and Greece. For almost all countries, the most recent surveys are from 2010 or 2013. The list of surveys is given in Annex 2.

One has to keep in mind, however, that despite the best efforts at harmonization conducted by the Luxembourg Income Study, the amount of capital incomes is probably underestimated in many cases. This is due to the fact that the original surveys out of which LIS data are built underestimate capital income, both because the rich (who receive a high share of income from capital) refuse to participate in surveys, or rich respondents, when participating, underestimate their capital income. LIS data for the United States, for example, give an average share of capital income (exclusive of capital gains) in total market income of 7 percent, which is about two-thirds of the value obtained from fiscal sources.[19] Despite that, comparisons of U.S. data obtained from the Luxembourg Income Study and from fiscal sources show very close correspondence between the values of the Gini coefficient for capital income and correlation ratios (R_c), the two factors that determine the transmission. The latter is therefore likely to be very similar whether calculated from household surveys or from fiscal sources (see Table 10-1).

TABLE 10-1.

Comparison of LIS survey and fiscal data for the United States

	2000		2004	
	Surveys	Fiscal	Surveys	Fiscal
Inequality of market income without capital gains (in Gini points)	53	55	54	55
Capital income share in market income (in %)	7	11	6	10
Gini of capital income (in Gini points)	90	92	92	94
Capital correlation ratio, R_c	0.63	0.76	0.64	0.78

Note: Calculations from household surveys are based on household per capita income; calculations from fiscal data are based on fiscal units (which are very close to households). The fiscal series ends in 2005. For comparison, I choose the two most recent years for which I had both survey and fiscal data. Source: LIS household surveys based on U.S. Current Population Surveys: my own calculations. Fiscal data: personal communication by Christoph Lakner.

Figure 10-4 shows the data on the elasticity of transmission (R_c) over time for four advanced economies. In addition to the United States, I selected Germany as an example of a continental-corporatist welfare state, Sweden as a prototype of a Scandinavian welfare state, and Spain as an advanced Mediterranean welfare state. The results show the United States with a rather high elasticity throughout. U.S. elasticity steadily increases, passing from 0.54 in the late 1970s to 0.64 in 2013. Most interesting, however, is Sweden, where the elasticity was as low as 0.2 in the mid-1970s but increased to 0.5 by 2000. This parallels the well-known increase in income inequality and especially wealth inequality in Sweden.[20] German elasticity also increased significantly, from 0.4 in the mid-1970s to the peak of 0.65 thirty years later. Finally, Spanish elasticity went up as well, from less than 0.3 in the 1980s to just short of 0.5 in 2010. In these four cases, there was a clear upward trend over the past thirty years. In addition, the gaps between countries' elasticities in the early 2010s are smaller than they were in the 1970s. We shall find very similar results for the whole sample of seventeen countries.

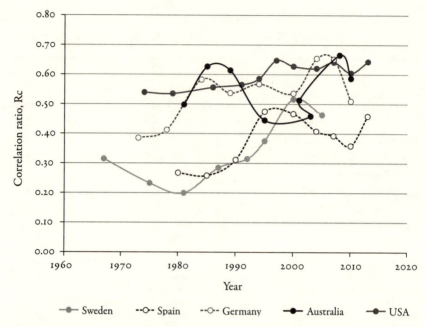

FIGURE 10-4: Elasticity of interpersonal income Gini to changes in capital income share, five advanced economies, 1967–2013.

Note: In all five countries except Australia, elasticity has clearly trended upward in the past three decades, and the gaps between countries' elasticities have become smaller.

Source: Calculated from household-level data available from Luxembourg Income Study (see Annex 2). All underlying variables normalized by household size, that is expressed in per-capita terms.

Figure 10-5 shows the average elasticity by country, ranked in increasing order. Italy, the United States, and Finland have the highest elasticities, around 0.6; at the other extreme are Belgium, Sweden, and Switzerland, with average elasticities of just under 0.35. Note that the period over which these elasticities are calculated is not identical across countries (the first data point for the United States goes back to 1979, and for Greece to only 1995), nor is the number of observations per country the same.

Figure 10-6 shows the scatterplot of elasticities obtained from 138 surveys against the capital shares calculated from the same surveys. As implied by our derivation in the previous section, higher capital share is associated with greater elasticity, but the scatterplot shows that the relationship is concave and that after the capital share reaches about 0.12, the elasticity increases

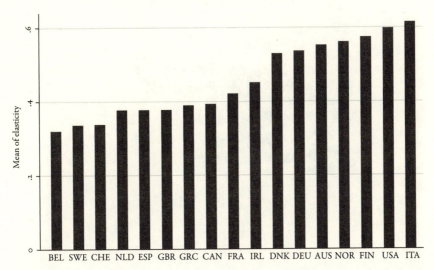

FIGURE 10-5: Average elasticity over the past approximately forty years, by country. Note: Italy, the United States, and Finland have the highest elasticities at around 0.6; at the other extreme are Belgium, Sweden, and Switzerland with average elasticities just under 0.35.

Source: See Annex 2.

by very little or is stable. This means that any increase in the capital share (say, by 1 percentage point) will be associated with a greater increase in interpersonal Gini at higher levels of capital share. But once that level is reasonably high, further increases in the capital share will produce about the same effect on interpersonal inequality.

Most elasticities are between 0.3 and 0.6, with both the median and the mean elasticity of 0.46 (implying a fairly symmetrical distribution of elasticities). The distribution of elasticities is shown in Figure 10-7.

How is elasticity related to the capital share? In other words, can we estimate the relationship shown in Figure 10-6 parametrically? Table 10-2 shows the regression results for several specifications. In the simplest linear specification where elasticity is regressed on capital share and time only, we find a steep slope on capital share of about 3, and a statistically significant positive coefficient on time. This former means that, on average, each percentage-point increase in the capital share is associated with an increase of elasticity of almost 3 points—for example, if the capital share increases from 0.05 to 0.06 (from 5 percent to 6 percent), the elasticity increases from 0.4 to 0.43. The

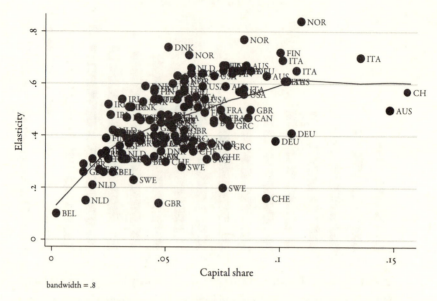

FIGURE 10-6: Elasticity with which capital share is "transmitted" into higher inter-personal inequality, and capital share, 17 advanced economies, 1967–2013.

Notes: All underlying variables normalized by household size, that is expressed in per-capita terms. Non-parametric *lowess* function in Stata with default bandwidth shown. Capital share is expressed as a ratio (0.05 = 5%) A single country abbreviation appears for all years for which surveys for such a country are available.

Source: Calculated from household-level data available from Luxembourg Income Study (see Annex 2).

positive sign on the *time* variable implies that the transmission function has recently become stronger. Perhaps more realistic (in light of the pattern in Figure 10-6) is a quadratic formulation, and indeed we find a significant quadratic term in regression 2. Another alternative is a country fixed-effect regression, which allows for heterogeneity between the countries (reflected in the country-specific intercepts). The coefficient on the capital share is quite similar (2.68) to what we have obtained in the simple pooled regression. The coefficient on time remains strongly positive. Finally, specification (4) repeats the squared capital share formulation, now in country-fixed effects, with basically unchanged results. We can draw two conclusions from this exercise: First, a rising capital share is associated with increasing (but concave) transmission into personal inequality, and second, the relationship has recently become stronger.

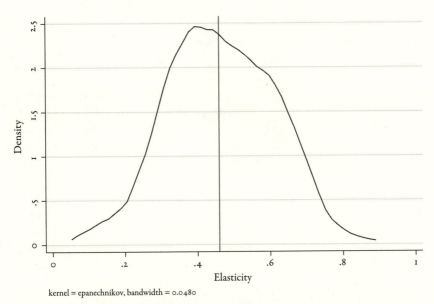

FIGURE 10-7: Distribution of elasticities (R$_c$) in advanced capitalist economies.

Note: Most elasticities are between 0.3 and 0.6. The straight line is drawn at the median and mean elasticity of 0.46 (implying a fairly symmetrical distribution of elasticities).

Source: Calculated from household-level data available from Luxembourg Income Study (see Annex 2).

We can now compare the elasticities from real life to those that we obtained earlier from our four ideal-typical social systems (Table 10-3). This enables us to see better where, compared to different ideal types, modern capitalist economies lie. Great Britain in 1969, Netherlands in 1987, Switzerland in 1982, and Sweden in 1981 had elasticities smaller or equal to 0.2 and were quite close to the socialist model. One-half of all observed elasticities fall between the values of 0.36 and 0.57 (with the median, as we have seen, of 0.46). This level of elasticity corresponds, within our ideal-typical world, to an intermediate position between socialism and classical or "new capitalism 1." Countries with the highest elasticities, which are Nordic countries in the years after 2000 and Italy in 1998 and 2000, have values above 0.7 and are thus closest to the classical or "new capitalism 1," and furthest from socialism.[21] The United States is close to these countries with its highest elasticity value of 0.65, reached in 1997, and its most recent 2013 elasticity at 0.64, just slightly below the previous peak.

TABLE 10-2.

Regression results: elasticity of transmission and capital share
Dependent variable: elasticity

	Pooled regressions		Country fixed effects (unbalanced panel)	
	1	2	3	4
Capital share	2.95	5.81	2.68	4.99
	(0.00)	(0.00)	(0.00)	(0.00)
Squared capital share		−20.69		−15.81
		(0.01)		(0.03)
Time	0.005	0.004	0.004	0.004
	(0.00)	(0.00)	(0.00)	(0.00)
Constant	−9.19	−8.45	−7.84	−7.17
	(0.00)	(0.00)	(0.00)	(0.00)
Adjusted (or within) R^2	0.41	0.43	0.43	0.45
(F-value)	(48)	(36)	(45)	(32)
Number of observations	138	138	138	138
Number of countries			17	17

Note: *p*-values between parentheses. *Time* is measured by the year when the survey was conducted (see Annex 2).

How much Gini will increase will depend not only on the elasticity but also on other parameters like Gini of labor and capital income and the correlation ratio for labor (R_l). Yet these parameters, and especially Ginis for labor and capital income, do not differ greatly between the countries, and we can make an easy approximation: The average Gini for labor income in our sample is 0.5 and the average Gini for capital income is 0.9. Taking these values and the average correlation ratio for labor gives us an estimated increase of 0.16 Gini point for each point increase in the capital share (see Table 10-3). A 5 percent increase in U.S. capital share (without any change in the underlying distribution of assets), as reported by Karabarbounis and Neiman[22] for the period 1975–2012, may be then expected to be associated with an approximately 0.8 Gini point increase in personal inequality.

TABLE 10-3.

Elasticity of transmission of rising share of capital income into personal income inequality

Economic system	Elasticity	Gini change
"New capitalism 1" (with $G_c > G_l$)	Around 1	$G_c - G_l$
Classical capitalism	<1	$R_c G_c - R_l G_l$
"New capitalism 2" (with $G_c = C_l$)*	1	0
Rich countries today	0.46	$R_c G_c - R_l G_l = (0.51)(0.9) -$ $(0.6)(0.5) = 0.16$*
Socialism	Around 0	Around 0 or negative **

* The mean Rc in the period after 2000 is 0.51; I also take the average values for other variables.
** Since Gini of labor income is supposed to be positive ($G_l > G_c = 0$).

Policy Implications

The implication of this analysis is that the way the rising share of capital income gets transmitted into greater interpersonal inequality varies between different social systems as a function of the underlying asset distribution. We are used to implicitly making the assumption that capital incomes are very concentrated and that the association between being capital-rich and overall-income-rich is very close. Both of these assumptions are reasonable given the empirical evidence. Indeed, as we see in the ideal-typical world of new capitalism, the increase in s_c almost directly translates into a higher Gini (because Gini of capital income is much greater than Gini of labor income). In classical capitalism, this is also true once the share of capitalists becomes sufficiently high. But in a socialist world, rising s_c does not imply rising interpersonal Gini; in effect, given our assumption of equal per capita distribution of capital assets, it implies a reduction in income inequality. Similarly, in "new capitalism 2," where every individual receives an equal share of his or her income from asset ownership, a rising capital share does not affect interpersonal income distribution.

This carries, I think, clear lessons for the rich societies in particular. The definition of rich societies is that they have high K/Y (β) ratios. As currently advanced societies become even richer, the $r > g$ dynamic will lead to rising beta and alpha. One way to ensure that this does not spill out into increased income inequality is through taxation, as advocated by Piketty, but another way—perhaps a more promising one or at least complementary— is to reduce the concentration of ownership of capital and thus of income from capital.

In the framework discussed here, reduced G_c will also reduce the association between (high) capital income and (high) overall incomes. Thus, both G_c and R_c would be reduced and an increase in capital share will have a small or even a minimal effect on personal income distribution. Ultimately, if $G_c = G_l$, it may have no effect at all on overall income Gini.

In turn, this means that much greater attention should be paid to policies that would redistribute ownership of capital and make it less concentrated. In principle, there are two kinds of such policies.

One would be giving greater importance to Employee Stock Ownership Plans and similar plans that would give a capital stake to workers who currently have none. A well-known Swedish trade union plan, for example, whereby companies would issue special shares to go into a fund that would support workers' pensions, was recently "resuscitated."[23] This approach, however, runs into the well-known problem of nondiversification of risk, where individuals' income depends entirely on working in a given company. This is indeed the case for most people today who have only labor incomes, so having both labor and capital income coming from the same company, it could be argued, does not expose them to more risk than they presently experience. While this may be true, it begs the question of why such pro-labor ownership would be introduced if it does not manifestly improve the situation of those who currently hold no capital assets. It therefore seems to me that this approach, while valuable, runs quickly into some limits.

A more promising approach may be to focus on wider share ownership divorced from one's workplace. This could be done through various incentives that would encourage small shareholdings, and penalize heavy concentration of assets. Indeed, Piketty's suggestion of a progressive wealth tax could be combined with implicit and explicit subsidies to those who hold small amounts of wealth.[24]

In rich societies whose capital / output ratio will tend to rise, the share of capital income in net income may be expected to go up as well.[25] If so, efforts should be directed toward ensuring that this inevitable upward movement in the K / Y ratio does not produce unsustainable levels of income inequality. A way to achieve this is to equalize as much as possible individuals' positions at the predistribution stage—or to put it in terms introduced in this paper, to move away from "new capitalism 1," which is in many ways similar to the actually existing capitalism today, and get closer to "new capitalism 2." This involves primarily lesser concentration of capital assets, but also (a topic that I did not discuss here) more equal access to education and deconcentration of the returns to skills.

Annex 1. Derivation of the Transmission Function in the Case of Classical Capitalism (with Two Nonoverlapping Income Classes)

$$s_c\left(p_w + p_k G_c - R_c G_c\right) = -s_l\left(-p_k + p_w G_l - R_l G_l\right)$$

$$s_c\left(p_w + p_k G_c - R_c G_c\right) = -\left(1 - s_c\right)\left(-p_k + p_w G_l - R_l G_l\right)$$

$$s_c\left(p_w + p_k G_c - R_c G_c\right) = -\left(1 - s_c\right)\left(A\right)$$

$$s_c\left(p_w + p_k G_c - R_c G_c - A\right) = -A$$

$$-s_c R_c G_c = -s_c\left(p_w + p_k G_c - A\right) - A$$

$$s_c R_c G_c = s_c\left(p_w + p_k G_c - A\right) + A$$

$$R_c G_c = \left(p_w + p_k G_c - A\right) + \frac{A}{s_c}$$

$$R_c = \left(\frac{p_w - A}{G_c} + p_k\right) + \frac{A}{s_c G_c}$$

$$\frac{dR_c}{ds_c} = -\frac{A}{s_c}\frac{1}{G_c^2} > 0$$

because $A = -p_k + p_w G_l - R_l G_l = -(1 - p_w) + p_w G_l - R_l G_l = p_w(1 + G_l) - 1 - R_l G_l$ will tend to be negative. In one extreme case, when $p_k \rightarrow 1$, this would be clearly the case. In the other extreme case, when $p_k \rightarrow 0$, $A = G_l(1 - R_l) \rightarrow 0$

This last case is clearly irrelevant because it implies that there are no capitalists at all. But for all sensible situations where $0 < p_k < 1$, $A < 0$.

The second derivative is

$$\frac{d^2 R_c}{ds_c^2} = \frac{2A}{s_c} \frac{1}{G_c^3} < 0$$

All symbols are as explained in the text.

Annex 2. List of Luxembourg Income Study Surveys Used

Country	Years
Australia	1981 1985 1989 1995 2001 2003 2006 2010
Belgium	1985 1988 1992 1995 1997 2000
Canada	1971 1975 1981 1987 1991 1994 1997 1998 2000 2004 2007 2010
Switzerland	1982 1992 2000 2002 2005
Germany	1973 1978 1984 1989 1994 2000 2004 2007 2010
Denmark	1987 1992 1995 2000 2004 2007 2010
Spain	1980 1985 1990 1995 2000 2004 2007 2010 2013
Finland	1987 1991 1995 2000 2004 2007 2010
France	1978 1984 1989 1994 2000 2005 2010
Great Britain	1969 1974 1979 1986 1991 1994 1999 2004 2007 2010
Greece	1995 2000 2004 2007 2010
Ireland	1987 1994 1995 1996 2000 2004 2007 2010
Italy	1986 1987 1989 1991 1993 1995 1998 2000 2004 2008 2010
Netherlands	1983 1987 1990 1993 1999 2004 2007 2010
Norway	1979 1986 1991 1995 2000 2004 2007 2010
Sweden	1967 1975 1981 1987 1992 1995 2000 2005
United States	1974 1979 1988 1991 1994 1997 2000 2004 2007 2010 2013

ELEVEN

Global Inequality

CHRISTOPH LAKNER

In *C21* Thomas Piketty looks at inequality within developed countries. But with increased globalization, another way to think about inequality is in terms of what it looks like across countries and across people around the world. In this chapter, Christoph Lakner shows that we have been living through a period of falling global inequality. He measures inequality across people around the globe and finds that in the 2000s, for the first time since the Industrial Revolution, global inequality fell. There are parallels to what Piketty found within countries: After pooling all the individuals around the world for whom he has data, Lakner finds that incomes grew the most for individuals within the global top 1 percent. While within-country inequality increased in population-weighted terms, for the average developing country the rise in inequality slowed in the second half of the 2000s. Lakner notes that this analysis is constrained by the data available, which likely misses top incomes, and points to the need for consistency in data across countries in order to understand the path of inequality around the world.

This chapter aims to complement Thomas Piketty's analysis in *Capital in the Twenty-First Century* by offering a twofold global perspective on inequality.[1] First, I review the trends in global inequality, defined as the inequality among all persons in the world regardless of their country of residence. Piketty's analysis, like most perspectives on inequality, concentrates on inequality among individuals *within* a country. Adopting a global (or cosmopolitan) perspective on inequality sheds light on another aspect of the world we live in. Although there exists no world government, international organizations play an increasing role, and the cosmopolitan view is the only one consistent with their mandates. Globalization has coincided with rapid growth in some of the poorest countries and with increasing inequality in many of these same countries. Global inequality captures the overall effect of these forces on persons, irrespective of where they might be living.

Second, I summarize the developments in within-country inequality in the developing world. This flows naturally from an analysis of the global income distribution, which can be broken up into differences between and within countries. An analysis of global inequality needs to separate the recognition of inequality from the capacity to reduce it, which largely remains at the country level.[2] *C21* documents a stark rise in inequality within developed economies in North America and Western Europe. Emerging economies do not feature prominently in the empirical work nor do they have an explicit role in Piketty's model. Milanovic argues that in Piketty's model, developed countries today are what developing economies will look like in the future.[3] China, for example, today is a wealth-young economy similar to the United States in the nineteenth century, but given China's fast demographic transition, it may be quite similar to today's France in fifty years. So the transition path is very much the same, just at a much faster pace.

Furthermore, Milanovic notes that emerging economies also affect *C21*'s inequality $r > g$.[4] On the one hand, given their lower capital stock, emerging markets continue to offer higher returns, pushing up r, which Piketty recognizes as one of the mechanisms behind the apparent stability in r. On the other hand, their higher growth rates push up g, thus delaying the point at which $r > g$ materializes.

Although Piketty's model deals almost exclusively with developed Western nations, this has not stopped the book from achieving a global appeal. The book has been widely translated, including into Chinese, Japanese, and Korean, and reported in the local press.[5] More generally, the concern with inequality goes beyond the developed countries. In a survey of fifteen developing countries, 77 percent of policy makers recognize that the current level of inequality threatens long-term development, while only 7 percent see inequality as conducive to long-term development.[6] Similarly, in a survey of more than 500 policy makers in Asia, 70 percent suggest that the concern with income inequality increased in the last ten years, while just over half disagreed that higher income inequality is acceptable as long as poverty is falling.[7]

A word of caution is needed right from the beginning. Expanding the analysis to a global level faces formidable data constraints. Due to the unavailability of administrative data for developing countries, the analysis in this essay will use household surveys. It is well known that household surveys do a poor job at capturing top incomes, and there is no reason this issue should be any less severe in developing countries.

Furthermore, as I will discuss in more detail below, household surveys in poor countries tend to use consumption expenditures—not income—which understates living standards at the top and thus understates levels (and possibly also trends) of inequality. Finally, those emerging economies that use income surveys typically do not capture capital incomes well, and information on wealth—the very topic of *C21*—is practically nonexistent. Paraphrasing Atkinson and Bourguignon, it is important to be very clear about what the data can and cannot say, while at the same time not rejecting all evidence on the grounds of imperfect measurement.[8]

The available evidence suggests that the Gini index of the global distribution of income has fallen for the first time since the Industrial Revolution, a development that is likely to continue. This decline was driven by falling inequality between countries, which means that average incomes converged across countries. This is likely to continue leading to further declines in global inequality. But this reduction was counteracted by an increase in (population-weighted) within-country inequality, such that the average person lived in a country where inequality was increasing. Looking at only developing countries, average national inequality increased during the 1980s and the 1990s, whereas it declined in the 2000s. This recent fall was driven by Latin America, while China appears to have plateaued. The changes in global and within-country inequality coincided with rapid globalization since the late 1980s, enabled by technological change. It seems that globalization has had important distributional effects, within countries and globally, and between skilled and unskilled labor, as well as between capital and labor.

This essay is structured in six main sections. I begin with describing the global distribution and trends in global inequality, drawing mostly on Lakner and Milanovic.[9] The second section moves from global inequality to inequality within countries, especially within developing countries. In the third section I discuss the role of globalization and technology in explaining some of these patterns.[10] Policy implications are presented in the fourth section. In the fifth section I offer some predictions on the likely future direction of global inequality. The sixth section outlines an agenda for future research on inequality in developing countries. I finish with a brief conclusion.

The Global Distribution and Trends in Global Inequality

The analysis of the global distribution presented in this essay is based on joint research with Branko Milanovic.[11] In our research we were interested in measuring the inequality of disposable income among all people in the world. Income is measured at the household level, and every household member is assigned an equal share. Incomes are compared across countries using purchasing power parity, or PPP, exchange rates to account for differences in price levels. Our data are based on household surveys that began to become widely available in the developing world only in the late 1980s. Therefore, our analysis begins in 1988, a much shorter time span than *C21* is considering.

Given our data sources, we need to make two further approximations: First, because some data come in grouped form (notably China), we use ten decile groups for every country-year.[12] That is, every individual is assigned the average income of her decile (in the within-country distribution). Second, because income is difficult to measure in an economy where own-consumption is widespread, developing countries tend to use consumption expenditure instead of income.[13] While this is a serious issue, as Anand and Segal write, "one simply has to live with the noncomparability" because "[t]here is no reliable way to infer an income distribution from an expenditure distribution."[14]

An important caveat is that we are likely to underestimate top incomes for a number of distinct reasons. First, we use household surveys, which do a poor job of capturing the richest households.[15] Second, even if the survey manages to interview the richest households, their income still may be understated. In particular, household surveys in developing countries often fail to capture entrepreneurial and capital incomes, which remain the main sources of incomes of the rich in developing countries, according to the few available data sources.[16] Third, consumption surveys—which are used in most developing countries outside Latin America—understate true living standards at the top because the rich save a higher proportion of their income than the poor do. Actual consumption expenditures at the top may also be underestimated because expenditure surveys poorly capture spending on durables.[17]

This suggests that household surveys are likely to underestimate the *level* of inequality. Yet if top incomes increase faster than the rest, then the surveys also would underestimate the *trend* in inequality. There is some suggestive evidence pointing in that direction. First, while the evidence from administrative data remains very limited, in some of the available countries (for example, Colombia and Malaysia) top income shares are rising, contrary to household-survey-based inequality measures.[18] Second, much has been written about the declining labor shares in many countries around the world.[19] In China, for instance, the labor share was falling at the same time that household savings recorded in national accounts were growing faster than GDP.[20] This suggests that the inequality in incomes grew faster than the inequality in consumption expenditures, which we use to estimate inequality in China. Third, a number of alternative data sources also point toward rising top incomes. In many developing regions of the world, billionaire wealth (according to the "rich list" published by Forbes magazine) increased faster than national income.[21] Between 2012 and 2015, a period of only three years, the number of billionaires in China doubled from 251 to 513.[22] Finally, account holdings leaked from a number of tax havens show considerable wealth in developing countries.[23]

According to our analysis, global inequality as measured by the Gini index has declined very slightly between 1988 and 2008. As the solid line in Figure 11-1 shows, the global Gini index fell from 72.2 percent in 1988 to 70.5 percent in 2008, a fall of almost 2 percentage points which was particularly strong since 2003. Not surprisingly, global inequality is much higher than what is found within individual countries. In 2008 the Gini index of South Africa, one of the most unequal countries, was 63 percent. The results are robust to using the same countries throughout, as shown by the dashed line in Figure 11-1.[24] But given the numerous margins of errors involved in these calculations, both sampling and non-sampling (for instance, PPP exchange rates), it would be premature to claim that global inequality declined robustly.[25] Furthermore, once we attempt to impute top incomes (Figure 11-1, dotted line), global inequality has remained almost unchanged over these twenty years, although the decline in the last five years remains.[26]

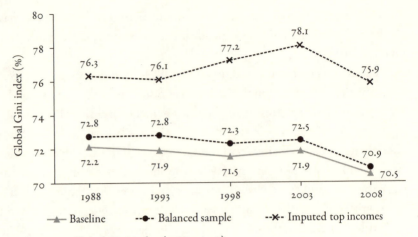

FIGURE 11-1: Global Gini index (1988–2008).

Source: Lakner and Milanovic, "Global Income Distribution: From the Fall of the Berlin Wall to the Great Recession."

Note: Solid line shows baseline results. Dashed line uses the same set of countries throughout. Dotted line imputes for missing top incomes using the household surveys-national accounts gap and a Pareto distribution, as explained in more detail in Lakner and Milanovic, "Global Income Distribution."

Taken together, this suggests that at the very least there is no evidence pointing toward *increasing* inequality at the global level. Although different methods and inequality measures disagree over the timing and size of the decline, the fall since the mid-2000s is robust across a number of sources.[27] Viewed over the long run, this is a remarkable development. Bourguignon and Morrisson find that global inequality rose steadily between 1820 and the 1990s, by some 15 percentage points.[28] Therefore, as Bourguignon and Milanovic point out, global inequality has stabilized or even declined for the first time since the Industrial Revolution.[29] Newer data for 2011 and 2013 find that the downward trend is accelerating.[30]

The decline in inequality has been driven by falling inequality between countries. Figure 11-2 decomposes global inequality into differences within and between countries. The total height of the bars shows total global inequality as measured by the GE(0) (or mean log deviation, Theil-L) inequality index.[31] The dark bars depict that part of total inequality that is due to differences within every country. The light bars capture the contribution of

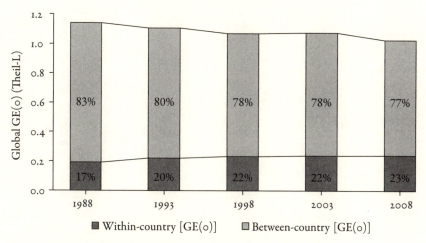

FIGURE 11-2: Country-decomposition of global inequality.

Source: Lakner and Milanovic, "Global Income Distribution."

Note: The height of the bars is the level of inequality (measured by Theil-L index). Within-country inequality captures inequality within countries, while between-country inequality consists of differences in average income across countries. The numbers in the bar chart refer to the contributions of between- and within-country differences to total inequality.

differences in mean incomes across countries. It is clear that the gap in mean incomes between countries has fallen while within-country inequality has increased to a more limited extent, although this conclusion no longer holds once you look within regions.[32] At the global level, the decline in the between-country component was clearly driven by the rapid growth in average incomes in China—the contribution of countries other than China, India, and the United States to between-country inequality almost doubled.[33] The decomposition also shows that the majority of the world's population lived in a country where inequality was increasing, which of course does not imply that inequality was going up everywhere, as I will discuss in the next section.

Between-country inequality can also explain the trend in global inequality in the long run. In the nineteenth century, global inequality was primarily due to differences within countries.[34] During the Industrial Revolution today's developed countries were pulling away from the global mean, thus increasing between-country inequality and in turn global inequality. Over the past couple of decades the gaps among countries have

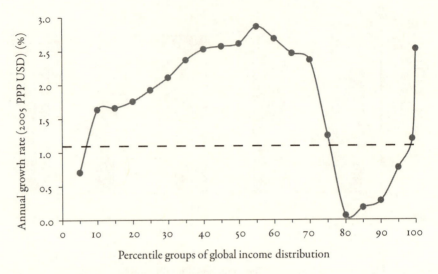

FIGURE 11-3: Global growth incidence curve, 1988–2008.

Source: Lakner and Milanovic, "Global Income Distribution."

Note: Y-axis shows annualized growth rate in average income (in 2005 PPP USD) of the fractile group. Growth incidence evaluated at ventile groups (e.g. bottom 5%); top ventile group split into top 1% and 4% between P95 and P99. The horizontal line shows the growth rate in the mean of 1.1% per year.

fallen for the first time.[35] At the same time, increasing within-country inequality has counteracted some of the fall in the between-country component. As Bourguignon and Milanovic discuss, these two developments could lead to a replacement of between-country differences with within-country differences, or an "internalization" of global inequality within countries, which would look more like the situation in the nineteenth century.[36] It is important to point out that between-country differences still account for most of global inequality (see Figure 11-2), so such a development would still take some time.

Instead of looking at the overall level of inequality, we might also be interested in how different parts of the global distribution have fared over time. Figure 11-3 shows the global growth incidence curve, which shows the growth rate of different percentile groups along the distribution.[37] This figure captures three developments in the global distribution: First, the rapid growth in China, especially in the upper parts of its distribution, creating the peak around the global median.[38] Second, the stagnation of incomes in the bottom parts of the rich countries, around the 85th global percentile. Third, the rapid growth of the very rich, giving rise to the second peak at the top of the global distribution. This seems to resemble the narrative on the distributional effects of globalization and technological change, whereby lower-paid workers in rich countries are being squeezed, the (urban) Chinese benefit from export-led growth, and the very top in rich countries have seen their income shares rise. This will be discussed in more detail below.

From the evidence presented thus far, the conclusion has been that global inequality on the whole has stopped increasing and might even have fallen while the gains were highest around the global median and the very top of the distribution. But it is important to bear in mind that this assessment has been based on comparing relative gains. The Gini index remains unchanged when all incomes grow at the same rate (or when Figure 11-3 is a flat line). But this implies very different absolute gains precisely because the underlying global distribution is so unequal. Although the growth rates of the global median and the top 1 percent are roughly similar, the former added $400 (2005 PPP) over this twenty-year period, compared with $25,000 (2005 PPP) for the latter (the initial average per capita incomes were $600 and $39,000, respectively). Put differently, the top 5 percent of the world's population received 44 percent of the increase in global income over this period. Therefore, while standard measures of inequality show a small decline between 1988 and 2008, absolute gaps between the rich and poor increased strongly.[39]

Within-Country Inequality around the World

The analysis so far has treated the entire world as a single unit. By contrast, most studies of inequality focus on within-country inequality, which remains the level at which most policies to address inequality operate. There is another reason to emphasize within-country inequality: Some commentators have used the evidence on falling global inequality to dismiss concerns about rising within-country inequality, such as in the United States. However, countries remain the relevant level for most concerns over inequality; in fact, studies show that well-being can be affected by very localized inequality.[40]

As the country decomposition in Figure 11-2 showed, between 1988 and 2008 the majority of the world's population lived in a country where inequality was increasing. In such an analysis every country is weighted by its population, so this conclusion does not imply that inequality increased in the average country. It is important to clarify this because trends can be different whether or not population weights are used. I will briefly review the trends in within-country inequality for all countries in the world, before discussing the trends in Latin America, East Asia, and sub-Saharan Africa in more detail. At the end, I present the most recent numbers on the developments since the onset of the Great Recession. Throughout this section, I concentrate on within-country inequality (typically measured by the Gini index) without using population weights. I will draw mostly on the reviews by Alvaredo and Gasparini and Morelli et al., as well as new up-to-date calculations based on data from the World Bank.[41]

In the *average developing country,* national inequality increased during the 1980s and 1990s and declined in the 2000s (largely driven by countries in Latin America). By contrast, the *average person* in the developing world (thus using population weights) lived in a country with steadily increasing inequality between the mid-1980s and 2010 (driven by the surge in China and more recently India). Despite the recent fall, inequality remains at a higher level than during the 1980s, and is substantially greater in the developing than the developed world. The overwhelming majority of developed countries experienced increasing inequality since the 1970s.

The decline in average inequality among developing countries in the 2000s was largely driven by the encouraging developments in Latin America, which have been widely documented.[42] This can be explained by a large number of factors, which certainly include more stable macroeconomics, the growth of low-skilled wages and purposive policy intervention more generally, such as conditional cash transfers, often made possible through booming commodity revenues.[43] But to avoid painting an overly optimistic picture of inequality in Latin America, two additional facts need to be borne in mind. First, inequality followed an inverse-U shape, such that the fall in the 2000s came after a prolonged increase during the 1980s and 1990s. By 2012 the average Gini index had returned to the level during the early 1980s, so viewed from this long-run perspective progress has been limited.[44] Second, even after the strong decline, Latin America remains one of the most unequal regions in the world (the other being sub-Saharan Africa).

East Asia shows a different pattern than Latin America, with inequality increasing during the 2000s on average, although with a lot of heterogeneity at the country level. Inequality increased in the two most populous countries in the region, China and Indonesia, but at different times. In China inequality surged in the 1990s but stabilized in the 2000s, whereas inequality increased in Indonesia during the 2000s. During the 1980s, South Korea and Taiwan managed the structural transformation toward becoming industrialized economies without major increases in inequality.[45] In contrast, Chinese inequality increased strongly during its transition, not dissimilar to the sharp rise in inequality in many Eastern European countries after the fall of the Berlin Wall.[46] Although data remain seriously limited, the available sources suggest a stabilization of inequality in China since the early to mid- 2000s, so the peak might have been reached.[47] Again, there are parallels with Eastern Europe, where inequality has been declining lately.

Data availability presents challenges in many developing countries, but it poses particular problems in sub-Saharan Africa. Over the past two decades, data availability and quality have improved drastically, yet researchers are invariably constrained when looking at long-term trends. Levels of inequality are high in the region, especially in the southern countries. Seven of the ten most unequal countries in the world are in Africa.[48] This is remarkable given that all other high-inequality countries use income surveys whereas sub-Saharan Africa uses expenditure surveys, which tend to produce lower levels of inequality. Furthermore, inequality in the region is high given its relatively widely shared land ownership.[49] Looking at trends, a set of sub-Saharan African countries with at least two strictly comparable and recent surveys (mostly in the 2000s) is split evenly into increasing and decreasing inequality.[50] Countries with increasing inequality are slightly larger, so around 57 percent of the population live in a country where inequality rose.

The levels and trends in within-country inequality reviewed thus far have covered a range of different time periods. This section ends by looking at the most recent past, which spans the Great Recession of 2007–2009. This is a rather special period, so any change in trend needs to be interpreted with caution. Figure 11-4 plots for every country the Gini coefficient around

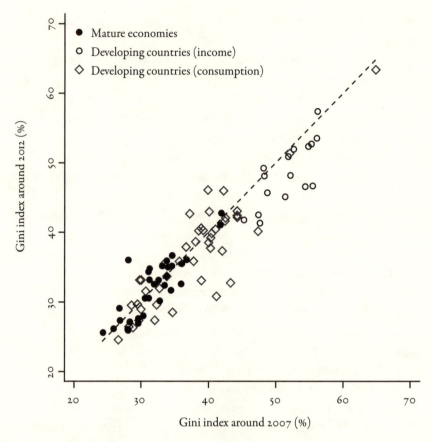

FIGURE 11-4: Gini index during the Great Recession.

Sources: "Indonesia's Rising Divide: Why Inequality Is Rising, Why It Matters and What Can Be Done," World Bank Working Paper 106070 (2016); "ECAPOV: Ex-post Harmonized Dataset Created by ECA Team for Statistical Development. Countries: Romania / 2008, Romania / 2013. As of April, 27 2016," World Bank (2016); "PovcalNet: the On-Line Tool for Poverty Measurement Developed by the Development Research Group," http://iresearch.worldbank.org/PovcalNet.

Note: Showing Gini indices around 2007 and around 2012 for 93 countries for which comparable surveys exist in both years ("Global Database of Shared Prosperity," World Bank Brief, October 6, 2015, http://www.worldbank.org/en/topic/poverty /brief/global-database-of-shared-prosperity). Initial year: 2003–2011; final year: 2009–2014; duration: 3–8 years, 5 years on average. Countries along the dashed line experienced no change in inequality. For countries below (above) the line, inequality fell (rose).

2012 against the Gini around 2007. Only countries with two comparable surveys in these years are included. A majority of countries appear to lie below the line, suggesting falling inequality. On average, the Gini index declined by approximately 1 percentage point from 38.1 to 37.1. Two-thirds of the countries (59 of the 93 countries included) experienced falling inequality. The moderation in the inequality trends comes from both sides: Inequality seems to have plateaued in China and the developed countries, which are both regions where previously inequality increased strongly.[51] In contrast, Latin America has seen a stagnation in inequality trends in recent years after the strong decline earlier.[52]

What does this mean for global inequality? The decline in inequality observed in Figure 11-4 was smaller for larger countries. Hence, the population-weighted Gini index fell only marginally from 39.4 in 2007 to 39.2 in 2012. Therefore, the within-country component of global inequality remained roughly stable.[53] At the same time, average incomes continued to grow faster in poorer countries, so the forces of economic convergence remained active. In sum, this suggests that global inequality continued to fall after 2008, which is confirmed by the 2011 results presented by Milanovic.[54]

The Role of Globalization and Technology

These changes in global inequality and within-country inequality around the world coincided with a period of rapid globalization, defined here loosely as an increase in international trade and increased movement of capital and people, as well as technological change, which in turn enabled much of the increased global integration and geographic spread of production processes. The evidence presented above is consistent with the following story line: China and other parts of Asia grew rapidly over this period, taking advantage of increased global integration and reducing between-country inequality. At the same time, within-country inequality increased in both developed and developing countries. Taken together, the winners of globalization appear to have been the middle and upper classes in China while the lower parts of the distributions in rich countries lagged behind. (See Figure 11-3.)

The remainder of this section will sketch a model of technological change that tries to explain some of these shifts—between skilled and unskilled labor and between labor and capital. Establishing a strict causal relationship between globalization or technological change and inequality, however, remains elusive, because income distributions are the outcome of a multitude of factors. Therefore, my discussion is perhaps best taken as "well-informed speculation."[55] At a basic level, the main takeaways are that the effects of trade on income distributions are more complicated than a simple Stolper-Samuelson effect, and while globalization has brought huge benefits, some have benefited more than others.[56]

In a recent paper, Basu distinguishes between two kinds of technical change—labor-saving and labor-linking.[57] The category of labor-saving technologies also includes skill-biased technical change as a result of which the demand for skilled labor was growing faster than the supply. This increased the premium for educated workers and thus the inequality within labor incomes, as in the original Tinbergen model.[58] Yet one also needs to recognize the role of capital, which gets to the core of the labor-saving technology argument. As Atkinson and Bourguignon argue, capital could be complementary to high-skilled labor, but a substitute for low-skilled labor.[59] This is hardly a new idea—Meade argued that automation would increase inequality.[60]

Labor-linking technological change captures how labor links up with demand in faraway places. This can happen through a number of channels, such as trade, outsourcing, or foreign direct investment. Maskin argues that advances in communication technology have led to an internationalization of the production process, such that a company can today employ workers on the opposite side of the world, thus creating a global labor market.[61] Labor-linking technological change has affected different parts of the distribution in different ways. In developed countries, low-skilled workers at the bottom of the wage distribution have been hurt by competition from abroad, with their "wages being set in Beijing," to paraphrase the title of Freeman's paper.[62] At the same time, this technological progress increased the global reach of the highest-paid individuals, thus raising the wages of the superstars in a winner-takes-all market.[63] As Bourguignon points out, the same is happening in developing countries, where Indian cricket stars or Chinese billionaires are profiting from their global reach.[64] Furthermore, some of the employees in developing countries who were serving customers in rich countries were demanding wages far above local rates, so it might appear that "top wages are being set in New York."[65]

What does this all mean for inequality in poor and rich countries? Low-skilled workers in rich countries are being squeezed by technological change that gets rid of their jobs and competition of lower-paid workers from abroad. While low- and middle-skilled workers in poor countries in Asia have seen their wages rise, further increases will be constrained by the threat of capital substitution. One case in point: The world's largest contract manufacturer, Foxconn Technology Group, is planning to add one million robots in the near future.[66] Top incomes in *both* rich and poor countries are benefiting in two ways. First, their wages are increasing with the size of the global market. Their incomes are being equalized due to the international tradability of high-skilled labor.[67] It appears this scale effect is particularly important for top incomes in poor countries where the general wage level is much lower. Second, top income recipients in both rich and poor countries own the capital, and the capital share has been rising over this period of global technological change.[68]

In summary, although the debate is often presented as a conflict between unskilled labor in poor and rich countries, or between skilled and unskilled labor within either set of countries, it is as much a conflict between shareholders and workers. It may "be that capital has been the main beneficiary of the globalization of trade and the resulting acceleration in economic growth . . . over the last two decades."[69]

Policy Implications

When discussing policy proposals, it is important to stress that it is not desirable to undo globalization. As Bourguignon points out, it is not clear that it would make people in rich countries better off, because higher trade barriers would increase prices and thus reduce their purchasing power.[70] But more importantly, a retrenchment may be bad for the poorest people on this planet. A globally integrated economy with easier movement of capital and labor complicates policy making because it points toward a race to the bottom, a policy problem that needs to be taken seriously. Yet it is also clear that countries are not powerless and that policy making at the country level matters. As I discussed above, inequality did not increase everywhere, although all countries were subject to the same technological change, at least to a first approximation. Furthermore, despite a global market for high-skilled workers, the salaries of the best-paid American chief executives are approximately four times the salaries of their German counterparts.[71]

The burgeoning literature on (global) inequality is not short of policy proposals to address inequality. Instead of offering a comprehensive review, I will outline a few that have received relatively little attention in the development literature. Developing economies have underdeveloped fiscal policies that largely rely on indirect taxes and withholding on formal-sector wages. According to Atkinson and Bourguignon, "no advanced economy achieved a low level of inequality . . . with a low level of social spending, regardless of how well that country performed on other dimensions that matter for poverty, notably employment."[72] Social spending in developing countries is constrained by low fiscal revenues. While state capacity continues to be limited in the poorest countries, middle-income or emerging countries are increasingly able to expand revenues. In these countries, households have bank accounts and credit cards, which create information flows that can be exploited for the purposes of taxation using new technologies. This is particularly true of Asia, where tax systems do not score highly on progressivity.[73] Across the region, effective progressivity is limited by very high tax thresholds, such that the highest rates apply to practically nobody.[74]

The taxation of capital incomes is another aspect I would like to highlight. First, capital incomes are typically taxed at lower rates than labor incomes (not only in developing countries), which creates horizontal inequity.[75] That is, individuals with the same incomes and assets face different tax rates.[76] Second, the revenue raised from property taxes is negligible, although they can be a relatively equitable, efficient, and implementable source of revenues.[77] Third, the issue of tax havens needs to be addressed. I am writing this at a time when the first details of the so-called Panama Papers are emerging, implicating numerous heads of state in using offshore accounts. Cracking down on tax havens is possible, but it requires coordination between countries—including rich countries, which account for the bulk of haven deposits.[78] Developing countries lose a significant share of their wealth to tax havens: Haven deposits account for 20 to 30 percent of financial assets in many African or Latin American countries.[79] Developing countries lose around $100 billion in corporate tax revenues to tax havens annually.[80]

Welfare states are coming under pressure in a global economy, though, so achieving redistributory objectives only through the fiscal system may not be feasible.[81] Instead, the distribution of market (or pre-fiscal) income also requires attention. Milanovic notes that while the levels of inequality in disposable income are similar between Western Europe and the advanced East Asian economies (Japan, South Korea, and Taiwan), the latter have much smaller redistribution through the fiscal system because they start from a less unequal distribution of market income. It is also striking that the East Asian countries that managed to create "growth with equity" during trade liberalization started from a relatively egalitarian land distribution and widespread basic education.[82] Market income is determined by an individual's endowments with assets (here defined as labor and capital) and the returns to these assets (wages and rents), which I will discuss in turn.

Latin America, which stands out as the region that managed to reduce inequality, has extensively used conditional cash transfers that are redistributive and are designed to build human capital through their conditionality.[83] Education has been a core part of the mainstream development economics toolkit; capital endowments have not received much attention. In the simple globalization model I outlined above, labor-saving technologies can have adverse distributional consequences precisely because capital is unequally distributed. If Bourguignon is right that capital has been a major beneficiary of globalization, then a more equal capital distribution would reduce some of globalization's adverse consequences.[84]

Policy proposals in this area fall into three areas: First, proposals that allow workers (or citizens more generally) to receive some of the benefits of automation, through either a profit-sharing arrangement or a sovereign wealth fund.[85] Second, policies that enable the poor and middle-class to build up financial assets, which includes the formalization of ownership titles in developing countries. Third, and most important, taxes on inheritance and *inter vivos* transfers, which play almost no role in current fiscal revenues. Besides overcoming the injustices associated with the intergenerational transmission of advantage, capital-receipt taxes are less distortionary than other wealth taxes because they do not tax one's own effort. To directly address the issue of capital endowments, Atkinson proposes to use some of the tax revenues to fund a minimum inheritance for every young adult independent of their family background.[86]

Affecting the returns to these endowments is more difficult, as returns are the direct result of the market process. But it is important to recognize that governments interfere in the market process in a number of ways, two of which I want to mention in this context. First, governments directly affect the development of new technologies—for example, through tax breaks for research and development or direct grants to universities and other research institutions.[87] Therefore, they can influence the direction of technological change, such as the use of labor-saving technologies and the relative returns of skilled and unskilled labor and capital. Second, the rapid development of some East Asian countries, such as South Korea, has often been explained by successful industrial policy. While this has not worked in many countries, where it enriched a small elite, it needs to remain part of the policy toolkit, especially in the poorest countries.[88] Freund summarizes the key elements of successful industrial policy, which include competition among multiple domestic firms and strict monitoring of export performance.[89]

The Future Direction of Global Inequality

Given that *C21* deals with long-run distributional forces, it is fitting to speculate about the long-run evolution of global inequality. According to Milanovic, the future trend for global inequality depends on three forces: Differences in mean income *across* countries (between-country inequality); differences in income *within* countries (within-country inequality); and differentials in population growth rates.[90] Any forecast has a significant margin of error, but population growth rates are substantially more accurate than the other two. Changing population patterns will put an upward pressure on global inequality, because the population in the poorest countries, notably in Africa, is growing faster than in the rest of the world.[91] Even though the most recent data on within-country inequality appears to show that it has reached a plateau, especially in the largest countries, such as China, it would be premature to interpret this as a change in trend. This is because the period straddles the Great Recession and as always there exist measurement issues. Milanovic proposes a theory of Kuznets waves, which captures the up and down of within-country inequality in the long run.[92] The bottom line is that within-country inequality is not immutable, but depends on deliberate policy choices, and while the Great Recession and globalization place some constraints, domestic policy remains powerful.

The largest changes to global inequality are likely to come from changes in the between-country component. Despite its decline, between-country inequality remains the dominant source of global inequality. Furthermore, in cross-country data, changes in country means tend to be larger than changes in within-country distributions.[93] In the long run, the powerful forces of economic convergence—faster growth in poorer countries—are likely to continue.[94] But there are at least three reasons to be cautious. First, growth in sub-Saharan Africa is volatile and has benefited from favorable terms of trade, without structural reform.[95] Second, growth outside China, especially in India, will become much more important for the continued reduction of global inequality.[96] Third, climate change places considerable uncertainty on any such growth projection.

Regarding the overall level of global inequality, Hellebrandt and Mauro predict a decrease in the global Gini of almost 4 percentage points by 2035, which is substantial but leaves global inequality at a high level.[97] Their results also show that growth (in GDP per capita proxying for survey incomes) will be crucial: In a scenario where poor countries grow slower than the baseline projections, the Gini index declines only by 1 percentage point. In contrast, overturning the decline in global inequality would require an increase of around 6 percentage points in within-country inequality in all countries, which is substantial.[98]

Research Agenda

More and better data have to be the top priority for future research on inequality in developing countries. First, good-quality data on living standards are still missing in a number of countries, especially in the Middle East, the African continent, the Caribbean, and the Pacific. Recently the World Bank committed to support countries such that all poor countries have a survey at least every three years.[99] Second, in middle-income countries, where agriculture and own-consumption are becoming less important, more attention ought to be paid to income data as opposed to consumption expenditure. Levels and trends in inequality can be different if they are measured in terms of income or consumption expenditure, especially if the growth has been concentrated at the top where expenditure might be a poor measure.[100] Third, very little is known about capital incomes in developing countries because many income surveys do not even attempt to collect this information.

Finally, and closely related, the measurement of top incomes needs to be improved in developing countries. The administrative records that have been used in developed countries are not available for the developing world. The most innovative approaches to inequality measurement combine income information from administrative records with household surveys for other questions.[101] Broad-based income taxes will generate these administrative records, similar to Piketty's proposal for introducing an even very modest wealth tax. But more needs to be done to exploit those opportunities. The World Bank and other international organizations, for example, often provide loans and technical assistance to support tax reforms in developing countries, so it would be relatively easy to require governments to release (suitably anonymized) distributional statistics to their citizens.

Armed with better data, a number of important research questions can be addressed, including some very basic ones: What is the "true" level and trend of inequality? Can the trends in the micro data and the national accounts be reconciled after accounting for capital incomes and the top of the distribution?[102] What do corporate tax data tell us about the true extent of economic concentration, and should it be a concern for competition authorities? How do capital-income dynamics compare with the more frequently analyzed dynamics of labor incomes? How does the current system of taxes and transfers affect the distribution of income? Is that fiscal system optimal? How do households in different parts of the income and skill distribution interact with the global economy—as consumers, sellers of their labor, owners of capital—and how is this different in poorer and richer countries?

Conclusion

This essay has provided a global perspective on inequality in an attempt to complement Piketty's analysis in *C21*. In contrast to the sharp increases in top incomes in Anglo-Saxon countries observed by Piketty and coauthors, inequality viewed from a global perspective appears to have stabilized or even fallen slightly, driven by convergence in average incomes across countries. After rising strongly in the 1980s and 1990s, inequality within the average developing country has fallen in the 2000s. These results are based on household surveys, which are known to underestimate top incomes, especially capital incomes. Furthermore, these surveys often use consumption expenditures, which might not capture increases in living standards at the top. Hence, although much more evidence has become available in poor countries, these results are subject to considerable uncertainty. Therefore, better data on developing countries remains a top priority to move forward the research agenda on inequality in these countries.

TWELVE

The Geographies of Capital in the Twenty-First Century: *Inequality, Political Economy, and Space*

GARETH A. JONES

Geographer Gareth Jones critiques the absence of "space" from C21, in which geography serves only as a "container for data" rather than a context for inequality and exploitation to play out. Jones discusses capital mobility and secrecy, and the international competition of cities to cater to a rootless global elite, as mechanisms by which geography enables and propagates inequality. He concludes that confronting the geography of inequality requires confronting its ideology ex ante, not ex post.

When the English translation of Piketty's *Capital in the Twenty-First Century* was published in 2014, its key message that inequality of income and wealth had increased since the early 1970s was hardly news to many economists, bankers, hedge-fund managers, or policy analysts, or to many interested social scientists, media opinion writers, think tanks, and activists.[1] Some considered inequality to be a "good thing," reflecting rewards for enterprise, and probably politically benign so long as living standards generally were rising or maintained.[2] Others had raised concerns for many years over the scale and implications of growing inequality for economic efficiency, social mobility, and democracy.[3]

Nevertheless, Piketty captured the zeitgeist and received numerous accolades as well as invitations to speak with an eclectic array of governments, international development and financial agencies, anticapitalist movements, and the popular press.[4] Inevitably, critics, including some contributors to this volume, also lined up to identify weaknesses with his analysis, especially focusing on Piketty's definition of capital,[5] embedded assumptions in his mathematical formula,[6] his lack of attention to gender and work,[7] and his "small c" conservative politics.[8] In this chapter I want to extend my earlier, limited contribution to these debates that had attempted to interrogate *C21* from the perspective of geography.[9]

My initial point of departure is how—in a book that claims to celebrate interdisciplinarity—an explicit concern with geography is largely absent. Conduct a word search for "space" and the first mention is page 246. Instead, as many others have rightly observed, Piketty offers a brilliant *longue durée* account of the distribution of incomes and wealth over time. He is able to do so, however, as Eric Sheppard noted, by relegating geography to being a container for data.[10] Piketty is explicit that, by his definition, capital refers to "national" wealth and capital—that is, the "total market value of everything owned by residents and government of a given country at a given point in time, provided that it can be traded on some market."[11]

Simply, variables are measured at the scale of the nation-state because that is how national accounts and tax records (for income, inheritance) are organized.[12] This practical decision conforms to the norms of economics, but it treats space as passive and implies that how we measure economic activity is consistent with how the economy itself is organized and operates. Consequently, Piketty's analysis of inequality is an exercise in measurement—the "basic facts," as he has claimed a number of times—which can be represented according to income deciles at the scale of nation-states and explained largely by the economic performance of those states, and irrespective of their relations with the global economy.[13]

The more substantive point, however, is that this inattentiveness to space speaks to a fundamental problem with Piketty's approach to political economy and policy. As David Soskice argues, throughout the pages of *Capital* Piketty promotes the need for a political economic analysis, yet the book is almost "devoid" of such an approach and "lacks any coherent foundations in comparative political economy" in order to explain the growth of inequality from the 1970s.[14] What Soskice calls a "parsimonious mathematical argument" (the famous $r > g$ that underpins Piketty's "central contradiction of capitalism") relies on a combination of assumptions, especially that savings are equal to investment and that savers (and not businesses) will invest despite the likelihood of low growth. As Soskice puts it, Piketty's analysis "almost completely ignores the interacting relations between politics, history and technological change," or the shift from Fordism to "weightless" economies driven by Internet and communications technologies, financial services, and consumption, in which the interests of capital firmly dictate decision making in advanced democracies, leading to the privatization of some profitable public services and to deregulation.

To this critique I would add that Piketty ignores shifts in the culture of the contemporary political economy, not least financial liberalization, which has changed the rationales by which remuneration is understood and the means by which it takes place.[15] Strangely, for an account that has courted controversy for its inclusion of property (real estate) in his definition of capital and holds progressive taxation as part of his self-proclaimed "utopian" policy correction to inequality, there is little attention, interdisciplinary or otherwise, to the complex role of finance, property, and the avoidance of taxation as drivers to contemporary inequality.

So, my argument is that an explanation of inequality in the twenty-first century requires an attention to spatial political economy. Consider the interface of the political economy and space in the following vignette that traces my actions in the sixty minutes after I decided to write this chapter. To get some inspiration I stepped into a branch of Starbucks, ordered an espresso, opened my iPad, searched Google for relevant texts on inequality, and ordered both a hard and a Kindle copy of Gabriel Zucman's *The Hidden Wealth of Nations* through Amazon.[16] A copy arrived to the Kindle app and a confirmation email pinged onto my mobile phone, which also told me that my electricity bill was due and that a friend had updated her Facebook page. I downed my coffee and made for home. I was eager to get going with Zucman's book before the kids got home. To make up time, I took a Santander Bank–sponsored "Boris Bike" to the station, swiped in using my "smart" Oyster card, caught a train to within a few hundred yards of my house, bought a loaf of bread from the bakery, and minutes later was through my front door, picking up a free "lifestyle" magazine from the mat—with pages full of articles and adverts for house refurbs, private schools, gallery exhibitions, and property for sale—and settled down on the Ikea sofa in the kitchen to start reading.

In the hour since having entered Starbucks, I had traveled less than five miles but in the process conducted transactions with a number of well-known companies, predominantly service providers, the geographies of which were highly obscure. The purchase of Zucman's book, for example, was conducted through Amazon.co.uk but the invoice would later indicate the seller to be Amazon SVS Europe, a subsidiary based in Luxembourg, even though the book itself was delivered from the fulfillment center in Swansea. So far as I can tell, the transactions described in the vignette involved companies that for tax management and regulatory purposes are registered in Luxembourg, Switzerland, the British Virgin Islands, the Cook Islands, and the Bahamas. Only a few of the companies mentioned or implied in the vignette pay much, if any, corporation tax in the United Kingdom, despite billions of dollars of sales: The exception seems to be Santander and of course the bakery.[17]

As Dani Rodrik argues, the ability of companies and owners of capital to avoid paying tax transfers the fiscal burden for public services (and debt) to labor (wages) and therefore contributes to inequality.[18] The registration of companies in low-tax jurisdictions was found by the OECD to cost the treasuries of G-20 nations as much as $240 billion annually, equivalent to 4 to 10 percent of global corporate tax revenues.[19] The trend over the past forty years has been for a significant readjustment in the distribution of economic activities and public obligations.

The aim of this chapter is to show that a political economic analysis of inequality must examine the geographies of capital. The economic geography of global capitalism for the past forty years shows that capital will seek out a spatial fix to the crises of under- / over-accumulation.[20] Fundamental to the power of capital, therefore, is its geographical mobility, to shape-shift from being something fixed to being a flow. The apotheosis of this transformation is finance capital.

Yet, as Karen Ho points out in her critique of *C21*, Piketty underplays the financialization of the economy in order to preserve the convention of capital and (versus) labor.[21] Thus, although he does describe the shift to hyper-remuneration of "supermanagers," as he calls them, and identifies this new elite with the financial sector, he does not attend to what Ho describes as the "seismic changes in the very nature and purpose of the corporation toward financial values, models, and practices."[22] In other words, *C21* avoids an analysis of what contemporary inequality tells us about the processes, including spatial processes, of capital accumulation that made this new form of extended inequality possible.

What I hope to show is that fundamental to the new political economy is the power of capital to appear on paper in locations distinct from a physical asset, or to locate in extra-legal spaces that are obscure to the purview of states and international governance protocols. The most obvious of these spaces are tax havens, but to these we can add other offshore and onshore jurisdictions, including zones, corridors, and many new science / knowledge / expo cities.[23] These spaces operate through forms of extra-legality that serve to decouple the economy from democratic politics—and to empower corporations and plutocrats whose moral obligations and fiscal responsibilities are minimized while an ability to ensure a return on capital is maximized. Spatially, extra-legality and secrecy work to enhance an uneven global economy in which, as Nils Gilman has suggested, "neoliberalism's wide-open, market-oriented rules may govern globalization, but the game gets played on a morally lumpy field."[24] To characterize this new political economy with a Piketty-like device: my proposal for a literary rapporteur for twenty-first-century capitalism would be J. G. Ballard.[25]

Capital Power: Extra-Legality, and Secrecy

Piketty is clearly and rightly angry about the capacity of high-income-and-wealth holders to extend their dominance over people in the middle and lower income deciles. But as a purely statistical relationship, we get little sense of how inequality is derived from an unequal distribution of power. As Marx pointed out, capitalism relies on social relations. His theory of class showed the ability of capital to dominate labor (wages), or what became a notion of class power. Inequality, therefore, might be measured by the relative percentages of income and capital held by deciles and quintiles, but these distributions are produced by the relative power of capital to extract value from labor.

The precise mechanisms through which capital power operates, however, changes over time and space. When Jane Austen was writing, inequality was being produced through extending and regulating laborers' workday, redistributing the commons to private property, incipient mechanization, and slavery. Since the 1970s the mechanism has been a profound pushback on the political regulation of capitalism.[26] From a geographical perspective, the contemporary global political economy has reworked its spatial dimensions such that although the nation-state is far from dead, according to Saskia Sassen, sovereignty has become decentered and territory denationalized.[27]

The contemporary political organization of space consists of ever more supranational organizations and international protocols, through which companies, trusts, funds, public-private partnerships, and civil society organizations are able to operate with what can seem like negotiated commitments to the nation-state.[28] In simple terms, the relations between capital and labor, as arranged through rules of trade, working conditions, corporate governance, and taxation, are interleaved or networked over multiple spaces. I call the resulting arrangements extra-legal spaces to capture the sense in which economic activity exists according to legal arrangements through which capital power is exerted via private rules and quasi-public agreements. Regulations, codes, and standards exist aplenty—but in terms of frameworks that prioritize private profit over public welfare or rights, and with the minimum of transparency to regulatory authorities, the media, trade unions, or even shareholders.

The first and best-known example of extra-legality is the zone, considered by Neilson to be the "paradigmatic space" for the contemporary global economy.[29] From a small handful in the 1960s, zones have proliferated in number to perhaps 4,000 by 2006, and in complexity and type from the export-processing and free-trade zone to corridors, enclaves, compounds, and new cities, employing in excess of 66 million people according to Keller Easterling.[30] Again according to Neilson, zones form a "new political topography of territory": "Exceptional forms of rule in zones tend to exist alongside domestic civil laws, opportunistic applications of international law, and diverse norms and standards promulgated by corporate actors. Zones can at once be spaces of exception and spaces saturated by competing norms and calculations."[31] Only in rare instances are zones "nonstate" spaces. Rather, they are created and operated according to what Stephen Krasner calls "hypocritical sovereignty" in which infrastructures that are often denied or unavailable beyond the zone are provided or enabled within it.[32]

But the state, although vital to the establishment of the zone, is not in command of it.[33] To Easterling, the zone is a "relaxed" form of extrastatecraft, with governance devolved to trusts or agencies often made up of the resident companies themselves, creating the possibility that decisions taken thousands of miles away in regional or global offices determine what happens in the zone with less, if any, recourse to the conditions expected by national or local polities, or even international law. Without recourse to democratic oversight, rule making and rule observance in the zone can take place according to the needs of capital. Laws and protocols on labor, environment, health, safety, and human rights, and of course taxation, can be modified or exemptions created.[34] Indeed, the zone is really governed by what Easterling calls the "dynamic systems of space, information, and power [that] generate de facto forms of polity faster than even quasi-official forms of governance can legislate them."[35]

The trick performed by the zone is to represent itself as a normative space for economic activity; that is, as a developmental space.[36] It achieves this through stressing a technocratic ethos—it is a space that works—and as a formula for what Bach summarizes as the "fantasies and aspirations of modernity."[37] Managers and marketing campaigns promote conditions in the zone as being better than in the economy generally. The factory floors are organized and clean, the workers are trained and often paid above minimum wage, and living conditions include company-provided crèches, health care, and even reasonable housing. Later-generation zones include leisure, entertainment, and high-culture institutions.[38]

But even though a zone might have the appearance of a city and be governed like a state, its modus operandi rests on secrecy and the absence of democracy. This infrastructure-rich urbanism, critics argue, is a "masquerade of freedom and openness [that] turns very easily to evasion, closure, and quarantine."[39] Free speech is monitored and forms of collective representation—especially trade unions—are prohibited, while labor, often migrant, is contracted with rights short of full citizenship, segregated in camps, and subject to long hours, toxic working conditions, and sexual predation.[40] Rules are enforced by private security, itself part of a global network that connects zones (enclaves / compounds / expo-cities / micro states), to each other and provides capital with quality control, certainty, and limits to state engagement.[41] Zones, according to Davis and Monk, are "evil paradises" that despite claims to being apolitical are quite the opposite—they are deliberately nondemocratic spaces that work hard to engineer an exceptional legal status.[42]

Under the conditions of low growth—as described by Piketty and critical to his empirical argument, especially in combination with austerity—the zone amplifies the power of capital. It provides a demarcated territory, far less messy than the nation-state, within which capital is able to "land" in ways that retain a capacity for mobility. Property is leased, buildings and machinery are rented, and services are contracted, while connectivity with suppliers, intermediaries, and markets are unencumbered by regulation and political demands. Roughly co-terminus with Piketty's observation of growing inequality from the 1970s through the measurement of "facts," thousands of zones have appeared across the world as spatial devices for the production and reproduction of inequality.

A second extra-legal space in contemporary capitalism is the offshore. However otherworldly the zone might seem to be, at one level it is a real space because the zone is located somewhere. In contrast, as Nicholas Shaxson argues, "offshore is fundamentally about being an 'elsewhere'" since offshore exists in space but only virtually in place.[43] A person, company, or investment vehicle such as a trust might be registered offshore in one of more than seventy tax havens—the quintessential offshore space—but they may have almost no relationship with that space, perhaps no more than a postal address (colloquially known as "letterboxes") that might be shared with hundreds of other individuals, companies, or trusts.

The success of offshore is almost undisputed. As Shaxson argues, "Offshore is how the world of power now works"; and John Urry even suggests that being onshore is the exception to the rule.[44] Urry's point seems to be backed up by Gabriel Zucman's careful empirical analysis, which suggests that around 55 percent of profits made abroad by U.S. corporations are recorded in just six tax havens, even though these corporations may have very limited economic relations with these locations in terms of production or sales.[45] Importantly, Zucman goes on to argue that the scale and nature of these relations with offshore tax havens is now large enough "to significantly affect measures of the inequality of wealth."[46]

As the release of the so-called Panama Papers indicates, tax minimization or evasion is not the only motive or effect of being offshore.[47] Indeed, as Gilman et al. note (and the Panama Papers seem to confirm), the offshore merges legitimate businesses with what they call "deviant globalization" such as informal or illegal trade in art, energy, environmental waste, arms,

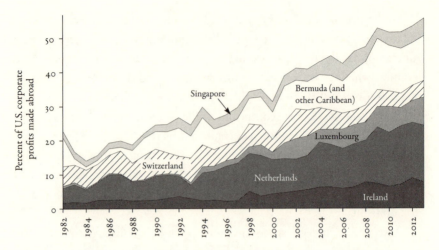

FIGURE 12-1: The share of tax havens in U.S. corporate profits made abroad. Author's computations using balance of payments data. See online Appendix.

Notes: This figure charts the share of income on U.S. direct investment abroad made in the main tax havens. In 2013, total income on U.S. direct investment abroad was about $500 billion. Seventeen percent came from the Netherlands, 8 percent from Luxembourg, etc.

drugs, people, animals, and financial crime.[48] Nevertheless, tax havens represent a particularly sharp lens through which to view the relationship of contemporary political economy with inequality as the ability of the world's largest corporations and rich individuals to organize their finances so that they are able to conduct a disproportionate amount of business with low-tax jurisdictions. (See Figure 12-1.)[49] The trend, moreover, is toward greater offshoring and the reduced capacity of the nation-state to capture taxes on profits, as well as income for high-earners. Zucman describes a tenfold increase in the percentage of corporate profits booked by U.S. corporations in tax havens from the 1980s to a figure that by the 2010s represents around 20 percent. The result is that the effective rate of tax paid by U.S. companies has fallen from 30 percent to 20 percent in around fifteen years.[50]

Offshore tax havens operate through what some observers identify as the modus operandi of the contemporary political economy—the ability of companies to keep their business affairs secret from competitors and regulators. Again, the advantages are not simply fiscal. As Zucman points out, "in the real world, tax evaders can combine countless holding entities in

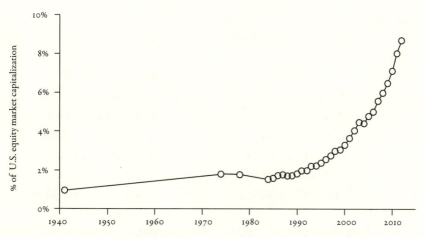

FIGURE 12-2: U.S. equities held by tax haven firms and individuals.

Source: Author's computations using U.S. Treasury international capital data. See the online appendix.

Note: In 2012, 9 percent of the U.S. listed equity capitalization was held by tax haven investors (hedge funds in the Cayman Islands, banks in Switzerland, mutual funds in Luxembourg, individuals in Monaco, etc.).

numerous havens, generating de jure ownerless assets or effectively disconnecting them from their holdings."[51] Attaining secrecy combines space and organizational complexity, which create the capacity to locate the appearance of activities in jurisdictions with limited transparency requirements and to do so in ways that are too complex for outside agents to unpick quickly or at all. Just one investment vehicle may be owned by hundreds of others, registered in numerous locations, and the principal vehicle will form just one entry in the portfolio of an investment company that may have upward of 2,000 Special Purpose Vehicles on its books. Understanding the precise composition of these vehicles and the identity of investors, which, if they use "bearer shares," for example, are virtually anonymous, is beyond the scope of a single regulatory authority.[52]

A classic device to "move" the appearance of assets and transactions offshore is inversion. In a typical example, a parent company establishes a subsidiary offshore in a location with lower tax rates and / or fewer transparency regulations. This subsidiary is then registered as the official head office of the parent company. (See Figure 12-2.) In practice this office may be no more than a shell with minimal requirements to host board meetings and no significant corporate functions performed from that site. The effect, however, is that companies and individuals can hide in plain sight, conducting substantial investments or expenditures in one location while appearing to have fewer assets recorded in that jurisdiction than is functionally the case. Business accounts and tax records significantly under-measure the wealth, revenues, and incomes that actually take place in one space and over-measure what is recorded as taking place in another. The important point here is that secrecy is enabled by the power to manipulate the spatial configuration of capital, transactions, and income, and how these are recorded.

From the perspective of secrecy, the contemporary political economy is not a simple binary of a transparent onshore and a murky offshore. Rather, as Cobham et al. argue, secrecy should be understood as a spectrum that is provided in different combinations in different locations.[53] They propose a Financial Secrecy Index to gauge the intensity of a jurisdiction's commitment to secrecy (or transparency). The most secret locations include the usual-suspect tax havens—Switzerland, Luxemburg, Hong Kong, the Cayman Islands, and Singapore—but also the United States (sixth) and Germany (eighth). (See Table 12-1.) Just as revealing, perhaps, is the finding that if the City of London were considered a separate entity from the United Kingdom, it would top the list as the single most important provider of financial secrecy worldwide (the United Kingdom is relatively transparent). (See Figure 12-3.)

The success of London in recent decades is partly attributable to its capacity to service a large number of highly skilled and well-remunerated accountants, investment advisers, and lawyers who, as Wójcik notes, have become complicit in making the geographies of global capital as opaque as possible.[54] Paradoxically, the evidence that "the City" has specialized and thrived on providing this service is public knowledge.[55] Indeed, as a U.K. Parliament Public Accounts Committee noted, four large accountancy firms employ 9,000 people in their tax management divisions and charge corporations £2 billion in fees.[56] The chair of the committee, Margaret Hodge MP, in her comments presenting the report described the activities of one company, PriceWaterhouseCoopers, as representing "nothing short of the promotion of tax avoidance on an industrial scale."

TABLE 12-1.

Top ten jurisdictions by FSI, FSI components, and other indices

Ranking by	FSI	Secrecy Score	GSW	BAMLI	CPI
1	Switzerland	Samoa	United States	Somalia	Afghanistan
2	Luxembourg	Vanuatu	United Kingdom	Afghanistan	Korea, DR
3	Hong Kong S.A.R. of China	Seychelles	Luxembourg	Iran, Islamic Rep.	Somalia
4	Cayman Islands	St. Lucia	Switzerland	Cambodia	Sudan
5	Singapore	Brunei Darussalam	Cayman Islands	Tajikistan	Myanmar
6	United States	Liberia	Germany	Iraq	Turkmenistan
7	Lebanon	Marshall Islands	Singapore	Guinea-Bissau	Uzbekistan
8	Germany	Barbados	Hong Kong S.A.R. of China	Haiti	Iraq
9	Jersey	Belize	Ireland	Eritrea	Venezuela, Rep. Bol.
10	Japan	San Marino	France	Myanmar	Burundi
Average Secrecy Score	69.0	83.4	59.3	n/a	n/a
Sum of GSW	58.9%	0.07%	80.4%	0.023%	0.014%

Note: FSI and BAMLI results for 2013, CPI results for 2012. Secrecy scores have not been calculated for any of the top 10 countries by BAMLI or by CPI.

Source: Cobham et al.

FIGURE 12-3: Wish Your Money Were Here.

A parody of a travel poster published by The Rules, an activist network that has as one of its key goals "to help spread radical and progressive memes into the mainstream." Source: AlJazeera.

The combination of moving the appearance of physical assets and transactions offshore—as is the case for many zones—and also buying the services of firms as alluded to by Margaret Hodge has profound consequences for how we must understand contemporary spatial political economy. It means, most obviously, that grasping the composition of economic activity through official tax records (which are unreliable under any circumstances) and at the scale of the nation-state is contrary to how contemporary economies actually work. The tax management divisions of London firms do not charge £2 billion per annum for companies and individuals to record transactions and assets, and accompanying tax liabilities, in the actual locations where these are undertaken. Zucman estimates, as a minimum, that offshore tax havens alone may account for around 8 percent of household financial holdings globally, although his data exclude nonfinancial wealth such as art, jewelry, and real estate, which he thinks might push the figure up to 11 percent, almost all of it avoiding tax.[57]

Audited company balance sheets are not likely to offer a more reliable and robust source of data. Balance sheets record the degree to which a company is "weightless," giving it the ability to conduct internal transfers, pay for intangible services (those that are not determined by market forces), especially intellectual property rights (trademarks, logos, or technologies) and marketing, and thereby shift net revenues and profits to specific jurisdictions.[58] Taken to its furthest extreme, a high-brand-recognition company that seems to be everywhere can appear to undertake economic activities nowhere.[59]

A good case in point is Apple Operations International. It reported a three-year net income of $30 billion, but through a complex network of affiliations and procedures that were essentially secret, it was able to avoid filing tax returns anywhere. Hence, secrecy is not a location-specific device—in a tax haven per se—but a networked extra-legal space that uses the opacity of legal systems and the imperfections of oversight across a range of different jurisdictions.[60]

Inequality, Class, and Citizenship in the Twenty-First Century

From a geographical perspective, the contemporary political economy and its relations with space disrupts the rather neat conceptualization of class that is portrayed in the pages of C21. Although Piketty is alive to the notion of class, and even rather inferentially to class warfare (although he never mentions exploitation explicitly), he associates class with income distribution. Hence, the working class is the lowest 50 percent of the income distribution and the upper class the top 10 percent, with the middle . . . in the middle. While admitting that these distinctions are arbitrary, schematic, and contestable, he also claims they allow comparative analysis that is rigorous and objective.[61]

This adherence to income as the principal indicator of class is loyal to the norms of economics and allows him to show rising inequality has been due to the gain of the top 1 percent or even the top 0.1 percent of income earners. Piketty does occasionally refer to the "elite" but stops short of concepts more commonly deployed by financial and lifestyle-service sectors as well as many government agencies, for example High Net Worth Individuals (HNWIs) or Ultra-High Net Worth Individuals (U-HNWIs).[62] The reliance on centiles as a proxy for class means that the concept loses analytical purchase. What does the upper class (top 10 percent) or the top 0.1 percent do? How do they live? What are their relations with or attitudes toward those not in their class group? And how do centiles qua elites combine their claims to citizenship, and even place identity, with the mobility of their financial capital?

The geographies (and sociologies) of class in the twenty-first century have documented that elites operate through mobile lives—moving, or being capable of doing so, for leisure but also to avoid harassment by political enemies, to avoid disclosure of business arrangements (and political connections) to governments, media, and civil societies, and obviously to avoid taxes and legal claims.[63] As elites have become hypermobile, they have decoupled from the nation and thus set out to challenge what Ong has called the "deep commitments required by classic citizenship."[64] Elites, like their capital (or its appearance), seem to be increasingly deterritorialized.

These elites are "becoming a transglobal community of peers who have more in common with one another than with their countrymen back home," according to Freeland. "Whether they maintain primary residences in New York or Hong Kong, Moscow or Mumbai, today's super-rich are increasingly a nation unto themselves."[65] Unlike most of Jane Austen's characters, whose social worlds were limited to country estates, occasional forays to London and Portsmouth, and seemingly invisible (and unspoken) economic relations with plantations in the Caribbean, the new plutocrats are highly mobile, globally networked, and yet placeless. The iconic winner in twenty-first-century capitalism is the "non dom," or occupants of what appears to be a liminal or imaginary space.[66]

These elites seem to be largely indifferent to and economically independent of the space in which they are located at any moment, a disposition that Elliott and Urry argue is deliberately nurtured as a badge of globalized pride and a tactic against feelings of entrapment.[67] Ong refers to them as "pied-à-terre" subjects, "a social form through which global capital inserts itself into the matrix of the national state, by establishing a residential presence in key urban nodes of global systems."[68] The implication I draw is that to understand elites—and perhaps do something about inequality—requires rejecting conventional economic geographies that are unable to synthesize "capital power" from percentages of national income.

As already noted, a critical power of the owners of capital is the capacity to negotiate their engagement with particular spaces. They attempt to have these arrangements kept secret and to construct or take advantage of extra-legality in business decisions. Yet, while the elites themselves may register a large part of their financial assets in multiple and possibly offshore locations, they nevertheless have to be physically present somewhere for work, leisure, health care, and children's schooling. In response, a central element of contemporary statecraft and the new political economy of capital accumulation attempts to "capture" elites within a particular space for as long as possible. The spatial net that most effectively captures elites is not, however, the nation-state but the city, or even the comparative advantage of particular boroughs and postal codes. It is in this sense that Cunningham and Savage describe London as an "elite metropolitan vortex" that pulls together a range of social and cultural forces demanded by elites, which are vital to their capital accumulation and the city's.[69]

Cities go to enormous lengths to entice elites' capital and consumption power. City mayors—political actors who have become empowered over the past thirty years—promote their cities as places to do business but also as livable places. A host of livability tables reflect their success, with composite indices ranking the qualities and costs of residential space, education, leisure activities—everything from Michelin-star restaurants, art festivals, galleries, ballet, and nightclubs, to prestige "sport" events such as Grand Prix—and "starchitect"-designed buildings.[70] The lifestyle magazine I picked up in haste from my doormat in a rush to read Zucman's Hidden Wealth of Nations shows that wealth is anything but hidden in London! The magazine's advertisements and articles on boutique hotels, organic home-delivery services, and fashion designer biographies are really about asserting London to be a city with an elite attitude, a city that works hard and deserves leisure, a city in which privilege can be attributed to merit and understanding the right mix of social and cultural capital, and in which the necessary co-presence of low-paid workers can be "cloaked" from intimate contact.[71]

To attract and nurture elites, a key power at the disposal of mayors and city managers, especially in a city such as London, is discretion within the planning and building system. A range of service providers negotiate with city authorities and lodge legal appeals so that elites can overbuild on floor-area ratios, install underground extensions under public streets,[72] close off public rights of way, install electric fences and private security, circumvent conservation restrictions, and incorporate self-governance arrangements.[73] As Webber and Burrows have recently shown, the return for enticing global elites to London has been contentious.[74] Neighborhoods historically linked with an older elite become modified to the tastes of a new class. Architectural styles are critiqued as signs of conspicuous consumption—architectural bling often ethnicized in popular discourse as the shift from a bucolic rustification of London villages to a "ruskification"—impacting on an area's sense of place (identity).[75]

The result: Not only is inequality in large, global cities quantifiably greater than in nation-states, but it also looks and feels greater, and perhaps has even challenged the notion of how class operates in the contemporary city.[76] Writing of London, for example, Atkinson has questioned whether the intense social connection that we associate with a city has given way to enhanced social distances, such that the air of cosmopolitanism is really something closer to a "plutocratic cloud" that in practice offers "null cosmopolitanism."[77]

An important part of the elite negotiation with place concerns the parameters of citizenship. As Ong observes (as part of what she calls emergent "graduations" in citizenship), "rights and entitlements once associated with all citizens are becoming linked to neoliberal criteria, so that entrepreneurial expatriates come to share in the rights and benefits once exclusively claimed by citizens."[78] Plutocratic elites can acquire the entitlements of doms even if they claim non-dom status for tax purposes. Importantly, however, elites are additionally well placed to claim what Sassen calls post-national citizenship—citizenship determined beyond the limiting requirements of the nation-state, such as respect for international human rights. Indeed, for elites, the ideal is a multi-sited citizenship, indicated by dual or multiple nationalities through which they may calculate the best combination of rights, entitlements, and protections across many locations, largely on their own terms and as a situation demands.[79]

Appropriately, this point was illustrated by numerous advertisements in the in-flight magazine en route to the original workshop convened by the Washington Center for Equitable Growth for the authors of this book, held in Bellagio, Italy, in late 2015. One of those advertisements, outlining the advantages of citizenship in Dominica, played up the country's "lush forests" and "tumbling waterfalls," attractive to adventurers, including "business adventurers" who might be attracted by an educated workforce but also the "benefits" of citizenship. These are then listed: a right to reside in Dominica and any Caribbean Community (CARICOM) country; visa-free travel to 110 other countries and territories; membership in the "Commonwealth of Nations"; citizenship granted within three months of application; "no interview, residence, education or business experience requirement"; and "life in a business-friendly jurisdiction."

Two routes to citizenship in Dominica are then outlined in the magazine piece, with prices for each, and available to an individual or their whole family. The first route is a contribution to Dominica's Economic Diversification Fund, which indicates that individual citizenship is likely to be provided for $100,000 and a "Due Diligence and Processing" fee of $10,500. The second route is acquisition of real estate, which requires an investment of $200,000 and a "Due Diligence Fee, Processing Fee and Government Fee" of $60,500. A few minutes on the Internet to find out more about these so-called Citizenship by Investment Programmes finds real estate developers across the Caribbean and Central America offering citizenship as part of luxury-condo or super-yacht facility packages, tax haven services, and legal intermediaries offering bespoke dual or multiple citizenship arrangements. An explicit advantage, according to some sites, was that the countries mentioned were subject to English law, and some offered "British-protected citizenship."

The arrangements that allow elites to hold multiple citizenships and to locate the appearance of wealth offshore yet be encouraged to reside, invest, and spend in particular locations, especially cities, are coproduced. Numerous Special Investment Vehicles provide the connecting thread, and again secrecy is a vital component. Market analysis by London Central Portfolio, an asset management company, suggests that 4,000 owner-occupied homes in England and Wales (in fact, almost all are in London) are held in "corporate envelopes" that allow property to be bought anonymously.[80] Yet even before the disclosures of the Panama Papers came to light, it was already clear that these figures were significant underestimates. In London, in what are called the "alpha territories," which concentrate high-value properties, more than 85 percent of properties with price tags of at least £5 million were bought by overseas buyers; in 2011–2013 the value of £5-million-plus house sales totaled £5.2 billion. And *The Guardian,* citing real estate company reports, claimed that around 50 percent of overseas buyers of alpha properties are not resident in the United Kingdom.

But what does overseas mean in the context of mobile elites? What is to prevent someone doing what is playfully called round-tripping? They work in London, register their financial holdings offshore, and invest in citizenship overseas, then set up a company that buys in the London property market. The company will pay stamp duty to the U.K. Treasury and property taxes to the local authority, but corporate taxes (on profit) can be reduced and the identity of the individual investors kept secret.

It is unclear from *C21* whether Piketty is proposing that rising inequality has produced new class relations. Yet this is the suggestion of most sociological analyses of contemporary political economy. Using an older vocabulary of class, inequality used to be discussed as a class divide. Sociological studies, especially from the 1960s, were concerned that a large group of people were falling out of the working class but they were not a lumpen proletariat but instead (euphemistically) an "underclass." By the 1990s the concern was that this group might be better understood as "outcasts," excluded or more ominously disconnected from the economy, the welfare state, and (especially in the United States, where class was more clearly combined with race) from the political process. The suggestion was the economic performance of elites was related to the increased poverty and suffering of others. Attending to the geographies of inequality demonstrates how this class relation may have become even more pronounced in the twenty-first century.

The financial crisis in 2007–2008 showed the connection between what Saskia Sassen has called the "savage sorting of winners and losers."[81] Sassen offers a compelling analysis, arguing that the crisis was set up by a financial deepening with origins going back at least to the 1980s to create a new frontier or "operational space for advanced capitalism." A crucial part of this deepening was the extension of mortgages to lower-income groups. In a well-regulated and transparent system, this would not be a bad thing. After all, Piketty shows that "at all times, the least wealthy half of the population own virtually nothing (and little more than 5 percent of total wealth)."[82] Indeed, Sassen suggests that the financial systems in most advanced economies were not vulnerable to conventional mortgage-lending problems, even though what became known as subprime mortgages represented 20 percent of all mortgages in the United States in 2006. What was not evident was the complexity and opacity caused, mostly quite legally, by what Sassen refers to as the "shadow banking system" that repackaged, bundled, coded, and connected simple financial instruments such as mortgage insurance policies into (unsecured) derivatives. When the mortgage market stumbled, the knock-on to credit-swap defaults translated to a near-systemic meltdown.

The nuance I would make to Sassen's argument is that instruments such as residential mortgage-backed securities (RMBSs) that were part of the complex maneuvers of shadow banking connected elites and the poor through space. Thus, the financial sector used offshore (and onshore) to reduce tax liabilities and protect assets, raise returns to capital, and pay high salaries and bonuses, sometimes as disbursements of share equity, benefiting further from increases in equity values and real estate prices in the world's major cities.[83] The performance of elites in the financial sector was related, to some extent, to the opening of new "operational spaces," such as the subprime market, and being protected from the risks of the crash through the mobilities of their capital. The analytical counterpoint to the elite mobilities that characterize inequality in the twenty-first century is how the losers have been "stuck." Neighborhoods with long histories of poverty and discrimination were back to owning "virtually nothing," to follow Piketty's phrase, but now partly through the practice of financial inclusion (not exclusion).[84] These neighborhoods have found it the hardest to bounce back once growth returned, embedding racial, income, and wealth inequalities.[85]

Conclusion

Piketty provides an important account of how holders of capital in the twenty-first century have come to prosper better than at any time since 1913, with those at the extremely high end doing especially well. Capital is highly concentrated, and those with the largest quantities gain disproportionately higher returns (rents) from capital than those with lower amounts.[86] Left unchecked, labor and capital markets will not find a new equilibrium, prompting Piketty in the closing pages of *Capital* to outline a number of approaches to pull back from even further inequality—namely, a coherent set of reporting structures in order to construct a global database of capital and a progressive global tax on wealth (capital).

These are, Piketty admits, "utopian proposals," but very much in line with proposals from other economists, and they have been mostly ignored.[87] A recent article penned for *Le Monde* and reproduced in *The Observer* was titled, "Why Have Governments Done So Little since 2008 to Address Financial Transparency?"[88] One might add, why have governments done so little to address inequality at all? The corridors of power, either in Whitehall, Davos, or The City, are not my world, so my conclusions reflect only what I can see as an outsider looking in. Nevertheless, based on the material presented in this chapter, a U.K.-centric viewpoint, and a few lessons from

Monty Python, there seem to be a couple of worthwhile concluding points, some of which are also distinctly utopian.

First, Piketty's proposals are ex-post solutions, in that they are correctives to the operation of capitalism as it stands and not reforms of capitalism itself. The limited discussions around a global register of financial securities and greater compilation of data on transactions and wealth holding have focused on voluntary declarations. The consensus position among most international financial agencies and government ministries about how markets work best with limited regulation has not shifted a great deal. There is no action to make taxation more progressive. Thresholds before income tax is payable have risen and tax breaks on pensions have been reformed, but sales taxes (mostly regressive) have risen, top-end marginal rates of income tax have come down, taxes on property have not kept pace with price increases, thresholds on inheritance have risen, and in the United Kingdom at least moves for super taxes on high-value properties were kicked into the long grass. Conversely, alternative approaches such as raising real wages, social transfers, and support for trade unions have gained modest political space.[89]

The second point is that this inertia is probably a realistic appraisal of the limited capacity of national and international agencies to measure income and wealth in the twenty-first century.[90] Piketty's proposals, when I first read them, reminded me of the Monty Python sketch that lampooned an imagined U.K. government meeting in which, in order to balance the books, civil servants contemplate a tax on "thingie" (sex) before cutting away to suggestions from the public, one of which is to tax "foreigners living abroad."[91] Piketty's proposals seem about as practical, but in the intervening four decades since the Python sketch the concept of abroad, or rather offshore, has become an even larger space and more fundamental to the operation of capitalism.

A spatial political economic approach suggests that individuals and companies are able to site actual production, as well as make financial services appear in, locations that operate under conditions of extra-legality, and to do so with great speed, complexity, and secrecy. Information-sharing treaties and greater scrutiny of tax havens are a good thing, but they are obviously clumsy and slow. An advertisement by the U.K. HM Revenue and Customs (HMRC) lists the "90 jurisdictions [that] will soon be sharing financial information with us ... [and after listing them] on UK residents

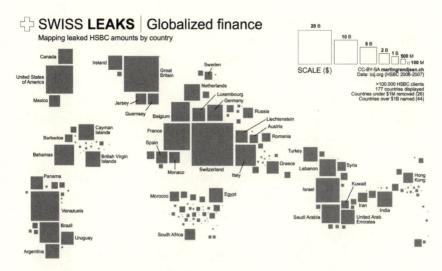

FIGURE 12-4: The globalization of tax evasion.
Source: Reproduced from www.martingrandjean.ch/swissleaks-map/.

with money, trusts or assets overseas." But the press is full of reports on how some well-known U.K. citizens are not "residents" for tax purposes, and how property and financial holdings are wrapped in envelopes that hide identities. In a ninety-minute flight from London to Milan, I was reading offers of dual citizenship from a number of Caribbean countries—no interview, no actual residence, and for an investment that would not buy me a one-bedroom apartment outside central London.[92]

The third point considers the alternatives, or at least what actions might either enforce compliance with international norms and regulations or reveal where capital appears to be located. The point has been somewhat preempted by the whistleblower leak of the so-called Panama Papers. As Easterling suggests, tax havens organized around networked infrastructures and the zone leaves capitalism vulnerable to hacking. Her argument is that "space has been available for manipulation."[93] It is not clear how spaces can be manipulated or hacked, nor what effects this might have on the economies of offshore or the strategies of elites. Nevertheless, advocacy groups such as the Tax Justice Network and International Consortium of Investigative Journalists, as well as groups such as Anonymous and the whistleblowing through WikiLeaks, SwissLeaks, and LuxLeaks have exposed the extent and routes of practices of dark-pool trading, explicit tax evasion, and links with politicians, banks, and criminal organizations.

The response of The City and Wall Street might be to develop even more complicated forms of shadow banking, but the exposures have posed political and moral questions at a time when the financial sector has been bailed out and austerity has undermined public services in many countries. They have also pointed to the asymmetry of legal systems that results in the conviction of whistleblowers but not those whose actions the leaks expose. In 2015, Hervé Falciani, who leaked personal data of 130,000 people involved in tax evasion through HSBC Private Swiss Bank to authorities in Argentina, India, France, Germany, and the United Kingdom, was sentenced to six years in prison for aggravated industrial espionage, data theft, and violation of banking secrecy laws.[94] Whistleblowing carries considerable personal risks, and legal reforms should take place to afford protections to those who provide information on activities that are in contravention of public law and regulation.

The fourth point is to ask why those in the bottom 50 percent or 99 percent of the income distribution are not more active and innovative in organizing the geographies of capital accumulation. Movements such as Occupy Wall Street drew from a pluralist political constituency that provided an oppositional voice to austerity and attempted to forward an agenda of social justice. But to paraphrase Easterling, and with a nod to Monty Python absurdism, other spaces are available for manipulation. How might governments or international agencies respond if everyone—or at least a lot of people—took the appearance of their economic activities offshore? Would it play into the hands of hypermarket theocrats? Or might it challenge the parameters of how finance ministers and economists think of the economy as still relatively contained?

Lots of people in the United Kingdom are already offshore without knowing it, probably through their pension funds. But what about a wider movement that threatened to move business offshore in order to reduce tax? According to a quick Internet search, law firms can set up a company in—as the Dominica advertisement put it—a "business-friendly jurisdiction" in just a few weeks. The idea is slightly ludicrous. Yet on November 10, 2015, the town of Crickhowell in South Wales submitted a proposal to HMRC to move its tax affairs offshore, citing Google and Starbucks as precedent, and using as a template the application of Caffè Nero when it registered to move its business registration to the Isle of Man. As one of the town's traders explained, his small family business pays seven times more tax in the United Kingdom than Facebook does. The town's trader association opened a campaign to get other towns to make similar applications to HMRC.

The shopkeepers of Crickhowell, if they were able to make a move offshore, would not likely be able to join Piketty's 0.1 percent anytime soon, but they are making a moral case for the equality of taxation and raising the kind of awkward questions about the new spatial political economy that governments need to consider if they are serious about tackling social and economic equality.

THIRTEEN

The Research Agenda after Capital in the Twenty-First Century

EMMANUEL SAEZ

Economist Emmanuel Saez plays a unique role in this volume. Saez is often a coauthor with Thomas Piketty and worked with him to develop much of the data in *Capital in the Twenty-First Century*. He is also, along with economists Anthony Atkinson, Facundo Alvaredo, and Gabriel Zucman, a co-manager of the World Top Incomes Database, where that data is housed. In this chapter Saez lays out a lifetime's worth of research ideas, much of which aims to empirically evaluate the documented rise in income and wealth inequality and what that means for economic outcomes—highlighting three themes for future research. First, he argues that researchers still have much to do on the issue of measurement. He argues that the next step is to disaggregate our systems of National Income Accounts to include distributional measures and devote more resources to measuring wealth inequality. Second, Saez points to the question of fairness. He argues that in order to judge whether current distribution outcomes are fair, we need to understand how they come about. Is today's wealth mostly self-made or inherited? Do incomes reflect productivity or rent? Finally, Saez pushes us to consider the role of policy in ameliorating or exacerbating inequality. He points specifically to the need to understand the effects of regulation and taxation, both of which seem to have been key in ushering in a unique and unfortunately ephemeral era of low inequality and high growth in the middle of the twentieth century.

The phenomenal success of Thomas Piketty's *Capital in the 21st Century* shows there is great interest in the issue of inequality among the public at large. Inequality matters because people have a sense of fairness. They care about not only their own economic situations but also how they stand relative to others in their communities. Such feelings go well beyond "envy," representing instead the very foundation of societies. In modern democracies, people have collectively decided to share a large fraction of their economic resources through government. In advanced economies, governments tax one-third to one-half of total national income to fund transfers and public goods. Hence, inequality is a people's issue and it is essential to bring the findings of research into the causes and consequences of inequality to the broader public—exactly what Piketty's book has succeeded in doing. How should economics and more broadly social science research capitalize on the success of the book and tackle some of the unanswered questions that have so fascinated the public?

To answer this question, it is useful first to understand why such a long and scholarly book could become a best-selling success. Such widespread readership is never predictable, of course, but three elements help us understand it, particularly for the United States.

First, the United States has experienced a very large increase in income inequality since the 1970s, with an ever-growing share of income going to the top of the distribution. Indeed, Piketty himself built the historical series on top income shares that had been widely discussed in U.S. public debates.[1] Furthermore, slow economic growth in the twenty-first century—particularly since the onset of the Great Recession in 2007—combined with still-growing income inequality implies that growth, excluding top incomes, is even slower. In a slow-growth economy where inequality increases, top incomes capture a disproportionate share of the fruits of economic growth. Prolonged inequitable growth raises deep concerns about the fairness of the U.S. economic system, which over time is not sustainable to the public.

Second, Piketty's book warns us that, absent any policy change, we should expect growing wealth concentration in the United States and other advanced democracies, with wealthy inheritors increasingly dominating the top of the economic ladder. This kind of "patrimonial economy" prevailed in Western European countries before World War I, something we know thanks to the patient gathering of data by Piketty alongside many colleagues. In the United States, of course, meritocracy is one of the nation's founding principles, so Piketty's prediction naturally struck a nerve with the American public.

Third, Piketty's book offers a way out. Drastic progressive policies enacted amid the Great Depression and World War II lowered wealth and income inequality durably in the post–World War II era in virtually all advanced economies. Similarly, restoring progressive policies in a modern form could again prevent the return of the "patrimonial economy" Piketty warns us about.

All three of these aspects of Piketty's book depend on economic phenomena that can be researched, analyzed, and better understood. Indeed, Piketty's book was made possible by a slow but systematic gathering of inequality data by a large number of researchers over the past twenty years, pioneered by Piketty himself in the case of France. Although this research agenda has made substantial progress, important gaps remain. We need to improve our measurements of inequality, and refine our understanding of its mechanisms and the policy remedies needed to address it. The numerous reactions, discussions, and criticisms of Piketty's book over the past two years give us an opportunity to identify the key issues outstanding. Progress in our understanding should come from a combination of data and research. The government plays a key role in collecting data and supplying it to researchers. Hence, in the same way that the government is key to implementing policies to remedy inequality, it is also key in helping build the data infrastructure needed to study inequality in the first place.

The theme of this chapter will follow the most important questions and controversies that have arisen in the commentary on Piketty's book. First, I discuss the issues involved in measuring inequality. Second, I look at the underlying mechanisms of inequality. And third, I examine policies that can remedy inequality. In all three cases, I highlight the most promising avenues for future research, focusing particularly on the United States, which provides the best evidence and is ground zero for the resurgence of inequality.

Measuring Inequality

The backbone of Piketty's book is a long and systematic collection of statistics on inequality and growth. Through his earlier long and scholarly book on France,[2] Piketty led the revival of the analysis of top income shares that had been famously pioneered by Kuznets's own long and scholarly book.[3] None of these two books made it to the bestseller lists, full as they are of long methodological details and even longer sets of tabulated statistics. Their long-term influence, however, has been enormous. Kuznets won the Nobel Prize, in large part due to the famous Kuznets curve theory of inequality he developed based on his statistics.[4] Piketty's older book revived the systematic analysis of top income shares. Since then, a World Top Incomes Database has been assembled by a large team of scholars. It covers more than thirty countries over long time periods, many for a century or more.[5] As Piketty's book shows so eloquently, this database has taught us a lot about inequality.[6] Yet it still has a number of shortcomings and gaps and that researchers will have to fill.

Income Inequality and Growth

First, there is a gap between the study of growth, which uses national accounts data that exclusively focus on economic aggregates, and inequality analysis, which focuses on distributions using micro data but without trying to be consistent with macro aggregates. Economists lack the measurement tools to analyze inequality, growth, and the role of the government together in a coherent framework. Historically, Kuznets was interested in both national income and its distribution and made pathbreaking advances on both fronts using administrative tabulated data.[7] But with the advent of micro-survey data in the postwar period, inequality analysis since the 1960s has lost the connection with national accounting and growth.

This creates two sets of issues. First, it is currently impossible to jointly analyze economic growth and inequality and answer simple questions such as: How is macroeconomic economic growth shared between income groups? Second, it creates comparability issues in inequality statistics computed with different datasets or in different countries. Survey data, for example, typically do not capture well capital income that is highly concentrated while individual tax data do. Individual tax data miss some forms of income that are nontaxable, such as fringe benefits, and do not provide systematic information on transfers. The comparison of inequality across countries is also particularly difficult as different countries have different tax bases or different ways of capturing incomes in survey data.[8]

National accounting has developed an international set of guidelines to make standardized and comparable measures across time and countries.[9] In the same way, economic researchers need to develop distributional national accounts (DINAs) that will use a common national income basis for analyzing inequality. Such a tool can integrate the analysis of growth and inequality and it will allow meaningful comparisons across countries.

Preliminary steps are being taken in this direction. The World Top Income Database (WTID) is being transformed into a World Wealth and Income Database (WID) that will offer distributional statistics on both income and wealth (instead of income only), cover the full population (as opposed to only top incomes), and be fully consistent with national accounts aggregates. Alvaredo et al. are laying out the preliminary guidelines.[10] Country-specific studies are being carried out for the United States,[11] France,[12] and the United Kingdom.[13] The goal of these studies is to start from available micro individual income tax data and survey data to construct annual synthetic micro-datasets that are representative of the full population of the country and consistent with national accounts.

This approach captures both labor and capital income. On the labor income side, wages and salaries are augmented by fringe benefits and employer payroll taxes to scale up to the full compensation of employees in national accounts. On the capital income side, corporate retained earnings are imputed to individual stockholders, returns to pension funds are assigned to individual pension owners, and rents are imputed to homeowners exactly as done at the aggregate level in national accounting when estimating national income. The goal is to produce measures of all the key income components (labor and capital income), wealth components, taxes, and transfers from national accounts in a microlevel database.

There are ongoing efforts to introduce distributional measures in the national accounts from government agencies. The U.S. Bureau of Economic Analysis (BEA), for instance, has a long-term plan to introduce distributional information in the national accounts. Fixler and Johnson and Fixler et al. describe this effort and make a first attempt to scale up income from the Current Population Survey to match personal income from national accounts.[14] The Organisation for Economic Co-operation and Development (OECD) is also starting to decompose national income by quintiles.[15] Hence, the time seems ripe for an academic and governmental partnership to push forward the creation of distributional national accounting data.

With distributional national accounting datasets, it is possible to compute inequality and growth statistics for both pretax incomes and post-tax incomes, and for specific demographic subgroups, such as the working-age population or male versus female. Preliminary estimates from Piketty, Saez, and Zucman show that from 1946 to 1980, the average real annual growth rates of pretax income per adult for the full population and the bottom 90 percent of income earners were the same, at 2.1 percent per year.[16] From 1980 to 2014, however, the growth rate for the bottom 90 percent is 0.8 percent. This is only about half of the growth rate for all adults, which is 1.4 percent, highlighting the effect of widening inequality on the distribution of economic growth. The bottom 90 percent captured 62 percent of overall economic growth from 1946 to 1980 but only 32 percent from 1980 to 2014. This shows that overall macroeconomic growth statistics can be very misleading when interpreting the economic growth experience of the vast majority of the population. It also suggests that using representative-agent models in macroeconomics can be misleading for analyzing many questions related to economic growth.

Comparing pretax incomes (before any taxes or government transfers) and post-tax incomes (where we subtract all taxes and add back all government transfers, including imputed spending on public goods) will provide the first overall and systematic picture of the direct redistributive effect of government.[17] Our preliminary results show that, indeed, post-tax inequality is lower than pretax inequality. However, the time trends in inequality pretax and post-tax are very similar. Transfers for lower-income families, such as Food Stamps, Medicare, and Medicaid, have grown over time, which reduces post-tax inequality. However, tax progressivity has declined over time, which increases post-tax inequality. In net, these two factors roughly cancel each other out.

Naturally the government also has an impact on pretax incomes through regulations, such as the minimum wage, and tax incidence, such as corporate taxation, which in the long run affects all capital owners and not only corporate stock owners. Therefore, the proper definition of pretax income already requires a conceptual framework. This is not just a pure accounting and measurement exercise, because it also involves economic thinking and drawing on the existing literature on the effects of taxes and transfers.

In the longer term, it is conceivable that distributional national accounts will be based on exhaustive population-wide data on earnings, income, wealth, and possibly even consumption. Indeed, the administration of government taxes and transfers already creates population-wide earnings and income data that have long been used for research.[18] Traditional national accounting also relies on such data, but typically in aggregated form, such as for specific industrial sectors. In principle, with expanding computing power it will become possible to have a fully integrated database that includes all individuals, businesses, and government entities, tracking down all income flows and payments at the micro level, which could be updated in real time as new data become available. Such a tool would be invaluable for economic analysis.

Wealth Inequality

Piketty's book focuses mostly on capital inequality, where capital is defined as net wealth, or the sum of assets minus debts for each individual. Unfortunately, statistics on wealth inequality are much weaker than statistics on income: Virtually all advanced economies have progressive individual income taxes that generate detailed information on income inequality, but very few have progressive and comprehensive individual wealth taxes. As a result, the quality and breadth of wealth data are much lower than for income data. This is particularly true in the United States, where the two most widely used sources to measure wealth inequality have been estate tax data available since 1916 and the Survey of Consumer Finances (SCF) available since 1989 (but only every third year). The two sources have generated very different results. According to estate tax data, U.S. wealth inequality has been low and stable since the 1980s, with the top 1 percent owning slightly less than 20 percent of total wealth, a level of wealth inequality that is very low by historical and international standards.[19] In contrast, according to SCF data, U.S. wealth concentration is pretty high, with the top 1 percent owning 36 percent of total wealth, and has been growing since the late 1980s.[20]

Piketty created a series for U.S. wealth concentration, patching together these two disparate sources (unfortunately, the only ones available then), trusting the estate tax data estimates for the pre-1980 period and using SCF data since the 1980s.[21] This led to the *Financial Times* controversy, because the rise in U.S. wealth concentration is partly an artifact of the change in sources.[22] Earlier on, Edward Wolff's famous book *Top Heavy: The Increasing Inequality of Wealth in America and What Can be Done about It* had similarly combined estate tax data and SCF data and hence also obtained an increasing level of U.S. wealth concentration.[23] The deeper issue here is that the United States does not produce systematic administrative wealth data, which is a glaring gap given the enormous public interest in this issue. An urgent task is to improve U.S. wealth statistics. This requires both more research exploiting alternative sources and improvements in administrative U.S. wealth data collection.

On the research front and after the publication of Piketty's book, Saez and Zucman used systematic capital income data, which is very well measured in individual tax data, to infer wealth from capital income (using the so-called capitalization method).[24] They find a very large increase in wealth inequality since the late 1970s, with the top 1 percent wealth share growing from 23 percent in 1978 to 42 percent in 2012. The increase since 1989 is even stronger than the one found in the SCF. This means these new estimates are fairly close to the earlier patched estate-SCF estimates by Wolff and Piketty in their respective books.[25] If anything, the resulting picture from the estimates by Saez and Zucman is an even stronger increase in wealth inequality than the one proposed by Piketty.[26]

In light of these discrepancies across estimates and the real possibility that U.S. wealth inequality is actually exploding, it is important to make progress on U.S. wealth data collection to settle the debate. First, it should be possible to mobilize the richness of existing tax data (particularly the internal tax data, available only within the U.S. tax administration agencies, which is now being used by external researchers with special agreements) to further improve the wealth estimates of Saez and Zucman.[27] Individual addresses in the internal tax data, for example, can be combined with third-party data on real estate prices (such as Zillow) to estimate precisely the value of homeowners' real estate. Similarly, pension wealth can be estimated more precisely using Individual Retirement Account (IRA) balances (systematically reported to the IRS) along with longitudinal information on past pension contributions, such as 401(k) contributions.

Second, enhanced information reporting could greatly improve the quality of U.S. wealth data. The most important step would be for financial institutions to report year-end wealth balances on the information returns they currently send to the IRS to report capital income payments. This requirement could be extended to student loans. Information returns on interest and dividend payments could report outstanding account balances as well. The existing universal balance reporting requirement of IRAs could be extended to all defined-contribution plans such as 401(k)s. The cost of collecting all this extra information would be modest because the information is already generated by financial institutions to manage their clients' accounts. In many cases, additional reporting could help better enforce existing taxes, and so would not necessarily require congressional action.

This discussion shows that government policy, research on inequality, and public awareness of the issue all go hand-in-hand. Without government policy—particularly tax policy—there is no systematic way to measure income inequality, particularly at the top of the distribution. Indeed, virtually all the top income share series discussed in Piketty's book start precisely when each country first implements a progressive individual income tax. Before that time, it was virtually impossible to measure income concentration accurately. Income inequality statistics using systematic administrative data can, in turn, powerfully shape public awareness of inequality, as Piketty's book has so eloquently shown. Naturally, even without systematic statistics, inequality looms large in society as reflected in political debates and literature. Piketty famously discusses representations of inequality and class in novels by Balzac and Jane Austen. Modern statistics help cast light on the issue but are not sufficient by any means to dispel all misconceptions on the issue.

Understanding Inequality Dynamics: Is Inequality Fair?

Piketty's book not only presents inequality statistics but also provides a framework for understanding the dynamics of inequality. This is important because not all inequalities are made equal. Some inequalities are perceived as fair. Almost everybody agrees it is fair that a hardworking person should earn and consume more than somebody with equal skills who prefers to work less and enjoy leisure. Other forms of inequalities are perceived as unfair. A high income obtained from a socially unproductive endeavor (such as rent seeking) is seen as unfair. Many people would view an idle and rich trust-funder as undeserving of his inherited wealth. Naturally, perceptions of unfair inequality then translate into demands for government action through the political process.

Capital Income: Inherited versus Self-Made Wealth

Wealth is quantitatively very important, on the order of four to five years of national income in the United States in recent years, and generates capital income, which is about 30 percent of national income.[28] Wealth is also highly concentrated, so that capital income plays a large role at the top of the distribution. Wealth comes from two sources: past savings, in which case wealth is self-made, and inheritance. This distinction is crucial because our modern meritocratic societies have a strong aversion toward privilege coming out of inheritance as opposed to one's own merit.

The central prediction of Piketty's book is that, absent policy changes, wealth will become more concentrated and will come mostly from inheritance, so that undeserving inheritors will dominate the top of the distribution. To test his central prediction, it is necessary to measure the share of inherited wealth in total wealth and its evolution. As explained in detail in *Capital,* Piketty and his coauthors, on the basis of underlying research, have been able to make progress on this important question in the case of France, by digitizing historical estate tax data and using current administrative estate tax data.[29]

Unfortunately, research on this question for the United States is particularly weak, in part due to the lack of adequate administrative data to measure savings and inheritances (and inter vivos gifts). This issue generated a controversial debate between Modigliani and Kotlikoff and Summers.[30] Modigliani argued that inherited wealth was relatively unimportant, whereas Kotlikoff and Summers argued that inherited wealth was very important. Unfortunately, little progress has been made on this question in the United States since this debate due to the lack of systematic administrative data. Therefore, getting a better measure of the fraction of inherited wealth in the United States should be a high priority.

The internal U.S. individual tax data track population-wide individual incomes, trusts, gifts, and large inheritances, offering a unique opportunity to provide better estimates for the United States. The analysis would nevertheless be challenging because estate tax is often avoided via use of early and undervalued gifts through trusts. U.S. internal individual tax data also track college attendance of children and college tuition effectively paid by parents. This is an important complementary data source, as college tuition has almost certainly become a very important fraction of the transfers made by parents to adult children.[31]

To measure self-made wealth accurately, it is necessary to measure savings precisely. Unfortunately, this is another critical area where measurement is poor, particularly in the United States. Savings data in the United States at the micro level are very limited. Only the Consumer Expenditure Survey (CEX) has the direct microlevel information on both income and consumption that is necessary to estimate savings. The CEX does not capture the top of the income distribution well, which is an issue because savings are also highly concentrated. Therefore, even the most basic fact that the savings rate (defined as the ratio of savings to income) increases with income or wealth is actually difficult to establish with precision in the United States. The best attempt is by Dynan, Skinner, and Zeldes, who do find savings rates sharply increasing with income.[32]

At the aggregate level, a very precise picture of aggregate savings and investment can be derived from the flow of funds and national accounts. Saez and Zucman construct a synthetic savings rate by wealth groups—defined as the savings rate needed to explain the dynamics of top wealth shares given the dynamics of income in top wealth groups and the price effects on assets (both of which can be measured well).[33] They also find the savings rate sharply increasing with wealth alongside plummeting middle-class savings since the 1980s. That is, the explosion in wealth concentration they obtain is explained both by an increase in income inequality and an increase in savings inequality. Savings inequality magnifies initial income inequalities into potentially enormous wealth inequalities: If the middle class does not save at all, then its share of total wealth will eventually fall to zero. This concern about wealth inequality exploding due to savings rate inequality is an old one and was already discussed by Kuznets.[34]

So in terms of data collection, it should be a priority to collect savings data systematically. With the improvements in wealth data collection through the tax administration proposed above, only a small extra step is needed to be able to compute savings. If we can observe end-of-year balances of financial accounts, then we only need to observe purchases and sales of assets to compute savings. The sale of an asset already generates an information return form for taxing realized capital gains; a purchase (or acquisition through a gift or inheritance) of an asset could generate a similar information return.

Such information on asset purchases is now already stored by financial companies because it is an information report requirement for administering realized capital gains taxation. Scandinavian countries collect comprehensive wealth information across many asset classes at the micro level, so that it is possible to compute very good microlevel savings rates. As a result, the most innovative research on savings and wealth is being done in Scandinavian countries.[35]

Labor Income: Fair versus Unfair Earnings

In a number of countries, particularly the United States and the United Kingdom, labor income inequality has also greatly increased since the 1970s. What is driving this increase in labor income inequality? There are two broad views.

Under the market view, labor is a standard good traded competitively on the labor market. In that case, pay is determined by the supply and demand for various labor skills, and reflects marginal productivity. Technological progress, for example, can drive up the demand for college-educated labor, leading to a higher wage premium for educated workers. Conversely, a rise in the supply of college graduates can depress the wage premium for educated workers. Under the market view, where pay reflects productivity, pay inequality can be seen as reflecting differences in productivity and hence as being consistent with meritocratic ideals of fairness.

Under the institutions view, labor is not a standard good. Instead, pay determination is the outcome of a bargaining process that can be affected by a number of institutions, among them labor market regulations, unions, tax and transfer policies, and more generally social norms regarding pay inequality. As a result, pay can depart significantly from productivity. In this scenario, if compensation is due in part to bargaining power, gains for some groups (such as top management) can come at the expense of others (such as regular workers). As a result, nothing guarantees that pay inequality resulting in part from bargaining power is always fair.

How can economic research cast light on which scenario is the most relevant in practice, and in particular at the top of the income distribution?

Piketty and Saez show that at the top of the distribution, a significant fraction of the surge in top income shares is due to large increases in wages and salaries as well as business income (partnership profits or closely held S-corporation profits).[36] Bakija, Cole, and Heim, using internal tax data, show that executives, managers, supervisors, and financial professionals account for about two-thirds of the increase in income going to the top 0.1 percent of the income distribution from 1979 to 2005.[37]

The surge in wages and salaries is due to the rise in executive compensation, which has been extensively discussed in the corporate governance literature. The key issue is whether this surge in executive compensation reflects increased value of top talent, as in the market view scenario,[38] or whether it reflects the ability of executives to extract more pay, as in the institution view scenario.[39]

Much less, however, is known about the surge in top business income, which is quantitatively even larger than wage and salary income at the top of the U.S. income distribution.[40] A number of large and highly profitable closely held businesses are organized as partnerships or S-corporations. Limited liability corporations (LLCs) can be organized as partnerships as well. Such businesses can sometimes be large and very profitable, but typically they have a small number of owners and hence can generate large profits for each owner. Traditionally, doctors and lawyers are organized as partnerships. In finance, hedge funds and private equity firms are generally organized partnerships as well. Most start-up firms are also typically LLCs before they become publicly traded (or are acquired by other, larger companies). Some of them might be quite large, like Uber today or Facebook before its initial public offering.

Whether such business profits are fair depends on the nature of the business as well as the regulatory environment. On the one hand, almost everybody agrees that hedge funds specializing in high-frequency trading do not add value but instead skim off gains at the expense of other, slower traders. On the other hand, there is agreement that a high-tech business that invents a new product that becomes widely used (such as a smart phone or an Internet search engine) or is a better way to provide existing services (such as Uber for taxis or Airbnb for housing rentals) adds real value to the economy. However, many high-tech businesses that succeed by developing a new product end up earning quasi-monopoly rents. In principle, monopoly rents should attract competitors. Many of the most successful high-tech firms, such as Microsoft, Google, and Facebook, have become natural monopolies through network effects. Facebook, for example, is valuable precisely because its enormous and unparalleled customer base gives it a decisive advantage against new entrants. Monopoly rents can also be protected by excessively long patent rights. Obviously, monopolies have very strong incentives to lobby government to entrench their position. As is well known, many of the fortunes of the Gilded Age originated from monopoly positions in railways or oil production.

It would naturally be very valuable to know more about the industrial composition of business income at the top of the U.S. income distribution to see whether it is dominated by information technology business profits, or financial firms in the form of S-corporations or LLCs, or biomedical research practices, or classical law firms. In principle, by merging individual tax data with business tax data it would be possible to trace the industrial composition of top business income and whether such profits come from quasi-monopoly situations, patents, or closely held businesses. Such information is central to enlighten the debate on the proper regulations or proper taxation of business profits at the top.

Policy Remedies: What Should Be Done about Inequality?

The issue of fairness and inequality discussed above naturally leads to the next question: How should unfair inequality be addressed by society?

An important lesson coming from Piketty's book is that government policy has played a key role in shaping inequality in the historical record. It is a striking finding that before World War I, pretty much all Western countries had small governments (typically raising 10 percent or less of national income in taxes) and very high levels of income and wealth concentration. By the 1970s the size of government had increased dramatically, to about one-third to one-half of national income in almost all advanced economies: Economically advanced societies had decided to share a much larger fraction of their income to fund a welfare state providing public education, public retirement and disability benefits, public health insurance, as well as a number of smaller income protection programs such as means-tested welfare and unemployment insurance.

This new and large welfare state was funded by taxation through the development of both broad and relatively flat taxes, such as social security contributions and value-added taxes, and progressive taxes such as progressive individual income taxes, corporate taxes falling primarily on capital, and progressive inheritance taxes. Interestingly, the United States and the

United Kingdom were the countries that implemented the most extreme progressive tax systems, with extremely high top tax rates on individual income and inheritances.[41] As the size of government (measured by taxes and spending) grew, there were also been drastic changes in regulation policies, including antitrust policies, financial regulation, consumer protection, and a vast array of labor and union regulations. The net effect of the large welfare state, progressive taxes, and progressive regulations has been a dramatic lowering of income and wealth concentration in almost all advanced economies from the early twentieth century to the post–World War II decades. Importantly, countries experienced drastic reductions in inequality both pretax and after taxes and transfers.

In recent decades, however, we have seen a comeback of inequality in some (but not all countries). Increases in inequality have been the largest in the United States and the United Kingdom, where the Reagan and Thatcher revolutions led to the sharpest policy reversals, particularly for progressive taxation, financial regulation, and labor regulations. The fact that the comeback in inequality happens in some (but not all) countries and that it is highly correlated with policy reversals strongly suggests that policy plays a key role. A phenomenon driven purely by technology and globalization would have affected all advanced economies similarly. Atkinson discusses these issues and makes bold policy proposals along many dimensions to curb inequality in the United Kingdom.[42]

There is a large body of work studying separately these various policy aspects, but we do not yet have a good comprehensive picture on how each element of the policy toolbox affects inequality and growth.

Remedies for Income Inequality

What does recent research say about the role of policy in shaping income concentration? Piketty, Saez, and Stantcheva show that the top 1 percent income share is highly correlated across countries and over time with top individual income tax rate, with no visible effects on growth.[43] Countries that experienced the largest reductions in the top marginal tax rates since the 1960s, among them the United States and the United Kingdom, are also the countries that experienced the largest increases in top income shares. Yet there is no compelling evidence that the countries that lowered their top marginal tax rates the most and experienced large increases in income concentration had a better growth experience since the 1960s. This suggests that high-income earners respond to lower top tax rates, not by increasing productive work effort as posited by the standard supply-side story, but instead by finding ways to extract a larger share of the economic pie at the expense of others in the economy.

Philippon and Reshef show that the size of finance in the U.S. economy and the relative compensation of financial workers are very highly and negatively correlated with the level of financial regulation: finance becomes large and pays very well when regulations are weak.[44] In the historical U.S. record, the period of tight financial regulation from 1933 to 1980 is actually associated with stronger economic growth, which shows that reining in finance does not seem to have detrimental effects on economic growth.

In the case of executive compensation, however, it seems that regulations on pay transparency and pay for performance have largely failed or been actually counterproductive. The 1993 U.S. tax law that limited to $1 million the deductibility of executive compensation (for corporate tax purposes) unless it was performance-related seems to have fueled the explosion of stock-option compensation. Stock options, which tie compensation to the stock value of the company, are a very blunt tool for compensation, as stock prices fluctuate for many reasons unrelated to the performance of executives. Hence, it is probably a very inefficient tool for compensation. Its success is likely due to the appearance of being performance-related and the fact that it is not as transparent and visible a form of compensation as regular salary.[45]

While there is a large literature in industrial organization on antitrust and patent regulations and their effects on abnormal profits and monopoly rents, this literature has not been connected to the analysis of inequality. Are such profits coming out of quasi-monopoly rents, thus fueling the increase in income and wealth concentration? If yes, then antitrust and patent regulation policy should take into account not only the classical efficiency effects but also the effects on inequality.

It would be particularly valuable to see more work analyzing specifically the relative advantages of regulations versus taxes and transfers to address inequality issues.

Remedies for Wealth Inequality

How could wealth disparity be reduced without hurting the aggregate savings and capital accumulation that is a key element of long-run economic growth? As famously proposed in Piketty's book, a progressive wealth tax seems like the most direct instrument to curb the accumulation of large fortunes. The advantage of the progressive wealth tax (as opposed to the progressive income tax) is that it specifically targets accumulated wealth rather than current income. In principle, if the concern is about inherited wealth, then inheritance taxation would be the best tool to prevent self-made fortunes from becoming inherited wealth.[46] In practice, however, inheritance taxation can be avoided through tax planning and undervaluation of gifts and transfers before death. It would be much more difficult to avoid an annual wealth tax where wealth is evaluated every year.

But because U.S. savings are very concentrated among top wealth holders, there is a concern that reducing top wealth through progressive wealth or inheritance taxation might negatively impact aggregate savings and hence capital accumulation. As we have seen, saving rates for the U.S. middle class have plummeted since the 1980s. So in order to maintain aggregate savings, it is important to pair progressive taxation with encouragement for savings for the broad middle class.

Which policies are best to encourage middle-class saving depends on the reasons for the observed drop in the middle-class saving rate. Middle-class saving might have plummeted because of the lackluster growth in middle-class incomes relative to top incomes, fueling demand for credit to maintain relative consumption.[47] In that case, policies to boost middle-class incomes would probably boost saving as well. Financial deregulation may have expanded borrowing opportunities (through consumer credit, mortgage refinancing, home equity loans, subprime mortgages) and in some cases might have left consumers insufficiently protected against some forms of predatory lending. In this case, greater consumer protection and financial regulation could help increase middle-class saving.

Another factor that may be inhibiting middle-class saving is the increase in college tuition, which may have increased student loans. This means that publicly funded higher education and limits on university tuition may have a role to play. Recent work in behavioral economics shows that individual savings decisions respond much more to frames and nudges (such as the default option in 401(k) employer pension plans) than to tax subsidies.[48] Therefore, the new and growing body of work in behavioral finance could be used to develop ways to promote middle-class savings and reduce wealth inequality in the longer run.[49]

FOURTEEN

Macro Models of Wealth Inequality

MARIACRISTINA DE NARDI, GIULIO FELLA,

AND FANG YANG

Economists Mariacristina De Nardi, Giulio Fella, and Fang Yang address wealth inequality, the ultimate end-state of the forecast for the future in *C21*. Even after *C21*, the mechanisms that cause both overall wealth inequality and individual outcomes within that distribution of wealth remain uncertain. The authors focus primarily on two sets of facts and hence two modeling traditions: One notes the extreme skewness of wealth holdings at a point in time (meaning that a large percentage of total wealth is held by the wealthiest few), as well as its increasing skewness over time. The other seeks to explain why some wealthy people stay wealthy (and become wealthier) while others become poorer. A recent body of research begins the process of uniting the two sets of theories. Altogether, data on wealth raise important questions for received wisdom in economics, questions that the research by these three authors is at the forefront of answering.

Piketty's *Capital in the Twenty-First Century* is, in the author's own words, "primarily a book about the history of the distribution of income and wealth." It documents the evolution of the distributions of income and wealth since the Industrial Revolution for a significant number of countries and offers a framework to account for the common patterns of the long-run evolution of within-country wealth inequality across a number of developed economies.

This chapter takes stock of the existing literature on models of wealth inequality through the lens of the facts and ideas in Piketty's book and highlights both what we have learned so far and what we still need to learn in order to reach more definitive conclusions on the mechanisms shaping wealth concentration. Differently from Chapter 4, by Devesh Raval, which discusses the determinants of *between* inequality related to the division of aggregate income between capital and labor, this chapter deals with the distribution of wealth (that is, with inequality *within* wealth).

The chapter starts by introducing some important stylized facts about the distribution of wealth:

1. Wealth is highly concentrated. Its distribution is highly skewed with a long right tail.
2. Overall, there is significant mobility within the wealth distribution, both within an individual's lifetime and across generations. Wealth mobility is substantially lower, though, at the top and the bottom of the distribution.
3. Wealth concentration—the share of aggregate wealth in the hands of the richest people—displays a U shape, trending downward for most of the twentieth century and then increasing from the 1980s onward.

The chapter then turns to a discussion of the main mechanisms affecting wealth inequality according to Piketty's book. More specifically, *Capital* stresses the importance of the difference between the post-tax rate of return on capital and the rate of aggregate output growth as the crucial force shaping wealth concentration.[1] It also discusses, to a lesser extent, the role of tax progressivity, top income shares, and heterogeneity in saving rates and inheritances.

Next we present a simple framework to better understand and categorize various mechanisms behind individual wealth accumulation that can account for wealth inequality. From there we move on to surveying the existing macroeconomic literature on wealth inequality with an emphasis on the forces that hold most promise to account for the high degree of wealth concentration observed in the data. More specifically, we discuss the (mostly analytical) literature aiming to account for the observation that the right tail of the wealth distribution is well approximated by a Pareto distribution. This strand of the literature provides the main theoretical underpinning for the mechanism, emphasized in Piketty's book, according to which wealth concentration increases with the difference between the average net rate of return on wealth, r, and the trend rate of growth of aggregate output, g. Multiplicative random shocks to the wealth accumulation process are the main mechanism that generates wealth concentration in this class of models.

Piketty sees the rate of output growth as unambiguously reducing wealth concentration, but according to some of these models, output growth due to total factor productivity (TFP) increases can either reduce or increase wealth concentration, depending on the environment.

For reasons of analytic tractability—with the exception of articles by Benhabib, Bisin, and Zhu, and Aoki and Nirei—the literature on models with multiplicative shocks abstracts from *endogenous* heterogeneity in saving rates and *endogenous* rates of return, in the form of entrepreneurial income, as a source of persistence in saving rates.[2] Furthermore, it does not consider life-cycle aspects and nonhomotheticity in bequest behavior, which affect wealth accumulation across generations and are important to explaining why rich people have higher saving rates during both their working life and retirement.[3]

Endogenous heterogeneity in saving to insure against earnings and expenditure shocks (including, possibly, medical and nursing home expenditures during retirement) is instead at the center of the quantitative models that we discuss next. The comparative advantage of this literature is its emphasis on understanding the forces that shape differences in saving behavior and rates of return and on quantifying the importance of such heterogeneity in accounting for wealth inequality in rich quantitative models. We argue that previous work has convincingly emphasized that entrepreneurial activity, voluntary bequests, heterogeneity in preferences across families, and compensation risk for top earners can help explain the high degree of wealth concentration. It is not clear, however, to what extent each of these forces quantitatively contributes to wealth inequality, because, at least so far, most of these forces have been studied in isolation. There is also much work to do in determining the extent to which these quantitative frameworks can match the observed large differences in wealth inequality both across countries and over time.

To go from the static understanding of what determines inequality at a point in time to how inequality changes over time, we next study the smaller literature that analyzes the transitional dynamics of the wealth distribution.

To quantitatively assess Piketty's conjecture that changes in the difference between the post-tax rate of return on wealth and the rate of output growth may drive the evolution of wealth concentration, we next perform some numerical simulations in a rich quantitative model that generates the observed inequality in both wealth and earnings. It shows that the effect of the rate of return on wealth concentration is small and that it is essential to distinguish between TFP and population when considering the effects of the output growth rate. Whereas the effect of the TFP growth rate is symmetric to that of the rate of return—both have a small effect on wealth inequality—changes in the rate of population growth have a very large effect on wealth concentration. Thus, the rate of return on capital and the rate of output growth are not perfect substitutes in their effect on wealth concentration when output growth is due to population growth.

We conclude with a discussion of fruitful areas for future research.

Stylized Facts

It is well established that the cross-sectional wealth distribution is right-skewed, unlike the normal distribution, and that its right tail is well approximated by a Pareto distribution. A Pareto distribution implies a linear relationship between the logarithm of wealth, w, and the logarithm of the proportion of individuals, $P(w)$, with wealth above w.[4] Figure 14-1 plots this relationship for the top 10 percent of the wealth distribution in a selected number of countries, with the circles denoting the actual observations and the dashed and solid lines denoting the fitted Pareto model for, respectively, the top 10 percent and top 1 percent of the distribution.

There is vast evidence that wealth is much more concentrated than labor earnings and income. Wold and Whittle cite early evidence for the United States. This fact has also been documented in several more recent articles by various authors.[5]

How wealth is distributed at a point in time is important, but equally important is how much churning there is within the distribution, both at the individual / household level and across generations. At the individual level, Hurst, Luoh, and Stafford document significant mobility across the 20th to 80th percentile range in the United States—they use the Panel Study of Income Dynamics (PSID) data over the 1984–1994 period—but substantial persistence in the top and bottom deciles.[6] For these two groups, the probability of remaining in the same decile ranged between 40 percent and 60 percent, depending on the subperiods.[7] This latter finding implies that 60 percent of total wealth—the share owned by the top decile in Hurst, Luoh, and Stafford—is quite persistent.

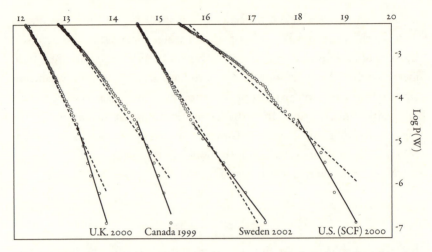

FIGURE 14-1: Pareto tails for selected countries: actual values (circles) and average slopes over the top 10 (dashed line) and 1 (solid line) percent of the distribution / protect (source: Frank K. Cowell, "Inequality among the wealthy," CASE Working Paper No. 150 (2011)).

Concerning the evidence on intergenerational wealth mobility, Mulligan estimates an elasticity of children's to parents' wealth for the United States between 0.32 and 0.43.[8] Charles and Hurst find a value of 0.37 in the PSID, which falls to 0.17 when controlling for children's age, education, and income.[9] Due to data limitations, these estimates are for the intergenerational wealth elasticity for parent-child pairs in which parents are still alive—that is, *before* the transfer of bequests.[10] For this reason, they possibly underestimate the overall degree of intergenerational wealth persistence. This problem is addressed in the studies by Adermon, Lindahl, and Waldenström for Sweden; Boserup, Kopczuk, and Kreiner for Denmark; and Clark and Cummins for England and Wales—all using wealth data spanning more than one generation. The first two studies use wealth tax data; Adermon, Lindahl, and Waldenström find a parent-child rank correlation of 0.3 to 0.4, while Boserup, Kopczuk, and Kreiner estimate a wealth elasticity between 0.4 and 0.5. Clark and Cummins instead exploit a long (1858–2012) panel of families with rare surnames whose wealth is observed at death and find an intergenerational elasticity of 0.4 to 0.5 for the subsample in which they can match parents and children and about 0.7 when grouping individuals by surname cohort.[11]

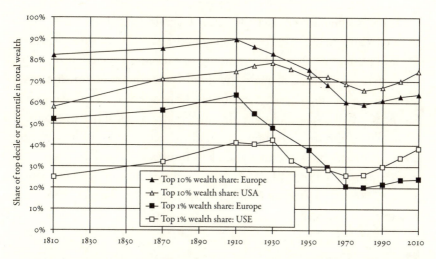

FIGURE 14-2: The evolution of wealth inequality in Europe and the United States (source: Thomas Piketty and Gabriel Zucman, "Wealth and Inheritance in the Long Run," Vol. 2B, chapter 15:1303—1368, ed. A. J. Atkinson and F. Bourguignon Handbook of Income Distribution (Elsevier B.V., 2014).

Overall, the evidence of significant wealth mobility suggests that shocks to economic circumstances are an important determinant of wealth dynamics. This feature lies at the heart of a large literature, which we survey in a later section, that emphasizes wealth accumulation as a way to smooth consumption in the face of idiosyncratic shocks to income.

A third important feature of the wealth distribution is its evolution over time. Until recently, studies documenting the evolution of wealth inequality over time were few and covered relatively short time spans.[12] One important contribution of Piketty's book is to bring together a number of recent studies and document the evolution of the wealth distribution since the Industrial Revolution for a significant number of countries. The main finding, common to the various countries, is that the share of aggregate wealth in the hands of the richest people displays a U-shaped curve starting from very high levels at the beginning of the twentieth century, falling dramatically during the two World Wars to reach its minimum, typically between the Second World War and the 1970s, and then increasing again from the 1980s onward (see Figure 14-2).

There is some debate over the actual magnitude of the increase in the share of wealth held by the top 1 percent of the distribution since the 1980s. Figure 14-2 reports the estimates from tax data in Saez and Zucman that imply that the share has increased by about 13 percentage points, effectively reverting to its 1930 peak.[13] Estimates from the Survey of Consumer Finances (SCF) imply a substantially smaller increase of about 5 percentage points.[14] Despite the uncertainty around the actual magnitude of the increase, understanding its causes and likely future evolution have become an important research topic. In a later section we discuss the extent to which alternative models of wealth inequality can account for the evolution of top wealth concentration.

Piketty's Mechanisms

Piketty's book offers a framework—rooted in the Pareto-tail literature—to explain the evolution of wealth inequality over the course of the twentieth century. According to this framework, wealth inequality increases with the difference between the net of tax average rate of return on wealth, r, and the trend rate of growth of aggregate output, g. This mechanism is consistent with the simultaneous fall in wealth concentration and $(r-g)$ over the course of the twentieth century. Between 1914 and the 1980s, the after-tax rate of return of capital fell, both as a result of the capital losses stemming from the Great Depression and the two World Wars and as a result of the progressive tax policies that have their roots in the shocks of the 1914–1945 period. At the same time, the rate of output growth over the second half of the twentieth century was dramatically larger than at the beginning of the century.

The intuition behind this "$(r-g)$" mechanism is that a higher rate of return, r, increases the rate at which existing wealth is capitalized, amplifying any initial heterogeneity in the wealth distribution. On the other hand, a higher rate of growth, g, increases the rate of accumulation of "new" wealth through saving out of labor earnings, which tends to reduce inequality. Whether existing wealth has been saved by current generations or inherited from previous ones, a higher rate of return increases the importance of wealth relative to current labor income.

Though this mechanism plays an important role in Piketty's book and has drawn a lot of attention, the book mentions other important forces. The first force—related to the previous one because it affects the *intergenerational* rate of wealth accumulation—is inheritance, of both financial and human wealth, and its interplay with demographics.

A second force is the heterogeneity of rates of return and the fact that wealthy people, who invest large amounts of capital, typically obtain higher returns—for instance, because they can take on riskier and less liquid investments, or because they have bigger incentives to hire financial managers and, more generally, to spend time and money to obtain higher returns. In addition, there is also heterogeneity in saving rates, with people with higher initial wealth saving more.

Another important aspect discussed in the book is the rise of the "supermanagers," high-level managers whose share of profits has increased faster than anyone else's, especially in the United States. Piketty argues that this is an important source underpinning the observed increase in inequality in total income. It should be noted that the United States is also the country in which wealth inequality increased the fastest over the same time period.

Finally, *Capital* highlights the importance of government taxes, transfers, government regulations, such as the minimum wage, and market structure in affecting income and wealth inequality across countries and over time for a given country.

Accounting for Wealth Concentration

We now introduce a simple accounting framework, originally due to Meade, to better organize our discussion both of Piketty's $(r-g)$ insight and of the literature on the determinants of wealth inequality.[15] To this end, consider an economy in which the aggregate capital stock grows at the exogenous rate g. At birth, individuals are endowed with a possibly individual-specific fraction of the contemporaneous, aggregate capital stock. The only source of income in the economy is an idiosyncratic rate of return on individual wealth.

In a given period, individual wealth, normalized by the average capital stock, accrues at the exponential rate $r_{it} - g + s_{it}$, where r_{it} is the realized rate of return for individual i of current age t and s_{it} is the ratio between the individual's flow of (dis)saving and her wealth at the beginning of the period.[16]

In this economy, there are three main forces that shape the distribution of individual wealth normalized by the average capital stock:

1. The individual history of saving rates, s_{it}, or equivalently the average saving rate over an individual's lifetime. Ceteris paribus, individuals with a higher average lifetime saving rate have accumulated wealth at a faster rate.

2. The individual history of the growth-adjusted rate of return $r_{it} - g$, or equivalently its average rate over the individual's lifetime. Ceteris paribus, individuals with a larger average lifetime return—that is, a history of high intra-period returns—have seen their wealth grow faster than individuals with a low average return. Conversely, for a given cross-sectional distribution of individual returns, r_{it}, a higher rate of growth, g, reduces the rate of growth of normalized individual wealth, by reducing the rate at which individual wealth grows relative to the aggregate economy.

3. The distribution of wealth at birth. Even abstracting from individual differences in rates of return and saving rates, the wealth differential between two individuals within the same cohort born with heterogeneous wealth endowments increases with age at the common rate of accumulation. An increase in the difference between the common rate of return, r, and the growth rate, g, increases this rate of divergence.

This last effect captures the essence of Piketty's $(r - g)$ insight. For given saving rates, the power of exponential compounding suggests that the persistent changes in the difference $(r - g)$ increase substantially the rate of divergence in the wealth distribution. Therefore, "growth or multiplicative" effects are crucial to account for why a minority of individuals hold a disproportionate share of aggregate wealth. This basic mechanism lies at the heart of the mostly analytical literature on multiplicative models of wealth accumulation, which we survey in a later section.

Analytical Models Generating Pareto Tails in the Wealth Distribution

Since Pareto, this feature of the wealth distribution has been further documented and has motivated a number of studies proposing economic mechanisms generating a wealth distribution with a right Pareto tail.

These mechanisms require multiplicative random shocks to the wealth accumulation process and fall into two main categories. The first type requires individual wealth to grow exponentially at some positive average rate until an exponentially distributed stopping time (for instance, death). In the absence of intergenerational transmission of wealth, this class of models implies counterfactually that all wealth heterogeneity is between, rather than within, age cohorts.[17] The individuals with higher wealth are the survivors from older cohorts that have accumulated wealth over a longer horizon. Allowing for stochastic intergenerational transmission of wealth, as in the article by Benhabib and Bisin, introduces additional heterogeneity: Within a cohort, individuals belonging to a dynasty with a longer history of bequests are wealthier.[18] To sum up, the general mechanism implies that the Pareto coefficient that indexes the thickness of the right tail of the distribution of wealth (relative to the size of the economy) is increasing in the growth rate of individual wealth relative to aggregate wealth, and decreasing in the probability of death and in those forces, such as redistributive estate taxation, that compress the wealth distribution at birth.

The second type of mechanism generating Pareto tails is, to some extent, conceptually opposite to the previous one and requires that the exponential rate of growth of individual wealth follows an appropriate stochastic process with a negative mean. The negative mean growth rate implies that, on average, individual wealth reverts to the mean of the distribution. Yet the lucky few with a long history of above-average positive rates of wealth growth escape this mean reversion force and accumulate large fortunes. Some inflow mechanism—such as transfers, positive additive income shocks, precautionary saving, and / or borrowing constraints—is necessary to provide a reflecting barrier that ensures that the mean of the wealth distribution is bounded away from zero. Models in this class generate both within- and between-cohort inequality.[19] They imply that the Pareto coefficient is larger, (1) the larger the variance of shocks, which increases the probability of long histories of positive shocks; or (2) the weaker the offsetting inflow mechanism, which increases the mean of the stationary distribution.

In common with the first class of models, these models imply that wealth concentration, as measured by the Pareto coefficient, is decreasing in the rate of wealth mean reversion—that is, it is increasing in the average rate of growth of individual relative to aggregate wealth. Such a rate equals the sum, on the one hand, of the difference $(r-g)$ between the average post-tax rate of return, r, and the rate of aggregate growth and, on the other hand, the average ratio sw between saving out of noncapital income and wealth. The logic of exponential growth implies that, in all models with multiplicative shocks, small variations in $(r-g)$ or sw generate large changes in the Pareto coefficient.

In their article, Benhabib, Bisin, and Zhu build a partial equilibrium, overlapping-generation model with a homothetic bequest motive in which individuals are born with independent and identically distributed (i.i.d.) earnings and rates of return to wealth, which remain constant over an individual's lifetime. They find that in their framework, it is rate-of-return shocks rather than earnings shocks across individuals that affect the shape of the right tail of the stationary wealth distribution. This is best understood in the case in which individuals have logarithmic preferences and wealth bequeathed equals a common share of wealth at birth but capitalized at the individual-specific rates of return. Wealthy dynasties have a long history of above-average rates of return. This mechanism is isomorphic to the model in the article by Piketty and Zucman, where each generation draws a bequest share and wealthy dynasties have a long history of above-average draws. For this reason, capital and bequest taxes can significantly reduce wealth inequality, the former through its effect on the net rates of return and the latter through the share of wealth that is transferred from one generation to the other. The propensity to leave bequests has a similar effect.[20]

In two articles, Benhabib, Bisin, and Zhu, and Aoki and Nirei show that a similar mechanism generates a wealth distribution with an asymptotically Pareto right tail in the general equilibrium of a Bewley model in which, in addition to the usual additive earnings risk, individuals face idiosyncratic multiplicative rate-of-return risk, in the form of shocks to their backyard production technology and can self-insure by lending and borrowing up to a limit, using a risk-free asset.[21] The introduction of individual-specific risk introduces a precautionary saving motive that is absent from all the models discussed above. Yet as wealth gets large enough, the precautionary saving motive goes to zero, as individuals can perfectly insure against the bounded earnings risk and saving is linear in wealth. Therefore, the multiplicative rate-of-return shock tends to dominate the distribution of wealth at high levels.

Because the presence of a borrowing constraint makes it difficult to characterize the Pareto coefficient in closed form, Aoki and Nirei use numerical simulations to confirm some of the insights from the article by Benhabib, Bisin, and Zhu in such a framework, but also obtain some new results.[22] First, they show that the presence of a precautionary saving motive implies that an increase in additive earnings risk reduces the thickness of the right tail of the wealth distribution by increasing the precautionary saving of low-wealth relative to high-wealth individuals. They also find that, contrary to the intuition from partial equilibrium models, an increase in the rate of TFP growth (which is zero in the articles by Benhabib, Bisin, and Zhu) has the effect of *increasing,* rather than reducing, wealth inequality.[23] In general equilibrium, a higher rate of TFP growth increases the steady-state capital stock, thus reducing the average return to detrended capital and reducing inequality. On the other hand, higher TFP growth increases the variability of the idiosyncratic return to the backyard technology, thus increasing inequality. This second effect prevails and implies that higher TFP growth increases inequality, as measured by the Pareto coefficient.

A similar reversal of the partial equilibrium insight into the effect of TFP growth on wealth inequality is also found by Jones, who studies a version of Blanchard-Yaari's model with logarithmic preferences and accidental bequests distributed uniformly to newborns.[24] The model generates a Pareto wealth distribution across cohorts through a deterministic, positive growth rate of individual wealth. In general equilibrium, the Pareto coefficient is independent of the rate of TFP growth and is fully determined by the demographic parameters.

The results in Aoki and Nirei and in Jones suggest that a negative relationship between the rate of growth and wealth concentration is not a robust feature of models with multiplicative shocks in general equilibrium.[25]

Bewley Models

In this framework, precautionary saving against earnings risk is the key force driving wealth concentration. The strength of the precautionary motive for saving, however, declines with wealth relative to labor earnings; it declines with one's ability to self-insure against earnings risk. It follows that if agents are impatient—a necessary condition to ensure stationarity of the wealth distribution—the saving rate is positive below, and turns negative above, the target value of net worth relative to labor earnings for which the precautionary saving motive is exactly offset by impatience. Hence, the saving rate in these models is declining in wealth.

In contrast, Saez and Zucman, among others, find that saving rates tend to rise with wealth, with the bottom 90 percent of wealth holders saving on average 3 percent of their income, compared with 15 percent for the next 9 percent and 20 percent to 25 percent for the top 1 percent of wealth holders.[26] The basic version of the model thus fails to generate the high concentration of wealth in the hands of the richest few—and therefore the emergence and persistence of their very large estates—because it misses the fact that rich people keep saving at high rates.

Saving behavior crucially depends on rates of return, patience, and earnings risk. High rates of return tend to increase savings. Rates of return are not exogenous, however, which raises the question of how rates of return are determined, especially at the top of the wealth distribution. For entrepreneurs, they are endogenous as a result of the decision to start a business and of the share of their wealth invested in their own risky activity. For investors, they are endogenous as a result of portfolio choice.

Patience is affected not only by how much people discount their utility from future consumption, but also by whether households care about leaving bequests to others after their own death and even how long they expect to live.

Taken together, the two points above imply that if people differ in their patience and risk tolerance, they might also select into different occupations and portfolio compositions and thus different returns, which will be correlated with their patience and risk attitude. As a result, more patient and less risk-averse people will take on riskier positions. While some of them will fail, some of them will succeed and enjoy very high returns. This implies that there will be a larger fraction of more patient and less risk-averse people among the rich, partly because they represent those who got lucky and partly because they have different preferences and their observed returns depend on their past occupational and saving decisions and on their preferences.

The third element in our list concerns high and heterogeneous earnings risk. Moderately persistent and skewed earnings shocks have the potential to generate heterogeneous savings rates. In fact, Castañeda, Díaz-Giménez, and Ríos-Rull show that a specific form of earnings risk for top earners can generate a very large wealth concentration in the hands of the richest few. This relates to the finding discussed by Piketty on the rising importance of the supermanagers, especially in the United States, and the volatility of their total compensation.[27]

In the rest of this section, we discuss the mechanisms that appear to hold the most promise for offsetting the fall of the saving rate as a function of wealth in the standard Bewley model and, therefore, can better account for the observed high top wealth share.

Endogeneity of Rates of Return

An important choice generating endogenous rates of return is entrepreneurial activity. Quadrini provides a nice survey of the factors affecting the decision to become an entrepreneur and the aggregate and distributional implications of entrepreneurship for saving and investment.[28] In addition, Quadrini, Gentry and Hubbard; De Nardi, Doctor, and Krane; and Buera argue convincingly that entrepreneurship is a key element in understanding wealth concentration among the richest households.[29]

Cagetti and De Nardi show that entrepreneurs constitute a large fraction of rich people in the data. In the 1989 Survey of Consumer Finances, for example, among the richest 1 percent of people in terms of net worth, 63 percent were entrepreneurs and they held 68 percent of the total wealth in the hands of the wealthiest 1 percent of people. Cagetti and De Nardi also build a model of entrepreneurship in which altruistic agents care about their children and face uncertainty about their time of death and thus leave both accidental and voluntary bequests. In every period, agents decide whether to run a business or work for a wage, and borrowing constraints generate a need for collateral and thus increase savings as long as the entrepreneur is constrained.[30]

In Cagetti and De Nardi's calibration, the optimal firm size is large and the entrepreneur is borrowing-constrained. Thus, even rich entrepreneurs want to keep saving to accumulate collateral to grow their firm and reap higher returns from capital. This is the mechanism that, in this framework, keeps the rich people's saving rate high and generates a high wealth concentration. As a result, their model generates wealth concentration that matches well that in the data, including the right tail of the distribution. In addition, the model implies plausible returns to capital in the range of those found by Moskowitz and Vissing-Jørgensen, and Kartashova. Finally, the model generates entry probabilities into the entrepreneurial sector as a function of one's wealth that are consistent with those estimated by Hurst and Lusardi on microlevel data and also implies that inheritances are a strong predictor of business entry.[31]

Kitao studies the effect of taxation on entrepreneurial choice in a model with multiple entrepreneurial ability levels.[32]

Among the models studying portfolio choice and wealth inequality, Kacperczyk, Nosal, and Stevens quantitatively evaluate portfolio choice in the presence of endogenous information acquisition and heterogeneity in investor sophistication and asset riskiness.[33] They show that an increase in aggregate information technology can explain the observed increase in wealth concentration among investors since 1990.

Earnings Risk and the Rise of the Supermanagers

There is a large literature studying precautionary savings as a mechanism to self-insure against earnings shocks. Carroll shows that the marginal propensity to consume out of a permanent income shock is close to, though lower than, one in a precautionary saving model with both transitory and permanent income shocks.[34] This implies that the saving rate out of wealth is hardly affected by permanent earnings shocks. Instead, in the case in which income shocks are purely transitory, consumption smoothing implies that individuals will save most of the income change. On the other hand, the transitory nature of the shocks, and therefore of the associated saving response, implies that the effect averages out. Hence, these forces do not imply a first-order persistent growth effect on savings and cannot generate substantial wealth concentration.

Precautionary saving behavior to self-insure against earnings risk, however, can generate a top wealth concentration (right skewness) if the stochastic process for labor earnings is appropriately skewed and persistent. Castañeda, Díaz-Giménez, and Ríos-Rull were the first to numerically generate this result in a model economy with perfectly altruistic agents going through a stochastic life cycle of working age, retirement, and death.[35] Their paper calibrates the parameters of the income process to match some features of the U.S. data, including measures of earnings and wealth inequality. The key force generating large wealth holdings in the hands of the richest is a productivity shock process calibrated so that the highest productivity level is more than 100 times higher than the second-highest. Thus, there is a large discrepancy between the highest productivity level and all of the others. Moreover, an agent in the highest productivity state has a roughly 20 percent chance of becoming more than 100 times less productive during the next period. Intuitively, high-earnings households have very high precautionary saving rates for two reasons. First, they face a large downside earnings risk and therefore they accumulate a large wealth buffer to self-insure against the possibly very large fall in earnings. As a result, they have a large target ratio of wealth relative to earnings. Second, a high wealth-to-earnings target corresponds to a very large target wealth *level* for agents with high earnings.

It is important to note that the steady-state fraction of high earners that drive the top wealth shares in Castañeda, Díaz-Giménez, and Ríos-Rull is extremely small (on the order of 0.04 percent). This feature is consistent with the following findings by Saez and Zucman: First, the large increase in wealth inequality in the United States over the past thirty years has been mostly driven by the threefold increase in the wealth share of the top 0.1 percent of wealth holders. Second, the main driver of the rapid increase in wealth at the top has been the large increase in the share of earnings earned by top wealth holders.[36]

From a theoretical standpoint, the "economics of superstars" (Rosen) rationalizes the emergence of a small number of highly compensated individuals and a highly skewed distribution of earnings with very large rewards at the top. Gabaix and Landier propose a model to rationalize increased CEO compensation between 1980 and 2003, while Lee develops a model of occupational choice for workers, entrepreneurs, and managers that endogenously generates high managerial wages.[37]

A series of papers by Thomas Piketty and Emmanuel Saez, together with a number of coauthors, have documented the skewness of the earnings and income distribution.[38] Recently, Guvenen, Karahan, Ozkan, and Song have exploited a large panel data set of earnings histories drawn from U.S. administrative records. They documented that earnings shocks display significant negative skewness and that for very high earners—individuals in the top fifth percentile of the income distribution—the increase in the absolute value of skewness over the lifetime is entirely driven by an increase in the risk of negative shocks, rather than a lower risk of positive ones.[39] Parker and Vissing-Jørgensen provide more empirical support for this modeling assumption and calibration, as they find that incomes at the top are highly cyclical because of the labor component and bonuses in particular.[40]

The Importance of Intergenerational Wealth Transmission

Piketty's book also stresses the importance of inherited wealth. Intergenerational transfers account for at least 50 to 60 percent of total wealth accumulation (Gale and Scholz) in the United States and potentially represent an important transmission channel of wealth inequality across generations. Furthermore, a luxury-good-type bequest motive can help explain why rich households save at much higher rates than the rest (Dynan, Skinner, and Zeldes; Carroll), why the portfolios of the rich are skewed toward risky assets (Carroll), and, possibly in conjunction with medical expenses, the low rates of dissaving of the rich elderly (De Nardi, French, and Jones).[41]

De Nardi introduces two types of intergenerational links in the overlapping-generation, life-cycle model used by Huggett: voluntary bequests and transmission of human capital. She models the utility from bequests as providing a "warm glow." In this framework, parents and their children are thus linked by voluntary and accidental bequests and by the transmission of earnings ability. The households thus save to self-insure against labor earnings shocks and life-span risk, for retirement, and possibly to leave bequests to their children. In De Nardi's model, therefore, voluntary and accidental bequests coexist and their relative size and importance are determined by the calibration. The calibration adopted implies that bequests are a luxury good, generates a realistic distribution of estates, and is also quantitatively consistent with the elasticity of the savings of the elderly to permanent income that has been estimated from microeconomic data by Altonji and Villanueva.[42]

De Nardi's work shows that voluntary bequests can explain the emergence of large estates, which are often accumulated over more than one generation and characterize the upper tail of the wealth distribution in the data. The calibration implies a much stronger bequest motive to save for the richest households, who, even when very old, keep some assets to leave to their children. The rich leave more wealth to their offspring, who in turn tend to do the same. This behavior generates some large estates that are transmitted across generations because of the voluntary bequests. Transmission of ability between parents and children also helps generate a concentrated wealth distribution. More-productive parents accumulate larger estates and leave larger bequests to their children, who in turn are more productive than average in the workplace. The presence of a bequest motive also generates lifetime saving profiles that imply slower wealth decumulation in old age for richer people, consistent with the facts documented by De Nardi, French, and Jones, using microlevel data from the Health and Retirement Survey.[43] Yet although modeling explicitly intergenerational links helps explain the savings of the richest, the model by De Nardi is not capable of matching the wealth concentration of the richest 1 percent without adding complementary forces generating a high wealth concentration for the rich.[44]

Thus, De Nardi and Yang merge a version of the model with intergenerational links with the high earnings risk for the top earners mechanism proposed by Castañeda, Díaz-Giménez, and Ríos-Rull (discussed in a later section) and find that these two forces together match important features of the data well.[45] Interestingly, they distinguish between the contribution to wealth inequality of the stochastic earnings process and that of bequests. They show that bequests account for about 10 percentage points in the share of wealth held by individuals in the top 20 percentiles.

As Piketty points out in *Capital,* wealth inequality is also large within various age and demographic groups. Venti and Wise, and Bernheim, Skinner, and Weimberg, for instance, show that wealth is highly dispersed at retirement, even for people with similar lifetime incomes, and argue that these differences cannot be explained only by events such as family status, health, and inheritances, nor by portfolio choice. Hendricks focuses on the ability of a basic overlapping-generations model to match the cross-sectional wealth inequality at retirement age. He shows that the model overstates wealth differences at retirement between earnings-rich and earnings-poor, while it understates the amount of wealth inequality conditional on similar lifetime earnings. Instead, De Nardi and Yang show that an overlapping-generations model augmented with voluntary bequests and intergenerational transmission of earnings also matches quite well the observed cross-sectional differences in wealth at retirement and their correlation with lifetime incomes.[46]

Preference Heterogeneity

An additional plausible avenue to help explain the vastly different amounts of wealth held by individuals is exogenous heterogeneity in saving behavior. The source of this heterogeneity in saving behavior is an important issue. There is enough microlevel empirical evidence of preference heterogeneity to suggest that preference heterogeneity might be a plausible avenue to help explain the vastly different amounts of wealth held by people. Lawrance and Cagetti, for example, find large heterogeneity in people's preferences.[47]

Krusell and Smith study the impact of preference heterogeneity, in the form of persistent (with an average persistence of one generation) shocks to the time-preference rate in an infinite-horizon model with idiosyncratic, transitory earnings shocks.[48] They find that a small amount of preference heterogeneity dramatically improves the model's ability to match the variance of the cross-sectional distribution of wealth.[49] While capturing the variance of the wealth distribution, however, their model and calibration fail to match the extreme degree of concentration of wealth in the hands of the top 1 percent of wealth holders.

Hendricks studies the effects of preference heterogeneity in a life-cycle framework with persistent earnings shocks and only accidental bequests.[50] He shows that time preference heterogeneity makes a modest contribution in accounting for high wealth concentration if the heterogeneity in discount factors is chosen to generate realistic patterns of consumption and wealth inequality as cohorts age.

In sum, previous work indicates that preference heterogeneity, and especially patience heterogeneity, can generate increased wealth dispersion. It would be interesting to deepen the previous analysis by both studying richer processes for patience and allowing for richer formulations of the utility function in which, for instance, risk aversion and intertemporal substitution do not have to coincide (see Wang, Wang, and Yang for some interesting findings on this).[51]

Transitional Dynamics of the Wealth Distribution

An important contribution of Piketty's book is to document the evolution of wealth inequality over a long span of time.

In the absence of big shocks, one may expect the concept of a stationary state to provide a useful reference to describe where an economy will settle down in the long run. In fact, the whole line of research discussed above studies the impact of alternative mechanisms on the shape of the *stationary* wealth distribution and mostly abstracts from both stochastic and deterministic aggregate changes in the economy's fundamentals in driving either the stochastic steady state or the transition of the economy as some force, such as government policy, changes over time.

Yet one question that naturally arises when observing, for example, the evolution of the top wealth shares for Europe and the United States reported in Figure 14-2 is the extent to which there were neither big shocks nor other deterministic changes in the fundamentals driving inequality during that long period. For instance, the top 1 percent and 10 percent wealth shares in Figure 14-2 display an upward trend up to 1910 for Europe and up to 1930 for the United States, and an upward trend for both areas after 1970. In addition, during the pre-1910 period the transitional dynamics seem to be quite slow, whereas the post-1970 U.S. experience points to rapid changes in the concentration of wealth in its upper tail. Two recent contributions tackle the question of whether existing models can account for the fast increase in U.S. top wealth inequality after 1970.

Gabaix, Lasry, Lions, and Moll study this question in a partial equilibrium model with multiplicative and idiosyncratic rate-of-return shocks that give rise to a wealth distribution with a Pareto right tail, of the type we discuss in a later section. They find that, without additional amplifying mechanisms, the model implies a transitional dynamic of wealth inequality in response to a one-off shock—for example, a change in the tax rate on capital that is too slow compared with the post-1980 rise in U.S. top wealth inequality as documented in the Survey of Consumer Finances, let alone compared with the much faster rate of increase documented by Saez and Zucman. On the basis of their findings, Gabaix et al. conjecture that a positive correlation between wealth and either saving rates or rates of return is necessary to account for the observed speed of the change in wealth inequality in terms of an increase in post-tax rates of returns or a fall in the aggregate rate of growth. As we have seen, models of entrepreneurship and of a nonhomothetic bequest motive can generate this type of correlation.[52]

Kaymak and Poschke study the transitional dynamics associated with the changes in the U.S. tax-and-transfer system over the past fifty years within a Bewley economy with an income process à la Castañeda, Díaz-Giménez, and Ríos-Rull, calibrated to match the income and wealth (including the top) distributions in the 1960s. They find that the increase in wealth inequality over the period can be accounted for by the increase in wage inequality, the changes in the tax system, and the expansion of Social Security and Medicare. More specifically, the increase in wage inequality accounts for more than half of the increase in top wealth inequality, as the increase in downside risk for workers in the top income states substantially boosts their precautionary saving. The remaining share of the increase in top wealth inequality is due to the fall in taxes (which increases the net return to saving) and the expansion of Social Security and Medicare (which reduces precautionary saving by poorer households). The latter effect increases the equilibrium interest rate and wealth accumulation by the rich. They also show that, assuming no further shocks after 2010, the top 1 percent wealth share would take roughly fifty years to increase by about 10 percentage points toward its new steady-state value of about 50 percent.[53]

One lesson to draw from comparing Kaymak and Poschke results with those by Gabaix, Lasry, Lions, and Moll and our earlier findings is that an important advantage of a quantitative framework is the ability to model in a more realistic way the evolution of important determinants of wealth inequality. On the fiscal side, for example, the *whole* set of changes to the progressivity of taxes and Social Security modeled by Kaymak and Poschke accounts for a substantially larger change in wealth inequality than our stylized experiments conducted in an earlier section and in Gabaix, Lasry, Lions, and Moll.[54]

A Simulation Exercise

This section uses the quantitative model of wealth inequality in De Nardi and Yang to test some of the predictions in *Capital*. The model is calibrated to the U.S. economy (see the Appendix for a description of the model and a discussion of the calibration choices), and the crucial features that allow it to match the U.S. wealth distribution are the combination of a voluntary bequest motive and a stochastic earnings process similar to that in Castañeda, Díaz-Giménez, and Ríos-Rull.[55]

TABLE 14-1.

Percentage of earnings in the top percentiles

		Percentile (%)					
	Gini	1	5	20	40	60	80
Data (SCF 1998)	0.63	14.8	31.1	61.4	84.7	97.2	100.00
Benchmark	0.62	14.7	31.3	63.0	85.0	93.4	100.00

Table 14-1 reports the earnings distribution at selected percentiles in the SCF data reported by Castañeda, Díaz-Giménez, and Ríos-Rull and in the data generated by the model.[56] Comparing the first two lines in the table reveals that benchmark calibration matches the earnings distribution very well.

Looking ahead to Table 14-3, we see the wealth distribution at selected percentiles in the SCF data and the various versions of the model studied. The comparison of the first two lines in the table shows that the benchmark calibration matches the wealth distribution in the SCF well. This is especially true for the share of wealth held by the top percentile. The model also matches, by construction, a bequest flow / GDP ratio of 2.8 percent[57] and the 90th percentile of the bequest distribution normalized by income. Thus, the model is capable of accounting for a number of data moments that should be informative on the contribution of the various motives for saving to individual wealth accumulation and to the cross-sectional wealth distribution.

We use the model to conduct two experiments to discuss the $(r-g)$ mechanism highlighted in *Capital*—in particular, the conjecture that it is only the difference between the average net rate of return on wealth and the rate of GDP growth that matters for wealth inequality. Note that the steady-state rate of GDP growth is the sum of the TFP growth rate and the rate of population growth. It is straightforward to verify that a change in the TFP growth rate is fully equivalent to an opposite change in the rate of return on wealth, at least in partial equilibrium. The same cannot be said for a change in the rate of population growth, because the latter changes the demographic composition. To investigate the quantitative importance of this distinction, we compare the effect of an increase in the post-tax rate of

TABLE 14-2.

Aggregate effects, adjusting the labor income tax. Aggregate labor is expressed as a ratio to that in the benchmark. Aggregate output is expressed as a ratio to that in the benchmark.

	τ_{SS}	τ_l	Y	A/Y	B/Y	$r-g$	r
Benchmark	0.12	0.19	1.0	3.1	2.8%	3.3	4.5
(1) $\Delta n = -1.2\%$	0.17	0.18	—	4.1	4.5%	4.5	4.5
(2) $\Delta r = 1.2\%$	0.12	0.14	—	4.7	5.1%	4.5	5.7

return to capital, r, and of a fall in the rate of population growth, n, by the same amount.

For simplicity, we conduct our experiments in partial equilibrium, keeping factor prices constant. Allowing for general equilibrium implies only minor quantitative differences in the equilibrium response of the wealth distribution. In all experiments, the proportional rate of contribution to Social Security adjusts to balance the Social Security budget, while the proportional labor income tax adjusts to balance the rest of the government budget. The calibrated value of the coefficient of relative risk aversion is 1.5, while the subjective discount factor $\beta = 0.945$. Table 14-2 reports the values of the Social Security tax τ_{SS}, the proportional labor tax rate τ_l, output Y, and the ratios of the aggregate stock of assets A and flow of bequests B to output, as well as factor prices, in the benchmark and the experiments. In what follows, r denotes the gross (pretax) rate of return on capital and $r = (1 - \tau_a)r$ the rate of return net of the proportional capital income tax $\tau_a = 0.2$. The value of τ_a is 0.2 in the benchmark calibration.

Lower Rate of Population Growth

In experiment (1), we consider the effect of reducing the rate of population growth n from 1.2 percent a year to zero.

Comparing the first two rows in Table 14-3 reveals that a fall in the population growth rate marginally increases overall wealth inequality as measured by the Gini coefficient and substantially increases the share of aggregate wealth accruing to the top 20th percentile of the wealth distribution. The effect is particularly pronounced for the top percentile, whose share

TABLE 14-3.

Percentage of total wealth held by households in the top percentiles

	Gini	Percentile (%)					
		1	5	20	40	60	80
Data (SCF 1998)	0.80	34.7	57.8	69.1	81.7	93.9	98.9
Benchmark	0.80	35.7	52.0	65.9	82.8	95.4	99.5
(1) $\Delta n = -1.2\%$	0.81	40.3	54.8	67.4	83.3	95.7	99.4
(2) $\Delta r = 1.2\%$	0.79	35.9	51.2	64.1	80.2	94.1	98.9

increases by about 5 percentage points. The fall in the rate of population growth increases the average age of the labor force and, because the share of the super-rich increases with age, the top shares of earnings and the wealth / GDP ratio. In addition, the higher ratio of deaths to births increases the aggregate flow of bequests to GDP (compare the first two rows in Table 14-2) and the average bequest size. Because the calibration implies that bequests are a luxury good, this last effect increases wealth concentration at the top.

Higher Return on Wealth

In experiment (2), we increase the yearly post-tax rate of return on wealth by 1.2 percentage points, so that the difference between the yearly post-tax rate of return on capital and the rate of population growth increases by the same amount as in the previous experiment. Given the partial equilibrium assumption, the increase in the interest rate is thus associated with a higher wealth / income ratio *and* share of capital relative to labor income. This is exactly the kind of scenario discussed in *Capital*.

Comparing rows 2 and 3 in Table 14-2 reveals that the increase in the return to capital has an even larger effect on the aggregate stock of wealth and the flow of bequests than the fall in population growth. Conversely, and contrary to the conjecture that it is the difference between the two rates that matters for inequality, the higher interest rate increases the share of wealth owned by the top 1 percent only marginally and actually *reduces* wealth concentration in the top 20th percentile.

Intuitively, the increase in the rate of return on capital reduces impatience by raising $\beta(1+r)$ and thus increases precautionary saving by individuals with low wealth relative to earnings. The negative wealth effect associated with the higher rate at which future earnings are discounted also boosts saving for these individuals. This increases the average wealth holding and reduces inequality. Conversely, in the case of wealthy savers for which capital is the main source of income, the precautionary saving and wealth effects are small and the income and substitution effects are roughly offsetting. As a consequence, the ratio between consumption and wealth is not much affected and the higher interest rate translates into a higher rate of capital accumulation.

What We Have Learned

To sum up, our findings confirm Piketty's insight that, qualitatively, an increase in the rate of return on capital or a fall in the rate of growth of output due to a demographic change both increase wealth concentration. Contrary to his conjecture, though, we find that the rate of return on wealth and the rate of population growth are not perfect substitutes in their effect on wealth concentration. For the same change in the difference between the two rates, an increase in the rate of return has a much smaller effect on wealth concentration than does a fall in the rate of population growth by the same amount. The intuition is that a lower rate of population growth is associated with a higher ratio of deaths to births and, as a consequence, a higher average bequest size. To the extent that bequests are a luxury good, this last effect has a significant impact on wealth concentration at the top.

Where Do We Go (in Terms of Modeling) and What Data Do We Need?

In addition to providing many important facts and ideas, Piketty's book has revitalized interest in inequality, especially wealth inequality, and in understanding the determinants of savings across all levels of the wealth and earnings distributions. This raises the question of where we go from here both in terms of modeling and in terms of data needed to better discipline these models.

As we have argued, quantitative Bewley models can generate realistic wealth inequality both in steady state and along the transition path. In addition, they offer the possibility of exploring quantitatively the contribution of various competing mechanisms shaping the dynamics of individual wealth accumulation, as well as of modeling detailed features of the institutional environment. In this framework, entrepreneurship, intergenerational links, earnings risk, medical expenses, and heterogeneous preferences have been shown to be important to understanding saving behavior and wealth inequality. They should be studied more closely so we can better understand how they work, and jointly, so we can better understand how they interact and their relative importance.

Thinking more about modeling entrepreneurial heterogeneity is both empirically reasonable and potentially important. Campbell and De Nardi find, for instance, that aspirations about the size of the firm that one would like to run are different for men and women and that many people who are trying to start a business also work for an employer and thus work very long hours in total.[58] It would be interesting to generalize the model to allow, for instance, for heterogeneity in entrepreneurial total factor productivity and optimal firm size (or decreasing-returns-to-scale parameters) and convincingly take the model to data to estimate those additional parameters. Given the data on time allocation, it would also be interesting to think more about the time allocation decision between working for an employer, starting and running one's own firm, working on home production, and enjoying leisure.[59]

More work is also warranted to evaluate the role of intergenerational links. How should we model bequests? How important are inter vivos transfers, and do they provide an important dimension of wealth heterogeneity early on in life that is then amplified by shocks and individual saving behavior later on?

De Nardi, French, and Jones have shown that medical expenses have large effects on old-age savings throughout the income distribution.[60] How do life-span risk and out-of-pocket medical expenses interact, and to what extent does heterogeneity in out-of-pocket medical expenses—which rise quickly with age and income during retirement—coupled with heterogeneous life-span risks contribute to wealth inequality?

Is the type of top-earnings risk necessary to account for the observed degree of top wealth concentration on the basis of precautionary behavior consistent with the empirical, microlevel evidence from earnings data? This question has been notoriously difficult to address, given that the usual survey data sets of individual earnings are either top-coded or do not oversample the rich. Comprehensive administrative data on earnings that have recently become available provide a way to address this problem. De Nardi, Fella, and Paz Pardo provide a first attempt to tackle this question by studying the implications for wealth inequality of an income process that is consistent with the skewness and kurtosis documented by recent studies (Guvenen, Karahan, Ozkan, and Song) relying on U.S. Social Security administrative data.[61]

Finally, to what extent does preference heterogeneity amplify and interact with the mechanisms above? How much preference heterogeneity is needed to understand the data once other observable factors, such as entrepreneurial choice, are accounted for and properly calibrated or estimated?

Appendix: The Model Used for Our Simulations in the Preceding Section

The model is a discrete-time, incomplete-markets, overlapping-generations economy with an infinitely lived government.

The Government

The government taxes capital at rate τ_a, labor income and Social Security pay-outs at rate τ_l, and estates at rate τ_b above the exemption level x_b to finance government spending G. Social Security benefits, $P(\tilde{y})$, are linked to one's realized average annual earnings $\tilde{y}$, up to a Social Security cap $\tilde{y}_c$, and are financed through a labor income tax τ_s. The two government budget constraints, one for Social Security and the other one for government spending, are balanced during each period.

Firm and Technology

There is one representative firm producing goods according to the aggregate production function $F(K; L) = K^\alpha L^{1-\alpha}$, where K is the aggregate capital stock and L is the aggregate labor input. The final goods can either be consumed or invested in physical capital, which depreciates at rate δ.

Demographics and Labor Earnings

Each model period lasts five years. Agents start their economic life at the age of 20 ($t = 1$). By age 35 ($t = 4$), the agents' children are born. The agents retire at age 65 ($t = 10$). From that period on, each household faces a positive probability of dying, given by ($1 - p_t$), which depends only on age.[62] The maximum life span is age 90 ($T = 14$), and the population grows at a constant rate n.

Total labor productivity of worker i at age t is given by $y_t^i = e^{z_t^i + \varepsilon t}$, in which ε_t is the deterministic age-efficiency profile. The process for the stochastic earnings shock z_t^i is: $z_t^i = \rho_z z_{t-1}^i + \mu_t^i, \mu_t^i \sim N(0, \sigma_u^2)$.

To capture the intergenerational correlation of earnings, we assume that the productivity of worker i at age 55 is transmitted to children j at age 20 as follows: $z_1^j = \rho_h z_8^i + v^j, v^j \sim N(0, \sigma_h^2)$, as parents are 35 years (seven model periods) older than their children.

Preferences

Preferences are time separable, with a constant discount factor β. The period utility function from consumption is given by $U(c) = (c^{1-\gamma} - 1) / (1 - \gamma)$.

People derive utility from holding onto assets because they turn into bequests upon death. This form of "impure" bequest motive implies that an individual cares about total bequests left to his / her children, but not about his / her children's consumption.

The utility from bequests b is denoted by

$$\phi(b) = \phi_1 \left[\left(b + \phi_2 \right)^{1-\gamma} - 1 \right].$$

The term ϕ_1 measures the strength of bequest motives, while ϕ_2 reflects the extent to which bequests are luxury goods. If $\phi_2 > 0$, the marginal utility of small bequests is bounded, while the marginal utility of large bequests declines more slowly than the marginal utility of consumption. In the benchmark model, we set b as bequest net of estate tax, b_n. We also consider the case in which gross bequests, b_g, enter the utility function. In that case, we set $b = b_g$. Our formulation is thus more flexible than in articles by De Nardi, and De Nardi and Yang, and Yang, because we allow for two kinds of bequest motives.[63] In the first one, parents care about bequests net of taxes. In the second one, parents care about bequests gross of taxes. A more altruistic parent would take into account that some of the estate is taxed away, but parents might just care about what assets they leave, rather than how much their offspring receive.

The Household's Recursive Problem

We assume that children have full information about their parents' state variables and infer the size of the bequests that they are likely to receive based on this information. The potential set of a household's state variables is given by $x = (t, a, z, \tilde{y}, S_p)$, where t is household age (notice that in the presence of a fixed age gap, one's age is also informative about one's parents' age), a denotes the agent's financial assets carried from the previous period, z is the current earnings shock, and $\tilde{y}$ stands for annual accumulated earnings, up to a Social Security cap $\tilde{y}_c$, which are used to compute Social Security payments. The term S_p stands for parental state variables other than age and, more precisely, is given by $S_p = (a_p, z_p, \tilde{y}_p)$. It thus includes parental assets, current earnings, and accumulated earnings. When one's parent retires, z_p or current parental earnings becomes irrelevant and we set it to zero with no loss of generality.

From 20 to 60 years of age ($t=1$ to $t=9$), the agent works and survives for sure to next period. Let $V_w(t, a, z, \tilde{y}, S_p)$ and $V_w^I(t, a, z, \tilde{y})$ denote the value functions of a working-age person whose parent is alive and dead, respectively, where I stands for "inherited." In the former case, the household's parent is still alive and might die with probability p_{t+7}, in which case the value function for the orphan household applies, and assets are augmented by inheritances in per-capita terms. That is,

$$V_w(t, a, z, \tilde{y}, Sp) = \max_{c, a'} \left\{ U(c) + \beta p_{t+7} E\left[V_w\left(t+1, a', z', \tilde{y}', S_p'\right)\right. \right.$$
$$\left. \left. + \beta\left(1 - p_{t+7}\right) E\left[V_w^I\left(t+1, a' + b_n / N, z', \tilde{y}'\right)\right]\right\} \tag{1}$$

subject to

$$c + a' = (1 - t_l) wy = t_s \min(wy, 5\tilde{y}_c) + [1 + r(1 = t_a)]a, \tag{2}$$

$$a' \geq 0, \tag{3}$$

$$\tilde{y}' = \left[(t-1)\tilde{y} + \min\left(wy/5, \tilde{y}_c\right)\right]/t, \tag{4}$$

$$\tilde{y}_p' = \begin{cases} \left[(t+6)\tilde{y}_p + \min((wy_p/5, \tilde{y}_c)\right]/(t+7) & \text{if } t < 3 \\ \tilde{y}_p & \text{otherwise} \end{cases} \tag{5}$$

$$b_n = b_n(S_p),\tag{6}$$

where N is the average number of children determined by the growth rate of the population. The expected values of the value functions are taken with respect to $\left(z', z_p'\right)$ conditional on (z, z_p). The agent's resources depend on labor endowment y and asset holdings a.

Average yearly earnings for children and parents evolve according to equations (4) and (5), respectively. Because current income y refers to a five-year period, current income is divided by five when the yearly lifetime average labor income ($\tilde{y}$) is updated. Equation (6) is the law of motion of bequest for the parents, which uses their optimal decision rule.

The value function of an agent who is still working but whose parent is dead is

$$V_w^I\left(t, a, z, \tilde{y}\right) = \max_{c, a'}\left\{U(c) + \beta E\left[V_w^I\left(t+1, a'z'\tilde{y}'\right)\right]\right\},\tag{7}$$

subject to (2), (3), and (4).

From 65 to 85 years of age ($t = 10$ to $t = 14$), the agent is retired and receives Social Security benefits and his parent is already deceased. He faces a positive probability of dying, in which case he derives utility from bequeathing the remaining assets.

$$V_r\left(t, a, \tilde{y}\right) = \max_{c, a'}\left\{U(c) + \beta p_t V_r\left(t+1, a', \tilde{y}\right) + \left(1 - p_t\right)\phi(b)\right\},\tag{8}$$

subject to (3),

$$c + a' = \left[1 + r\left(1 - \tau_a\right)\right]a + \left(1 - \tau_l\right)P\left(\tilde{y}\right),\tag{9}$$

$$b_n = \begin{cases} a' & \text{if } a' < x_b, \\ \left(1 - \tau_b\right)\left(a' - x_b\right) + x_b & \text{otherwise,} \end{cases}\tag{10}$$

and, in the case of net bequest motives,

$$b = b_n,\tag{11}$$

while in the case of gross bequest motives,

$$b = b_g = a'\tag{12}$$

regardless of the structure of the estate tax.

We focus on a stationary equilibrium concept in which factor prices and age-wealth distribution are constant over time. Due to space constraints, the definition of a stationary equilibrium for our economy is in the online appendix in De Nardi and Yang.[64]

Calibration

Table 14-4 summarizes the parameters that are either taken from other studies or can be solved independently of the endogenous outcomes of the model. See De Nardi and Yang for a discussion of these choices.[65]

Our calibration of the labor earnings process is based on the observation that the Panel Study of Income Dynamics (PSID) provides excellent data on the earnings dynamics for much of the population, but not for those of the richest households.[66] To match the earnings dynamics of all the population, we thus proceed as follows.

TABLE 14-4.
Exogenous parameters used in the benchmark model

	Parameters		Value
Demographics	n	annual population growth	1.2%
	p_t	survival probability	see text
Preferences	γ	risk aversion coefficient	1.5
Labor earnings	ε_t	age-efficiency profile	see text
	ψ	labor earnings levels	see text
	Q_y	labor earnings transition matrix	see text
	ρ_h	AR(1) coef. of prod. inheritance process	0.50
	σ_h^2	innovation of prod. inheritance process	0.37
Production	α	capital income share	0.36
	δ	depreciation	6.0%
Government policy	τ_a	capital income tax	20%
	$P(\hat{y})$	Social Security benefit	see text
	τ_s	Social Security tax	12.0%

TABLE 14-5.

Parameters calibration for the benchmark model and the model with no voluntary bequests

Moment	Data	Benchmark	No Bequest Motives
Wealth-output ratio	3.10	3.10%	3.10%
Bequest-wealth ratio	0.88–1.18%	0.87%	0.56%
90th perc. bequest distribution	4.34	4.36	4.53
Fraction of estates paying taxes	2.0%	1.85%	1.89%
Revenue from estate tax / output	0.33%	0.33	0.11%
Government spending / output	18%	17.99%	17.76%

Parameters				
β	discount factor		0.9453	0.9513
φ_1	bequest utility		−5.3225	0.0000
φ_2	bequest utility shifter (in \$ 2000)		1116K	0.0000
τ_b	tax on estates		21.52%	21.52%
x_b	estate exemption level (in \$ 2000)		782K	782K
τ_l	tax on labor income		19.19%	19.19%

1. We assume four possible earnings states: low, middle, high, and super-high. We take the support of the earnings shocks from Castañeda, Díaz-Giménez, and Ríos-Rull.[67] The resulting grid points for ψ are [1, 3.15, 9.78, 1,061].

2. We take the persistence ρ_b of the earnings inheritance process to be 0.5 and the variance σ_b^2, both are from the article by De Nardi. We then discretize the earnings inheritance process as proposed by Tauchen.[68]

3. We take PSID estimates on the persistence (0.92) and variance (0.38) over five-year periods from table A.1 in appendix A in the article by De Nardi; and we discretize this process for the lowest three grid points using the method in the article by Tauchen to make sure that our process accurately represents the estimated earnings dynamics for much of the population. This gives us a three-by-three transition matrix.[69]

4. We pick the remaining six elements of our four-by-four transition matrix to match the following aspects of the earnings distribution: The Gini coefficient and the share of total earnings earned, respectively, by the top 1, 5, 20, 40, and 60 percent, and an earnings persistence at the top of 80 percent. The latter is consistent with work by DeBacker, Panousi, and Ramnath, which reports that the persistence of both labor and business income at the top of the labor and business income distributions is high and that, in particular, the probability of staying there, both after one year and five years (the latter results are available from the authors on request), is around 80 percent.[70] We also impose adding-up restrictions.

The transition matrix for Q_y is:

$$\begin{bmatrix} 0.8239 & 0.1733 & 0.0027 & 0.000112 \\ 0.2171 & 0.6399 & 0.1428 & 0.000200 \\ 0.0067 & 0.2599 & 0.7334 & 0.000000 \\ 0.0720 & 0.0000 & 0.1252 & 0.802779 \end{bmatrix}$$

The transition matrix for Q_{yb} in the benchmark model is

$$\begin{bmatrix} 0.8272 & 0.1704 & 0.0024 & 0.0000000000 \\ 0.5000 & 0.4696 & 0.0304 & 0.0000000000 \\ 0.1759 & 0.6513 & 0.1728 & 0.0000000051 \\ 0.0000 & 0.0018 & 0.9678 & 0.0304357624 \end{bmatrix}$$

The transition matrices induce an initial distribution of earnings with probability masses over the respective earnings levels, given by [59.89% 35.88% 4.24% 0.00154845%].

Table 14-5 lists the parameters we use to calibrate the model; see De Nardi and Yang for a discussion of these targets and the implied parameter values.[71]

FIFTEEN

A Feminist Interpretation of Patrimonial Capitalism

HEATHER BOUSHEY

Economist Heather Boushey takes us into a different dimension on inequality. Piketty's thesis is that we're living in a new age of "patrimonial capitalism" and Boushey asks what feminist economics can tell us about what this era looks like and the trajectory moving forward. The optimistic view is that inclusion promotes economic growth and, thus, given the importance of women's contributions to the economy and the egalitarian nature of today's inheritance patterns, even as inequality rises, this should not necessarily reduce women's economic or political rights. However, a more pessimistic assessment is that alongside inequality moving back to nineteenth-century levels, there will be forces pushing toward a reduction in women's economic options and political power.

The field of academic economics has recently moved toward recognizing how important institutions are understanding economic outcomes. Thomas Piketty is no exception. In 2015 he wrote: "One should be wary of any economic determinism in regard to inequalities of wealth and income. . . . The history of the distribution of wealth has always been deeply political, and it cannot be reduced to purely economic mechanisms. . . . It is shaped by the way economic, social, and political actors view what is just and what is not, as well as by the relative power of those actors and the collective choices that result. It is the joint product of all relevant actors combined. . . . How this history plays out depends on how societies view inequalities and what kinds of policies and institutions they adopt to measure and transform them."[1]

In *Capital in the Twenty-First Century* (*C21*), Piketty singles out one area for particular scrutiny: inheritance. In the first part of the book, Piketty shows that among those with the highest incomes, the majority of that income currently comes from labor. But he argues that over time this will change into what he calls "patrimonial capitalism," whereby the richest will—like in the nineteenth century and before—earn most of their income from capital, not labor. As he puts it in the beginning of chapter 11, "Almost inevitably, this tends to give lasting, disproportionate importance to inequalities created in the past, and therefore to inheritance."[2] Therefore, he devotes that entire chapter to how inheritances are making a comeback.

But what institutions matter for inheritance? Like much of the other work in economics, the interesting institutions get thrown into a black box, the edges of which are somewhat arbitrarily determined. What micro institutions make up the macro institution of inheritance? How is inheritance connected to broader social structures? How will today's institutions affect inheritance patterns? Piketty argues that just because inheritance is coming back, it will not look exactly like it did in the nineteenth century, "in part because the concentration of wealth is less extreme (there will probably be more small to medium rentiers and fewer extremely wealthy rentiers, at least in the short term), in part because the earned income hierarchy is expanding (with the rise of the supermanager), and finally because wealth and income are more strongly correlated than in the past. In the twenty-first century it is possible to be both a supermanager and a 'medium rentier': the new meritocratic order encourages this sort of thing, probably to the detriment of low- and medium-wage workers, especially those who own only a tiny amount of property, if any."[3] Piketty also makes the argument that today's supermanager positions are being passed on from one generation to the next. While inheritance of wealth remains important, today's elites bequest high-paying jobs by getting their progeny into the right schools and giving them the right connections. In this way, even in our supposedly merit-based labor market, parents can ensure that their children become as firmly ensconced into elite circles as the heirs and heiresses of days past.

It is here that feminist economics can serve as a useful complement to Piketty's analysis. Since its inception, the field has focused on seeing the gendered (and racialized) nature of the social and economic system.[4] This kind of analysis is critical to a fuller understanding of the descriptive and predictive accuracy of Piketty's central points. It allows us to see how the gendered nature of institutions and social norms affect inheritance patterns and how the shift to capital mattering more than labor income among those at the very top could very well undermine recent trends toward gender equity. In the nineteenth century, inheritance was ruled by male primogeniture.[5] Within marriage, women had dower rights but otherwise had no legal authority over their finances. Today we have much more egalitarian inheritance laws and norms in terms of financial and physical assets, but what parents pass on is more about human and social capital. The path to becoming a supermanager has its own set of gender dynamics that affects today's inheritance patterns.

This chapter will explore the plausibility of Piketty's arguments from a feminist perspective. In the first section I describe the optimistic neoclassical views connecting growth to inclusive economic growth. I then recount Piketty's challenge to this view—namely, that structural features in capitalism will lead to a permanent divergence in the welfare of groups in society, hinging on inheritance. In my recounting, I note the ways Piketty's concerns here overlap with the concerns of feminist economics. That leads naturally into a description of Piketty's predictions of the role inheritance will play in twenty-first-century capitalism. I then assess his predictions through the more optimistic lens of standard neoclassical theory, where the trends he describes are not particularly worse for women than men, and the more pessimistic lens of feminist economics, which predicts a dystopian future of male supremacy. In my concluding section, I suggest how these tensions could be reconciled and directions for future research.

The Optimistic View: Growth Is, by Nature, Inclusive

In the middle of the twentieth century, economists were optimistic that growth would reduce inequality and be good for all of us. In 1955, in his American Economic Association presidential address, Simon Kuznets famously argued for his "Kuznets curve" analysis, based on his meticulous data work, that inequality would fall as economies became more developed. Yet it turns out that educational opportunities and marriage patterns have had an impact on distributional outcomes that Kuznets did not foresee.

Although he said, "The paper is perhaps 5 per cent empirical information and 95 per cent speculation, some of it possibly tainted by wishful thinking," his conclusions gained wide acceptance.[6] Thomas Piketty uses this Kuznetsian moment in economic thinking—and the view on the relationship between growth and inequality it engendered—as the intellectual foil for *C21*. He says in the introduction, "The philosophy of the moment was summed up in a single sentence: 'Growth is a rising tide that lifts all boats.'"[7]

The optimism of that era runs deep. Twentieth-century economics was built on a set of theorems contending that market forces, left to their own logic, would generate outcomes that were in some sense economically optimal and to some degree fundamentally fair. At the turn of the twentieth century, John Bates Clark, the namesake of one of the most sought-after prizes in economics, developed the marginal productivity theory of distribution. This gave economists a mathematically beautiful model predicting that, in a competitive economy (one where no individual player has power over other buyers or sellers), an individual's wage would be a function of their productivity. As he put it, "What a social class gets is, under natural law, what it contributes to the general output of industry."[8] Productivity, both of the individual and of the assets to which he or she holds rightful title, still sits at the core of mainstream economic thinking. An individual's human capital—that is, the education and skills a person brings to the production process—is presumed to drive the lion's share of differences in wages across individuals in similar occupations and industries. And those who invest not in human but in physical capital similarly earn a return based on the usefulness of what their assets bring to the production process.

Standard economics reaches its glorious, optimistic pinnacle in the unification of a theory of prices, distribution, and growth. As Piketty points out, the Solow-Swan growth model showed a "trajectory along which all variables—output, incomes, profits, wages, capital, asset prices, and so on—would progress at the same pace, so that every social group would benefit from growth to the same degree, with no major deviations from the norm."[9] This brought together human capital and population growth, alongside technological change, as the key drivers of growth in economic output. In the textbook Solow-Swan growth model, the economy grows when the population increases or when productivity rises.

Empirical research since the 1950s supports the theory that improving labor supply and ensuring broad-based education are good for growth. In a now-famous 1992 paper, Gregory Mankiw, David Romer, and David Weil found that the effect of human capital investment on economic growth rates was roughly equivalent to or larger than the effect of investment in physical capital.[10] Thus, improvements in knowledge and skills boost productivity. This means that society's educational investments are critical for growth, because more education spurs innovation and economic dynamism.[11] The idea that creating broadly shared opportunity for education and training is good for the economy flows from this decades-old body of scholarship.

Paul Romer's development and extension of endogenous growth theory extended the standard model further, showing that educational investments create benefits that go beyond improving outcomes for the person with the higher skill set. In his approach, the key determinants of growth include not just the boost to one's own productivity generated by improvements in one's own human capital but also the spillovers of one's innovations and ideas as those boost the human capital of others. Romer thus goes much farther than J. B. Clark by arguing that the market-produced wealth of the idea- and innovation-generating minority is but a small part of how their additions to the human stock of knowledge have boosted economic productivity. Most of the income and productivity they generate flows to the suppliers of raw labor as free-riders on the productivity-growth process.[12]

Microeconomic theory also provides a strong foundation for the idea that "equality of opportunity" and a strong economy go hand in hand because matching skills to jobs and rewarding merit is economically optimal. Differences in pay across similar jobs are due to differences in human capital. Jacob Mincer's wage model, which remains one of the most-used tools in the economist toolbox, regresses wages on education and experience, controlling for job and demographic characteristics, and finds that the level of human capital—both formal education and on-the-job experience—can explain differences in wages across individuals. The implication is that armed with a good education and hard work, anyone can get close to the top of the income ladder within their lifetime.[13]

A second implication of the Mincer model is that discrimination is not economically efficient, and so it should not persist in a fully competitive market. An individual's earnings flow from his or her marginal contribution to production and thus distortions in compensation due to characteristics unrelated to productivity will be eliminated by the market. When people—employers, customers, or other workers—bestow preferences on one group or person over another based on characteristics that are not tied to that person or group's economic contribution, this will lower productivity and profits. Successful employers would hire the best, most productive person for the job.[14] Firms that practice discrimination would be driven out of business because they are not making rational economic decisions. The only way discrimination continues to exist is through state action that blocks win-win exchanges between the discriminated-against and those who do not share majority prejudices. Nobel laureate Kenneth Arrow went so far as to say that, with the erosion of legal structures that promote discrimination, exclusion along the lines of race and gender would disappear.[15]

All of this leads to the conclusion that promoting growth means reducing inequality, especially if we think that talent follows anything akin to a normal distribution. The economy grows when people find a more efficient match of skills to jobs, and therefore policy makers—and businesses—should be naturally encouraged, not toward categorically excluding people based on non-productivity-related factors, but instead toward finding ways of increasing human capital and its availability to freely find economic outlets across the society. It should come as no surprise that opening jobs to women and people of color can improve economic outcomes at the macro level. Research by Chang-Tai Hsieh et al. finds that between 1960 and 2008, 16 to 20 percent of growth in output per worker was due to both a decrease in explicit discrimination and a subsequent increase in the willingness of women and people of color to make the human capital investments necessary to enter professional occupations that make better use of their talents.[16] And this process is presumably far from its end.

Yet even in the face of this strong theoretical argument for inclusion, gender equity obviously remains an unfinished project, despite the legal strictures promoting it and the consequences for economic growth. In the United States, women continue to earn 79 cents on the male dollar. The extent to which we devalue women—and their contribution to the economy—has widespread and often underappreciated effects. One example in the United States is the ongoing consternation over "teacher quality," without a concomitant commitment to raising teacher pay. In an economy where women had little or no opportunity enter professions, many of the best and the brightest women used their talents as mothers or, if they worked, teachers or nurses. Thus, our economy benefited from a class of workers with few other options. Now, of course, women have more options, but teacher pay woefully lags other comparable professions. Students who make the best marks in school won't choose teaching on the basis of pay (or social respect) unless it's a calling; more likely, they'll choose a profession that can offer pay and social esteem.

Even setting aside the importance of human capital improvements, increasing the supply of labor by groups that had been categorically excluded based on nonproductivity factors should increase growth. There is ample economic evidence for this. In the United States between 1948 and 2000, women's labor force participation grew sharply, rising from 32 to 60.3 percent, only to fall slightly in recent years; as of April 2016, it stood at 56.8 percent.[17] Looking at the effect of rising women's labor supply on growth, the International Monetary Fund pointed out that in the United States, increasing women's labor force participation rate to that of men would increase total economic output by 5 percent.[18] In a recent paper I coauthored with Eileen Appelbaum and John Schmitt, we estimated the economic benefits of women's employment and found that gross domestic product, or GDP, would have been roughly 11 percent lower in 2012 if women had not increased their working hours as they did. In today's dollars, this translates to more than $1.7 trillion less in output—roughly equivalent to combined U.S. spending on Social Security, Medicare, and Medicaid in 2012.[19] Of course, this is just a measure of standard GDP; it does not take into account value of time and stress, as women typically find themselves doing half of external-to-the-household wage work and still the lion's share of internal-to-the-household home production. According to research by Benjamin Bridgman et al., if home production were taken into account, in 1965, GDP would have been 37 percent higher and in 2014, 23 percent higher.[20]

Therefore, standard economic theory tells an optimistic story about why inclusion should be—and, in fact, has been—good for growth. As the economy moved toward a greater emphasis on labor than land or other fixed capital, this created economic pressure for greater inclusion. Armed with the empirical evidence that human capital drives economic growth, economic logic reinforced the idea of promoting equal access to education, training, and jobs across people, based on their aptitudes and skills, not solely on their family name, gender, or birth order. In an economy driven by human capital, it's not cost effective to allow talent to lie fallow. This is why if you ask most any economist what's the best policy for improving someone's life, they will give an answer that includes improving skills.[21] This set of economic ideas also easily incorporates feminist concerns. Some standard theorists were slow to see women's value added outside the home (see Gary Becker's 1956 *Treatise on the Family*), but the logic pushed toward the conclusion that if women or people of color have aptitude or talent that could be economically useful, then there's an incentive to access it. It also supported the argument that merit matters; if you improve your skills, work hard, and play by the rules, you can earn a well-paid job.

The implications of this set of ideas about how the economy works were clear. So long as policy makers focused on promoting economic growth and removing legal barriers to inclusion, discrimination-driven race and gender inequality would fall and, in turn, this will strengthen the economy. The economics of the day allowed midcentury thinkers and doers to believe in the idea that economic growth would easily, straightforwardly, and naturally solve social and political problems. It should be no surprise, then, that it coincided with optimism about our ability to eradicate poverty and exclusion along the lines of gender, race, and ethnicity. If growth could reduce inequality—and if reducing economic exclusion promotes growth—then policymakers could end poverty and should open the economy to those traditionally excluded—women, African Americans, and recent immigrants.

It was in this era that Robert Kennedy pushed for a War on Poverty, President Lyndon Johnson sought to establish a Great Society, Dr. Martin Luther King called for "jobs *and* freedom," and second-wave feminism sought equal civil and economic rights for women. These calls to action occurred within the context of an economic framework that suggested that greater inclusion was not only possible but also economically optimal and would promote productivity and growth.

But even as the standard economic argument created pressure to expand economic opportunity, it also encouraged and legitimated rising salaries at the top of the income distribution. If inequality continues to persist, it must because it's economically optimal. If pay is tied to what a person contributes to the production process, then we must each be paid what we deserve, right?

The Pessimistic View: Growth Is Not (Necessarily) Inclusive

The optimistic view that a growing economy will move seamlessly toward less social and economic inequality did not turn out to be true. Here is the purpose of *C21:* Piketty wants us to understand that the economy does not naturally push toward greater economic equity. He looks at the data and eschews putting our hopes in market forces to fix the social and political problems of inequality.

Piketty's argument that optimistic faith in the market is misplaced stems from his (untraditional) methods. He makes three related breaks with the standard economic methodology. As we will see, these dovetail with ideas developed in feminist economics. First, Piketty builds his theory up from the first-order empirical regularities of the data to fit them, rather than following the Procrustean methodology of chopping and stretching the data until they fit the theory. Second, Piketty eschews a narrow focus on modeling to the exclusion of an understanding of history and real-world data and problems. Third, Piketty incorporates the interaction between institutions and practices—refusing to take the property-rights and bargaining-power setups underlying the market as exogenous. Plus, Piketty pursues a much greater array of engagement with the social sciences more generally than an economist typically undertakes.[22]

The data that underlie *C21* were mostly already known, at least within the economics community. In 2003 Piketty and Emmanuel Saez published a pathbreaking paper in the *Quarterly Journal of Economics,* documenting that income inequality has widened more than had been previously recognized, and that the top 1 percent now captures a higher share of income than at any time since the early twentieth century's Gilded Age.[23] In *C21,* Piketty takes the data to what he sees as the logical conclusion: As incomes accumulate into capital and then calcify into inheritances, the wealth of the dead takes on greater importance than that of the living. We will see ever-increasing inequality so long as the growth rate of the economy is below the rate at which the wealth of the rich compounds itself via the rate of profit.

Piketty predicts that this will long be the case, because the process is self-reinforcing: "When the rate of return on capital exceeds the rate of growth of output and income, as it did in the nineteenth century and seems quite likely to do again in the twenty-first, capitalism *automatically* generates arbitrary and unsustainable inequalities that radically undermine the meritocratic values on which democratic societies are based."[24]

Piketty rejects the idea that highly developed economies can do much to improve growth—and that even if they could, that would only begin to reduce, rather than simply slow, the growth of inequality insofar as growth rises above the rate of return on capital.[25] He ends *C21* with what he sees as the only reasonable policy conclusion: policy makers should implement a global wealth tax to reduce the rate of return on capital. To describe the system he identifies, Piketty coins a new term: "What we are witnessing is a strong comeback of private capital in the rich countries since 1970, or, to put it another way, the emergence of a *new patrimonial capitalism*."[26] He argues that this system will be based on inherited wealth, and thus similar in salient respects to that of the northwest European economies prior to the twentieth century.

But the idea that we are moving to an inheritance-based economy is at odds with the trends in the data that show that today's rich receive the majority of their income from labor, not capital. The optimists can point to this as evidence that there is still hope that Piketty's predictions will not come true. Figures 15-1 and 15-2 reproduce two figures from the work of Piketty and his coauthors (all shown only for the United States). There has been a sharp rise in income inequality since the 1980s. In the United States, inequality is now higher than at any time since before the Great Depression in the 1930s (Figure 15-1). However, the composition of income of those at the top differs from in the early twentieth century. In the early part of the twentieth century, capital income was the largest component of the income of the top 0.1 percent, today, about half of all income for the top 0.1 percent is from labor. Even as income from wealth rose sharply starting in 1980, the proportion of income from earnings also continued to rise (Figure 15-2).

It's not until we get to the very top—the top 0.01 percent—that income from capital plays as large a role today as earnings from labor. Figures 15-3A and 15-3B show the share of income from salaries, businesses, and capital for those in top 10 percent in 1929 and 2007, the year before the financial crisis. Figure 15-3A shows that in 1929, wage income accounts for a smaller share of

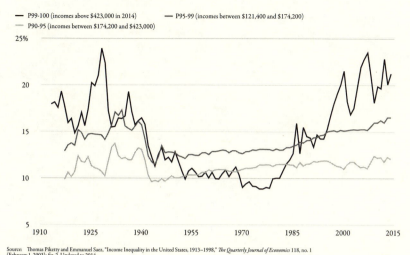

Source: Thomas Piketty and Emmanuel Saez, "Income Inequality in the United States, 1913–1998," *The Quarterly Journal of Economics* 118, no. 1 (February 1, 2003): fig. 2. Updated to 2014.

FIGURE 15-1: Decomposing top 10 percent into three groups, 1913–2014.

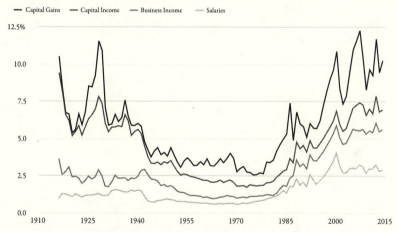

Source: Thomas Piketty and Emmanuel Saez, "Income Inequality in the United States, 1913–1998," *The Quarterly Journal of Economics* 118, no. 1 (February 1, 2003). Tables A3, A7, and A8, col. P99.9-100. Updated to 2014.

FIGURE 15-2: Share and source of income for the top 0.1 percent.

total income among all of those in top decile. In Figure 15-3B, for 2007, those at the top have markedly shifted their sources of income. Taxpayers in the top 10 percent earn upward of 85 percent of their income from salaried employment, including stock options and other kinds of nonwage remunerations directly tied to employment. This means that for today's high earners,

Income composition within the top decile, 1929 and 2007

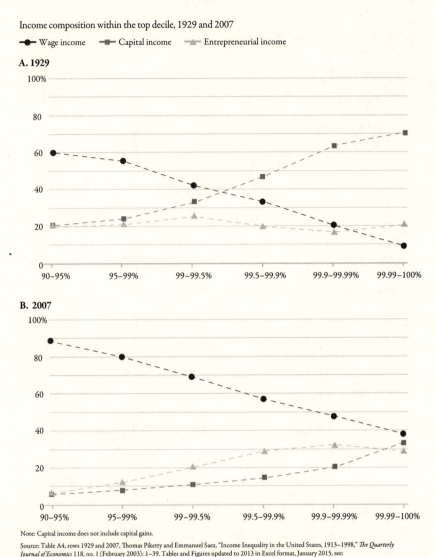

A. 1929

B. 2007

Note: Capital income does not include capital gains.

Source: Table A4, rows 1929 and 2007, Thomas Piketty and Emmanuel Saez, "Income Inequality in the United States, 1913–1998," *The Quarterly Journal of Economics* 118, no. 1 (February 2003): 1–39. Tables and Figures updated to 2013 in Excel format, January 2015, see: http://eml.berkeley.edu/~saez/TabFig2013prel.xls.

FIGURE 15-3: Salaries are a much larger share of income for today's super-rich: Income composition within the top decile, (A) 1929 and (B) 2007.

their job is the most important source of high income, even for those at the top. And even for the high earners whose income comes from capital, the bulk of that is the result of their own luck or their own previous work. It is only with the descent of Sam Walton's wealth to his heirs that we have begun to see at the very top the return of Piketty's patrimonial capitalism.

This is, of course, markedly different from a century or two ago; then, if you grew up in a super-rich family in northwest Europe, you were most likely the child of property owners—probably part of the landed gentry—or living off of business investments made by your ancestors.

Putting Figures 15-1, 15-2, 15-3A, and 15-3B together, for Piketty's pessimistic prognosis that the "past devours the future" to be true, we need to see a shift in income source for those at the top from labor back to capital. Piketty argues that this will happen over time through inheritances.[27] Today's recipients of larger incomes will save more than do those with lower incomes and so, over time and generations, higher-income families will amass greater stocks of wealth and pass that on to their children so that the capital income from a growing stock of wealth will overtake labor income. Thus, even if the standard model is correct and all pay—even at the very top—is merit-based, bequests will, over time, move us toward a world where income from capital—not labor—will again comprise the majority of income of those at the very top.

Piketty argues that the incorporation of institutions is important for understanding the dynamics of the economy that will inevitably lead to this return to patrimonial capitalism. He pushes economists to move beyond the standard model's theoretical predications and aims to develop a model that builds up to a system by identifying the dynamic interactions between labor and capital markets, something that economists have traditionally viewed as separate issues. By including institutions in what he calls "the capitalist system," Piketty implies that any theory of growth that excludes the institutional context will ultimately prove inadequate. He appears to bristle at the idea that his analysis is "deterministic," that is, the idea that the inequality $r > g$ is set in stone rather than a description of current reality and future trends without changes in institutions, social practices, family structures, and norms that drive capital accumulation over time. In a 2015 article in the *Journal of Economic Perspectives* where he reacted to the reception of *C21* within the economics community, Piketty argues, "Ultimately, what really matters is the interaction between economic forces and institutional responses, particularly in the area of educational, labor, and fiscal institutions."[28] He concludes the article by saying, "More generally, one of the lessons that I draw from this work is that the study of inequality dynamics and institutional change are intimately related."[29]

Yet even as Piketty makes some sharp breaks with standard economic theory and points to the importance of institutions, he doesn't let go of the standard model. Many chapters in this volume this point out, perhaps Suresh Naidu (Chapter 5) most strongly. This is, in no small part, because in Piketty's analysis the role of institutions is, as Daron Acemoglu and James Robinson put it, "ad hoc."[30] We can see this in his analysis of the labor market. He notes the failure of marginalist thinking to explain wages at the top, but he agrees that the demand for skills depends on the state of technology available in the production of goods and services. He also agrees that the supply of skills depends on access to education, without reference to the large literature showing that institutional factors play a role in wage setting up and down the income ladder.[31] Thus, while he concedes that the standard model cannot explain wage setting at the top of the wage ladder, he doesn't concede that the model is flawed at other points along the wage spectrum. This is puzzling because it creates logical inconsistencies.

Luckily, feminist economics provides a plausible path out of at least some of these difficulties. And so we now turn to it.

The Feminist View

Let us consider what the body of scholarship in feminist economics can add to the analysis of the interplay between r and g.

The field itself is fairly young. The International Association for Feminist Economics and the accompanying journal, *Feminist Economics,* were launched only in 1993. One top purpose of the association and journal is to "advance feminist inquiry into economic issues." Julie Nelson, one of the founding scholars of IAFFE, summed up the key ideas in a recent encyclopedia entry: "Feminist economics is a field that includes both studies of gender roles in the economy from a liberatory perspective and critical work directed at biases in the economics discipline."[32]

Like Piketty, feminist economics tends to put data and measurement before theory building. A top concern has been the value of women's unpaid labor within the home and the role of home production in the economy more generally. Along these lines, an early important contribution to feminist economics was Marilyn Waring's 1988 landmark study (with an introduction by Gloria Steinem), *If Women Counted,* where she examined national income accounts. She elaborated how women's unpaid contributions are missed in national economic data and what this means for how we think about women's contributions to the family and the economy more generally. She provided tools to revise the data to include unpaid labor.[33] This push to include unpaid labor in national accounts continues: in 2016 the Bureau of Economic Analysis provided data showing that incorporating "nonmarket household production" raises the measure of gross domestic product by 37 percent in 1965 and 23 percent in 2014.[34] Notably, this research is conceptually similar to work Piketty is now doing along with Emmanuel Saez and Gabriel Zucman as they seek to incorporate distributional data into national accounts.[35]

Also like Piketty, feminist economics seeks to move beyond the limitations of the standard model and to pay attention to institutions and interdisciplinary research. Feminist economics incorporates the idea that the market functions within social structures; therefore, uncovering the nature of how the market works within these structures is important. As Nelson writes, "Recognition of the importance of social beliefs and structures of power in creating gendered economic outcomes has remained a hallmark of feminist economics."[36] One important early contribution was a rethinking of "rational economic man," dovetailing with the greater emphasis more generally on behavioral economics. In *Beyond Economic Man,* a 1993 compilation edited by Julie Nelson and Marianne Ferber that helped launch the field, scholars probed the importance of social beliefs and structures of power in economics.[37] Much scholarship in feminist economics concludes that institutions and social norms shape employment outcomes, but go further than Piketty is willing to go. Specifically, feminist economics has long been concerned with the institutions that continue to generate differences in economic outcomes by gender and race that are unassociated with productivity differences.

It may be that Piketty's lack of attention to demographic differences is driven by his data selections. While Piketty's data set is unique and provides a historical view of income and wealth, like any data set it has limitations that affect the derivation of his key concepts. The unit of analysis for the data that Piketty and his colleagues rely on most heavily for the United States is the "tax unit," which is typically a family, although family members can file separately. On its own, this administrative data does not provide detailed information on demographics—in particular, race and ethnicity—or family relationships. Researchers may be able to match it to other data using an individual's unique identifying information, but few scholars have access to this level of detail. In general, the data Piketty relies on obscures what happens inside families and how wealth is accumulated by race and ethnicity and, as such, it's quite difficult—if not impossible—to see how it is embedded in social institutions on this data alone.

The lack of attention to demographics is quite different from how scholars had been thinking about inequality prior to Piketty and Saez's groundbreaking research, and there may be something to learn from combining the two. The scholarship on inequality from the 1980s and 1990s typically focused on understanding the human capital explanations for disparities across individuals or families with attention to race and gender. This research sought to reconcile the optimism of the standard model against the emerging reality of ongoing disparities in outcomes that could not be explained away by identifiable differences in productivity. This research exploited greater access to computing power and focused on large-scale national surveys, which for the United States most often meant the U.S. Census Bureau's Current Population Survey and other national-level surveys.[38]

A deeper concern is that Piketty fails to investigate the gender component of institutions and norms that directly affect the dynamics he argues to be most important. Even though Piketty himself says that inequality is related to institutions, he fails to think through how marriage and the family affect the transmission of wealth in the modern economy. One indication of this lack of attention is his choice (in his native French language) to label the current system "patrimonial capitalism." Piketty uses this term to describe an economy based on inheritance, but to an English speaker the word "patrimony" does not mean inheritance; in English, words that begin with "pater" imply father. The word "patrimony" means a system of inheritance *through the male line*—and so the phrase "patrimonial capitalism" implies a set of institutions and practices that would systemically exclude women from this transfer of wealth.[39]

While this is not Piketty's point, is there an underlying revelation here? While Piketty clearly does not mean that inheritance is only through the "pater," he never explores the gender context of inheritance, as Jane

Humphries pointed out in her review in *Feminist Economics*. For instance, he includes many storytelling vignettes from the early nineteenth century in order to elevate the role of institutions or cultural norms around marriage and inheritance patterns, but he does not comment on their gendered nature. The only place where the word "gender" comes up in *C21* at all is when he discusses inequality in labor income for those in the bottom half of the labor market.[40]

It is understandable that some concepts cannot be translated across languages without some loss of meaning—but the role that gender plays in inheritance today and historically is highly relevant to Piketty's thesis. In the United States, we continue to have high levels of inequality across gender and race, and the idea that we are moving to a new patrimonial capitalism cannot be stripped of the gender implications. We cannot ignore how the economy looks by gender as it relates to stocks of wealth, wealth inherited, and particularly the labor market.

This inquiry is also important because, so far, there has been very little feminist scholarship explicitly engaging with *C21*. In the spring of 2014, as the coeditors of this book were preparing to pull together a list of potential contributing scholars, we searched for all the available reviews of *C21*. We found over 700 pages of text online, but very few women—in the low single digits—had shared their reactions at that time. By the following August, Kathleen Geier wrote that she was aware of only one published feminist critique, by Zillah Eisenstein, and set out to change that by asking five women (myself include) to take on this question.[41] This was quickly followed by Diane Perrons's piece in *The British Journal of Sociology* where she highlights how gender identity plays a role both in the experience of inequality and in the social processes through which it plays out.[42]

Adding a Gender Lens to Piketty

We have seen how attention to gender affected standard economic theory. What does it mean for Piketty? Specifically, what would Piketty's predictions for the twenty-first century look like through a feminist lens? Recall that in Piketty's view, we are entering a new age of patrimonial capitalism where, over time, the super-rich will shift the source of their income from labor to capital and bring us back to the kind of inheritance-based economy that characterized the nineteenth century and before. But, as Piketty acknowledges, the world has changed. A key institutional change is that women have legal and economic rights on a par with men. Today Jane Austen could earn a high salary and also receive an inheritance shared with her brother. Indeed, shifts in primogeniture mean that there could be women of leisure alongside men of leisure. I begin by exploring what implications adding a gender lens means for the data, then move on to what questions this poses for assessing the validity of Piketty's pessimistic predictions.

Data: Gender Matters

I begin, as Piketty does, with the data. Piketty's descriptive analysis focuses on inequality trends using data from tax records. But this analysis fails to consider how the meritocratic economy and assortative mating affect the path of inequality for both those at the very top and the rest of the distribution. In chapter 11, "Merit and Inheritance in the Long Run," Piketty does not discuss the role of higher women's employment or assortative mating in shaping inheritance patterns, nor does he discuss the gender (or race) dynamics of who gets to be a supermanager. However, is not possible to understand patterns of inheritance without understanding the social, economic, and cultural institutions surrounding marriage, gender relations, and the family.

Historically, marriage markets were created so that families could not only pass on their wealth, but also secure their place in society. Piketty often points to Jane Austen's novels, where many of her heroines visit London or Bath in the spring to participate in British society's mating rituals. According to Lawrence Stone's history of marriage in England: "The development of a national marriage market in London and Bath in the second half of the eighteenth century greatly widened the pool of potentially satisfactory spouses from the point of view of upper-class parents, because it increased the number of potential spouses who would meet the necessary financial and social qualifications."[43]

It wasn't only the upper classes; lower-class families also used marriage as a means of maintaining a family's place. A peasant could expand his land holdings by having his son marry a neighbor's daughter with a dowry of land or livestock. Piketty of course recognizes this dynamic, which is why he includes the many quotes from Balzac and Austen and other eighteenth- and nineteenth-century authors. These novels illustrate how marriage markets worked under the old patrimonial capitalism: those without inherited wealth were encouraged to focus on marrying into families who could improve their station in life—which often meant seeking to marry someone just a bit wealthier than oneself.[44]

Piketty uses passages from historical fiction, yet he does not focus on the gender (or race) implications of these stories. These stories also bring to the fore the importance of family for determining one's place in society and whether the individual can pass into elite society. For instance, he points to Honoré de Balzac's character Eugène de Rastignac. In *Père Goriot,* a shady character named Vautrin tells Rastignac that to be truly wealthy, he must not devote himself to studying the law and setting up a practice; instead, he must marry a rich woman. Vautrin suggests a woman who is neither pretty nor appealing, but who would be willing. It turns out that the heiress Vautrin suggests is a not the legitimate child of her wealthy father, so in order to access her inheritance, Rastignac must murder her brother, who had the foresight (or not, as it turned out) to be born within the strictures of legal marriage.[45] This example illustrates three significant points about the institution of marriage and wealth. First, in the novel's day, capital, not labor, was the source of future wealth. Second, wealth accumulation affected the choice of marital partner. And third, this coincided with specific strictures policing sexuality. If having a high income comes from inheriting a stock of capital, knowing who is the legitimate heir is critical. Piketty focuses on the first point, but doesn't take on the second or third.

While Piketty relies on cultural documents to show how the old patrimonial capitalism was embedded in a specific social context, he morphs into the staid economist when it comes to describing today's social context. He says next to nothing about today's cultural or social norms, nor does he extensively reference modern novels—or reality TV shows—or discuss how one's race, ethnicity, or gender affects how today's wealth is earned and accumulated. Just as in the past, finding the right mate remains key to accumulating wealth, as does securing one's children's place in society. Today, those mating rituals look very different. Now, individuals are focused not only on getting the education and training to get the jobs at the top of the income ladder but also on looking at whether a potential mate has the "right" job or the educational credentials to get that job in the future. For all but the wealthiest of families, women's earnings have become ever-increasingly important to family incomes. Further, families pass on their place in society through making sure their children (largely regardless of their gender) accumulate the right human capital and have the connections to access the top jobs.[46]

Whom one marries continues to be important for determining one's economic situation. What's different—and what Piketty's data tell us nothing about—is how families are combining incomes. The literature on assortative mating tells us that high-earning men and women are increasingly marrying each other. This is consistent with research on what people look for in a spouse, which shows an increase in preferences for high earnings potential and that this is true both of women and men. Men still tend to value looks more than women do, but both men and women increasingly value a partner who is also a potential breadwinner. These preferences, alongside higher levels of education and earnings among women overall, have led to an increase in assortative mating, with like marrying like in terms of partners' earning power.[47]

There is also the issue of geography. Marriage markets tend to be local—people marry others who live in their city or town—and as rising income inequality plays out across place, this can also exacerbate assortative mating. In the United States the highest-paying jobs are concentrated in a few cities—New York City, San Francisco, Boston, Washington, DC—and these cities attract the ambitious and highly educated.[48] Geographic concentration of good jobs spurs the concentration of marriage markets in those locations. Then, of course, there's college, where the young prepare for those good jobs. These, too, serve as places where marriage markets operate in twenty-first-century America. Case in point: 1977 Princeton alumna Susan Patton recently wrote an open letter to Princeton graduates encouraging them to "find a husband on campus before you graduate." She pointed out that their classmates at school were probably going to be the most impressive group of marriageable partners that they would ever be among. She made the point that in today's economy, whom you marry may have just as big an effect on your life prospects as your career decisions, but for very different reasons than those made by the better-off in society a century or more ago.[49]

Marriage patterns tend to reinforce one's place in the economic hierarchy, affecting inequality patterns and economic mobility. Research shows that the individual earnings of husbands and wives are as highly correlated with the incomes of their *in-laws* as with the incomes of their own parents. Laura Chadwick and Gary Solon find that "spouses' earnings appear to be just as elastic as the offspring's own earnings with respect to the parents' income."[50] In the United States the elasticity of daughters' family earnings with respect to their parents' income is about 0.4.[51] In a study on Germany and Great Britain, John Ermisch, Marco Francesconi, and Thomas Siedler found that about 40 to 50 percent of the covariance between parents and their own permanent family income can be attributed to the person to whom one is married. This effect is driven by a strong spousal correlation in human capital.[52] Piketty dismissed economic mobility as a way to reduce inequality, but his data do not allow him to see the role played by marriage patterns.

The high correlation of incomes across families sounds similar to the marriage markets described in a Jane Austen novel. We can see the same kinds of cultural invocations in today's culture. Consider the words of Facebook's chief operating office, Sheryl Sandberg, who in her book, *Lean In,* tells how finding the right partner can make all the difference. She pulls examples from her own marriage to Dave Goldberg (who tragically died soon after) to show how having a partner who is supportive of your career can help you succeed in the workplace. Sandberg is speaking specifically to young women, but this advice certainly goes both ways.[53]

There is also, however, evidence that higher women's employment has reduced inequality across families, slowing the process of moving to an inheritance-based society. In a recent study, Brendon Duke uses the method developed by Maria Cancian and Deborah Reed to measure how changes in married women's earnings affect changes in inequality.[54] Cancian and Reed estimated what the level of inequality would have been in 1989 if married women's earnings had not changed since 1979. Duke extends this analysis to the period from 1963 to 2013 and finds that "inequality would have grown 38.1 percent between 1963 and 2013 if married women's earnings had not changed, compared with the observed 25 percent growth. Without changes in women's earnings during that 50-year span, inequality would have grown 52.6 percent faster."[55]

Marriage patterns also affect bequests, as does the fact that what many families are giving their children is access to the right job, rather than (or on top of) a stock of financial or physical capital, as was more likely the case prior to the twentieth century. One of the striking things about the U.S. economy in recent decades is the sharp divide that has emerged in family patterns across income. It used to be that most—but certainly not all—children were raised in married-couple families, at all levels of the income ladder.[56] According to analysis by Philip Cohen, in 1960, among families in the bottom third of the income distribution, just under one in five children aged fourteen and under lived with a single mom, compared to just over two in five in 2012.[57] Now, though, families at the top continue to raise children inside marriage—typically with both Mom and Dad holding down a fairly high-paying job—while children in families at the bottom of the income distribution, and now many in the middle, are living with a single, working parent, most often a mother.[58]

These changes in family patterns, alongside the need to invest heavily in children's human capital, have opened up a divide across families. Sara McLanahan documents that professional families delay marriage and children, are less likely to divorce or have children outside marriage, and have high maternal employment. Relative to their counterparts forty years ago, their mothers are older and more likely to be working at well-paying jobs. They are also investing heavily in their children's upbringing.[59] Annette Lareau documents that upper-middle-class families in her study focus on what she terms "concerted cultivation," or an emphasis on developing a child's talents, which requires a great deal of time and can be challenging for dual-earning professional families. Thus, those who can afford to often outsource this work to tutors or enroll children in expensive afterschool or summer enrichment activities, on top of investing time in their children's development.[60] All of this means that children born into the most advantaged families have much higher economic resources, as well as high levels of parental involvement in their emotional needs and development, compared to children in low-income or even middle-class families.

Predictions: Does Gender Matter?

Like any good economic theory, the shift in gender relations has two possible implications for Piketty's predictions. These push in opposite directions. First, although we may be moving toward an inheritance-based society, the pools of capital passed on will be smaller than in the nineteenth century, when most of the inheritance went to the eldest male, even though

TABLE 15-1.

Inheritance-based economies and gender norms

	19th century	20th century	21st century
Income source for top 10 percent	Capital	Labor	Capital
Inheritance pattern for rich	Jane Austen	Sheryl Sandberg	???
Women's civil / economic rights	Limited civil rights; no property rights	Equal civil rights; full property rights	???

he also had a social—if not legal—obligation to his siblings or widowed mother. This is no longer the case for today's young heirs; parents typically leave bequests equally across children, and even if one child inherits more, in general they are not obligated to provide for other family members, legally or otherwise. Breaking up family wealth across children will slow the rate of concentration of capital, but it can still produce Piketty's "return to the nineteenth century" in due time. Second is the question of how rich men will act. Piketty points out that economic elites have political power and that supermanagers have economic power, but he does not lay out whether or how these powers may be used to revert to rules that (re)empower men's elevated seat in the economic hierarchy.

Table 15-1 summarizes the basic outlines of the nineteenth-, twentieth-, and twenty-first-century inheritance-based economic systems and what this means for women's civil and economic rights today and into the future. It seems to me that there are two scenarios. The first is that gender identity doesn't matter. Wealthy parents will bequeath their estates in equal measure to daughters and sons. The amount each child inherits will be smaller than in economic systems where a single child inherits, but this new practice—combined with continued economic pressures to maintain high productivity and make use of male and female talent in the workplace—will promote continued gender equity at the top. The second is a dystopian future where women lose civil and economic rights. In this scenario, the wealthy—who are predominantly men—use their enhanced economic and political power to dismantle gender-equity protections. Is this plausible? Yes, because seizing inheritance is easier than seizing human capital. Ironically, this is a gender-driven mechanism to get us back to Austen's world, even though Piketty doesn't mention gender in his analysis of the nineteenth or twentieth century.

The implications for our prognosis about g could be significant, and it's worth pausing a moment to lay them out. As Piketty notes in chapter 2 of *C21* (and as has been well documented in standard economics), growth depends on demographics and especially population growth, along with human capital and technological innovation. The dystopian path not only reduces economic and political equity, it will drag down economic growth, hastening Piketty's prediction of ever-rising inequality.

First let's consider population growth. The level of women's economic and political rights plays a well-documented role in fertility patterns. Where women have greater civil rights and economic opportunity, they have fewer children and the children they have tend to live longer. This happens in part because as women gain economic rights, they gain access to health care and other services that increase the probability of any one child living into adulthood. Further, women with economic and political power have a greater capacity as individuals to control their own fertility as well as to promote policies that give women this right more generally.

Second, and just as importantly, women with greater control over fertility and the ability to contribute to the economy have a direct effect on what kinds of investments are made in future human capital, including future innovation. As families have fewer children, they invest more in each child. Girls are given access to education when it will lead to greater future economic returns—which also improves child development even if a woman never ends up in the labor force. In a more gender-equal society, where women are full participants in the economy, women will be able to demand government and social support to address work-life conflict *and* promote human capital investments in the next generation, all of which, as noted above, improve g.

Piketty emphasized the importance of capital transfers vis-à-vis investments in children's educations, but he doesn't consider the family side of the equation, noting only that childbearing decisions "are influenced by cultural, economic, psychological, and personal factors related to the life goals that individuals choose for themselves. These decisions may also depend on the material conditions that different countries decide to provide, or not provide, for the purpose of making family life compatible with professional life: schools, day care, gender equality, and so on. These issues will undoubtedly play a growing part in twenty-first-century political debate and public policy."[61] Whether we have this policy conversation depends on whether we are going down the path of continued gender equity or dystopia.

The Optimistic Scenario: Continued Gender Equity

In the heyday of patrimonial capitalism in the eighteenth and nineteenth centuries, inheritance was by law patrilineal. Historically, women in the United States (and under English common law) were subject to what was called "coverture," meaning that they forfeited all rights to assets once married. In the United States, some of these laws were undone by Married Women's Property Acts, a series of state laws passed starting in 1839 and expanded upon in subsequent decades, but it wasn't until the 1960s that all aspects of this forfeiture were eliminated. Up until the 1960s, married women in the United States could not open a bank account without their husband's permission, and it was not until the Equal Credit Opportunity Act was passed in 1974 that it became illegal to discriminate against women in matters of access to credit.[62] The slow pace of change in inheritance laws isn't only a U.S. problem. It wasn't until the implementation of the Perth Agreement across the British Commonwealth of Nations in 2015 that the laws of primogeniture were changed from male-preference primogeniture to absolute primogeniture.[63] Thus, had Prince William and the Duchess of Cambridge Kate's first child been a daughter, she would have been the legitimate heir to the throne even if eventually she had a younger brother.

One can argue that the egalitarian nature of today's inheritance laws and patterns is likely to have a strong path dependency. Certainly within families, we do not see parents choosing to bestow more on their sons than on their daughters. Economic research finds that—at least within the United States—parents bestow fairly equal bequests on their male and female children. According to research by Paul Menchik, this pattern isn't altered for very valuable estates: "The bequest proportion received by males does not significantly increase with the size of the estate bequeathed, and the wealth elasticity of bequests to males is equal to unity. First- or earlier-born children do not receive larger bequests than their later born siblings."[64]

Piketty acknowledges that today's inheritance patterns are more broadly dispersed. In his analysis of France, he finds that although the stock of inheritances has risen back to high levels, this is dispersed across more people, thus any single inheritance is smaller. This keeps up the pressure on individuals to focus on labor market earnings, alongside any inheritance they might receive. This, in turn, encourages the kind of high investments in human capital and assortative mating described above, which temper Piketty's conclusions and which are worthy of future study. The more equitable the patterns of bequests among men and women, the greater equity in the overall wealth distribution, which could keep the pace of growth of r slower than otherwise over time.[65]

Yet there is evidence that parents bestow different kinds of wealth on their sons and daughters, and there is some—scant—evidence that daughters receive less human capital investment than sons. While women are just as likely as men to inherit wealth from their parents, men are more likely to inherit the family business. According to Paul Menchik (in an admittedly old paper), "The evidence on devolution patterns of business assets suggests that the son is more likely to inherit a family business if it is owner-operated, but wealth per se is inherited equally by sex."[66] The sociological literature documents that parents make higher financial investments in the education of male children, even in modern-day America. Seth Stephens-Davidowitz uses the novel method of studying Google searches and finds that parents in the United States who turn to Google are two and a half times more likely to ask "Is my son gifted?" than "Is my daughter gifted?" They are also twice as likely to ask how to get their daughters to lose weight than they are to ask about their son's weight.[67] It seems that the focus on their daughter's appearance remains more concerning to parents than her ability to be the smartest in the class.

One worry is that if a woman's value again becomes more closely tied to her ability to catch a capital-rich husband—like in Jane Austen's day—will this negatively affect women's political or economic rights? There is a path dependency to women's political power, so that might be unlikely. With women outpacing men in earning college, and now graduate degrees, women are in the queue for professional jobs and may not be easily moved back into primarily working inside the home.[68] But given the importance of this path dependency for half the population, its stickiness needs to be thought through within the context of the rising importance of capital over labor income. Piketty notes, "[Today's inheritance pattern in France] is also more difficult to represent artistically or to correct politically, because it is a commonplace inequality opposing broad segments of the population rather than pitting a small elite against the rest of society."[69] Feminist voices are certainly part of both the "small elite" and the "rest of society" Piketty refers to, with real implications for women's economic and social power. If there are feminist reasons to encourage broad bequests, this may be another avenue of political discourse to investigate.

The Dystopian Scenario: Patriarchy's Return

But we also have to consider that gender identity may matter for politics. Currently men continue to occupy the highest rungs of power in business and politics. Piketty points out that these men make the rules in ways that suit themselves. Supermanagers have been able to be paid based not on "estimate[s] of each manager's contribution to the firm's output," but by processes "largely arbitrary and dependent on hierarchical relationships and on the relative bargaining power of the individuals involved."[70] What's to stop them from using this power to push toward greater exclusion of women—or to oppose policies that would encourage women's inclusion?

First, some facts. Among the highest earners, there has been very little progress in terms of gender or racial equity. According to research by Wojciech Kopczuk, Emmanuel Saez, and Jae Song using U.S. Social Security Administrative data, the top 1 percent of earners in 1970 were only 2.5 percent female, and the top 0.1 percent of earners were less than 1 percent female. By 2004, the female composition of these groups stood at 13 percent for the top 1 percent of earners, and 7.8 percent for the top 0.1 percent. So there has been progress, but it has fairly slow and small. Further, white men dominate in the jobs that pay the most.[71]

Things are no better in terms of wealth equity. Kopczuk, in research with Lena Edlund, finds that the share of women in the top 0.1 percent and top 0.01 percent of wealth holders in the United States has decreased from around half to approximately one-third from the late 1960s to 2000. Caroline Freund and Sarah Oliver find that as of 2014, only 58 of 492 (11.8 percent) of U.S. billionaires were female. Further, rich women are more likely than men to have inherited, rather than earned, their wealth. In their analysis, Freund and

Oliver find that the self-made female share of this group's wealth was 3.1 percent. And while that number is likely skewed downward because of higher and higher wealth levels as you travel up the rankings, Edlund and Kopczuk show that pattern holds when you count self-made women as a share of the wealthiest people. In 2003, only 22 of the 400 richest Americans were self-made women; the other 30 women on the list inherited their wealth. As for men, 312 of the 348 on the list were self-made. Thus, today's wealthy women are more likely to be like Paris Hilton, who inherited her wealth from her father, Mr. Hilton, rather than Oprah Winfrey, the self-made billionaire.[72]

The reality is that economic and social and political power go together. Piketty encourages his readers to focus on taxing capital as the entry point to reduce r, because he sees limited routes to raise g. However, g may be raised by focusing on ensuring equal access to and economic and political rights for men and women—and for those with and without caregiving responsibilities. In the old patriarchal system, women had far fewer political rights. An economic determinist might argue this was because wealth was accumulated and transferred in a manner that was intended to preserve capital stocks. Within elite families, rules that encouraged sharing would diminish that stock—and one "easy" way to keep the pie whole was elaborate rules that excluded women—except via dowries, of course.

Standard economic theory gave us a strong reason to support inclusive political and economic rights, but how much does this hinge on labor being the primary source of wealth generation? Will powerful men seek ways to limit the need to share highly paid jobs with women? Will they fight for women's inclusion in political and economic leadership, and what implications would there be for a host of other rights for women? In the United States we still debate whether women have the right to choose to continue a pregnancy or whether access to contraception is an important part of women's health care.

Conclusions

A year after the publication of *C21*, Piketty wrote, "All economic concepts, irrespective of how 'scientific' they pretend to be, are intellectual constructions that are socially and historically determined, and which are often used to promote certain views, values, or interests."[73] In this chapter I have sought to show how feminist economics can shed light on the key dynamics in his model. There are important policy implications that can be derived from this analysis. Piketty's conclusion that a global tax on wealth is the most important policy tool still stands, but does this address the gendered nature of how inheritance works? If policy makers focus now on policies that support women's economic independence, then will they both support g and reduce the rate of accumulation, slowing the rise of r? Policies that Piketty casually notes once in his 800+ page book that have "the purpose of making family life compatible with professional life: schools, day care, gender equality, and so on" may actually be another arrow in the quiver to reduce the potential for ever-rising inequality.[74]

SIXTEEN

What Does Rising Inequality Mean for the Macroeconomy?

MARK ZANDI

Economist Mark Zandi—one of the world's leading macroeconomic forecasters—here considers the implications of inequality for macroeconomic growth and stability. He presents the key channels by which inequality of income and wealth enters the model he's developed and undertakes counterfactual analysis of a scenario of constant inequality since 1980. He concludes that the main channel by which inequality affects the macro economy is through the threat it poses to economic stability, rather than economic growth.

The nation's income and wealth have become much more concentrated in recent decades. While many Americans find this disquieting, most macroeconomists—at least those that think about the economy's future performance—have largely ignored it.

Macroeconomists' complacency comes largely because connecting the dots between the skewing of the income and wealth distribution and the economy is difficult—particularly when those linkages must be quantified, as they must in the models these economists typically use to make their projections.

This chapter describes work to account for the changing income and wealth distribution in the Moody's Analytics' econometric model of the U.S. economy. This model is used for a range of purposes, including forecasting, scenario construction, bank stress testing, and policy analysis.[1] The factors determining the income distribution are identified and modeled, as are the channels through which changes in the distribution impact the economy. The model is then used to forecast the outlook for the income distribution and its implications for the economy's future performance.

The most likely outlook is generally sanguine. The income and wealth distributions are not expected to become appreciably more skewed going forward than they are today—the gap between the haves and the have-nots is not expected to grow any wider. Moreover, even if the income and wealth distribution were to become more skewed, under most conditions this would likely not significantly impact the economy's long-term potential growth rate.

However, the more skewed income and wealth distribution has increased the downside risks to this benign outlook, as it has likely resulted in a less stable financial system and a more cyclical economy. This is especially problematic given the slowdown in the economy's long-run potential growth rate, which means that the odds of suffering a recession will be greater in the future than in the nation's past, and the constraints on the Federal Reserve and fiscal policy makers' abilities to respond to future recessions will be more binding.

How Unequal?

There is little debate that the economic pie in the United States is being divided much more unequally than in times past. Well over half of the income earned goes to those in the top quintile of income earners, and more than one-fifth of income goes to the top 5 percent of earners. Moreover, the share of income going to the top has surged in the past thirty years, with the share going to the top quintile increasing by 7 percentage points, while falling for everyone else. The Gini coefficient based on market incomes—a popular measure of the distribution of before-tax income, not including government transfers—has increased sharply over the same period (see Figure 16-1).

Wealth is even more skewed. Nearly three-fourths of household net worth is held by those in the top quintile of income earners.[2] This share has also increased by an outsized 10 percentage points in just the past twenty years. This reflects the increasing concentration of stock wealth among the wealthiest, and the greater indebtedness of lower- and middle-income households.

It is important to note that while incomes and wealth are more skewed, government policies have significantly mitigated the skewing. The Gini coefficient based on before-tax income, which includes government transfers, has not changed much in the past fifteen years. And based on after-tax

TABLE 16-1.

Explaining income inequality across states

Dependent Variable	Mean-to-Median Inequality	Gini Coefficient
Model	First Difference	First Difference
Fixed Effects	Year	Year
Years	80, '90, '00, '10	80, '90, '00, '11
Sample size	153	153
Explanatory Variables:		
Technology share of employment		
Coefficient	0.0526	ns
P-Value	0.0005	ns
Manufacturing share of employment		
Coefficient	−0.0098	−0.001
P-Value	0.0281	0.0085
Working age share of population		
Coefficient	ns	−0.0046
P-Value	ns	0.0005
Share of population with college degree		
Coefficient	ns	0.0013
P-Value	ns	0.0341
Low-skilled immigration share		
Coefficient	0.0189	0.0016
P-Value	0.067	0.0013
High-skilled immigration share		
Coefficient	0.0486	ns
P-Value	0.0332	ns
Unionization rate		
Coefficient	ns	−0.0012
P-Value	ns	0
Adjusted R-square	0.191	0.753

Note: ns is not statistically significant.

Sources: Census, BEA, BLS, Moody's Analytics.

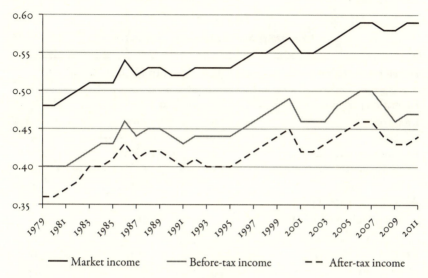

FIGURE 16-1: More unequal income distribution.
Sources: Congressional Budget Office, Moody's Analytics.

income, the Gini has been more or less unchanged over the past twenty years. Recent changes to tax policy, which have increased tax burdens on high-income and wealthier households, have likely further mitigated the skewing, although this will take some time to show up in the numbers.

Also important is that while household consumption as measured by personal outlays is also very skewed—the top quintile accounts for well more than half of spending, and the top 5 percent of income earners account for almost one-third of spending—it hasn't become more skewed in the past fifteen years.[3] Increased leverage by lower- and middle-income households propped up spending before the financial crisis, but these households have maintained their share of spending postcrisis, despite substantial deleveraging.

Explaining Inequality

The forces driving the increasingly unequal distribution of income are complex and difficult to identify quantitatively. To help inform the modeling of the national income distribution in the Moody's Analytics model, various econometric analyses were conducted at a state level. The greater variability in income inequality across states over time allows for a more refined analysis.

TABLE 16-2.

Explaining national income inequality

Dependent Variable	Mean-to-Median Inequality	
Estimation period	1967q1 to 2014q4	
Estimation	Least Squares	
Explanatory Variables:	Coefficient	t-Statistic
Constant	5.296	29.97
Working age share of population	−0.061	−17.49
Growth in info processing equipment deflator	−0.025	−9.11
Net export share of GDP	−0.026	−7.19
Manufacturing share of employment	−0.011	−2.25
Unionization rate	−0.051	−8.48
Unemployment gap	0.006	1.91
Adjusted R-square	0.98	
Durbin-Watson statistic	0.365	

Note: The variables in this model are cointegrated. Since this is a long-run model of income inequality, this allows the use of least squares estimation.

Note: Newey-west standard errors are used.

Sources: Census, BEA, BLS, Moody's Analytics.

Both state Gini coefficients and the ratio of average household income to median income—mean-to-median inequality—are modeled. The state Ginis are more stable, with a correlation across decades (1980–1990, 1990–2000, 2000–2010) averaging 0.91, compared to 0.66 for mean-to-median inequality.

Simple cross-sectional models attempting to explain both measures of income inequality do not show many statistically significant factors. The exception is unemployment, which has a strong effect on the Gini. This is intuitive and is evident graphically (see Figure 16-2).

First-difference models examining changes in both measures of inequality over longer periods are more productive in identifying other factors impacting inequality. These models are based on a panel of the 50 states plus the District of Columbia, with changes by decade from 1980 to 2010, for a total sample of 153 observations. These models include year fixed effects, and

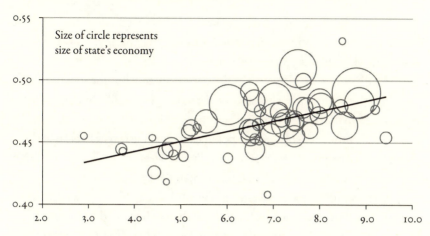

FIGURE 16-2: Inequality and unemployment are linked.
Source: BLS, Moody's Analytics.

so focus on relative changes among states within the decade. Regressions are weighted using state population.

Manufacturing employment is a consistent determinant of income inequality in the state models. Manufacturing is a source of generally good middle-paying jobs, and factory workers who lose them have had a tough time finding comparable jobs, particularly because they are generally older and less likely to move for new work. Manufacturing employment is also a proxy for the broader effects of globalization, which has been hard on the nation's manufacturers in recent decades.

The skill level of foreign immigrants, as measured by American Community Survey micro data on the educational attainment of the foreign born, also significantly impacts inequality. The share of the immigrant population that is low-skilled—with less than a high school degree—is especially important, as a rising share weighs on the incomes of those in the lower part of the income distribution.

Factors that impact inequality, but depend on the measure of inequality modeled, include the technology share of employment, the share of workers that are unionized, the share of the population with at least a college degree, and high-skilled immigrants with at least a college degree (see Table 16-1). The share of the population that is of working age also matters for inequality, and likely reflects the impact of an aging population, as retirees have less income and spend down their assets, exacerbating inequality. It also captures changes in the dependency ratio; a declining ratio is a plus for economic growth and prosperity in general.

Causality can run both ways in these state models, but for some variables the effect runs most plausibly in one direction. It is unlikely that high inequality led to the decline of manufacturing employment or unionization or a larger tech sector and working-age population, making it very likely that these factors drive inequality. However, causality between inequality and foreign immigration and educational attainment may run in both directions.

Other factors are likely measuring the same thing. High-skilled immigration increases mean-to-median inequality, whereas higher education levels increase the Gini. It is likely that both are picking up the effect of a more skilled population on inequality. Both are also closely related to technological change, which is proxied by the share of employment in technology industries.

Overall, the state modeling results suggest that the skewing of the income distribution in recent decades has been shaped by demographic factors, the pace of technological change and globalization, and labor market conditions.

Modeling National Inequality

The state models are useful for identifying factors driving income inequality, but they are less useful for forecasting purposes. Many of the factors are difficult to forecast at a state level, and some factors, like technological change and globalization, can only be weakly proxied at a state level. The model of the national income distribution in the Moody's Analytics model is thus consistent with the state models, but differs given the limitations of the state models and other modeling constraints.

Income inequality in the Moody's Analytics national model is measured by mean-to-median inequality, and the impact of demographics on inequality is captured by the share of the population that is of working age (see Table 16-2). It is the most statistically significant factor in the model, highlighting its importance to future changes in inequality.

Technological change is captured in the model by changes in the price deflator for information-processing equipment. Growth in this deflator reflects in part quality changes in this important technology.[4] Rapid technological improvements during the tech boom of the late 1990s and early 2000s resulted in rapid declines in the deflator. More recently, the deflator has stopped declining, suggesting that the pace of technological improvement has slowed, although other factors are also playing a role.

The faster the pace of technological change, as measured by a more rapidly declining deflator, results in a more skewed income distribution. This is consistent with evidence that technological improvements are particularly hard on those working in occupations with pay that puts them in the middle of the income distribution. In a metaphorical if not real sense, these jobs can be replaced by computer code, and those losing their jobs as a result generally move down the income distribution, as they lack the skills and education to move up. Of course, those writing the computer code do fabulously well.[5]

Globalization's impact on the income distribution is captured in the model by the net export share of GDP and manufacturing's share of employment. The U.S. economy became much more globally oriented beginning in the early 1980s, the last time the United States ran a trade surplus. Advances in logistics and transportation technologies, along with a series of trade deals, helped open the U.S. economy to the rest of the world. The trade deficit had ballooned to a record share of GDP just prior to the Great Recession. However, in the wake of the recession and the inability of policy makers to strike any new major trade deals, the globalization of the U.S. economy has stalled. Moreover, with the nation's manufacturing base already fully integrated into the global economy, further globalization will need to occur in the information and other service-oriented industries.

The model captures the impact of labor market conditions on the income distribution through the unemployment gap—the difference between the unemployment rate and the natural rate of unemployment—and the share of the workforce that is unionized. Not surprisingly, the unemployment gap was more or less positive for the thirty-year period extending from the mid-1970s to the mid-2000s, when income inequality was worsening (see Figure 16-3).

This is due in significant part to the conduct of monetary policy, which was focused on reining in the period's uncomfortably high inflation. Federal Reserve Chairman Paul Volker induced the severe recessions of the early 1980s to kibosh the period's runaway inflation, and Alan Greenspan, who followed Volker as chairman, followed a stated policy of "opportunistic disinflation." Under this policy, the Fed was slow to respond to a weaker economy and

TABLE 16-3.

Inequality and consumption

	1980	2015
Aggregate Consumer Spending (Tril$)	1.7	12.4
Consumer spending due to household income (Tril $)		
Top 20%	0.42	3.30
Bottom 80%	0.84	4.96
Marginal propensity to consumer out of income	0.63	0.61
Top 20%	0.48	0.48
Bottom 80%	0.75	0.75
Household Income (Tril$)	2.0	13.5
Top 20%	0.9	6.9
Bottom 80%	1.1	6.6
Consumer spending due to household wealth (Tril $)		
Top 20%	0.41	4.09
Bottom 80%	0.00	0.00
Marginal propensity to consume out of wealth	0.041	0.048
Top 20%	0.065	0.065
Bottom 80%	0.000	0.000
Household Wealth (Tril$)	10	85
Top 20%	6	63
Bottom 80%	4	22

Sources: BEA, Federal Reserve, Moody's Analytics.

higher unemployment in order to dampen inflation expectations and wage demands. The policy was successful in reducing inflation, but the wages of lower- and middle-income workers were significant casualties of this policy.

The collapse in unionization during these decades also swung the balance of power from workers to their employers in the negotiations over wages and other compensation. Union workers accounted for some one-fourth of wage and salary workers in the 1960s. That share had fallen to about one-fifth of

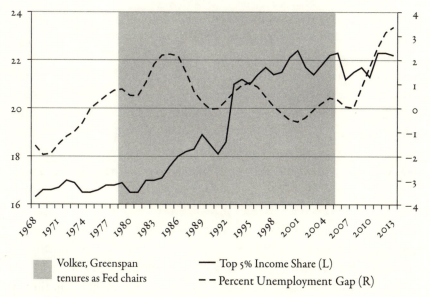

FIGURE 16-3: Wider unemployment gap, more inequality.
Source: Census, BLS, Moody's Analytics.

workers in 1980 when then-president Ronald Regan broke the air-traffic controllers union, a significant symbolic blow to unionization. Today, closer to only one-tenth of workers are unionized, although the share has stabilized over the past decade.

Low- and high-skilled foreign immigration, which were found to be important factors driving income inequality in the state models, are not included in the national model of inequality, given the difficulties in forecasting them. Moreover, they should have somewhat offsetting effects on inequality going forward, as immigration flows are expected to become increasingly high-skilled.

Consumer Spending Behavior

There are several potential channels through which a more skewed income and wealth distribution could potentially impact the economy. Most direct is the impact on aggregate consumer spending and saving. But just how is hard to disentangle, as lower-income households have a higher propensity to spend out of their income and wealthier households have a higher propensity to spend out of their wealth. It is thus unclear how a more unequal distribution affects aggregate spending and saving behavior.

To see this, consider the thought experiment shown in Table 16-3. Based on the consumer spending equations across income quintiles in the Moody's Analytics model, which will be described soon in more detail, consumer spending in 1980 (before the increase in inequality) and 2015 are decomposed into the spending driven by household income and wealth for the top quintile and everyone else. The marginal propensities to consume (MPCs) out of income and wealth (the wealth effect) differ for these income groups: The MPC out of income is much larger for the lower-income groups, but the wealth effect is much larger for higher-income groups. The MPCs are assumed to remain unchanged between 1980 and 2015, although as is also discussed later, there is evidence that the wealth effect varies substantially over time, and has increased substantially since the financial crisis.

Multiplying the MPCs out of income and wealth for those in the top quintile and the bottom four quintiles by their income and wealth determines spending by these income groups. Aggregate consumer spending, which is the sum of the spending by the income groups, totaled $1.7 trillion in 1980, rising to $12.4 trillion in 2015.

Now consider what happens if it is assumed that the share of income and wealth that went to the different income groups remained unchanged between 1980 and 2015—that is, if the income and wealth distributions didn't actually become more skewed. The impact on aggregate spending is very modest, with spending in 2015 totaling $12.0 trillion. This suggests that the skewing of the income and wealth distribution between 1980 and 2015 had only a very modest impact on aggregate consumer spending and saving behavior.

Moreover, even if inequality were to diminish spending by more than this analysis suggests, this would mean that aggregate saving would be greater. In the long run, with an economy at full employment, the increased saving would presumably support greater investment and long-term economic growth.

As an important sidebar based on this analysis, policy makers working to end recessions should probably focus on policies that lift the after-tax income of low-income households and the net worth of wealthy households. Indeed, this is what fiscal policy makers did with the various stimulus measures implemented during the Great Recession, including increased unemployment insurance benefits and payroll tax holidays. The Federal Reserve's quantitative easing programs also worked to buoy the economy by supporting stock prices and house values, to the direct benefit of wealthier households.

Modeling Spending by Income

The connection between inequality and aggregate consumer spending and saving may be tenuous, but it is explicitly modeled in the Moody's Analytics model. Spending by consumers in each quintile of the income distribution is modeled based on more than a quarter century of data through 2014 from the Bureau of Labor Statistic's Consumer Expenditure Survey (see Table 16-4).[6]

Consumer spending per capita by income quintile is determined by income per capita by quintile, stock wealth, homeowners' equity, and the household debt service burden. The model is log linear and has fixed effects for each income quintile. The income and wealth distribution are linked to consumer spending in the model as income and wealth by quintile are determined by aggregate income and wealth and mean-to-median inequality.

The marginal propensity to consume out of after-tax income is, as expected, much larger for lower-income groups than for higher-income groups. For those in the bottom quintile of the income distribution, the MPC out of income is estimated to be .86, while it is only .48 for those in the top quintile of the distribution.

Stock prices only affect the spending of consumers in the top quintile with a wealth effect of 9.4 cents. That is, for each $1 dollar increase in stock wealth, consumer spending in the top quintile increases by nearly a dime. The implied aggregate stock wealth effect among all consumers is closer to 2 cents, which is consistent with other econometric estimates of this effect.[7]

The housing wealth effect affects spending decisions by consumers in the top two quintiles of the distribution, and is estimated at close to 7 cents. The implied aggregate housing wealth effect across all consumers is thus almost 3 cents. This is smaller than most estimates of the housing wealth effect, although these estimates are based on data prior to the housing bust and financial crisis.

Debt service burdens—the share of after-tax income that households must devote to servicing their debt to remain nondelinquent—also impact consumer spending, but only for those in the bottom quintile. It is somewhat

TABLE 16-4.

Explaining consumer spending by income quintile

Dependent Variable	Consumer expenditures per capita	
Estimation period	1987 to 2014	
Estimation	Linear estimation after one-step weighting matrix	
Explanatory Variables:	Coefficient	t-Statistic
Constant	3.044	19.370
Income per capita, First Quintile	0.861	21.840
Income per capita, Second Quintile	0.759	24.710
Income per capita, Third Quintile	0.743	30.210
Income per capita, Fourth Quintile	0.622	9.350
Income per capita, Fifth Quintile	0.485	8.080
Stock Wealth, Fifth Quintile	0.094	4.600
Debt Service Burden, First Quintile	−0.023	−1.890
Housing Wealth, Fourth and Fifth Quintiles	0.072	1.650
Fixed Effecs, First Quintile	−0.733	
Fixed Effecs, Second Quintile	−0.412	
Fixed Effecs, Third Quintile	−0.349	
Fixed Effecs, Fourth Quintile	0.252	
Fixed Effecs, Fifth Quintile	1.250	
Adjusted R-square	0.995	
Durbin-Watson statistic	0.733	

Note: The variables in this model are cointegrated. Since this is a long-run model of income inequality, this allows the use of least squares estimation.

Note: Newey-west standard errors are used.

Sources: Census, BEA, BLS, Moody's Analytics.

surprising, given the massive household leveraging and deleveraging before and after the financial crisis, that debt burdens don't explain spending for other income groups. Other measures of household financial stress that are part of the Moody Analytics' model were also tested for inclusion in the model of consumer spending, but to no avail.

Public Spending

A more skewed income and wealth distribution could also impair economic growth if it were to constrain public spending on education and infrastructure. The educational attainment of the population is important to productivity and the economy's long-run potential. So too is the quality of the infrastructure upon which all businesses and households rely, from the highways and water systems to the telecommunication network and air traffic control.

However, identifying the links between income inequality, public infrastructure, and productivity and the economy's potential are difficult. Perhaps the wealthy bend the political process to favor fewer taxes, resulting in less government revenue to support spending on all public goods and services? After all, many of them send their children to private schools and their lives are less impacted by potholes and long waits at airports. This is hard to prove, given that government revenues as a share of GDP are close to their long-run norms, and it is all but impossible to quantify, even if true.[8]

Or perhaps inequality results in the underfunding of public education via the uneven redistribution of property taxes within states? Property taxes are a key funding source for public education, and income and wealth across communities have become increasingly uneven. The ratio of per capita income between the richest counties in the nation, those in the 95th percentile, and the median county has continued to grow steadily since the late 1970s, suggesting the richest communities continue to pull away from the pack (see Figure 16-4). And although the ratio of the income of the median county to income in counties in the 5th percentile declined through 1990, suggesting convergence as low-income counties caught up, that improvement has stalled in the last twenty years. Lower-tail inequality between counties has kept the poorest from catching up to the rest. These trends of continually increasing upper-tail inequality and unchanged lower-tail inequality mirror national income inequality trends.

The educational attainment of U.S. counties is also drifting apart. Higher-income counties have higher education levels, and this has grown over time. This is evident graphically using county-level data on per capita

397

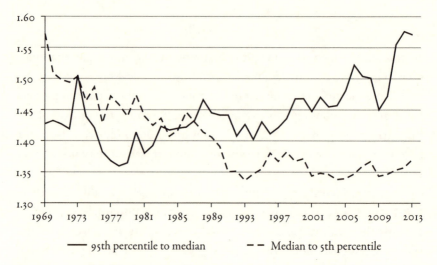

FIGURE 16-4: Wealth counties pull away.
Source: BEA, Moody's Analytics.

income and college attainment based on the 1990 and 2000 decennial Census and the 2010 American Community Survey (see Figure 16-5). This is also supported by a regression model that shows that counties with higher per capita income in 2000 experienced a greater increase in the share of 25- to 34-year-olds with a college degree in the subsequent decade.

However, it is likely that the causality between inequality and educational attainment across counties runs in both directions. Households in the highest-income communities send more of their children to college, and these communities attract more college-educated workers and thus experience stronger economic growth. Disentangling this relationship is problematic, and quantifying to what degree it impacts productivity and the economy's potential is even more of a problem.

Despite this significant econometric concern, educational attainment in the Moody's Analytics model is modeled in part by mean-to-median inequality. Educational attainment in turn drives productivity growth and the economy's long-term growth potential in the model. Increasing mean-to-median inequality slows the growth in educational attainment, and thus productivity and long-term potential growth.

TABLE 16-5.

Big swings in savings by high income households

	Personal Saving Rate					Change in the Personal Saving Rate			
	Pre-bubbles 1990–94	Stock bubble 1995–99	Housing Bubble 2000–07	Great Recession 2008–2009q2	Recovery 2009q2–2015q3	1995–99 vs. 1990–94	2000–07 vs. 1995–99	2008–2009q2 vs. 2000–07	2009q2–2015q3 vs. 2008–2009q2
Total Population	10.2	7.1	3.0	9.9	8.7	–3.0	–4.2	7.0	–1.2
Part of the Income Distribution:									
Income: 0%–39.9%	5.7	6.7	3.0	3.8	4.8	1.0	–3.8	0.8	1.0
Income: 40%–59.9%	4.6	3.0	–0.3	2.5	5.6	–1.6	–3.3	2.8	3.1
Income: 60%–79.9%	6.1	3.3	0.0	2.9	6.5	–2.8	–3.3	3.0	3.5
Income: 80%–94.9%	10.1	6.4	1.7	7.3	9.9	–3.7	–4.7	5.6	2.6
Income: 95%–100%	17.5	12.4	6.7	19.2	11.0	–5.2	–5.6	12.4	–8.2
	Savings (Billions $)					Change in Savings (Billions $)			
Total Population	483.0	435.3	269.1	1127.7	1060.9	–47.6	–166.2	858.6	–66.8
Part of the Income Distribution:									
Income: 0%–39.9%	27.6	43.2	20.7	40.8	58.0	15.6	–22.5	20.1	17.2
Income: 40%–59.9%	27.5	24.0	–8.3	33.1	76.3	–3.6	–32.3	41.4	43.2
Income: 60%–79.9%	59.7	40.3	–2.9	61.0	143.6	–19.4	–43.2	63.9	82.6
Income: 80%–94.9%	126.1	100.4	34.8	190.6	303.2	–25.6	–65.6	155.8	112.6
Income: 95%–100%	242.0	227.4	224.7	802.1	479.7	–14.7	–2.7	577.4	–322.4

Note: A description of the methodology used to construct estimates of the personal saving rate by income is available upon request.

Sources: BEA, Federal Reserve, Moody's Analytics.

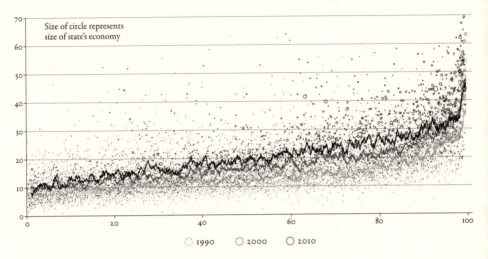

○ 1990   ○ 2000   ○ 2010

FIGURE 16-5: High-income counties are highly educated.
Source: Census Bureau, Moody's Analytics.

Financial Stability

The connection between inequality and the economy's performance may also run through the financial system. There is no argument that the recent financial crisis and Great Recession were due in significant part to the dramatic increase in leverage among lower-income households during the housing bubble.

This leveraging is evident in the dramatic decline in personal saving in the years leading up to the financial collapse. Based on estimates of personal saving rates for households in different parts of the income distribution, constructed by combining data from the Federal Reserve's Survey of Consumer Finances and Financial Accounts of the United States, saving fell sharply across all income groups in the early 2000s (see Table 16-5). However, those in the bottom 80 percent of the income distribution effectively saved nothing, and those in the middle quintiles of the distribution actually dis-saved. That is, they spent beyond their incomes by increasing their borrowing or selling assets. Given the rapid growth in debt during the period, it is likely the former.

Whether this saving and borrowing behavior is linked to rising income and wealth inequality is hard to determine. Some have posited that there was a "keeping up with the Joneses" dynamic at work, with lower-income households willing to shred their finances in order to maintain their spending relative to their wealthier neighbors. However, what empirical study there is on this suggests that there was no such dynamic during this period.[9]

Another possibility is that increasing income and wealth inequality during the 1980s and 1990s created more credit-constrained households. When those credit constraints were relaxed in the 2000s, as they were when mortgage and other consumer lenders substantially eased their underwriting standards prior to the financial crisis, this resulted in a massive and unsustainable increase in household leverage and ultimately a catastrophic increase in financial instability.

The economic damage wrought by the Great Recession is impossible to overstate. It took nearly a decade for the economy to return to full employment after the downturn struck, and the economy was permanently smaller when it finally did. Recessions reduce the economy's potential, by crimping productivity and the labor force, and severe recessions reduce the economy's potential by a lot.

The risk of a similar financial crisis, with massive household leveraging and deleveraging, playing out in the future has been significantly reduced, at least for a while, by regulatory changes to the financial system implemented in response to the crisis. The Dodd-Frank regulatory reform requires the nation's banks to hold much more capital, be more liquid, and underwrite their lending substantially more cautiously. Lower income and wealth households will continue having a more difficult time getting approved for a loan than they did prior to the crisis.

Of course, the fast-evolving, lightly regulated shadow financial system is working to find ways to extend more credit to these households. This combined with a further skewing of the income and wealth distribution and a growing number of credit-starved households could ultimately sow the seeds of the next financial crisis.

This potential scenario is captured in the Moody's Analytics model in the equations for single-family residential mortgage debt outstanding, revolving credit outstanding, and nonrevolving credit outstanding. Mean-to-median inequality is interacted with underwriting standards as measured by the Federal Reserve's Senior Loan Officer Survey results in the equations. Rising inequality combined with an easing in standards results in stronger growth in household debt. This in turn results in higher debt service burdens, and ultimately more delinquencies and losses in the financial system.

Under most conditions, inequality does not significantly impact credit growth, the health of the financial system, and the economy's performance. But it can, especially in scenarios in which rising inequality conflates with increasingly poor underwriting, fueling stronger credit growth and rising household leverage. If the economy then suffers a recession, for whatever reason, the result would at the very least be a more severe downturn.

Bigger Business Cycles

The economy may also be more cyclical, with more frequent recessions, as a result of the skewed income and wealth distribution. Behind this is the more pro-cyclical saving behavior of high-income, high-net-worth households. That is, their saving rate rises more (and their consumption weakens) in recessions and falls more (with consumption strengthening) in economic recoveries.

This behavior is evident in the saving rate data shown in Table 16-5. For those households in the top 5 percent of the income distribution, who account for the bulk of personal saving, their saving rate fell significantly during the 1990s technology stock bubble and also during the housing bubble. Between the early 1990s and early 2000s, this group's saving rate declined by more than 10 percentage points.

When the Great Recession hit, these panicked high-income households battened down the proverbial hatches, significantly curtailing their spending and increasing their saving. Their saving jumped to just under 20 percent of their income. It was this sharp reversal in their spending that was behind the severity of the downturn.

The subsequent economic recovery is also due in significant part to more relaxed high-income households. Their saving rate has normalized. In contrast, saving rates for all other income groups have continued to increase, reflecting the deleveraging these groups have been engaged in since the recession. The aggregate saving rate across all income groups has declined only marginally since the recession.

The cyclicality of saving by the wealthy is consistent with large wealth effects; as the value of the assets they own go up and down, so too does their spending and saving. All of this is especially true in the current context. The stock wealth effect appears to be especially large by historical standards, as the large baby-boom generation is in or near retirement. This cohort's spending and saving seems especially sensitive to movements in stock prices, perhaps given how much their stock portfolios mean to their financial well-being in retirement.

The seemingly larger stock wealth effects post financial crisis are evident via econometric analysis. Metropolitan-area consumption functions are estimated based on metro-area retail sales data constructed using the Census of Retail Trade and retail trade employment. Metro-area financial wealth, including stockholdings, fixed-income assets, and deposits, is based on data collected by IXI Services (a division of Equifax) from the nation's largest financial institutions. Metro-area homeowners' equity is estimated based on data on house prices, the housing stock, and mortgage debt available from credit bureau Equifax.[10]

The stock wealth effect estimated based on data prior to the financial crisis ranges between 1.6 cents and 3.6 cents, depending on the model specification (see Table 16-6). As previously described, this is similar to the size of the wealth effect in the Moody's Analytics model, after adjusting for the use of retail sales, which are approximately half of total consumer spending. Post crisis, the stock wealth effect ranges from a much larger 11.7 cents to 14 cents. Not surprisingly, the housing wealth effect has been cut approximately in half before and after the financial crisis. Homeowners clearly have been chastened by the housing bust and less willing to pull equity from their homes to finance spending. They are also less able, given much tighter underwriting on home equity borrowing and cash-out refinancing.

A reasonable criticism of this analysis is that this division of the data into pre- and postcrisis periods using the end of 2007 as a cutoff is arbitrary. House prices peaked in early 2006, while the full brunt of the financial crisis did not strike until mid-2008. To address that criticism, we performed a rolling regression of the consumption function over a span of 28 quarters, which is the length of the current expansion, and near the average length of expansion over the period considered.

Prior to the Great Recession, the housing wealth effect was always greater than the stock wealth effect, save for a very brief period at the height of the technology stock bubble in the late 1990s (see Figure 16-6). In recent years the stock wealth effect has been as large as it has ever been and meaningfully larger than the housing wealth effect. In contrast, the housing wealth effect is currently as low as it has been since the early 1990s.

TABLE 16-6.
Changing wealth effects

	Simple Model		Metro-specific time trends	
	Pre 2008	Post 2007	Pre 2008	Post 2007
Lagged consumption				
Stock wealth	0.016	0.117	0.036	0.140
	(4.26)	(22.46)	(10.90)	(53.20)
Value of Housing Stock	0.092	0.051	0.126	0.053
	(9.91)	(6.08)	(14.79)	(6.52)
Income	0.523	0.591	0.619	0.603
	(14.03)	(7.41)	(3.07)	(12.76)
Constant	8.851	7.341	12.704	7.023
	(24.68)	(8.13)	(28.34)	(14.03)
N	12448	10500	12448	10500
Within-metro R2	48.8%	60.2%	84.0%	77.5%

The Pre 2008 sample spans 2000Q1 through 2007Q4.
The Post 2007 sample spans 2008Q1 through 2014Q4.
All specifications have 389 metropolitan areas (panels).
t statistics are in parentheses and are robust to arbitrary within-state correlation.
All variables are in log real per-household units.

Sources: BEA, IXI, Census, Moody's Analytics.

The total wealth effect, derived by weighting stock and housing wealth effects by households' stock and housing wealth, has fluctuated significantly since the Great Recession. At its peak in late 2010, the total wealth effect based on retail sales reached 18 cents (see Figure 16-7). This includes the 28-quarter period beginning in early 2004 and encompasses the housing bubble and the crash in house and stock prices. The total wealth effect has since receded, and is currently just under 8 cents, approximately equal to the decade prior to the housing bubble.

The pro-cyclicality of spending by the wealthy may also be exacerbated by the seemingly greater volatility in asset prices post crisis. Stock market volatility appears especially elevated, given high valuations and increasing

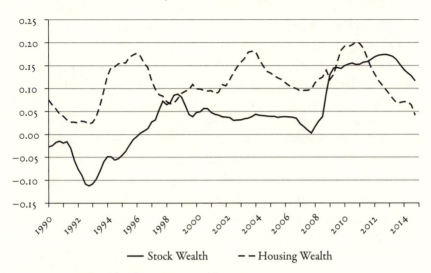

FIGURE 16-6: Wealth effects are not stable.

Sources: IXI, Federal Reserve, Census, Moody's Analytics.

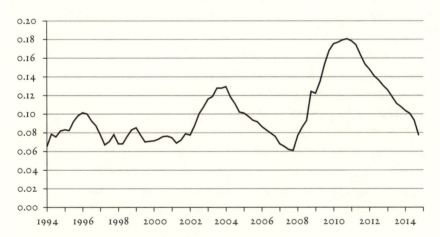

FIGURE 16-7: Aggregate wealth effect normalizes.

Sources: IXI, Federal Reserve, Census, Moody's Analytics.

connections to the highly variable global economy and currency movements. Asset markets also appear to be affected by less-liquid trading. Large
systemically important banks have scaled back their broker-dealer operations since the crisis due to heightened regulation and stiffer capital and liquidity requirements. This is especially evident in fixed-income markets.

Any given change in economic fundamentals thus appears to be creating greater swings in stock, bond, currency, and commodity markets.

Given that the economy currently has a much lower potential growth rate, the greater cyclicality suggests that the economy is more likely to suffer recessions. The economy's slower potential growth rate has been partly expected, given the retiring boomers and resulting slowdown in labor force growth, but the persistently weak productivity growth has been a surprise.

Further adding to the recession odds is that interest rates are still not far from the zero lower bound, creating difficulties for any monetary policy response to a soft economy. Other monetary policy tools such as quantitative easing and negative interest rates are much less efficacious. The nation's high federal government debt load and the poisoned political environment in Washington, D.C., also make any fiscal policy response to a troubled economy less likely.

A more cyclical economy with more recessions will only exacerbate the skewed income and wealth distribution. Incomes of low- and even middle-income households are also more likely to decline, further weighing on the educational attainment of these groups, and even undermining financial stability, as it may lead to greater, unsustainable credit use by these groups. A self-reinforcing, negative dynamic may set in.

Capturing all of this in the Moody's Analytics model is intractable. The model is not designed to handle complex time-varying relationships, such as the stock and housing wealth effects, or the implications of more volatile asset prices. Gauging how the Federal Reserve and fiscal policy makers will react to future recessions is also very difficult. Instead, to gauge the implications of these kind of dynamics, the model is simulated under different scenarios, which allows for adjusting the model to account for them.

Inequality Peaks

There is much reasonable handwringing over the prospects of a further erosion in income and wealth inequality and the implications for the economy's performance. Extrapolating from the trend lines of the past thirty years and considering the economy's tough road since the Great Recession, it is easy to be pessimistic about the future. Indeed, the deep angst evident in

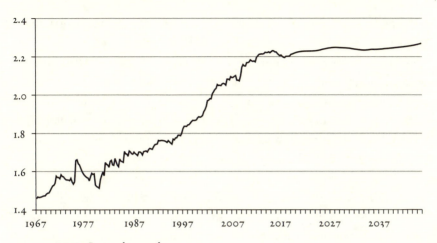

FIGURE 16-8: Inequality peaks.
Source: BLS, Moody's Analytics.

surveys of how people view their financial situation and in the nation's fractured politics likely reflects this pessimism, at least in part.

These worries are likely misplaced; prospects are good that inequality has peaked. That is, income and wealth inequality is not expected to be any worse a decade or even a quarter century from now. Not that the gulf between the haves and have-nots will narrow to any significant degree, but simply that it won't widen further.

Based on a simulation of the Moody's Analytics model under the most likely set of assumptions—the baseline scenario—mean-to-median income inequality is expected to remain essentially unchanged going forward (see Figure 16-8). This is despite what will be a steady decline over the next fifteen years in the share of the population that is of working age, as the large baby-boom generation retires. All else being equal, this should exacerbate inequality, given the large increase in dependent seniors.

Inexorable improvements in technology will also aggravate inequality, as more rote middle-paying jobs vanish and most of the displaced workers move down the income ladder. Indeed, the pace of technological change, as measured by the growth in the deflator for information-processing equipment, should be meaningfully faster in the future than it is today. The deflator, which has been essentially unchanged in recent years, is projected to decline by approximately 5 percent per annum over the next thirty years. This isn't the 10 to 15 percent annual declines experienced during the late 1990s technology boom, but it is a relatively heady pace of technological change by any other historical standard.

Offsetting the negative impact of demographics and technological change on inequality is an expected positive shift in the impact of globalization. This is measured by a narrowing in the U.S. trade deficit as a share of GDP, and a stabilization in manufacturing's share of total employment.

Behind this optimism is the perspective that there is very little remaining economic fallout from industries and companies that have struggled with global competition. They have long since moved their operations overseas, downsized, or failed. Those businesses in operation are hypercompetitive, with a global market niche, superior technology or other intellectual property, or a very low cost structure.

Moreover, the U.S. economy is well poised to benefit from expected strong growth in global trade in services. This includes everything from media and entertainment, to educational and financial services, to management consulting and other professional services. U.S. businesses have long been active in these activities, and businesses and households in the fast-developing emerging world have finally become wealthy enough to want and afford them. Selling these services to the rest of the world should be the source of a significant number of new well-paying U.S. jobs.

Globalization's full promise depends on the ability of policy makers to reach new trade deals like the Trans Pacific Partnership, and the Transatlantic Trade and Investment Partnership. These deals, which are currently hung up in the U.S. political process, are especially important in protecting the intellectual property that American companies are increasingly selling overseas.

Prospects for a generally tight labor market should also support less inequality. With persistently weak inflation, disinflation, and even deflation since the Great Recession, the Federal Reserve has pursued a highly accommodative monetary policy. While the Fed has begun to normalize monetary policy, policy makers have stated that they will raise rates cautiously and that interest rates will fully normalize well after the economy is operating at full employment. The unemployment gap is likely to be negative—actual unemployment will be less than the natural rate—for the foreseeable future.

Retirement of the baby-boom generation also suggests that the nation's labor force will grow extraordinarily slowly over the next fifteen years, arguing for a perennial tight labor market. Labor shortages will likely be a problem, especially if the nation's immigration laws aren't significantly overhauled to allow many more immigrants into the country. These shortages will be especially pronounced in the manufacturing, construction, and transportation sectors, suggesting that the rate of unionization will stabilize. The balance of power between workers and employers, which has strongly favored employers over the past thirty years, will be much more balanced going forward. The long-running skewing in the income and wealth distribution is over.

Macroeconomic Nonevent?

There is evidence that extreme inequality, as prevails in some parts of the world, weakens economies, but inequality in the United States doesn't appear to be significant enough for it to make a substantial difference to the economy's prospects. That is, despite the skewing of the distribution of income and wealth in recent decades, it has likely not significantly diminished the American economy's growth rate, nor is it expected to in the future.

Of course, this results from the expectation that inequality has peaked. But even if this proves too optimistic, and inequality continues to erode, its impact on the economy's long-run growth potential should not prove too significant. To see this, consider a simulation of the Moody's Analytics model under the assumption that mean-to-median income inequality increases over the next thirty years similarly to its increase over the past thirty years. The simulation is agnostic with regard to the factors behind the worse inequality.

In this simulation, real GDP falls almost $300 billion short of GDP in the baseline scenario by 2045. To put this into context, consider that real GDP is expected to increase by nearly $13 trillion between now and then. Thus, an erosion in inequality in the future on a par with what has happened in the past, reduces real GDP by less than 1 percent, thirty years from now. This largely reflects the lower educational attainment of the population, and its impact on productivity and the economy's potential; the shortfall in GDP is mostly due to less consumer spending by lower-income households.

Dark Scenario

Despite this sanguine outcome, it is not difficult to construct scenarios that result in a much darker outcome for the U.S. economy. Consider a scenario in which mean-to-median inequality erodes over the next decade similar to the erosion that occurred in the 1980s, again for indeterminate reasons. However, in this scenario the economy suffers a recession early in the next decade. This scenario also assumes that the stock wealth effects are larger than those in the Moody's Analytics model, consistent with those described earlier for the post-financial-crisis period.

That another recession might occur early in the next decade would be consistent with the dynamics typical in modern business cycles. Given the currently accommodative monetary policy, the economy will soon be operating beyond full employment and wage and price pressures will develop. Asset prices rise strongly and credit growth is robust, as capital markets turn euphoric and lenders ease their underwriting standards. The Fed, worried that inflation and inflation expectations are becoming untethered, finally responds by accelerating its interest rate hikes. As the decade comes to a close, the Treasury yield curve inverts. A recession invariably follows, generally after there is some type of seemingly exogenous shock that undermines the lofty asset prices and confidence.

The growing income inequality in this scenario significantly exacerbates the severity of the recession. Wealthy households sharply curtail their spending in the face of falling asset prices, as do lower-income households encumbered with higher levels of debt.

Interest rates decline quickly, and short-term rates fall back to the lower zero bound. The Moody's Analytics model allows for quantitative easing when short rates hit the zero lower bound and thus lower long-term interest rates, but monetary policy soon loses its effectiveness. Fiscal policy is also assumed to be confined to the automatic stabilizers built into government spending and tax policy. Given the still-acid politics surrounding the use of fiscal stimulus in the Great Recession, the scenario assumes that policy makers do not implement stimulus measures.

The economy ultimately recovers in this scenario, but it is much diminished. A decade from now, real GDP still remains a consequential 2.6 percent lower than it is in the baseline scenario. This is a very dark, but plausible, scenario.

Conclusions

For many Americans, the growing chasm between the wealthy and the poor is one of the most disturbing features of the U.S. economy's performance in recent decades. This sentiment goes to the fairness of our economic system, and the ability of those less well-off to better their economic fortunes.

In odd juxtaposition to these concerns, most macroeconomists, at least those focused on the economy's prospects, have all but ignored inequality in their thinking. Their implicit, if not explicit, assumption is that inequality doesn't matter much when gauging the macroeconomic outlook.

For the most part this chapter suggests that macroeconomists probably have it roughly right. Namely, the links between inequality and economic growth are tenuous, at least in the case of the United States, and even though greater inequality hurts long-term growth, it hurts it only a little bit. Given the errors inherent in making long-term economic projections, not accounting for increasing inequality likely adds little to those errors.

Having said this, it isn't said with much confidence. Greater inequality likely makes the financial system less stable, as credit-constrained low-income households are potentially significant risks, and the economy more cyclical, as wealthier households that account for the bulk of the spending are sensitive to swings in increasingly volatile asset markets. This may not be a big deal if financial markets and the economy move in a more or less straight line, but it could be a huge deal if they don't.

This is especially true given that the economy's potential growth will be much slower going forward than in the past, suggesting that recessions will be more likely. With monetary and fiscal policy almost certainly rendered more impotent by the zero lower bound and tighter political fetters, future recessions could be more severe.

A critical lesson of the Great Recession is that recessions do permanent damage to the economy, diminishing its potential. Few, if any, macroeconomists have models that account for this in their long-term projections. Macroeconomists should thus not be comfortable that they have a good grip on what inequality means for our economic prospects.

SEVENTEEN

Rising Inequality and Economic Stability

SALVATORE MORELLI

For a long time, the distribution of income or wealth was not a critical factor for understanding economic performance. Part of this is due to the separate treatment, in economics, of the conceptual issues of equity and efficiency. A key question to consider, however, is the role of rising inequality—especially in the wake of the financial crisis and the ensuing recession felt worldwide. Does inequality affect economic stability? If so, how? What do we know and what more do we need to know to advise policy makers on this question?

These are the questions asked by economist Salvatore Morelli. In this chapter Morelli critically surveys the existing body of evidence and hypotheses on the link between inequality and macroeconomic instability in order to ascertain what guidance, if any, the literature can offer us. He drills down specifically on the question of economic instability. He argues that a new hypothesis has emerged (or perhaps reemerged) that excessive inequality can have negative macrolevel impacts. At the same time he warns us that such a hypothesis cannot be robustly demonstrated without qualifications, and many empirical and theoretical caveats need to be solved by future research.

He makes three contributions. He begins by showing that definitions matter. There are many ways to conceive of inequality, and these differing definitions often lead to divergent conclusions. Level of inequality or changes? Personal income or wealth? Factor incomes? Inequality of opportunity? Inequality of other resources? Top or bottom inequality? Middle class? This issue will also likely rise in importance, because researchers now have access to a seemingly ever-expanding set of distributional data. Morelli then examines the theoretical and empirical evidence on whether and how inequality affects macroeconomic outcomes. He concludes by identifying avenues of future research.

The ongoing and future increase in wealth inequality within countries stems from the macroeconomic circumstance where the average return to capital exceeds the rate of growth of the broader economy. This is, at the most general level, one of the main arguments of Thomas Piketty's book *Capital in the Twenty-First Century*.[1]

This chapter looks at things the other way around and analyzes what possible macro consequences may have occurred, or are likely to occur in the future, from changing levels of inequality. In particular, this chapter focuses on the role inequality plays in generating economic instability, providing an important instrumental reason to focus on the concentration of economic resources that goes beyond classic concerns about distributional equity and fairness.[2]

After some time in which inequality was largely overlooked within macroeconomics, a new hypothesis has emerged (or perhaps reemerged) in the wake of the 2008 financial crisis that excessive inequality can have negative macrolevel impacts. Quoting Nobel Prize–winner Joseph Stiglitz: "For years, the dominant paradigm in macroeconomics . . . ignored inequality—both its role in causing crises and the effect of fluctuations in general, and crises in particular, on inequality. But the most recent financial crisis has shown the errors in this thinking, and these views are finally beginning to be questioned."[3]

If it is true that inequality has negative effects on the economy, that would clearly add force to the case for coordinated intervention to reduce it, a case that of course is often made on moral grounds alone. In connection with making such efforts, Piketty's book discusses the importance of "regaining control of the dynamics of accumulation" and of "regulating the globalized patrimonial capitalism of the twenty-first century."[4] In order to keep inegalitarian pressure in check, Piketty proposes a progressive global tax on wealth, arguing that the social state and the progressive income tax "must continue to play a central role in the future."[5]

My purpose in this chapter is to present and critically survey the existing body of evidence and hypotheses on the link between inequality and macroeconomic instability in order to ascertain what guidance, if any, the literature can offer us in this area. Along the way, I hope to make three contributions to this end. First, I seek to assess what grounds—theoretical and empirical—exist to support the claim that inequality has negative macroeconomic consequences. Second, by highlighting gaps in our understanding of these issues and the associated empirical evidence, I attempt to identify potential avenues of future research. Third, I aim to clarify the concept of inequality and to point out the diversity of concepts that have been used by researchers, given that inconsistency can lead to conflicting conclusions in relation to the questions above. Empirical works can now rely on an ever-expanding set of distributional data in order to shed further light on these controversies and to identify the relevant mechanisms at work in shaping the distribution of economic resources. Piketty's book analyzes how national income is distributed to factors of production (functional income distribution). The relationship between functional income distribution and personal income distribution, as well as the distribution of wealth among individuals and households, also have a prominent role within the book.

Although the concept of human well-being is clearly multidimensional in nature, this chapter also focuses mostly on its economic and monetary dimensions. Among the nonmonetary dimensions (health, education, nutrition, and so on), political power and influence may clearly play an important role and should not be neglected. Finally, people may worry about the persistent differences that exist within a society among specific groups, whether these groupings are based on race, ethnicity, gender, religion, or location. Such horizontal inequality can be the result of systematic discrimination and exclusion and is commonly analyzed in relation to concerns about political stability and the fragmentation of society. This naturally leads us to the problem of creating a "level playing field" and to highlighting the role of inequality of ex-ante opportunities. Generally speaking, however, inequality of outcomes and inequality of opportunities are not two distinct phenomena. Anthony Atkinson, a leading scholar in the field, puts this clearly: "Today's ex-post outcomes shape tomorrow's ex ante playing field: the beneficiaries of inequality of outcome today can transmit an unfair advantage to their children of tomorrow."[6]

The assertion that, generally speaking, economic inequality can "destabilize" our economies has typically fallen into two separable, though linked, sub-assertions and lines of enquiry. First, inequality can, through a variety of channels—consumption, investment, or rent-seeking behavior—affect various aspects of economic performance and growth. Indeed, a large part of what we mean by economic instability relates in some way to economic performance. Indeed, the investigation of the inequality and growth nexus has a very long tradition in economics and it is now again under active scrutiny. Although sluggish growth is not typically associated with what we would call "instability," it does play an important role in, for instance, weakening macroeconomic fundamentals, and therefore it acts as a root cause of financial turmoil.[7]

In this way it can present a destabilizing factor. Other aspects of economic performance constitute in and of themselves more direct manifestations of macroeconomic instability broadly defined: volatile growth, growth persistence and sustainability, the occurrence of recessions as well as their magnitude and duration, and the ability of an economy to get back to growth after a crash. All these aspects have rarely been systematically investigated and discussed in relation to excessive economic inequality.

The second line of investigation pertains to the link between inequality and financial instability. In particular, excessive inequality may also contribute to the creation of macroeconomic imbalances, rendering our financial system fragile to the point that any small perturbation may result in its collapse. For instance, recent contributions in the literature discuss the hypothesis that inequality might be a driving factor behind the overaccumulation of household indebtedness, leaving great segments of families in a precarious (and therefore unstable) situation. In fact, even small changes in their personal economic circumstances, or in broader economic conditions, such as interest rates or house prices, can trigger insolvencies and financial losses to banks' assets. An over-leveraged economy can also hasten or deepen a crisis triggered by some other cause or external shock, or perhaps hinder any subsequent recovery.

Inequality and Economic Performance

As noted above, economists have typically focused on the channels by which economic inequality can affect the level or growth of economic activity (as measured by gross domestic product). These aspects are extensively analyzed below, but there are also other dimensions of economic performance and growth that have not been given enough attention in the literature: the volatility of growth itself; its persistence and sustainability; and the duration and the magnitude of recessions. This section begins by investigating these aspects, given their relative neglect within the literature as well as their more direct relevance to macroeconomic instability. I will then move to survey the proposed standard mechanisms by which inequality is argued to negatively affect economic activity and growth.

Inequality and Unstable Performance

In this section I investigate three questions: Is inequality leading to volatile aggregate performance? Are recessions in more unequal countries deeper and do they last longer? Does inequality lead to unsustained and short-lived growth?

Inequality, Cycles, and Volatility

Economic inequality can be relevant for growth cycles, as theorized within the dynamic representation of the economy by Aghion et al.,[8] which, in particular, brings inequality of investment opportunities, wealth inequality, and credit market imperfections to the center of the creation of endogenous business cycle fluctuations and short-run macroeconomic volatility.[9] In this model, instability in the economy ultimately is promoted by a dualism between investors and non-investors, not by the classic inequality between rich and poor.

This distinction is more pertinent to an explanation, in terms of income inequality, of volatility and cycles in aggregate demand, rather than of economic growth. This idea was present in Galbraith's account of the 1929 Great Crash in which he argued that a highly unequal distribution of personal income and wealth renders the aggregate demand more fragile and volatile, as it has to rely strongly on high levels of either investments or spending on luxury goods, or both.[10] The argument would easily carry through in the context of our modern economies, where the share of total economic resources in the hands of the richest individuals is growing within most of the countries and is becoming more volatile and responsive to business cycles.[11] Robert Frank summarized this well for the case of the United States when he observed that "America's dependence on the rich plus great volatility among the rich equals a more volatile America."[12] A recent IMF discussion paper supports this hypothesis, estimating that 70 percent of changes in U.S. consumption during the decade 2003–2013 came from the action of the top 10 percent richest individuals.[13]

In other words, the rich are driving the aggregate dynamics of consumption and savings, countering the standard narrative that associates the post-2008 drop in U.S. aggregate demand to lower-middle-class losses in housing wealth. Indeed, the important work by Mian and Sufi argues that poorer U.S. households were highly leveraged before 2007 and therefore took the largest hit from the drop in house prices.[14] This was, in turn, responsible for the large drop in aggregate consumption and subsequent employment losses, as poorer households tend to have a relatively higher marginal propensity to consume (MPC).[15]

Inequality, Sustained Growth, Depth, and Length of Recessions

Are recessions in more unequal countries deeper and do they last longer? Does inequality lead to unsustained and short-lived growth? Recent empirical research seems to answer these in the affirmative. For instance, on the one hand, recent IMF empirical work finds that countries with higher income inequality (using the Gini coefficient) would not be able to sustain GDP growth for long, once it started, as it would soon be undermined by the instability forces unleashed by the unequal distribution of resources.[16] On the other hand, support for the idea that income inequality can retard full economic recovery following recessions, is found in studies for the case of the United States.[17]

In order to understand why inequality affects the duration and depth of a recession, economist Dani Rodrik suggested focusing on the interaction between the domestic social conflicts generated by inequality and poor institutions.[18] Most importantly, Rodrik argues that in the presence of high social division ("along the lines of wealth, ethnic identity, geographical region or other divisions") and weak institutions of conflict management, the magnitude of the collapse of growth due to external shocks can be higher and the resilience of the economy to external shocks can be damaged. In particular, Rodrik finds that countries with greater social cleavages and weaker institutions of conflict management experienced the sharpest drops in GDP growth after 1975 (a highly turbulent period from the macroeconomic point of view).

Moreover, latent social conflict (proxied by income inequality) and "bad institutions" (proxied by public spending on social insurance, measures of civil liberties and political rights, the quality of governmental institutions, the rule of law, and the competitiveness of political participation) explained most of the cross-country differences in growth performances between 1960–1975 and 1975–1989—even controlling for government policies at the outset of the crisis. Indeed, policies that have to be put in place to face the external shock usually carry substantial distributional implications, while the latent social conflict that permeates the economy may delay their implementation and lead to "macroeconomic mismanagement," with each independent group seeking to bargain a lower burden of a negative shock and the share of resources devoted to counterproductive rent-seeking activities increases.[19]

Furthermore, as argued by Stiglitz, inequality can preempt the use of standard tools of countercyclical fiscal policy. Indeed, greater inequality also leads to the growing political influence of the elites, which in turn tends to counter the expansion of government expenditures, such as investments in education and public infrastructure.[20] As a consequence, economic recovery that follows the occurrence of a large downturn can be delayed.

Inequality, Economic Activity, and Growth

Piketty's book clearly underlines that the social burden of inequality, and in particular the importance of inheritance within the economy, may be exacerbated in the context of low growth.[21] The book, however, does not dwell on the endogenous response of economic growth to increasing levels of wealth and income inequality. In fact, investigation of the relationship between inequality and economic growth has a long tradition in economics, notwithstanding the relative indifference of the neoclassical economists.[22] Over time, a wide variety of theoretical positions have been taken within the literature.[23]

Modern theories typically share the idea that the relationship between inequality and growth is complex in nature and that different forms of inequality can have different impacts on economic growth. On the one hand, income and wealth dispersion stemming from differences in effort, productivity, and risk attitude are clearly seen as a prerequisite for investment and innovation incentives. On the other hand, high levels of inequality may hinder growth by promoting rent-seeking behaviors.[24]

Similarly, the extent to which the economic outcomes of individuals depend on circumstances outside their own control, such as family background, race, and gender, is thought to be particularly detrimental to growth and incentives.[25] According to Galor and Moav, the effect of income inequality on growth varies over the course of development as an economy endogenously moves from a model of physical capital accumulation to that of human capital accumulation.[26] At the early stage of development, unequal income distribution—with the resulting higher aggregate propensity to save—fuels the accumulation of capital and economic growth (this idea dates back to Kaldor and Pasinetti).[27] But as the economy grows richer, capital / skill complementarities stimulate the accumulation of human capital, which now becomes the main determinant of growth. The latter can be then hindered by the presence of credit constraints, so that policies of income redistribution can become efficiency- as well as equity-enhancing.

The empirical investigation of whether economic inequality affects economic growth has been at the center of the inequality literature and, as recalled in recent work by the World Bank, has followed three main waves since the beginning of 1990s, with disparate findings pointing in different directions.[28] In the first wave, inequality measures were proved to be negatively associated with growth, whereas the second wave pointed toward a positive relationship. Such heterogeneity of findings partly reflected the evolution of the available data sets as well as the empirical methods of investigations.[29] Unsurprisingly, the subject has fallen again under active scrutiny (and likely will in the future) as more and more consistent data become available to researchers (see also Chapter 13 of this volume, where Saez refers to the project of distributional national accounts). Importantly, it is worth noting that the third wave of empirical studies gives particular credit to the complex nature of the relationship between inequality and growth. Indeed, such a relationship can be changing over time and be non-linear in nature. Moreover, conflating all aspects of growth and inequality in an individual index can mask the true relationship between these two variables.

First of all, and moving beyond the concerns for the nonlinear relationship between inequality and growth, one can explore different dimensions of the growth process.[30] For instance, as noted in the previous section, recent works have found that countries with higher income inequality have relatively more unstable GDP growth and tend to experience more prolonged recessions.

Secondly, one can add a further element of complexity by exploring different dimensions of inequality. The shape of the income distribution, for instance, matters in the work by Voitchovsky, who found that only inequality at the top end is positively associated with economic growth whereas inequality at the bottom impairs growth.[31] These findings are also in line with recent OECD work by Cingano, who claims that what matters most for the estimated negative relation between inequality and subsequent growth "is the gap between low-income households and the rest of the population. In contrast, no evidence is found that those with high incomes pulling away from the rest of the population harms growth."[32]

Along similar lines, Martin Ravallion, the former director of the research department at the World Bank, the poverty rate is a useful predictor of negative future growth.[33] Yet another approach was taken by Marrero and Rodríguez, who used micro income for the United States in order to attribute a portion of inequality to opportunities and a portion to "effort." The findings they report are in line with the above-stated intuition that inequality of opportunity harms growth whereas unequal reward of different effort and merit tends to favor the growth process.[34]

Although these results appear not to be entirely robust if one applies this framework to a broader set of countries, it is fair to say that the empirical findings of this "third" phase (in which I also include the work by Ferreira et al., who coined the terminology)[35] show that specific dimensions of inequality can be detrimental for economic growth and that, more precisely, a less unequal society is not bad for growth.

Given that this issue is likely to attract much attention in the future, I turn now to explore in more depth the most important mechanisms justifying the view that inequality plays a detrimental role with respect to economic activity and economic growth.

Inequality, Economic Activity, and Growth: The Political Economy Channel

Income and wealth distribution are key variables to link economics to politics, as witnessed by the literature of political economy. It is generally argued that excessive inequality in income and wealth can create political and social instability, lowering in turn the growth prospects of an economy. Piketty himself put this fundamental issue at the start of his first chapter of *Capital*. He writes, "The question of what share of output should go to wages and what shares to profits has always been at the heart of distributional conflict." In particular, it is the "extreme concentration of the ownership of capital" that fosters distributional conflict in the presence of unequal factor income distribution.[36]

According to various models in political economy, inequality can harm growth because it can discourage investments in productive capital and risky activities via expropriation and confiscatory policies. Interestingly, such expropriation actions can be undertaken by government or relatively poor or rich people alike, depending on the specific model we have in mind. The works conducted in the 1990s by Persson and Tabellini, and Alesina and Rodrik, for instance, posited that excessive inequality produces a bias of government policies toward redistribution and confiscatory fiscal policies.[37] The latter disincentivizes richer individuals to invest in physical capital and in riskier and more rewarding activities.[38] This result follows from the tension between unequal distribution of income and equal distribution of de jure voting rights. Moreover, the fact that preference for redistribution increases as we move down in the income scale—assuming that the higher the income, the higher the net contribution to the government—implies that the result of a democratic vote will reflect the preference of the median voter. As inequality of income increases for any level of mean income, the median income falls, so that the resulting socially desirable tax rate is higher. This latter prediction, however, does not have strong empirical support, as top income shares and top marginal tax rates are actually strongly negatively correlated, as shown in Piketty's book.[39] This calls for alternative explanations.

The growing level of inequality, for instance, implies that increasingly more people remain locked in poverty and excluded from better future economic prospects, which increases resentment toward the rich and creates incentives to expropriate their wealth through either revolutions or theft.[40] As in the case of confiscatory fiscal policy, the risk of expropriation impairs growth-enhancing investments by richer individuals and distorts the allocation of resources toward the protection of property rights.[41]

Most importantly, it is increasingly acknowledged that inequality of wealth begets unequal de facto political power and that this can promote rent-seeking behavior, so that expropriation can also be perpetrated by wealthy individuals by "subverting legal, political and regulatory institutions to work in their favor."[42] This may create inefficient allocation of resources and may harm the security of property rights of small entrepreneurs, reducing their incentives to invest and hence holding back economic growth.[43]

These considerations lead to important questions that are the central focus of current research and hopefully will be subject to further scrutiny. Can wealth inequality promote rent-seeking behavior (lobbying activity)? Is economic rent, the excessive return to factors of production compared to that of a purely competitive market, the main source of wealth inequality?

The answer to the first question may seem obvious, but it is nonetheless important to quantify it empirically. A recent work by Bonica and Rosenthal found that the wealth elasticity of U.S. campaign contributions is around 0.6–1 for the Forbes 400 listed individuals between 1982 and 2012.[44] This is equivalent to saying that U.S. wealthy individuals donate, on average, $10,000 to political campaigns for each $1 million increase in their wealth. Such a high propensity to political activism of wealthy Americans was also documented in an interesting work by Page, Bartels, and Seawright.[45] Despite strong limitations in empirical work that attempts to survey super-wealthy individuals, using a representative sample of wealthy households from communities in the Chicago metropolitan area (mostly zeroing in on the top 1 percent of U.S. wealth holders), the three authors reported that almost half of wealthy respondents made at least one contact with a congressional office within the previous six months of the interview. Most surprisingly, their research found that about half of the contacts that could be coded "acknowledged a focus on fairly narrow economic self interest." It is therefore not surprising that a work by Bagchi and Svejnar finds that the main driver of the negative relationship between wealth inequality and economic growth is the fraction of wealth inequality ascribed to political connections.[46]

Recent work by Stiglitz also goes as far as suggesting that economic rent has also been one of the main drivers of wealth inequality dynamics in recent decades.[47] In particular, Stiglitz argues that economic rents have been increasing in the United States over the past decades. Moreover, economic rents shifted away from labor and toward capital (rents are also increasing due to the increase in land rents, intellectual property rents, and monopoly power), which partly explains the contemporaneous rise in income and wealth inequality and productivity stagnation. "As a result," says Stiglitz, "the value of those assets that are able to provide rents to their owners like land, houses and some financial claims is rising proportionately. So overall wealth increases, but this does not lead to an increase in the productive capacity of the economy."[48]

Inequality, Economic Activity, and Growth: The Imperfect Credit Market Channel

The size distribution of initial wealth endowments can also generate short-run and long-run suboptimal economic performance if coupled with imperfections in the credit markets (not everyone can borrow). In the well-known work by Galor and Zeira, for instance, this happens because only those who inherit sufficiently high wealth are able to pay the fixed cost of education, becoming more productive and better-paid skilled workers.[49] In particular, in this "overlapping generation" model, the distribution of wealth coincides with the distribution of inheritances and essentially represents the inequality of education opportunity faced by individuals who otherwise have similar talent and characteristics. In addition, the initial level of wealth inequality influences income inequality (through wages resulting from differential investment in human capital), which in turn affects inheritance and therefore future wealth distribution. As less wealthy individuals are cut off from highly productive investments in education, their economic and social mobility is permanently harmed, paving the way to a poorer society in which inherited fortunes and advantages dominate. Economic growth can also be harmed permanently if a reduction in the amount of skilled labor also leads to a lower technological innovation rate. Generally speaking, a bigger middle class can guarantee higher economic output and better economic performance.

Moreover, the assumptions of imperfect credit markets and fixed costs of investments can also apply to investment technologies other than education and human capital. For instance, Banerjee and Newman have shown that unequal wealth distribution has similar negative effects on economic activity when one assumes that less-wealthy individuals are systematically rationed out of investments in entrepreneurial activity.[50]

In light of the increasing importance of inheritance in modern society, as documented by Piketty's book, these are mechanisms of renewed importance through which inequality may affect economic development. Such problems become even clearer to the extent that human capital is accounted as an integral component of the intergenerational transfer of economic advantages, as discussed elsewhere in this volume. Moreover, as discussed by Jason Furman and Joseph Stiglitz, it is important to stress that the lack of specific insurance markets can amplify the problems induced by credit constraints.[51] In fact, poorer individuals may still underinvest in education and entrepreneurial activity as a reflection of the riskiness of future investment returns—even if they are able to borrow the necessary funds. As a consequence, efficiency and potential for growth are undermined as inequality increases.

Inequality, Economic Activity, and Growth: Under-Consumption?

Over time, perhaps the most commonly suggested mechanism by which inequality is proposed to have a negative impact on economic performance is by its effect on aggregate consumption (the "under-consumption" hypothesis). The idea that an increase in income inequality (represented as a "mean-preserving spread") can bring about a reduction in aggregate consumption was formalized by Blinder under the condition that the consumption function is concave with respect to income (the marginal propensity to consume decreases with income).[52] Given its prominence in the literature, and the renewed significance of aggregate demand and fiscal policy for economic stabilization, I now discuss the argument at some length.[53]

The concavity of the consumption function is very well supported by theoretical models of consumption decisions, at least once the appropriate version of each model is considered.[54] Similarly, the assumption enjoys strong empirical support. For instance, Figure 17-1 shows the median saving rates of U.K. households ranked by income decile (defined over household equivalized disposable income) and clearly highlights that the saving rate increases as we move up the income ladder.[55] Other works provided similar estimations for the U.S. and Italian cases.[56]

Therefore, there does indeed seem to be a prima facie reason to expect decreasing aggregate consumption with rising inequality. Joseph Stiglitz argues along these lines about the United States in his book *The Price of Inequality:* "Moving money from the bottom to the top lowers consumption because higher-income individuals consume a smaller proportion of their income than do lower-income individuals (those at the top save 15 to 25 percent of their income, those at the bottom spend all their income)."[57]

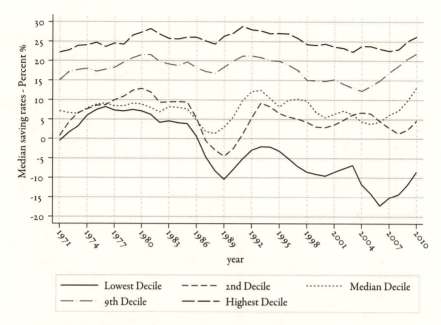

FIGURE 17-1: Median savings rates of U.K. households, ranked by income decile.

Note: Savings rates clearly increase with income levels. Data source: Family Expenditure Survey for years 1984 to 2000–2001; Expenditure and Food Survey for years 2000–2001 to 2007; Living Costs and Food Survey for years after 2007.

It must be noted, however, that it is not easy to reconcile this general hypothesis—that increased inequality lowers consumption—with the available empirical evidence. For instance, taking the case of the United Kingdom, Figure 17-2 makes use of national accounts data to show the trend, from 1963 to 2010, in the aggregate proportion of total U.K. household disposable income that is consumed. The figure shows that over the past decades, and net of short-term fluctuations linked to economic cycles, the U.K. aggregate household consumption rate appears *positively* correlated with the share of total gross income held by the richest 1 percent of the population (a measure of income inequality). This appears evident also across the income distribution shown in Figure 17-1, as the average saving rate of every income decile declined during the 1980s and from the early 1990s to the eve of the crisis (periods of strong increase in or very high levels of income inequality).[58] In addition, it is worth noting that no significant association between income inequality (as measured by the Gini coefficient) and average

425

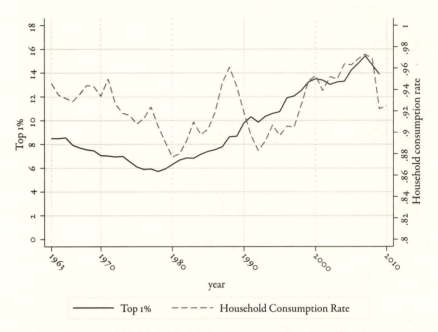

FIGURE 17-2: Household consumption rates correlate with inequality.

Note: Using U.K. data, shifting shares of total gross income held by the richest 1 percent of the population correlate with changes in the country's aggregate household consumption rate. Data source: National Account data.

saving rates or average propensity to consume is found using a wider set of countries.[59]

What, then, can we conclude from such empirical evidence in relation to the under-consumption hypothesis? There are a number of possibilities. First, it might be that the hypothesis is just straightforwardly wrong—that, in fact, there is no tendency for increasing levels of inequality to reduce consumption. Yet given the robustness of the evidence supporting the assumption that the consumption function is concave, it seems reasonable to reject this possibility and conclude that while this tendency is generally present, there must be additional factors present, capable of working in the opposite direction at the same time.

Indeed, continuing the above quotation from Stiglitz, we see that he too is arguing with a ceteris paribus clause firmly in mind: As inequality increases, "total demand in the economy will be less than what the economy is capable of supplying . . . until and unless something else happens, such as an increase in investment or exports." From the concavity of the consumption function, we can expect a negative effect on consumption from increased inequality, all other things being equal. But clearly, in general, other things are not equal. For instance, in order to compensate for the reduced pressure on aggregate demand, a central bank might decrease interest rates and government might promote deregulation of the financial sector to prop up the availability of credit to households and support consumption.[60]

Putting debt aside (it will be discussed in detail in the next section), the rise in inequality may occur contemporaneously with a variety of other factors, affecting in turn the optimal consumption decision. In particular, the more conventional explanation derived from life-cycle and permanent-income models of consumption choices can also replicate the empirical evidence detailed above. For instance, in theory, periods of increasing inequality can coincide with periods in which income growth trickles down to lower-income households or simply periods in which individuals are optimistic about their future income prospects, leading to lower savings.[61] Similarly, a decline in the willingness to bequeath fortune or an increase in the discount rate (an increase in the impatience and "short-sightedness" features of consumers) would reduce the incentive for households to save. The same may happen if wealth assets increase in value or if credit conditions improve (financial integration and development may have improved both the price and the quantity of available credit).[62]

Disentangling the direct impact of inequality on consumption from coincidental confounding factors as described above is a very challenging question for future research. A step toward the solution of this important issue has been undertaken by Bertrand and Morse, who have investigated the reasons the consumption share of the middle class (between the 20th and 80th percentiles) has been positively associated with changes in upper income (a cruder measure of income dispersion) in the United States since the early 1980s.[63] The authors do not find any support for some of the conventional explanations presented above in which inequality is simply coincidentally associated with the increase in consumption. Hence, their findings point to the relevance of direct behavioral responses of consumers to changes in upper income, which are not usually contemplated in conventional consumer theories.[64]

In particular, they find strong evidence for two hypotheses. The first suggests that the growth of income at the top of the income distribution increases the supply of "rich" goods in the economy, which automatically leads to an increase in demand for those goods by poorer individuals. The second hypothesis the two authors support is the "relative income hypothesis," which suggests that greater consumption by relatively richer households sets consumption standards also for the rest of the population, who are then pushed to consume a greater share of their income in order to imitate their wealthier peers and to "keep up with the Joneses." This happens, it is argued, because the consumption of different individuals is interdependent; one's personal well-being reflects not only one's own consumption but also one's consumption relative to a reference group of peers. Therefore, under this assumption, "disequalization can conceivably lead to more rather than less consumption," justifying a positive association between inequality and aggregate consumption.[65]

Most importantly, the two authors say that "this interdependence in consumption can be viewed as an externality, which can compel individuals to work harder and consume more to keep up with neighbors. It is individually rational behavior, but collectively sub-optimal."[66] Furthermore, growth and stability can also be affected and, broadly, there are two main suggestions. On the one hand, as further discussed in the next section, when inequality goes hand in hand with stagnation of income at the bottom, this argument can be then translated into one of overindebtedness, because higher credit is needed to finance the desired additional consumption, thus causing instability in the economy. On the other hand, inequality can lead to an inefficient allocation of resources in the economy, as people direct their spending toward forms of wasteful consumption at the expense of more important investments whose benefits are, however, more intangible, such as education.[67]

Inequality and Financial Instability

Whereas the previous section focused on the linked income or wealth inequality and economic performance and macroeconomic stability, here I discuss in turn its relation to financial stability, broadly defined. The distinction, although not necessarily stark, it is conceptually useful. In particular, I first briefly discuss the suggested association between inequality and banking crises. I then move to the discussion of the inequality-and-indebtedness nexus.

Inequality and Banking Crises

The high level of income inequality (broadly seen as a combination of stagnation of average incomes at the middle and bottom of the distribution and an increase in average incomes at the top) has been singled out as one of the structural causes of the recent crisis, especially in the United States.

A recent body of empirical literature has investigated this conjecture, but found no strong supportive evidence on the inequality-and-crises nexus across a broad range of countries, years, and different inequality measures.[68] More specifically, the analysis carried out in Morelli and Atkinson claims that neither growing levels nor high levels of inequality may be systematically associated with the occurrence of banking crises.[69] Pooling as much data as possible over the period 1900–2012, the analysis was conducted for 26 countries, on five different indicators of economic inequality, ranging from relative poverty measures, to top wealth measures and the Gini coefficient of equivalized disposable household income.[70] Nonetheless, the authors also remark that "the apparent statistical insignificance of the findings does not rule out the economic relevance of the question at hand, given that the hypotheses cannot be rejected for important crises and countries such as the US and the UK."[71] Moreover, excessive inequality may contribute to the creation of macroeconomic imbalances without necessarily leading to a crisis.

Before the recent financial meltdown, the concept of macroeconomic stability was normally associated with price stability and output-gap stability. The postcrisis awakening, however, revealed that the apparent pre-crash macroeconomic stability was hiding the accumulation of economic imbalances, such as the remarkable rise in household indebtedness and the occurrence of bubbles in the financial and real estate markets.[72] Interestingly, as argued in the recent literature, a highly unequal distribution of income and wealth can be one of the structural determinants for the buildup of the above-mentioned imbalances, which may render the economy more unstable and inherently fragile.[73]

Inequality and Indebtedness

Arguments have also been put forward invoking an explicit link to the increasing levels of economic inequality witnessed in the run-up to the crisis, especially in the United States. Inequality, it is argued, created both an additional demand for and a supply of credit that led to an unstable level of debt.

Reduced pressure on aggregate demand or lower aggregate economic performance resulting from increasing economic inequality may have stimulated the government to deregulate financial markets and the central bank to decrease interest rates. These actions served in principle to prop up the *supply* of credit to households in order to compensate for poor economic performance. Further pressure to deregulate the financial markets may in turn have come directly from wealthy individuals who captured and lobbied the regulators to further accumulate financial benefits. Similarly, the increasing share of richer individuals, with high saving rates and in search of new financial investments, may have increased the supply of funds available in the economy, providing credit to the rest of the population as well as fueling asset bubbles.[74]

Increasing income inequality also may have directly generated higher *demand* for credit as well as the supply of credit. Indeed, as discussed in the previous section in relation to the relative income hypothesis, individuals left behind may have taken on more debt in order to keep up with the rising standards of living and satisfy their increased consumption desires. Higher demand for credit may have also been driven by concerns to smooth out consumption in the face of increasing income volatility, driving the upward trends in income inequality.

Whatever is the main driver of household debt accumulation (and our knowledge is still very limited on this front), unequal over-leveraging may leave great segments of the population in a precarious situation so that small changes in their personal economic circumstances—or in broader economic conditions, such as interest rates or housing prices—could now trigger insolvencies and financial losses to banks' assets.[75]

Models like the one proposed by Aghion et al., discussed within the previous section, can replicate an endogenous cycle of income distribution, debt, and growth and are particularly relevant to the discussion of the role of inequality in both macroeconomic and financial instability.[76] Yet no role for consumption-led borrowing—an important feature of the recent crisis—is contemplated in such a model. Instead, works by Iacoviello, Khumof, Rancière, and Winant are among the few studies available in the literature that link the distribution of income or earnings to the increase in either supply or demand of household indebtedness.[77]

Iacoviello constructs a simulated model where agents are infinitively lived and optimally choose their level of consumption and debt, following the classic Permanent Income Hypothesis framework. Within such a framework, individuals respond to increased inequality, measured as earnings patterns that become more erratic over time, by resorting to the credit market in order to smooth consumption, thereby increasing their stock of debt. The ultimate practical relevance of this model, then, rests on the empirical evidence about the incidence of transitory shocks compared to the permanent difference in earnings across different agents. In fact, recent empirical evidence suggests that increases in earnings inequality were largely driven by increases in the dispersion of permanent incomes across households. For instance, Kopczuk and Saez, for the case of the United States, wrote that "virtually all of the increase in the variance in annual (log) earnings since 1970 is due to increase in the variance of permanent earnings (as opposed to transitory earnings)."[78] Similar results are found for the United Kingdom.[79]

Differently from Iacoviello, the key heterogeneity in Kumhof, Rancière, and Winant's model is between two groups in the economy—workers and investors—and workers' loss of bargaining power (because of increases in inequality) compensated for by an increase in investors' borrowing in order to sustain consumption levels. Moreover, it is the distribution of income between two different groups that matters in their model and not just the volatility of earnings over time.

But do data support the hypothesis that inequality and household indebtedness rise in tandem? Figure 17-3 summarizes the aggregate evidence for the U.K. household debt-to-income ratio since the early 1960s. The two U.K. debt-cycle episodes occurred from 1980 until the economic recession of 1990–1992 and from the end of the 1990s until the onset of the recent financial crisis in 2007. Interestingly, periods of debt accumulation also tended to occur during periods of increasing inequality (measured by both the Gini coefficient of household equivalized disposable income and the top share of the richest 1 percent of U.K. individuals) or high levels of income inequality.[80] These findings were corroborated in a recent investigation by Perugini, Hölscher, and Collie using a panel of top income shares for 18 countries for between 1970 and 2007.[81] In a similar work, Scognamillo et al. claim that higher income inequality, measured by the Gini coefficient

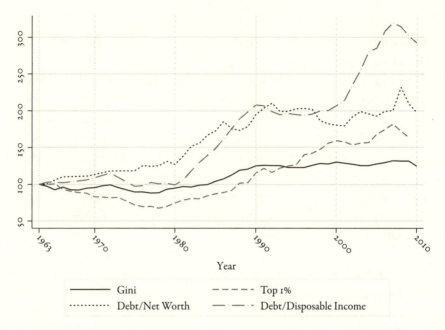

FIGURE 17-3: Debt accumulation correlates with inequality.

Note: Periods of debt accumulation in the U.K. (from 1980 until the economic recession of 1990-1992, and from the late 1990s till the 2007 financial crisis) coincided with periods of increasing inequality, as measured by both Gini coefficient of household equivalized disposable income and the top share of the richest 1 percent of individuals. The correlations between debt and inequality measures are substantially above .8 and are significant at the 1 percent significance level.

Data source: Debt series assembled by T. Atkinson and S. Morelli from a variety of historical sources.

of disposable household income, is systematically associated with higher household indebtedness at the aggregate level.[82]

Nonetheless, there are several reasons to believe that the evidence is not as clear-cut as it might at first appear. First of all, the overindebtedness trend during the past several decades is less clear if one uses a debt-to-net-worth measure of leverage. The use of wealth as a scaling factor of total household liabilities is seldom analyzed and highlights the substantial role of household assets, especially housing. It can be argued, in fact, that such a measure can carry more useful information about the overall sustainability of debt, because it can represent the extent to which debt can be covered by asset liquidation (to the extent that assets are marketable).

Second, the use of micro data does not unequivocally suggest the existence of a positive correlation between inequality and indebtedness, let alone a causal association. For instance, Coibion et al. show that, during the period from 2001 to 2012, low-income households in high-inequality regions accumulated less (not more) debt relative to income than their counterparts in lower-inequality regions (zip codes and states).[83] On the other hand, Carr and Jayadev instead use PSID data to show that lower-income and lower-relative-income households, within similar education and race classes, tend to leverage more.[84] This divergence of findings highlights the importance of a proper identification of the relevant peer group of reference, to the extent that the relevant mechanism supporting the positive correlation between inequality and indebtedness is a concern with relative standing in social circles. For instance, Georgarakos, Haliassos, and Pasini exploit an important feature of the DNB Household Survey, representative of the Dutch population, that elicits the "perceptions of respondents regarding the average income of their social circle and ability of their peers to spend."[85] This avoids arbitrary assumptions about the nature of the social circle of reference and allowed them to estimate that individuals tend to borrow more, the higher the perceived income of their peer group. Most importantly, the effect is stronger for those respondents who perceive themselves as poorer than the average individual within their social circle.

Conclusions

This chapter has aimed at assessing the theoretical and empirical grounds that exist to support the claim that inequality has negative macroeconomic consequences. These issues are not explicitly explored in Piketty's *Capital*, and this chapter attempted to complement his analysis of the concentration dynamics as intrinsically resulting from the so-called fundamental laws of capitalism.

There is growing evidence that different dimensions of economic inequality may negatively affect various aspects of economic performance and growth. Inequality can be responsible for the lack of resilience of the economy as well as of the prolonged duration of economic recessions once the economy is hit by external shocks. Similarly, recent works found that countries with higher income inequality have relatively more unstable GDP growth.

But it is important to stress that, until recently, very little attention was devoted to these important issues and more empirical research is warranted to corroborate these important findings also outside of the U.S. context. Inequality, it has been argued, also can negatively affect growth and economic activity per se via the political economy, imperfect credit market, or consumption channels. More effort, however, should be devoted to disentangle the real determinants of economic inequality. Negative association between inequality and growth can be more likely to occur if a greater component of wealth inequality is due to an increase in inherited advantage of heirs or to rent seeking and regulatory capture activities by wealthy elites.

Similarly, this may happen if the income inequality we observe is mostly due to the inequality of opportunity among individuals, which constrains their potential and aspirations and distorts the efficient allocation of resources within the economy. The ongoing effort by independent researchers and by institutions to produce better and more comprehensive data on the evolution of income and wealth inequality will clearly shed more light on these important issues.

Secondly, and contrary to standard textbook assumptions in economics, recent research has emphasized how relative income and spending comparisons may have important influences on what people spend their money on, how much they save, and even how much debt they accumulate. These considerations suggest that the degree of inequality should have a direct effect on aggregate savings, debt accumulation, and thus on economic activity. The investigation of the alleged relationship between inequality and private debt becomes particularly relevant in light of the fact that the latest crisis was largely the result of the burst of a debt-financed housing and consumption bubble that involved the private sector of the economy. Findings, mostly based on aggregate data and cross-country analysis, emphasize positive correlations between inequality, household over-consumption, and indebtedness. But the evidence based on micro data is less consistent, and additional empirical investigation is required to establish the validity of this hypothesis.

Moreover, it is important to stress that the hypothesis that individuals' relative income comparisons affect their economic behavior is subject to a series of theoretical and empirical caveats that need to be addressed in future research. For instance, a precise identification of the social circle of influence to which relative comparisons are made is of crucial importance. The best way to identify the individual's peer group of reference is to ask the individual directly. But it is very rare for household surveys to have information on their networks of influence.[86] Administrative micro data allows for an alternative, refined, and precise definition of the peer group identified as co-workers and / or neighbors.[87] In addition, the available theories based on the relative income hypothesis do not always formally link a measure of dispersion of incomes per se to optimal consumption and indebtedness decisions. Rather, it is common to assume that, for instance, individual utility and welfare are affected by per capita consumption or by the relative distance of personal consumption from the average consumption of peers in the reference group.

Finally, some models have already attempted to tackle this issue, but the concerns about the social nature of consumption and the interconnectedness of utility functions often fail to proper account for the forward-looking nature of the consumption decision. This is an important component of consumption decisions and needs to be properly accounted for.

The available evidence to date demonstrates that inequality, in a variety of dimensions, can play an important role in generating macroeconomic and financial instability. But no relationships have been robustly demonstrated without qualification. It is also important to stress, as recalled by Dani Rodrik, that "the relationship between equality and economic performance is likely to be contingent rather than fixed, depending on the deeper causes of inequality and many mediating factors." Therefore one has to be very careful not to draw easy conclusions leading to a new "consensus" on the detrimental effects of inequality on economic stability that "is as likely to mislead as the old one was."[88]

Notwithstanding this important caveat, recent research has made important initial steps in linking inequality to economic underperformance and instability. To the extent that it succeeds in doing so, it presents an instrumental justification—alongside other, more direct justifications in terms of fairness or social inclusion—for effective coordinated actions by governments to reduce income and wealth inequality. As such, further research to generalize existing results and resolve remaining inconsistencies is of the utmost significance.

[IV]

THE POLITICAL ECONOMY OF CAPITAL AND CAPITALISM

EIGHTEEN

Inequality and the Rise of Social Democracy: An Ideological History

MARSHALL I. STEINBAUM

A central element of Piketty's historical argument is that mass enfranchisement was insufficient to alter the social and economic hierarchy when inequality reached its height in the major economies of Western Europe and the United States in the late nineteenth and early twentieth centuries. Instead, Piketty argues, it took massive capital destruction and war-induced taxation to accomplish that.

In this chapter, economist Marshall Steinbaum complicates the historical picture: The wars (and the Great Depression) were indeed decisive, but because they discredited the ideology of capitalism in a way that mere mass enfranchisement had been unable to do. Instead, a series of political events in major economies eventually empowered left-wing movements, because the wars and the Depression discredited the policies and continuing power of the political establishment—policies it had undertaken precisely to counter rising domestic political threats from the left.

Capital in the Twenty-First Century reads like a history book, and it makes a clear argument about inequality in history. Universal suffrage does not check the tendency to divergence inherent in capitalism.[1] Instead, war, and the taxes needed to pay for it, do.

World War I may have destroyed property, but along with the Great Depression, it also destroyed an ideology: the free market economics that sustained inequality well into the era of mass enfranchisement. That ideology maintains that the free market operates for the best when left to itself, and hence that incumbent wealth and power, originating in the market, ought not to be challenged in the political realm. It was this free market ideology that sustained conservative politics through the nineteenth century, because it facilitated an alliance between the old aristocracy, whose continuing political power it justified, and the propertied class of entrepreneurs and professionals, who saw their wealth as arising out of their mastery of the newly industrialized economy. The World Wars and the Depression resulted from the conscious strategy of the representatives of that class in formal politics, who sought to manipulate both foreign and domestic policy to serve their interests against a rising left-wing threat.

What closed the book on the Gilded Age, therefore, was not the World Wars per se, but rather that the realized disaster of those wars and the Depression finally discredited capitalist ideology and its associated policies and political movement between the advent of universal male suffrage and the Nazi takeover of Europe. Social democracy grew out of mass enfranchisement, but it did not win until capitalist claims about the origin and just distribution of wealth in an industrial economy were finally put to rest thanks to the discredit of the elite.

I argue here that the decline and fall of an ideology is what precipitated the egalitarian era of the mid-twentieth century. This chapter is organized in terms of the countries that were the world's leading economies at that time: the United States, Britain, France, and Germany. Each had its own, sometimes temporally inconsistent, political history, and each of these countries had its own institutional and societal background against which its politics operated. That means that a different set of political events assumes importance in each country's history, given the bad (or good) decisions its incumbent rulers were perceived to have made, and in light of the differing array of external and internal threats recognized by its political parties and alliances. But the themes that unite increasingly egalitarian economic policymaking across Western Europe and the United States during that period shine through:

- Income and wealth taxes became a permanent element of public budgeting and of economic policy, both to finance war and expanding social obligations and explicitly to encourage egalitarian pre- and post-tax income distributions.[2]
- States recognized collective bargaining rights and enacted other measures such as social insurance that interfered in what had previously

been conceptualized as the "freedom of contract" between employers and their employees.[3]

- The public sector made provision for universal health and education, including public infrastructure. Social commitments displaced war-making as the chief obligation of the state.[4]
- The gold standard ceased to be the norm for national monetary policy.[5]

Each of these themes was controversial and threatening to the political and economic status quo when it was first voiced by left-wing political movements. Together they constituted a radical departure, aimed directly at overturning established wealth and power. In the process of enacting them, or not, political systems strained almost to their breaking point—and in Germany, beyond it.

The political phenomena that punctuated the process of ideological discrediting differ across the four countries, but they can be categorized. The first category is mass enfranchisement itself, and the second is the formation of a national political party of the industrial working class, usually in coalition with older political groups, then either displacing former partners or joining and radically altering them.[6] A third category is de facto constitutional reform that removed a nondemocratic instrument of government from power over economic policy. The fourth category is the election of the working-class, left-wing coalition to power on a platform consisting of the four planks named above.

In recounting a narrative history of ideological failure, though, especially one that transpired across countries, it may be tempting to understand the process as inevitable and each step of it as fitting into a larger, predetermined story. That could not be farther from the truth, and luckily (at least for the purpose of proper historical interpretation), from the vantage point of the present, we benefit from the knowledge of what has happened since: near-complete reversal, as *Capital in the Twenty-First Century* lays out in great detail. There was nothing inevitable about the discrediting of free market ideology, as we know because a different set of historical and intellectual circumstances resurrected it. Nor was that discrediting gradual, or, in mathematical terms, monotonic. It was chaotic, with important, notable reversals, which themselves need not have been reversed. In particular, as ostensibly democratic governments and their elite constituencies attempted to face down the rising left-wing political threat during the Depression, and in so doing entered into alliance with the non-democrats of the right, it appeared to many left-wing observers that the great ideological struggle of their lives had been lost and that the future had been won by totalitarians. World War II very well could have been the final catastrophe, rather than the cause of their ultimate triumph.

Capital in the Twenty-First Century argues that the income and wealth distributions in capitalist economies tend to diverge thanks to the structure of the macroeconomy, unless it is knocked off course by violence. Instead, I argue that they tend to diverge because the ideological commitments of capitalism prohibit policies that would check divergence, unless that ideology is knocked off course by political failure and the discredit it brings to the elites, factions, and social groups who espouse that ideology.[7]

United States

I begin with the United States, even though its history in some ways diverges from that of the three Old World countries considered as a group. Its income and wealth distributions never achieved the heights of inequality during the Gilded Age that the others did. It also never achieved universal male suffrage during the period in question, because a substantial share of the unpropertied working class—southern blacks—was effectively excluded from the franchise from 1877 until the 1960s.

Eric Foner, among many others, has argued that this legacy of white supremacy exerted a profound influence on national political history, beyond the subjugation of a racial minority: when the rest of the developed world was implementing egalitarian policies, the analogous policies in the United States were less egalitarian because they were designed to exclude the poorest. Ira Katznelson's book *Fear Itself* highlights this with regard to the New Deal and the labor market regulation of the Roosevelt administration.[8] On the other hand, franchise restrictions on the unpropertied were removed earlier in the United States than elsewhere, and nineteenth-century immigrants received the vote more or less instantaneously upon arrival, which explains the outburst of nativism in the mid-1850s following the Irish potato famine and the influx of European political refugees from the Revolutions of 1848.

Reconstruction and the aftermath of the Civil War is the logical place to begin the account of the rise of social democracy in the United States, even though universal male suffrage was rolled back by the negotiated termination of inter-sectional conflict in 1877. There was nascent labor unrest before the Civil War, but the period from 1873 until 1896—and especially from 1886 to 1896—stands out for the rapid growth of militant trade unionism and the widespread sense that the social order was threatened by mass industrialization. It is also the period during which the intellectual elite rallied to what might be called the ideology of capitalism, which grew out of the Free Labor concept that emerged from the war.

Free Labor as initially conceived referred to the ideal in which a man born as an employee could, through hard work and thrift, rise through the social hierarchy to end up as an employer of others. Before the war, in the eyes of the Union's partisans, the future of a northern Free Labor–based economy was threatened by the westward expansion of slavery, which displaced remunerated labor by white men. Therefore, confining slavery to the South was necessary to secure Free Labor in the future, by making sure it had scope to expand and predominate in the U.S. economy. That was the nature of the inter-sectional conflict that led to war—though the abolitionist movement had certainly attracted public opinion to the cause of humanitarian intervention on behalf of slaves, that was not the reason the North went to war. But as the war was actually fought, especially following emancipation and the enlistment of black soldiers in the Union Army, Free Labor was gradually extended to include the freed slaves themselves.

The aim of Radical Reconstruction between 1866 and 1877 was to secure the economic and political freedom of black people in the South. The major vehicle by which this was to be accomplished was the Fourteenth Amendment, which guaranteed to each person due process and equality before the law and committed the federal government to intervention in the southern economy and political system to secure those ends. The Civil Rights Acts that enforced the amendment bound southern legislatures and local administrations not to impair the right of black people to supply or withhold their labor at will.

Reconstruction and the extension of federal authority into southern localities became more and more controversial in the North and in national politics, especially following the Panic of 1873, when the Free Labor coalition of the Republican Party fractured and elitists dissatisfied with the Grant administration retreated to orthodox economic policies of free trade, the gold standard, small government, and eventually the view that the state had no role in what they called "class legislation"—anything designed to alter the "natural" social hierarchy established by the working of the market. During the recession that followed the financial crisis and lasted through most of the 1870s, the problems of immiserated, industrial wage labor and the subjugation of small farmers at the hands of railroads, banks, and other increasingly powerful "trusts" became more prominent in the national debate, culminating in the 1877 railroad strike that followed collusive wage cuts and shut down most railway lines.

The publication of Henry George's *Progress and Poverty* in 1879 gave voice to the puzzle of rapid economic growth and industrialization coinciding with the immiseration of anyone who worked for a living. And the remedy George proposed—a tax on land values designed to socialize natural resource endowments—gained millions of adherents inside and outside the labor movement, along with the extreme enmity of the cadre of professional economists who felt he had usurped their expertise with simplistic snake-oil medicine.[9]

The 1877 Supreme Court case *Munn v. Illinois* was the first hearing for the idea that the Fourteenth Amendment contained a right to economic due process—that legislation could not "interfere" with the functioning of the free market—in contrast with the original interpretation of the Fourteenth Amendment precisely as protecting freedmen from exploitation in the labor market. In that case the court sided with the state of Illinois, which had legislated to regulate the price of storing and transporting grain in response to the demands of the Grange, an organization of proto-populist farmers. Over the following thirty years, the Court gradually expanded the immunity of corporations and other employers from regulation at the state and federal level, at the same time as it restricted the protection the Fourteenth Amendment offered to blacks in the South, indigenous people of the United States' expanding empire of overseas possessions, and the like. When in 1885 the New York State Court of Appeals struck down a regulation restricting the manufacture of cigars from tenement houses on the grounds that it impaired the freedom of contract, one labor publication blared, "Slavery declared to be liberty!"

The threat of militant unionism reached its peak between 1886, when the Haymarket Square Riot scared public opinion away from immigrant-dominated trade unions, and the Pullman Strike in 1894. In the latter case, President Grover Cleveland ordered federal troops to suppress the sympathy strikes that shut down the national railway network, and in so doing ruined his chance of renomination by his own Democratic Party, which was increasingly sympathetic to the cause of industrial workers after Cleveland's hard-money, business-backed policies (particularly the repeal of the Sherman Silver Purchase Act) exacerbated the Panic of 1893. Both Haymarket and Pullman also represented a great divide in the union movement, because they were opposed by the moderate craft unions of the American Federation of Labor, which favored industrial action only as a last resort in wage negotiations, not as a vehicle for social change. Eugene Debs's American Railway Union, the instigator of the Pullman Strike, was far more radical and ambitious.

During the same period of urban labor strife, the Farmers' Alliance and its successor, the Populist Party, swept rural areas where farmers had been immiserated by overproduction, high transportation costs, and the crop-lien system that left them permanently indebted, with nominal obligations becoming more onerous over time thanks to a strengthening dollar. Starting in the early 1890s they succeeded in challenging the "Redeemer" governments that had dominated southern states since the end of Reconstruction, and eventually they formed an alliance with western Populists who gained many state-level offices in their own right in 1892 and 1894. The Populists' issues were the domination of agriculture by railroads and banks, tight monetary policy, and oppressive tariffs that drove up the cost of inputs.

An 1893 meeting of the American Economic Association featured a telling debate over the issue of Populism, pitting a well-known and controversial left-wing economist, Edward A. Ross, against a prominent conservative, Franklin Giddings. Ross: "A great cause of the farmers' difficulty is that he is selling at competitive prices and buying a great many things, including transportation, at monopoly prices." Giddings replied: "Why, throughout the long years of his affliction, has [the farmer] always come off worse in the contest? There must be something wrong in his own make-up ... he controls more votes than other men control. . . . The failing is in himself. If you want to reach the root of the farmers' difficulties, you will have to begin with the farmers' minds."[10]

Giddings's assertion that if any man or class of people remains impoverished over a long enough time, he or they have only themselves to blame, is a core belief of the free market ideology that enabled Pikettian divergence in the nineteenth century. And similar sentiments have been expressed (with varying degrees of frankness) over the history of economic thought. For instance, Gary Becker's assertion that a meritocracy based on human capital accumulation displaced patrimonial capitalism in the mid-twentieth century is the heir to Giddings's point of view, because it implies that long-standing group inequality persisting across generations, even under supposedly meritocratic conditions, reflects inherent characteristics rather than unjust power structures.[11]

Thanks to the disaster of the Cleveland administration, power in the Democratic Party shifted away from the gold-standard-supporting, business-friendly "Bourbon" faction to John Peter Altgeld, the immigrant governor of Illinois who supported the Pullman strikers (and had pardoned anarchists convicted of the Haymarket bombing). Altgeld engineered the party's split with the Cleveland administration and supported a political marriage of convenience with the Populist Party for the presidential election of 1896. That led the Democrats to nominate the Populist candidate, William Jennings Bryan, but there were two main problems with that jury-rigged alliance. First, Bryan had no interest in altering his strategy or political stances, which were avowedly rural, agricultural, and Protestant, to fit his status as nominee for the Democratic Party, whose northern voters were overwhelmingly urban, industrial, and Catholic. Bryan's famous "Cross of Gold" speech at the 1896 Democratic Convention openly denigrated the morality of the industrial economy, and by extension, the militant workers who labored therein, and Republican operatives had an easy time goading Bryan into xenophobic anti-Catholic bigotry when he campaigned in front of urban audiences. The second problem with the Democratic-Populist alliance was that it made no political sense in the South, where Populists had come to power in the previous two elections as the long-awaited challenge to the Democratic Redeemer one-party governments that had ended Reconstruction and subsequently ruled state governments in the interest of local economic elites. Sympathetic Populist voters were being asked to split their tickets in the name of reform, which turned out not to be a sound basis for constructing a durable political movement.

Bryan's defeat, and with it the defeat of the Democratic-Populist alliance, set back overtly left-wing politics in the United States for decades and left intact the core ideological doctrines of capitalism in both major parties. The radical element within organized labor continued to operate on the margins, eventually forming the Industrial Workers of the World (IWW), as the AFL continued to shun organizing unskilled workers. Debs founded a series of European-style Social Democratic parties in the aftermath of 1896, and he ran for president repeatedly on the Socialist ticket. Most importantly, the high pitch of left-wing politics between 1886 and 1896 subsided into a more moderate progressivism that had an appeal for both major parties and outside the radicalized working class. In the South, the backlash to Populism's brief moment in the sun came when the political heirs to the Redeemers successfully broke the movement by racist appeals to poor whites. In the late 1890s the final vestiges of black voting and political power disappeared in the South, generally due to the use of literacy and property tests, which also served the purpose of restricting the franchise of poor whites. Statutory segregation also dates to this period of retrenchment.

Politics was characterized by moderate Progressivism alongside racial reaction between Theodore Roosevelt's ascension to the presidency in 1901 and the end of Woodrow Wilson's administration in 1920. The federal government was aggressive in the matter of breaking up some of the monopolies whose predations had radicalized politics in the 1890s, but they let others stand. The Panic of 1907 gave impetus to the founding of the Federal Reserve System in 1913, which amounted to the financial establishment partly taking on board the Populists' critique of tight money. Although the new central bank did not depart from the gold standard, its aim was to have a system for resolving credit crunches at the ready, to avoid the series of disastrous panics that made the late nineteenth century so economically turbulent. This was the period in which large-scale investments in public infrastructure started to be made, to the benefit of public sanitation and health among the urban poor and as a means of undermining exploitative monopolies in transportation and housing. Most importantly, the U.S. Constitution was amended to pass a federal income tax in 1913 after the Supreme Court struck down an earlier statutory attempt in the 1890s, on the grounds that income from capital was outside the bounds of congressional power of direct taxation.

The political process that culminated in the federal income tax relied on a coalition between progressives and prohibitionists, since the main impediment to the latter's cause had always been that the federal government's second-largest source of revenue (after tariffs) was excise taxes on liquor. Thus, the advent of the income tax was one of the great examples of coalition-building in the history of a political system that requires compromise. Outside politics, there was recurrent labor unrest coming from the IWW and similarly independent, radical elements of the labor movement, but the AFL supported the Wilson administration and was happy to see the radical wing of the labor movement decimated by the Palmer Raids and deportation of some of its notable leaders in 1919–1920.

This was also the era in which state governments began enacting elements of the progressive platform designed to regulate the labor market and begin the provision of social insurance. During this so-called Lochner era (named for a 1905 case in which the Court blocked a New York maximum hours law for bakers), the Supreme Court became increasingly aggressive at using the Fourteenth Amendment's guarantee of "liberty" to strike down such regulation on the grounds that it interfered with individual freedom of contract. That doctrine was deployed in *Hammer v. Dagenhart* to strike down the Keating-Owen Act of 1916, a federal ban on child labor, and in 1923 in *Adkins v. Children's Hospital,* which struck down a District of Columbia minimum wage law. While some new state regulations were upheld, the Court continued to hold the line on regulating the labor market in favor of workers on the federal level.

American entry into World War I split the Democratic Party and the progressive movement, generally along class lines because it had the flavor of a fanciful, elite foreign adventure that distracted from domestic policy priorities. That was especially true after the Versailles Treaty departed decisively from President Wilson's stated war aims, embodied in his Fourteen Points. That, in combination with the Russian Revolution, created a political backlash that made the 1920s a period of retrenchment, and also of de-unionization as the remnants of unskilled workers' unions faded and the AFL had no interest in making up for them by expanding its reach. Most rural areas were left out of the economic boom of the period, and the doctrine of laissez-faire continued to be deployed against aiding them, most notably in Calvin Coolidge's veto of the McNary-Haugen Farm Relief Bill.

Andrew Mellon spent nearly the entire decade as Treasury secretary, overseeing an orthodox economic policy that ultimately came to grief after the stock market crashed in 1929 and the continuing credit crunch played out through successive bank failures and runs on the gold supply.

The crash, and the Depression that followed, eviscerated Mellonism at the national level. Far from ending the economic turbulence of the nineteenth century through judicious monetary regulation by the Fed and national economic policy in the hands of a seasoned banker, the crisis could only be ended by abandoning the gold standard and inaugurating a new era of economic policy that included Keynesian fiscal expansion and policies to prevent deflation and lift the burden of debt on households, firms, farms, and financial institutions, as well as extremely progressive taxation. Roosevelt's inauguration in 1933 is thus labeled a "regime change" by the economic historians Peter Temin and Barry Wigmore.[12] Although those policies were successful at reversing the contraction, they did not relieve the most acute miseries of unemployment and poverty, so the "second New Deal" of 1935 enacted Social Security and unemployment insurance, and vastly expanded public employment.

The Supreme Court, however, continued to bedevil left-wing economic policies by striking down laws establishing New Deal agencies and regulations. Finally, having won reelection in a landslide in 1936, Roosevelt threatened to act on the so-called court-packing plan, by which he would have appointed sufficient additional justices to approve his priorities. That threat more or less induced the Supreme Court to concede defeat in the case *West Coast Hotel v. Parrish,* which approved a minimum wage law and overturned *Adkins.* That paved the way for the 1938 Fair Labor Standards Act (FLSA), which imposed national labor regulations that had previously been able to survive only at the state level, if at all. The FLSA, however, exempted the agriculture and domestic sector, excluding the vast majority of black workers in the South by design of the still-segregationist New Deal coalition. The closing of racial economic gaps awaited the integration of the military industrial complex and the postwar economic boom.

With its overt departures from laissez-faire orthodoxy, the Roosevelt administration constituted the ideological transformation of the twentieth century in the context of the United States, with the caveat that black people remained excluded from national economic policy and from the body politic because they still lacked the franchise. In the United States, the occasion for ideological discrediting was the Depression rather than the two World Wars. Although American involvement in the World War I was controversial, it was not a regime-shaking disaster brought on by reactionary connivance against domestic left-wing movements, as it was for the European powers. Instead, it appeared as a foreign policy blunder brought on by the bumbling of an overly idealistic center-left administration that was out of its depth in international Old World politics. As for the Second World War, it further cemented the discrediting of the right because Roosevelt's most prominent opponents compounded their political problems with isolationism, convinced throughout that the Soviet Union was the greater threat than fascism. Those business leaders who were flexible enough to take advantage of the wartime economic bonanza made their peace with the quid pro quo that required them to accept the New Deal's political supremacy, at least for a time. The war itself prompted the beginnings of the civil rights revolution in the United States, and the labor shortage convinced the Roosevelt administration of the need for racial integration of the military's supply chain, and under his successor, Harry Truman, the military itself was integrated. Thus, the United States emerged from the war with a chastened conservative politics and an empowered, increasingly ideologically left-wing Democratic Party intent on using federal power to reduce inequality.

Britain

Britain moved toward universal male suffrage with the Reform Acts of 1832, 1867, and 1884, which enfranchised men of the middle class, urban working class, and rural peasantry, respectively.[13] The politics of their adoption were dramatic, but also anticlimactic in their time. Predictions of social cataclysm attending each piece of legislation (and the failed attempts in the interim) turned out to be overblown. Yet they did eventually bring down the party system that had prevailed since the Wars of the French Revolution and replace it with one based on the class system of the Second Industrial Revolution.

On economic policy, the old party system adhered to a liberal consensus: Between the repeal of the Corn Laws in 1846 and the Unionist adoption of protectionism as "imperial preference" in 1903, both parties espoused free trade. The gold standard was never seriously questioned in this period—it was an article of faith that the Treasury should run a surplus each year sufficient to sink the enormous Napoleonic debt at stable nominal values. The Poor Law Amendment Act 1834 required residence in workhouses to obtain aid, which was designed to be penal to deter indolence, in line with Malthusian population theory and David Ricardo's "iron law of wages." Those were the core doctrines underlying classical liberalism and its hostility to political solutions to inequality and destitution.

Radical movements, most famously the Chartists, bubbled up throughout the nineteenth century, but they found no purchase in the established political system. Despite being criminalized, trade unions grew during the second half of the century, and their activities were legalized by the Trade Union Act 1871. Although a few union-aligned members were elected to Parliament and a political affiliation of different unions formed in 1899 as the Labor Representation Committee (LRC), the galvanizing moment that brought labor into the national political system was the 1901 court case known as *Taff Vale,* in which a railway union was found liable for inflicting economic damages following a successful strike.

The judgment in *Taff Vale* threatened to undermine the whole idea of industrial action, so unions, which had generally backed Liberal candidates when they involved themselves in politics at all, embarked on an independent path. The LRC's membership ballooned as unions increasingly affiliated with it, and in 1903 the LRC formed a strategic noncompete pact with the Liberal Party to be allowed thirty seats in the next Parliament in exchange for the LRC's support for Liberal candidates in the other constituencies. At the following 1906 election, a decade-long Conservative government was swept away in a Liberal landslide (with the LRC's support), and the government that assumed office in 1906 under the leadership first of Henry Campbell-Bannerman and then of H. H. Asquith was well to the left of any of its predecessors. The House of Commons almost immediately passed a bill overturning *Taff Vale*—affirming the immunity of union funds from legal claims by employers, and enacting a right to strike.

The forces of capital struck back in 1908, with another case against the Amalgamated Railway Union, this time aimed at preventing it from using funds for political activities (namely, the financing of the LRC). The House of Lords decided the case in favor of an employer-financed union member, and this time the Liberal government did nothing directly to overturn the ruling, greatly offending both its supporters in the parliamentary LRC and rank-and-file workers, who came to see the LRC as a sellout.

But the government was stoking its own challenge to the House of Lords, which had repeatedly operated at the limits of its traditional authority to stymie the Liberal program. In 1909 the Chancellor of the Exchequer, David Lloyd George, proposed what became known as the "People's Budget," which for the first time taxed large landholdings (at 20 percent of appreciated value when ownership changed hands). That was a direct threat to the aristocracy's source of wealth and its plans for a graceful decline financed by the continual, gradual sale of hereditary holdings. It also made the income tax much more progressive at the top of the distribution and raised the inheritance tax as well. Lloyd George framed the People's Budget as explicitly redistributionist, though it was also motivated by the need to pay for the naval arms race with Germany that had commenced a few years earlier.

In violation of the unwritten norms of the British constitution, which held that the Commons alone held the power of the purse, the House of Lords vetoed the 1909 budget, triggering a political standoff long in the making. By winning two 1910 elections on the platform of disempowering the Lords and passing the budget, the Liberal government convinced the king to threaten to appoint new members of the Upper House sufficient to uphold the government. Instead the Lords acceded to the Parliament Act of 1911, which greatly curtailed their own power over legislation. The Parliament Act was the British equivalent to *West Coast Hotel v. Parrish,* the 1937 Supreme Court case that ended the Lochner era in the United States, in that it disempowered an unelected branch of government that had blocked the adoption of progressive legislation. And it transpired in a similar way: The body essentially chose to disempower itself, under political pressure that threatened to expand its membership such that its traditional social authority would be undermined. In essence, faced with defeat by another hand, both the U.S. Supreme Court and the British House of Lords chose suicide.

Furthermore, conditional on losing, in both cases suicide actually worked, in the sense that it inflicted substantial political harm on the adversary, whereas the antagonist's outright victory would have done the opposite. FDR lost authority within his own congressional party and around the country due to his the court-packing threat, and following the Parliament Act, the Liberal government in office until 1914 essentially lost control of the country between the protests over women's suffrage, rampant labor unrest, and Irish home rule, in part because the Liberal party found it impossible to recoup the political capital it had expended on taming the House of Lords, and it ended up essentially welcoming the coming of war in 1914 as a political savior.

War was not simply thrust upon the United Kingdom, however, much though its government framed the *casus belli* as a treaty obligation to defend the Belgian territorial sovereignty. Nor was the United Kingdom drawn into the war simply through the diplomatic bumbling of its foreign policy officialdom. Protecting and expanding its profitable empire was a policy the post-1906 Liberal government largely shared with its Conservative predecessor, notwithstanding their disagreements over the Boer War, and as the threat shifted from Russian encroachment in the Middle East and South Asia to German encroachment, the United Kingdom joined the Entente Cordiale and refigured its military posture to contain the threat to overseas holdings posed by the growing German fleet, at enormous expense. But the Great War had its genesis in domestic politics as well: It offered a reprieve from the ongoing crises that had paralyzed the country and its politics since 1911. All three revolts—of the unions, of women's suffragists, and of Irish unionists—abandoned their open challenge to the government at the start of war.

The legacy of the women's suffrage movement is particularly notable here: The movement had a conservative, upper-middle-class leadership and a strong working-class component, and both were equally targeted by the Liberal government's repressive policies of 1911–1914. The vulgar and even violent sexism of those policies (alongside the government's official nonpolicy on the underlying question of women's suffrage) turned both factions against the Liberal party forever, contributing to the cratering of the party's support after equal suffrage finally passed, since the two factions divided neatly between Conservative and Labour. The prewar union militancy also did not just disappear with the coming of war. Dissatisfaction with its conduct accumulated at the grassroots and eventually sent Labour's cabinet members into opposition to the national government by 1917.

The war turned out to be a disaster for all involved. First of all, paying for it required taxation of income and wealth far in excess of what had been levied by the People's Budget of 1909. The gold standard was abandoned during the war, causing rampant inflation that further eroded the real value of wealth. The conduct of the war itself discredited the traditional elite, both on a macro scale (with the seeming futility of both prewar diplomacy in avoiding what everyone expected to be calamitous ex ante and of the disposition of national resources during the war) and at the micro level (with costly military tactics by which the aristocracy ordered commoners to their deaths en masse). The political imperative in the postwar settlement was to save the leaders responsible for the coming of war and its conduct from facing the electoral music, which seemed to be accomplished by the general election of 1918, when the National (primarily Conservative) Coalition that had ruled since 1916 was reelected, with Labour and the anti–Lloyd George Liberals pushed to the sidelines. The 1919 Versailles Treaty exacted enormous concessions from Germany, way beyond Woodrow Wilson's Fourteen Points, which had been the basis for the armistice that ended hostilities in the autumn of 1918. The lion's share of the reparations were to go to France and a smaller chunk to Poland. Where Britain ostensibly gained was in the loss of its main prewar industrial competitor, as the German capital stock and manufacturing base was to have been dismantled.

Notwithstanding that initial triumph for Lloyd George's postwar government, the war killed off the Liberal Party as an electoral force and polarized British politics between Labour and the Conservatives. The result actually moved politics substantially to the right of where it had looked to be headed in the immediate prewar years. What happened was that the war, alongside the prewar failure of the Asquith government (the most left-wing government the United Kingdom had ever had to that point), made nineteenth-century classical liberalism, even in its proto-welfare-statist tendencies, untenable as an electoral vehicle for the working class. But that did not (yet) mean it ceased to be the ideology of government for the country as a whole. After all, Britain had won, and in the meantime the Russian Revolution presented the threat of violence and radical upheaval—a threat the right-wing press played up throughout the inter-war decades. The war had fractured the ideological foundation of capitalism in Britain, but the foundation didn't fail until the end of the 1930s.

In 1925 the Conservative Chancellor of the Exchequer, Winston Churchill, resumed the gold standard at the prewar exchange rate, which had the effect of revaluing accumulated wealth substantially while driving up the cost of British exports to foreigners and the cost of servicing Britain's war debt. The motivation, as Churchill later admitted, was essentially political: By returning to the prewar monetary policy, he somehow anticipated a return to its politics as well. The effect of the deflation was a recession unique to Britain, resulting in mass layoffs as domestic price levels were supposed to adjust downward. As Keynes argued in "The Economic Consequences of Mr. Churchill," the mechanism whereby that happens is layoffs and unemployment, not "immaculate transfer," and when coal miners were hit with a nominal wage reduction in 1926, they went on strike. All the unions followed suit in a general strike that proved unsuccessful, but the crisis created by an unnecessarily draconian monetary policy got worse with the Great Depression. In 1929 a Labour-led government came to power, but fearing it would be labeled radical, that government felt bound to uphold the previous government's monetary policy at all costs, imposing fiscal retrenchment as the global contraction persisted, and breaking the Labour Party in the process. The resulting National Government, reliant on Conservative support, ended up withdrawing from the gold standard, but rejected most further left-wing-originating reform policies—most notably, public employment and nationalization of industry, both aimed at eliminating what came to be seen as capitalism's inherently wasteful by-product of unemployment.

Throughout the 1930s, both high politics and societal conflict pitted the middle-class defenders of traditional economic policy against working-class proponents of industrial nationalization to eliminate unemployment and the enactment of a comprehensive welfare state that would meet all other instances of deprivation. At the same time, the reaction against the punitive treatment of Germany that characterized Conservative foreign policy in the 1920s migrated to appeasement of fascism in the 1930s, based largely on the assumption that the greater threat to continental peace was the Soviet Union and that fascism was at least a bulwark against it, one that had the benefit of enjoying popular legitimacy in Germany, Italy, and Spain (unlike traditional liberal parties) and that did not threaten to end private capital ownership through democratic rather than violent means (unlike social democratic parties). The fate of that foreign policy is well known. And during the war itself, the Conservative government of appeasement and "sound" economic policy was replaced by a coalition led by the one dissident Conservative who dared challenge appeasement in the 1930s, Winston Churchill, but whose other ministers were for the most part the Labourites who had long advocated for a planned economy. The one they implemented during the war itself validated their prior claims that it could be done to great productive effect, totally eliminating the endemic unemployment of the 1930s. Thus, the Second World War finished the process started by the First: undermining the credibility of Britain's traditional rulers, because the electorate saw the working class as having saved the country from those rulers' incompetence at both foreign and economic policy.

The coming and conduct of the war put the final nails into the coffin of Britain's classical liberal consensus of the nineteenth century: Prolonged high unemployment and material deprivation were endemic to a modern, industrialized economy. The elites that sustained the ideology long into the era of mass enfranchisement were discredited by the failure of their policies in the decades prior to the war. For those reasons, immediately after the war ended, Labour finally swept to power with a popular majority and enacted its longtime program of peacetime industrial nationalization, the welfare state, and confiscatory income and wealth taxation—the central reasons for the ultimate reduction of inequality in midcentury.

France

France achieved universal male suffrage during the Revolution of 1848, which created the Second Republic, and in its first election it replaced the radical politicians who had overthrown the previous July Monarchy with a National Assembly in which the balance of power was held by rural moderates with monarchical sympathies. A presidential election that year brought Prince Louis Napoleon to power against a divided Republican left, with the socialists of the Parisian working class a distinct minority, and their rival government in the Parisian city hall menaced the National Assembly throughout the government's short existence. The president bided his time, and in 1851 he took advantage of widespread dissatisfaction with political upheaval to claim the monarchy by overwhelming plebiscite, bringing down the Second Republic and ruling the Second Empire as the Emperor Napoleon III for the next twenty years. Thus, in the French case not only was universal suffrage insufficient to overthrow laissez-faire capitalism, it was insufficient to guarantee democratic government.[14]

The Second Empire, which was already facing increased labor unrest in its final years, collapsed with the Prussian invasion of 1870–1871. One immediate consequence was the Paris Commune, which became the international byword for the dangers of radicalism for many decades thereafter. Thus, the Second Empire was born out of extreme political polarization and also died in it, bequeathing to the Third Republic a polarized politics that never really dissipated. On the other hand, the politics of the Third Republic drifted to the left only gradually and in the context of a parade of coalition governments with compromise agendas, not, as happened in Britain (and eventually in France in 1936), with dramatic new departures. The other difference was that clericalism was a major political issue in France throughout the Third Republic, providing an additional dimension over which political conflict played out—one that complicates the picture of elite capitalist discredit. A similar drama transpired in Germany with the Kulturkampf.

Republican (that is, democratic) government in the Third Republic only won out when its monarchist first president, Patrice de MacMahon, lost an 1877 election for the Chamber of Deputies (the lower house of the French legislature under the Third Republic) he had called on the question of whether the government should be accountable to the legislature or to the president. In 1879 the Republican parties gained control of the Senate, whose existence as presumed monarchical bastion had been the royalists' condition for agreeing to the constitution that established the Third Republic, and in the early 1880s the education minister, Jules Ferry, passed his series of namesake laws that nationalized public education, which was a huge loss of influence for the Catholic Church. The same government, led by Leon Gambetta, legalized trade unions in 1884, though they did not formally affiliate with any political party. The political left in those years was split between a number of socialist factions advocating a range of positions on the proper way to overthrow capitalism (and to interact with the rest of the capitalist political system), and the so-called Opportunist Republicans of Gambetta, Ferry, and their successors, who eventually gave way to the Radical Party, which was even more explicitly anticlerical and began to broach the possibility of taxing income. The right was fractured by its long association with monarchism and then with the middle-class populist / revanchist nationalism of the would-be dictator General Boulanger, who swept onto the political scene in the late 1880s with monarchist support and then flamed out under sustained assault from united Republican forces.

The most notorious political event of the prewar Third Republic was the Dreyfus Affair, which brought to the surface all the sublimated conflict of the period. Once again monarchism, clericalism, and militant nationalism reared their collective head in politics, while the pro-Dreyfus factions unified behind Republican politicians and parties. Amid the larger crisis, a debate raged on the left about whether the socialist Alexandre Millerand should take part in the Republican, pro-Dreyfus ministry of Pierre Waldeck-Rousseau in 1899, which also included a nobleman who had suppressed the Paris Commune. Between 1902 and 1905, French socialism came into political being with the formation of the Section Française de L'Internationale Ouvrière (SFIO), the democratic vehicle of the nonrevolutionary socialists led by Jean Jaurès. 1905 also saw the enactment of the Law of Secularism, which totally excluded the church from public education and other state functions, and the successive ministries thereafter enacted some labor reforms, including social insurance and maximum hours legislation. Although the income tax managed to pass the Chamber of Deputies in 1909 following a long debate about the anti-egalitarian character of the existing regressive tax system, it languished in the Senate until the eve of war in July 1914, when it was passed only in expectation of the expensive impending conflict. The historian Arno Mayer described the French Senate in this period as "the rock on which inchoate cabinets kept foundering."[15]

Foreign policy ended up driving a wedge between the Radicals of the Republican Left and the SFIO, with the latter opposed to military buildup and confrontation with Germany. On the eve of war, Jaurès, who favored an international general strike to avert it, was assassinated by a monarchist in a Paris café, and the war was conducted by moderate Republicans of the left until they were replaced by the archnationalist Clemenceau in 1917. The war was even more disastrous for France than for Britain, so the absolute imperative at the Versailles conference was to salvage the reputation of the political elites who had spent the prewar decades inviting it—hence the punitive reparations schedule imposed on Weimar Germany. All the same, as in Britain, the moderate left that ruled at the outset of war emerged crippled, and postwar politics was dominated by a working-class left and a middle-class right.

In the French case, however, the left was almost immediately confronted by the implications of the Russian Revolution for domestic politics. The pre-Jaurès debate about whether it was proper to participate in bourgeois governments gave way to a tug-of-war between Jaurès's disciples and the proponents of overt alliance with and subservience to Soviet Communism. The SFIO was subverted for good at its 1920 Tours conference, when the majority Communists joined the Soviet "Third International" and took control of the party's journalistic outlets and a large chunk of its labor union affiliates, while the rump Socialists remained, led by Leon Blum. That faction supported governments led by the Left Radicals in the 1920s and 1930s, the so-called Lefts Cartel governments that vied with the National Front. France was more or less in economic crisis throughout the period, thanks to the failure of German reparations to materialize, creating a fiscal crisis until the end of the 1920s, followed by the Great Depression in 1929–1936. (Though, as Piketty writes, the two crises, with very different causes and characters, had very different distributional and therefore political impacts.) Eventually the weakness that attended factional conflict in the Chamber of Deputies provided a pretext for the riots of February 1934, the only time a Third Republic government was overthrown by street demonstrations. That and, more importantly, a change in Soviet foreign policy following Fascist successes in Germany, Italy, and Spain, set the stage for the Popular Front.

The Popular Front brought the Communist Party, which had more or less sat on the sidelines of French politics since 1921, into government and brought their unions into coordination with more moderate ones, setting the stage for the Matignon Agreements that finally enacted the full panoply of labor reforms the SFIO had advocated for its whole existence, including the forty-hour workweek, statutory collective bargaining, immediate wage increases, and mandatory paid vacation, all as part of a government-mediated settlement between the unions and employers to end a general strike called immediately after the Popular Front's electoral victory in May 1936. The new government also finally abandoned the gold standard, the final major economy to do so during the Depression. All of this transpired in the midst of high political tension, ongoing street violence, and widely expressed doubt about the political legitimacy of the current government and the entire Third Republic.

Thus, the Popular Front's two governments in the mid- to late 1930s did not signal the final victory of leftism in France. Far from it. The cooperation of the Communists with bourgeois parties did not last, due to further machinations in Moscow. Meanwhile, the worsening security situation in light of German rearmament empowered reactionary elements that claimed France had been sold out to its enemies from within. As with Britain, France more or less opted for appeasing Nazi Germany—knowing that it wouldn't work, but without a workable alternative in the absence of political consensus of any kind. When the Nazi invasion, occupation, and puppet Vichy regime finally came, the invaders found willing collaborators among what had been the prewar right—those factions that had spent the prior decades warning that the left threatened to sell France out from within—which was the final discredit that set the stage for postwar enactment of the welfare state. While portions of the center-right establishment joined the Free French, it was the left and especially the Communists who animated the Resistance left within France, and consequently it was the remaining shards of the Popular Front that held the political initiative in the Fourth Republic, when they enacted a more comprehensive welfare state.

Germany

Modern Germany only came into its political existence in 1871, with the culmination of Prussia's wars of unification, uniting the fragmented political order established by the Congress of Vienna. The political motive for that order had been to preserve the European balance of power, which tilted in Prussia's favor with its victory over France and the establishment of the Second German Empire. Revolutionary politics played a role in bringing about unification, which had been a liberal aim under the "Congress System." But in the aftermath of the Revolutions of 1848, German liberalism and nationalism diverged (and many liberals went into exile). For that reason, Germany had a substantial history of left-wing politics, the most developed in Europe, even before it became a unified political entity. Each of its constituent states had a liberal reformist faction in its internal politics, as well as a growing working-class movement, though they didn't all have universal male suffrage.

By the 1860s the cause of German unification itself united the traditional aristocracy and modern bourgeoisie—the classic nineteenth-century political alliance that prevailed in Britain and France as well. The liberals in the constituent states largely supported the Prussian takeover as a counterweight to their traditional, aristocratic domestic political opponents, because the Prussian state government embodied the constitutional monarchy then considered the ideal end-state of liberal politics. As in France, religion retained a major presence in politics, as the Catholic Church was one of the major loci of opposition to unification, and for that reason Bismarck's anti-Catholic Kulturkampf was the most controversial political issue following unification. Liberals largely supported unification, and the Prussian constitutional monarchy gave them an outsize influence on domestic policy, equivalent to what they attained under the Theodore Roosevelt and Wilson administrations in the United States several decades later. In 1891, Prussia legislated a pioneering income tax, and throughout the period natural monopolies were regulated, and in some cases outright turned over to state administration. The national government also enacted the first instances of social insurance for health, retirement, and workers' compensation, as well as tax advantages for middle-class savings explicitly aimed at ensuring loyalty from property holders for the regime in the face of a political threat from below.[16]

On the other hand, and despite the universal suffrage for the Reichstag included in the constitution of 1871, the traditional aristocracy and its allies retained a strong influence, even a stranglehold, over politics at both the state and national levels. The imperial government was responsible to the Kaiser, not the Reichstag, though it was required to obtain the latter's approval for its budget. The state governments, rather than the people, were represented in the Bundesrat (federal counsel), where Prussia exercised a de facto veto over major areas of policy. And the franchise within Prussia was far from universal: Seats in the lower house were determined by votes allocated in thirds by share of total tax revenue, rather than population, meaning that in most constituencies, a tiny elite controlled a third of the votes, a larger middle class controlled a third, and the vast underclass the final third. The upper house there was populated by the hereditary aristocracy and appointees of the king. In summary, then, the mass politics ostensibly included in the 1871 constitution was continually thwarted even as left-wing politics grew in organization and popular support.

What became (and remains) the German Social Democratic Party (SPD) assembled itself from labor unions and working-class political movements in the constituent states during the 1860s. As Germany unified, so did the SPD. At its party conference in 1875, the party developed its Gotha Program, calling for democratic government, free speech, and universal social insurance, health care, and education, all funded by progressive income and wealth taxes. What it notably did not advocate was nationalizing industry, garnering a famous critique from Karl Marx for its incrementalism and adhesion to bourgeois democratic politics. On the basis of its antimonarchism as well as several (independent, needless to say) assassination attempts on the kaiser, Bismarck had the party outlawed by the German Reichstag in 1878, a ban that lasted until 1890. Even when the SPD was legalized, several constituent states reverted to class-based voting that weighted property owners more heavily in the franchise in order to thwart the SPD's rising power.

The expiration of the Reichstag's ban in 1890 occasioned the ideological struggle on the left that persisted across Europe until the Popular Front policies of the mid-1930s. Initially, socialist-affiliated labor unions launched a wave of strikes, and the SPD effectively adopted the Marxist critique of its earlier Gotha Program by pledging to nationalize industry in its Erfurt Program of 1891 (partly in a bid to tame immediate union militancy, in expectation of a more auspicious political moment shortly to come). But over the course of the 1890s, the SPD split into revisionist and orthodox factions, with the former starting to question the desirability of a capitalist overthrow from both a theoretical and a practical perspective. Eduard Bernstein wrote a series of pamphlets, "Problems of Socialism," rejecting lofty rhetoric in favor of a movement of gradual worker liberation in a democratic and essentially capitalist context. Though the party remained formally politically united, Bernstein's revisionism became its default ideology for most of the twentieth century, during which it repeatedly acquiesced to the maintenance of the political and social status quo on the occasions when it accepted the mantle of power, and indeed sought popular acceptance precisely through its willingness to confront the task of governing and clean up the messes made by the traditional parties.

In the meantime, the policy of both Germany and of constituent states was evolving in the shadow of the SPD's rising membership and power. In the early 1900s the Reichstag enacted worker protections, including social insurance, limits on working hours, and factory inspections. But as left-wing influence grew, a political backlash favored militarization as a bid to redirect national politics. Traditional elements in the state bureaucracy, military, and high counsels thus directed their attention to provoking a series of crises with the congealing Triple Entente, despite the widespread realization that a grand conflagration risked losing everything. On the one hand, by amassing what was widely known to be an overwhelmingly powerful military machine thought capable of defeating France and Russia in sequence, some in the German leadership, including Imperial Chancellor Theobold von Bethmann-Hollweg and Chief of the Military Staff Helmuth von Moltke, imagined they were killing two birds with one stone: empowering conservative forces in domestic politics while cowing foreign adversaries into reluctance to actually go to war. The effect was to put in place a series of switches that could be triggered more or less automatically, a disastrous scenario that unfolded in 1914.

War split the SPD immediately, with the former left faction leaving to form the Spartacists. The remaining SPD at first acquiesced to military budgets in the Reichstag, but its parliamentarians gradually turned against it, such that by 1916 the cabinet could no longer command majority support for continuing to fund the conflict in the Reichstag. At that point the kaiser executed a de facto military coup, passing civil authority to the military high command, which put into place its strategy of total war. That nearly achieved its objective in the spring of 1918, but in so doing, it strained the home front beyond the breaking point, and once the Allies turned the tide on the western front just short of Paris, the Second German Empire was effectively finished. By September the high command of Paul von Hindenburg and Erich Ludendorff appealed to the kaiser to install a civilian government and seek an armistice from the United States, knowing that was Germany's only hope for staving off collapse from within and that the Wilson administration would need some sign of internal political reform to justify any break with the policies of its more war-ravaged allies. As part of that, the inequitable Prussian suffrage law was finally reformed, not thanks to the fact that for twenty years the SPD had been the largest party and yet excluded from the government of the Empire, but instead to appease an outside power. Ludendorff especially already had his sights on postwar politics, in which it was imperative to obscure responsibility for impending defeat in order that the establishment live to fight another day.

In that, Ludendorff had no greater ally than the SPD, eager to show itself as a credible party of government. Its leader, Friedrich Ebert, willingly took the baton the high command more or less offered, in return ceding its political allies the period of abstention they needed to regroup. Ludendorff even ordered the military officers in command at the front not to attend the armistice ceremony so as to keep the armed forces' signatures off the document and out of the picture. The government that came together following the armistice of November 1918 immediately enacted universal suffrage, including for women, as well as freedom of speech, and of the press, which had been vastly curtailed during the war. It also enshrined legal protection for collective bargaining and abolished the upper house's veto over federal legislation. In that sense, the so-called German Revolution of 1919 and the Weimar Constitution were clear political departures resulting from the discredit of the prewar and wartime governments. But the new regime faced the dissolution of the country. To preserve the country, it required the cooperation of what remained of the military and professional elite in order to tame an uprising fomented by the Spartacists, who elected workers' councils to civil government in many major cities, along the lines of what had happened in the first stage of the Soviet Revolution the previous year. Those councils managed to extract major concessions on wages, working conditions, and union recognition from employers as a condition of keeping factories open. But the new civilian government, its uniformed military allies, and groups of armed irregulars, mostly decommissioned soldiers returning defeated from the front, easily defeated the leftists. That anti-democratic taint never left the Weimar political scene, though its eventual overthrow by those same elements fifteen years later was not inevitable in 1919.

The Treaty of Versailles finally produced in the summer of 1919, was an utter disaster for the government, and the effect in Germany was to locate blame for the impending economic catastrophe with the Weimar government. The continuation of the Allies' food blockade more or less forced the government to the table, a consideration that gave strength to the argument that Germany was subsequently under no obligation to honor the treaty.

Furthermore, prior to the negotiations Ebert had assured the public that Germany's evident economic prostration from the collapse of the wartime economy would paradoxically serve to strengthen its negotiating position, as it evidently could not finance reparations.[17] That strategic and rhetorical error failed to account for the fact that France and Britain were also hobbled and their leadership desperate for German blood, and that Wilson, who had been weakened politically by his controversial war of choice, was in no position to rein in his allies who had suffered far greater casualties. The treaty they imposed at Versailles was thus untenable from the start and opposed at least rhetorically by the entire political system, but the Allies made it clear that if the government rejected it, they would remobilize and occupy at least Western Germany, and after soliciting the views of the high command that the military was in no shape to resist, the government acquiesced.

The Weimar political system consisted of the Communist Party, the heir to the Spartacists who eventually became closely tied to the Soviet Union; the SPD; democratic bourgeois parties of the moderate left; the Catholic Center, which had left- and right-wing factions itself; two parties of the right, one democratic and one aristocratic; and eventually the Nazis. The Communists challenged the republic from the left three times between 1919 and 1923, and each attempt fared worse than the previous. The antidemocratic right also attempted to overthrow the government, first in 1920 with the Kapp Putsch and again in 1923 with the Beer Hall Putsch, and in 1919 its paramilitaries assassinated the Spartacist leaders Rosa Luxemburg and Karl Liebknecht. These events garnered no outright support from the formal political system, but conservative elements in the bureaucracy and judiciary shielded the paramilitary right from punishment and persuaded the government that an aggressive crackdown would only inflame an unstable situation. However, Weimar's congenital political instability and the constant "threat" of establishment-enabled political extremism on the right have given rise to an unfortunate historiographic tradition: that its fall into Nazism was inevitable. That style of argument serves a counterintuitive purpose: to obscure the blame properly attributed to the forces that actually caused it—namely, the right flank of the formal political system that preferred autocracy to democracy and thought paramilitary violence a useful tool to neutralize and intimidate political threats to its social and economic position.

The historiography of Weimar is at its worst in analyzing the crisis that characterized its first stage: hyperinflation.[18] The hyperinflation was caused, at root, by Versailles' preposterous reparations schedule and the clearly erroneous though politically necessary belief that German workers could be made to toil indefinitely to save the political careers of the foreign politicians whose reputations had been devastated by the costly war they had engineered. The dynamics of the hyperinflation exactly mirrored the Allies' efforts to secure payment: The crisis spiked when France occupied the Ruhr in an attempt to coerce German factories into high productivity, and it subsided when that tactic proved unable to induce German workers to show up. The refusal of Western German factory workers to cooperate in securing reparations—specifically, whether those actions were coordinated from above in Berlin, and how much the government's policy, whatever it was, mattered on the ground—is a matter of debate. Whatever the case, the government's preliminary agreement to halt overt noncooperation while France withdrew its forces late in 1923 set the stage for the series of negotiations that finally ended the hyperinflation, with the introduction of the new "Rentenmark" backed by U.S. loans, and most importantly a more sustainable reparations schedule embodied in the Dawes and Young Plans.

The hyperinflation was massively destructive to the value of the German capital stock, but it also cost organized labor some of its hard-fought gains from the 1919 revolution when, as part of the renegotiation of reparations, the government imposed austerity measures on the private sector designed to elicit greater tax revenues at the expense of labor rather than of capital. Eric Weitz described the result: "The Weimar Republic lost the middle class in the inflation and the working class in the stabilization."[19] As a result, the SPD lost ground to the center of the political spectrum during Weimar's second phase after 1924, though when it regained power in 1927, it enacted a yet-more-generous social insurance system, including (unpaid) leave and job protection for pregnant workers, superseding the patchwork that had gradually been built on Bismarck's foundation.[20] It was that expanded social insurance system that triggered Weimar's final political crisis.

The recovery from hyperinflation had hinged on American financial backing, and when the U.S. stock market crashed in 1929, American banks began calling in their debts in panic, propagating the financial crisis to Germany as its first overseas victim. The Nazi Party had existed on the fringes since 1920, and the resulting Depression stoked its membership and convinced its enablers inside the formal political system that the time was ripe to launch the counterrevolution they had been fomenting since the first stages of the Republic. The first step was to demand austerity as the solution to crisis, a policy that first doomed the SPD government that had backed social insurance, when it tried to raise business taxes to bail out the system after the Depression bankrupted it. Then President Hindenburg tapped the Center Party's Heinrich Bruning for the chancellorship in 1930, and when he too failed to get a majority in the Reichstag, he ruled by decree under Article 48 of the constitution. In effect, this was the end of the Weimar Republic, though at the time its remaining adherents thought it was but a temporary measure.

Through two years of government by decree, Bruning implemented one austerity program after another, cutting unemployment and other social welfare benefits, civil servants' salaries, and eventually agricultural subsidies—the last of which was the final straw that caused the right-wing parties representing Prussia's rural aristocracy to withdraw support. In the meantime, several elections failed to provide him a parliamentary majority, instead polarizing representation to the benefit of the Communists and especially the Nazis. The system failed because the regime's only supporters were in the shrinking SPD, and they opposed the government's policies. Meanwhile, the right, which had long sought to overthrow the republic even as they ruled it undemocratically, saw in the Nazis the vehicle by which they might accomplish their end, since the Nazis were able to mobilize a mass political movement the representatives of the right-wing elite have historically been unable to do—making the far right a vital ally in a time of acute political and ideological crisis. In fact, the Nazis came closest to electoral success in Hitler's two bids for power in 1932 (when he ran against Hindenburg for the presidency, and when he sought the chancellorship after Bruning was forced to step down). Neither worked, and the Nazi tide was ebbing by the last of three elections in 1932. It was only then that a cadre of aides around Hindenburg persuaded him to name Hitler chancellor and eventually to ensure his domination of the Reichstag through the passage of the Enabling Act the following year (after the orchestrated Reichstag fire and the ensuing atmosphere of political terror), which bestowed a majority of seats upon the winner of a plurality of the vote.

The Nazi takeover was very much a counterrevolution to the events that transpired at the end of the First World War and immediately following it, during the German Revolution of 1918–1919. That revolution proved insufficient to finally remove the old elite from power, and it came roaring back thanks to the instability and policy failure of Weimar politics and, specifically, the failure of the democratic left to completely destroy its old antagonists when it had the chance. To be sure, the SPD was always being attacked from behind by the Communists, who were operating under orders from the Soviet Union not to legitimize a democratic government of the left in Germany through its cooperation, and at that time Germany would have been the only country in the world to have had such a thing. And the anti-Weimar right, both the heirs to the old regime and, needless to say, the Nazi upstarts, never accorded a basic legitimacy to democratic government. In that way, the fact that left-wing politics in Germany was most advanced among the four countries discussed here, and the old elite most discredited by having begun and lost the first war (rather than having fought it to at least a victory, if a pointlessly costly one, as in Britain and France), ended up costing the SPD, its voters, and Germany the most—there was as yet no international precedent for the politics they wanted, only the Soviet Union's cautionary tale. Unwilling or unable to implement a final and unprecedented victory over capitalist ideology and power by democratic means in 1919, the party was condemned to destruction at the instigation of those antagonists in 1933 and thereafter, in the early years of the Nazi takeover. The Nazis themselves accomplished the final destruction of capitalist politics at home, and the Allies were the agents of left-wing democratic revolution when they finally won the war, wrote Germany's modern constitution, and reengineered its politics and economy to never again pose an expansionist military threat. By the time modern Germany emerged from the Allied occupation, it already had the policies and politics of an advanced democratic economy with an empowered working class.

Conclusion

This essay attempts to plot the ideological history of capitalism from mass enfranchisement through to the policies that finally succeeded in taming the inequality of the Gilded Age. At some level, though, the historical narrative doesn't quite answer the question "Why isn't mass enfranchisement sufficient?," or alternatively "What is it about the ideology of capitalism that allows it to persist?" In *The Road to Wigan Pier* (1937), an investigation into and rumination on the continuing misery of the Great Depression in the coal fields of northern England, George Orwell turns to those same questions.[21] At that point, socialism, broadly defined, had been on the political stage for fifty years or more, alongside near-universal male suffrage, and the economic depredations it assailed had only worsened, by that point dramatically. In the meantime, fascism was on the march internationally, and the Spanish loyalist government fighting for its survival had been abandoned by its international allies and was on the verge of being subverted by Soviet agents who evidently desired its demise as a means to discredit democratic socialism. In other words, to Orwell things appeared to be getting worse, the great struggle of the age on the verge of being lost forever.

Orwell blamed the socialists themselves, along with their natural allies in the left intelligentsia. Given all the suspect baggage socialism carried, Orwell conjectured, no self-respecting working man could ever imagine himself a socialist. On the other hand, plenty of people who had much to gain from an egalitarian policy agenda hesitated to label themselves working class on account of snobbery. Either way, Orwell's explanation concerned itself with the ideology of individuals, and in that sense it was woefully inadequate. At some level, it rests on the assumption that political outcomes reflect what *the people* want, and the failure of political egalitarianism amounts to a failure to convince enough people to support it. But political outcomes reflect more than the aggregation of individual preferences—they reflect the consequences of actions, events, and movements, and the ideologies that history engenders.

The narrative here complicates Orwell's intuitive understanding of political change. Reducing inequality required social movements interacting with political environments in which the ideology of individuals is insufficient to the explanatory task at hand. The ideology of systems—in particular, of capitalism—plays a crucial role, because it serves to organize diverse interests and political actors. Within eight years of the publication of Orwell's book, a social democratic government was elected in a landslide and enacted the welfare state and industrial nationalization, overturning the hierarchy of well-being heretofore inextricably linked with Britain's ancient class system. But in those eight years, European civilization collapsed and 50 million people died around the world. The crucial element in explaining that turnaround was not the material destruction, nor the taxes levied to pay for it, but the ideological revolution. *How* it achieved that, though, has yet to be satisfactorily interpreted.

NINETEEN

The Legal Constitution of Capitalism

DAVID SINGH GREWAL

Legal philosopher David Singh Grewal traces the development of Piketty's laws of capitalism to the political philosophy of the seventeenth and eighteenth centuries, which first theorized the capitalist economy as the natural form of human society. Grewal shows how this concept became the basis for a new legal order, generating the historical dynamics of wealth accumulation Piketty discusses.

Thomas Piketty's *Capital in the Twenty-First Century (C21)* deserves great credit for having sparked an unusually rich and important set of debates about the consequences of capitalist development over several centuries.[1] In summarizing his argument, both Piketty and his reviewers have focused on the divergence between the return to capital and the average growth rate, the inequality $r > g$, as the condensation of his broader analysis. Piketty argues that, over several centuries, with the exception of the social-democratic era following the Second World War, the return on capital has consistently outpaced the average growth of the economy as a whole.[2] Much follows: an increased accumulation of capital and concentration of its ownership; a higher share of capital's take of overall national income; an increase not only in inequalities of wealth but also of incomes, given the portions of income coming from capital; and the possibility of "super-salaries" for the managers of capital assets. Fundamentally, $r > g$ signals a preponderance of capital over labor: "Capital reproduces itself faster than output increases."[3]

But what is behind $r > g$? The inequality serves as shorthand for a theory of capitalism understood as a socioeconomic system with seemingly autonomous macroeconomic dynamics. Economic debate has accordingly concentrated on the mechanisms by which such inequality is generated and maintained. A different approach to the inequality $r > g$ is to view it as an empirical discovery—that the rate of return to capital has, in general and across a wide variety of societies, outpaced average growth—and then conduct an institutional analysis into the historical causes of this fact.

Standard economic theories suggest that as the economy's "capital / output" ratio rises, the profit rate will fall more than proportionately, reducing the salience of the income received by capital owners. This is bound to occur in standard neoclassical analyses, under which factors of production are paid their marginal product and subject to diminishing returns. Likewise, Keynes's prediction of the "euthanasia of the rentier" as capital becomes abundant—albeit through deliberate monetary policy aimed at maintaining full employment—supposes a similar dynamic.[4] Finally, although somewhat different dynamics generate the "falling rate of profit" discussed in the third volume of Marx's *Capital,* even there we find an analysis (of the self-undermining trajectory of capitalist development) predicated on a decline in profits.[5]

Yet Piketty finds, empirically, that the rate of profit has remained stubbornly at around 5 percent a year even as capital's abundance relative to labor has varied widely over the centuries. This finding flatly contradicts the economic theories described above. Piketty himself has not attempted to provide an institutionally detailed historical explanation for this regularity. Yet such an approach is arguably necessary to bring to light the underlying dynamics of capitalist expansion that he identifies.

In this chapter, I adopt such an historical and institutional approach. I focus not on the macroeconomic dynamics but rather on the legal foundations that generate the persistent dominance of capital over the rest of the economy, as summarized in $r > g$. I take Piketty's major claim—that capitalist societies exhibit a trend of increasing inequality—as a prompt to examine the underlying legal and institutional foundations of capitalism.

The account I offer here characterizes capitalism as a legal ordering, a juridical regime derived from what we may call the "constitution of capitalism," which has existed in each society analyzed by Piketty, beginning with revolutionary France and persisting into the nineteenth-century "Gilded Age," the exceptional postwar era, and the present reassertion of

$r > g$. My analysis concerns therefore the "laws" of capitalism, understood not as its statistical regularities, but as its underpinning legal foundations.

By way of preface, we should note that Piketty discusses two "laws" of capitalism in a nonjuridical sense. Piketty "first"[6] and "second"[7] laws prove useful in organizing economic statistics. But neither explains why inequality has returned following the exceptional postwar period, during which the Kuznets curve appeared so plausible. In addressing that question, Piketty arrives at the inequality $r > g$, which many reviewers of his work have termed the "law" of capitalism, and which perhaps should be dubbed "Piketty's law," though he does not claim it as such. Indeed, he seems divided as to whether it presents any lawlike necessity at all. He sometimes discusses it as a quasi-natural fact; at other times he emphasizes that it obtains only in particular political contexts.[8]

Tellingly, he gives it a variety of names:

- a "fundamental inequality,"
- a "fundamental force for divergence,"
- a "mechanism of wealth divergence,"
- a "historical fact,"
- a "contingent historical proposition,"
- the "central contradiction of capitalism," and
- the "fundamental structural contradiction of capitalism."[9]

It is, of course, all these things. But it is neither an actuarial identity (like the first law) nor a long-run condition (like the second). It is a historical generalization drawing on his empirical analysis. And it is a conceptual frame in which to make sense of his data.

Why, then, has r > g held across the periods it has? Having tracked this inequality, Piketty has offered suggestions as to how it generates such highly visible inequalities of income and wealth.[10] Its ultimate causes, however, remain unclear. We must treat Piketty's book as a catalyst for further research on the legal, social, political, and economic dimensions of inequality under capitalism, as he himself hopes it will be.[11] This chapter attempts to historicize the laws of capitalism understood *as laws*. It closes with a puzzle concerning the continued dominance of capital in liberal-democratic societies today.

Commercial Society and Modern Inequality

C21 is a study of "modern" inequality—of differences in income and wealth among people of equal juridical status. That modern market societies produce prodigious inequality of this kind was taken for granted by the classical political economists. Adam Smith's *Wealth of Nations,* for instance, opens with a comparison of the rich and poor in Europe set against the inequality of primitive society: "The accommodation of a European prince does not always so much exceed that of an industrious and frugal peasant as the accommodation of the latter exceeds that of many an African king, the absolute master of the lives and liberties of ten thousand naked savages."[12]

It was never doubted that the new reliance on the market would generate new kinds of inequality. Early market advocates, however, simply argued that even the smallest share of what was produced through the modern division of labor had already compensated for the loss of primitive natural equality.[13] More subtly, these early market advocates also noted that primitive natural equality had already been undermined by human conventions—for example, slavery and other formal hierarchies. They hoped that increasing reliance on the market would generate juridical equality, because market exchange was thought to be predicated upon and reinforce particular forms of mutual regard among contracting agents.[14] But although the transition to juridical equality and market reciprocity may have helped to dissolve vestigial feudal relations, it left unsolved the problem of economic inequality among a legally equal citizenry.

Borrowing Henry Maine's famous description of this social emancipation as the movement from "status to contract,"[15] the decline of inequality based on status in no way precluded a dramatic rise in economic inequality produced through formally consensual contractual relations. All that was required was the backdrop of an unequal initial division of property and other resources. It was this form of "modern" inequality that concerned later critics, such as John Stuart Mill and Karl Marx. They argued that the organization of production and the distribution of wealth had to be understood as political issues and advocated more equitable social and economic arrangements within societies already transformed by commerce.[16]

One of the prime virtues of *C21* is that it returns us to these classical debates on capitalism and inequality. Of course, it is neither Smith nor

Marx but rather the twentieth-century economist Simon Kuznets who serves as Piketty's main foil.[17] Over the longer time-horizon that Piketty studied, the Kuznets curve is revealed as a temporary aberration: the postwar moderation of economic inequality turned out to have been the exception rather than the trend. With Kuznets dispatched, as Piketty recognizes, the study of economic inequality opens once again to the consideration of the deeper theoretical issues that concerned nineteenth-century classical political economy and the earlier discourse of eighteenth-century moral philosophy. *C21* shows us the way back to these debates—indeed, to the necessity of reengaging them—via the recognition that the decline in inequality during the mid-twentieth century was an anomaly.

To recover these earlier debates and understand how they influenced state policy and became juridical norms (rather than remaining merely theoretical positions), we must first note that the term "capitalism" was popularized (though not coined) by Marx and successor Marxists to describe modern societies in which the majority of the population meets its needs through specialized production in a complex division of labor determined through commercial exchange.[18] In Marx's analysis, of course, it further signified the domination of the owners of one factor of production, capital, over those who work for wages. Marx's key insight was that equality of legal status and a formally consensual wage bargain did not prevent the owners of capital from extracting surplus from workers—under the compulsion of unmet need, however, rather than, as in earlier episodes of such extraction, through the use of direct coercion. Marx's analysis of capitalism was thus simultaneously a description and a critique of a socioeconomic order that was fairly well established in the dominant states of the North Atlantic when he was writing.

Before the term "capitalism" became prevalent, the more general term for the socioeconomic order in which most people secure material needs through market exchange was "commercial society."[19] The fundamental transformation that marked commercial societies off from earlier ones was, as Adam Smith famously argued, the general economic interdependence of the advanced division of labor. As Smith explained: "Every man thus lives by exchanging, or becomes in some measure a merchant, and the society itself grows to be what is properly a commercial society."[20] The advantages and disadvantages of commercial society were the subject of ongoing debate in several places in the eighteenth century, notably France and Scotland, where the theories that would later be identified as foundational to classical political economy emerged.[21]

These debates focused on a newly articulated domain of "society" thought to arise naturally out of private property and commercial exchange.[22] The institutions of private property and commerce were themselves argued to reflect deep features of human nature. In fact, they were argued to be developmentally and normatively prior to the political state, unlike in earlier accounts, such as Aristotle's or Hobbes's, which in their different ways foregrounded the role of politics in organizing human society. There is a point of complexity here, however, in that the commercial society envisaged did presuppose a juridical order: a juridical order without a state. Specifically, the eighteenth-century theorists of commercial society began with what Hobbes had called the "state of nature," but reimagined it as a "state of natural liberty" in which a social condition in which property was not insecure, and life was not "nasty, brutish, and short," as Hobbes had argued.

The beginning of this theoretical move can be identified in the work of the German jurist Samuel Pufendorf, who posited a rich domain of "natural law" in the pre-political state, the content of which he took largely from Roman private law.[23] Pufendorf's innovations influenced John Locke's famous arguments concerning pre-political commercial activity, and a further host of figures who constituted a bridge between seventeenth-century contract theory and eighteenth-century political economy, including Shaftesbury, Frances Hutcheson, and David Hume.[24]

Commercial society was thus theorized as ordered through laws that had, in fact, been produced originally in an established political society (Rome), and which were in the process of being deliberately revived as part of the consolidation of early modern European states.[25] Yet these laws were widely touted as the product of society before or without the state—an ordering at once natural and divine. This theoretical move allowed Pufendorf to posit a private "economic status" that rested on self-interested commercial exchange, rather than on the noncontractual hierarchies of family and slavery familiar to the ancient *oikos,* and from which the term *oeconomy* came into modern European languages.[26]

A new account of how markets operate was central to this conceptualization of the economy. In fact, while markets and commerce long predated this period, it is only in the late seventeenth century that we find the explicit theorization of the market as an institution of reciprocal exchange, driven by individual self-interest, and yet, perhaps paradoxically, producing collective benefits.[27] This idea, made famous in Bernard de Mandeville's "private vices, public virtue" argument (in his *Fable of the Bees*), first emerged in the work French Jansenists, Pierre Nicole and Pierre de Boisguilbert, who theorized the market mechanism as a system of divine benevolence that transforms the sin of individual egoism into the collective benefit of material abundance.[28] The metaphor of an "invisible hand" regulating the market system has its origins in this theological discourse. Its first use was in articulating the program of laissez-faire as an ideal of governmental nonintervention in the operation of markets against the consolidation of the French state under Louis XIV.[29]

Legal Power and Commercial Society

The laissez-faire ideal was articulated in initial opposition to state power. But by the mid-eighteenth century, establishment intellectuals and monarchical advisors alike counseled deploying newly centralized state powers to transform French society in a liberalizing direction. As Michel Foucault noted of the emergence of economic liberalism, the limits to state power initially justified by alleged prerogatives of property and conscience became rationalized as an internal self-limitation on an otherwise undisciplined extension of *raison d'état*.[30] Most prominently, the midcentury circle of economists around a royal administrator, Vincent de Gournay, as well as the school known as "Physiocracy," advocated the strategic use of monarchical power to construct and defend markets against both popular and elite opposition.[31]

Through these later eighteenth-century articulations, the commercialized "state of natural liberty" became what Smith called the "*system* of natural liberty."[32] System coherence was provided by what was initially thought to be a paradoxical mechanism (the reciprocal exchange of utilities), which was itself maintained through consolidated laws of property and contract in the early modern state. The familiar intellectual history of classical political economy from Adam Smith to John Stuart Mill suggests an origin that is secular, British, and affiliated to popular government (of a more or less robust kind). A better understanding, however, locates its beginning at least two generations before Smith, in a discourse that is theological, French, and affiliated to monarchical government (of a more or less "moderate" kind).

Crucially, these ideas did not remain merely the subject of debate among the *philosophes.* In addition to becoming the object of relatively extensive discussion among an increasingly literate and urban society, the new discourse of political economy was used in the advocacy of legal reforms. Indeed, the legal underpinnings of commercial society were a central concern of its early observers. From the writings of Norman administrator Pierre de Boisguilbert[33] and the *économistes'* appeals to monarchical advisors on tax and grain policy through Smith's *Lectures on Jurisprudence* in the early 1760s and Marx's study of labor regulations, the ambition was not to study markets in the abstract, but instead to uncover the legal foundations of what was understood to be a new type of socioeconomic regime.[34] In this pursuit, these economists were not merely observers but advocates of reform of one kind or another. To use a limited (and anachronistic) vocabulary, their concerns were inextricably "normative" and "positive"—in part for the general reason that there is never a clean analytic separation between these orientations,[35] but also because the "economy," which was the object of their study, was under active construction.[36]

In that construction, two markets were of overwhelming concern to these early theorist-advocates: grain and labor. Reforming them required eliminating price controls and supply requirements on grain—which constituted what has been called the "moral economy" in food. The state or local community largely abandoned to the self-regulating mechanism of the market the ultimate responsibility for the provision of even the bare minimum of subsistence. Deregulating the labor market meant abolishing guild restrictions on entry into trades, as well as feudal dues and related obligations in the countryside.[37] It was believed that the labor and grain markets were linked: a reorientation in one both required, and pushed along reciprocally, a corresponding reorientation in the other. According to its advocates, the results of this liberalized grain-labor market would be progress for the poor, productivity in agriculture, the enhancement of the power and wealth of the state (owing to a larger tax base), and the dissolution of vestigial feudal relations, all through the commercialization of labor relations and the free rental or sale of farmland.[38]

At the heart of this argument was the claim that higher grain prices would stimulate agricultural production and raise wages, ultimately helping the poor. Defenders of the moral economy resisted this conclusion. Some resisted on the ground that this claim, like many others in the discourse of political economy, with its focus on unintended emergent properties of systems, was paradoxical. Others resisted by arguing that higher grain prices might indeed prompt farmers to more production, but that the increased long-run provision of food would do nothing to alleviate the short-term dearth that was the target of government regulation.[39] The focus on liberalizing grain and labor markets dates from the birth of political economy in the work of Boisguilbert through Smith's *Wealth of Nations*. Its prominent impact on European society continued to be felt in subsequent centuries.[40]

In fact, a relatively direct line of influence runs from Boisguilbert to the political economy of the *économistes* Quesnay and Turgot, from whom Hume and Smith borrowed a great deal.[41] Full recognition of this influence has been complicated by the fact that what began under Boisguilbert and the Jansenists as a program of laissez-faire opposed to the centralizing French monarchy became, over the course of the eighteenth century, a program of top-down economic liberalization pursued by royal advisors and administrators keen to deploy central power to promote and protect market relations.[42]

Reforming markets in grain and labor required both reconceptualizing property and contract law and developing new state regulations and public infrastructures.[43] The "freeing" of the grain and labor markets was not a simple hydraulic process (though it was often depicted as such) in which the dead weight of state regulation was removed, allowing a wellspring of commercial sociability to bubble up. Rather, the new market regime was understood from its inception to be a positive legal construction, requiring centralized power to enact and enforce it. It thus required the creation of a new legal order: what we may call the drafting of the laws of capitalism.

At the foundation of these laws was a new conception of juridical equality based on freedom of contract and private property, in which no formal distinctions among parties would be recognized. Corresponding to this equality before law was the delegation of productive activity to private agents linked through markets—that is, to agents understood to be acting in their "private" capacity.[44] With variation in tempo and means, legal changes along these lines were pursued by successive British governments, by the French monarchy, later by the French revolutionaries, and then across the Continent in countries that received the Napoleonic Code following French conquest.[45] In the process, a new domain of "private" law was constructed. It adapted earlier Roman law on property and contracts, and it brought newly centralized state power to the enforcement of private rights, which were theorized as appropriately limning state power in late seventeenth-century natural jurisprudence and the political economy that followed it.

This process was nowhere more evident than in the construction of the French Civil Code. A large part of the reform agenda of the French *écono-mistes* was realized through this Jansenist-influenced project of legal codification. Codification began with the centralization of power in the French monarchy, which promulgated unifying national legal codes—a practice that found its apogee in the post-revolutionary promulgation of the *Code Napoléon*. While the early monarchical codes were heavily indebted to Roman law, their drafting was executed by jurists with links to the Jansenists: first, under Louis XIV, by the Jansenist jurist Jean Domat;[46] and second, in the mid-eighteenth century, by Jean-Etienne-Marie Portalis, sometimes called the "father of the civil code," whose own links to Jansenist thought were obscured (because Jansenism was banned in the early eighteenth century and had to be drawn on with delicacy).[47]

These early codification efforts provided much of the foundation for the major codification schemes during the French Revolution, culminating in the Napoleonic Code.[48] Through that Code and the power of Napoleon, the Directory and successor French governments achieved the long-sought goal of the *économistes:* the legal foundation of economic liberalism and the central authority capable of enforcing it.[49] The Code consolidated the revolutionary overturning of feudalism, which the centralizing monarchs of the later eighteenth century had been unable to realize. It thus built on the changes that the French National Constituent Assembly brought about in the famous August decrees, including the abolition of personal servitudes and feudal dues, the seigneurial rights of the nobility, and the tithes to the clergy, as well the consolidation of the legal system away from the regional *parléments*.[50] Formal juridical equality was likewise guaranteed with the abolition of all status distinctions for offices, lawsuits, and taxation.

The negation of the old order in the early years of the Revolution, however, remained juridically underdetermined until it was instantiated in the positive legal enactments of the Code, which took the postfeudal order as its explicit normative baseline. It was thus Napoleon, not the French monarchs or early revolutionaries, who achieved what the *économistes* had theorized as "legal despotism," the centralized power capable of sweeping away the vestiges of feudalism on behalf of commercial society.[51]

The consequence of these policy changes—which were perhaps clearest in France but had analogues and extensions over a longer period in England and elsewhere—was the creation of the modern industrial economy. In it, urban workers sell their labor in competitive markets for wages. They then use this money to purchase foodstuffs produced by a much smaller number of farmers. The generalization of such wage work in the eighteenth and nineteenth centuries made European states (and subsequently their colonies) into "capitalist" societies, in which markets and the division of labor are central to the distribution of essential goods and services. As was understood at the time, this new socioeconomic order was in significant contrast to earlier regimes, in which markets played a less central role in the production and distribution of basic resources.

The Constitution of Capitalism

This historical juncture is where Piketty's narrative begins in earnest: the data made available following the French Revolution allows him to trace the economic consequences of commercial society from its revolutionary inception to the present. He finds that, with relatively wide national variations, capitalism has generated persistent economic inequalities owing to the privileged position that the owners of capital assets have within their societies. How has this privileged position been maintained?

As a preliminary matter, we should note that to ask this question is to presuppose that capital is a "social relation"—that it is not, as on the neoclassical view, simply a stock of assets, whose equilibrium rental price may be established through conventional supply and demand considerations.[52] In his analysis, Piketty adopts the neoclassical conception of capital as a measurable stock generating a flow. However, he also presents it as a social relation produced through political contest. He thus offers what might be considered a hybrid position in the controversy over capital theory.[53]

According to the critics of the neoclassical position, capital is not homogeneous, but consists in a variety of resources that people use to produce things. Moreover, the market value of this heterogeneous capital stock cannot be determined without examining the distribution of the returns to capital, which is necessarily given by political and social conditions rather than through a strictly technical process.[54] Owing to his use of standard neoclassical formulations, some critics have argued that Piketty missed the stakes of this controversy. But it may nonetheless be possible to interpret his conclusions sympathetically. What he has estimated is not a physical stock of stuff so much as the market valuation of the extent of capitalist privilege, as it is ramified across a range of assets from houses to machines to software programs. Piketty recognizes that the set of assets called "capital" includes much more than the productive machines of neoclassical economic theory, and that it has varied across historical periods as a result of changing governmental policy.[55]

What juridical regime, if any, has protected and legitimated this privileged position of asset-holders?

With the exception of Great Britain, which maintained both its medieval representative structure and customary law, the majority of European and later postcolonial states have been organized through written constitutions, usually legitimated through some form of popular or revolutionary ratification, often accompanied by projects of legal codification that rationalized customary law. Piketty's France offers the paradigmatic example here, with its revolutionary constitutions and civil code. But we may discern in France and beyond a more general juridical form, an organization of state authority that legitimates and consolidates the legal basis of commercial society.[56] This "constitution of capitalism" may be understood in a double sense. It is the constitutional order that most capitalist societies have adopted historically. It is also the legal foundation underpinning the social processes that comprise the economic system of capitalism.[57]

With significant national and historical variation, the constitution of capitalism institutionalizes two key distinctions. The first is a division between "public" and "private," drawn so as to secure a functional separation between the allegedly distinct domains of politics and economics.[58] The second is a division between "sovereignty" and "government" in the structure of modern constitutional lawmaking.

The first, the division between public and private, is a long-running feature of contemporary liberal-democratic societies and their antecedent regimes. It is based on adaptations of Roman and natural law conceptions of the division between a "natural" realm of property and contract and the public power of the state. It is this division that produces the familiar opposition expressed variously as the separation of "politics" or "the state" from "civil society" or "the economy." At the heart of this distinction between publicly accountable power and decentralized commercial activity is a conception of individual property rights as providing relative insulation from direct political control—though, of course, that insulation is itself achieved only through the careful deployment of political power to enforce those rights in the first place.

The distinction between "sovereignty" and "government" is less familiar. However, it is arguably more crucial in defining modern constitutional regimes. In France and the United States—and then elsewhere—the legal construction of commercial society was ultimately given public legitimation through new constitutional orders. These constitutional orders were predicated on a revolutionary distinction between "sovereignty" and "government" that solved the puzzle of how to create a political whole out of the legally equal, discrete individuals of commercial society.[59] They had the effect of ratifying formal equality among persons while providing special protections to the rights of contract and property.

While the distinction between sovereignty and government would prove crucial to the democratic legitimation of modern constitutional regimes, it first appeared in the work of the sixteenth-century French jurist Jean Bodin in his study of monarchical sovereignty.[60] In articulating the foundational concept of "sovereignty," Bodin distinguished it from "government" or "administration." The will of the sovereign was the ultimate source of all mundane law. However, the will of the sovereign could be kept functionally distinct from the ongoing administrative operations that the sovereign might authorize. Only *fundamental* law had to be issued by the sovereign. It could then authorize others (the "government" or "administration") to make lesser rules on its behalf.

As Richard Tuck has shown, this distinction made democracy in modern times seem newly possible, at least at the level of sovereignty. It allowed for direct popular legislation on matters of fundamental law, even if only intermittently. But it lodged ongoing administrative powers—including those regulating economic matters—in the hands of a government bound by constitutional mandates to uphold the legal basis of commercial society.[61]

The division between direct democracy at the level of sovereignty and representation at the level of government means that the source of ultimate constitutional authority in a modern democracy—the people—will often be "asleep" (to use a metaphor that Hobbes devised) for long spells. This sleep of the sovereign, however, may be punctuated by brief bouts of constitutional lawmaking when awake.[62] Governmental activity authorized by the constitution proceeds in the interim. Control of this government by the popular sovereign rests on a variety of mechanisms, most obviously elections and other techniques meant to induce accountability.

In practice, the sovereignty / government distinction has provided for the periodic reaffirmation of the sovereignty of the people in the form of direct ratification of fundamental legislation, either at the moment of constitutional inauguration, through ongoing processes of formal amendment, or through "constitutional moments" of various sorts. By the same token, however, these constitutions put limits on the ability of the people to revise the entrenched legal rules underlying commercial society and given effect through ongoing governmental operations, since they usually contain a wide variety of countermajoritarian mechanisms hobbling the majority of the day. These are only to be overcome, if at all, in extraordinary moments of popular constitutional lawmaking.[63]

How do these two features of modern constitutionalism work to entrench the privileged place of capital, and so generate the persistent inequality $r > g$?

The role of the public / private divide in insulating the economy from public control is straightforward. That it rests on substantive protections for individual rights of property and contract is straightforward. The economy is never, of course, fully insulated. The governments of the day retain important powers of taxation and regulation as part of their normal activities. More generally, the division between public and private—that is, between activities regulated as public matters and those which are in effect delegated to private actors—is itself historically variable and shifting. The "economy" constructed in this way proves a variable product of public power and its strategic abstinence.

This brings us to the important role of the distinction between sovereignty and government in enabling the ongoing governmental construction of the economy. The resuscitation of democracy at the level of popular sovereignty provides an opportunity for public legitimation of the constitutional regime. But it also means that direct popular rule is limited to exceptional moments. Thus, most public actions that limit—or buttress—the prerogatives of capital come through the ongoing initiatives of government. And governments will be limited in their power and will to tackle inequality for many reasons. These include the pressures of international competition, the class interests of the civil service and military, and so on,[64] but more importantly they also include the higher-order constitutional protections for property and contract ratified initially by the popular sovereign but then rendered difficult to change. These mandates were rationalized as inaugurating a new (postfeudal) era of equality, the very basis of the modern rule of law, but then largely insulated from ongoing popular modification.

From this perspective, capitalism is not (or not merely) a socioeconomic system. It is a juridical regime. It is a form of the modern "rule of law." It is legitimated through constitutional ratification by an ultimate popular sovereign that then rules in theory, without in practice surrendering governmental administration to ongoing popular control. The effect of this regime is that emanation of commercial sociability we now call "the economy." It is produced as the outworking of legal rights and duties that offer special protections to asset-holders legitimated through a constitutional order. The population is episodically organized into a unified popular sovereign, but it is mostly treated as the disparate subjects of ongoing governmental oversight.

We can interpret Piketty's data as revealing that the fundamental tendency of this kind of regime is toward accelerating inequality of the modern kind, an inequality produced through formally consensual relations among persons enjoying juridical equality. Reframed in this way, it is not Piketty's discovery that the rate of return to capital outpaces average growth that should be surprising, but rather Kuznets's earlier supposition that he was tracing anything other than a temporary aberration. And because the juridical regime establishing capitalism had not been altered in its fundamentals during the postwar period, the presumption should be that capitalist inequality would eventually return. Indeed, perhaps unsurprisingly, recent social science research suggests that the American government has functioned in an increasingly "oligarchic" manner over the time period in which Piketty has diagnosed a return to Gilded Era levels of inequality.[65]

The Legal Analysis of Capitalism

Understanding why $r > g$ has generally held—and why it briefly did not—requires an account of capitalism as a socioeconomic system structured through law. This should not be an unfamiliar inquiry, because capitalism is undeniably a legal ordering: the bargains at the heart of capitalism are products of law. Yet the postwar economic circumstances that led to the Kuznets curve had the further effect of sidelining the study of the legal and institutional foundations of capitalist economic systems, on the supposition that the economy constituted a social subsystem that could be managed by experts in line with the political choices of an informed electorate.[66] Precisely why these conditions no longer hold—whether for contingent or deep reasons—is a centrally important question to which Piketty's analysis points us.

The idea that capitalism is not just an economic system but also a juridical regime was familiar to early commentators on commercial society. Perhaps the most developed contemporary discussions have been in Marxist circles, where both a theoretical-deductive and a historical-institutional approach to capitalism have been pursued. In Marx's original analysis, capitalism was depicted as a system with its own logic, which could be made the subject of a deductive analysis, but it was also presented as a form of "class rule," instantiating a particular historical configuration of domination by some people over others (through legal institutions such as private property and wage work). The precise connection between these two accounts—of capitalism as system and capitalism as regime—remains the subject of debate, both within and outside Marxist circles. Attempts to reconcile them have turned on the question of whether the "logic" of capitalism or its form of "rule" is ultimately held to be foundational.[67]

Much the same argument might be had about Piketty's $r > g$. Is it a condition that holds as a systemic requirement of capitalism's logic? Or is it an outgrowth of the historical development of capitalism as a form of class antagonism—namely, the domination of labor by capital? It can be both. But to describe it as both requires an account that is at once a genealogy of capitalism and a structural account of the economy. Such an account would require some reconciliation of "structure" and "struggle" in the analysis of capitalism.[68]

Providing that reconciliation is beyond the scope of this chapter, but some preliminary remarks about how legal analysis might contribute to it are possible. In the broadest framing, the effort should accomplish four tasks. It should show how the legal arrangements undergirding commercial society prompt an ongoing, multidimensional social contestation over the terms of shared economic life. It should show how they influence the settlement of any episode of social contestation. It should show how the settlement of any episode of contestation is, in turn, given legal and institutional form. And it should show how that legal and institutional settlement regenerates the structural foundation of "the economy" while also setting the stage for the next iteration of contestation.

Both legal scholarship and institutional political economy may be usefully adapted to this task.[69] For example, as Wolfgang Streeck has recently argued, the "institutionalist turn" in social science has produced general insights that can, with a few "parametric specifications," be put to use in the study of capitalism as a "specific type of social order," undergirded by distinct legal arrangements.[70] Supplementing Marx's insights about the organization of wage-labor, Streeck suggests a variety of other empirical features characterizing capitalism. These include: first, the presumed legitimacy of pursuing private gain without, for the most part, being constrained by traditionalist "supernorms" like expectations of social solidarity, restraints on competition, or elite duties to ensure "system survival"; second, the expectation that rule followers are "rational-egoistic" in their orientation rather than norm-internalizers with respect to the purpose of a rule (consider, for example, manipulations of financial regulations); and, third, a "differential endowment of classes with resources," which results in classes having different capacities for effective agency, including disparate ability to mobilize political coalitions to advance their interests.[71] It is not difficult to appreciate that these aspects of capitalist societies have their basis in law and, in turn, that they help to define the context in which the "fundamental inequality of capitalism" has mostly held across the past few centuries.

The puzzle to which Piketty's analysis points us is understanding the exceptional post-war period. Were the mixed economies of the postwar period still capitalist, if what Piketty calls the "central contradiction of capitalism" had been overcome, albeit temporarily? Note that the mid-twentieth-century reversal of $r > g$ led some contemporary observers, such as the Labour Party theoretician Anthony Crosland, to wonder whether their societies were still capitalist.[72] More generally, was it inevitable that the organized interests of capitalists would succeed in re-creating "capitalism"? How can mobilized publics maintain a mixed economy of the social-democratic kind in spite of the demobilization and privatization that is intrinsic to the constitution of capitalism as described above?

Understanding the movement from what Piketty calls patrimonial capitalism to the postwar "mixed economy" and back requires a nuanced account of what John Commons long ago analyzed as the "legal foundations of capitalism." In an earlier generation, legal realists from Robert Hale to Karl Llewellyn to Jerome Frank put these legal foundations at the center of their analyses.[73] A return to Hale-style legal realism in the analysis of public institutions and "private" law would be a welcome turn. It might help stimulate a law-and-economics approach to the study of capitalism as a historical system, supplementing the standard law-and-economics approach in which markets tend to be considered in the abstract as mechanisms of social choice.

Particularly important subjects for future research include: the causes and consequences of the postfeudal reconstitution of property law; the ways in which labor, public benefits, and corporate law together structure the modern labor market as an arena of "contested exchange"; and the ways in which "economic power" arises via specific contractual mechanisms.[74] These and related inquiries would help us understand the conditions under which formal equality of contract proves compatible with widening economic inequality. We must also consider the way that law structures not only particular bargains in capitalist societies (most prominently, the sale of labor for wages), but also the broader social and political setting of the market. Here the dynamics of public and private debt, the regulation of finance in an age of "financialization," and the constraints placed on democratic control of the economy through international economic integration may prove especially salient.[75]

In studying these issues, Piketty's work should lead us to consider how the legal foundations of capitalism influence the rate of return on capital and its consistent outpacing of overall growth. The ways different areas of law interact to produce the inequality $r > g$ may be complex. For example, Piketty analyzes the demographic contribution to the inequality by focusing on the impact of inherited wealth, which is more concentrated in low-growth demographic regimes; by contrast, in growing populations, the return to labor proves more important than inheritance.[76] Yet, under some legal conditions, slower demographic growth may also lead to increased bargaining power for labor, because the availability of fewer workers means that those present can demand more from employers—a dynamic that John Stuart Mill emphasized in his social reform agenda.[77] Indeed, the *trente glorieuses* may have achieved their exceptionally high ratio of g to r—and their relatively egalitarian distribution of that average growth—at least partly because of relative labor scarcity in the advanced industrial world. In support of that possibility, we should note that it was not only Europe that enjoyed rapid and shared growth in the postwar period, but also the United States, which was already at the "technological frontier"—and therefore not merely in a phase of "catch-up" and reconstruction.[78] Likewise, the end of the exceptional postwar period coincided with the beginning of "globalization," through which multinational companies gained the ability to resist wage demands by offshoring or threatening to offshore industrial jobs.[79]

Further study of these dynamics may suggest that the dominance of capital over labor that Piketty has observed rests, at least partly, on unanalyzed demographic preconditions. The globalization of the last few decades has had the effect of reconstituting what Marx called the "reserve army" *across* countries, and thus partly within them, leading to a downward pressure on wages, the decline of organized labor as a political force, and the resultant rise in oligarchic policies that exacerbate the trends.[80] Perhaps much of the difference between Kuznets's and Piketty's studies may be attributed to this changing demographic context: the postwar capitalist core experienced relative labor scarcity, and a consequent moderation of inequality, which was later reversed with the incorporation of new labor pools from abroad.

Likewise, these demographic considerations might allow us a different forecast of trends in twenty-first-century capitalism. Instead of projecting $r > g$ into the future, as Piketty suggests, we may interpret this inequality as reflecting the differential bargaining power of capital as against labor under some demographic conditions but not others. Just as capital is no longer national, neither are the demographic determinants of $r > g$. Looking ahead, the dynamics of what might be called a demographic contradiction of capitalism are now becoming visible: both capitalism and the stabilization of fertility rates that accompanies it are manifestly intensifying on a global scale.[81] It is not hard to imagine that an economist working through Piketty's argument fifty years hence (much as Piketty worked through Kuznets's numbers) will focus on the neglected demographic context of his claims. *Capital in the Twenty-First Century* may thus have arrived at the precise moment when capitalism has gone truly global, but before the demographic consequences of this expansion have become obvious. And yet understanding more fully how demographic change might contribute to economic inequality will require a study of its broader legal and institutional context, taking in labor law, reproductive rights, corporate strategy, and international economic integration. Inquiries into other possible determinants of $r > g$—for example, the impact of technological change—will likely prove just as complex and just as legally structured.

Alongside this research into the legal foundations of capitalism, there remains the work of understanding the institutional structure of democracy, which Piketty presents as the counterpoint to capitalism. In brief, the problem is to understand why neither the intermittent constitutional referenda of popular sovereignty nor the elected representation of modern liberal-democratic societies have proven able to tame inequality, at least outside the exceptional period of the postwar boom. That nineteenth-century societies with severely restricted suffrage and oligarchic state bureaucracies were unable to moderate levels of economic inequality is not hard to explain. Marx may have been perfectly correct when he wrote, in his analysis of the Paris Commune in 1871, that "the working class cannot simply lay hold of the ready-made state machinery, and wield it for its own purposes."[82] But why this should remain so today in societies with mass suffrage is a puzzle that requires a deeper inquiry, which is only now beginning in earnest, spurred by Piketty's important book.[83]

TWENTY

The Historical Origins of Global Inequality

ELLORA DERENONCOURT

Economist Ellora Derenoncourt addresses the deep historical and institutional origins of wealth inequality, which she argues may be driven by what Daron Acemoglu and James Robinson identify as "extractive" versus "inclusive" institutions. Derenoncourt's core point is that while institutions underlying wealth accumulation may be inclusive for "citizens," or those individuals granted rights in the body politic, they may at the same time be extractive for "subjects," including slaves, members of historically marginalized racial and ethnic groups, and others not accorded equal legal status. Derenoncourt discusses several examples of this dichotomy playing out, with documented ramifications for the current distribution of wealth.

History has shaped and continues to shape global inequality, and violent encounters between different parts of the globe are far from the least part of that history. From the 1500s to the 1960s, global integration in the form of the Atlantic slave trade and direct and indirect European colonial rule over the Americas, Africa, and Asia has been defined by extraction and a stark imbalance of power. These exploitative economic activities nonetheless contributed to patterns of modern economic growth—or at the very least, to the stark enrichment of some at the expense of others—to warrant their study in the context of contemporary global inequality.

This paper presents a framework that partitions the effect of history on global inequality into an effect on endowments, or the initial distribution of wealth in a society, and institutions, or the rules that have typically governed economic, political, and social behavior.[1] Both endowments and institutions have been powerfully shaped by the extractive encounters that are the focus of this chapter. North Atlantic slavery and European colonization each generated two distinct groups of economic actors, whom I term "citizens" and "subjects" after the work of political scientist Mahmood Mamdani.[2] At the risk of anachronism I simply define citizens and subjects as being on the winning and losing side, respectively, of history's extractive encounters. At least on average, global citizens enjoy larger initial endowments, the economic and political rights guaranteed by long-standing democratic institutions, and the opportunities to accumulate thereby generated. By contrast, global subjects start with little if any endowment, with economic and political lives hemmed in by coercive, undemocratic institutions, with no due-process rights, susceptible to coercive labor practices, and a distinct lack of opportunities to accumulate wealth.

De Nardi, Fella, and Yang, in Chapter 14 of this volume, have already provided one theoretical treatment of factors that shape incentives for wealth accumulation. The authors add bequest motives and heterogeneous preferences into Piketty's formal model of dynamic output growth and the return on capital. Their approach extends what Naidu, in Chapter 5 of this volume, describes as the "domestic Piketty" reading of *Capital in the Twenty-First Century*—one that wields the standard language of macroeconomics and public finance to understand patterns in wealth accumulation.[3] My reading instead follows from Naidu's alternative vision of a "wild Piketty," placing power and politics at center stage. Indeed, given that much of the economic activity considered here takes place outside the realm of competitive markets or rule of law, this chapter evaluates historically determined institutions and endowments as drivers of long-run inequality.

I will start by sketching a simple model of intergenerational wealth transmission with group-level heterogeneity. The model allows past endowments and institutions to influence individual wealth and thus inequality within and between two groups—citizens and subjects. The model yields the insight that the effect of endowment differences erodes over the centuries. By contrast, institutions shape not only the incentives for wealth accumulation, but also the capacity for redistribution. These institutions persist and continue to influence inequality long after the effect of initial endowment differences has died away. I compare this approach to the literature on the importance of slavery and colonialism in the Great Divergence and the Industrial Revolution, where a focus on endowments has missed sight of the more pernicious effect of institutions.

I illustrate this problem by turning to the context of U.S. slavery. The Civil War and emancipation sounded a death knell for slave wealth as a form of wealth, but this shock to wealth was far from sufficient to remove either the advantage that slaveholders enjoyed in Southern society or slavery's hold on Southern politics. Institutional persistence opened other avenues for their dynasties to regain prominence in the decades after the Civil War. The evidence suggests some resurgence of the antebellum southern dynasties. One compelling channel for persistence is through elite capture of political institutions.

I next turn to examining the persistent effects of the institutions of European colonial rule on inequality, broadening both the geographic and the temporal scope of the analysis. Acemoglu, Johnson, and Robinson have provided a method for identifying the causal effect of institutions on economic outcomes via the use of exogenous variation in disease environments as an instrumental variable for colonial institutions.[4] These variations affected the ability of Europeans to settle in potential colonies and arguably shaped the types of institutions they subsequently built. Although institutional persistence affects inequality through numerous channels, I primarily focus on tax infrastructure, and the resulting selection into global inequality databases like the World Wealth and Income Database maintained by Piketty and collaborators. Societies with extractive institutions have more recent and less stable tax infrastructure, on average, and this matters for inequality within formerly colonized societies today.

In the final section, I discuss paths for future research and the policy implications of history's continued influence on global inequality. The most distinctive policy proposal in the context of historical extraction is reparations. I briefly discuss the pitfalls of this policy instrument as conceived and implied by the literature focused on endowments. I conclude with an alternative approach to reparations that focuses on the problem of institutional segregation rather than merely the initial divergence in endowments.

A Model of Group Inequality with History

To model intergenerational wealth transmission in a world where groups of individuals have faced different sets of institutions historically, I work off of Mulder et al.'s model of intergenerational wealth transmission in small-scale societies.[5] Mulder et al. are interested in the average levels of inequality generated by the different economic production systems in small-scale societies whose institutions range from the highly egalitarian to the strongly stratified. Their estimates of intergenerational transmission for each of these societies suggest, first, that inequality between the groups is significant and larger than fluctuations around long-run inequality within groups and second, that inequality between societies is largely a function of the institutions that come along with each type of production technology. Here, I modify their model to take into account the interrelation between the institutions of citizens and subjects stemming from the historical encounters discussed in the previous section. I focus my interpretation on the effects of endowments versus institutions on inequality within and between these two groups.

As mentioned, groups that have historically enjoyed inclusive political and economic institutions I label "citizens" while groups that have historically faced extractive institutions I label "subjects." In the model, an individual's wealth is determined by three components: institutions that determine the degree of transmission of wealth from the individual's parents; endowments, or the average wealth for the individual's group, which in turn depend on the institutions; and idiosyncratic shocks, which capture unanticipated fluctuations in the individual's wealth. For citizens, strong inclusive institutions limit the degree of wealth determined by the individual's parents, whereas for subjects, extractive institutions ensure that one's status is largely transmitted from the previous generation. Further, citizens enjoy greater endowments and subjects lower endowments due to historical encounters that have transferred wealth between the two groups, including the Atlantic slave trade, slave-based plantation agriculture in the Americas, and resource extraction in the colonies from Africa to Asia. The final term in the wealth equation captures unpredictable economic shocks that are beyond the control of the individual. These include macrolevel shocks, such as wars and economic downturns, or individual-level idiosyncratic shocks, including illness or death in the family.

Global inequality in this setting is captured by the variance in individual wealth in the combined population of citizens and subjects. The model's main insight, which is shown below after some technical manipulation, is that while initial endowments matter for global inequality in the short and medium run, in the long run only the effect of institutions remains. This is because idiosyncratic shocks dampen the effect of endowments passed on, generation to gen-

494

eration, eventually making them irrelevant for global inequality. Once wealth stabilizes between generations, in an equilibrium known as the steady state, only institutions continue to determine the level of global inequality.

I show this formally by letting citizens and subjects have population frequencies ρ and $1-\rho$, respectively, and face the following group-specific wealth accumulation processes:

$$W_{it+1}^C = \beta^C W_{it}^C + \left(1-\beta^C\right)\bar{W}_t^C\left(\beta^C,\beta^S\right) + \varepsilon_{it}^C,$$

$$W_{it+1}^S = \beta^S W_{it}^S + \left(1-\beta^S\right)\bar{W}_t^S\left(\beta^S,\beta^C\right) + \varepsilon_{it}^S,$$

Here, β^G captures historically determined institutions for group G, $\bar{W}_t^G$ is average wealth for group G in period t and thus represents endowments, W_{is}^G is the wealth of individual i in group G in time period s, and ε_{is}^G is the idiosyncratic shock to i's wealth in group G in time period s, where the shock has mean zero with variance $\sigma_{\varepsilon G}^2$. Thus, an individual's wealth tomorrow is a function of their individual wealth in the previous period, the average wealth of the group in the previous period, and an idiosyncratic shock during each period at the individual level. Initial endowments can be thought of as group-level average wealth in time period zero.

The second term represents regression to the mean, or the group-level average endowment from the previous period, weighted by $\left(1-\beta^G\right)$. If β^G represents institutions, then a lower β^G implies inclusive economic and political institutions that increase equality of opportunity and compress the distribution within a group—for example, constraints on elites, strong public goods provision, and social safety nets. High β^G s capture the extractive institutions that emerged under colonialism and slavery: a political system that favors elites, conflict, and coercive labor markets. Extractive institutions in the past engender low intergenerational mobility as well as higher levels of contemporaneous inequality through institutional persistence. Importantly, I allow group-level endowments to depend on institutions in other groups to capture the consequences of historical encounters between citizens and subjects.

In places with inclusive institutions, endowments may be even higher due to resource extraction or the practice of slavery in overseas colonies. In this model, both differences in endowments and differences in institutions are purely determined by these historical encounters. Though this abstracts from other factors that influence institutions and initial endowments, the purpose here is to highlight the relative importance of endowments versus institutions in determining contemporary global inequality. The model provides a convenient way of relating global inequality to the divergence in endowments and institutions that comes about through extractive historical encounters. These historical encounters create groups of citizens and subjects, both globally and within a country or region.

For any group G, with the other group represented as $-G$, under shocks that are independently and identically distributed (i.i.d.), the steady-state variance of wealth can be derived as follows:

$$\text{Var}\left(W_{it+1}^{G}\right) = \text{Var}\left(\beta^{G} W_{it}^{G} + \left(1-\beta^{G}\right)\bar{W}_{t}^{G}\left(\beta^{G}, \beta^{-G}\right) + \varepsilon_{it}^{G}\right)$$
$$= \beta^{G^{2}} \text{Var}(W_{it}^{G}) + \sigma_{\varepsilon^{G}}^{2}$$

In the steady state where $W_{it+1}^{G} = W_{it}^{G}$, $\text{Var}\left(W_{it+1}^{G}\right) = \text{Var}\left(W_{it}^{G}\right) = \sigma_{W^{G}}^{2}$

$$\sigma_{W^{G}}^{2} = \beta^{G^{2}}\sigma_{W^{G}}^{2} + \sigma_{\varepsilon^{G}}^{2} \Rightarrow \sigma_{W^{G}}^{2} = \sigma_{\varepsilon^{G}}^{2} / \left(1-\beta^{G^{2}}\right)$$

Thus, in the steady state, initial endowments have no effect on group G's variance of log wealth. Instead, steady-state variance is purely a function of group G's institutions and the variance of the individual-level idiosyncratic shocks.

In what sense do institutions matter for inequality within and between citizens and subjects? Global wealth accumulation is a sum of the two wealth accumulation processes for citizens and subjects, weighted by population frequencies:

$$W_{it+1}^{WORLD} = \rho W_{it+1}^{C} + \left(1-\rho\right)W_{it+1}^{S} = \rho\left(\beta^{C}W_{it}^{C} + \left(1-\beta^{C}\right)\bar{W}_{t}^{C}\left(\beta^{C}, \beta^{S}\right) + \varepsilon_{it}^{C}\right)$$
$$+ \left(1-\rho\right)\left(\beta^{S}W_{it}^{S} + \left(1-\beta^{S}\right)\bar{W}_{t}^{S}\left(\beta^{S}, \beta^{C}\right) + \varepsilon_{it}^{S}\right)$$

This can be rewritten as follows:

$$W_{it+1}^{WORLD} = \rho\beta^{C}W_{it}^{C} + \bar{W}^{WORLD} + \left(1-\rho\right)\beta^{S}W_{it}^{S} + \varepsilon_{it}^{WORLD}$$

where $\bar{W}^{WORLD}$ is the appropriately weighted mean of the two group-level endowments, normalized across periods.

Global inequality is defined as the variance of W_{it+1}^{WORLD}:

$$\mathrm{Var}\left(W_{it+1}^{WORLD}\right)=\mathrm{Var}\left(\rho\beta^C W_{it}^C+\bar{W}^{WORLD}+\left(1-\rho\right)\beta^S W_{it}^S+\varepsilon_{it}^{WORLD}\right)$$
$$=\rho^2\beta^{C^2}\mathrm{Var}\left(W_{it}^C\right)+\left(1-\rho\right)^2\beta^{S^2}\mathrm{Var}\left(W_{it}^S\right)+2\rho\left(1-\rho\right)$$
$$\mathrm{Cov}\left(W_{it}^C,W_{it}^S\right)+\sigma_{\varepsilon WORLD}^2$$

Because shocks are i.i.d., the covariance of W_{it}^C and W_{it}^S is zero. Thus, we have that global inequality in time period t is

$$\mathrm{Var}\left(W_{it+1}^{WORLD}\right)=\rho^2\beta^{C^2}\mathrm{Var}\left(W_{it}^C\right)+\left((1-\rho)^2\beta^{S^2}\mathrm{Var}\left(W_{it}^S\right)\right)$$

In the steady state, global inequality can be written as

$$\mathrm{Var}\left(W_i^{WORLD}\right)=\rho^2\beta^{C^2}\sigma_{\varepsilon C}^2/\left(1-\beta^{C^2}\right)+(1-\rho)^2\beta^{S^2}\sigma_{\varepsilon S}^2/\left(1-\beta^{S^2}\right)$$

What this tells us is that in the long run, global inequality is a function of each group's institutions, population frequencies, and the variance in individual-level shocks for each group. Importantly, initial endowments do not explain global inequality in the long run.

Thus, we can think of history acting in two ways: Institutions affect the degree of mobility in the wealth distribution within a group, and institutions affect group-level endowments for both groups through extractive historical encounters between the two. The latter are important if we believe group outcomes are not at the steady state. Ultimately, however, the model suggests that shocks can wipe away the initial endowment differences so that they do not characterize global inequality in the long run. We may reasonably think of institutions as more persistent than endowment differences, and in the model this is indeed the case. In the long run, institutional divergence holds more explanatory power for global inequality than endowments. Nonetheless, as I will show in the following section, much of the scholarship on historical encounters and subsequent inequality tends to emphasize divergence in endowments rather than in institutions.

Endowments

In his watershed 1944 work *Capitalism and Slavery,* historian Eric Williams proposed that profits from the slave trade and slave plantations funded the

British Industrial Revolution. When slavery no longer served the interests of capital, he argued, the alliance of capitalists and abolitionists brought the institution down. But the first part of his thesis launched an inquiry into the importance of slavery for British economic development. Although Williams's detractors argued that the profit rates from the slave trade were overestimated, or that the size of the sector was too small to have a significant effect on the rest of the economy, economic historians tend to accord some role for slavery in British growth during this period.[6] Furthermore, if as Inikori argues, African or West Indian demand for key industrial products ran high, then even a small sector can contribute to the restructuring of the British economy.[7] A similar argument has been made in the context of British colonization of the African continent.[8]

The mechanisms for slavery's effects range from the direct influx of profits from the slave trade and plantation production in the Americas to a spillover effect of slavery on related industries in the economy, including shipping, textiles, maritime insurance, and finance.[9] These spillover effects may imply a large effect of slavery on growth even if direct profits from the trade and plantations were small.

Newer arguments in global history have focused on spillovers, including into innovation, thus challenging the notion that a small trade or sector can only have small effects on the economy. If cheap access to raw inputs fueled innovation, then political and economic ties to extractive institutions abroad can lead to sustained economic growth, amplifying the divergence in endowments. This is no better illustrated, perhaps, than by the textile industry in the United Kingdom. The key commodity that highlights these spillover connections and the importance of overseas colonies is cotton. Cotton produced by slave labor in the United States, or in India under increasing colonial control, played a major role in British economic development. Hanlon documents, for example, how the Civil War shock to the supply of U.S. cotton dramatically reduced the relative price of Indian to U.S. cotton. Imports of Indian cotton increased dramatically, but technological innovations that reduced the cost of processing Indian cotton kept pace. The result was that Indian cotton prices rebound despite no corresponding decrease in the import ratio. Britain's secure access to Indian cotton thus played a role in ensuring that these innovations took place at a time when the end of slavery in the United States threatened to remove a critical input into the British textile industry.[10] Indeed, after the U.S. Civil War, Britain continued to dominate cotton production into the early twentieth century.[11]

Others have looked at the role of slavery on financial market development. Gonzalez, Marshall, and Naidu use historical business reports for Maryland to show that slave owners were more likely to start new businesses than were their nonslaveholding peers, supporting a model where lenders prefer slaves as collateral, due to their greater liquidity and mobility when compared to land.[12] Rosenthal studies the rise of accounting as a science in the United States and locates the early influence of accountants on plantations. The professionalization of accountants and bookkeepers and the development of accounting as a field was spurred by planter demand for bookkeeping and the expertise that accountants developed through working on plantations.[13]

Less discussed in the economic history literature are the effects of slavery on the advancement of modern medicine. In the eighteenth century, physicians inoculated patients against smallpox by transferring bodily material from a mildly infected person into an open puncture wound on an uninfected individual. In Cuba and other parts of Spanish America, both orphans and slaves were used as vessels for the transmission of vaccines, carrying the vaccine in pustules on their arms. Gonzalez documents the high correlation between slaves and number of persons vaccinated in Cuba during the early nineteenth century. Fears of disease spreading from slaves to the rest of the population induced rigorous vaccination procedures at the ports. The rising importance of slavery in the Cuban economy spurred demand for physicians and surgeons, leading to very high per capita levels of medical professionals. When the stock of orphans used for vaccine transmission ran out, slaves could be purchased to ensure that the chain of human transmission would not be broken. Slave ships and trading routes provided a natural avenue for scaling the vaccination of populations in Spanish America.[14] These pieces of evidence suggest a potentially large total-factor-productivity effect of slavery. Spurring medical advancement and management science affects all factors, making all more productive.

Economist William Darity characterizes this relationship between growth and extraction in Africa and the Americas as modern Europe's "original sin." But for how long do "original sins" matter? According to the model described in the previous section, although endowment differences matter in the short and medium run, in the long run these endowment differences are wiped out by repeated shocks to the wealth accumulation process. In the end, the rules that incentivize wealth accumulation and govern redistributive policy (the β term in the model) persist while endowment differences fade. In other words, if Europe's original sins are its initial endowment divergence, the claim on these endowments from a globally redistributive perspective grow infinitely small with time. Eventually, once the economy reaches steady state, only institutional differences matter.[15] But at what point does an economy reach steady state? I explore this puzzle in the context of U.S. slavery in the following section.

Shocks versus Persistence

Piketty documents the blow that the two World Wars dealt to the capital / income ratio, but perhaps no modern war managed to eradicate an entire form of wealth as effectively as the American Civil War did. In a matter of years, the most dynamic form of capital held by southern wealth holders, slave capital, became a historical artifact. Thus, the Civil War serves as the quintessential shock to historical endowments as defined in the previous section. What was the effect of abolition on the distribution of wealth in the postbellum period? Was this shock sufficient to blur the lines between "citizens," the southern elites, and "subjects," including poor whites and freed persons, in the U.S. South?

The data for answering this question have become increasingly available due to the ongoing digitization of historical U.S. Census returns by genealogical societies and the Integrated Public Use Microdata Series (IPUMS). Using the IPUMS census data, Dupont and Rosenbloom test the extent to which slaveholders remain in the top end of the southern wealth distribution after the Civil War.[16] In contrast to earlier scholars, who, using more limited data, find the strong persistence of a southern planter class after the Civil War, Dupont and Rosenbloom report more mixed results. In the South, less than half of the top 5 percent of southern wealth holders in 1870 were in the top 10 percent in 1860, suggesting a moderate degree of churn in the Southern wealth distribution. Ultimately, with the wiping out of slave wealth, a somewhat modified set of individuals rose to the top by 1870. Importantly, wealth mobility was lower in the North over the same period.

Still, Dupont and Rosenbloom report that about a third of wealthy south-erners from 1860 retained their status in 1870, a seemingly high number given the extent of the shock that the Civil War precipitated.[17] The authors' results suggest a society on the path to a steady state where initial endowment differ-ences between citizens and subjects in this context cease to matter for the distribution of wealth. Further, Ager, Boustan, and Eriksson find that slave wealth, which is persistent before the Civil War, ceases to predict wealth in 1870 while real estate wealth continues to do so.[18]

In a working paper, I find results that are nevertheless consistent with the persistence of some form of southern slaveholder advantage on a much longer time scale.[19] Drawing on the complete-count U.S. slave schedule from 1860, which enumerates approximately 430,000 slaveholders, and the complete-count U.S. Census from 1940, I run an initial test inspired by Clark's work on socioeconomic mobility and surnames.[20] I find a positive correlation between slave wealth and modern income for the nearly 40,000 surnames from the 1860 slave schedules matched to southern surnames in 1940. The combination of this evidence with Dupont and Rosenbloom raises a puzzle. Did former slaveholders in the South experience an eco-nomic resurgence in the decades after the Civil War?[21]

A persistent effect of slavery on the wealth and income distribution would not be out of place amid ample evidence suggesting that extractive institutions cast long shadows—an empirical pattern I discuss in greater de-tail in the following section. In the context of U.S. slavery, Blackwell and coauthors find nonlinear effects of slavery on twentieth-century political and cultural outcomes that plausibly fit in with slaveholding dynasties re-turning to prominence long after the Civil War. Using variation in cotton suitability as a source of random variation in large-scale slave plantation ag-riculture, the authors find that a higher proportion enslaved in 1860 pre-dicts greater identification with the pre-southern-realignment Democratic Party and negative racial attitudes toward African Americans today. The re-lationship peaks in the early twentieth century, consistent with southern redemption and reversals of Reconstruction being strongest in previously slave-intense parts of the South. These political realities may carry over into the income distribution, resurrecting slaveholder dynasties and entrenching them in the structure of southern elites.[22] After their most important form of personal wealth transformed into a free labor force, formerly slaveholding dynasties may have substituted into obtaining political power, which could then be used to subjugate recently freed slaves anew and restore their economic status in future periods.[23]

These recent advances in the literature on slaveholding and mobility after the Civil War suggest that endowments are indeed susceptible to shocks, recalling Du Bois's obituary to the slaveocracy: "With the civil war, the planters died as a class." Yet in 1940, slaveholdings of surnames from 1860 appear to be correlated with income. Furthermore, the long legacy of slavery in southern politics is clear: places with more slaves in 1860 were less likely to vote for Barack Obama in 2008. Thus, even if endowment advantages fade, the institutions that produce those advantages can have a lasting impact on economic and political outcomes long after the institution has officially ceased to exist. In the next section, I discuss the relationship between institutions and inequality in more depth. In particular I look at the relationship between extraction during colonization and subsequent tax infrastructure in former European colonies.

Institutions and Inequality

Why do institutions matter for global inequality? First, institutions are key for understanding comparative economic development: historical encounters have produced institutional divergence that affects inequality both between and within groups of global citizens and subjects. I review the former, which has received a fair amount of attention in the institutions literature. Next I analyze in depth the relationship between institutions and inequality through the impact of colonization on tax infrastructure. In addition to serving as a key redistributive policy tool, income taxation yields gold-standard data regarding the distribution of income within a country, primarily because they are not top-coded as many household surveys are. Using a common proxy for the type of colonial institutions in a country from the institutions literature, I measure the effect of historical institutions on data I have collected regarding the introduction of an income tax in thirty-two former colonies and on the coverage of income taxes in the world wealth and income database maintained by Piketty and collaborators. Using these data, I demonstrate a systematic relationship between institutions and tax infrastructure that emphasizes the detrimental legacy of extractive institutions on the distribution of income as well as the very government structures that might let us measure it.

Institutions, or the rules that govern economic, social, and political behavior, have profound explanatory power for uneven global development over time, a theory that economists, including Douglass North and Acemoglu, Johnson, and Robinson, have developed at length.[24] Over the past couple of decades, economists have increasingly leveraged natural experiments in history to measure the impact of institutions on economic development.[25] In one highly cited work, Acemoglu, Johnson, and Robinson approach disease mortality at the time of European colonization as a large-scale version of one such natural experiment in institutional variation. Given the lack of European knowledge about how infectious diseases such as yellow fever or malaria spread, the natural environments faced in different would-be colonies provides in their view an exogenous source of variation in where Europeans could settle. The ability to settle determined the incentives for Europeans to build particular kinds of institutions. Where high mortality rates prevailed, settlement was unlikely, and extractive institutions were characterized by slave-based production of cash crops and limits on the franchise. Where mortality rates were lower, Europeans tended to settle and establish relatively inclusive institutions, including checks and balances in the political system and an emphasis on private property protection.[26]

This initial institutional divergence determined by disease environments is predictive of economic institutions and performance today. Among former colonies, places where the disease environment prevented Europeans from settling have less secure property rights and lower GDP per capita today. By contrast, places where mortality rates for Europeans were lower performed relatively better. Thus, the authors interpret these empirical results as supporting a hypothesis that inclusive institutions improve long-run economic performance while extractive institutions do the opposite.

The difficulty is that institutional innovation and initial spurts of economic growth in Europe did not occur in a vacuum, but instead precisely during the period of European exploration and conquest of much of the rest of the world. The boost in wealth from colonial acquisitions and the slave trade helped secure inclusive institutions in Europe by empowering a merchant middle class with the ability to offset the power of the crown.[27] This pattern extends to later periods of growth in the New World. Within the

Americas, places with more inclusive institutions benefited from extractive activity along extensive frontiers, including appropriation of indigenous land and annihilation of local populations.[28] In short, growth relies on inclusive institutions, but it may also be linked to the availability of extractive economic opportunity elsewhere.

Consider Britain's rising merchant class, which placed checks on monarchical power at home and also had the distinction of being the most prolific slave traders in all of Europe. Similarly, the expansion of democracy in the Netherlands coincided with their brutal campaigns to establish monopoly control of the spice trade in Southeast Asia. These periods of history serve as "critical junctures," watershed historical periods where initial institutions determine how societies respond to sources of economic opportunity. But the fodder for inclusive institutions in one society may be the foreclosing of those same institutions in another; this was the case in particular for West Africa, the Caribbean, and Southeast Asia, subsequent to British and Dutch incursions.

One straightforward way to measure the impact of colonization on within-group inequality is to look at the effect of colonial institutions on tax infrastructure. A government's capacity to tax income is a strong signal of its ability to provide public goods and to redistribute income to mitigate inequality. Lack of a tax infrastructure corresponds to states where social programs are sparse, barriers to entry are rampant, and elite incomes go unbridled.

A key barrier in examining the effect of different institutions on inequality is that the types of institutions in a region may be correlated with the availability of data on economic outcomes. Atkinson attempts to fill in some of these gaps using colonial tax data for several former British colonies in Africa. The data are themselves a legacy of an extractive arrangement between the British metropole and the colonies. They only allow an analysis of the very upper echelon of the wealth distribution and generally shed light on settler colonial officials as opposed to the native residents. Studying these numbers at the top reveals that inequality was high in a number of these colonies, even among the very elite segment of society for which tax data were available. While this work fills in a void for understanding income inequality dynamics globally, we are left with the glaring absence of more than 90 percent of the population who are not represented in these data. Further, we still do not know what the effect of the colonial system on the distribution of wealth implies for colonies versus noncolonies. I explore this issue in the last part of this section.[29]

Focusing on formerly colonized countries, I provide some direct suggestive evidence on the institutional persistence mechanism behind weaker tax and statistical infrastructure in poor countries. Specifically, I look at the relationship between historical European settler mortality rates in former colonies (the measure created by Acemoglu, Johnson, and Robinson) and the first year of income taxation for thirty-two former colonies. Recall that these disease-mortality figures provide as-if random variation in the ability of Europeans to settle in the areas encountered during the age of exploration. This ability to settle subsequently determined the type of institutions set up in the colony. Places with low settlement tended toward extractive institutions with little accountability to the local populace. In places with greater settlement, colonists faced incentives to set up inclusive institutions that favored their own prospects for economic success. For the outcome variable, I collect data on the first year of income taxation from a variety of academic sources. I am able to find the first year of income tax legislation for thirty-two former colonies for which I also have European settler mortality rates.[30]

Figure 20-1 plots the relationship between colonial institutions as proxied by logged settler mortality rates and the first year of income taxation. Observations are grouped by equally sized bins of settler mortality rates, and the y-axis shows the average first year of income taxation for each bin. The plot indicates a positive correlation: the more extractive the colonial institutions, the later the introduction of the income tax in that country. Because personal income taxation is a key government tool for curbing inequality, extractive colonial institutions persist through contemporary institutions that have limited capacity for redistribution or revenue generation for social programs. Within-group inequality thus depends on the types of institutions set up during the historical encounter of colonization.

The second way that institutions matter for global inequality is in determining the quality of our information about inequality. The World Wealth and Income Database (WID) maintained by Piketty and collaborators aims to track the evolution of income and wealth for more than 40 countries throughout the world.[31] This leaves about 150 countries unrepresented in the database, and these are concentrated in South America, Africa, and Eastern Europe. The lack of data for many formerly colonized countries prevents a

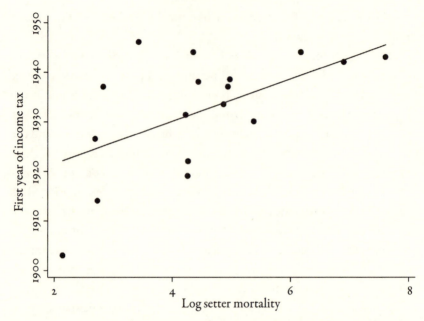

FIGURE 20-1: Relationship between colonial settler mortality rates and introduction of income tax.

Note: Personal income taxation is a key government tool for curbing inequality. The positive correlation here indicates that the more extractive a country's colonial institutions, the later its introduction of the income tax.

full assessment of the impact of historical institutions on inequality and wealth. But lack of coverage is itself a form of data. Coverage in the database requires a well-developed tax infrastructure. Typically, early implementation of a personal income tax is a prerequisite for a country to offer a long series of wealth and income data.

Figure 20-2 relates settler mortality to years of coverage in the WID. The plot, which bins observations in the same manner as Figure 20-1, indicates that the more extractive the institutions in the colonial era, the lower the country's coverage in the WID. The perverse takeaway here is that the more extractive the colonial institutions in a place, the less we know about the distribution of income in those places today. The knowledge we produce on inequality thus suffers from a bias of focusing on places where information about inequality is available. Yet clearly the availability of data is systematically influenced by institutions. Lack of coverage is prob-

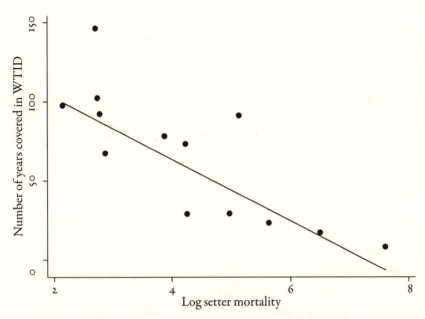

FIGURE 20-2: Relationship between colonial settler mortality and years of coverage in the WTID.

Note: Countries with more extractive institutions in the colonial era tend to have lower coverage in the World Wealth and Income and Database. Knowledge of inequality thus suffers from a bias of focusing on places where information about inequality is available.

ably related to shorter duration of the tax system and lower redistributive capacity, while quantitative analysis may unconsciously shy away from places where we lack detailed data on the income distribution. Thus, our understanding of what determines inequality is shaped by the places where we can measure it.

The findings discussed above suggest a direct role for historically extractive institutions in shaping the wealth distribution through their impact on subsequent tax infrastructure as well as our production of knowledge about that inequality. Because taxation is a key redistributive policy tool of governments, these results suggest an impact of extractive institutions on inequality in formerly colonized countries. Institutions have direct bearing on property rights and the degree of mobility within a society. Institutional change may lead to tax or land reform that redistributes assets and lowers inequality directly. Such change could level the political playing field so that the poor have a mechanism for improving their economic position relative to elites. There is also a value to information. Transparency about the income distribution makes gross inequalities more politically costly and could galvanize support for redistribution.

Finally, policies that seek to address global inequality without acknowledging the role of history may be limited in their efficacy. We may need more flexible global redistributive instruments, tailored to diverse betas, in order to account and compensate for the historical trajectories that affect inequality between and within groups of citizens and subjects.

Global Redistribution with History

This chapter offers a framework for relating history, through initial endowments and institutional legacies, to contemporary patterns of global inequality. Wealth accumulation is by its nature dynamic, but history plays a larger role than simply providing us with an initial capital stock. If we parameterize past institutions with β, the intergenerational persistence coefficient from the model introduced earlier, and allow one group's initial wealth to depend on its own past institutions and those of other groups, we capture the effects of the many critical junctures throughout history discussed earlier in this chapter, where one group's extractive practices have contributed to a stark divergence in outcomes between groups today.

I have called these groups the world's "citizens" and "subjects," terminology I have borrowed from Mamdani's work on institutional segregation in colonial Africa. Those with representation in the political system that governs them, who do not live under constant fear of expropriation, for whom the rules of the game are clear and consistently applied, are the world's citizens. They broadly enjoy the returns to their economic activity and have a decent chance of moving up the economic ladder because of the openness and inclusivity of their society's political and economic institutions. Those who remain at the mercy of powerful individuals instead of under rules that apply to all, where expropriation is the norm rather than the exception, are the world's subjects. There is little mobility; instead, even survival may come at the cost of subjugation to an elite.

As we have seen, it is not enough to understand the impact of extractive activity on the distribution of past endowments. In the long run, these differences in endowments will have limited explanatory power for global in-equality. But whether an economy has reached steady state is up for debate. I explored this question in the context of slaveholding in the United States. Economic historians have debated the extent to which slave wealth con-tinued to confer advantages on the descendants of slaveholders after the Civil War. Dupont and Rosenbloom find that the Civil War resulted in higher churning of the wealth distribution in the South compared to the North. Still, I find evidence that wealth advantages may persist well into the twentieth century by looking at slaveholder surnames in the 1860 slave schedule and the 1940 complete count U.S. Census. The evidence can be interpreted in a couple of different ways. On the one hand, the evidence suggests the United States is not at a steady state when it comes to groups that grew in prominence from historical extraction. On the other hand, there is some evidence that slave-holder dynasties, having lost their primary form of wealth due to the war and changes in the political system, substituted into politics and may have re-gained power during the early twentieth century.

This is just one of the many ways that past institutions condition con-temporary wealth distributions. Furthermore, this example highlights the fact that institutions are the result of the strategic action of agents. The ability of a group of elites to hold onto or regain power is contingent on a number of factors. In the case of the U.S. South, the civil rights movement may have suc-ceeded in turning the tide against the southern elite by removing the teeth of institutional approaches to subjugation in the region. Thus, while southern wealth endowments under slavery were hit hard by the Civil War, an institu-tional channel of persistence can explain the reconstituted wealth inequality between citizens and subjects in the postbellum South.

In the next section, I drew on the institutional theory of growth to dem-onstrate why historical extractive institutions have bearing on global wealth patterns between and within citizen and subject categories. In former colo-nies, institutions directly condition inequality through tax infrastructure. Income taxes were introduced later in countries that faced historically extractive institutions. Taking coverage in the WID as an alternative measure, I show that coverage in the database is lower for places with historically ex-tractive institutions. With income taxation as one of the government's key tools to raise revenue for social programs or redistribute, this institutional legacy may have direct explanatory power for wealth inequality. Without a tax infrastructure, even a benevolent state that wishes to redistribute will be unable to do so. This redistribution can further politically empower poorer individuals in society. Without such an infrastructure, society remains up for capture by a narrow elite. These institutional effects may be much longer lasting than endowment differences. According to the model presented earlier in the chapter, in a steady state it is past institutions, rather than endowment differences, that continue to influence the contemporary distribution of wealth. From a policy perspective then, the question is less about addressing Europe's "original sin" than about confronting the legacy left by extractive institutions, particularly those that emerge out of critical junctures.

What would it mean to redistribute across institutional differences? A global wealth register such as Zucman has proposed would help piece together the owners of wealth in the parts of the world where capital is primarily foreign-owned.[32] But this still leaves the blank spots in the WID that nothing other than incorporation into an income tax infrastructure can mend. These blank spots are sure to correlate with underdevelopment and massive inequality within these societies, where income and capital returns flow to the top echelon, which also forms part of the global elite that a potential global wealth tax would help identify.

Rather than merely redistributing endowments through a global wealth tax, globally redistributive policy ought to force citizens to reckon with the arbitrary historical forces that prevented subjects from realizing the fruits of economic growth. Strengthening and improving institutions in the places in the world where "subjects" are most at the mercy of a powerful elite could have ripple effects. Global labor standards, for example, could do well to begin shifting the surplus from global capital to global labor in, say, the textile and smart phone industries. Intellectual property, migration, and health and educational policies could be reweighted toward the losing geographies of the past 500 years. Thus, what this chapter aims to convey is that beyond redistribution of wealth, integrating the institutions faced by the world's citizens and subjects, given their shared history, is a step toward reducing global inequality that merits study and implementation.

Going forward researchers need to focus on two things. One, we need more quantitative analyses of historical encounters and institutional divergence. When and how have historical encounters between groups of economic actors produced institutional divergence? Two, we need policy proposals that take into account institutional divergence and work toward extending institutional privileges to global subjects. The question that should be asked is, "What can be done to tether the rising institutions of citizens to those of subjects?" Reparations based on endowments will be insufficient and their effect transitory. The redistribution that will have a lasting impact is institutional desegregation: an extension of economic and political rights to citizens and subjects alike.

TWENTY-ONE

Everywhere and Nowhere: Politics in Capital in the Twenty-First Century

ELISABETH JACOBS

Capital in the Twenty-First Century is at once a work of radical political economy and an argument rooted in deeply traditional economic assumptions. Politics is everywhere and nowhere in Piketty's story of the relationship between economic inequality and growth. In this chapter sociologist Elisabeth Jacobs examines this tension. She asks: How can we have both fundamental laws of economics and historically contingent, institutionally bound processes that shape the relationship between the distribution of economic gains and the pace of economic growth? How does research from political science, political sociology, and related disciplines shed light on the apparent contradictions inherent in Piketty's rough theory of politics in *C21*? What questions remain unanswered, and how should policy makers be thinking about political reform in the context of an economic policy agenda to spur equitable economic growth going forward?

Politics are everywhere and nowhere in Thomas Piketty's *Capital in the Twenty-First Century.* On the one hand, there is Piketty the radical political economist. Early in his introduction, he declares that "the history of the distribution of wealth has always been deeply political, and it cannot be reduced to purely economic mechanisms," suggesting that the history of inequality "is shaped by the way economic, social, and political actors view what is just and what is not, as well as by the relative power of those actors and the collective choices that result."[1] These are deeply political claims, broadly supported by decades of research in political science and political sociology. Yet, as *Capital* unfolds over nearly 700 pages, Piketty returns repeatedly to the idea of a "fundamental force for divergence," the fact that the rate of return to capital (r) consistently outpaces the growth rate for the economy as a whole (g).[2] This dynamic makes it "almost inevitable that inherited wealth will dominate wealth amassed from a lifetime's labor by a wide margin, and the concentration of capital will attain extremely high levels— levels potentially incompatible with the meritocratic values and principles of social justice fundamental to modern democratic societies."[3]

How can these two claims be simultaneously true? How can we have both a fundamental force for divergence (r > g) while simultaneously understanding the history of inequality as actively shaped by political mechanisms? In other words, what is the role of politics in Piketty's *Capital*, how does it mesh with the current state of the literature on the politics of economic inequality, and what questions does Piketty's game-changing volume leave unanswered? My goal in this chapter is to provide an overview that touches on all three of these broad questions. In the first section, I provide a brief analysis of the role of politics in *Capital*, with an eye toward assessing both the strengths and the weaknesses in his theoretical approach, and the implications for the strengths and weaknesses of his empirical analyses. In the second section, I provide a review of the contemporary research on the politics of inequality, with an eye toward assessing how Piketty's arguments both inform and are informed by (or not) this growing field of study, and attention to opportunities for future research based on the issues raised by Piketty. In the third, concluding section, I provide suggestions for a political reform agenda informed by Piketty's work in *Capital*.

Politics and *Capital in the Twenty-First Century*

Piketty traces the rise in inequality in wealthy countries over the course of the twentieth century to an increase in the share of income claimed by the top 1 percent. In explaining rising inequality in rich nations, Piketty's decomposition highlights an increasing share of income accruing to capital ownership, and an increasing share of labor income accruing to corporate executives and financiers. He argues that this increased share of labor income going to top earners is not economically useful but instead a rent in the classic economic sense, in that it is not increasing economic growth and is generally above and beyond its productive value. Piketty defines the return on capital as the pure return to passive ownership, which in turn means that both the labor income and capital income accruing to the top 1 percent are arguably not "productive" in the sense of generating broadly shared growth.

Piketty repeatedly shows that, except for the brief period between the two World Wars and the 1970s, the rate of return on investments has tended to be greater than the rate of economic growth. In other words, the great period of the growing middle class, the golden age of prosperity for all, amounts to what one magazine reviewer calls "a historical blip."[4] The analysis in *Capital* is not the first to note that the distribution of economic resources during the intra-war period may have been a historical anomaly rather than the norm. For instance, labor economists Claudia Goldin and Larry Katz's historical analysis of wage inequality suggests that earnings were uniquely "compressed" between the 1940s and 1960s as compared to later periods, and term the intra-war period "The Great Compression."[5] Where Piketty shines is in his careful empirical documentation of the rise of capital inequalities. Piketty argues that social democrats and others who believe that the state played a role in creating and sustaining this golden age are largely delusional. For Piketty, the central reason the balance between inequality and growth seemed in check during the postwar era was simply the sheer levels of destruction of capital in the war. This annihilation of capital temporarily wiped out the ability of rentiers to collect on their assets, and allowed for the illusion of a new, friendlier form of capitalism that benefited all while simultaneously growing the economy. In other words, rising tides don't really lift all boats. As the impacts of World War II began to wane, capitalism picked up again where it left off, and the inexorable march toward inequality continued.

Specifically, *Capital* carefully illustrates the share of income going to the very top of the distribution from 1900 through 2010, in what is perhaps the most comprehensive treatment of cross-national income data to date. While the share of income taken by the upper decile has varied across a wide range of countries, the general trajectory is essentially the same—falling rates across the globe between the Gilded Age and the 1970s, and then a fairly relentless upward climb. Notably, however, some countries (such as Sweden) are still below their 1900 levels, while others are well on their way toward returning to those peaks. In some cases, notably the United States, the top decile's income share was higher in 2010 than at the peak of the

Gilded Age. Some of this increase in inequality reflects the astronomical earnings accorded to "supermanager" corporate executives and money managers, especially in the United States. Much of it, however, reflects a widening gap in nonwage income driven by corresponding trends in wealth inequality. Wealth inequality in the United States has been steadily increasing since the 1970s, with the top decile of the income distribution holding about three-quarters of the nation's assets in 2010. European trends roughly mirror those in the United States, though wealth inequality dropped more sharply in Europe following the wars, and the return to prewar levels has occurred at a slower pace. Piketty attributes this to the violence of the European midcentury experience, and the slower pace of postwar socioeconomic transformation.[6]

For decades, policy thinking in the United States and beyond has been dominated by what one sharp-penned commentator deems "magical thinking"—a belief that, left to its own devices, capitalism naturally generates broadly shared growth and prosperity.[7] Piketty's careful empirical assessments suggests that, with rare exceptions, the rate of return on rewards to capitalism accrue highly unevenly, concentrate advantage among the few, and ultimately outpace the rate of growth. In other words, growth doesn't automatically translate into shared prosperity. In the very long run, based on Piketty's projections, the inequalities generated by the natural dynamics of capitalism will ultimately overwhelm growth entirely, societies will stagnate, and progress will ultimately stop completely.

Where are politics in the story laid out by *Capital in the Twenty-First Century*? Everywhere, and nowhere.

Capitalism has its own fundamental logic, according to Piketty. On the very first page of his treatise, he declares: "Capitalism automatically generates arbitrary and unsustainable inequalities that radically undermine the meritocratic values on which democratic societies are built."[8] The key tell here is Piketty's use of the word "automatically," which betrays the author's deep roots in the economics profession. The popular press—some in mainstream economics as well—labeled Piketty as a radical, but the political economy of *Capital* is in fact in many ways a deeply traditional economist's view of the interaction between economics and politics.

Important critiques of this idea of an "underlying market dynamic" come from within economics. For instance, economist Daron Acemoglu and political scientist James Robinson note that "the quest for general laws of capitalism is misguided because it ignores the key forces shaping how an economy functions: the endogenous evolutions of technology and of the institutions and political equilibrium that influence not only technology but also how markets function and how the gains from various different economic arrangements are distributed."[9] Moreover, they argue, though Piketty "discusses the role of certain institutions and policies, he allows neither for a systematic role of institutions and political factors in the formation of inequality, nor for the endogenous evolution of these institutional factors."[10] Acemoglu and Robinson point out that the focus on the ownership and accumulation of capital distracts from key societal characteristics that are fundamental to determining their economic development and the extent of inequality. For instance, both Uzbekistan and Switzerland have private ownership of capital, but these societies have little in common in terms of prosperity and inequality because their political and economic institutions differ so sharply. In fact, Uzbekistan's capitalist economy has more in common with avowedly noncapitalist North Korea than with Switzerland.[11]

Acemoglu and Robinson's arguments echo the turn toward comparative institutionalism and the development of a rich literature on the "varieties of capitalism" that took flight in political science circles in the early 2000s. For instance, political scientists Peter Hall and David Soskice argue that capitalist economies are characterized by two distinct types—coordinated market economies (such as Germany and Sweden) that rely heavily on nonmarket interactions for coordination between firms, and liberal market economies (such as the United States and the United Kingdom) that coordinate actions primarily through markets.[12] Institutions—not only legal structures, but also informal rules and common knowledge acquired by actors through history and culture—shape firm strategy, capacity for innovation, social protections, as well as the employment and income distribution. In the next section I will offer a more in-depth review of the ways in which the varieties of capitalism literature has investigated the cross-national rise in economic inequality. For now, however, suffice it to say that *Capital*'s sweeping generalizations about the fundamental laws of capitalism gloss over some significant differences between market economies that come about vis-à-vis the institutional foundations for managing the inequalities generated by capitalism.

Piketty makes a concerted effort to take the role of the state seriously. Indeed, he introduces *Capital* as a book of political economy, and the title alone indicates that Piketty could be read as the successor to Karl Marx, introducing a theory of political economy meant to describe the contemporary dilemmas of our time that has the heft to provide a framework for policy solutions. He repeatedly suggests that policies and institutions play a central role in explaining economic trends, and thumbs his nose at his fellow economists for their insularity and obsessions with mathematics, which he views as "an easy way of acquiring the appearance of scientificity without having to answer the far more complex questions posed by the world we live in."[13] Government is a major player in *Capital,* because it is government that imposes taxes and provides social insurance—key components for taming capitalism, protecting meritocracy, and allowing democracies the freedom to achieve their best purposes. Piketty's statistics document the role of the "social state," and he dedicates a full chapter to exploring the key question "What is the role of government in the production and distribution of wealth in the twenty-first century, and what kind of social state is most suitable for the age?"[14] His analysis traces the rise of the role of the state in the decades following World War II.

And yet, Piketty offers no systematic analysis of or explanation for why the state has contracted and expanded over the course of time in terms of its interventions in economic and social life. *Capital's* treatment of politics is description, not theory. In short, "government" is not synonymous with politics. Ultimately, what is missing from Piketty's analysis is a systematic analysis of the relationship between civil society and the state, in order to understand how high inequality in wealth translates into high inequalities in power.[15] How do the wealthy operate to translate their economic interests into political interests? Under what circumstances do the nonwealthy have voice and influence?

Moreover, Piketty's analysis of the role of the state is remarkably sanitized of any questions of power dynamics. Take, for example, his concession, "Of course, the role of government has been constantly challenged since the 1970s."[16] The use of passive voice here is telling. Who has been challenging the role of government, why, and to what end? These are questions that political science has made a great deal of progress toward answering in the last decade, as I detail in the next section. Yet Piketty's perspective on power in society glosses over much of this work. To the extent that Piketty takes politics into consideration in his analysis, it is through his conviction that a majority of citizens must be convinced that government can and does work on behalf of their interests, in order for democracies to implement the new policy tools necessary for tackling the problems created by capitalism: "New instruments are needed to gain control over a financial capitalism that has run amok . . . [b]ut it will be impossible to convince the majority of citizens that our governing institutions (especially at the supranational level) need new tools unless the instruments already in place can be shown to be working properly."[17]

Piketty's implied political theory appears to be deeply rooted in faith in the power of deliberative democracy. In his discussion of the role of the state in mitigating inequality through taxes and social insurance, he notes that "questions [of abstract principles of social justice] will never be answered by abstract principles or mathematical formulas. The only way to answer them is through democratic deliberation and political confrontation. The institutions and rules that govern democratic debate and decision-making therefore play a central role, as do the relative power and persuasive capabilities of different social groups."[18] Deliberative democracy is certainly a powerful and important goal for strong democratic societies. Indeed, as political theorist Amy Gutman argues, "deliberative democracy affirms the need to justify decisions made by citizens and their representatives," with this "reason-giving imperative" driven by a need for democracies to implement policies with "reasons that are accepted by free and equal persons seeking fair terms of cooperation."[19] Piketty's Habermasian faith in the power of deliberative democracy reflects a desire for inclusive critical discussion, and an uncomplicated belief that such a discussion is possible in light of the social and economic power structures, including institutions, of our time.[20]

Political scientist Miriam Ronzoni astutely notes that *Capital* reflects a friction between Piketty's diagnosis, "which seems to draw a rather bleak picture of the power of capital in the early 21st century" and his suggested cure, "which seems to rely on the optimistic hope that, once well-minded citizens will have recognized the problem, the only hurdle will be to find the right policy to fix it."[21] Ronzoni has a "suspicion that Piketty seems to hold on to a social-democratic optimism of sorts at all costs, whereas his findings push him in a different direction." By social-democratic optimism, she means "on the one hand, optimism about the role of policies and institutions in taming capital ... ; on the other, the persuasion that what politics is fundamentally about is making citizens understand what the problems are in a well-minded, reasoned dialogue, and then they will be persuaded to do the right thing."[22]

Take, for instance, Piketty's proposed policy panacea: a wealth tax. After spending 500 pages describing the forces that drive capitalism toward inexorable inequality and, ultimately, unsustainable slow rates of growth, Piketty suggests that the best possible solution for taming capitalism's ill effects is a progressive global tax on capital, coupled with high levels of international financial transparency. Piketty acknowledges that this is a "utopian idea," and argues for incrementalism. While a global tax on wealth may or may not be an advisable policy goal, the point here is that Piketty's proposal belies the space between his own analytic lens and that of students of the impacts of inequality on power, institutions, and representation. Given the interplay between economic inequality and political power, what is the path toward creating a global tax on capital? In Piketty's view, citizens simply need to understand his ideas regarding the dark side of unfettered capitalism, and then they will demand better twenty-first-century solutions from their governments. In practice, economic inequality generates durable political inequalities that cast a long shadow over Piketty's optimism regarding the feasibility of a global capital tax.

Piketty is motivated by a deep concern for the consequences of economic inequality on democracy. He says this repeatedly, yet he gives us only hints of why we should care. For instance, he warns of the potential for violence stemming from extreme inequality: "There will always be a fundamentally subjective and psychological dimension to inequality, which inevitably gives rise to political conflict that no purportedly scientific analysis can alleviate. Democracy will never be supplanted by a republic of experts—and that is a very good thing. ... Expert analysis will never put an end to the violent political conflict that inequality inevitably instigates."[23] In other words, inequality is uncomfortable—potentially dangerously so for democracies. But can we say more? Why, exactly, is Piketty so concerned with the implications of economic inequality for democracy? And why should we care?

Piketty's concerns for democracy in the context of capitalism's inherent drive toward excessive economic inequality fall under three loose categories.

First, Piketty worries that inequality violates basic principles of equity in voice and representation. It is morally reprehensible in a democracy for citizens not to have equal voice and influence, and he suggests that the skewed nature of control over economic resources may be poisoning the promise of equality representation. Second, if inequality means government is less able to provide for public goods, respond to public problems, and in turn less capable of promoting broadly shared prosperity, then we should be deeply concerned about the impact of economic inequality on the political process. Finally, Piketty worries that excessive inequality creates violence. It is not clear whether this is in fact the case so long as levels of economic well-being remain high enough, however. This is a long-running debate in America, beginning with political commentator Werner Sombart's suggestion in "Why Is There No Socialism in the United States?" that relatively high levels of absolute well-being in America mean that "on the reefs of roast beef and apple pie, socialist utopias of every sort are sent to their doom."[24] Suffice it to say that contemporary political debates in Europe and the United States suggest that although revolution may not be imminent, levels of vitriol and anger are remarkably high.[25]

Putting *Capital* in Conversation with the Research

While Piketty may believe economic inequality poses a threat to democracy, he does little to spell out the mechanisms through which inequality might erode the promise of democratic governance. This is a rapidly evolving field, with research advances from political science and political sociology that help inform Piketty's perspective on the relationship between economic and political inequality. In this section I borrow a conceptual framework from Albert Hirschman's classic *Exit, Voice, and Loyalty* in order to provide an overview of the literature organized across three broad channels through which the economic inequality detailed by Piketty may be creating durable political inequalities.[26] First, economic inequalities create inequalities in *voice* that in turn undermine the promise of democracy. Second, economic inequalities create inequalities in the opportunity for *exit,* creating spatial inequalities that undermine shared prosperity and commitments to shared principles. Finally, economic inequalities create inequalities in *loyalty* that pose a fundamental challenge to the very concept of the nation-state on which democracy is premised. Note that while Piketty's focus skews toward France, mine for the purposes of this chapter is on the United States, and particularly with an eye toward the utility of Piketty's ideas for the period from the 1970s through the present. My focus on the American case is in no small part because American political science has been especially aggressive in researching the connection between economic and political inequality, which means that much of the available data on the politics of inequality comes from the United States.

Voice

Economic inequality has translated into unequal voice in American democracy. For decades political scientists viewed American democracy as characterized by Ronald Dahl's inclusive pluralism: individuals are represented by interest groups, many interest groups compete in the political sphere, and government's main role is to act as a mediator between those groups.[27] Today's reality is far more reflective of political theorist E. E. Schattschneider's pathbreaking critique of pluralism, encapsulated in his astute observation that "the flaw in the pluralist heaven is that the heavenly chorus sings with a strong upper-class accent."[28] As is perhaps obvious to any casual observer of American politics, the voices of the wealthy are far more powerful than those farther down the income distribution.

Political voice matters for democracy for two key reasons. First, political voice communicates information to policy makers. Second, political voice provides incentives to policy makers.[29] In a democracy characterized by highly unequal political voice, as is the case in America today, policy makers are thus receiving both flawed information and distorted incentives. The result is a dysfunctional democracy that perpetuates the very economic inequalities that marred it in the first place. Political inequality of voice occurs through two main channels: individuals and organized interests.

Well-educated and affluent individuals are active in many ways that provide voice and influence, while less-advantaged Americans are not. Consider the political activity of the wealthy as reported by the Survey of Economically Successful Americans (SESA), which, as the only representative sample of affluent Americans to date, presents a unique window into the political preferences, beliefs, and behavior of truly affluent Americans. Wealthy Americans tend to be far more politically active and engaged than the average citizen. About 48 percent report that they "attend to politics most of the time," and 99 percent reported voting in the most recent election. 41 percent attended a political meeting, rally, speech or dinner, 68 percent contributed money to politics, and a remarkable 21 percent either helped solicit or actively bundled political contributions—not a common act among ordinary citizens. About half of SESA respondents had initiated contact with an elected official or their staff in the last six months, with a particular focus on members of Congress. Over 40 percent had contacted their senator, 37 percent had contacted their representative, and, perhaps most remarkably, about a quarter had contacted a senator or legislator from another state. In total, 47 percent of the wealthy had made contact with at least one federal legislator's office in the last six months. Contacts with executive department officials, White House officials, and officials at regulatory agencies were less frequent, but not uncommon. Most respondents supplied the first name of the officials with whom they were in the most frequent contact (as in "Rahm" for former White House Chief of Staff and current Chicago mayor Rahm Emanuel). 44 percent responded to an open-ended question about the nature of the contact with a description of a specific and narrow economic self-interest (such as "to try to get the Treasury to honor their commitment to extend TARP funds to a particular bank in Chicago," "I own stock in several banks. I was concerned about legislation he was drafting that I think could be harmful for the banks.")[30]

Voice matters. Policy outcomes are far more responsive to the preferences of the wealthy than to anyone else. Sociologist Marty Gilens and political scientist Ben Page analyze nearly two thousand policy outcomes over a period of more than two decades and conclude that "economic elites and organized groups representing business interests have substantial independent impacts on U.S. government policy, while mass-interest groups and average citizens have little to no independent influence."[31] Indeed, the collective preferences of economic elites were fifteen times as important as those of ordinary citizens. Similarly, political scientist Larry Bartels finds that the behavior of senators as measured by congressional roll call votes aligns more closely with the preferences of the rich than the poor.[32] An implication of this work is that one reason inequality has risen so much over the last thirty years is simply that democracy does not respond to the preferences of those at the bottom of the economic distribution.

If elite Americans and ordinary citizens had the same policy preferences, then perhaps this inequality in representative voice would not be an issue. Yet data suggest that this is very much not the case. Page and his collaborators catalog a host of differences between the policy preferences of the wealthy versus those of the general public, and the overall picture presented is one where the wealthy (a definition that arguably includes Piketty's patrimonial middle class) are substantially more economically conservative (though also more socially liberal) than the general public.[33]

Perhaps most notable in the context of Piketty's work are the attitudes of the wealthy toward economic inequality and their preferences for what ought to be done (and not done) about it. Fully 86 percent of wealthy Americans are aware of the fact that income and wealth have grown more concentrated. And half (56 percent) did not accept the proposition that "large differences in income are necessary for America's prosperity." About two-thirds (62 percent) said that differences in income are too large. While wealthy Americans believe that pay for hedge fund managers and CEOs of large corporations should be reduced, and that pay for low-wage occupations should be increased, they emphatically (87 percent) do not view it as the role of government to "reduce the differences between those with high incomes and those with low incomes." 83 percent said that the government should not redistribute wealth by heavy taxes on the rich. In contrast, 46 percent of the general public say that reducing income differences should be the role of the government, and 52 percent say the government should accomplish as much by heavy taxes on the rich.[34] In short, the wealthy aren't going to go for Piketty's global wealth tax, or even for a more modest domestic version.

Note that social science is badly in need of better data on the political and policy attitudes and behavior of the very wealthy. Median wealth of a SESA respondent is $7,500,000, and the average (mean) was over $14,000,000. Respondents' average income is $1,040,140. About a third of SESA respondents report income of $1,000,000 or more. Other political attitudinal data sources top-code top incomes above the 90th percentile, making it impossible to distinguish between the merely rich and the super-rich. The fact that the SESA is literally the only known representative data source for studying exactly those high-flying elites that Piketty spends time focused on suggests a major future research agenda, beginning with data collection efforts aimed at better understanding the political behavior and preferences of the super-rich in a far more rigorous and richly textured way.[35]

An individual lens on redistributive politics is too simple a version of the story, however. The political voices of organized interests are even less representative than those of individual voices. This is where an institutional perspective comes in, framing politics as a complex game in which organizations with competing interests use whatever tools the political system offers to shape the terms of the country's basic governing institutions, especially its economic institutions. This battle, which plays out not only through individual preferences and actors but also on an institutional level, has profound impacts on the distribution of income and wealth. And it helps explain the particular shape of the growth in economic inequality over the last several decades in ways that competing explanations cannot.

Political scientists Jacob Hacker and Paul Pierson argue this case cogently in *Winner-Take-All Politics,* which takes seriously Piketty and Emmanuel Saez's data on the rise of the top 1 percent, much of which was released prior to the publication of *Capital.*[36] Hacker and Pierson note that the skills-biased technical change argument that dominated economics departments throughout the 1990s and 2000s cannot explain the pulling away of the very top of the income distribution, and look to politics and policy to help make sense of the unique shape of rising income inequality. It is worth noting that Hacker and Pierson were not the first to question the skills-biased technical change argument, which posited that the development of personal computers and related information technologies had privileged certain types of skill above and beyond others, and that the resulting differences in labor demand in turn resulted in rising earnings inequality. As economists David Card and John DiNardo note, the skills-biased technical change argument fails to explain why wage inequality stabilized in the 1990s despite continued advances in computer technology, among other things.[37] Hacker and Pierson take the critique one step further and suggest that skills-biased technical change does little to explain the runaway-rich phenomenon, an observation that Piketty makes as well. Unlike Piketty, however, Hacker and Pierson's theory of the case for the rise in inequality hinges on politics, and a theory of how politics serves as a channel through which markets are shaped.

Hacker and Pierson make three main claims. First, rather than focusing narrowly on the "electoral spectacle," research needs to also focus on the politics of agenda-setting. Second, organizations are central to under-standing which policy changes happen—and, in a nod to the undeniable importance of electoral politics, organizations are key for understanding the dynamics of electoral contests as well. Third, understanding the importance of the rules of the game is key to making sense of the politics of agenda-setting. Each of these arguments demands a bit more clarification.

First, elections are not the only moments of policy choice. As political scientist Henry Farrell aptly notes, "While elections clearly play a role in determining *who* can set policy, they are not the only moment of policy choice, nor necessarily the most important. The actual processes through which policy gets made are poorly understood by the public, in part because the media are not interested in them."[38] Contemporary political scientists, including students of the relationship between economic inequality and political inequality, have focused mainly on electoral politics rather than on broader forces that shape the political landscape. This is likely in part because of the broad-based availability of electoral data, as well as mass opinion data from individuals based on survey data. But looking at ques-tions of the role of politics in shaping inequality requires a broader focus, which is Hacker and Pierson's main project. The key question is not the final two or three specific policy options on the table at a given moment, but in-stead the prior question of whose preferred range of options forms the "choice set" from which actors are allowed to select.[39] Attention to agenda-setting makes clear the importance in the shifts in the organization of American political life that have happened over the course of the last half century, as they've changed who sets the agenda and therefore what battles actually play out in the political arena.

Second, understanding the organizational structure of a given polity is key for understanding how economic inequalities are created and sustained through politics. The weakening of key organizational pillars of American civic life has played an important role in the transformation of political economy over the last half century. Middle-class democracy rested on unions and cross-class civic organizations that served two central functions. First, these organizations gave working families information about what was at stake in central policy debates. Second, they offered political leverage to in-fluence those debates. In the absence of strong civic institutions, working fam-ilies face serious challenges connecting policy makers' actions and rhetoric with the strains in their own economic lives—and they are ill-equipped to receive a narrative for how policy might ease those strains.

Sociologist Theda Skocpol summarizes: "Voluntary civic federations have both pressured for the creation of public social programs, and worked in partnership with government to administer and expand such programs after they were established."[40] The decline in civic federations that began in the 1960s was ushered in by numerous social and economic forces, including the rise in television advertising, polling, and focus groups, and the orchestration by consultants paid huge sums of money raised from big donors and impersonal mass mailings. At the same time that civic federations were on the decline, so were unions. The decline in labor was ushered in by both active political forces and changes in the structure of the economy, and represented a shift in bargaining power that has arguably both lowered wages in the bottom half of the distribution and enhanced the ability of those at the top to command rents. These factors come together to mean minimal voice for the concerns of working families. Skocpol archly concludes: "Among elites, new kinds of connections are alive and well. Privileged Americans remain active in think tanks, advocacy groups, and trade and professional associations, jetting back and forth between manicured neighborhoods and exotic retreats. Everyone else has been left to work two or three poorly paid jobs per family, coming home exhausted to watch TV and answer phone calls from pollsters and telemarketers."[41]

The unraveling of civic society in America is not the only factor affecting the power structures that influence politics and in turn inequality. At the same time that the organizational life of every-day middle-class families has fundamentally shifted and eroded, the organizational prowess of narrow corporate interests has grown. As political scientist Lee Drutman's research documents, corporate interests are dramatically overrepresented in Washington by nearly every measure. Corporate lobbying expenditures total about $2.6 billion per year, more than the combined budget required to operate the House and Senate. For every $1 spent on lobbying by labor unions and public interest groups, large corporations and their associations spend $34. Of the 100 organizations that spend the most on lobbying, 95 consistently represent business. In other words, the organized voice of American business dramatically overshadows those who speak primarily for working families. And, as Drutman argues, corporations now increasingly focus on bringing government in as a partner, instead of advocating primarily on behalf of keeping government out of business's affairs (as they once did).[42] Increasingly, Congress relies on corporate lobbyists for information. And in a time when corporate power so dwarfs that of working families, this has real implications for democratic politics.

A long tradition in political science has focused on the importance of organized interests in informing the power dynamics that influence policy outcomes, much of it coming from historical institutionalist scholars contributing to the growing body of literature on the varieties of capitalism. Contrary to most economics (including, at times, Piketty), historical institutionalists view policy and political outcomes as the result of a complex, interdependent set of historically embedded factors—not a product of a parsimonious linear model along the lines of what Piketty presents.[43] As political scientists Bo Rothstein and Sven Steinmo put it, "As humans build, adapt, and change social, political, and economic institutions, they can—and do—change history. In short, there is no singular set of laws that apply to all actions at all times with which one can predict all past— or even less, future—events. Humans, unlike atoms, planets, and clouds, make their own history, in part by deliberately creating different social, economic, and political institutions."[44] The power dynamics that go into creating these various institutions are informed by organized interests. For instance, political sociologists Francis Castles, Walter Korpi, and others have argued that politics are the pursuit of economic self-interest, and suggest that various democracies pursue different public policy regimes because different organized interests possess different "power resources" with which to fight for their constituencies' self-interest.[45]

Steinmo's cross-national comparison of tax regimes is an instructive example of what the historical institutional perspective can add to our understanding of how organized interests may play a key role in shaping economic inequality over time. Steinmo demonstrates that cross-national differences in these three tax regimes are best explained by an examination of the institutional structures through which the tax systems were created. In particular, Steinmo focuses on the concentration of power within both labor and the business community. These organizational structures "provide the context in which interest groups, politicians, and bureaucrats define their policy preferences."[46] In Sweden, both business and labor interests are represented by highly concentrated, highly organized, powerful interest groups with a strong voice in government decision making. In the United States, business and labor interests are diffuse—and, as documented by Hacker and Pierson, among others, organized labor's role in politics has further diffused and dissipated at the same time as organized corporate interests have grown.[47]

The resulting tax policies reflect the different countries' organized interest structures. Sweden's tax regime is "a broadly-based, financially-lucrative tax system that carefully generates maximum revenues while impinging on Sweden's capacity for economic growth and profit generation as little as possible. Efficiency and revenue-yield considerations permeate the system as a whole."[48] In contrast, taxation in the United States is characterized by a fragmented, complex, and loophole-ridden process that reflects organized interests' ability to manipulate and take advantage of the opportunities provided by America's unique and highly diffuse political institutions.

Understanding why organized interests in the United States have been able to take advantage of the political process requires taking seriously the institutional structure of politics in a second way as well. American politics is generally characterized as an institutional setting in which power is fragmented and authority is broadly dispersed. As political sociologists Margaret Weir and Theda Skocpol summarize, the United States "possesses a distinctive complex of weak national administration, divided and fragmentary public authority and non-programmatic political parties."[49] Particularistic tax expenditures in the United States are a direct result of the fragmentation of political authority in the United States. Unlike parliamentary regimes' centralized powers to make tax policy, in the United States tax policy is written by Congress, a highly fragmented decision-making institution. And, absent strong political parties that can decisively influence representatives' electoral fortunes, members of Congress are responsive to their local constituencies in a way that make them uniquely vulnerable to locally defined demands and special interest group pressures. This fragmentation magnifies the power of the wealthy, further contributes to their outsized influence on policy, and perpetuates a cycle of inequality whereby economic inequality leads to political inequalities.

In the absence of strong institutional support and linkages to a strong national party, individual members of Congress have become "independent political entrepreneurs" in search of support for election from groups that are often particularly interested in specific legislative outcomes—including tax amendments.[50] Fragmentation is inherent to American political institutions, woven into the Constitution beginning with James Madison's vision of a political system whereby conflict between a multiplicity of interests generated compromise and a lack of extremism.[51] As Steinmo summarizes, the unanticipated consequences of Madisonian factionalism are a key explanatory factor: "Madison's fragmented political institutions provide a profoundly important variable for explaining the complexity, low revenue yield, and ultimately the distribution of effective tax in the United States."[52] As a result, the U.S. tax code is complex and highly skewed toward the interests of the wealthy and powerful.

The overarching point here is that the structure of organized interests combined with the nature of a country's political institutions can play a key role in shaping policy, which in turn can play a key role in shaping inequalities. Tax policy is but one example; one could trace out a similar story for regulatory policy, including both labor market and financial regulation, both of which would have meaningful implications for economic inequality. Politics create markets, to return to a recurring theme. Indeed, the literature on the varieties of capitalism has a great deal to say about how institutions have shaped the income distribution in different ways across different political systems (aka countries)—but the focus to date has been nearly entirely on the ways in which different social protection regimes have shaped the poverty rate and the fate of the middle class.[53] Virtually no scholarship, to the best of my knowledge, has focused on the implications of the "varieties of capitalism" thesis for top-end inequality. *Capital* opens this up as a question with important implications for researchers committed to understanding the role of political institutions in shaping economic distribution, particularly in light of Piketty's findings suggestive of capital concentration across diverse types of capitalist regimes.

Hacker and Pierson's third main argument around understanding the influence of politics on inequality emphasizes the importance of the "rules of the game," a fundamental component to any institutional account. The rules of the game make it more or less easy to get policy through the system, by shaping veto points. Institutional rules provide policy actors with opportunities to both try to get policies that they want through the system, and to stymy policies that they do not want to see enacted.

This perspective illustrates the importance of understanding, not only which decisions are made, but which decisions are not made because they are opposed by parties or interest groups. These nondecisions are particularly underappreciated and understudied, because of the strong bias against "nonresults" in the social sciences—in fields dominated by statistical analysis and an increasing focus on big data, it is very difficult to successfully build a research agenda around studying cases where nothing happened. Yet understanding those cases of inaction are critically important to understanding the rise of economic inequality in the context of American politics over the last half century.

Over time, legislation can become untethered from its intended purposes, as society changes. Alternately, policies can turn out to have significant unanticipated loopholes. This "policy drift" is a classic example of what sociologist Steven Lukes calls the second face of power: non-decision-making.[54] In the face of power imbalances, these changes over time can have a meaningful impact on the shape of economic policy both as it pertains to addressing the problems of working families and as it pertains to enhancing the power of the superwealthy. How the wealthy exert political power (and continue to enhance their economic status) via policy drift can happen through a number of channels. One is the agenda-setting channel described above: organized combat via organized interests.

Another is more subtle and (arguably) less calculated: research tells us that economic inequality has resulted in dramatically higher rates of political polarization, polarization in turn creates gridlock, which in turn privileges the status quo.[55] For instance, economists John Duca and Jason Saving build on political scientist Nolan McCarty's groundbreaking work on the relationship between income inequality and political polarization to show that income inequality has resulted in a more polarized Congress, and a more polarized Congress has in turn resulted in greater income inequality.[56] Note, however, that a research agenda connecting the dots between political polarization and wealth inequality (the capital inequality that Piketty carefully lays out) remains virtually untapped, and future research would do well to mine this vein.

In short, economic inequality translates into unequal political voice. And unequal political voice not only shifts the policy priorities of government, but arguably erodes the capacity of the government to actually get much of anything done at all. For those who are actively interested in preserving the status quo, this is a great deal. But for those who are looking for change—and for whom an active state serves a key role in facilitating economic well-being—this is a gloomy situation. The research on this front is nearly unequivocal, though this does not mean that there aren't important new avenues for work, particularly for those looking to understand the channels through which capital inequalities translate into unequal voice and in turn shape markets vis-à-vis politics.

Exit

Inequalities in voice are one path through which political inequalities translate into economic inequalities and back again into political inequalities. Inequalities in options for political exit are another key pathway through which the feedback loop between economic and political inequalities may operate.

Albert Hirschman recognized the importance of exit for socioeconomic cohesion and healthy political institutions nearly fifty years ago, as the engines of the contemporary age of inequality were just beginning to rev up. It is worth quoting at length:

> The traditional American idea of success confirms the hold which exit has had on the national imagination.... Success is in fact symbolized and consecrated by a succession of physical moves out of the poor quarters in which [a successful individual] was brought up into ever better neighborhoods.... [T]he ideology of exit has been powerful in America. With the country having been founded on exit and having thrived on it, the belief in exit as a fundamental and beneficial social mechanism has been unquestioning. It may account for the strength of the national faith in the virtues of such institutions as the two-party system and competitive enterprise; and, in the latter case, for the national disbelief in the economist's notion that a market dominated by two or three giant firms departs substantially from the ideal competitive model. As long as one can transfer his allegiance from the product of firm A to the competing product of firm B, the basic symbolism of the national love affair with exit is satisfied.[57]

Hirschman's instincts about exit have played out in dramatic ways over the last half century. For the purposes of this section, I use "exit" as a proxy for place-based segregation and its impacts on the feedback loop between economic and political inequalities. In other words, economic inequality has come along with dramatic segregation whereby rich Americans live highly separate lives, distinct from those of the rest of the country. In a sense, the rich have taken advantage of the opportunity for "exit" from all manner of public institutions, which has the potential to erode a collective vision of what "counts" as a public good.

Economic inequality has translated into dramatic economic segregation in the United States. Americans increasingly live lives segregated by class, and experience public goods in an increasingly disparate way. The unrest in Ferguson, Missouri, in 2014 and Baltimore in 2015 highlighted in dramatic fashion the place-based experience of inequality and government. Multiple days of protests and collective civil disobedience in these two primarily African-American communities in the wake of police brutality elevated the disparate experiences of government lived on a daily basis in America, in ways that map onto racial and economic inequalities. The rise in economic inequality has coincided with a similarly dramatic rise in economic geographic segregation.

Numerous studies have documented this trend. Geographers Richard Florida and Charlotte Mellander find that Americans are increasing sorting by class—defined by income, education, occupation, and a composite measure of socioeconomic status—between cities and metro areas, and also within those cities. Moreover, economic segregation is largely conditioned by the decisions of more advantaged groups. The wealthy are even more segregated than the poor, and by a substantial margin.[58] Middle-income neighborhoods have disappeared, and been replaced by concentrated poverty and concentrated affluence. Sociologists Kendra Bischoff and Sean Reardon have documented the rise in geographic economic segregation. They found that in 1970 roughly two-thirds (65 percent) of Americans lived in middle-class neighborhoods, and that today that figure is just slightly more than 40 percent. Over the same period, the share of families living in affluent neighborhoods rose from 7 to 15 percent, while the share living in poor neighborhoods grew from 8 to 18 percent.[59]

As social commentator Ta-Nehisi Coates cogently argues, the geography of inequality in America did not simply arise out of nowhere. Nor was it entirely the consequences of "free market" dynamics at play. To the contrary, the geography of inequality was, and remains, politically generated, and po-litically sustained. In the United States, the geography of inequality maps tightly onto the geography of racial segregation, which intertwines with economic inequality to cast an enduring shadow over the promise of shared prosperity in the United States. Racial segregation was baked into the New Deal, an underappreciated dark underside of the policy package lauded for reducing economic inequalities and bolstering economic growth in the wake of the Great Depression. The New Deal–created Federal Housing Ad-ministration (FHA) was key to building up the capital stocks of millions of middle-class Americans by providing mortgage insurance that contributed to a drop in interest rates and a reduction in the amount of money required for a down payment. At the same time, the FHA played a key role in gener-ating enduring capital inequalities and neighborhood inequities by estab-lishing the principle of "redlining"—essentially boxing African-American home buyers into less-desirable neighborhoods and excluding them from the primary mortgage market. In a classic example of policy creating mar-kets, the private insurance industry then adopted the government's policy as standard practice.[60]

Sociologists Mel Oliver and Tom Shapiro summarize the consequences of politically created durable capital inequalities: "Locked out of the greatest mass-opportunity for wealth accumulation in American history, African-Americans who desired and were able to afford home ownership found themselves consigned to central-city communities where their investments were affected by the 'self-fulfilling properties' of the FHA appraisers: cut off from sources of new investment[,] their homes and communities deterio-rated and lost value in comparison to those homes and communities that FHA appraisers deemed desirable."[61] Even though redlining is now illegal, the consequences for capital accumulation—wealth inequality—reverberate today. For instance, residential segregation fostered by redlining artifi-cially lowers demand, placing a forced ceiling on home equity for African-Americans who own homes in nonwhite neighborhoods. Because whites are far more able to give inheritances or family assistance for down pay-ments, due to historical wealth accumulation, white families buy homes and start accumulating capital on average eight years earlier than similarly situ-ated black families. And because whites are more able to give financial as-sistance, larger up-front payments typically lower interest rates and lending costs for white families as compared to blacks.[62] Much of this inequality in capital accumulation can be traced back to an early policy decision, which shaped access to capital in important ways.

The broader points to keep in mind here are threefold. First, capital is continually subject to definition and redefinition by political actors, and access to capital is governed by institutions. Second, early policy decisions regarding the rules of capital accumulation and who has access can have long-term reverberating effects, not only in terms of accumulation but also in terms of the absence of accumulation. And, third, those dynamics are often located in specific places, creating a political geography of inequality with enduring consequences for political power and economic opportunity.

Economist Raj Chetty and his colleagues' widely cited study on the geography of economic mobility offers another indication of the important of place-specific mechanisms through which economic inequities may be perpetuated. Using administrative records on the incomes of millions of children and their parents to describe three decades of intergenerational mobility, Chetty and his coauthors find that mobility prospects vary dramatically across U.S. localities (defined by "commuting zone" for the purposes of this study). High-mobility areas have less income inequality, less residential segregation, better primary schools, greater social capital, and higher levels of family stability.[63] All of these factors are potentially shaped in important ways by local political institutions, and by enduring legacy of earlier political and policy decisions.

This economic segregation—and the "exit" option for the rich—has potentially huge consequences for public service investment, and for the role of government more generally. Economic inequality may reduce the provision of public goods because heterogeneous societies are unable to compromise on common public goods and services. There is some empirical evidence to support this hypothesis, though most of the literature investigates the consequences of racial segregation rather than the consequences of economic segregation—an indication of the need for more work looking at the implications of economic segregation as distinct from the implications of racial segregation.

For instance, economist Alberto Alesina and his colleagues find that shares of spending on productive public goods (such as education, roads, sewers, and trash pickup) in American cities are inversely related to the city's ethnic fragmentation, independent of other socioeconomic and demographic characteristics of the city as a whole. Alesina and his coauthors conclude that "ethnic conflict is an important determinant of local public finance."[64] More recently, research by political scientist Daniel Hopkins suggests that racial and ethnic diversity reduces localities' willingness to raise taxes only when localities are undergoing sudden demographic changes, suggesting that what matters is not diversity per se, but instead the ways in which demographic changes can destabilize residents' expectations and influence local elites.[65]

These recent empirical studies suggest that rising inequality may be eroding the ability of local communities to provide adequate public goods and services (or to provide the tax base necessary for financing such goods and services). But it is worth pausing for a moment to consider the geographic unit of analysis in the context of the aforementioned point regarding rising economic segregation occurring alongside rising economic inequality. Depending on the unit of analysis, rising economic segregation may not necessarily translate into more economically heterogeneous places. Indeed, segregation may mean *less* heterogeneity. This need not translate into more social cohesion or stronger public institutions, however, given the power differentials between low-income communities and wealthier communities. Far more research remains to be done into understanding the relationship between growing levels of economic segregation in an era of high inequality, and the provision of public services. And the channels through which these public services are provided are distinctly political—political institutions, influenced through political power.

Economic segregation has implications for modeling how the provision of public services may function, too. For instance, economists David Cutler, Douglas Elmendorf, and Richard Zeckhauser explore the relationship between the demographic characteristics of a community and the quantities of goods and services provided by its government. They adjudicate between three models of public spending: a traditional "selfish" public choice model in which individuals care only about themselves, a "community preference" model in which an individual's preferred level of spending depends on the characteristics of his or her community, and a sorting process, perhaps best thought of as a "choice" model where individuals choose communities according to their taste for public spending.[66] Note that none of these models take into account the fact that individuals' ability to act in accordance with their preferences may be constrained by their economic status—that is, low-income individuals may be far less able to "choose" their geographic location than those with greater resources. In an age of high inequality, the distribution of the ability to act according to one's preferences may fundamentally alter the relationship between demographic characteristics and the provision of public goods. Given that we know that the provision of public goods has strong ties to future economic growth—education, for example, is a classic public good with strong ripple effects across generations into the healthy growth of the economic as a whole—understanding the implications of economic segregation for the provision of public goods seems a worthy future line of work.

In contrast to earlier work suggesting a role for the geography of inequality in the provision of public goods and services, however, economist Leah Platt Boustan's work finds that growing income inequality is associated with an expansion in government revenues and spending on a wide range of services in United States municipalities and school districts.[67] The contrast between Boustan and her colleagues' work and earlier research, along with the remaining need for additional theoretical clarity about the unit of analysis and the channels through which inequality might translate into public goods provision suggest that much more research is needed on this potential feedback loop between economic and political inequalities.

Loyalty

In Hirschman's classic essay, loyalty is the key ingredient determining whether citizens (or institutions) choose to exercise voice or exit. "The presence of the exit option can sharply reduce the possibility that the voice option will be take up widely and effectively," writes Hirschman, but "Loyalty rais[es] the cost of exit."[68] Hirschman presciently wondered about the impact of globalization on loyalty, writing: "Only as countries begin to resemble each other because of advances in communication and all-around modernization will the danger of premature and excessive exits arise," and suggested that "at that point, a measure of loyalty would keep us in good stead."[69] Hirschman notes as well that "the detail of institutional design can be of considerable importance for the balance of exit and voice."[70] What do high levels of inequality portend for loyalty, and in turn for the politics of inequality? This line of inquiry remains largely unexplored and presents an important open set of questions for researchers committed to better understanding the politics of economic inequality.

Extreme wealth puts a small yet incredibly well-resourced slice of the global population in a position to test various nation-states for their loyalty. Global elites can essentially shop for the destination that will treat their resources most favorably, and exercise the political power that comes with their economic power across national borders. In an era of global capitalism, where capital is highly mobile while labor is substantially less so, global capitalists can shop for the most favorable place to park their money.[71] The political power indicated here is substantial—and potentially distinct from the high levels of capital inequality witnessed prior to the Belle Époque (also sometimes called the Great Moderation) that Piketty notes. In a highly globalized economy, has nation-state loyalty eroded to the point where global flows of capital mean that national governments are consistently held hostage by the threat of exit by moneyed interests?

The recent political debates in the United States over corporate inversions are a concrete example of the erosion of loyalty heightening the likelihood of the exit option and infusing American politics. The practice of inversion involves moving the paper address of a company's residence overseas, typically to a low-tax country, so that the company can avoid paying its fair share of taxes at home. When multinational corporations exploit these tax loopholes, they enjoy the benefits of the American political system (political stability, skilled workers, and so on) but avoid paying the full cost for those benefits. Those decisions erode the American tax base, which in turn may undercut future economic growth by consistently chipping away at the pot of funding available for investments in public goods. The U.S. Treasury department under the Obama administration proposed new regulations aimed at making corporate inversions more difficult, and the public outcry over such practices has gone from a murmur to a full-throated rally cry. At the same time, however, congressional action is necessary to fully put a stop to the practice of corporate inversion in the United States—action that is highly unlikely, given the power dynamics of voice discussed above. Economic policies designed to mitigate high levels of inequality might be straightforward, but the politics of inequality consistently throws a wrench into best-laid plans.

Piketty recognizes that the global nature of capital makes a borderless policy regime desirable, if not necessary. This is part of the motivation for his global wealth tax. Yet the proposal that he sketches out in *Capital* is just that—a sketch—and ignores many of the key details of power and politics detailed in the preceding pages. To put in place the economic policy solutions necessary for jumpstarting growth and slowing the rise of economic inequality, analysts and policy makers would do well do train an analytic lens on the politics of inequality as well as the economics.

Why Care? And What to Do?

Politics, and political institutions, matter a great deal for creating, growing, and sustaining economic inequalities. Politics create markets. Economic inequality poses a threat to democracy, for a variety of somewhat more specific reasons that Piketty illuminates in his book. Research suggests that achieving the promise of democracy may in fact require acting to reduce extreme economic inequalities. Successful interventions on behalf of democracy require thinking hard about political reforms, not simply about economic policy prescriptions. In short, economic and political inequality are trapped in a feedback loop. Breaking this cycle requires smart reforms to political processes, in addition to smart economic policy thinking.

The most promising ideas for political reform focus not on limiting voice at the top, but rather on amplifying voices below the top. Traditional political reform efforts have focused on "getting big money out of politics," because big money is drowning out everyone else. Instead, reform efforts ought to focus on the concept of expanding "political opportunity." Political opportunity focuses on elevating people and ideas to a point where they can be heard amidst all the noise. Somewhere after that threshold is reached, there are likely to be diminished returns to additional spending. As democracy scholar Mark Schmitt summarizes, "Efforts to limit spending at the top end are likely to have less of an impact on opportunity than reforms that help others be heard."[72]

Political opportunity as characterized by Schmitt is characterized by four key dimensions. First, any candidate with a broad base of support, or who represents a viewpoint that wouldn't otherwise be represented, should have the chance to be heard in elections and other contexts, without the support of big-donor dollars. Second, every citizen should have the opportunity to participate meaningfully, not just as a voter, but as a donor, a volunteer, and / or an organizer, or by expressing his or her own views. Third, individuals should feel free to express their own political views, protected from coercion by an employer or other institution. Finally, the system should be structured in a way that encourages organizing people, not just money, especially around issues affecting low- and moderate income voters.[73]

The key to a political opportunity framework is that it serves two important functions for unraveling the deleterious consequences of political inequality. First, it makes the system fairer—by giving voice to the currently voiceless and helping to offset the political influence of wealth. Second, it holds the promise of restoring fluidity and creativity to the political process, as candidates are forced to compete on new axis of conflict and new compromises emerge.

Unlike the prior generation of campaign finance, which aimed to "get money out of politics," political opportunity efforts recognize that money is likely to find its way into politics no matter what. The key is to give those without resources the opportunity to build countervailing power by expanding opportunity. Thus, a movement for a constitutional amendment protecting the right to vote (which, contrary to popular opinion, doesn't actually exist in the U.S. Constitution) would have far more power than a constitutional amendment overturning Citizens United decision, which gave corporations the right to unlimited spending on elections. Why? Because the right to vote is a positive right—rather than a prohibitive, limiting one such as restricting campaign spending—and as such builds focus for movement-building around political participation. Like the failed Equal Rights Amendment movement, a right-to-vote amendment movement could build incremental power by focusing efforts on all of the reasons so many Americans today are disenfranchised, and along the way might contribute to movement-building power for policy efforts to allow for same-day voter registration and to overturn restrictive voter identification laws.[74]

To be sure, efforts focused on electoral reform are only the tip of the iceberg in terms of political reform efforts aimed at reversing the feedback loop between political and economic inequality. The aim is to build countervailing political power such that political equity in turn makes possible reforms to unravel the pernicious economic inequality detailed by Piketty in *Capital*. Until we focus on such solutions, promising economic policy ideas such as Piketty's utopian vision of a global wealth tax are likely to remain a fantasy.

[v]

PIKETTY RESPONDS

TWENTY-TWO

Toward a Reconciliation between Economics and the Social Sciences

Lessons from Capital in the Twenty-First Century

THOMAS PIKETTY

I would like to see *Capital in the Twenty-First Century* as a work-in-progress of social science rather than a treatise about history or economics. It seems to me that too much time is lost within the social sciences on petty quarrels about boundaries and often rather sterile methodological positions. I believe that these oppositions between disciplines can and should be overcome, and that the best way to do so is to address big issues and see how far we can take them, using whatever combination of methods and disciplinary traditions seems appropriate. I could not have hoped for a greater homage to my approach than this group of texts written by specialists from very different horizons and methodological perspectives.[1] Within the framework of such a short article, it is impossible to respond to all of the points raised in this book and to do justice to the richness of these essays. I would simply like to attempt to clarify a small number of issues and refine certain elements that were undoubtedly insufficiently developed in my book, in particular from the perspective of the multidimensional history of capital and power relations, and regarding the role played by belief systems and economic models in my analysis. I will then turn to another important limitation of my book—namely, the fact that it is too Western-centered.

Capital and the Social Sciences

First of all, I would like to briefly summarize what I have tried to do in *Capital* and how the book fits into the history of the social sciences, where several research traditions and schools of thought intersect. It is above all a book about the history of capital, the distribution of wealth, and the conflicts raised by this unequal distribution. My main objective was to bring together historical sources relating to the evolution of wealth and income in over twenty countries since the eighteenth century, thanks to the combined work of some thirty researchers (notably Anthony Atkinson, Emmanuel Saez, Gilles Postel-Vinay, Jean-Laurent Rosenthal, Facundo Alvaredo, and Gabriel Zucman). The primary ambition of my book was to present this historical material coherently. I began with sources and proposed an analysis of the economic, social, political, and cultural processes that could make it possible to account for the evolutions observed in the various countries since the Industrial Revolution. In doing so, I attempted to return the issues of distribution and the inequalities between social classes to the center of economic, social, and political thought.

Nineteenth-century political economy—particularly the works of Thomas Malthus, David Ricardo, and Karl Marx—already placed the issue of distribution at the heart of its analysis. These authors were often motivated by the profound social changes they perceived around them. Malthus was marked by Arthur Young's accounts of poverty in the French countryside on the eve of the Revolution and feared more than anything else that overpopulation would bring about poverty and revolutionary chaos everywhere. Ricardo based his analysis on clear-sighted intuitions about the price of land and the impact of the public debt accumulated by Great Britain following the Napoleonic Wars. Marx accurately observed the profound imbalance between the evolution of profits and salaries in the booming industrial capitalism of the first two-thirds of the nineteenth century. Even though they did not have at their disposal systematic historical sources for studying such evolutions, these authors at least had the merit of asking the right questions. Throughout the twentieth century, economists all too often sought to remove themselves from the social sciences (an illusory temptation, if ever there was one) and to pass over the social and political foundations of economics. Some authors—particularly Simon Kuznets and Anthony Atkinson—nonetheless patiently embarked on the meticulous task of collecting historical data on the distribution of income and wealth. My research directly stems from these studies and has largely consisted of extending the collection of historical data to a broader geographical and temporal scale (an extension that has been greatly facilitated by information technologies, which have made available to us data that was inaccessible to previous generations of researchers).[2]

In my work I also attempt to renew a tradition that used to be very prominent in economic and social history, and in particular in the French-language school of history and sociology that between the 1930s and the 1970s generated numerous studies devoted to the history of prices, salaries, income, and wealth in the eighteenth and nineteenth centuries. I am thinking especially of the major works by François Simiand, Ernest Labrousse, François Furet, and Adeline Daumard.[3] Unfortunately this history (sometimes qualified as "serial") died out before the end of the twentieth century—largely for the wrong reasons, it seems to me.[4] My approach is also inspired by sociological studies on inequalities of cultural capital and disparities in wages, notably those conducted by Pierre Bourdieu and Christian Baudelot (in different but, I think, complementary registers).[5]

Furthermore, in *Capital* I tried to show that it is possible—and, in fact, indispensable—to simultaneously study the evolution of collective representations of social inequality and money in both public debates and political conflicts as well as in literature and cinema. I am convinced that such an analysis of the systems of representations and beliefs about the distribution of income and wealth, however incomplete and preliminary it is within my book, is essential when it comes to understanding the dynamic of inequality. To me this is the central interaction between belief systems and inequality regimes that should be studied more extensively in future research, and which I plan to further study in the years to come. Money and its unequal distribution constitute the supreme social object and cannot be studied from an exclusively economic perspective. In this respect my work is akin to and feeds off the many studies devoted to perceptions of equality and inequality issuing from the fields of political sociology and intellectual history.[6]

In fact, the main conclusion of this work is this: "One should be wary of any economic determinism in regard to inequalities of wealth and income. The history of the distribution of wealth has always been deeply political, and it cannot be reduced to purely economic mechanisms. . . . The history of inequality is shaped by the way economic, social, and political actors view what is just and what is not, as well as by the relative powers of those actors and the collective choices that result. It is the joint product of all relative actors combined."[7]

The central role of politics and the changing representations of the economy is particularly evident when studying the evolution of the distribution of income and wealth throughout the twentieth century. The reduction of inequality observed in Western countries between the 1900s–1910s and the 1950s–1960s is largely explained by the wars and revolutions that marked this period, as well as by the new social and institutional compromise that emerged following such upheaval. Similarly, the rise in inequality observed since the 1970s–1980s owes much to the political and institutional reversal of recent decades, notably in fiscal and financial matters. I also tried to show that the belief systems surrounding the distribution of income and wealth as a function of the economy and society play a central role in our understanding of the structure of inequality in the eighteenth and nineteenth centuries and, in fact, within all societies. Each country has its own intimate history with inequality, and I tried, for example, to show that national identities and the representations each country has of its own economic and historical trajectory play an important role in the complex interaction between the dynamics of inequality and the evolution of perceptions and institutions.[8]

In particular, the "Social Democratic Age in the Global North (1945–1980)" (as it is aptly labeled by Brad DeLong, Heather Boushey, and Marshall Steinbaum in their introductory essay) can certainly be viewed as an unstable historical episode, but it is also a product of deep transformations in belief systems about capitalism and markets. I fully agree with Marshall Steinbaum (Chapter 18) when he stresses that the World Wars and the Great Depression were decisive, not so much in themselves, but because they "discredited the ideology of capitalism in a way mere mass enfranchisement had been unable to do so [in the decades preceding World War I]." The crisis of the 1930s and the complete collapse of the European inter-state competition system during the two World Wars led to the end of the nineteenth-century political regime, which was based upon the laissez-faire ideology and the quasi-sacralization of private property. This radical change in dominant belief systems is of course nothing else than the "Great Transformation" famously analyzed by Karl Polanyi in his 1944 book.[9]

In his illuminating essay, David Grewal (Chapter 19) also stresses the central interactions among ideology, the legal system, and institutional change. In particular, he emphasizes how the political philosophy of the seventeenth and eighteenth centuries first theorized private property as a legal construct and built up an ideology of capitalism to protect it. In my own research, I was particularly impressed by the way the French republican elite in the late nineteenth and early twentieth centuries used the reference to the French Revolution and the rise of modern property rights to oppose progressive taxation (an issue to which I will return at the end of this essay).

This interaction between belief systems and inequality regimes results in a wide variety of political and institutional forms that are often only briefly touched upon within the framework of my book but that play a fundamental role in the dynamics of inequality and warrant further study in terms of their intellectual and political genesis and how they were established in practice. I particularly insisted upon the role of educational institutions and the ways in which they can sometimes reduce or, on the contrary, amplify inequalities,[10] as well as on the role of fiscal institutions, particularly the difficult and fragile emergence of the progressive tax on income, inheritance, and wealth.[11] A large number of other public and sociopolitical institutions also play an important role. These include: the development of the social state in the broad sense;[12] monetary regimes, central banks, and inflation; labor legislation, the minimum wage, and collective bargaining; nationalization, expropriation, and privatization; slavery and forced labor; corporate governance and the rights of salaried workers; the regulation of rent and other forms of control over prices and usurious interest rates; financial deregulation and the flow of capital; commercial and migratory policies; inheritance regulations and property regimes; demographic and familial policies; and so on. I will return to some of these aspects later in this essay.

A Multidimensional History of Capital and Power Relations

Let us now turn more precisely to the notion of capital that I attempt to develop in my book. I have tried to write a multidimensional history of capital as well as of the relations of ownership and domination that accompany different forms of possessions and assets. I attempted to show how, at each stage, the different metamorphoses of capital lead to new social and institutional compromises that enable the relationships between social groups and

547

the relations of production to be regulated. It should be clarified from the outset that this is ultimately just an introduction to such a multidimensional history, because numerous aspects are only outlined in my book.

Unidimensional economic models describing the accumulation of capital, abstract concepts, and equations (such as the inequality r > g, which I think makes it possible to better grasp certain invariables within these metamorphoses) also play a certain part in my analysis. However, this is only a relatively modest and limited role—one that, in my view, corresponds to what theoretical modeling and equations can bring to research in the social sciences. This kind of extreme simplification of the real occasionally isolates some interesting logical relationships between two given abstract concepts. It can be useful, but only provided that one does not overestimate the scope of this type of abstract operation, nor lose sight of the fact that all the concepts in question are ultimately nothing more than socially and historically determined constructions. Theoretical models form a sort of language that is useful only when it is solicited in conjunction with other forms of expression that participate in the same deliberative and conflictual process. I will return below to the specific and limited role that economic models play in my framework—an issue on which I was probably not sufficiently clear in my book, and that has generated some confusion. In my view, capital is best viewed as a complex, multidimensional set of property relations.

As I note as early as the first chapter of *Capital,* where I define the main notions explored in the book, "The boundary between what private individuals can and cannot own has evolved considerably over time and around the world, as the extreme case of slavery indicates. The same is true of property in the atmosphere, the sea, the mountains, historical monuments, and knowledge. Certain private interests would like to own these things, and sometimes they justify this desire on the grounds of efficiency rather than mere self-interest. But there is no guarantee that this desire coincides with the general interest. Capital is not an immutable concept: it reflects the state of development and prevailing social relations of each society."[13]

The fact that the forms assumed by the possession of capital and the nature of ownership rights are historically determined is clearly demonstrated in my analysis of the importance of slavery and slave capital in forms of wealth in the southern United States before 1865, without a doubt the most extreme example of relations of ownership and domination by owners over others.[14] As Daina Ramey Berry rightly stresses in Chapter 6, my book does not devote sufficient attention to the crucial role of slavery in the formation of modern capitalism. I should point out, however, that the estimates of total slave value in the pre–Civil War United States that are reported my book, as well as the comparison with other forms of private wealth, are to my knowledge the first explicit computations attempting to do this kind of comparison and to point out in this manner the central role of slave capital.[15]

The fact that property rights are historically and socially determined is equally evident when I examine the relatively low stock-market capitalization of German companies compared to their Anglo-American counterparts,[16] a phenomenon undoubtedly linked to the fact that German shareholders are less omnipotent than shareholders elsewhere and must to some degree share power with employees, regional governments, and other stakeholders (though this evidently does not prevent a certain level of productive efficiency). This clearly demonstrates that the market value and the social value of capital are two quite distinct things, and the importance of the legal system in shaping property relations.

More generally, I tried to show the multitude of forms assumed by capital and its market valuations throughout history, from agricultural land to real estate and professional, financial, and immaterial modern capital. Each type of asset has its own economic and political history and involves relations of power and specific social compromises. Thus, large-scale movements in real-estate prices and rent levels, whether upward or downward, have played a decisive role in the evolution of real-estate capitalization over the course of the last few decades, just as they did during the first half of the twentieth century.[17] These movements are themselves the result of a complex group of institutional, social, legal and technological forces, including the contrasting evolution of rent control policies and other rules governing relations between landlords and tenants; the changes in economic geography and residential segregation; and the varied rhythms of technical change in construction and transportation compared to other sectors. There are, however, other examples. On several occasions in *Capital,* I examine the importance of petroleum capital and its distribution worldwide, the accompanying relations of domination and military protection (notably in the Middle East), and the impact of this on the sometimes unusual financial investment strategies employed by corresponding sovereign wealth funds.[18]

The hypertrophy of gross asset positions between countries, which has been one of the main characteristics of the process of financial deregulation during the last few decades, is another recurring theme in the book.[19] I also analyze the extremely high levels of foreign assets held by Great Britain and France during the late nineteenth and early twentieth centuries, a time when both countries possessed an important share of the rest of the world. The very substantial rents, dividends, and interest that this brought in—the equivalent, in Belle Époque France, of the production of the country's industrial east— enabled them to finance a permanent commercial deficit while continuing to acquire a growing share of the rest of the world (which did not fail to stimulate tensions between colonial powers). I compare these levels with those reached in the early twenty-first century by the net asset positions of Germany, Japan, China, and the oil-rich countries, which to date remain markedly lower but are rising very rapidly (prompting, in countries such as France, fears of one day becoming that which is owned rather than the power that owns).

On a number of occasions I insisted on the fact that relations of international ownership always come charged with multiple tensions and are light-years away from the calm theoretical models of economists, regulated by natural harmony and mutually profitable exchange. In general, relations of ownership are always complex and difficult to organize calmly within the framework of a political community. It is never simple, for example, to pay rent to one's landlord and peacefully agree on the institutional framework of the relationship and the perpetuation of the situation (hence the multiple systems in place for controlling rent, lengthening leases, and taxing inheritance). But when an entire country is paying rents and dividends to another country, the situation can become even more tense and the means of regulating this relationship are generally less peaceful. This often results in relations based on military domination by those in the position of ownership. Or else the country in the position of being owned goes through unending political cycles in which phases of triumphant ultraliberalism and authoritarianism alternate with brief periods of chaotic expropriation—a phenomenon that has consistently undermined the development of numerous countries, particularly in Latin America and Africa. The peaceful regulation of social inequality and relations of ownership is one of the most important stakes in the construction of a rule of law and legitimate public power, and involves developing norms of justice and complex institutional structures. When inequality and ownership are largely external to a given political community, this construction can find itself lastingly impaired. Economic rationality in fact tolerates the perpetuation of inequality rather well, and in no way leads to democratic rationality.

Public capital also plays a central role in my analysis of the history of capital.[20] This can be positive or negative, depending in particular on political and ideological cycles of public investment and nationalization or, on the contrary, public deficit and privatization. In the former case, public capital diminishes the hold of private capital over national capital and society; in the latter, it reinforces it by adding government bonds to private assets as an additional element of ownership and domination. I also analyze the importance of inflation when it comes to the dynamic of public debt and, more generally, the role of monetary creation and the different operations involving the redistribution of national capital performed by central banks.[21] I stress the diversity of national experiences and trajectories when it comes to public debt, in particular by contrasting the cases of France and Great Britain in the eighteenth and nineteenth centuries and then Germany in the twentieth century—a development that is of interest for the current European context, as countries that never reimbursed the public debts they incurred during the twentieth century (notably France and Germany) explain to countries in southern Europe that they must pay more in interest to bondholders than they invest in their school system for decades to come (just as the British did in the nineteenth century). Phases in which evolutions converge can also be observed. For example, public capital was a significant portion (between a quarter and a third) of national capital in most European countries during the postwar period and has fallen to very low levels over the course of the last few decades (and even to negative levels, as in Italy). In many instances these movements of public debt and privatization favored particularly rapid private enrichment, not only within developed countries, as one would expect, but also and above all in post-Communist countries, beginning with Russia and China.

Throughout *Capital* I tried to show that the history of capital is multidimensional and that each of these categories of assets and possessions involves a wide variety of institutional mechanisms and compromises. Ownership assumes multiple forms that are historically and socially determined and that trace just as many social relationships. The fact that it is also possible to add up all these forms of wealth—by using, for example, the current market prices for the different assets (supposing that they are well defined, which is not always evident)—in order to calculate the total monetary value of the stock of capital in no way changes this manifold reality. This abstract operation can certainly be useful; it enables us, for example, to observe that despite multiple metamorphoses in the forms that capital takes, in the early twenty-first century this total market valuation (expressed in years of national income) appears to have returned to a level nearing that observed in the patrimonial societies that prospered from the eighteenth and nineteenth centuries up until the Belle Époque. This provides a language that enables the overall scale of market valuations to be compared in societies that are otherwise very different from one another. However, such an overarching measurement does not make it possible to take into account the multiplicity of relations of ownership and production that develop in these different societies.

The approach that I develop in my book is in fact only an introduction to a multidimensional history of capital and forms of possession—it neglects a large number of essential aspects and touches on others only briefly. For instance, as Gareth Jones (Chapter 12) rightly points out, it would be beneficial to further examine the geographical and spatial dimensions of capital. Much attention is paid to possessions outside of France and Great Britain, but nothing has been said about possessions within countries—for instance, comparing the northeastern United States and the rest of the country. More generally, it would be useful to vary the scale of analysis, from the national level to the imperial level up to the world economy. In particular, this would make it possible to examine much more directly than I do in my book the impact of colonization on development and the overall effects of domestic and international inequality on the construction of a legitimate public power. As Ellora Derenoncourt (Chapter 20) emphasizes, global integration in the form first of the Atlantic slave trade, and then of direct and indirect European colonial rule over the Americas, Africa, and Asia, has been defined by extraction and a stark imbalance of power, from the 1500s up to the 1960s. My analysis of foreign possessions is largely Western-centered and neglects to study the impact on inequality regimes and state formation in the Global South (an issue on which I will return below).

The Limited Role of Economic Models:
"Domesticated Capital" versus "Wild Capital"

I would now like to clarify what I mean by the *limited* role played by economic models (and in particular by the neoclassical model of capital accumulation and the notion of a production function) in my book and in my research. Suresh Naidu (Chapter 5) offers an interesting distinction between two forms of narratives and interpretative frameworks which (according to Suresh) are simultaneously present in my book: on the one hand, the "domesticated" *Capital* (based on the neoclassical model and the assumption of perfect competition); and on the other hand, the "wild" *Capital* (emphasizing the role of power relations, political conflict and institutional change). Let me make very clear that I feel much closer to the "wild" interpretation than to the "domesticated." Had I believed that the one-dimensional neoclassical model of capital accumulation (based upon the so-called production function $Y = F(K,L)$ and the assumption of perfect competition) provided an adequate description of economic structures and property relations, then my book would have been 30 pages long rather than 800 pages long. The central reason my book is so long is that I try to describe the multidimensional transformations of capital and the complex power patterns and property relations that come with these metamorphoses (as the examples given above illustrate). I should probably have been more explicit about this issue, and I am grateful to Suresh for giving me the opportunity to clarify this important point.

In particular, as David Grewal (Chapter 19) aptly notes, the "two fundamental laws of capitalism" that I present in chapters 3–6 of my book should be viewed as "a way of organizing the data," and nothing more. The "first law" is nothing more than a definition: it says that the capital share α can be decomposed as the product of the average rate of return r and the capital / income ratio β. The objective is simply to help the reader to remember the basic orders of magnitude and logical relations between core concepts (for example, $\alpha = 30\%$ in case $r = 5\%$ and $\beta = 6$). But this does not alter in any way the fact that capital is fundamentally multidimensional, and that rates of return vary enormously across types of assets, societies, and epochs, depending in particular on the institutional and legal environment, the balance of power between owners and workers, and so forth, as the historical narrative provided in my book amply illustrates.

To summarize: models should be used with parsimony—that is, only when we really need them—and their role should not be exaggerated. Models can be useful to organize the data and clarify simple logical relations between basic concepts; but they cannot replace the historical narrative, which in my view must be the real core of the analysis (and which I consider to be the core of my book). The complexity and multidimensionality of historical, social, and political processes in real-world societies are so great that there is no way they can be adequately described by mathematical language alone: one needs to use primarily the natural language of the social sciences (and sometimes the language of literature and movies, which, as I try to show in my book, can be viewed as an additional and complementary way to grasp social and historical realities, just like mathematical language).

The same remarks also apply to the "second law" (according to which the capital / income ratio β tends to approach the ratio s/g between the saving rate and the growth rate, under certain conditions—no change in relative asset prices, no natural resources—and in the very long run) and to the discussion about rising capital shares. According to best available historical series, aggregate capital / income ratios and aggregate capital shares tend to move together: they were both relatively low in the mid-twentieth century, and they were both relatively high in the nineteenth century and the early twentieth century, as well as in the late twentieth century and the early twenty-first century. If we were to use the language of aggregate production functions and the assumption of perfect competition, then the only way to explain the fact that β and α tend to move together in the long run would be to assume an elasticity of substitution that is somewhat larger than 1 over long periods (so that the rate of return r falls less than proportionally as β rises). Standard estimates suggest smaller elasticities (as rightly argued by Devesh Raval in Chapter 4), but they are typically not long-run estimates. It is also possible that technical change and the rise of new forms of machines, robots, and capital-intensive technologies (along the lines described by Laura Tyson and Michael Spence in Chapter 8) will lead to a gradual increase of the elasticity of substitution over time.

Let me make clear, however, that this is not my favored interpretation of the evidence, or at least of the long-run historical evidence. Maybe robots and high capital-labor substitution will be important in the future. But at this stage, the important capital-intensive sectors are more traditional sectors like real estate and energy. I believe that the right model for thinking about why capital-income ratios and capital shares have moved together in the long run is a multisector model of capital accumulation, with substantial movements in *relative* prices, and most importantly with important variations in bargaining power and institutional rules over time.[22] In particular, large upward or downward movements of real estate prices have played an important role in the evolution of aggregate capital values during recent decades,[23] as they did during the first half of the twentieth century. This can in turn be accounted for by a complex mixture of institutional and technological forces, including rent control policies and other rules regulating relations between owners and tenants, the transformation of economic geography, and the changing speed of technical progress in the transportation and construction industries relative to other sectors. More generally, the main reason capital values and capital shares are both relatively high in the late twentieth and early twenty-first centuries is that the institutional and legal systems have gradually become more favorable to capital owners (both owners of real estate capital and owners of corporate capital) and less favorable to tenants and workers in recent decades, in a way that is broadly similar (but with different specific institutional arrangements) to the regime that prevailed in the nineteenth century and early twentieth century. In contrast, the legal and institutional regimes prevailing in the mid-twentieth century and during the "Social Democratic Age (1945–1980)" was more favorable to tenants and workers, which can help explain why both capital values and capital shares were relatively low by historical standards. This does not mean that changing production functions and elasticities of substitution are not important: I am convinced that this form of mathematical language can be useful to clarify certain concepts and logical relations between concepts. But these notions need to be embedded into a broader social-institutional framework and historical narrative if we want to be able to account for observed evolutions. In some cases, institutional change directly interacts with technological change—as in, for example, the decline of unions and the evolution toward a "fissured workplace" analyzed by David Weil in Chapter 9.

Finally, the same remark applies to the relation between $r-g$ and inequality. In my view, the gap between r and g is determined by a complex set of historical, legal, and social forces. In particular, the rate of return is largely influenced by bargaining power and changing institutions, while the growth rate depends upon fertility and innovation, which are themselves determined by a broad set of social and institutional factors. In standard economic models, the fact that r is always bigger than g is mechanically determined by simple technological or psychological factors. For instance, in the benchmark dynastic model of economic growth, the equilibrium rate of return is well known to be given by the modified "golden rule" $r = \theta + \gamma g$ (where θ is the rate of time preference and γ is the curvature of the utility function). For example, if $\theta = 3\%$, $\gamma = 2$, and $g = 1\%$, then $r = 5\%$. In this framework, the inequality $r > g$ always holds true, and it follows mechanically from supposedly universal psychological laws (namely, the existence of human impatience, which implies that r has to be positive even if $g = 0$, and also the fact that $r < g$ would lead utility-maximizing agents to borrow infinite amounts from their future incomes, thereby leading r back above g). Such models certainly capture some of the basic psychological reasons r is bigger than g in historical series. However, the full story is much more complicated and involves a broad set of institutional and social factors, with large historical variations in both the rate of return and the growth rate.

In the same way, dynamic models of wealth accumulation with multiplicative shock can be very useful to understand and quantify why a higher r and a lower g lead to higher steady-state levels of wealth concentration. For instance, as Mariacristina De Nardi, Giulio Fella, and Fang Yang show in Chapter 14, the impact of higher rate of return and lower population growth rate or productivity growth rate is not fully symmetrical. But these models must not overshadow the fact that the relation between rates of return, growth rates, and inequality dynamics is determined by a broad set of political and legal factors that are largely outside the model (and on which formal models have little to say).

Financial Capital and Cultural Capital: Reconciling Marx and Bourdieu

I would now like to turn to another essential aspect of the multidimensionality of capital. Throughout the book, I distinguish between two social hierarchies, that of wealth and that of labor income. Both hierarchies are, of course, closely related and in some societies they largely coincide. However, they are never exactly the same, because the 50 percent at the bottom (some-times designated within the framework of my book as the "lower class" for clarity and to allow for comparisons across time and space), the 40 percent in the middle (the "middle class"), and the 10 percent at the top (the "upper class," within which I frequently distinguish the 1 percent at the very top, or the "dominant class") do not exactly correspond to the same social groups, depending on which of the two hierarchies is being examined. Sometimes they are even completely different, as in traditional patrimonial societies where those in possession of large fortunes are unembarrassed about not working and dominate most of society.

Above all, in each society these two hierarchies mobilize quite distinct mechanisms of domination and inequality production that are potentially complementary as well as cumulative. The hierarchy of wealth is deter-mined by multiple processes that contribute to the accumulation of real-estate, professional, and financial capital, already mentioned above. These include placement and investment strategies, inheritance regulations and property regimes, the functioning of financial and real-estate markets, and so on. The hierarchy of labor income notably depends on rules and institu-tions contributing to the formation of salaries and different work statuses and contracts; the inequality of skills and relations; the functioning of the education system; and, more generally, the hierarchy of cultural capital. Both hierarchies—that of financial capital and that of cultural capital, to put it simply—also correspond to different systems of discourse and justifi-cation. Traditional patrimonial inequality generally does not seek to base its domination in merit or in cultural superiority, at least not primarily. On the contrary, modern inequality aims to justify itself through an ideology resting on merit, productivity, and virtue. This system of justification, based on stigmatizing the "undeserving poor" and what I call "meritocratic extremism,"[24] has ancient origins. It can be traced back to the Middle Ages and perhaps even to the end of slavery, forced labor, and the pure and simple ownership of the poor classes by the rich classes (when the poor person becomes a subject and not just an object, he or she must be pos-sessed by other means).[25] However, it reaches its maximum extension in the modern era. A particularly distinct expression of this can be found in an astounding declaration by Émile Boutmy, who created the École Libre des Sciences Politiques (commonly known as Sciences Po, one of the most elitist French schools) in 1872 and set out its mission: "Obliged to submit to the rule of the majority, the classes that call themselves the upper classes can preserve their political hegemony only by invoking the rights of the most capable. As traditional upper-class prerogatives crumble, the wave of democracy will encounter a second rampart, built on eminently useful talents, superiority that commands prestige and abilities of which society cannot sanely deprive itself."[26]

Are we witnessing in the twenty-first century the emergence of a new inegalitarian model that combines a return to the patrimonial and capitalistic inequalities of the past with extreme forms of domination based on cultural capital, symbolic capital, and blaming the victims of the system? That is in any case one of the hypotheses I formulate in my book. In particular, I note the gaping hypocrisy of contemporary meritocratic discourses. For example, the average income of parents of students at Harvard University currently corresponds to the average income of the wealthiest 2 percent of Americans. In France, the most elitist educational programs recruit their students from among social pools that are barely any larger, and three or four times more public resources are invested in them than in programs open to ordinary students, without anyone batting an eyelid.[27] Besides this privileged access to cultural and symbolic capital, over the last few decades these ruling groups have increased their capacity to award themselves extravagant pay packages and bonuses—with weakened unions and fiscal policies incapable of providing effective resistance.[28]

Recent work by Raj Chetty and Emmanuel Saez in the context of the "Equality of Opportunity" project[29] have shown the extreme inequality of access to higher education in the United States: the probability of going to college rises almost linearly from barely 20 percent for children with lowest-decile parental income to over 90 percent for those with upper-decile parental income. The gap with the official meritocratic discourse and values is particularly abyssal. I fully agree with Eric Nielsen (Chapter 7) that strongly egalitarian policies at the level of early education are part of the solution, probably in conjunction with more transparency and affirmative action policies in higher education admission systems.[30] Note also that the extreme inequality of the U.S. education system is probably a big part of the explanation as to why income inequality increased so much more in the United States than in Europe and Japan in the recent decades. In turn, it is likely that rising inequality has a number of negative long-run consequences, not only from the viewpoint of financial stability, as rightly stressed by Salvatore Morelli (Chapter 17) and Mark Zandi (Chapter 16), but also from the viewpoint of long-run growth potential.

This combination of the effects of both financial capital and cultural capital appears to constitute something new on this scale—particularly in comparison with the postwar period, when patrimonial inequality played a lesser role following the military, political, and social upheaval of the years 1914–1945. It was precisely during this time—more precisely in the 1960s—that Pierre Bourdieu developed his analysis of forms of domination based on cultural and symbolic capital. These concepts have clearly lost none of their relevance in the early twenty-first century—in fact, quite the contrary. It is simply that now they are combined with the return of real estate and financial capital to a level comparable to that observed in the late nineteenth and early twentieth centuries. To understand the relationship between production and power in the twenty-first century, it seems to me that it is necessary to combine Marx's observations with those of Bourdieu in order to develop a real political and historical economics of capital and inequality between social classes.

Moving beyond a Western-Centered Approach to Inequality Regimes

Let me now turn to what I view as the most important limitation of my book, namely the fact that it is too much Western-centered. This is partly due to a data problem: historical data sources on income, inheritance, and wealth are much more numerous and accessible for Western Europe, North America, and Japan than for the rest of the world. One positive impact of the global success of the book (which, as Art Goldhammer notes in Chapter 1, is relatively balanced over the planet, with about one-third of total sales in the English language, one-third in European languages other than in English, and one-third in Asian languages) is that it induced more governments and tax administrations in emerging countries to make their fiscal files and financial archives more accessible. Thanks to this, many important countries that were not covered by the World Wealth and Income Database (WID)[31] at the time of the book, such Brazil, Korea, Taiwan, Mexico, Chili, Ivory Coast, and many others, are not part of the WID (or about to be part of WID). More data was also released by South Africa, India, and China, although in this latter case progress is very slow.

More generally, as emphasized by Emmanuel Saez (Chapter 13), we are permanently trying to update and extend the WID, first in the direction of emerging countries, and also in order to better cover both the bottom part and the top part of the distribution of both income and wealth (with the development of distributional national accounts), and to include other dimensions of inequality that have not been properly addressed so far (such as gender inequality, which as Heather Boushey rightly points out in Chapter 15 is largely absent from my book). By covering more and more countries, we will also be able to aggregate inequality measures at broad regional levels or even at the world level, following and extending the pioneering work of Christophe Lakner and Branko Milanovic. In the future, we will all have access to a much more developed global inequality database, and this will make it much easier to go beyond Western-centered approaches, and also to go beyond *Capital in the Twenty-First Century*.

It should be recognized, however, that the lack of data is not the only reason my book is excessively Western-centered (although this is certainly a big part of the explanation). In part, my book is Western-centered, or even European-centered, for deeper reasons. To a large extent, this is a book that tells the story of inequality in the West during the twentieth century: it is centered around the central role played by the two World Wars in the reduction of inequality during the past hundred years. It is centered around the fact that it took violent political shocks, wars, and revolutions in order to force Western elites, and particularly the French, German, and British elites, to accept fiscal and social reforms that they largely refused until World War I, and that finally led to a prolonged compression of inequality in the postwar period. This is an important fact, and it carries lessons for the rest of the world as well—whether in India, Brazil, South Africa, or China (and of course for the United States today). But this is not the end of the story. It is important to move beyond Western-centered approaches, first and foremost because inequality regimes can take very different forms in various parts of the world. The basic structure of inequality is not the same in postapartheid South Africa, ex-slave societies like Brazil, oil-rich kingdoms and Islamic republics like in the Middle East, or post-caste societies like India. Lessons from European, North American, and Japanese inequality trajectories during the twentieth century are certainly useful for understanding inequality dynamics in these other countries; but to be honest, they are not necessarily hugely useful.

In any case, it is important to reverse the perspective and ask the opposite question: What can the West learn from these other historical experiences with inequality regimes? According to dominant Western ideology, modern inequality in the West takes a radically different form: it is supposed to be based upon individual merit and equality of rights and opportunities, as opposed to ancient inequality regimes (the inequality regimes that existed prior to the Atlantic Revolutions in the West, and that supposedly still exist in non-Western countries), which are supposed to be based upon rigid inequalities of status or ethnicity or caste. In practice, this set of beliefs clearly includes strong self-serving elements: the rise of the West came with violent forms of colonial domination and coercion (which had little to do with equality of rights and opportunities), and modern hypermeritocratic discourses often look more like a device used by the winners to justify their position than an objective description of reality. In addition, postcolonial societies are often plagued with massive labor market discrimination—witness the discrimination against populations with Muslim names in Europe. It is common in the West to look down on the kind of explicit affirmative-action policies that have been developed in a country like India in order to improve access to education, jobs, and political office on the basis of gender, parental caste, or parental income. These policies are certainly not perfect. But Western countries also suffer from massive gender, racial, and social discrimination, and they are not in a position to give lessons to the world as to how to solve these difficult problems. On the contrary, Western countries have to learn from looking at the experience of India or other parts of the world. More generally, all countries in the world have a lot to learn from adopting a global historical approach to the study of inequality regimes. For all these reasons, it is urgent to move beyond a Western-centered approach to inequality, and to move beyond *Capital in the Twenty-First Century.*

The Regulation of Capital and Institutional Change

To conclude, let me reiterate that one of the main weaknesses of my book is undoubtedly that—in addition to the limited geographical and historical scope—I did not analyze in great enough depth the social and political conditions of institutional change and their impact on inequality dynamics. As Elisabeth Jacobs (Chapter 21) rightly observes, changes in social norms and political outcomes often appear exogenous and exterior to my analysis: "politics is everywhere and nowhere in Piketty's story." I have tried to show that changes in representations and belief systems involve both the short and the long term, but my analysis of political change would without a doubt benefit from further exploration.

In particular, I insisted upon the role of violent political shocks (wars, revolutions, and economic crises) as well as the role of longer learning curves and the cross effects of national identities when it comes to perceptions of inequalities and the economy. In the early 1920s, one of the most right-wing Chambers of Deputies in the history of the French Republic, the Bloc National (National Bloc), voted the most heavily progressive tax on the rich (with rates reaching 60 percent for the highest incomes), even though these very same political groups had stubbornly refused to adopt an income tax with a top rate of 2 percent before the summer of 1914. The ideology whereby France—a country of small landowners rendered egalitarian through the Revolution, according to the dominant ideology held by French elites at that time—had no need for a progressive and spoliating tax (contrary to the aristocratic and inegalitarian United Kingdom) played an important role in this refusal, or at least in the intellectual system that made it possible to justify it. Yet inheritance data unambiguously demonstrate that the concentration of capital had reached extreme levels in France in 1914, not so different from those observed at the same time in the United Kingdom or even in the France of 1789. Although the nature of capital had completely changed (land-based fortunes had become real-estate, manufacturing, financial, and international fortunes), the degree of concentration was scarcely different from what it had been on the eve of the Revolution, firm proof that formal equality before property laws and the market is not enough to lead to equality itself. The French republican elite, for better or for worse, did not completely change their point of view concerning fiscal progressivity in the early 1920s simply because of the human and financial impact of the war: the Bolshevik Revolution and social movements had also completely transformed the political and intellectual landscape.

In a different way, I tried to show that the neoconservative revolutions of the 1980s were fed not only by the financial crises of the 1970s and the end of the exceptional growth that had followed the war, but also and perhaps above all by certain countries' fear of losing their leading position—or at least the fear that those who had been defeated during the war would catch up. This fear was especially pronounced in the United States and the United Kingdom, and Ronald Reagan and Margaret Thatcher knew how to use it to announce a return to pure capitalism, freed from elements of the mollifying social and fiscal state imposed by interventionists at the end of the Great Depression and World War II.

However, it is clear that the role of long-term, underground movements in these changes should have been more strongly emphasized. For example, the role of the ideological debates about progressive taxation that took place in the late nineteenth and early twentieth centuries should not be underestimated, for in many respects they laid the groundwork for later developments. It nonetheless seems to me that without wars, revolutions, and social movements, the political and economic elites in both France and other countries would have continued to deploy their persuasive skills and their influence over the media in order to oppose any substantial move toward progressivity. Nor would it be outrageous to consider that the inequality and extreme social tensions that characterized European societies in the twentieth century could have contributed to the rise in nationalism and even the war itself, which certainly should not be considered exogenous to the socioeconomic dynamic of the accumulation and distribution of capital during the previous decades.

Given the essential role played by financial crises, revolutions, and social movements in the history of inequality over the past centuries, it would be surprising if the same elements did not exert the same influence in the future. The advent of the modern social and fiscal state, which made it possible to develop a system of fundamental social rights that profoundly altered the logic of the capitalist system during the twentieth century, was not the product of a peaceful electoral process. In my book, I did not seek to study the forms that social movements and political reversals will assume in the future, but I have proceeded as if they will play an essential role. I also hope that the democratization of economic knowledge can contribute to the overall process of the democratization of the economy and society. I should also stress that the project for economic and fiscal democracy I support cannot be fully achieved without a change in the system of political representation itself. Democratic institutions must be continually reinvented. For example, within the framework of current European institutions, it is strictly impossible to put in place policies for fiscal justice at a European level, for the simple reason that fiscal decisions are taken according to the rule of unanimity. This is why it is essential to debate the concrete organization of democracy on both the local level and the European level.[32]

Another important limitation of the book relates to the fact that I have not analyzed in sufficient depth the possible ways that forms of ownership themselves might evolve. I insisted above all upon the social state and its system of rights as well as on the progressive tax on income and capital. It should be noted that, correctly applied, the progressive tax on capital would enable capitalism and private property to be surpassed in a relatively profound way, because it would transform the latter into a temporary rather than a permanent reality—particularly when it comes to the most sizable possessions, which could be taxed at very significant rates (for example, 5 percent or 10 percent each year, perhaps even more according to the reproduction rates observed and the desired social objective). This tax is in many ways the equivalent of a permanent agrarian reform. Furthermore, the financial transparency that would accompany a true progressive tax on capital would contribute in a key way to a democratic reappropriation of capitalism. Finally, I have not sufficiently studied the way in which new forms of ownership and participatory governance lying between private property (which would itself be democratized, thanks to the increased participation of salaried workers in the wielding of economic power) and public property (which must continue to play a role in numerous sectors—not easy when public debt exceeds meager public assets) could be developed in the future (for example, in education, health care, and even the media).[33]

The final chapter of my book concludes with the following statement: "Without real accounting and financial transparency and sharing of information, there can be no economic democracy. Conversely, without a real right to intervene in corporate decision-making (including seats for workers on the company's board of directors), transparency is of little use. Information must support democratic institutions; it is not an end in itself. If democracy is someday to regain control of capitalism, it must start by recognizing that the concrete institutions in which democracy and capitalism are embodied need to be reinvented again and again."[34] The fact that I did not explore these new forms more thoroughly in the chapters that precede this statement is undoubtedly the main reason my book is, at best, simply an introduction to the study of capital in the twenty-first century. Imperfect as it is, I hope this work can contribute to make a little progress on the long road toward a gradual reconciliation between economics and the social sciences.

Notes

Introduction

1. Thomas Piketty, *Capital in the Twenty-First Century,* trans. Arthur Goldhammer (Cambridge, MA: Belknap Press of Harvard University Press, 2014).

2. On wealth, see Thomas Piketty and Gabriel Zucman, "Capital Is Back: Wealth-Income Ratios in Rich Countries, 1700–2010," *Quarterly Journal of Economics* 129, no. 3 (August 1, 2014): 1255–1310, doi:10.1093/qje/qju018.

3. Thomas Piketty, Thomas, Emmanuel Saez, and Gabriel Zucman (2016) "Distributional National Accounts: Methods and Estimates for the United States," working paper, http://gabriel-zucman.eu/files/PSZ2016.pdf.

4. Piketty, *Capital,* 571, Kindle location 10107.

5. John Maynard Keynes, *The General Theory of Employment, Interest, and Money* (New York: Harcourt Brace Jovanovich, 1953), 376.

6. See Robert J. Gordon, *The Rise and Fall of American Growth: The U.S. Standard of Living since the Civil War* (Princeton, NJ: Princeton University Press, 2016).

7. Matthew Rognlie, "A Note on Piketty and Diminishing Returns to Capital," working paper, 2014.

8. Tyler Cowen, "Capital Punishment," *Foreign Affairs,* June 2014, https://www.foreignaffairs.com/reviews/review-essay/capital-punishment.

9. Daron Acemoglu and James Robinson, "The Rise and Decline of General Laws of Capitalism," *Journal of Economic Perspectives* 29, no. 1 (Winter 2015): 9.

10. Allan Meltzer, "The United States of Envy," in *Defining Ideas: A Hoover Institution Journal,* April 17, 2014, http://www.hoover.org/research/united-states-envy.

11. Anne Case and Angus Deaton, "Rising Morbidity and Mortality in Midlife among White Non-Hispanic Americans in the 21st Century," *Proceedings of the National Academy of Sciences* 112, no. 49 (December 8, 2015): 15078–15083, doi:10.1073/pnas.1518393112.

12. Derek Neal and Armin Rick, "The Prison Boom and the Lack of Black Progress after Smith and Welch," NBER Working Paper No. 20283 (2014), http://home.uchicago.edu/~arick/prs_boom_201309.pdf.

13. Richard V. Reeves and Kimberly Howard, "The Glass Floor: Education, Downward Mobility, and Opportunity Hoarding," Brookings Institution (November 2013), http://www.brookings.edu/~/media/research/files/papers/2013/11/glass-floor-downward-mobility-equality-opportunity-hoarding-reeves-howard/glass-floor-downward-mobility-equality-opportunity-hoarding-reeves-howard.pdf.

14. Nelson Schwartz, "In an Age of Privilege, Not Everyone Is in the Same Boat," *New York Times,* April 23, 2016, http://www.nytimes.com/2016/04/24

/business/economy/velvet-rope-economy.html?em_pos=large&emc=edit_nn
_20160426&nl=morning-briefing&nlid=74144564.

15. Arthur M. Okun, *Equality and Efficiency: The Big Tradeoff,* 2nd ed. (Washington, DC: Brookings Institution Press, 2015).

16. Thomas Piketty, "Putting Distribution Back at the Center of Economics: Reflections on Capital in the Twenty-First Century," *Journal of Economic Perspectives* 29, no. 1 (Winter 2015): 75–76.

1. The Piketty Phenomenon

I am grateful to Nicolas Barreyre, Mark Blyth, Gary Gerstle, Alex Gourevitch, Peter Gourevitch, David Grewal, Peter Hall, Deborah Mabbett, Noam Maggor, Ian Malcolm, Jedediah Purdy, George Ross, Waltraud Schekele, William Sisler, and Michael Zakim for discussions that helped to shape this essay. An early version was presented at the Université de Montréal in November 2014 at the invitation of Pierre Martin and George Ross, to whom I wish to express my gratitude.

1. Sales figures are approximate, based on private communication from Harvard University Press.

2. Piketty presented his findings publicly in many countries, including China, Japan, India, South Africa, and Argentina. On one occasion his travels had to be postponed because there were no more blank places for stamps in his passport and border officials would not let him board his flight.

3. http://www.bloomberg.com/bw/articles/2014-05-29/businessweeks-thomas -piketty-cover-how-we-made-it.

4. Craig Lambert, "The 'Wild West' of Academic Publishing," *Harvard Magazine,* January–February 2015, http://harvardmagazine.com/2015/01/the-wild-west -of-academic-publishing. See also *Business Week,* May 29, 2014, cover, http:// www.businessweek.com/printer/articles/203578-pikettys-capital-an-econo mists-inequality-ideas-are-all-the-rage.

5. Chris Giles, "Piketty Findings Undercut by Errors," *Financial Times,* May 23, 2014, http://www.ft.com/intl/cms/s/2/e1f343ca-e281-11e3-89fd-00144feabdc0 .html#axzz3mfDs2OBq. Piketty's reply effectively disposed of Giles's critique, however. There have been other, more substantive critiques of Piketty's findings, most notably Matt Rognlie, "Deciphering the Fall and Rise in the Net Capital Share," *Brookings Papers on Economic Activity,* March 19, 2015, http://www.brook ings.edu/about/projects/bpea/papers/2015/land-prices-evolution-capitals -share; and Odran Bonnet et al., "Capital Is Not Back," Vox EU, June 2014, http://www.voxeu.org/article/housing-capital-and-piketty-s-analysis.

6. Andrew Hill, "Thomas Piketty's *Capital* Wins Business Book of the Year," *Financial Times,* November 11, 2014, http://www.ft.com/intl/cms/s/0/b9e03c5c -6996-11e4-9f65-00144feabdc0.html.

7. Private communication.

8. Private communication.

9. Private communication.

10. Thomas Piketty, *Les hauts revenus en France au 20e siècle: Inégalités et re-distribution, 1901–1998* (Paris: B. Grasset, 2001). An English translation of this 800-page work has been commissioned, following on the success of *Capital.*

11. Jordan Ellenberg, "The Summer's Most Unread Book Is ...," *Wall Street Journal,* July 3, 2014, http://www.wsj.com/articles/the-summers-most-unread -book-is-1404417569.

12. http://www.dailymotion.com/video/xgs61l_hollande-piketty-et-la-revolution -fiscale-1-2_news.

13. Olivier J. Blanchard, "The State of Macro," NBER Working Paper No. 14259 (August 2008), http://www.nber.org/papers/w14259.

14. O. Blanchard, G. Dell'Ariccia, and P. Mauro, "Rethinking Macroeconomic Policy," IMF Staff Position Note (February 12, 2010), https://www.imf.org /external/pubs/ft/spn/2010/spn1003.pdf.

15. Paul Krugman, "The Profession and the Crisis," *Eastern Economic Journal* 37, no. 3 (May 2011): 307–312, http://www.palgrave-journals.com/eej/journal/v37 /n3/full/eej20118a.html.

16. Thomas Piketty and Emmanuel Saez, "Income Inequality in the United States, 1913–1998," *The Quarterly Journal of Economics* 118, no. 1 (February 2003); Thomas Piketty and Emmanuel Saez, "The Evolution of Top Incomes: A His-torical and International Perspective," *American Economic Review: Papers and Proceedings* 96, no. 2 (May 2006): 200–205.

17. In a speech hosted by the Center for American Progress, President Obama pointed to "dangerous and growing inequality and lack of upward mobility" in the United States and called it "the defining challenge of our time." He pledged that "over the course of the next year and for the rest of my presidency, that's where you should expect my administration to focus all our efforts." Barack Obama, "Remarks by the President on Economic Mobility" (speech, Wash-ington, DC, December 4, 2013), https://www.whitehouse.gov/the-press-office /2013/12/04/remarks-president-economic-mobility.

18. Lawrence H. Summers, "The Inequality Puzzle," *Democracy,* no. 33 (Summer 2014), http://www.democracyjournal.org/33/the-inequality-puzzle.php?page =all.

19. Eugene Robinson, "Elizabeth Warren Makes a Powerful Case," *Washington Post,* October 20, 2014, https://www.washingtonpost.com/opinions/eugene-robin son-elizabeth-warren-makes-the-case-on-income-inequality/2014/10/20/ba54 c68e-588a-11e4-8264-deed989ae9a2_story.html.

20. Eric Alterman, "Inequality and the Blind Spots of the Democratic Party," *The Nation,* May 14, 2015, http://www.thenation.com/article/bill-de-blasio-crisis -inequality-and-blind-spots-democratic-party/.

21. Lawrence Mishel, "Chair Yellen Is Right: Income and Wealth Inequality Hurts Economic Mobility," Economic Policy Institute, Working Economics Blog, http://www.epi.org/blog/chair-yellen-income-wealth-inequalities/.

22. Alan B. Krueger, "The Rise and Consequences of Inequality in the United States," speech (January 12, 2012), https://www.whitehouse.gov/sites/default/files/krueger_cap_speech_final_remarks.pdf.

23. Raj Chetty, Nathaniel Hendren, Patrick Kline, Emmanuel Saez, and Nicholas Turner, "Is the United States Still a Land of Opportunity? Recent Trends in Intergenerational Mobility," NBER Working Paper No. 19844, http://www.nber.org/papers/w19844: "We find that all of these rank-based measures of intergenerational mobility have not changed significantly over time. For example, the probability that a child reaches the top fifth of the income distribution given parents in the bottom fifth of the income distribution is 8.4 percent for children born in 1971, compared with 9.0 percent for those born in 1986. Children born to the highest-income families in 1984 were 74.5 percentage points more likely to attend college than those from the lowest-income families. The corresponding gap for children born in 1993 is 69.2 percentage points, suggesting that if anything intergenerational mobility may have increased slightly in recent cohorts. Moreover, intergenerational mobility is fairly stable over time in each of the nine census divisions of the US even though they have very different levels of mobility." Nevertheless, because of growing inequality, the authors also stress that "the consequences of the 'birth lottery'—the parents to whom a child is born—are larger today than in the past."

24. Jerome Karabel, *The Chosen: The Hidden History of Admission and Exclusion at Harvard, Yale, and Princeton* (New York: Houghton Mifflin Harcourt, 2005).

25. Nicholas Lemann, *The Big Test: The Secret History of American Meritocracy* (New York: Farrar, Straus and Giroux, 2000).

26. Theda Skocpol and Vanessa Williamson, *The Tea Party and the Remaking of American Conservatism* (New York: Oxford University Press, 2012).

27. Branko Milanovic, "The Return of 'Patrimonial Capitalism': A Review of Thomas Piketty's *Capital in the Twenty-First Century*," *Journal of Economic Literature* 52, no. 2 (2014): 1–16.

28. *The Economist,* May 2014.

29. Thomas Edsall, "Capitalism vs. Democracy," *New York Times,* January 28, 2014, http://www.nytimes.com/2014/01/29/opinion/capitalism-vs-democracy.html.

30. Krugman, "Why We're in a New Gilded Age," *New York Review of Books,* May 8, 2014. (Krugman's article is Chapter 3 in this volume.)

31. Robert M. Solow, "Thomas Piketty Is Right," *New Republic,* April 22, 2014 (Chapter 2, this volume).

32. See Lambert, "The 'Wild West,'" n. 3.

33. Thomas Piketty, *Capital in the Twenty-First Century,* trans. Arthur Goldhammer (Cambridge, MA: Belknap Press of Harvard University Press, 2014), 32, 15.

34. Thomas Edsall, "Thomas Piketty and His Critics," *New York Times,* May 14, 2014, http://www.nytimes.com/2014/05/14/opinion/edsall-thomas-piketty-and-his-critics.html.

35. James K. Galbraith, "*Kapital* for the Twenty-First Century?," *Dissent,* Spring 2014, https://www.dissentmagazine.org/article/kapital-for-the-twenty-first-century.

36. Timothy Shenk, "Apostles of Growth," *The Nation,* November 5, 2014, http://www.thenation.com/article/apostles-growth/.

37. It should be noted that the second lecture took place at Harvard Law School, and one of the commentators was a law professor. Interest in Piketty's work among legal scholars has been high, as exemplified in reviews by Jedediah Purdy of Duke Law School and David Grewal of Yale. Purdy's review appeared in the *Los Angeles Review of Books,* April 24, 2014. For Grewal's, see *Harvard Law Review* 128, no. 626 (December 10, 2014).

38. I am grateful to Noam Maggor for this point.

39. Krugman, "New Gilded Age."

40. *Lire* Le capital de *Thomas Piketty,* special issue, *Annales: Histoire, Sciences sociales* 70, no. 1 (January–March 2015): 5.

41. Nicolas Delalande, "Vers une histoire politique de capital?," *Annales: HSS* 70, no. 1 (January–March 2015): 50.

42. Alexis Spire, "Capital, reproduction sociale et fabrique des inégalités," *Annales: HSS* 70, no. 1 (January–March 2015): 61.

43. Piketty, *Capital,* 573.

44. Spire, "Capital," 63.

45. Nancy Partner, "*Les mots et les choses* and Beyond," paper delivered at a colloquium on the work of Michel Foucault at Harvard's Center for European Studies, April 17–18, 2015.

46. After the success of *C21,* Harvard University Press alone published an early work of Piketty's and a book by Anthony Atkinson, a pioneer in the economics of inequality, and signed a work by Piketty reviewer Branko Milanovic—moves that gave the press "a lead position as the 'inequality' publisher" (private communication from press chief William Sisler). As Piketty's translator, I was contacted by several publishers asking if I knew any other French economists or social scientists working in the field of inequality. And as mentioned earlier, a translation of Piketty's *Hauts revenus en France* has been commissioned. There is no question that the field is "hot" thanks to Piketty's success.

47. Zhou apparently believed he was being asked about the political consequences of the May 1968 uprising in Paris, not about the French Revolution, when he made his famous remark.

48. Galbraith, "*Kapital.*"

49. For example, see Peter Spiegel, "EU Agrees Laws to End Banking Secrecy," *Financial Times,* October 14, 2014, http://www.ft.com/intl/cms/s/0/0ca39924-53b3-11e4-929b-00144feab7de.html#axzz3mfDs2OBq.

50. Piketty, *Capital,* 570.

4. *What's Wrong with* Capital in the Twenty-First Century's *Model?*

All opinions and conclusions expressed herein are those of the author. I would like to thank Chris Adams, Miguel Leon-Ledesma, Eric Nielsen, Ezra Oberfield, Dave Schmidt, Marshall Steinbaum, and Nathan Wilson for their comments.

1. Robert M. Solow, "A Contribution to the Theory of Economic Growth," *Quarterly Journal of Economics* 70, no. 1 (1956): 65–94; Trevor W. Swan, "Economic Growth and Capital Accumulation," *Economic Record* 32, no. 2 (1956): 334–361.

2. Krusell and Smith criticize Piketty's assumption of a constant net savings rate, and point out that either a constant gross savings rate or an endogenous rate of savings would reduce how much the capital / output ratio rises with a fall in the growth rate, and eliminate the explosion of the capital / output ratio when growth falls to zero. The qualitative implications of Piketty's model on a rise in the capital / output ratio with a fall in the growth rate would remain unchanged, however. See Per Krusell and Tony Smith, "Is Piketty's 'Second Law of Capitalism' Fundamental?," *Journal of Political Economy* 123, no. 4 (August 2015): 725–748.

3. The CES production function nests a number of special cases, including a Leontief fixed proportions production function when σ is 0, a linear production function when σ is infinite, and a Cobb-Douglas production with capital coefficient a when σ is one.

4. See page 39 of Thomas Piketty, "Technical Appendix of the book *Capital in the Twenty-First Century*," 2014, http://piketty.pse.ens.fr/files/capital21c/en/Piketty2014TechnicalAppendix.pdf.

5. Robert Rowthorn, "A Note on Piketty's *Capital in the Twenty-First Century*," *Cambridge Journal of Economics* 68, no. 1 (2014): 1275–1284; Matthew Rognlie, "Deciphering the Fall and Rise in the Net Capital Share," *Brookings Papers on Economic Activity*, March 2015, https://www.brookings.edu/bpea-articles/deciphering-the-fall-and-rise-in-the-net-capital-share/.

6. Rognlie, "Deciphering the Fall and Rise"; Odran Bonnet et al., "Does Housing Capital Contribute to Inequality? A Comment on Thomas Piketty's *Capital in the 21st Century*," Sciences Po Economic Discussion Paper 2014-07 (2014), http://econ.sciences-po.fr/sciences-po-economics-discussion-papers.

7. Rognlie derives the relation between the net and gross elasticity:

$$\frac{\sigma^N}{\sigma^G} = \frac{r^N K / Y^N}{r^G K / Y^G} = \frac{\alpha^N}{\alpha^G} \tag{10}$$

Here, N stands for the net value and G for the gross value. The ratio of net to gross elasticity is equal to the ratio between the net capital share and the gross capital share. The net elasticity is always below the gross elasticity because the net capital share is always below the gross capital share. The intuition here is that any change in the gross return is a larger change in the net return, so, given that the change in K/L is the same, the net elasticity must be smaller than the gross elasticity. Using data collected by Piketty and Zucman, the gross capital share has been about 30 percent higher than the net capital share for the United States on average over the 1970–2010 period. Thomas Piketty and Gabriel Zucman, "Capital Is Back: Wealth-Income Ratios in Rich Countries, 1700–2010," *Quarterly Journal of Economics* 129, no. 3 (2014): 1255–1310. For the difference between net and gross capital share, see Benjamin Bridgman, "Is Labor's Loss Capital's Gain? Gross versus Net Labor Shares" (2014), https://bea.gov /papers/pdf/laborshare1410.pdf.

8.   Robert S. Chirinko, "Sigma: The Long and Short of It," *Journal of Macroeconomics* 30 (2008): 671–686; Miguel A. Leon-Ledesma, Peter McAdam, and Alpo Willman, "Identifying the Elasticity of Substitution with Biased Technical Change," *American Economic Review* 100, no. 4 (2010): 1330–1357.

9.   Peter Diamond, Daniel McFadden, and Miguel Rodriguez, "Measurement of the Elasticity of Factor Substitution and Bias of Technical Change," chap. 5 in *Production Economics: A Dual Approach to Theory and Applications,* ed. Melvyn Fuss and Daniel McFadden (Amsterdam: North-Holland, 1978).

10. Daron Acemoglu, "Labor- and Capital-Augmenting Technical Change," *Journal of the European Economic Association* 1, no. 1 (2003): 1–37.

11. Pol Antras, "Is the US Aggregate Production Function Cobb-Douglas? New Estimates of the Elasticity of Substitution," *Contributions to Macroeconomics* 4, no. 1 (2004). Klump, McAdam, and Willman estimate a *rise* of about 0.4 percentage points per year. However, the main difference between these estimates is that Antras uses a capital deflator series from Krusell et al., based on earlier work by Gordon, that declines more steeply over time than the NIPA deflators used by Klump, McAdam, and Willman. See Rainer Klump, Peter McAdam, and Alpo Willman, "Factor Substitution and Factor Augmenting Technical Progress in the US," *Review of Economics and Statistics* 89, no. 1 (2007): 183–192; Antras, "Is the US Aggregate"; Per Krusell et al., "Capital-Skill Complementarity and Inequality: A Macroeconomic Analysis," *Econometrica* 68, no. 5 (2000): 1029–1053; Robert J. Gordon, *The Measurement of Durable Goods Prices* (Chicago: University of Chicago Press, 1990).

12. Klump, McAdam, and Willman, "Factor Substitution." The Box–Cox transformation implies that $d \log \varphi = \gamma t^{\lambda}$; λ allows the rate of biased technical change to vary over time.

13. In addition, see Klump, McAdam, and Willman, "Factor Substitution"; Berthold Herrendorf, Christopher Herrington, and Ákos Valentinyi, "Sectoral Technology and Structural Transformation," *American Economic Journal: Macroeconomics* 7 no. 4 (2015): 104–133; Francisco Alvarez-Cuadrado, Ngo Van-Long, and Markus Poschke, *Capital-Labor Substitution, Structural Change and the Labor Income Share* (Munich: CESifo, 2014); Miguel Leon-Ledesma, Peter McAdam, and Alpo Willman, "Production Technology Estimates and

Balanced Growth," *Oxford Bulletin of Economics and Statistics* 77, no. 1 (February 2015): 40–65; Lawrence, "Recent Declines in Labor's Share in US Income: A Preliminary Neoclassical Account," NBER Working Paper No. 21296, http://www.nber.org/papers/w21296.

14. Leon-Ledesma, McAdam, and Willman, "Identifying the Elasticity of Substitution."

15. Robert Chirinko and Debdulal Mallick, "The Substitution Elasticity, Factor Shares, Long-Run Growth, and the Low-Frequency Panel Model," CESifo Working Paper No. 4895 (2014).

16. Loukas Karabarbounis and Brent Neiman, "The Global Decline of the Labor Share," *Quarterly Journal of Economics* 129, no. 1 (2014): 61–103.

17. Piyusha Mutreja, B. Ravikumar, and Michael J. Sposi, "Capital Goods Trade and Economic Development," FRB of St. Louis Working Paper No. 2014-012A (2014).

18. Robert S. Chirinko, Steven M. Fazzari, and Andrew P. Meyer, "A New Approach to Estimating Production Function Parameters: The Elusive Capital-Labor Substitution Elasticity," *Journal of Business and Economic Statistics* 29, no. 4 (2011): 587–594.

19. Sebastian Barnes, Simon Price, and María Sebastiá Barriel, "The Elasticity of Substitution: Evidence from a UK Firm-Level Data Set," Bank of England Working Paper No. 348 (2008).

20. Devesh Raval, "The Micro Elasticity of Substitution and Non-Neutral Technology" (2015), http://www.devesh-raval.com/MicroElasticity.pdf.

21. Doraszelski and Jaumendreu estimate a structural model in which the elasticity of substitution is equal between capital, labor, and materials. While the estimating variation in factor prices is due to differences between labor and materials prices, their elasticity estimates also range between 0.45 and 0.65, in line with the estimates discussed above. See Ulrich Doraszelski and Jordi Jaumendreu, "Measuring the Bias of Technological Change" (2015), http://economics.yale.edu/sites/default/files/ces20150319.pdf.

22. Hendrik Houthakker, "The Pareto Distribution and the Cobb-Douglas Production Function in Activity Analysis," *Review of Economic Studies* 23, no. 1 (1955): 27–31. Houthakker demonstrated that if A^K and A^L have independent Pareto distributions, an economy of firms with an elasticity of zero has a Cobb-Douglas aggregate production function.

23. See Piketty and Zucman, "Capital Is Back," 1271.

24. Ezra Oberfield and Devesh Raval, "Micro Data and Macro Technology," NBER Working Paper No. 20452 (September 2014); Kazuo Satō, *Production Functions and Aggregation* (Amsterdam: Elsevier, 1975).

25. Oberfield and Raval, "Micro Data," generalize this case to allow for many inputs and industries.

26. Rainier Klump and Olivier De La Grandville, "Economic Growth and the Elasticity of Substitution: Two Theorems and Some Suggestions," *American Economic Review* 90, no. 1 (2000): 282–291.

27. Olivier De La Grandville, "In Quest of the Slutsky Diamond," *American Economic Review* 79, no. 3 (1989): 468–481.

28. Christophe Chamley, "The Welfare Cost of Capital Income Taxation in a Growing Economy," *Journal of Political Economy* 89, no. 3 (1981): 468–496.

29. Data on U.S. imports as share of GDP are from the World Bank Development Indicators; data on the Chinese share of goods trade are from the U.S. Census.

30. Michael W. L. Elsby, Bart Hobijn, and Aysegul Sahin, "The Decline of the U.S. Labor Share," Brookings Papers on Economic Activity (2013).

31. They define import exposure as the percentage increase in value added if all output were to be produced domestically. Payroll is one component of labor income in addition to self-employment income.

32. Daron Acemoglu, David Autor, David Dorn, Gordon Hanson, and Brendan Price, "Import Competition and the Great US Employment Sag of the 2000s," *Journal of Labor Economics* 34 (2016): S141–S198.

33. David Autor, David Dorn, and Gordon Hanson, "The China Syndrome: Local Labor Market Effects of Import Competition in the United States," *American Economic Review* 103, no. 6 (2013): 2121–2168.

34. They define Chinese exports per worker by dividing Chinese imports across regions based on industry employment shares in the initial period. They examine changes between 1990 and 2000 and between 2000 and 2007.

35. Denis Chetverikov, Bradley Larsen, and Christopher Palmer, "IV Quantile Regression for Group-Level Treatments, with an Application to the Distributional Effects of Trade," *Econometrica* 84, no. 2 (2016): 809–833.

36. Andrew B. Bernard, J. Bradford Jensen, and Peter K. Schott, "Survival of the Best Fit: Exposure to Low-Wage Countries and the (Uneven) Growth of US Manufacturing Plants," *Journal of International Economics* 68, no. 1 (2006): 219–237.

37. James Schmitz, "What Determines Productivity? Lessons from the Dramatic Recovery of the U.S. and Canadian Iron Ore Industries Following Their Early 1980s Crisis," *Journal of Political Economy* 113, no. 3 (2005); Tim Dunne, Shawn Klimek, and James Schmitz, "Does Foreign Competition Spur Productivity? Evidence From Post WWII U.S. Cement Manufacturing" (2010), https://www.minneapolisfed.org/~/media/files/research/events/2010_04-23/papers/schmitz8.pdf?la=en.

38. Nicholas Bloom, Mirko Draca, and John Van Reenen, "Trade Induced Technical Change? The Impact of Chinese Imports on Innovation, IT and Productivity," *Review of Economic Studies* 83, no. 1 (2015): 87–117.

39. Timothy F. Bresnahan and Manuel Trajtenberg, "General Purpose Technologies 'Engines of Growth'?," *Journal of Econometrics* 65, no. 1 (1995): 83–108. For the historical effect of electricity adoption on the labor share in the concrete industry, see, for example, Miguel Morin, "The Labor Market Consequences of Electricity Adoption: Concrete Evidence from the Great Depression" (2015), http://miguelmorin.com/docs/Miguel_Morin_Great_Depression.pdf.

40. David H. Autor, Frank Levy, and Richard J. Murmane, "The Skill Content of Recent Technological Change: An Empirical Exploration," *Quarterly Journal of Economics* 118, no. 4 (2003): 1279–1333.

41. Ibid.

42. James Bessen, "Toil and Technology," *Finance and Development* 52, no. 1 (2015).

43. Emek Basker, Lucia Foster, and Shawn Klimek, "Customer-Labor Substitution: Evidence from Gasoline Stations," U.S. Census Bureau Center for Economic Studies Paper No. CES-WP- 15-45 (2015).

44. David Autor, David Dorn, and Gordon Hanson, "Untangling Trade and Technology: Evidence from Local Labor Markets," *Economic Journal* 125 (May 2015): 621–646.

45. Paul Beaudry, David A. Green, and Benjamin Sand, "The Great Reversal in the Demand for Skill and Cognitive Tasks," *Journal of Labor Economics* 34, no. S1 (2016): S199–S247.

46. Daron Acemoglu, "When Does Labor Scarcity Encourage Innovation?," *Journal of Political Economy* 118, no. 6 (2010): 1037–1078.

47. Acemoglu, "Labor- and Capital-Augmenting Technical Change."

5. A Political Economy Take on W / Y

1. Joan Robinson, "Open Letter from a Keynesian to a Marxist," *Jacobin,* July 17, 2011, https://www.jacobinmag.com/2011/07/joan-robinsons-open-letter-from-a-keynesian-to-a-marxist-2/.

2. Paul Krugman, "Wealth over Work," *New York Times,* March 23, 2014; Daron Acemoglu and James A. Robinson, "The Rise and Decline of General Laws of Capitalism," NBER Working Paper No. w20766 (2014).

3. José Azar, Martin C. Schmalz, and Isabel Tecu, "Anti-competitive Effects of Common Ownership," Ross School of Business Paper No. 1235 (2015); Einer Elhauge, "Horizontal Shareholding," *Harvard Law Review* 129 (2016): 1267–1811.

4. Jason Furman and Peter Orszag, "A Firm-Level Perspective on the Role of Rents in the Rise in Inequality," paper presented at "A Just Society" Centennial Event in Honor of Joseph Stiglitz Columbia University (2015).

5. Simon Kuznets, "Economic Growth and Income Inequality," *American Economic Review* 45, no. 1 (1955): 1–28, quotation at 9.

6. Wojciech Kopczuk, "What Do We Know about the Evolution of Top Wealth Shares in the United States?," *Journal of Economic Perspectives* 29, no. 1 (2015): 47–66, discussing the capitalization estimates of wealth inequality created by Emmanuel Saez and Gabriel Zucman, "Who Benefits from Tax Expenditures on Capital? Evidence on Capital Income and Wealth Concentration," IRS Statistics of Income Working Paper Series (2014).

7. Filipe R. Campante, "Redistribution in a Model of Voting and Campaign Contributions," *Journal of Public Economics* 95 (August 2011): 646–656, http://scholar.harvard.edu/files/campante/files/campanteredistribution.pdf.

8. Adam Bonica and Howard Rosenthal, "The Wealth Elasticity of Political Contributions by the Forbes 400" (2015), https://papers.ssrn.com/sol3/papers.cfm?abstract_id=2668780.

9. Lee Drutman, *The Business of America Is Lobbying: How Corporations Became Politicized and Politics Became More Corporate* (Oxford: Oxford University Press, 2015).

10. Joshua Kalla and David Broockman, "Congressional Officials Grant Access to Individuals Because They Have Contributed to Campaigns: A Randomized Field Experiment," *American Journal of Political Science* 33, no. 1 (2014): 1–24.

11. Gabriel Zucman, "Taxing across Borders: Tracking Personal Wealth and Corporate Profits," *Journal of Economic Perspectives* 28, no. 4 (2014): 121–148; and "What Are the Panama Papers?," *New York Times*, April 4, 2016, http://www.nytimes.com/2016/04/05/world/panama-papers-explainer.html?_r=0.

12. Matthew Ellman and Leonard Wantchekon, "Electoral Competition under the Threat of Political Unrest," *Quarterly Journal of Economics* (May 2000): 499–531.

13. Nicos Poulantzas, "The Problem of the Capitalist State," *New Left Review*, November–December 1969, 67; Ralph Miliband, "Poulantzas and the Capitalist State," *New Left Review*, November–December 1973, 83.

14. It has long been thought that slave owners thought of their assets much as homeowners think of theirs, where preservation of value reigns supreme. Hence the furor over the fugitive slave law, despite a relatively small number of actual runaways.

15. Alexander Hertel-Fernandez, "Who Passes Business's 'Model Bills'? Policy Capacity and Corporate Influence in US State Politics," *Perspectives on Politics* 12, no. 3 (2014): 582–602.

16. Marion Fourcade, Etienne Ollion, and Yann Algan, "The Superiority of Economists," *Journal of Economic Perspectives* 29, no. 1 (2015): 89–114.

17. Ibid., 17.

18. Brad DeLong, "The Market's Social Welfare Function," Semi-Daily Journal (blog), October 9, 2003, http://www.j-bradford-delong.net/movable_type/2003_archives/002449.html.

6. The Ubiquitous Nature of Slave Capital

1. Southern Railroad Ledger, Purchases for 1848, Natchez Trace Slaves and Slavery Collection, no. 2E775, Dolph Briscoe Center for American History, University of Texas at Austin.

2. Robert S. Starobin, *Industrial Slavery in the Old South* (New York: Oxford University Press, 1970), 221–223; William G. Thomas, "Been Workin' on the Railroad," *Disunion: New York Times*, February 10, 2012. Economic historians and economists have published work on railroads and slavery and have been writing about this topic from the early 1960s until today. See Robert Evans Jr., "The Economics of Negro Slavery, 1830–1860," in *Aspects of Labor Economics*, ed.

Universities-National Bureau for Economic Research (Princeton, NJ: Princeton University Press, 1962), 185–256; Robert Fogel, *Railroads and Economic Growth: Essays in Econometric History* (Baltimore: Johns Hopkins University Press, 1964); Mark A. Yanochik, Bradley T. Ewing, and Mark Thornton, "A New Perspective on Antebellum Slavery: Public Policy and Slave Prices," *Atlantic Economic Journal* (February 2006): 330–340.

3. Thomas Piketty, *Capital in the Twenty-First Century,* trans. Arthur Goldhammer (Cambridge, MA: Belknap Press of Harvard University Press, 2014), 46.

4. Ibid., quotation at 46, discussion at 158–163.

5. Ibid., 46.

6. See the database Legacies of British Slave-Ownership, http://www.ucl.ac.uk/lbs/; and "Britain's Forgotten Slave Owners," BBC Media Centre, http://www.bbc.co.uk/mediacentre/proginfo/2015/28/britains-forgotten-slave-owners/.

7. Sir Hilary Beckles, a historian of Caribbean slavery, leads the efforts in the West Indies. See Beckles, *Britain's Black Debt: Reparations for Caribbean Slavery and Native Genocide* (Kingston: University of West Indies Press, 2013). See also, "CARICOM Reparations Commission Press Statement," http://caricom.org/jsp/pressreleases/press_releases_2013/pres285_13.jsp.

8. California Department of Insurance, "Slavery Era Insurance Registry," Report to the California Legislature, May 2002. The city of Chicago and other states, such as Maryland, implemented similar legislation.

9. Jenny Bourne, "Slavery in the United States," EH-Net, https://eh.net/encyclopedia/slavery-in-the-united-states/. See also Robert William Fogel and Stanley L. Engerman, *Time on the Cross: The Economics of American Negro Slavery* (1971; reprint, New York: W. W. Norton, 1989); Stanley L. Engerman, Richard Sutch, and Gavin Wright, eds., *Slavery: For Historical Statistics of the United Sates Millennial Edition* (Riverside, CA: Center for Social and Economic Policy, 2003), 1–15; and Ira Berlin and Philip Morgan, *Cultivation and Culture: Labor and the Shaping of the Americas* (Richmond: University Press of Virginia, 1993).

10. Piketty, *Capital,* 162.

11. Walter Johnson, *Soul by Soul: Life in an Antebellum Slave Market* (Cambridge, MA: Harvard University Press, 1999).

12. Piketty, *Capital,* 46.

13. W. E. B. Du Bois, *The Suppression of the African Slave Trade to the United States of America* (New York: Longmans, Green and Co., 1896), preface.

14. Ibid.

15. Ibid., 12.

16. Ibid., 196.

17. Ulrich Bonnell Phillips, *American Negro Slavery* (New York: D. Appleton and Co., 1918), xxiii.

18. Eric Williams, *Capitalism & Slavery* (1944; reprint, Chapel Hill: University of North Carolina Press, 1994), xi.

19. Ibid., 197.

20. Alfred H. Conrad and John R. Meyer, "The Economics of Slavery in the Ante Bellum South," *Journal of Political Economy* 66 (April 1958): 95–130.

21. Fogel and Engerman, *Time on the Cross,* 39. The scholarship on African history contains several studies on slavery economics, but they are beyond the scope of this essay. See David Eltis, *The Rise of African Slavery in the Americas* (Cambridge: Cambridge University Press, 2000).

22. Key texts and articles include: Claudia Goldin, *Urban Slavery in the Antebellum South* (Chicago: University of Chicago Press, 1976); Roger Ransom and Richard Sutch, "Capitalists without Capital: The Burden of Slavery and the Impact of Emancipation," *Agricultural History* 62 (Summer 1988): 133–160; Laurence J. Kotlikoff, "The Structure of Slave Prices in New Orleans, 1804 to 1862," *Economic Inquiry* 17 (1979): 496–517; Richard Steckel, "Birth Weights and Infant Mortality among American Slaves," *Explorations in Economic History* 23 (April 1986): 173–198; Robert Margo and Gavin Wright, *The Political Economy of the Cotton South* (New York: W. W. Norton, 1978); and Jonathan Pritchett, "Quantitative Estimates of the United States Interregional Slave Trade, 1820–1860," *Journal of Economic History* 61 (June 2001): 467–475.

23. Walter Johnson, *River of Dark Dreams: Slavery and Empire in the Cotton Kingdom* (Cambridge, MA: Harvard University Press, 2013).

24. Joshua Rothman, *Flush Times and Fever Dreams: The Story of Capitalism and Freedom in the Age of Jackson* (Athens: University of Georgia Press, 2012); Edward Baptist, *The Half Has Never Been Told: Slavery and the Making of Modern Capitalism* (New York: Basic Books, 2014); Sven Beckert, *Empire of Cotton: A Global History* (New York: Knopf, 2014); and Calvin Schermerhorn, *The Business of Slavery and the Rise of American Capitalism, 1815–1860* (New Haven, CT: Yale University Press, 2015).

25. "Blood Cotton," *The Economist,* September 4, 2014.

26. See Editor's Note, "Our Withdrawn Review 'Blood Cotton,'" *The Economist,* September 4, 2014; and Edward Baptist, "What *The Economist* Doesn't Get About Slavery—and My Book," *Politico,* September 7, 2014.

27. Alan Olmstead and Paul Rhode have been working on studies of cotton productivity and argue that the cotton crop changed, as did technological improvements to ginning and other devices used during production. See Alan L. Olmstead and Paul W. Rhode, "Biological Innovation and Productivity Growth in the Antebellum Cotton Economy," *Journal of Economic History* 68 (December 2008): 1123–1171.

28. Herman Freudenberger and Jonathan B. Pritchett, "The Domestic United States Slave Trade: New Evidence," *Journal of Interdisciplinary History* 21, no. 3 (1991): 447–477; Freudenberger and Pritchett, "A Peculiar Sample: The Selection of Slaves for the New Orleans Market," *Journal of Economic History* 52 (March 1992): 109–127; Kotlikoff, "The Structure of Slave Prices"; B. Greenwald and R. Glasspiegel, "Adverse Selection in the Market for Slaves: New Orleans, 1830–1860," *Quarterly Journal of Economics,* 98, no. 3 (1989).

29. Sowande' Mustakeem, "'She Must Go Overboard & Shall Go Overboard': Diseased Bodies and the Spectacle of Murder at Sea," *Atlantic Studies* 8, no. 3 (Fall 2011): 301–316; Mustakeem, "'I Never Have Such a Sickly Ship Before': Diet, Disease, and Mortality in 18th-Century Atlantic Slaving Voyages," *Journal of African American History* 93 (Fall 2008): 474–496; Marcus Rediker, *The Slave Ship: A Human History* (New York: Viking Books, 2007); and Stephanie Smallwood, *Saltwater Slavery: A Middle Passage from Africa to American Diaspora* (Cambridge, MA: Harvard University Press, 2007).

30. See Seth Rothman, *Scraping By: Wage Labor, Slavery and Survival in Early Baltimore* (Philadelphia: University of Pennsylvania Press, 2009); Jessica Millward, *Finding Charity's Folk: Enslaved and Free Black Women in Maryland* (Athens: University of Georgia Press, 2015); Wilma King, *The Essence of Liberty: Free Black Women during the Era of Slavery* (Columbia: University of Missouri Press, 2006); Amrita Chakrabarti Myers, *Forging Freedom: Black Women and the Pursuit of Liberty in Antebellum Charleston* (Chapel Hill: University of North Carolina Press, 2011); Judith Schafer, *Slavery, the Civil Law, and the Supreme Court of Louisiana* (Baton Rouge: Louisiana State University Press, 1997); and Leslie Harris and Daina Ramey Berry, *Slavery and Freedom in Savannah* (Athens: University of Georgia Press, 2014).

31. Richard Wade, *Slavery in the Cities: The South, 1820–1860* (New York: Oxford University Press, 1964), 44.

32. "Request for Slaves to Build Levee during Flood," Concordia Parish, LA, March 1815, Slaves and Slavery Collection, Mss. 2E777, no. 3, Dolph Briscoe Center for American History, University of Texas at Austin.

33. Savannah City Council Minutes, "Municipal Slavery," City of Savannah website, http://savannahga.gov/slavery.

34. Ibid., August 14, 1820, http://savannahga.gov/slavery. For the closing of the slave trade, see Du Bois, *Suppression*, as well as Erik Calonis, *The Wanderer: The Last American Slave Ship and the Conspiracy That Set Its Sails* (New York: St. Martin's Press, 2006); Sylvianne Diouf, *Dreams of Africa in Alabama: The Slave Ship Clotilda and the Story of the Last Africans Brought to America* (New York: Oxford University Press, 2007); and Ernest Obadele Starks, *Footbooters and Smugglers: The Foreign Slave Trade in the United States after 1808* (Fayetteville: University of Arkansas Press, 2007).

35. Savannah City Council Minutes, August 14, 1820, http://savannahga.gov /slavery.

36. Ibid., February 24, 1831.

37. Ibid., June 2, 1842. For the value of enslaved laborers, see Daina Ramey Berry, *The Price for Their Pound of Flesh: The Value of the Enslaved from the Womb to the Grave in the Building of a Nation* (Boston: Beacon Press, 2017).

38. Wade, *Slavery in the Cities,* 45.

39. Robert S. Starobin, *Industrial Slavery in the Old South* (New York: Oxford University Press, 1970), 18–19.

40. "Slaves Subject to Road Duty," Slaves and Slavery Records, Mss. 2E777, Natchez Trace Collection, Dolph Briscoe Center for American History, University of Texas at Austin, Ashford Family, 5, 407, 410, 480, and 481.

41. See Jonathan Martin, *Divided Mastery: Slave Hiring in the American South* (Cambridge, MA: Harvard University Press, 2004); John J. Zaborney, *Slaves for Hire: Renting Enslaved Laborers in Antebellum Virginia* (Baton Rouge: Louisiana State University Press, 2012). For the labor of newly freed blacks in urban spaces, see Jennifer Hull Dorsey, *Hirelings: African American Workers and Free Labor in Maryland* (Ithaca, NY: Cornell University Press, 2011).

42. Savannah City Council Minutes, August 25 and 30, 1842.

43. Craig Steven Wilder, *Ebony & Ivy: Race, Slavery, and the Troubled History of America's Universities* (New York: Bloomsbury Press, 2013), 9.

44. *Hillsborough Recorder,* Hillsborough, NC: Dennis Heartt, 1820–1879, November 29, 1829, http://dc.lib.unc.edu/cdm/singleitem/collection/vir_museum /id/421.

45. For the conference hosted by Brown University and Harvard University in the spring of 2011, see the proceedings, *Slavery's Capitalism: A New History of America's Economic Development* (Philadelphia: University of Pennsylvania Press, 2016). Also in 2011, Emory University hosted the conference "Slavery and the University" (http://shared.web.emory.edu/emory/news/releases/2011 /01/slavery-and-the-university-focus-of-emory-conference.html# .VhVKvUVrUvg), for which an edited volume of the proceedings is forthcoming. For more information about Kitty, see Mark Aslunder, *The Accidental Slaveholder: Revisiting a Myth of Race and Finding an American Family* (Athens: University of Georgia Press, 2011).

46. See the multipart documentary "The Ultimate Guide to the Presidents," on the History channel, http://www.history.com/shows/the-ultimate-guide-to-the-presidents; and the website compiled by Grand Valley State University: http://hauen steincenter.org/slaveholding/.

47. Piketty, *Capital*, 159.

48. His website does not clarify the sources used to compile these figures.

49. See, for example, Ira Berlin, *Many Thousands Gone: The First Two Centuries of Slavery in North America* (Cambridge, MA: Harvard University Press, 1998); Leslie M. Harris, *In the Shadow of Slavery: African Americans in New York City, 1626–1863* (Chicago: University of Chicago Press, 2003); Graham Russell Hodges, *Root and Branch: African Americans in New York and East Jersey, 1613–1863* (Chapel Hill: University of North Carolina Press, 1999); Leon Litwack, *North of Slavery: The Negro in the Free States, 1790–1860* (Chicago: University of Chicago Press, 1961); Joan Pope Melish, *Disowning Slavery: Gradual Emancipation and "Race" in New England, 1780–1860* (Ithaca, NY: Cornell University Press, 1998); Wade, *Slavery in the Cities;* and Shane White, *Somewhat More Independent: The End of Slavery in New York City, 1770–1810* (Athens: University of Georgia Press, 1991).

50. Beckles, *Britain's Black Debt;* Mary Frances Berry, *My Face Is Black Is True: Callie House and the Struggle for Ex-Slave Reparations* (New York: Vintage Books, 2006); Ta-Nehisi Coates, "The Case for Reparations," *The Atlantic,* June 2014, 1–65.

51. Du Bois, *Suppression,* 197.

7. Human Capital and Wealth before and after
Capital in the Twenty-First Century

I would like to dedicate this essay to the memory of Gary Becker, a wonderful mentor who dramatically improved my understanding of the concepts discussed herein. I thank Michael Palumbo, Marshall Steinbaum, Devesh Raval, and other contributors to this volume for helpful feedback on this chapter. The views and opinions expressed here are mine alone and do not in any way reflect the views or policies of the Board of Governors or the Federal Reserve System.

1. Slavery does reveal human capital prices, and historically slaves functioned much like other forms of wealth; slaves were traded, invested in, and used as collateral. In Chapter 6 of this volume, Daina Berry discusses the historical importance of slaves as form of capital.

2. Thomas Piketty, *Capital in the Twenty-First Century,* trans. Arthur Goldhammer (Cambridge, MA: Belknap Press of Harvard University Press, 2014), 46, 163.

3. Ibid., 305–308.

4. Ibid., 163.

5. Ibid., 223–224. Capital's share of income has traced a U-shape over the last century. The share is currently 25 to 30 percent of national income, which is still below the 35 to 40 percent that prevailed a century ago.

6. Lawrence Katz and Kevin M. Murphy, "Changes in Relative Wages, 1963–1987: Supply and Demand Factors," *Quarterly Journal of Economics* 107 (1992): 35–78.

7. Alan Krueger, "Measuring Labor's Share," *AEA Papers and Proceedings* 89, no. 2 (1999): 45–51. Krueger estimates that raw labor's share of national income increased from 0.1 to 0.13 between 1939 and 1959 before falling to 0.049 by 1996, with most of the decline taking place after 1979. In contrast, human capital's share of national income follows a U-shaped pattern over the twentieth century, climbing from a nadir of 0.63 in 1959 to 0.72 in 1996.

8. Mariacristina De Nardi, Eric French, and John Jones, "Saving after Retirement: A Survey," NBER Working Paper No. 21268 (2015). See also Karen Dynan, Jonathan Skinner, and Stephen Zeldes, "Do the Rich Save More?," *Journal of Political Economy* 112, no. 2 (2004): 397–444.

9. Mariacristina De Nardi, "Quantitative Models of Wealth Inequality: A Survey," NBER Working Paper No. 21106 (2015).

10. Michael Hurd, "Savings of the Elderly and Desired Bequests," *American Economic Review* 77, no. 3 (1987): 298–312. See also Wojciech Kopczuk and Joseph

Lupton, "To Leave or Not to Leave: The Distribution of Bequest Motives," *Review of Economic Studies* 74, no. 1 (2007): 207–235. Hurd finds that people with children actually run down their wealth faster than those without children. Kopczuk and Lupton estimate substantial heterogeneity in bequest motives and argue that children do not seem to be the primary determinant of who leaves a bequest. Dynan et al., "Do the Rich Save More?," similarly find no evidence that households with children save more or have a steeper gradient of savings with respect to income than households with no children.

11. Lena Edlund and Wojciech Kopczuk, in "Women, Wealth, and Inequality," *American Economic Review* 99, no. 1 (2009): 146–178, argue that inherited wealth has become less important over the last several decades because the share of women among the very wealthy, a proxy for inherited wealth, has fallen by 40 percent since 1960. Piketty argues that the destruction of great fortunes in the first half of the twentieth century explains the relative decline in the importance of inherited capital and that the fundamental economic mechanisms at work are no different now than in the past. Piketty's argument relies on the untested assumption that high-income individuals will adopt savings and bequest behaviors similar to those that prevailed prior to World War I.

12. Greg Duncan and Richard Murnane, "Figure 1.6: Enrichment Expenditures on Children, 1972–2006," Russell Sage Foundation (2011), http://www.russellsage .org/research/chartbook/enrichment-expenditures-children-1972-to-2006. For trends in parental time allocation, see Jonathan Guryan, Erik Hurst, and Melissa Kearney, "Parental Education and Parental Time with Children," *Journal of Economic Perspectives* 22 (2008): 23–46. See also Anne Gauthier, Timothy Smeedeng, and Frank Furstenberg Jr., "Are Parents Investing Less Time in Children? Trends in Selected Industrialized Countries," *Population and Development Review* 30 (2004): 647–671; Mark Aguiar and Erik Hurst, "Measuring Trends in Leisure: The Allocation of Time over Five Decades," *Quarterly Journal of Economics* 122 (2007): 969–1006.

13. Susan Mayer, *What Money Can't Buy: Family Income and Children's Life Chances* (Cambridge, MA: Harvard University Press, 1997). See also David Blau, "The Effect of Income on Child Development," *Review of Economics and Statistics* 81, no. 2 (1999): 261–276, as well as Gordon Dahl and Lance Lochner, "The Impact of Family Income on Child Achievement: Evidence from the Earned Income Tax Credit," *American Economic Review* 102, no. 5 (2012): 1927–1956.

14. Sean Reardon, "The Widening Academic Achievement Gap between the Rich and the Poor: New Evidence and Possible Explanations," in *Whither Opportunity? Rising Inequality, Schools, and Children's Life Chances,* ed. Greg J. Duncan and Richard J. Murmane, 91–116 (New York: Russell Sage Foundation, 2011). For a contrasting view, see Eric Nielsen, "The Income-Achievement Gap and Adult Outcome Inequality," Finance and Economics Discussion Series, Board of Governors of the Federal Reserve System (2015).

15. Douglas Almond and Janet Currie, "Killing Me Softly: The Fetal Origins Hypothesis," *Journal of Economic Perspectives* 25, no. 3 (2011): 153–172. See also, among many others, Sandra Black, Paul Devereaux, and Kjell Salvanes, "From the Cradle to the Labor Market? The Effect of Birth Weight on Adult Outcomes," *Quarterly Journal of Economics* 122, no. 1 (2007): 409–439.

16. Some of this literature is surveyed in James Heckman and Stefano Mosso, "The Economics of Human Development and Social Mobility," *Annual Review of Economics* 6 (2014): 689–733. See also Flavio Cunha, James J. Heckman, and Susan Schennach, "Estimating the Technology of Cognitive and Noncognitive Skill Formation," *Econometrica* 78 (2010): 883–931.

17. Gary Becker and Nigel Tomes, "Human Capital and the Rise and Fall of Families," *Journal of Labor Economics* 4 (1986): S1—S39. See also Bhashkar Mazumder, "Fortunate Sons: New Estimates of Intergenerational Mobility in the United States Using Social Security," *Review of Economic and Statistics* 87 (2005): 235–255; Miles Corak, Matthew Lindquist, and Bhashkar Mazumder, "A Comparison of Upward and Downward Intergenerational Mobility in Canada, Sweden, and the United States," *Labour Economics* 30(C) (2014): 185–200. By using many years of income data, Mazumder finds much lower mobility estimates than early papers such as Becker and Tomes, which used a single year of adult earnings for each generation. However, Corak et al. obtain mobility estimates only slightly lower than those of Becker and Tomes even after controlling for transitory income variability.

18. For an excellent overview of the various intergenerational mobility literatures, see Sandra Black and Paul Devereux, "Recent Developments in Intergenerational Mobility," in *Handbook of Labor Economics* 4, pt. B (2011): 1487–1541. Estimates of the relative importance of genetic inheritance in explaining intergenerational correlations are mixed; some papers find quite a large role for genes, while other papers suggest smaller effects. Attempts to measure the causal effects of parental education on mobility likewise produce widely varying estimates. Finally, estimates of wealth mobility, which is most directly related to *C21*'s concerns, are also all over the place, with various authors disagreeing about the importance of bequests, environmental influences, and genetic inheritance. See Casey Mulligan, *Parental Priorities and Economic Inequality* (Chicago: University of Chicago Press, 1997); Kerwin Charles and Erik Hurst, "The Correlation of Wealth across Generations," *Journal of Political Economy* 111, no. 6 (2003): 1155–1182; and Sandra Black, Paul Devereux, Petter Lundborg, and Kaveh Majlesi, "Poor Little Rich Kids? The Determinants of the Intergenerational Transmission of Wealth," NBER Working Paper No. 21409 (2015).

19. Susan Mayer and Leonard Lopoo, "Has the Intergenerational Transmission of Economic Status Changed?," *Journal of Human Resources* 40, no. 1 (2005): 169–185. See also Daniel Aaronson and Bhashkar Mazumder, "Intergenerational Economic Mobility in the United States, 1940–2000," *Journal of Human Resources* 43, no. 1 (2008): 139–172; Chul-In Lee and Gary Solon, "Trends in

Intergenerational Income Mobility," *Review of Economics and Statistics* 91 (2009): 766–772. Mayer and Lopoo estimate that mobility was likely increasing for cohorts born between 1949 and 1956 and then likely decreasing up to cohorts born in 1965. Aaronson and Mazumdar argue that mobility increased in the United States from 1950 to 1980 and declined sharply thereafter. In contrast, Lee and Solon find no significant time trend. A major new addition to this literature is Raj Chetty, Nathaniel Hendren, Patrick Kline, and Emmaniel Saez, "Where Is the Land of Opportunity? The Geography of Intergenerational Mobility in the United States," *Quarterly Journal of Economics* 129, no. 4 (2014): 1553–1623. Chetty and coauthors find that mobility was roughly constant for Americans born between 1971 and 1993, although they also find substantial geographic heterogeneity across different geographies. Mobility over much longer time horizons is studied by Joseph Ferrie, "The End of American Exceptionalism? Mobility in the U.S. since 1850," *Journal of Economic Perspectives* 19 (2005): 199–215; and Gregory Clark, *The Son Also Rises: Surnames and the History of Social Mobility* (Princeton, NJ: Princeton University Press, 2014). Ferrie finds that occupational mobility in the United States was very high in the second half of the nineteenth century before declining markedly after about 1920. Clark uses unusual surnames to track social status over many generations to argue that intergenerational persistence is both much higher than others have estimated and also much more stable over time and across geographies.

20. Becker and Tomes, "Human Capital." See also Gary Becker and Nigel Tomes, "An Equilibrium Theory of the Distribution of Income and Intergenerational Mobility," *Journal of Political Economy* 87 (1979): 1153–1189.

21. Gary Solon, "A Model of Intergenerational Mobility Variation over Time and Place," in *Generational Income Mobility in North America and Europe,* ed. Miles Corak (Cambridge: Cambridge University Press, 2004). Solon develops a model in which parents choose how much to invest in the human capital of their children. A child's human capital depends also on governmental investments and an inherited endowment. Solon shows in this model that mobility is lower when (1) government investment is less progressive, (2) investments in human capital (from either the government or the parent) are more efficient, (3) the earnings return to human capital is higher, or (4) ability is more heritable. Ideally, one could take these theories to data to test the relative importance of various factors in determining intergenerational mobility.

22. Anders Bjorklund, Mikael Lindahl, and Erik Plug, "The Origins of Intergenerational Association: Lessons from Swedish Adoption Data," *Quarterly Journal of Economics* 121 (2006): 999–1028. These authors use data on both the biological and adopted parents of adopted children to argue that prebirth environment seems to interact positively with postbirth factors.

23. Harry Frankfurt, "Equality as a Moral Ideal," *Ethics* 98, no. 1 (1987): 21–43. Frankfurt argues that what matters morally is not equality per se but rather that the poor "have enough."

24. See, among many others, James Heckman, Seong Moon, Rodrigo Pinto, Peter Savelyev, and Adam Yavitz, "The Rate of Return to the High / Scope Perry Preschool Program," *Journal of Public Economics* 94, nos. 1–2 (2010): 114–128; Frances Campbell, Gabriella Conti, James Heckman, Seong Hyeok Moon, Rodrigo Pinto, Elizabeth Pungello, and Yi Pan, "Early Childhood Investments Substantially Boost Adult Health," *Science* 343 (2014): 1478–1485. Prof. Heckman's website, http://heckmanequation.org/, is an excellent source for evidence on the effectiveness of early childhood education.

25. Janet Currie and Duncan Thomas, "Does Head Start Make a Difference?," *American Economic Review* 85 (1995): 341–364. See also Eliana Garces, Duncan Thomas, and Janet Currie, "Longer-Term Effects of Head Start," *American Economic Review* 92 (2002): 999–1012. Currie and Thomas find that Head Start leads to persistent gains in test scores and grade completion for white students, whereas black students experience smaller and more fleeting gains. Garces, Thomas, and Currie find large effects of Head Start on high school graduation, college enrollment, earnings, and criminal activity, although the effects differ substantially by race. For research that looks at differences in treatment effects between very deprived and moderately deprived children, see Marianne Bitler, Hilary Hoynes, and Thurston Domina, "Experimental Evidence on Distributional Effects of Head Start," NBER Working Paper No. 20434 (2014); David Deming, "Early Childhood Intervention and Life-Cycle Skill Development: Evidence from Head Start," *American Economic Journal: Applied Economics* 1 (2009): 111–134. Bitler et al. argue that the gains to Head Start are highly heterogeneous, with the largest treatment effects accruing to the most deprived recipients, a result consistent with Deming's findings.

8. Exploring the Effects of Technology on Income and Wealth Inequality

1. Erik Brynjolfsson and Andrew McAfee, *The Second Machine Age: Work, Progress, and Prosperity in a Time of Brilliant Technologies* (New York: W. W. Norton, 2014).

2. Ezra Oberfield and Devesh Raval, "Micro Data and Macro Technology," NBER Working Paper No. 20452 (September 2014); Loukas Karabarbounis and Brent Neiman, "The Global Decline of the Labor Share," NBER Working Paper No. 19136 (June 2013).

3. David Michael, Antonio Varas, and Pete Engardio, "How Adding More Mobile Subscribers Will Drive Inclusive Growth," a proposal for discussion, submitted to the Symposium on Inclusive Growth, Harvard University, October 2, 2015.

4. Thomas Piketty, "Putting Distribution Back at the Center of Economics: Reflections on *Capital in the Twenty-First Century*," *Journal of Economic Perspectives* 29, no. 1 (Winter 2015): 67–88.

5. Claudia Goldin and Lawrence Katz, *The Race between Education and Technology: The Evolution of U.S. Educational Wage Differentials, 1890–2005* (Cambridge,

MA: Belknap Press of Harvard University Press, 2010); David Autor, Lawrence Katz, and Melissa Kearney, "The Polarization of the U.S. Labor Market," *American Economic Review* 96, no. 2 (2006): 189–194; and David Autor, "Polanyi's Paradox and the Shape of Employment Growth," NBER Working Paper No. 20485 (September 2014).

6. Maarten Goos and Alan Manning coined this use of the term "polarization" in their paper "Lousy and Lovely Jobs: The Rising Polarization of Work in Britain," *Review of Economics and Statistics* 89, no. 1 (2007): 118–133. For a summary of recent research on polarization, see David Autor, "Why Are There Still So Many Jobs? The History and Future of Workplace Automation," *Journal of Economic Perspectives* 29, no. 3 (Summer 2015): 3–30.

7. *Hard Times Reports,* Center on Education and the Workforce, Georgetown University, 2014 and 2015.

8. James Manyika et al., "Digital America: A Tale of the Haves and the Have-Mores," McKinsey Global Institute, December 2015.

9. David Autor, "Skills, Education and the Rise of Earnings Inequality among the Other 99%," *Science,* May 23, 2014, 843–851.

10. Gini coefficients calculated from World Bank data and reported in Wikipedia. See https://en.wikipedia.org/wiki/List_of_countries_by_income_equality. Comparisons of wage inequality in the United States and other developed countries reported in James Gornick and Branko Milanovic, "Income Inequality in the United States in Cross-National Perspective: Redistribution Revisited," Research Brief, Luxembourg Income Study Center, Graduate Center, City University of New York, May 2015.

11. Josh Bivens, Elise Gould, Lawrence Mishel, and Heidi Shierholz, "Raising America's Pay: Why It's Our Central Economic Policy Challenge," Briefing Paper No. 378m, Economic Policy Institute, June 4, 2014.

12. Lawrence Mishel and Alyssa Davis, "Top CEOs Make 300 Times More than Typical Workers," Issue Brief No. 399, Economic Policy Institute, June 21, 2015.

13. Kevin Murphy, "Executive Compensation: Where We Are and How We Got There," in *Handbook of the Economics of Finance,* ed. George Constantinides, Milton Harris, and Rene Stulz (Amsterdam: Elsevier Science North-Holland, 2012).

14. Erik Brynjolfsson, Heekyung Kim, and Guillaume Saint-Jacques, "CEO Pay and Information Technology," MIT Initiative on the Digital Economy Working Paper, February 2016. Earlier draft reported in ICIS 2009 Proceedings, AIS Electronic Library (AISeL), http://aisel.aisnet.org.

15. Jon Bakija, Adam Cole, and Bradley Heim, "Jobs and Income Growth of Top Earners and the Causes of Changing Income Inequality: Evidence from U.S. Tax Returns, William College," April 2012, https://web.williams.edu/Economics/wp/BakijaColeHeimJobsIncomeGrowthTopEarners.pdf.

16. Ulrike Malmendier and Geoffrey Tate, "Superstar CEOs," NBER Working Paper No. 14140 (June 2008).

17. Marianne Bertrand and Sendhil Mullainathan, "Are CEOs Rewarded for Luck? The Ones without Principals Are," *Quarterly Journal of Economics* 116, no. 3 (2001): 901–932.

18. Recent work on the role of rents in income and wealth inequality in the United States and the links between rents, technology, and intellectual property protection includes the following: Joseph Stiglitz, *The Price of Inequality* (New York: W. W. Norton, 2012); Robert Reich, *Saving Capitalism: For the Many, Not the Few* (New York: Knopf, 2015); Paul Krugman, "Challenging the Oligarchy," *New York Review of Books,* December 2015; Jason Furman and Peter Orzsag, "A Firm-Level Perspective on the Role of Rents in the Rise of Income Inequality," White House Council of Economic Advisers, October 2015; and Dean Baker, "The Upward Redistribution of Income: Are Rents the Story?," Working Paper, Center for Economic and Policy Research, December 2015.

19. Robert M. Solow, "Thomas Piketty Is Right," *New Republic,* April 22, 2014 (this volume, Chapter 2).

20. Daron Acemoglu and David Autor, "Skills, Tasks and Technologies: Implications for Employment and Earnings," Handbook of Labor Economics, 2011.

21. Autor, "Polanyi's Paradox"; Manyika et al., "Digital America"; and Carl Frey and Michael Osborne, "The Future of Employment: How Susceptible Are Jobs to Computerization?," Oxford Martin School (September 2013).

22. Autor, "Why Are There Still So Many Jobs?"

23. Nir Jaimovich and Henry E. Siu, "The Trend Is the Cycle: Job Polarization and Jobless Recoveries," National Bureau of Economic Research, Working Paper No. 18334 (2012).

24. Daron Acemoglu, David Autor, David Dorn, Gordon Hanson, and Brendan Price, "Import Competition and the Great US Employment Sag of the 2000s," *Journal of Labor Economics* 34 (2016): S141–S198; and David Autor, David Dorn, and Gordon Hanson, "Untangling Trade and Technology: Evidence from Local Labor Markets," *Economic Journal* 125, no. 584 (2015): 641–646.

25. Manyika et al., "Digital America."

26. Lawrence Mishel, Elise Gould, and Josh Bivens, "Wage Stagnation in Nine Charts," Report, Economic Policy Institute (January 6, 2015).

27. Autor, "Skills, Education."

28. Lawrence Mishel, "Unions, Inequality and Faltering Middle-Class Wages," Economic Policy Institute, Issue Brief No. 342 (August 2012).

29. Florence Jaumotte and Carolina Osorio Buitron, "Inequality and Labor Market Institutions," International Monetary Fund Staff Discussion Note, July 2015.

30. David Cooper, "Raising the Minimum Wage to $12 by 2020 Would Lift Wages for 35 Million American Workers," Economic Policy Institute, EPI Briefing Paper No. 405 (July 2015), http://www.epi.org/files/2015/raising-the-minimum-wage-to-12-dollars-by-2020-would-lift-wages-for-35-million-american-workers.pdf.

31. Michael Spence and Sandile Hlatshwayo, "The Evolving Structure of the American Economy and the Employment Challenge," Working Paper, Council on Foreign Relations (2011); Michael Spence, "The Impact of Globalization on Income and Employment," *Foreign Affairs,* July / August 2011.

32. Economy-wide productivity growth, measured by changes in value added per person over time, is a weighted average of the change in value added per person in the tradable and nontradable sectors (where the weights are the starting employment shares) minus the difference between tradable and nontradable value added per person times the increment in the employment share of the nontradable sector.

33. David Autor, David Dorn, and Gordon Hanson, "The China Syndrome: Local Labor Market Effects of Import Competition in the United States," *American Economic Review* 103, no. 6 (2013): 2121–2168.

34. Robert Lawrence, "Recent Declines in Labor's Share in US Income: A Preliminary Neoclassical Account," Working Paper No. 15-10, Peterson Institute for International Economics (June 2015), http://hks.harvard.edu/fs/rlawrence /wp15-10PIIE.pdf.

35. Josh Bivens and Lawrence Mishel, "Understanding the Historic Divergence between Productivity and a Typical Worker's Pay," Economic Policy Institute, EPI Briefing Paper No. 406 (September 2015), http://www.epi.org/files/2015 /understanding-productivity-pay-divergence-final.pdf.

36. For a more detailed discussion of trends in robotics, artificial intelligence, additive manufacturing, and other technological breakthroughs and their impact on jobs and wages, see Carl Benedikt Frey and Michael Osborne, "Technology at Work: The Future of Innovation and Employment," Oxford Martin School and Citi GPS, February 2015, http://www.oxfordmartin.ox.ac.uk/downloads /reports/Citi_GPS_Technology_Work.pdf.

37. Dani Rodrik, "Premature Industrialization," NBER Working Paper No. 20935 (February 2015), http://www.nber.org/papers/w20935.

38. Carl Benedikt Frey and Michael Osborne, "Technology at Work v.2.0: The Future Is Not What It Used to Be," Oxford Martin School and Citi GPS (January 2016), http://www.oxfordmartin.ox.ac.uk/downloads/reports/Citi_GPS _Technology_Work_2.pdf.

39. Michael Greenstone, Adam Looney, Jeremy Patashnik, and Muxin Yu, "Thirteen Economic Facts about Social Mobility and the Role of Education," The Hamilton Project (June 2013), http://www.hamiltonproject.org/assets/legacy /files/downloads_and_links/THP_13EconFacts_FINAL6.pdf.

40. Autor, "Why Are There Still So Many Jobs?"

41. Martin Ford, *Rise of the Robots: Technology and the Threat of a Jobless Future* (New York: Basic Books, 2015).

42. Laura Tyson, "Intelligent Machines and Displaced Workers," Project Syndicate, March 7, 2014.

9. Income Inequality, Wage Determination, and the Fissured Workplace

The views expressed in this paper do not necessarily reflect the views of the U.S. Department of Labor. No government resources were expended in the writing or research of this chapter.

1. See Larry Mishel, Josh Bivens, Elise Gould, and Heidi Shierholz, *The State of Working America,* 12th ed. (Ithaca, NY: Cornell University Press, 2013).

2. Along with Thomas Piketty, *Capital in the Twenty-First Century,* trans. Arthur Goldhammer (Cambridge, MA: Belknap Press of Harvard University Press, 2014), for overall facts and surveys of theoretical work in the area, see David Autor, Lawrence Katz, and Melissa Kearney, "Trends in U.S. Wage Inequality: Revising the Revisionists," *Review of Economics and Statistics* 90, no. 2 (2008): 300–323; and Daron Acemoglu and David Autor, "Skills, Tasks and Technologies: Implications for Employment and Earnings," in *Handbook of Labor Economics,* vol. 4, pt. B, ed. David Card and Orley Ashenfelter (Amsterdam: Elsevier, 2011), 1043–1166.

3. See David Weil, *The Fissured Workplace: Why Work Became So Bad for So Many and What Can Be Done to Improve It* (Cambridge, MA: Harvard University Press, 2014).

4. The development of these standards—the "glue" that keeps the mechanisms of the fissured workplace together—have become more available as digital technologies have lowered the costs of monitoring. See ibid., chap. 3.

5. These estimates are from Kevin Hallock, "Job Loss and the Fraying of the Implicit Employment Contract," *Journal of Economic Perspectives* 23, no. 4 (2009): 40–43. They are based on data from the National Compensation Survey for 2011. The averages mask differences in the components of employer hourly costs across workers, occupations, and industries. For example, wages and salaries for service workers account for 71 percent and legally required benefits account for 9.3 percent of employer hourly costs because employees in service industries typically receive far lower insurance and retirement benefits than workers in other industries.

6. Sidney Webb and Beatrice Webb, *Industrial Democracy* (London: Macmillan, 1897), 281.

7. This assumes that the supply of labor is upward sloping—that is, in order to induce additional people into a labor market, employers must pay an increasingly higher wage rate as they increase employment. How quickly the wage needs to increase to entice additional people in the market (measured as the elasticity of labor supply) affects the degree to which a labor market is affected by a monopsonistic employer. For a complete discussion, see Alan Manning, *Monopsony in Motion: Imperfect Competition in Labor Markets* (Princeton, NJ: Princeton University Press, 2003), chap. 4.

8. In a competitive labor market, the supply of labor facing a firm is totally elastic, meaning that the firm can purchase as much labor at a certain skill level as it

wants at the market price. But search frictions reduce the willingness of workers to move, which means the supply of labor slopes upward and firms have an ability to set wages (William Boal and Michael Ransom, "Monopsony in the Labor Market," *Journal of Economic Literature* 35, no. 1 [1997]: 86–112). Ransom and Oaxaca estimate elasticity of labor supply for men and women in the grocery store industry and show that the supply of labor for women is less elastic than for men, and as a result their wages are more affected by the monopsony position of employers in that industry—specifically, that the relative pay of women is lower. See Michael Ransom and Ronald Oaxaca, "New Market Power Models and Sex Differences in Pay," *Journal of Labor Economics* 28, no. 2 (2010): 267–315.

9. Another reason for employer-side power, they argued, was that leisure is a normal good at the household level, and hence in response to wage cuts male workers would supply their wives and children to the labor market. For that reason— namely, sustaining a high wage rate for men—the Institutionalists supported statutory limits on child labor and working hours for women, and championed the nascent concept of minimum wages. See Richard Ely, *The Labor Movement in America* (New York: Thomas Y. Crowell and Co., 1886).

10. See Sumner Slichter, "Notes on the Structure of Wages," *Review of Economics and Statistics* 32, no. 1 (1950): 80–91; Sumner Slichter, James Healy, and Robert Livernash, *The Impact of Collective Bargaining on Management* (Washington, DC: Brookings Institution, 1960).

11. Fred Foulkes, *Personnel Policies in Large Non-Union Workplaces* (Englewood Cliffs, NJ: Prentice Hall, 1980).

12. Gary Becker and Walter Oi proposed models to help explain why, as John Dunlop often commented, "labor markets are not a bourse" and instantaneous wage rates do not allocate labor efficiently on their own. The presence of either quasi-fixed costs of labor or the need to provide specific training (i.e., training that benefits a worker at a specific employer) creates a compensation problem that firms must find a way to solve by acting as if, in the Oi model, only a portion of compensation costs are variable or, in the case of Becker, thinking about compensation policy as part of a human capital investment that the firm must recover over time. See Gary Becker, *Human Capital: A Theoretical and Empirical Analysis with Special Reference to Education* (New York: Columbia University Press, 1964); and Walter Oi, "The Fixed Employment Costs of Specialized Labor," in *The Measurement of Labor Costs*, ed. Jack Triplett (Chicago: University Chicago Press, 1983), 63–122.

13. In this view, the overall employment relationship creates value that the parties then must figure out a way to share in the course of ongoing employment. These contracts reflect both conditions in the external labor markets and relative bargaining power within the firm. This view is developed in Paul Milgrom, "Employment Contracts, Influence Activities, and Efficient Organization Design," *Journal of Political Economy* 96, no. 1 (1988): 42–60. For an overview of

implicit contract theory in employment, see Sherwin Rosen, "Implicit Contracts: A Survey," *Journal of Economic Literature* 25, no. 4 (1988): 1144–1175.

14. The ultimatum game and a wide variety of variants of it (e.g., the "dictator game," where the proposer's split is imposed without the consent of the second player) have been used both as experiments, where people play the game with real money but in a decision laboratory, and in the field, where experimenters try to create similar conditions but with more realistic setups. They have also been replicated at different levels of payoffs—that is, with much larger pots of money at stake. In general, the same results hold up. Detailed discussions and extensive references about these results can be found in Ernst Fehr and Klaus Schmidt, "A Theory of Fairness, Competition, and Cooperation," *American Economic Review* 114, no. 3 (1999): 177–181; Fehr and Schmidt, "Theories of Fairness and Reciprocity," in *Advances in Economics and Econometrics,* ed. Matthias Dewatripont, I. Hansen, and S. Turnovsly (New York: Cambridge University Press, 2002), 208–257; Fehr and Schmidt, "A Theory of Fairness, Competition, and Cooperation," *Quarterly Journal of Economics* 97, no. 2 (2007): 817–868; and Colin Camerer, *Behavioral Game Theory* (Princeton, NJ: Princeton University Press, 2003).

15. The vast majority (87 percent) of managers in Bewley's study of compensation policies agreed with the statement "Most or all employees know one another's pay." See Truman Bewley, *Why Wages Don't Fall during a Recession* (Cambridge, MA: Harvard University Press, 1999), table 6.6, p. 80.

16. I discuss two types of equity notions—horizontal fairness versus vertical fairness—in greater depth in *The Fissured Workplace,* chap. 4.

17. Just under 50 percent cited "job performance" and only 7 percent cited "avoidance of discrimination suits" as the major reason for internal pay equity. Bewley quotes a human resources manager in a unionized manufacturing company with 27,000 employees remarking: "Unfairness can cause upheaval within an organization and lead to dysfunctional activities. People want to be treated fairly and to see that their contributions are recognized and that this is done on a consistent basis from one location to another and from one profession to another." See Bewley, *Why Wages Don't Fall,* 79, 81. For a related formal model of how fairness concerns play out in workplaces, see Oded Stark and Walter Hyll, "On the Economic Architecture of the Workplace: Repercussions of Social Comparisons among Heterogeneous Workers," *Journal of Labor Economics* 29, no. 2 (2011): 349–375.

18. See Ernst Fehr, Lorenz Goette, and Christian Zehnder, "A Behavioral Account of the Labor Market: The Role of Fairness Concerns," *Annual Review of Economics* 1 (2009): 355–384, quotation at 378. The literature on loss aversion and "framing" in psychology is extensive. Kahneman provides an overview of the extensive research in the field in the decades following his landmark work with Amos Tversky. See Daniel Kahneman, *Thinking Fast and Slow* (New York: Farrar, Straus and Giroux, 2011).

19. Fred Foulkes in his study of large nonunion workplaces in the 1970s found that "the pay policies of the companies [large nonunion employers] are designed to provide and demonstrate equity" (Foulkes, *Personnel Policies in Large Non-Union Workplaces* [Englewood Cliffs, NJ: Prentice Hall, 1980], 185). Bewley similarly found that although executives acknowledged that differences in pay between grades proved useful as incentives, 69 percent of the businesses interviewed cited "internal equity, internal harmony, fairness, and good morale" as the principal justification. See Bewley, *Why Wages Don't Fall,* table 6.4 and discussion at 75–79.

20. For an overview of this literature, see Walter Oi and Todd Idson, "Firm Size and Wages," in *Handbook of Labor Economics,* vol. 13, ed. Orley Ashenfelter and David Card (New York: Elsevier, 1999), 2165–2214. Two groundbreaking studies of the effects are Charles Brown and James Medoff, "The Employer Size-Wage Effect," *Journal of Political Economy* 97, no. 5 (1989): 1027–1059; and Charles Brown, James Hamilton, and James Medoff, *Employers Large and Small* (Cambridge, MA: Harvard University Press, 1990). See also Erica Groshen, "Five Reasons Why Wages Vary across Employers," *Industrial Relations* 30, no. 1 (1991): 350–381. A more recent study finds that large firm-effect on wages declined by about one-third between 1988 and 2003; see Matissa Hollister, "Does Firm Size Matter Anymore? The New Economy and Firm Size Wage Effect," *American Sociological Review* 69, no. 5 (2004): 659–676. Binnur Balkan and Semih Tumen find larger firm size effects in informal jobs than in formal jobs in the Turkish economy, raising interesting organizational questions around wage-setting differences within firms. See Binnur Balkan and Semih Tumen, "Firm-Size Wage Gaps along the Formal-Informal Divide: Theory and Evidence," *Industrial Relations* 55, no. 2 (2016): 235–266.

21. A recent set of empirical papers estimating the degree of monopsony power provide interesting evidence. The papers are summarized in Orley Ashenfelter, Henry Farber, and Michael Ransom, "Labor Market Monopsony," *Journal of Labor Economics* 28, no. 2 (2010): 203–210.

22. Jim Rebitzer and Lowell Taylor summarize literature on problems arising from more complex monitoring / agency where workers have multiple aspects of effort to monitor. If there are two aspects of effort, for example, and they are complementary, but one aspect is not observable, the employer faces a difficult problem in creating a compensation model. Shifting this work to an independent contractor is desirable in such cases, in that the payment becomes more directly related to output of the provider than to the input of the worker. See James Rebitzer and Lowell Taylor, "Extrinsic Rewards and Intrinsic Motives: Standard and Behavioral Approaches to Agency and Labor Markets," in Card and Ashenfelter *Handbook of Labor Economics,* vol. 4, pt. B.

23. Ironically, it would also remove the resource distortion introduced by monopsony, because under these circumstances the employer would end up hiring additional workers to the point that would be found in a competitive market.

However, unlike the situation in a competitive market, the monopsonist would capture the "bonus" received by workers whose wage rate exceeded their marginal contribution to production (i.e., the rents of inframarginal workers).

24. More technically, successful core competency in branding or product development means less-elastic demand for those companies (and therefore a greater ability to price at higher levels for a given level of costs). In those cases, the reduction of labor costs arising from fissuring can go primarily to investors. In core competency areas of coordination (think retailing) or with economies of scale, lead companies may still face more competition in their product markets. Labor cost savings are more likely to flow into reduced prices for consumers (as well as to higher returns for investors).

25. See Matthew Dey, Susan Houseman, and Anne Polivka, "What Do We Know about Contracting Out in the United States? Evidence from Household and Establishment Surveys," in *Essays in Labor in the New Economy,* ed. Katherine Abraham, James Spletzer, and Michael Harper (Chicago: University of Chicago Press, 2010), 267–304.

26. Abraham and Taylor demonstrate that the higher the typical wage for the workforce at an establishment, the more likely that establishment will contract out its janitorial work They also show that establishments that do any contracting out of janitorial work tend to shift out the function entirely. See Katherine Abraham and Susan Taylor, "Firms' Use of Outside Contractors: Theory and Evidence," *Journal of Labor Economics* 14, no. 3 (1996): 394–424, esp. tables 4 and 5 and pp. 407–410.

27. Samuel Berlinski, "Wages and Contracting Out: Does the Law of One Price Hold?," *British Journal of Industrial Relations* 46, no. 1 (2008): 59–75.

28. Arandajit Dube and Ethan Kaplan, "Does Outsourcing Reduce Wages in the Low-Wage Service Occupations? Evidence from Janitors and Guards," *Industrial and Labor Relations Review* 63, no. 2 (2010): 287–306. The cited differences control for a variety of factors that might be associated with differences in the workforce as well as the places where the work is done. The Dube and Kaplan study provides a particularly rich set of estimates that allow the authors to rule out a number of potentially "unmeasured" characteristics of contract versus in-house workers.

29. See Deborah Goldschmidt and Johannes Schmieder, "The Rise of Domestic Outsourcing and the Evolution of the German Wage Structure," Working Paper, Boston University (2015). The authors also show that food, cleaning, security, and janitorial workers receive wage premiums comparable to those of the overall workforce prior to outsourcing. This result, like the earlier Abraham and Taylor study ("Firms' Use of Outside Contractors"), have significant incentives to outsource work that are not central to core competencies, particularly where they can find other methods to monitor the output of subordinate providers of those services.

30. See Peter Cappelli and Monika Hamori, "Are Franchises Bad Employers?," *Industrial and Labor Relations Review* 61, no. 2 (2008): 146–162.

31. Franchisees (independent businesses who pay royalties to be a part of a franchised system) have significantly lower rates of return than do the franchisors (the owners of the brand—the core competency—and sometimes operators of a limited number of "company-owned" outlets). See Patrick J. Kaufmann and Francine Lafontaine, "Costs of Control: The Source of Economic Rents for McDonald's Franchisees," *Journal of Law and Economics* 37, no. 2 (1994): 417–453; and Weil, *The Fissured Workplace*, chap. 6.

32. Alan Krueger found that managers of franchisees earned significantly less than managers of comparable fast-food outlets owned by the company (Alan Krueger, "Ownership, Agency, and Wages: An Examination of Franchising in the Fast Food Industry," *Quarterly Journal of Economics* 106, no. 1 [1991]: 75–101). MinWoong Ji and I found in a related vein far higher violations of labor standards in terms of frequency and severity among franchisees than in the company-owned units of the franchisors (MinWoong Ji and David Weil, "The Impact of Franchising on Labor Standards Compliance," *Industrial and Labor Relations Review* 68, no. 5 [2015]: 977–1006). For consistent evidence of the impacts of fissuring on overall earnings in the hotel industry, see Richard Freeman, "The Subcontracted Labor Market," *Perspectives on Work* 18 (2014): 38–42.

33. The authors use a combined data set of the March Current Population Survey, the Census Longitudinal Business Data Base, and the Longitudinal Employer-Household Dynamics data set. This provides them detailed data on both workers and the firms for which they work. Because most workers stay at the same establishment in any given year, the approach of looking at the sources of growing inequality "around" the stayers provides a useful mooring post to explore the causes of growing earning dispersion around them. See Erling Barth, Alex Bryson, James Davis, and Richard Freeman, "It's Where You Work: Increases in Earnings Dispersion across Establishments and Individuals in the U.S.," *Journal of Labor Economics* 34, no. 2 (2016): S67–S97.

34. The authors use administrative data from the confidential Master Earnings File (MEF), compiled and maintained by the U.S. Social Security Administration, for their analysis. The MEF contains labor earning data, which, unlike other sources of earnings data, is not capped and also includes nonsalary forms of compensation such as bonuses, exercised stock options, and estimated dollar values of restricted stock grants provided to employees (executives, in most cases). See Jae Song, David Price, Nicholas Bloom, Faith Guvenen, and Till von Wachter, "Firming Up Inequality," NBER Working Paper No. 21199 (2015).

35. See David Card, Jörg Heining, and Patrick Kline, "Workplace Heterogeneity and the Rise of West German Wage Inequality," *Quarterly Journal of Economics* 128, no. 3 (2013): 967–1015. A more recent paper by this team (along with Cardoso) builds a model where firms exercise some monopsony power arising from

heterogeneity in workers' preferences for different employers (with no particular model of the source of that heterogeneity). Their model precludes price discrimination based on idiosyncratic preferences of the workers, but still allows firms to "post a common wage for each skill group that is marked down from marginal product in inverse proportion to their elasticity of labor supply to the firm." See David Card, Ana Rute Cardoso, Jörg Heining, and Patrick Kline, "Firms and Labor Market Inequality: Evidence and Some Theory," Working Paper, University of California, Berkeley (2016).

36. John Dunlop articulated this view—and in many ways founded a new area that sought to wed economic principles to the realities of wage determination—in his book *Industrial Relations Systems,* first published in 1957. The book set out a theoretical framework for assessing the market, institutional, technological, and social forces driving actors in industrial relations systems (both union and nonunion) to the outcomes observed in the labor market. See Dunlop, *Industrial Relations Systems,* rev. ed. (Cambridge, MA: Harvard Business School Press Classic, 1993).

37. Indicative of the wedding of economic theory and mathematics, Paul Samuelson's groundbreaking book *Foundations of Economic Analysis* begins with the following statement: "The existence of analogies between central features of various theories implies the existence of a general theory which underlies the particular theories and unifies them with respect to those central features. This fundamental principle of generalization by abstraction was enunciated by the eminent American mathematician E. H. Moore more than thirty years ago. It is the purpose of the pages that follow to work out its implications for theoretical and applied economics." See Samuelson, *Foundations of Economic Analysis* (Cambridge, MA: Harvard University Press, 1947).

38. Ronald Coase commented on the ascendency of neoclassical approaches over Institutionalists, "Without a theory they had nothing to pass on except a mass of descriptive material waiting for a theory, or a fire." Coase quoted in Richard Posner, "Nobel Laureate: Ronald Coase and Methodology," *Journal of Economic Perspectives* 7, no. 4 (1993): 195–210, quotation at 206.

39. Piketty, *Capital,* 333.

40. See, for example, Patrick Bayer, Stephen Ross, and Giorgio Topa, "Place of Work and Place of Residence: Informal Hiring Networks and Labor Market Outcomes," *Journal of Political Economy* 116, no. 6 (2008): 1150–1196; Judith Hellerstein, Melissa McInerney, and David Neumark, "Neighbors and Coworkers: The Importance of Residential Labor Market Networks," *Journal of Labor Economics* 29, no. 4 (2011): 659–695; and Yves Zenou, "A Dynamic Model of Weak and Strong Ties in the Labor Market," *Journal of Labor Economics* 33, no. 4 (2015): 891–932.

41. See Freeman, "The Subcontracted Labor Market," 42. In a similar vein, David Card and co-authors note, "Finally, the idea that even highly advanced labor markets like that of the United States might be better characterized as

imperfectly competitive opens a host of questions about the welfare implications of industrial policies and labor market institutions such as the minimum wage, unemployment insurance, and employment protection" (Card et al., "Firms and Labor Market Inequality," 24).

42. The fissured workplace phenomenon is also being documented in countries around the world. A number of the aforementioned studies focused on the impact on earnings for specific occupations and job types in Germany and Turkey. Another set of studies discussed by David Card and co-authors examines the growth in earnings inequality in Germany, Portugal, the United Kingdom, Italy, and other countries. For a summary of studies, see Card et al., "Firms and Labor Market Inequality," appendix table 1. The *Comparative Labor Law and Policy Journal,* volume 27, provides articles on the growth and impact of the fissured workplace in nine countries, including France, the United Kingdom, Israel, Brazil, and Japan.

43. Piketty, *Capital,* 333.

10. Increasing Capital Income Share and Its Effect on Personal Income Inequality

I am grateful for comments by Healther Boushey, Brad DeLong, Christoph Lakner, Salvatore Morelli, Eric Nielsen, Marshall Steinbaum, and other participants at the conference in Bellagio, December 2015.

1. The terms "personal" and "interpersonal" income distribution will be used interchangeably.

2. Loukas Karabarbounis and Brent Neiman, "The Global Decline of the Labor Share," *Quarterly Journal of Economics* 129, no. 1 (October 24, 2013): 61–103; Michael Elsby, Bart Hobijn, and Ayşegül Şahin, "The Decline of the U.S. Labor Share," Brookings Papers on Economic Activity, Brookings Institution (Fall 2013), http://www.brookings.edu/~/media/Projects/BPEA/Fall%202013/2013b _elsby_labor_share.pdf.

3. Erik Bengtsson and Daniel Waldenström, "Capital Shares and Income Inequality: Evidence from the Long Run," Discussion Paper Series, Institute for the Study of Labor, Bonn, Germany (December 2015), table 5, http://ftp.iza .org/dp9581.pdf.

4. Margaret Jacobson and Filippo Occhino, "Labor's Declining Share of Income and Rising Inequality," Economic Commentary, Federal Reserve Bank of Cleveland, Ohio (September 25, 2013), https://www.clevelandfed.org/newsroom-and -events/publications/economic-commentary/2012-economic-commentaries /ec-201213-labors-declining-share-of-income-and-rising-inequality.aspx.

5. Maura Francese and Carlos Mulas-Granados, "Functional Income Distribution and Its Role in Explaining Inequality," IMF Working Paper WP/15/244 (November 2015), https://www.imf.org/external/pubs/ft/wp/2015/wp15244.pdf.

6. Ibid., 15.

7. A slightly different approach to this issue is adopted by Anthony Atkinson, "Factor Shares: The Principal Problem of Political Economy?," *Oxford Review of Economic Policy* 25, no. 1 (2009): 3–16, see esp. 10–11. I assume here a model of homogeneous capital. Probably reacting to the critiques (e.g., Joseph Stiglitz, "New Theoretical Perspectives on the Distribution of Income and Wealth among Individuals: Part 1. The Wealth Residual," NBER Working Paper No. 21189 [May 2015], http://www.nber.org/papers/w21189.pdf, and several other follow-up papers) that have pointed out that it is the heterogeneous nature of capital, more particularly the role of housing, that is responsible for the rise in the capital / income ratio, Thomas Piketty ("Capital, Predistribution and Redistribution," Crooked Timber, January 4, 2016, http://crookedtimber.org /2016/01/04/capital-predistribution-and-redistribution/) now prefers multi-sector models of capital accumulation. Such models allow relative prices of various capital goods to vary differently and, as in the case of rising real estate prices, to drive the observed K / Y ratio. They also do not depend on the greater than uni-tary elasticity of substitution between capital and labor to generate an increasing capital share. Although that approach certainly has the advantage of being more realistic, it fails to provide the powerful and focused simplicity of the one-sector model.

8. Debraj Ray, "Nit-Piketty: A Comment on Thomas Piketty's *Capital in the Twenty-First Century*," Chhota Pegs, May 25, 2014, http://debrajray.blogspot .co.uk/2014/05/nit-piketty.html; Ray, "Ray on Milanovic on Ray on Piketty," Chhota Pegs, June 3, 2014, http://debrajray.blogspot.com/2014/06/ray-on -milanovic-on-ray-on-piketty.html.

9. Yew-Kwang Ng, "Is an Increasing Capital Share under Capitalism Inevitable?," discussion paper, Nanyang Technological University, Singapore, August 13, 2014.

10. Michał Kalecki, "A Theory of Profits," *Economic Journal* 52, nos. 206 / 207 (1942): 258–267; Robert Solow, "A Contribution to the Theory of Economic Growth," *Quarterly Journal of Economics* 70, no. 1 (February 1956): 65–94. Branko Milanovic, "Where I Disagree and Agree with Debraj Ray's Critique of Piketty's *Capital in the 21st Century*," Globalinequality, June 2, 2014, http:// glineq.blogspot.com/2014/06/where-i-disagree-and-agree-with-debraj.html. In his two recent papers (Thomas Piketty and Gabriel Zucman, "Wealth and Inheritance in the Long Run," in *Handbook of Income Distribution*, ed. Anthony Atkinson and Bourguignon François, vol. 2B (Amsterdam: North-Holland, 2015), 1303–1368; and Piketty, "Capital, Predistribution and Redistribution"), Piketty addresses this point explicitly. He allows for capitalists' consumption out of r but notes that a family needs only to "reinvest a fraction g / r of its capital income . . . to ensure that its capital stock will grow at the same rate . . . as the . . . economy" (Piketty, "Capital, Predistribution, and Redistribution," 3). Obvi-ously, any greater saving will increase the capital stock and make capital's income share in net product go up. Both papers also deemphasize, compared to the

book, the importance of the r > g relationship in explaining the increase in income inequality, but see its role as having mostly to do with the long-run level of wealth inequality: "Specifically, a higher r-g gap will tend to greatly amplify the steady-state inequality of wealth distribution" (ibid., 3).

11. s_c is the same as Piketty's alpha.

12. The condition is $R_c G_c > R_l G_l$.

13. In its implications, this is similar to the situation where capital is privately owned but the return on capital is assessed at confiscatory (100 percent) tax rates and the proceeds are distributed equally per capita. Obviously, endowments of capital will not be equalized, but income from capital would be. I owe this idea to Christoph Lakner.

14. James Meade, *Different Forms of Share Economy* (London: Public Policy Centre, 1986); Anthony Atkinson, *Inequality: What Can Be Done?* (Cambridge, MA: Harvard University Press, 2015).

15. We implicitly assume that the amount of randomly distributed capital income is equal to the usual share of capital income in total net income (say, up to 30 percent). Obviously, if randomly distributed capital dwarfs labor income, then it could happen that people who have randomly "drawn" a large allotment of capital income become also total income rich. In that rather extravagant case, R_c could be high and indeed even approach 1.

16. Obviously, having just one capitalist (low s_k) does not ensure that s_c will be also low: it could be that that sole capitalist is so rich that the capital share is high. In the rest of the discussion, I assume, however, that s_k and s_c move broadly together.

17. For the evidence on new capitalism, see Anthony Atkinson and Christoph Lakner, "Wages, Capital and Top Incomes: The Factor Income Composition of Top Incomes in the USA, 1960–2005," paper presented at Sixth ECINEQ Meeting in Luxembourg, July 2015, http://www.ecineq.org/ecineq_lux15/FILES x2015/CR2/p196.pdf, which shows an increasing association of high labor and capital income in the United States during the past half century. Such a society is also evoked by Piketty (*Capital,* chap. 7, p. 416 in French edition).

18. These features of "new capitalism" are similar to the point repeatedly made by Piketty that the postwar period is distinguished by the emergence of a property-owning middle class even if its share of capital ownership has remained relatively small; see Piketty, *Capital in the Twenty-First Century* (Cambridge, MA: Belknap Press of Harvard University Press, 2014), 410, 552.

19. Personal communication by Christoph Lakner.

20. "In It Together: Why Less Inequality Benefits All," OECD (May 21, 2015), http://www.oecd.org/social/in-it-together-why-less-inequality-benefits-all -9789264235120-en.htm; Piketty, *Capital,* 549.

21. Note that we cannot judge how close they come to "new capitalism 2" because under "new capitalism 2" R_c would be still equal 1 even though the transmission link between greater capital income share and interpersonal inequality is severed.

22. Karabarbounis and Neiman, "Global Decline of the Labor Share," fig. 2.

23. Lance Taylor, Özlem Ömer, and Armon Rezai, "Wealth Concentration, Income Distribution, and Alternatives for the USA," Working Paper No. 17, Institute for New Economic Thinking (September 2015), https://ineteconomics.org/uploads /papers/WP17-Lance-Taylor-Income-dist-wealth-concentration-0915.pdf.

24. Piketty notices the need for complementarity between taxation and re-distribution policies in general and the need to change forms of governance of private capital. He closes the last chapter of his book by stating that "without a real right to intervene in corporate decision-making (including seats for workers on the company's board of directors), [financial] transparency (brought about by taxation of wealth) is of little use" (*Capital*, 570).

25. Assuming some stickiness in the rate of return.

11. Global Inequality

Christoph Lakner is an economist in the Development Economics Research Group at the World Bank. I am very grateful to Espen Prydz and Matthew Wai-Poi for help with the data, and Heather Boushey, Francisco Ferreira, La-Bhus Fah Jirasavetakul, Branko Milanovic, and Carmen Ye for very helpful comments. The findings, interpretations, and conclusions expressed in this chapter are entirely those of the author. They do not necessarily represent the views of the International Bank for Reconstruction and Development / World Bank and its affiliated organizations, or those of the Executive Directors of the World Bank or the governments they represent.

1. T. Piketty, *Capital in the Twenty-First Century,* trans. Arthur Goldhammer (Cambridge, MA: Belknap Press of Harvard University Press, 2014).

2. S. Anand and P. Segal, "The Global Distribution of Income," in *Handbook of Income Distribution,* vol. 2, ed. A. B. Atkinson and F. Bourguignon (Amsterdam: Elsevier, 2015).

3. B. Milanovic, "The Return of 'Patrimonial Capitalism': A Review of Thomas Piketty's *Capital in the Twenty-First Century,*" *Journal of Economic Literature* 52, no. 2 (2014): 519–534.

4. Ibid.

5. P. Brasor, "The Economics Book Everyone Is Talking About, but Has Anyone Read It?," *Japan Times,* February 14, 2015, http://www.japantimes.co.jp/news /2015/02/14/national/media-national/economics-book-everyone-talking -anyone-read; S. Denney, "Piketty in Seoul: Rising Income Inequality in South Korea," *The Diplomat,* November 4, 2014, http://thediplomat.com/2014/11 /south-koreas-shocking-inequality/.

6. United Nations Development Programme (UNDP), Bureau for Development Policy, "Humanity Divided: Confronting Inequality in Developing Countries" (2014).

7. R. Kanbur and J. Zhuang, "Confronting Rising Inequality in Asia," in *Asian Development Outlook* (Washington, DC: Asian Development Bank, 2012).

8. A. B. Atkinson and F. Bourguignon, "Introduction: Income Distribution Today," in Atkinson and Bourguignon, *Handbook of Income Distribution*.

9. C. Lakner and B. Milanovic, "Global Income Distribution: From the Fall of the Berlin Wall to the Great Recession," *World Bank Economic Review* 30, no. 2 (2016): 203–232.

10. In Chapter 8 of this volume, Tyson and Spence discuss in more detail the role of technology in explaining U.S. income inequality.

11. Lakner and Milanovic, "Global Income Distribution."

12. As a result, our results would tend to underestimate within-country and thus global inequality. However, Anand and Segal, in "The Global Distribution of Income," argue that the differences are very small. We find that moving from percentile to decile groups in a slightly different global distribution reduces the global Gini index by half a percentage point.

13. The difference between income and expenditure is net savings; A. Deaton and S. Zaidi, "Guidelines for Constructing Consumption Aggregates for Welfare Analysis," World Bank (2002), http://documents.worldbank.org/curated/en /20656146878115332o/Guidelines-for-constructing-consumption-aggregates -for-welfare-analysis.

14. Anand and Segal, "The Global Distribution of Income."

15. A. B. Atkinson, T. Piketty, and E. Saez, "Top Incomes in the Long Run of History," *Journal of Economic Literature* 49, no. 1 (2011): 3–71; F. Alvaredo and J. Londoño Vélez, "High incomes and personal taxation in a developing economy: Colombia 1993–2013," Commitment to Equity Working Paper No. 12 (March 2013), http://www.commitmentoequity.org/publications_files/CEQWPNo12%20 HighTaxationDevEconColombia1993-2010_19March2013.pdf.

16. F. Alvaredo and L. Gasparini, "Recent Trends in Inequality and Poverty in Developing Countries," in Atkinson and Bourguignon, *Handbook of Income Distribution*.

17. M. Aguiar and M. Bils, "Has Consumption Inequality Mirrored Income Inequality?," *American Economic Review* 105, no. 9 (2015): 2725–2756.

18. Alvaredo and Gasparini, "Recent Trends."

19. L. Karabarbounis and B. Neiman, "The Global Decline of the Labor Share," *Quarterly Journal of Economics* 129, no. 1 (2014): 61–103.

20. Household savings as a percentage of GDP increased from 17.5 in 2000 to 23.4 in 2008 (G. Ma and W. Yi, "China's High Saving Rate: Myth and Reality," Bank for International Settlements Working Papers No. 312 [2010]).

21. C. Lakner and C. Ruggeri Laderchi, "Top Incomes in East Asia: What We Know, Why It Matters and What to Do About It," World Bank, forthcoming.

22. Hurun Report, "The Richest People in China," http://www.hurun.net/en /HuList.aspx, accessed November 16, 2015.

23. International Consortium of Investigative Journalists, "Giant Leak of Offshore Financial Records Exposes Global Array of Crime and Corruption," April 3, 2016, https://panamapapers.icij.org/20160403-panama-papers-global-overview .html.

24. The baseline results use the largest possible sample of countries in every year. A closely connected issue, which cannot be addressed, is the unavailability of surveys for some countries. This problem is most acute for the Middle East and Africa. The affected countries account for around 5 percent of global GDP and 10 percent of global population.

25. Anand and Segal, "The Global Distribution of Income."

26. Anand and Segal, ibid., use a different approach to account for missing top incomes, which results in an upward adjustment to the level of the global Gini index that is approximately half of the difference presented in Figure 11-1. They assume that the household survey fails to capture the top 1 percent. They then append the top 1 percent income share either directly from tax record data or predict it from a cross-country regression that uses the survey-based top 10 percent share and the survey mean income. While their procedure also increases a country's mean, this effect is smaller than the national-accounts-based adjustment in Lakner and Milanovic, "Global Income Distribution" (shown in Figure 11-1). Regarding the time trend, Anand and Segal ("The Global Distribution of Income") also find a fall in the most recent period (between 2002 and 2005 in their data), although the level remains marginally higher in 2005 than in 1988 (72.7 percent and 72.6 percent, respectively).

27. According to the review by Anand and Segal, "The Global Distribution of Income," methodologies differ primarily in their (1) use of GDP per capita or average incomes from household surveys, (2) adjustments for differences between income and consumption surveys, and (3) PPP exchange rates. F. Bourguignon, *The Globalization of Inequality* (Princeton, NJ: Princeton University Press, 2015), who rescales survey incomes to GDP per capita, finds a faster decline than what is presented in Figure 11-1, beginning in the early 1990s.

28. F. Bourguignon and C. Morrisson, "Inequality among World Citizens: 1820–1992," *American Economic Review* 92, no. 4 (2002): 727–744.

29. Bourguignon, *The Globalization of Inequality*; B. Milanovic, *Global Inequality: A New Approach for the Age of Globalization* (Cambridge, MA: Belknap Press of Harvard University Press, 2016).

30. Milanovic, *Global Inequality*, 120. World Bank, *Poverty and Shared Prosperity 2016: Taking on Inequality* (Washington, DC: World Bank, 2016).

31. I use an alternative measure of inequality because the Gini index cannot be decomposed in this manner.

32. In both sub-Saharan Africa and East Asia, regional inequality increased. But whereas in Africa this increase was driven by increasing between-country inequality, in East Asia it was driven by rising within-country inequality (L. F. Jirasavetakul and C. Lakner, "The Distribution of Consumption Expenditure in

Sub-Saharan Africa: The Inequality among All Africans," Policy Research Working Paper Series 7557, World Bank [2016]).

33. Of course, the two aspects are not independent. The between-country contribution is computed as the difference between the country mean and the global mean, which China's rapid growth would have also tended to increase. A poor country that is growing slower than the global mean would tend to increase between-country inequality, as long as its mean is below the global mean.

34. Bourguignon and Morrisson, "Inequality among World Citizens."

35. Milanovic, *Global Inequality.*

36. Bourguignon, *The Globalization of Inequality;* Milanovic, *Global Inequality.*

37. The pattern remains very similar with data after the global financial crisis (Milanovic, *Global Inequality*). The pattern is also very similar when using a non-anonymous growth incidence curve (not shown). In Figure 11-3, which is an anonymous growth incidence curve, the composition of the global percentiles with different country-groups may change over time. In other words, we do not track the evolution of a particular country-group (e.g., the bottom 10 percent in the United States) over time, although this is sometimes implicit in the interpretation. However, as it turns out, the two graphs are very similar (see Lakner and Milanovic, "Global Income Distribution").

38. Milanovic, *Global Inequality.*

39. Relative measures of inequality obey the scale invariance axiom, which says that an inequality measure ought to be independent of any transformation that multiplies all incomes by the same constant, such as a simple rescaling from euro to U.S. dollar. On the one hand, perceptions about rising income gaps often carry absolute connotations, and experiments with university students in Germany, Israel, the U.K., and the United States show an approximately equal split between absolute and relative concerns (M. Ravallion, *The Economics of Poverty: History, Measurement, and Policy* [Oxford: Oxford University Press, 2016]). On the other hand, Milanovic, *Global Inequality,* argues strongly for keeping inequality measures relative while recognizing that an analysis of the absolute differences provides a complementary perspective. Atkinson and Brandolini also argue that a global analysis especially needs to consider both absolute and relative differences (A. B. Atkinson and A. Brandolini, "On Analyzing the World Distribution of Income," *World Bank Economic Review* 24, no. 1 [2010]: 1–37).

40. In the United States, Luttmer finds that an increase in neighbors' earnings reduces reported happiness after controlling for individual income, where the spatial unit has 150,000 residents on average (E. Luttmer, "Neighbors as Negatives: Relative Earnings and Well-Being," *Quarterly Journal of Economics* 120, no. 3 [2005]: 963–1002). By contrast, in Malawi such relative differences are not the dominant concern, except for the better-off (M. Ravallion and M. Lokshin, "Who Cares about Relative Deprivation?," *Journal of Economic Behavior & Organization* 73, no. 2 [February 2010]: 171–185).

41. There are notable differences between these three sources, so they need to be compared carefully. The World Bank data are also used by Alvaredo and Gasparini. However, Alvaredo and Gasparini cover only developing countries and adjust for differences between income and consumption surveys. Morelli et al. cover only rich and (some) middle-income countries and tend to use equivalence scales and a mix of primary data and secondary sources. The updated calculations based on World Bank data (see Figure 11-4) cover all income groups and mix per capita income or consumption without any adjustment. Alvaredo and Gasparini, "Recent Trends"; S. Morelli, T. Smeeding, and J. Thompson, "Post-1970 Trends in Within-Country Inequality and Poverty: Rich and Middle-Income Countries," in Atkinson and Bourguignon, *Handbook of Income Distribution*; "PovcalNet: The On-Line Tool for Poverty Measurement Developed by the Development Research Group," http://iresearch.worldbank.org/PovcalNet, accessed April, 16 2016.

42. For example, L. F. Lopez-Calva and N. Lustig, eds., *Declining Inequality in Latin America: A Decade of Progress?* (Washington, DC: Brookings Institution and UNDP, 2010); N. Lustig, L. F. Lopez-Calva, and E. Ortiz-Juarez, "Declining Inequality in Latin America in the 2000s: The Cases of Argentina, Brazil, and Mexico," *World Development* 44 (2013): 129–141.

43. L. Cord, O. Barriga Cabanillas, L. Lucchetti, C. Rodriguez-Castelan, L. D. Sousa, and D. Valderrama, "Inequality Stagnation in Latin America in the Aftermath of the Global Financial Crisis," Policy Research Working Paper Series 7146, World Bank (2014); R. Kanbur, "Poverty and Distribution: Thirty Years Ago and Now," in *Inequality and Fiscal Policy,* ed. B. Clements, R. de Mooij, S. Gupta, and M. Keen (Washington, DC: International Monetary Fund, 2015).

44. M. Székely and P. Mendoza, "Is the Decline in Inequality in Latin America Here to Stay?," in *Inequality and Human Development in Latin America: A Long-Run Perspective* (special issue), *Journal of Human Development and Capabilities* 16, no. 3 (2015): 397–419; see also the introduction to this special issue, L. F. Lopez-Calva, N. Lustig, and E. Ortiz-Juarez, "A Long-Term Perspective on Inequality and Human Development in Latin America," at 319–323.

45. R. Kanbur, "Globalization and Inequality," in Atkinson and Bourguignon, *Handbook of Income Distribution*.

46. B. Milanovic and L. Ersado, "Reform and Inequality during the Transition: An Analysis Using Panel Household Survey Data, 1990–2006," Working Paper Series wp2010-62, World Institute for Development Economic Research (2010).

47. Milanovic, *Global Inequality*.

48. K. Beegle, L. Christiaensen, A. Dabalen, and I. Gaddis, *Poverty in a Rising Africa: Africa Poverty Report* (Washington, DC: World Bank, 2016).

49. B. Milanovic, "Is Inequality in Africa Really Different?," World Bank Policy Research Working Paper Series 3169 (2003).

50. Beegle et al., *Poverty in a Rising Africa*. Changes in survey design (such as urban or national coverage), implementation (such as effects of seasonality), or

questionnaires (such as recall periods for consumption expenditures) can make surveys hard to compare. This pattern of within-country inequality trends is confirmed for a longer time period by G. A. Cornia, "Income Inequality Levels, Trends and Determinants in Sub-Saharan Africa: An Overview of the Main Changes," Università degli Studi di Firenze, Florence, 2014.

51. Milanovic, *Global Inequality;* Morelli, Smeeding, and Thompson. "Post-1970 Trends."

52. Cord et al., "Inequality Stagnation"; L. Gasparini, G. Cruces, and L. Tornarolli, "Chronicle of a Deceleration Foretold: Income Inequality in Latin America in the 2010s," CEDLAS Working Paper No. 198 (2016).

53. Figure 11-4 includes only comparable spells and thus covers a smaller set of countries than a pure cross-sectional analysis. The comparable sample covers 84 percent of global GDP and population, which is smaller than the coverage of Lakner and Milanovic, "Global Income Distribution" (93 percent of global GDP and 91 percent of global population in 2008).

54. Milanovic, *Global Inequality.*

55. F. H. G. Ferreira, "Kuznets Waves and the Great Epistemological Challenge to Inequality Analysis," World Bank Development Impact Blog (April 27, 2016), http://blogs.worldbank.org/impactevaluations/kuznets-waves-and-great -epistemological-challenge-inequality-analysis.

56. According to the Stolper-Samuelson theory, trade will increase the relative return of the abundant factor—unskilled labor in developing countries. The experience of the East Asian economies (South Korea and Taiwan) that pursued trade liberalization after World War II and managed to create growth with equity is consistent with this theory (A. Wood, "Openness and Wage Inequality in Developing Countries: The Latin American Challenge to East Asian Conventional Wisdom," *World Bank Economic Review* 11, no. 1 [1997]: 33–57). But this theory has been challenged by the increasing inequality in the 1980s and 1990s in both labor-abundant and labor-scarce countries that liberalized. Furthermore, the East Asian experience coincided with supportive initial conditions, such as land reforms and widespread basic education, which may be at least as important as trade liberalization by itself (Kanbur, "Globalization and Inequality").

57. K. Basu, "Globalization of Labor Markets and the Growth Prospects of Nations," World Bank Policy Research Working Paper Series 7590 (2016).

58. J. Tinbergen, *Income Distribution: Analysis and Policies* (Amsterdam: North-Holland, 1975).

59. Atkinson and Bourguignon, "Introduction: Income Distribution Today."

60. J. E. Meade, *Efficiency, Equality and the Ownership of Property* (London: Allen and Unwin, 1964).

61. E. Maskin, "Why Haven't Global Markets Reduced Inequality in Emerging Economies?," *World Bank Economic Review* 29 (suppl. 1) (2015): S48–S52.

62. R. B. Freeman, "Are Your Wages Set in Beijing?," *Journal of Economic Perspectives* 9, no. 3 (1995):15–32.

63. A. B. Atkinson, *The Changing Distribution of Earnings in OECD Countries* (Oxford: Oxford University Press, 2008).

64. Bourguignon, *The Globalization of Inequality.*

65. Basu, "Globalization of Labor Markets."

66. W. H. Davidow and M. S. Malone, "What Happens to Society When Robots Replace Workers?," *Harvard Business Review,* December 10, 2014.

67. Bourguignon, *The Globalization of Inequality.*

68. Karabarbounis and Neiman, "Global Decline of the Labor Share." See also Raval, Chapter 4 in this volume.

69. Bourguignon, *The Globalization of Inequality.*

70. F. Bourguignon, "Inequality and Globalization: How the Rich Get Richer as the Poor Catch Up," *Foreign Affairs,* January / February 2016, 11–15.

71. Bourguignon, *The Globalization of Inequality.*

72. Atkinson and Bourguignon, "Introduction: Income Distribution Today."

73. Kanbur, "Globalization and Inequality."

74. Lakner and Ruggeri Laderchi, "Top Incomes in East Asia."

75. For instance, in Indonesia dividends and interest income are taxed at 10 percent and 20 percent, respectively, which is substantially lower than the 30 percent top marginal tax rate that many dividend earners would face for their earned income. While capital gains are subject to standard personal income taxes, there is no withholding, so compliance is limited (World Bank, "Indonesia's Rising Divide," [Jakarta: World Bank, 2016]). As a result, only 5 percent of personal income tax revenues in Indonesia are from capital incomes, with the rest coming from withholding on salaries.

76. Warren Buffett has famously said that he faces a lower tax rate than his receptionist (N. G. Mankiw, "Defending the One Percent," *Journal of Economic Perspectives* 27, no. 3 [2013]: 21–34), which can be explained by most of his income being in the form of dividends and capital gains.

77. J. Norregaard, "Taxing Immovable Property: Revenue Potential and Implementation Challenges," in Clements et al., *Inequality and Fiscal Policy,* 191–222.

78. G. Zucman, "Taxing across Borders: Tracking Personal Wealth and Corporate Profits," *Journal of Economic Perspectives* 28, no. 4 (2014):121–148.

79. Ibid.

80. United Nations Conference on Trade and Development, "World Investment Report 2015: Performing International Investment Governance," http://unctad.org/en/PublicationsLibrary/wir2015_en.pdf.

81. Milanovic, *Global Inequality.*

82. Kanbur, "Globalization and Inequality."

83. At the same time, it is important to be clear that conditional cash transfers by themselves are too small to explain the trend reversal in Latin America (ibid.). Instead, the growth of low-skilled wages appears to explain most of the decline (Lopez-Calva and Lustig, *Declining Inequality in Latin America;* Lustig et al.,

"Declining Inequality in Latin America in the 2000s"; Cord et al., "Inequality Stagnation").

84. Bourguignon, *The Globalization of Inequality.*

85. Basu, "Globalization of Labor Markets"; Milanovic, *Global Inequality;* A. B. Atkinson, "How to Spread the Wealth: Practical Policies for Reducing Inequality," *Foreign Affairs,* January / February 2016, 29–33.

86. A. B. Atkinson, *Inequality: What Can Be Done?* (Cambridge, MA: Harvard University Press, 2015).

87. Ibid.

88. Bourguignon, *The Globalization of Inequality.* South Korea's chaebol are also a case in point. Although they played an important developmental role during industrialization (T. Khanna and Y. Yafeh, "Business Groups in Emerging Markets: Paragons or Parasites?," *Journal of Economic Literature* 45, no. 2 (2007): 331–372), they often use opaque pyramidal holding structures, and the chairmen of the three largest chaebol have all been charged with crimes ("To Those That Have—The Dark Side of Family Capitalism" [April 18, 2015], http://www.economist.com /news/special-report/21648178-dark-side-family-capitalism-those-have).

89. C. Freund, *Rich People Poor Countries: The Rise of Emerging-Market Tycoons and Their Mega Firms* (Washington, DC: Peterson Institute for International Economics, 2016).

90. Milanovic, *Global Inequality.*

91. Bourguignon, "Inequality and Globalization."

92. Milanovic, *Global Inequality.*

93. A sizable literature discusses the relationship between poverty reduction and growth and inequality, as reviewed in F. H. G. Ferreira, "Distributions in Motion: Economic Growth, Inequality, and Poverty Dynamics," in *The Oxford Handbook of the Economics of Poverty,* ed. P. N. Jefferson (Oxford: Oxford University Press, 2012).

94. One reason, though an unwelcome one, is that the outlook for productivity growth in the developed countries is gloomy; see R. J. Gordon, *The Rise and Fall of American Growth: The U.S. Standard of Living since the Civil War* (Princeton, NJ: Princeton University Press, 2016).

95. In 2015 it weakened to 3.5 percent, the lowest level in the last fifteen years (Bourguignon, *The Globalization of Inequality*).

96. Roughly speaking, when the average income in China exceeds the global average, growth in China will have a disequalizing effect on the global distribution. This is likely to happen very soon, as Milanovic, "Global Income Distribution," explains in detail.

97. T. Hellebrandt and P. Mauro, "The Future of Worldwide Income Distribution," Working Paper Series WP15-7, Peterson Institute for International Economics (2015).

98. It is not unprecedented for individual countries over a twenty-year period, but this is unlikely to happen in all countries in the world.

99. World Bank, "World Bank's New End-Poverty Tool: Surveys in Poorest Countries," press release, October 15, 2015, http://www.worldbank.org/en/news /press-release/2015/10/15/world-bank-new-end-poverty-tool-surveys-in -poorest-countries.

100. This does not necessarily apply to the measurement of absolute poverty, such as the $1 per day poverty estimated by the World Bank. Even though the importance of the agricultural sector is declining in these emerging economies, many of the poorest individuals will continue to live in rural areas and work in agriculture. Furthermore, monetary and nonmonetary transfers may be underreported at the bottom in an income survey. For example, the U.S. Current Population Survey fails to capture many transfer payments at the very bottom, when compared with administrative records (B. D. Meyer, W. K. C. Mok, and J. X. Sullivan, "Household Surveys in Crisis," *Journal of Economic Perspectives* 29, no. 4 [2015]: 199–226). As a result, consumption is often surprisingly high for individuals on very low or even zero incomes (see M. Brewer, B. Etheridge, and C. O'Dea, "Why Are Households That Report the Lowest Incomes So Well-Off?," Economics Discussion Papers 8993, University of Essex, Department of Economics [2013]).

101. France, for example, recently began using register-based information (including tax records) for some questions in its EU-SILC survey; see C. Burricand, "Transition from Survey Data to Registers in the French SILC Survey," in *The Use of Registers in the Context of EU-SILC: Challenges and Opportunities,* ed. M. Jäntti, V. Törmälehto, and E. Marlier, Eurostat Statistical Working Papers (2013), http://ec.europa.eu/eurostat/documents/3888793/5856365/KS-TC-13 -004-EN.PDF.

102. Similarly, Saez (Chapter 13, this volume) calls for integrating surveys and income tax data in a manner that is consistent with national accounts.

12. The Geographies of Capital in the Twenty-First Century

1. Thomas Piketty, *Capital in the Twenty-First Century,* trans. Arthur Goldhammer (Cambridge, MA: Belknap Press of Harvard University Press, 2014).

2. The financial crash and subsequent recession challenged this view, prompting even the IMF to contemplate capital controls and enhanced regulation. See International Monetary Fund, *The Liberalization and Management of Capital Flows: An Institutionalist View* (Washington, DC: IMF, 2012), www.imf.org /external/np/pp/eng/2012/111412.pdf.

3. S. Armstrong, *The Super-Rich Shall Inherit the Earth: The New Global Oligarchs and How They're Taking Over Our World* (London: Constable and Robinson, 2010); A. Atkinson, "Income Distribution in Europe and the United States," *Oxford Review of Economic Policy* 12, no. 1 (1996): 15–28; M. Davis and D. B. Monk, eds., *Evil Paradises: Dreamworlds of Neoliberalism* (New York: New Press, 2007); G. Irvin, *Super Rich: The Rise of Inequality in Britain and the United States* (Cambridge: Polity, 2008); J. Stiglitz, *Freefall: Free Markets and*

the Sinking of the Global Economy (London: Allen Lane, 2010); Oxfam, *Working for the Few: Political Capture and Economic Inequality* (Oxford: Oxfam International, 2014).

4. T. Piketty and E. Saez, "Top Incomes and the Great Recession: Recent Evolutions and Policy Implications," *IMF Economic Review* 61, no. 3 (2013): 456–478; T. Piketty and G. Zucman, "Capital Is Back: Wealth-Income Ratios in Rich Countries, 1700–2010," *Quarterly Journal of Economics* 129, no. 3 (2014): 1255–1310.

5. As Galbraith points out, Piketty's "measure of capital is not physical but financial," which allows Piketty, albeit inconsistently, to include real estate within his definition, and thus consider capital as both productive ("real" capital) and a store of value. See J. K. Galbraith, "*Kapital* for the Twenty-First Century?," *Dissent,* Spring 2014, 77–82, at 77.

6. D. Soskice, "*Capital in the Twenty-First Century:* A Critique," *British Journal of Sociology* 65, no. 4 (2014): 650–666.

7. D. Perrons, "Gendering Inequality: A Note on Piketty's *Capital in the Twenty-First Century,*" *British Journal of Sociology* 65 (2014): 667–677.

8. Peter Lindner, "Problematising Inequality," *Geopolitics* 21, no. 3 (2016): 742–749, doi: 10.1080/14650045.2016.1139998.

9. G. A. Jones, "Where's the Capital? A Geographical Essay," *British Journal of Sociology* 65, no. 4 (2014): 721–735.

10. E. Sheppard, "Piketty and Friends: Capitalism, Inequality, Development, Territorialism," *AAG Review of Books* 3, no. 1 (2015): 36–42.

11. Piketty, *Capital,* 48.

12. This restrictive database means that Piketty has little to say about inequality in most of the world and especially in the Global South where inequality is both higher than the North but fell, albeit briefly, in some countries, notably in Latin America during the 1990s and 2000s. He does briefly comment on China regarding capital controls.

13. T. Piketty and E. Saez, "Inequality in the Long Run," *Science,* May 23, 1014, 838–843.

14. Soskice, "*Capital,*" 661, 650.

15. K. Ho, *Liquidated: An Ethnography of Wall Street* (Durham, NC: Duke University Press, 2009.

16. G. Zucman, *The Hidden Wealth of Nations* (Chicago: University of Chicago Press, 2015).

17. *The Daily Mail* reported that 47 of the FTSE 100 companies appear to pay no or little tax in the United Kingdom, 12 declare that they paid no tax, and 6 received tax credits. In some cases there are legitimate reasons for the low or negative figures, through allowances on R&D, investment, and, with more skepticism, losses brought forward. Yet the companies are recording billions in sales and even recording billions in profits at the corporate (global) level, without paying corporation tax. Amazon paid £1.8 million tax on £3.35 billion U.K. sales

in 2011 (£11.9m on £5.3bn 2014), eBay £1 million on £800 million sales in United Kingdom, Starbucks was revealed to have paid just £8.6m in U.K. corporation tax in the fourteen years between 1998 and 2012, despite making more than £3bn in U.K. sales in the same period.

18. D. Rodrik, *The Globalization Paradox: Why Global Markets, States, and Democracy Can't Coexist* (Oxford: Oxford University Press, 2011). Also see R. Reich, *Saving Capitalism: For the Many, Not the Few* (New York: Knopf, 2015).

19. OECD / G20, *Base Erosion and Profit Shifting Project Final Report* (Paris: OECD, 2015).

20. D. Harvey, *The Enigma of Capital: And the Crises of Capitalism* (London: Profile Books, 2011).

21. K. Ho, "Supermanagers, Inequality, and Finance," *HAU: Journal of Ethnographic Theory* 5, no. 1 (2015): 481–488.

22. Ibid., 483.

23. R. Palan, "Tax Havens and the Commercialization of State Sovereignty," *International Organization* 56 (2002): 151–176; N. Shaxson, *Treasure Islands: Tax Havens and the Men Who Stole the World* (New York: Random House, 2012); J. Urry, *Offshoring* (London: Polity Press, 2014); Zucman, *Hidden Wealth of Nations*.

24. N. Gilman et al., eds., *Deviant Globalization: Black Market Economy in the 21st Century* (New York: Continuum Books, 2011), 5.

25. See *Vermillion Sands* (1971), *Cocaine Nights* (1996), *Super-Cannes* (2000), all published by HarperPerennial.

26. S. Gill, "Constitutionalizing Inequality and the Clash of Globalizations," *International Studies Review* 4, no. 2 (2002): 47–65. Also see Harvey, *The Enigma of Capital*.

27. S. Sassen, *Territory, Authority, Rights: From Medieval to Global Assemblages* (Princeton, NJ: Princeton University Press, 2008).

28. B. Chalfont, "Global Customs Regimes and the Traffic in Sovereignty: Enlarging the Anthropology of the State," *Current Anthropology* 47 (2006): 243–276; Sassen, *Territory, Authority, Rights*.

29. B. Neilson, "Zones: Beyond the Logic of Exception?," *Concentric: Literary and Cultural Studies* 40, no. 2 (2014): 11–28.

30. K. Easterling, *Extrastatecraft: The Power of Infrastructure Space* (London: Verso, 2014). While zones appear to be intercompetitive pods in a global economy, they are networked through corporations, information technologies, and international standards agencies to form what Easterling regards analogously as a "global spatial operating system" (173).

31. Neilson, "Zones," 18, 11.

32. Cited in Easterling, *Extrastatecraft,* 49. And in sub-Saharan Africa especially, zones often bring together multiple nation-states into a space as a means to extend economic and political interests through partnerships. See D. Bräutigam and T. Xiaoyang, "African Shenzhen: China's Special Economic Zones in Africa,"

Journal of Modern African Studies 49, no. 1 (2011): 27–54; L. Bremner, "Towards a Minor Global Architecture at Lamu, Kenya," *Social Dynamics* 39, no. 3 (2013): 397–413.

33. As Levien has shown for India, the state is an active agent in the creation of zones and corridors through the dispossession of land (often from peasants) in the "public interest." See M. Levien, "The Land Question: Special Economic Zones and the Political Economy of Dispossession in India," *Journal of Peasant Studies* 39, nos. 3–4 (2012): 933–969.

34. J. Bach, "Modernity and the Urban Imagination in Economic Zones," *Theory, Culture and Society* 28, no. 5 (2011): 98–122; S. Opitz and U. Tellmann, "Global Territories: Zones of Economic and Legal Dis / Connectivity," *Distinktion: Scandinavian Journal of Social Theory* 13, no. 3 (2012): 261–282.

35. Easterling, *Extrastatecraft*, 15.

36. See Bräutigam and Xiaoyang, "African Shenzhen"; Bremner, "Minor Global Architecture"; and I. Dey and G. Grappi, "Beyond Zoning: India's Corridors of Development and New Frontiers of Capital," *South Atlantic Quarterly* 114, no. 1 (2015): 153–170.

37. Bach, "Modernity," 99.

38. See Easterling, *Extrastatecraft*; Davis and Monk, *Evil Paradises*.

39. Easterling, *Extrastatecraft*, 67.

40. S. Ali, *Dubai: Gilded Cage* (New Haven, CT: Yale University Press, 2010).

41. R. Abrahamsen and M. C. Williams, *Security beyond the State: Private Security in International Politics* (Cambridge: Cambridge University Press, 2010).

42. Easterling suggests the zone is "perfectly apolitical" as a technocratic space "decoupled from its reality on the ground." In this sense she is right—the zone is perceived by those that run it as apolitical—but it is not "without politics."

43. Shaxson, *Treasure Islands*, 8.

44. Urry, *Offshoring*.

45. The six are The Netherlands, Bermuda, Luxembourg, Ireland, Singapore, and Switzerland. The situation may be worse in Europe, where Urry calculates that 99 of the top 100 largest companies use offshore subsidiaries to minimize their tax exposure.

46. G. Zucman, "Taxing across Borders: Tracking Personal Wealth and Corporate Profits," *Journal of Economic Perspectives* 28, no. 4 (2014): 121–148, at 140. See also D. Haberly and D. Wójcik, "Tax Havens and the Production of Offshore FDI: An Empirical Analysis," *Journal of Economic Geography* 15, no. 1 (2014): 75–101.

47. More than 11.4 million documents were leaked from the law firm Mossack Fonseca in April 2016 to the German newspaper *Süddeutsche Zeitung*. The papers purport to show how individuals, from politicians to celebrities, and companies, moved assets (from real estate to works of art) through trusts and funds through Panama, with the assistance of banks and legal firms. Investigators in over seventy countries are currently assessing the value of the assets, the legality

of the transactions, and the potential loss of tax revenue. See the International Consortium of Investigative Journalists (https://panamapapers.icij.org).

48. Highlighting the problem of relying on tax and national accounts, Piketty omits any attention to informality or illegality, despite estimates for many parts of the world that the majority of economic activity is "off the books." Yet Gilman et al. observe that "deviant globalization" challenges "traditional notions of wealth, development, and power" via entrepreneurs who "use the technical infrastructure of globalization to exploit gaps and differences in regulation and law enforcement of markets for repugnant goods and services" (*Deviant Globalization,* 3).

49. Zucman identifies Switzerland as the historically leading offshore site, followed by Luxembourg and the Virgin Islands to form what he calls a "sinister trio."

50. Zucman, "Taxing across Borders," 121.

51. Ibid., 144.

52. D. Wójcik, "Where Governance Fails: Advanced Business Services and the Offshore World," *Progress in Human Geography* 37, no. 3 (2013): 330–347.

53. A. Cobham, P. Janský, and M. Meinzer, "The Financial Secrecy Index: Shedding New Light on the Geography of Secrecy," *Economic Geography* 91, no. 3 (2015): 281–303.

54. Wójcik, "Where Governance Fails." Also J. V. Beaverstock, S. Hall, and T. Wainwright, "Servicing the Super-Rich: New Financial Elites and the Rise of the Private Wealth Management Retail Ecology," *Regional Studies* 47, no. 6 (2013): 834–849.

55. T. Wainwright, "Tax Doesn't Have to Be Taxing: London's 'Onshore' Finance Industry and the Fiscal Spaces of a Global Crisis," *Environment and Planning A* 43, no. 6 (2011): 1287.

56. House of Commons Committee of Public Accounts, "Tax Avoidance: The Role of Large Accountancy Firms (Follow-Up)" (2015), HC 860, available at www.publications.parliament.uk/pa/cm201415/cmselect/cmpubacc/1057 /1057.pdf.

57. Zucman, *Hidden Wealth of Nations,* 44–45. He notes that if Switzerland is representative of the "tax haven set," then at least 80 percent of wealth is undeclared for tax purposes.

58. The best-known example is Starbucks, which appears to buy its coffee from Switzerland, although the beans actually go to The Netherlands for roasting, and are then bought by national affiliates at large premiums, which also pay fees for use of brand and logo, and thus shift profits and tax liabilities to Switzerland.

59. Cobham et al., "The Financial Secrecy Index."

60. Access to and optimum operation within this space seems more restricted than the open-market discourse of the early twenty-first century would imply. A now-famous study by the Swiss Federal Institute of Technology that looked at the relationships between 37 million companies and investors worldwide

discovered a "super-entity" of just 147 highly networked companies that controlled 40 percent of the total wealth.

61. Piketty, *Capital*, 180.

62. High Net Worth Individuals (HNWIs), people with around $1million or more available to invest, are the largest and fastest-growing category of rich—at about 11 million globally in 2011—but their total income and wealth is far surpassed by the estimated 100,000 Ultra-High Net Worth Individuals (U-HNWIs) with disposable wealth in excess of $42 trillion. As Beaverstock and Faulconbridge note, the boundaries in these elite categorizations are arbitrary, with U-HNWIs defined as having between $40 million and tens of billions of dollars. See J. V. Beaverstock and J. R. Faulconbridge, "Wealth Segmentation and the Mobilities of the Super-Rich," in *Elite Mobilities*, ed. T. Birchnell and J. Caletrío (New York: Routledge, 2013), 40–61.

63. Birchnell and Caletrío, *Elite Mobilities;* Urry, *Offshoring*.

64. A. Ong, "Please Stay: Pied-a-Terre Subjects in the Megacity," *Citizenship Studies* 11, no. 1 (2007): 83–93.

65. C. Freeland, "The Rise of the New Global Elite," *The Atlantic,* January / February 2011, 2.

66. This liminality is captured semiplayfully by Robert Frank whose typology of the new elites distinguishes between those that live in Upper Richi$tan and those in Lower Richi$tan, in his book *Richistan: A Journey Through the American Wealth Boom and the Lives of the New Rich* (London: Piatkus Books, 2007).

67. A. Elliott. and J. Urry, *Mobile Lives* (New York: Routledge, 2010).

68. Ong, "Please Stay," 89.

69. N. Cunningham and M. Savage, "The Secret Garden? Elite Metropolitan Geographies in the Contemporary UK," *Sociological Review* 63 (2015): 321–348.

70. See L. Sklair, and L. Gherardi, "Iconic Architecture as a Hegemonic Project of the Transnational Capitalist Class," *City* 16, nos. 1–2 (2012): 57–73; also Cunningham and Savage, "The Secret Garden?"

71. For an interesting study of elite ideas toward privilege and how it can misrecognized as merit, or what Piketty might term "luck" (Piketty, *Capital*, 315–321, 333–335), see S. Khan, "Privilege: The Making of an Adolescent Elite at St. Paul's School" (Princeton, NJ: Princeton University Press, 2012). Use of the term "cloaking" to describe the hidden presence of a service economy on which elites depend is from R. Atkinson, "Limited Exposure: Social Concealment, Mobility and Engagement with Public Space by the Super-Rich in London," *Environment and Planning A* 48, no. 7 (2016): 1302–1317, doi 10.1177/0308518X15598323.

72. *The Guardian* (January 24, 2016) reported that in 2013 the borough of Kensington and Chelsea had granted permission for 450 "mega basement extensions"—some of more than one floor, and including swimming pools and home cinemas—compared with just 46 in 2001.

73. Reich noted in the early 1990s that the "fortunate fifth" had managed to secede from the nation through physical enclaves and lack of commitment to wider senses of community. See R. B. Reich, *The Work of Nations: Preparing Ourselves for 21st-Century Capitalism* (New York: Vintage Books, 1992); also Davis and Monk, *Evil Paradises*.

74. R. Webber and R. Burrows, "Life in an Alpha Territory: Discontinuity and Conflict in an Elite London 'Village,'" *Urban Studies* 53, no. 15 (2015): 3139–3154.

75. For New York, see the *Financial Times,* "Global Elite Buys Trophy Apartments," September, 29, 2015, http://www.ft.com/cms/s/0/dd7ac2f2-472d-11e5 -af2f-4d6e0e5eda22.html#axzz46kKTUoqH; for London, see *The Guardian,* July 22, 2013, www.theguardian.com/commentisfree/2013/jul/22/london -wealth-global-elite-home.

76. The 2012 U.S. Census data show that 31 of the largest 50 cities are more unequal by income compared with the United States generally and are becoming more so over time. The rich in the 50 largest cities are richer than in cities generally and proportionally better off than the poor, who are poorer in the largest 50 cities than cities generally.

77. Atkinson, "Limited Exposure," 1315.

78. A. Ong, "Mutations in Citizenship," *Theory, Culture & Society* 23, no. 2–3 (2006): 499–505.

79. S. Sassen, "Towards Post-National and Denationalized Citizenship," in *Handbook of Citizenship Studies,* ed. E. F. Isin and B. S. Turner (London: Sage, 2002).

80. Cited in K. Jefford, "Homes Owned through Companies Falls Below 4,000, HMRC Figures show," *City AM,* February 15, 2016.

81. S. Sassen, "A Savage Sorting of Winners and Losers: Contemporary Versions of Primitive Accumulation," *Globalizations* 7, no. 1 (2010): 23–50.

82. Piketty, *Capital,* 336.

83. This is the supermanager scenario described by Piketty, but also the culture of financial capitalism analyzed by Ho, *Liquidated.*

84. See M. Aalbers, ed., *Subprime Cities: The Political Economy of Mortgage Markets* (Chichester, U.K.: Wiley, 2012); J. Crump, K. Newman, E. S. Belsky, P. Ashton, D. H. Kaplan, D. J. Hammel, and E. Wyly, "Cities Destroyed (Again) for Cash: Forum on the U.S. Foreclosure Crisis," *Urban Geography* 29, no. 8 (2008): 745–784.

85. E. Raymond, K. Wang, and D. Immergluck, "Race and Uneven Recovery: Neighborhood Home Value Trajectories in Atlanta before and after the Housing Crisis," *Housing Studies* 31, no. 3 (2016): 324–329.

86. Piketty, *Capital,* 244–246, 395.

87. Also Stiglitz, *Freefall;* Zucman, *Hidden Wealth of Nations.*

88. *The Observer,* April 10, 2016, 7.

89. See Galbraith, *"Kapital";* Lindner, "Problematising Inequality"; Perrons, "Gendering Inequality."

90. Zucman points out that legal and regulatory constraints mean that U.S. Treasury Department statisticians have no way of knowing who owns U.S. stocks and bonds held in Swiss (or other) bank accounts. They have to assume that wealth in Geneva bank accounts is an asset of Switzerland, and hence data "reveal not who possesses the world's wealth, but where it is being managed—the geography of tax havens more than that of the actual wealth" (*Hidden Wealth of Nations,* 21). The observation highlights how objective measures of real wealth and geography are in combat with each other when the latter is instrumental to the creation and holding of the former.

91. See https://www.youtube.com/watch?v=4S9AwO-rkJs.

92. See M. Everest-Phillips, "When Do Elites Pay Taxes? Tax Morale and State-Building in Developing Countries," paper presented at WIDER Elites conference, June 12, 2009; also Wainwright, "Tax Doesn't Have to Be Taxing."

93. Easterling, *Extrastatecraft,* 232.

94. *The Guardian,* November 27, 2015, http://www.theguardian.com/news/2015/nov/27/hsbc-whistleblower-jailed-five-years-herve-falciani.

13. *The Research Agenda after* Capital in the Twenty-First Century

1. Thomas Piketty and Emmanuel Saez, "Income Inequality in the United States, 1913–1998," *Quarterly Journal of Economics* 118 no. 1 (2003): 1–39. Series updated to 2014 in June 2015.

2. Thomas Piketty, *Les hauts revenus en France au 20ème siècle—Inégalités et redistributions, 1901–1998* (Paris: Grasset, 2001).

3. Simon Kuznets, *Shares of Upper Income Groups in Income and Savings* (New York: National Bureau of Economic Research, 1953).

4. Simon Kuznets, "Economic Growth and Economic Inequality," *American Economic Review* 45 (1955): 1–28.

5. See Thomas Piketty and Emmanuel Saez, "Top Incomes in the Long Run of History," *Journal of Economic Literature* 49 (2011): 3–71, for a survey of this body of work. The data are online at http://www.wid.world/.

6. Thomas Piketty, *Capital in the Twenty-First Century,* trans. Arthur Goldhammer (Cambridge, MA: Belknap Press of Harvard University Press, 2014).

7. Simon Kuznets, *National Income and Its Composition, 1919–1938* (New York: National Bureau of Economic Research, 1941); Kuznets, *Shares of Upper Income Groups.*

8. The Luxembourg Income Study (LIS) project has made an admirable effort at creating harmonized international micro data using existing micro survey data across countries (see http://www.lisdatacenter.org/). The LIS data are very useful but cannot capture well the top of the distribution.

9. The latest version of the System of National Accounts is the SNA 2008; see *System of National Accounts 2008* (New York: European Communities, International Monetary Fund, Organisation for Economic Co-operation and Development, United Nations, and World Bank, 2009). The United States National

Income and Product Accounts has still not incorporated all the SNA 2008 guidelines but is slowly moving in this direction.

10. Facundo Alvaredo, Anthony B. Atkinson, Lucas Chancel, Thomas Piketty, Emmanuel Saez, and Gabriel Zucman, "Distributional National Accounts (DINA) Guidelines: Concepts and Methods used in the W2ID," Paris School of Economics Working Paper (December 2016).

11. Thomas Piketty, Emmanuel Saez, and Gabriel Zucman, "Distributional National Accounts: Methods and Estimates for the U.S.," NBER Working Paper No. 22945 (December 2016).

12. Bertrand Garbinti, Jonathan Goupille, and Thomas Piketty, "Inequality Dynamics in France, 1900–2014: Evidence from Distributional National Accounts (DINA)," Paris School of Economics (2016).

13. Facundo Alvaredo et al., "Distributional National Accounts: Methods and Estimates for the UK," Paris School of Economics and Oxford University (2016).

14. Dennis Fixler and David S. Johnson, "Accounting for the Distribution of Income in the US National Accounts," in *Measuring Economic Stability and Progress,* ed. D. Jorgenson, J. S. Landefeld, and P. Schreyer (Chicago: University of Chicago Press, 2014); Dennis Fixler, David Johnson, Andrew Craig, and Kevin Furlong, "A Consistent Data Series to Evaluate Growth and Inequality in the National Accounts," Bureau of Economic Analysis Working Paper (2015).

15. Maryse Fesseau and M. L. Mattonetti, "Distributional Measures across Household Groups in a National Accounts Framework: Results from an Experimental Cross-Country Exercise on Household Income, Consumption and Saving," OECD Statistics Working Papers (2013).

16. Piketty, Saez, and Zucman, "Distributional National Accounts."

17. The Piketty and Saez U.S. top income series has often been criticized for ignoring government transfers; see, e.g., Richard Berkhauser, Jeff Larrimore, and Kosali Simon, "A Second Opinion on the Economic Health of the American Middle Class and Why It Matters in Gauging the Impact of Government Policy," *National Tax Journal* 65 (March 2012): 7–32. In reality, both pretax and post-tax distributions are of great value. Distributional National Accounts is the sound conceptual way to do this thoroughly. Many official statistics on income, such as those created by the Census Bureau from the Current Population Survey, blur the pretax vs. post-tax concepts by adding some (but not all) transfers and subtracting some (but not all) taxes from their official income definition; see Carmen DeNavas-Walt and Bernadette D. Proctor, U.S. Census Bureau, *Income and Poverty in the United States: 2014* (Washington, DC: U.S. Government Printing Office, 2015).

18. In addition to governments, a number of institutions such as credit bureaus and educational institutions produce administrative micro data that can be merged to supplement government micro data. The Scandinavian countries have the most advanced central statistical agencies, able to merge datasets from

many different sources for research. For a discussion on improving U.S. administrative data access for research, see David Card, Raj Chetty, Martin Feldstein, and Emmanuel Saez, "Expanding Access to Administrative Data for Research in the United States," White Paper for NSF 10-069 call for papers on "Future Research in the Social, Behavioral, and Economic Sciences" (2010).

19. Wojciech Kopczuk and Emmanuel Saez, "Top Wealth Shares in the United States, 1916–2000: Evidence from Estate Tax Returns," *National Tax Journal* 57 (2004): 445–487.

20. Arthur Kennickell, "Tossed and Turned: Wealth Dynamics of US Households 2007–2009," Finance and Economics Discussion Series Working Paper, Board of Governors of the Federal Reserve System (2011); Edward Wolff, "Household Wealth Trends in the United States, 1962–2013: What Happened over the Great Recession?," NBER Working Paper No. 20733 (2014).

21. Piketty, *Capital.*

22. Chris Giles, "Data Problems with *Capital in the 21st Century*," *Financial Times,* May 23, 2014.

23. Edward Wolff, *Top Heavy: The Increasing Inequality of Wealth in America and What Can Be Done about It* (New York: New Press, 2002).

24. Emmanuel Saez and Gabriel Zucman, "Wealth Inequality in the United States since 1913: Evidence from Capitalized Income Tax Data," *Quarterly Journal of Economics* 131 (2016): 519–578.

25. Wolff, *Top Heavy.*

26. Saez and Zucman, "Wealth Inequality."

27. Ibid.

28. For detailed statistics, see Thomas Piketty and Gabriel Zucman, "Capital Is Back: Wealth-Income Ratios in Rich Countries, 1700–2010," *Quarterly Journal of Economics* 129 (2014): 1255–1310; and Saez and Zucman, "Wealth Inequality."

29. Thomas Piketty, Gilles Postel-Vinay, and Jean-Laurent Rosenthal, "Inherited versus Self-Made Wealth: Theory and Evidence from a Rentier Society (1872–1927)," *Explorations in Economic History* 51 (2013): 21–40; Thomas Piketty and Gabriel Zucman, "Wealth and Inheritance in the Long Run," in *Handbook of Income Distribution,* vol. 2, ed. A. Atkinson and F. Bourguignon (Amsterdam: Elsevier, 2014), 167–216.

30. Franco Modigliani, "The Role of Intergenerational Transfers and Lifecycle Savings in the Accumulation of Wealth," *Journal of Economic Perspectives* 2 (1988): 15–40; Lawrence Kotlikoff and Lawrence Summers, "The Role of Intergenerational Transfers in Aggregate Capital Accumulation," *Journal of Political Economy* 89 (1981): 706–732.

31. Chetty et al. use this comprehensive data to document, college by college, the distributions of parental income and the earnings of students later in life (see Raj Chetty, John N. Friedman, Emmanuel Saez, Nicholas Turner, and Danny Yagan, "The Distribution of Student and Parent Income across Colleges in the United States", working paper, 2016). Their results show that elite schools

disproportionately serve high-income families, suggesting that higher education plays a large role in the transmission of economic privilege in the United States.

32. Karen Dynan, Jonathan Skinner, and Stephen Zeldes, "Do the Rich Save More?," *Journal of Political Economy* 112 (2004): 397–443.

33. Saez and Zucman, "Wealth Inequality."

34. Kuznets, *Shares of Upper Income Groups.*

35. See, e.g., Raj Chetty, John Friedman, Soren Leth-Petersen, T. Nielsen, and Torre Olsen, "Active vs. Passive Decisions and Crowd-Out in Retirement Savings Accounts: Evidence from Denmark," *Quarterly Journal of Economics* 129 (2014): 1141–1219. Some recent research studies in the United States have started using data from financial institutions such as banks, credit card companies, or other financial service providers (see, e.g., Michael Gelman et al., "Harnessing Naturally Occurring Data to Measure the Response of Spending to Income," *Science,* July 11, 2014, 212–215). Although these data can be valuable for many research questions on savings behavior, they are not representative samples of the U.S. population and hence cannot be used to provide an overall picture of the U.S. wealth and savings distributions.

36. Piketty and Saez, "Income Inequality."

37. Jon Bakija, Adam Cole, and Bradley Heim, "Jobs and Income Growth of Top Earners and the Causes of Changing Income Inequality: Evidence from U.S. Tax Return Data," unpublished working paper (2012).

38. Xavier Gabaix and Augustin Landier, "Why Has CEO Pay Increased So Much?," *Quarterly Journal of Economics* 123 (2008): 49–100.

39. Marianne Bertrand and Sendhil Mullainathan, "Are CEOs Rewarded for Luck? The Ones without Principals Are," *Quarterly Journal of Economics* 116 (2001): 901–932; Lucian Bebchuk and Jesse Fried, *Pay without Performance: The Unfulfilled Promise of Executive Compensation* (Cambridge, MA: Harvard University Press, 2006).

40. Piketty and Saez, "Income Inequality."

41. Thomas Piketty, Emmanuel Saez, and Stefanie Stantcheva, "Optimal Taxation of Top Labor Incomes: A Tale of Three Elasticities," *American Economic Journal: Economic Policy* 6 (2014): 230–271.

42. Anthony Atkinson, *Inequality: What Can Be Done?* (Cambridge, MA: Harvard University Press, 2015).

43. Piketty, Saez, and Stantcheva, "Optimal Taxation."

44. Thomas Philippon and Ariell Reshef, "Wages and Human Capital in the U.S. Finance Industry: 1909–2006," *Quarterly Journal of Economics* 127 (2012): 1551–1609.

45. Brian Hall and Kevin Murphy, "The Trouble with Stock Options," *Journal of Economic Perspectives* 17 (2003): 49–70.

46. The estate tax in the United States is not popular and was almost entirely repealed during the Bush administrations. The current U.S. estate tax affects only

about the top 1 / 1000 of the wealthiest decedents each year. However, unpopularity of the estate tax seems largely due to misinformation (and the success of conservatives in framing it as a death tax negatively affecting family businesses). Kuziemko et al. show that support for the estate tax doubles when people are informed that it is a tax on very wealthy decedents only; see Ilyana Kuziemko, Michael I. Norton, Emmanuel Saez, and Stefanie Stantcheva, "How Elastic Are Preferences for Redistribution? Evidence from Randomized Survey Experiments," *American Economic Review* 105 (2015): 1478–1508.

47. Marianne Bertrand and Adair Morse, "Trickle-Down Consumption," NBER Working Paper No. 18883 (2013).

48. Chetty et al., "Active vs. Passive Decisions."

49. Richard Thaler and Cass Sunstein, *Nudge: Improving Decisions about Health, Wealth, and Happiness* (New Haven, CT: Yale University Press, 2008).

14. Macro Models of Wealth Inequality

1. Thomas Piketty, *Capital in the Twenty-First Century,* trans. Arthur Goldhammer (Cambridge, MA: Belknap Press of Harvard University Press, 2014). In this respect Piketty writes, "In a sense, it sums up the overall logic of my conclusions" (25).

2. Jess Benhabib, Alberto Bisin, and Shenghao Zhu, "The Wealth Distribution in Bewley Models with Capital Income Risk," *Journal of Economic Theory* 159 (2015): 459–515; Shuhei Aoki and Makoto Nirei, "Pareto Distribution in Bewley Models with Capital Income Risk," Hitotsubashi University (2015).

3. Karen E. Dynan, Jonathan Skinner, and Stephen P. Zeldes, "Do the Rich Save More?," *Journal of Political Economy* 112 (2004): 397–444.

4. It was this very observation that prompted Pareto to propose his eponymous distribution. Vilfredo Pareto, *Cours d'économie politique,* vol. 2 (Lausanne: F. Rouge, 1897).

5. Anthony B. Atkinson, *The Economics of Inequality* (Oxford: Clarendon Press, 1983); Javier Díaz-Giménez, Vincenzo Quadrini, and José-Victor Ríos-Rull, "Dimensions of Inequality: Facts on the U.S. Distributions of Earnings, Income and Wealth," *Federal Reserve Bank of Minneapolis Quarterly Review* 21 (1997): 3–21; Arthur B. Kennickell, "A Rolling Tide: Changes in the Distribution of Wealth in the U.S., 1989–2001" (2003), https://www.federalreserve.gov/pubs/feds/2003/200324/200324pap.pdf; Santiago Budria Rodriguez, Javier Díaz-Giménez, Vincenzo Quadrini, and José-Victor Ríos-Rull, "Updated Facts on the U.S. Distributions of Earnings, Income, and Wealth," *Federal Reserve Bank of Minneapolis Quarterly Review* 26 (2002): 2–35; Herman O. Wold and Peter Whittle, "A Model Explaining the Pareto Distribution of Wealth," *Econometrica* 25 (1957): 591–595; Edward N. Wolff, "Changing Inequality of Wealth," *American Economic Review* 82 (1992): 552–558; Wolff, "Recent Trends in the Size Distribution of Household Wealth," *Journal of Economic Perspectives* 12 (1998): 131–150.

6. Erik Hurst, Ming Ching Luoh, and Frank P. Stafford, "The Wealth Dynamics of American Families, 1984–94," *Brookings Papers on Economic Activity* 29 (1998): 267–338.

7. Klevmarken, Lupton, and Stafford find that the *overall* wealth-quintile mobility, though not wealth inequality, in Sweden is comparable to that in the United States. See N. Anders Klevmarken, Joseph P. Lupton, and Frank P. Stafford, "Wealth Dynamics in the 1980s and 1990s: Sweden and the United States," *Journal of Human Resources* 38 (2003): 322–353.

8. Casey B. Mulligan, *Parental Priorities and Economic Inequality* (Chicago: University of Chicago Press, 1997).

9. Kerwin Kofi Charles and Erik Hurst, "The Correlation of Wealth across Generations," *Journal of Political Economy* 111 (2003): 1155–1182.

10. The age of children in Mulligan's sample is below thirty-five, and the number of parent-child pairs in which both parents have died is very small in the Charles and Hurst sample. Charles and Hurst, "Correlation of Wealth"; Mulligan, *Parental Priorities*.

11. Adrian Adermon, Mikael Lindahl, and Daniel Waldenström, "Intergenerational Wealth Mobility and the Role of Inheritance: Evidence from Multiple Generations," IZA Discussion Paper No. 10126 (2015); Simon Halphen Boserup, Wojciech Kopczuk, and Claus Thustrup Kreiner, "Stability and Persistence of Intergenerational Wealth Formation: Evidence from Danish Wealth Records of Three Generations," 2015, http://eml.berkeley.edu/~saez/course131/WealthAcrossGen.pdf; Gregory Clark and Neil Cummins, "Intergenerational Wealth Mobility in England, 1858–2012: Surnames and Social Mobility," *Economic Journal* 125 (2015): 61–85.

12. Early efforts to document the evolution of the wealth distribution in the twentieth century are Lampman for the United States and Atkinson and Harrison for the U.K. See Robert J. Lampman, *The Share of Top Wealth-Holders in National Wealth, 1922–1956* (Princeton, NJ: Princeton University Press, 1962); Anthony B. Atkinson and Allan J. Harrison, *Distribution of Personal Wealth in Britain, 1923–1972* (Cambridge: Cambridge University Press, 1983).

13. Emmanuel Saez and Gabriel Zucman, "Wealth Inequality in the United States since 1913: Evidence from Capitalized Income Tax Data," 2015, http://gabriel-zucman.eu/files/SaezZucman2015.pdf.

14. Kopczuk discusses differences among the available estimates and possible explanations for their divergence. Wojciech Kopczuk, "What Do We Know about the Evolution of Top Wealth Shares in the United States?," *Journal of Economic Perspectives* 29 (2015): 47–66.

15. James E Meade, *Efficiency, Equality and the Ownership of Property* (London: Allen and Unwin, 1964).

16. To be precise, the flow of savings out of noncapital income equals minus the flow of consumption in the present setup with zero noncapital income.

17. The article by Wold and Whittle is an early example featuring an exogenous rate of wealth accumulation. The latter is endogenized in the optimizing models in articles by Benhabib and Bisin, and Jones. Jess Benhabib and Alberto Bisin, "The Distribution of Wealth and Redistributive Policies," 2006, http://www.econ.nyu.edu/user/benhabib/parvolt3.PDF; Charles I. Jones, "Pareto and Piketty: The Macroeconomics of Top Income and Wealth Inequality," *Journal of Economic Perspectives* 29 (2015): 29–46; Wold and Whittle, "Pareto Distribution of Wealth."

18. Benhabib and Bisin, The Distribution of Wealth."

19. The article by Champernowne is an early, purely statistical, contribution. Articles by Benhabib, Bisin, and Zhu, Aoki and Nirei, Piketty and Zucman, and Gabaix, Lasry, Lions, and Moll exploit the original insight in the context of economic models with optimizing agents. D. G. Champernowne, "A Model of Income Distribution," *Economics Journal* 63 (1953): 318–351; Jess Benhabib, Alberto Bisin, and Shenghao Zhu, "The Distribution of Wealth and Fiscal Policy in Economies with Finitely Lived Agents," *Econometrica* 79 (2011): 123–157; Benhabib, Bisin, and Zhu, "The Wealth Distribution"; Aoki and Nirei, "Pareto Distribution"; Thomas Piketty and Gabriel Zucman, "Wealth and Inheritance in the Long Run," in *Handbook of Income Distribution,* vol. 2B, ed. A. J. Atkinson and F. Bourguignon (Amsterdam: Elsevier, 2014), 1303–1368; Xavier Gabaix, Jean-Michel Lasry, Pierre-Louis Lions, and Benjamin Moll, "The Dynamics of Inequality," NBER Working Paper No. 21363 (2015).

20. Benhabib, Bisin, and Zhu, "The Distribution of Wealth"; Piketty and Zucman, "Wealth and Inheritance."

21. Benhabib, Bisin, and Zhu, "The Wealth Distribution"; Aoki and Nirei, "Pareto Distribution."

22. Aoki and Nirei, "Pareto Distribution"; Benhabib, Bisin, and Zhu, "The Distribution of Wealth."

23. Benhabib, Bisin, and Zhu, "The Distribution of Wealth"; Benhabib, Bisin, Zhu, "The Wealth Distribution."

24. Jones, "Pareto and Piketty."

25. Aoki and Nirei, "Pareto Distribution"; Jones, "Pareto and Piketty."

26. Saez and Zucman, "Wealth Inequality."

27. Ana Castañeda, Javier Díaz-Giménez, and José-Víctor Ríos-Rull, "Accounting for U.S. Earnings and Wealth Inequality," *Journal of Political Economy* 111 (2003): 818–857.

28. Vincenzo Quadrini, "Entrepreneurship in Macroeconomics," *Annals of Finance* 5 (2009): 295–311.

29. Francisco Buera, "Persistency of Poverty, Financial Frictions, and Entrepreneurship," Working paper, Northwestern University, 2008, http://www.iadb.org/library/repository/paper120071217.pdf; Mariacristina De Nardi, Phil Doctor, and Spencer D. Krane, "Evidence on Entrepreneurs in the United States: Data from the 1989–2004 Survey of Consumer Finances," *Economic Perspectives* 4 (2007): 18–36; William M. Gentry and R. Glenn Hubbard,

"Entrepreneurship and Household Savings," *Berkeley Economic Journal: Advances in Macroeconomics* 4 (2004); Vincenzo Quadrini, "Entrepreneurship, Saving and Social Mobility," *Review of Economic Dynamics* 3 (2000): 1–40.

30. Marco Cagetti and Mariacristina De Nardi, "Entrepreneurship, Frictions and Wealth," *Journal of Political Economy* 114 (2006): 835–870.

31. Cagetti and De Nardi, "Entrepreneurship, Frictions and Wealth"; Erik Hurst and Annamaria Lusardi, "Liquidity Constraints, Wealth Accumulation and Entrepreneurship," *Journal of Political Economy* 112 (2004): 319–347; Katya Kartashova, "Private Equity Premium Puzzle Revisited," *American Economic Review* 104 (2014): 3297–3394; Tobias J. Moskowitz and Annette Vissing-Jørgensen, "The Returns to Entrepreneurial Investment: A Private Equity Premium Puzzle?," *American Economic Review* 92 (2002): 745–778.

32. Sagiri Kitao, "Entrepreneurship, Taxation, and Capital Investment," *Review of Economic Dynamics* 11 (2008): 44–69.

33. Marcin Kacperczyk, Jaromir Nosal, and Luminita Stevens, "Investor Sophistication and Capital Income Inequality," 2015, http://econweb.umd.edu/~stevens/KNS_Sophistication.pdf.

34. Christopher D. Carroll, "Precautionary Saving and the Marginal Propensity to Consume out of Permanent Income," *Journal of Monetary Economics* 56 (2007): 780–790.

35. Castañeda, Díaz-Giménez, and Ríos-Rull, "Accounting for U.S. Earnings."

36. Ibid.; Saez and Zucman, "Wealth Inequality."

37. Sherwin Rosen, "The Economics of Superstars," *American Economic Review* 71 (1981): 845–858; Xavier Gabaix and Augustin Landier, "Why Has CEO Pay Increased So Much?," *Quarterly Journal of Economics* 123 (2008): 49–100; Sang Yoon (Tim) Lee, "Entrepreneurs, Managers and Inequality," 2015, http://lee.vwl.uni-mannheim.de/materials/ent_mgr_ineq.pdf.

38. The complete set of studies is collected in Atkinson, Piketty, and Saez. The data set is available at Alvaredo, Atkinson, Piketty, and Saez. See Anthony B. Atkinson, Thomas Piketty, and Emmanuel Saez, "Top Incomes in the Long Run of History," *Journal of Economic Literature* 49 (2010): 3–71; Facundo Alvaredo, Anthony B. Atkinson, Thomas Piketty, and Emmanuel Saez, "The World Top Incomes Database," http://topincomes.g-mond.parisschoolofeconomics.eu/, 2015; Thomas Piketty and Emmanuel Saez, "Income Inequality in the United States, 1913–1998," *Quarterly Journal of Economics* 118 (2003): 1–39.

39. Fatih Guvenen, Fatih Karahan, Serdar Ozkan, and Jae Song, "What Do Data on Millions of U.S. Workers Reveal about Life-Cycle Earnings Risk?," Federal Reserve Bank of New York Staff Report, 2015, https://www.newyorkfed.org/medialibrary/media/research/staff_reports/sr710.pdf.

40. Jonathan A. Parker and Annette Vissing-Jørgensen, "Who Bears Aggregate Fluctuations and How?," *American Economic Review* 99 (2009): 399–405.

41. William G. Gale and John Karl Scholz, "Intergenerational Transfers and the Accumulation of Wealth," *Journal of Economic Perspectives* 8 (1994): 145–160;

Dynan, Skinner, and Zeldes, "Do the Rich Save More?"; Christopher D. Carroll, "Why Do the Rich Save So Much?," in *Does Atlas Shrug? The Economic Consequences of Taxing the Rich*, ed. J. B. Slemrod (Cambridge, MA: Harvard University Press, 2000); Carroll, "Portfolios of the Rich," in *Household Portfolios: Theory and Evidence,* ed. L. Guiso, M. Haliassos, and T. Jappelli (Cambridge, MA: MIT Press, 2002); Mariacristina De Nardi, Eric French, and John B. Jones, "Why Do the Elderly Save? The Role of Medical Expenses," *Journal of Political Economy* 118 (2010): 39–75.

42. Mariacristina De Nardi, "Wealth Inequality and Intergenerational Links," *Review of Economic Studies* 71 (2004): 734–768; Joseph G. Altonji and Ernesto Villanueva, "The Effect of Parental Income on Wealth and Bequests," NBER Working Paper No. 9811 (2002); Mark Huggett, "Wealth Distribution in Life-Cycle Economies," *Journal of Monetary Economics* 38 (1996): 469–494.

43. De Nardi, French, and Jones suggest that medical expenses are another important mechanism that can generate this kind of slow decumulation. Lockwood argues that both medical expenses and a luxury bequest motive are necessary to account for both the low rate of asset decumulation *and* the low rate of insurance against medical expenses. De Nardi, French, and Jones, "Why Do the Elderly Save?"; Lee M. Lockwood, "Incidental Bequests: Bequest Motives and the Choice to Self-Insure Late-Life Risks," NBER Working Paper No. 20745 (December 2014).

44. Nishiyama obtains similar results in an overlapping-generation model with bequests and inter vivos transfers in which households in the same family line behave strategically. Shinichi Nishiyama, "Bequests, Inter Vivos Transfers, and Wealth Distribution," *Review of Economic Dynamics* 5 (2002): 892–931.

45. Castañeda, Díaz-Giménez, and Ríos-Rull, "Accounting for U.S. Earnings"; Mariacristina De Nardi and Fang Yang, "Wealth Inequality, Family Background, and Estate Taxation," NBER Working Paper No. 21047 (2015).

46. Steven F. Venti and David A. Wise, "The Cause of Wealth Dispersion at Retirement: Choice or Chance?," *American Economic Review* 88 (1988): 185–191; B. Douglas Bernheim, Jonathan Skinner, and Steven Weimberg, "What Accounts for the Variation in Retirement Wealth among U.S. Households?," *American Economic Review* 91 (2001): 832–857; Lutz Hendricks, "Retirement Wealth and Lifetime Earnings," *International Economic Review* 48 (2007): 421–456; Mariacristina De Nardi and Fang Yang, "Bequests and Heterogeneity in Retirement Wealth," *European Economic Review* 72 (2014): 182–196.

47. Marco Cagetti, "Wealth Accumulation over the Life Cycle and Precautionary Savings," *Journal of Business and Economic Statistics* 21 (2003): 339–353; Emily Lawrance, "Poverty and the Rate of Time Preference: Evidence from Panel Data," *Journal of Political Economy* 99 (1991): 54–77.

48. Though the model also allows for aggregate shocks, these do not have quantitatively important implications for the wealth distribution. Per Krusell and Anthony Smith Jr., "Income and Wealth Heterogeneity in the Macroeconomy," *Journal of Political Economy* 106 (1998): 867–896.

49. They also find that heterogeneity in risk aversion does not affect the results much. However, Cagetti shows that this result is sensitive to chosen utility parameter values. Marco Cagetti, "Interest Elasticity in a Life-Cycle Model with Precautionary Savings," *American Economic Review* 91 (2001): 418–421.

50. Lutz Hendricks, "How Important Is Preference Heterogeneity for Wealth Inequality?," *Journal of Economics Dynamics and Control* 31 (2007): 3042–3068.

51. Chong Wang, Neng Wang, and Jinqiang Yang, "Optimal Consumption and Savings with Stochastic Income and Recursive Utility," NBER Working Paper No. 19319 (2013), http://www.nber.org/papers/w19319.

52. Gabaix, Lasry, Lions, and Moll, "The Dynamics of Inequality"; Saez and Zucman, "Wealth Inequality."

53. B. Kaymak and M. Poschke, "The Evolution of Wealth Inequality over Half a Century: The Role of Taxes, Transfers and Technology," *Journal of Monetary Economics* (2015), http://dx.doi.org/10.1016/j.jmoneco.2015.10.004i; Castañeda, Díaz-Giménez, and Ríos-Rull, "Accounting for U.S. Earnings."

54. Gabaix, Lasry, Lions, and Moll, "The Dynamics of Inequality"; Kaymak and Poschke, "Evolution of Wealth Inequality."

55. Castañeda, Díaz-Giménez, and Ríos-Rull, "Accounting for U.S. Earnings"; De Nardi and Yang, "Wealth Inequality."

56. Castañeda, Díaz-Giménez, and Ríos-Rull, "Accounting for U.S. Earnings."

57. In the data, this fraction increases to 3.8 percent if inter vivos transfers and college expenses are also included.

58. Jeffrey R. Campbell and Mariacristina De Nardi, "A Conversation with 590 Entrepreneurs," *Annals of Finance* 5 (2009): 313–327.

59. For quantitative works that highlight the importance of home production in life-cycle settings, see, for example, Michael Dotsey, Wenli Li, and Fang Yang, "Consumption and Time Use over the Life Cycle," *International Economic Review* 55 (2014): 665–692; and Michael Dotsey, Wenli Li, and Fang Yang, "Home Production and Social Security Reform," *European Economic Review* 73 (2015): 131–150.

60. De Nardi, French, and Jones, "Why Do the Elderly Save?"

61. Mariacristina De Nardi, Giulio Fella, and Gonzalo Paz Pardo, "Fat Tails in Life-Cycle Earnings and Wealth Inequality," 2015; Guvenen, Karahan, Ozkan, and Song, "What Do Data on Millions."

62. To reduce computational time, we make the assumption that people do not die before age sixty-five. This assumption does not affect the results, because in the United States the number of adults dying before age sixty-five is small.

63. De Nardi, "Wealth Inequality and Intergenerational Links"; De Nardi and Yang, "Bequests and Heterogeneity"; Fang Yang, "Social Security Reform with Impure Intergenerational Altruism," *Journal of Economic Dynamics and Control* 37 (2013): 52–67.

64. De Nardi and Yang, "Wealth Inequality."

65. Ibid.

66. See, for example, Barry P. Bosworth and Sarah Anders, "Saving and Wealth Accumulation in the PSID, 1984–2005," NBER Working Paper No. 17689 (2011).

67. Castañeda, Díaz-Giménez, and Ríos-Rull, "Accounting for U.S. Earnings."

68. De Nardi, "Wealth Inequality and Intergenerational Links"; George Tauchen, "Finite State Markov-Chain Approximations to Univariate and Vector Autoregressions," *Economic Letters* 20 (1986): 177–181.

69. De Nardi, "Wealth Inequality "; Tauchen, "Finite State Markov-Chain Approximations."

70. Jason DeBacker, Vasia Panousi, and Shanthi Ramnath, "The Properties of Income Risk in Privately Held Businesses," Federal Reserve Board Working Paper No. 2012-69 (2012).

71. De Nardi and Yang, "Wealth Inequality."

15. A Feminist Interpretation of Patrimonial Capitalism

This chapter was also presented at a conference at the Rockefeller Bellagio Retreat Center, December 1–4, 2015. I thank the participants at the conference and especially Todd Tucker, Art Goldhammer, Brad DeLong, and Branko Milanovich for very helpful comments; All errors remain mine alone.

1. Thomas Piketty, "Putting Distribution Back at the Center of Economics: Reflections on *Capital in the Twenty-First Century*," *Journal of Economic Perspectives* 29, no. 1 (Winter 2015): 69, quoting himself in *C21,* 20, 35.

2. Thomas Piketty, *Capital in the Twenty-First Century,* trans. Arthur Goldhammer (Cambridge, MA: Belknap Press of Harvard University Press, 2014), 378.

3. Ibid.

4. From its inception, feminist economics has purposefully been attentive to issues of intersectionality. Inheritance patterns differ greatly across racial groups, especially in the United States with our history of slavery of African Americans. Chapters 6 and 20 in this volume specifically grapple with racial equity issues.

5. Bradford DeLong, "Bequests: An Historical Perspective," University of California, Berkeley (2003). http://www.j-bradford-delong.net/econ_articles /estates/delongestatesmunnell.pdf

6. Simon Kuznets, "Economic Growth and Income Inequality," *American Economic Review* 45, no. 1 (March 1955): 26.

7. Piketty, *Capital,* 11.

8. J. B. Clark, "Distribution as Determined by a Law of Rent," *Quarterly Journal of Economics* 5, no. 3 (1891): 289–318, at 313.

9. Piketty, *Capital,* 11.

10. N. Gregory Mankiw, David Romer, and David N. Weil, "A Contribution to the Empirics of Economic Growth," *Quarterly Journal of Economics* 107, no. 2 (1992): 407–437.

11. J. Bradford DeLong, Claudia Goldin, and Lawrence Katz, "Sustaining U.S. Economic Growth," in *Agenda for the Nation,* ed. Henry J. Aaron, James M. Lindsay, and Pietro S. Nivola (Washington, DC: Brookings Institution, 2003).

12. Paul M. Romer, "Human Capital and Growth: Theory and Evidence," Working Paper (National Bureau of Economic Research, November 1989), http://www.nber.org/papers/w3173; Paul Romer, "Increasing Returns and Long-Run Growth," *Journal of Political Economy* 94, no. 5 (October 1986): 1002–1037, http://www.apec.umn.edu/grad/jdiaz/Romer%201986.pdf.

13. Jacob A. Mincer, *Schooling, Experience, and Earnings* (New York: Columbia University Press, 1974), http://papers.nber.org/books/minc74-1; see also Thomas Lemieux, "The 'Mincer Equation' Thirty Years after *Schooling, Experience, and Earnings,*" in *Jacob Mincer: A Pioneer of Modern Labor Economics* (New York: Springer Science and Business Media, 2006), 127–145.

14. Gary S. Becker, *The Economics of Discrimination,* 2nd ed. (Chicago: University of Chicago Press, 1971).

15. Kenneth Arrow, "Some Mathematical Models of Race in the Labor Market," in *Racial Discrimination in Economic Life,* ed. A. H. Pascal (Lexington, MA: Lexington Books, 1972).

16. Chang-Tai Hsieh, Erik Hurst, Charles Jones, and Peter Klenow, "The Allocation of Talent and U.S. Economic Growth," NBER Working Paper No. 18639 (January 2013), http://www.nber.org/papers/w18693.

17. U.S. Bureau of Labor Statistics, "Civilian Labor Force Participation Rate: Women" (LNS11300002), https://research.stlouisfed.org/fred2/series/LNS11300002, accessed May 16, 2016.

18. Katrin Elborgh-Woytek et al., "Women, Work, and the Economy: Macroeconomic Gains from Gender Equity," IMF Staff Discussion Note, September 2013, http://www.imf.org/external/pubs/ft/sdn/2013/sdn1310.pdf; DeAnne Aguirre et al., "Empowering the Third Billion: Women and the World of Work in 2012" (Booz & Company, October 15, 2012), http://www.strategyand.pwc.com/reports/empowering-third-billion-women-world-2.

19. Eileen Appelbaum, Heather Boushey, and John Schmitt, "The Economic Importance of Women's Rising Hours of Work," Center for Economic and Policy Research and Center for American Progress, April 2014.

20. Benjamin Bridgman, Andrew Dugan, Mikhael Lal, Matthew Osborne, and Shaunda Villones, "Accounting for Household Production in the National Accounts, 1965–2010," Bureau of Economic Analysis, May 2012, https://www.bea.gov/scb/pdf/2012/05%20May/0512_household.pdf; Bridgman, "Accounting for Household Production in the National Accounts: An Update, 1965–2014," Bureau of Economic Analysis, February 2016, https://www.bea.gov/scb/pdf/2016/2%20February/0216_accounting_for_household_production_in_the_national_accounts.pdf.

21. IGM Forum "Inequality and Skills," panelist poll, University of Chicago, Booth School of Business, The Initiative on Global Markets, January 24, 2012,

http://www.igmchicago.org/igm-economic-experts-panel/poll-results?SurveyID=SV_oIAlhdDH2FoRDrm.

22. In the introduction to *C21,* where he outlines his methodology, Piketty doesn't mince words in his criticism of modern-day economics: "To put it bluntly, the discipline of economics has yet to get over its childish passion for mathematics and for purely theoretical and often highly ideological speculation, at the expense of historical research and collaboration with the other social sciences." Piketty, *Capital,* 32.

23. Thomas Piketty and Emmanuel Saez, "Income Inequality in the United States, 1913–1998," *Quarterly Journal of Economics* 118, no. 1 (February 2003): 1–39.

24. Piketty, *Capital,* 1, italics added.

25. I leave it to other chapters to consider whether $r > g$ will in fact describe our economy.

26. Ibid., 173, italics added. This is the second mention of the term; the first is at 154.

27. Ibid., 571.

28. Piketty, "Putting Distribution Back at the Center," 84.

29. Ibid.

30. Daron Acemoglu and James Robinson, "The Rise and Decline of General Laws of Capitalism," *Journal of Economic Perspectives* 29, no. 1 (Winter 2015): 9.

31. For a classic read on labor markets, see David Card and Alan Krueger, *Myth and Measurement: The New Economics of the Minimum Wage* (Princeton, NJ: Princeton University Press, 1995).

32. Julie Nelson, "Feminist Economics," in *The New Palgrave Dictionary of Economics,* ed. Steven N. Durlauf and Lawrence E. Blume (New York: Palgrave Macmillan, 2008), http://www.sdum.uminho.pt/uploads/palgrave1.pdf.

33. Marilyn Waring, *If Women Counted: A New Feminist Economics,* with an introduction by Gloria Steinem (San Francisco: Harper, 1990).

34. Bridgman et al., "Accounting for Household Production in the National Accounts, 1965–2010"; Bridgman, "Accounting for Household Production in the National Accounts: An Update, 1965–2014"; Bridgman, "Home Productivity," Bureau of Economic Analysis, February 2013, http://bea.gov/papers/pdf/homeproductivity.pdf. See also Duncan Ironmonger and Faye Soupourmas, "Output-Based Estimates of the Gross Household Product of the United States 2003–2010: And Some Interactions of GHP with Gross Market Product during the Great Financial Crisis (2008–2009)," paper presented at the 32nd General Conference of the International Association for Research in Income and Wealth, Boston, 2012, http://www.iariw.org/papers/2012/IronmongerPaper.pdf.

35. Thomas Piketty, Emmanuel Saez, and Gabriel Zucman, "Distributional National Accounts: Methods and Estimates for the United States," Working Paper (December 2, 2016), http://gabriel-zucman.eu/files/PSZ2016.pdf.

36. Nelson, "Feminist Economics."

37. Julie A. Nelson and Marianne A. Ferber, *Beyond Economic Man: Feminist Theory and Economics* (Chicago: University of Chicago Press, 1993).

38. There's a rich literature here, but see, for example, Sheldon Danziger and Peter Gottschalk, *America Unequal* (New York: Russell Sage Foundation, 1995).

39. I reached out to Art Goldhammer, who translated *C21* from French into English, about whether or not the word "patrimony" had a gendered meaning in French. He said no; in the original French, "patrimonie" "is a gender-neutral term . . . 'Patrimoine' simply means wealth, inheritance, or heritage. 'Le patrimoine national' refers to national wealth in both an economic and cultural sense. Museums, for example, are said to preserve 'le patrimoine national.'" Goldhammer also noted that the translation of patrimony was a concern; however, "After some back-and-forth, [they] decided it would be best just to keep it close to the French and let the text define how Thomas uses it."

40. Jane Humphries, "Capital in the Twenty-First Century," *Feminist Economics* 21, no. 1 (January 2, 2015): 164–173, doi:10.1080/13545701.2014.950679.

41. Kathleen Geier, "How Gender Changes Piketty's 'Capital in the Twenty-First Century,'" *The Nation*, August 6, 2014, http://www.thenation.com/article/how-gender-changes-pikettys-capital-twenty-first-century/.

42. Diane Perrons, "Gendering Inequality: A Note on Piketty's *Capital in the Twenty-First Century*," *British Journal of Sociology* 65, no. 4 (2014): 667–677, doi:10.1111/1468-4446.12114.

43. Quote taken from John Ermisch, Marco Francesconi, and Thomas Siedler, "Intergenerational Mobility and Marital Sorting," *Economic Journal* 116 (July 2006): 659–679; see also Lawrence Stone, *The Family, Sex and Marriage: In England, 1500–1800* (New York: Harper and Row, 1977).

44. Stone, *Family, Sex and Marriage;* Roger Chatier, ed., *Passions of the Renaissance,* trans. Arthur Goldhammer, vol. 3 of *A History of Private Life* (Cambridge, MA: Belknap Press of Harvard University Press, 1993), http://www.hup.harvard.edu/catalog.php?isbn=9780674400023; Michelle Perrot, ed., *From the Fires of Revolution to the Great War,* trans. Arthur Goldhammer, vol. 4 of *A History of Private Life* (Cambridge, MA: Belknap Press of Harvard University Press, 1990), http://www.hup.harvard.edu/catalog.php?isbn=9780674400023.

45. Piketty, *Capital,* 240.

46. For more on this argument, see chapter 4 of Heather Boushey, *Finding Time: The Economics of Work-Life Conflict* (Cambridge, MA: Harvard University Press, 2016).

47. David M. Buss et al., "A Half Century of Mate Preferences: The Cultural Evolution of Values," *Journal of Marriage and Family* 63, no. 2 (May 1, 2001): 491–503, doi:10.1111/j.1741-3737.2001.00491.x.

48. U.S. Bureau of Economic Analysis, "Table CA1. Personal Income Summary: Personal Income, Population, Per Capita Personal Income," http://www.bea.gov/iTable/iTableHtml.cfm?reqid=70&step=30&isuri=1&7022=20&7023=7&7024=non-industry&7033=-1&7025=5&7026=xx&7027=2014&7001

=720&7028=-1&7031=5&7040=-1&7083=levels&7029=20&7090=70 (accessed May 17, 2016).

49. Susan Patton, "Letter to the Editor: Advice for the Young Women of Princeton: The Daughters I Never Had," *Daily Princetonian,* March 29, 2013, http://dailyprincetonian.com/opinion/2013/03/letter-to-the-editor-advice-for-the-young-women-of-princeton-the-daughters-i-never-had/.

50. Laura Chadwick and Gary Solon, "Intergenerational Income Mobility among Daughters," *American Economic Review* 92, no. 1 (March 2002): 343.

51. Ibid.

52. Ermisch, Francesconi, and Siedler, "Intergenerational Mobility and Marital Sorting."

53. Sheryl Sandberg, *Lean In: Women, Work, and the Will to Lead* (New York: Alfred A. Knopf, 2013).

54. Brendan Duke, "How Married Women's Rising Earnings Have Reduced Inequality," Center for American Progress, September 2015, https://www.americanprogress.org/issues/women/news/2015/09/29/122033/how-married-womens-rising-earnings-have-reduced-inequality/; Maria Cancian and Deborah Reed, "Assessing the Effects of Wives' Earnings on Family Income Inequality," *Review of Economics and Statistics* 80, no. 1 (February 1, 1998): 73–79.

55. Duke, "Married Women's Rising Earnings."

56. Philip Cohen, "Family Diversity Is the New Normal for America's Children," Council on Contemporary Families Brief Reports, September 4, 2014.

57. Boushey, *Finding Time,* fig. 3.2.

58. Andrew J. Cherlin, *Labor's Love Lost: The Rise and Fall of the Working-Class Family in America* (New York: Russell Sage Foundation, 2014).

59. Sara McLanahan, "Diverging Destinies: How Children Are Faring under the Second Demographic Transition," *Demography* 41, no. 4 (2004): 607–627, doi:10.1353/dem.2004.0033. According to data from Andrew Cherlin, Elizabeth Talbert, and Suzumi Yasutake, among women aged twenty-six to thirty-one who gave birth by 2011, of those with a college degree, fewer than one in three women were unmarried, compared with 63 percent of those without a college degree. Andrew J. Cherlin, Elizabeth Talbert, and Suzumi Yasutake, "Changing Fertility Regimes and the Transition to Adulthood: Evidence from a Recent Cohort," Johns Hopkins University, May 3, 2014.

60. Annette Lareau, *Unequal Childhoods: Class, Race, and Family Life,* 2nd ed. (Berkeley: University of California Press, 2011).

61. Piketty, *Capital,* 80.

62. Linda Speth, "The Married Women's Property Acts, 1839–1865: Reform, Reaction, or Revolution?," in *The Law of Sex Discrimination,* ed. J. Ralph Lindgren et al., 4th ed. (Boston, MA: Wadsworth, 2010), 12–17; Equal Opportunity Credit Act, 15 U.S. Code § 1691.

63. Nick Clegg, "Commencement of Succession to the Crown Act 2013," U.K. Parliament, March 26, 2015, http://www.parliament.uk/business/publications

/written-questions-answers-statements/written-statement/Commons/2015
-03-26/HCWS490/.

64. Paul Menchik, "Primogeniture, Equal Sharing, and the U.S. Distribution of Wealth," *Quarterly Journal of Economics* 94, no. 2 (March 1980): 314.

65. Menchik, ibid., 301, points out, "Though the models [Blinder, Stiglitz, Pryor] presented differ considerably in terms of methodologies and assumptions, they are similar in one respect. For all of them, equal sharing predicts less distributive inequality than primogeniture, and in general, the smaller the within-family degree of bequest inequality, the smaller the predicted degree of distributive inequality."

66. Ibid., 314.

67. Seth Stephens-Davidowitz, "Google, Tell Me. Is My Son a Genius?," *New York Times,* January 18, 2014, http://www.nytimes.com/2014/01/19/opinion/sunday /google-tell-me-is-my-son-a-genius.html.

68. Council of Economic Advisers, "Women's Participation in Education and the Workforce," October 14, 2014, https://www.whitehouse.gov/sites/default /files/docs/womens_slides_final.pdf.

69. Piketty, *Capital,* 421.

70. Ibid., 332.

71. Since 1978 the Social Security earnings data are not top-coded; from 1951 to 1977, the authors are able to use quarterly earnings information to extrapolate earnings up to 4 times the annual cap. Wojciech Kopczuk, Emmanuel Saez, and Jae Song, "Uncovering the American Dream: Inequality and Mobility in Social Security Earnings Data since 1937," NBER Working Paper No. 13345 (August 2007), http://www.nber.org/papers/w13345.pdf.

72. Lena Edlund and Wojciech Kopczuk, "Women, Wealth, and Mobility," NBER Working Paper No. 13162 (June 2007), http://www.nber.org/papers/w13162 .pdf; Caroline Freund and Sarah Oliver, "The Missing Women in the In-equality Discussion," *Realtime Economic Issues Watch,* August 5, 2014, http:// blogs.piie.com/realtime/?p=4430.

73. Piketty, "Putting Distribution Back at the Center," 70.

74. Piketty, *Capital,* 80.

16. What Does Rising Inequality Mean For the Macroeconomy?

I am grateful to Adam Ozimek for his insight, expertise, and hard work in researching and writing this chapter.

1. A detailed description of the Moody's Analytics model of the U.S. economy is available upon request.

2. Net worth by income group is based on the Federal Reserve's Survey of Consumer Finance.

3. Personal outlays by income group is based on the Federal Reserve's Survey of Consumer Finance and the Financial Accounts of the United States. The methodology used to derive this is available upon request.

4. Other factors also drive the deflator for information-processing equipment investment, most notable in recent years being the import share of this equipment.

5. A good exposition of this thesis is found in Frank Levy and Richard Murane, "Dancing with Robots: Human Skills for Computerized Work," Third Way white paper, July 17, 2013, http://www.thirdway.org/report/dancing-with -robots-human-skills-for-computerized-work.

6. The CES data serve a range of purposes, most notably the construction of the U.S. Consumer Price Index. For reference, according to the 2014 CES survey, those in the first quintile made less than $15,500 during the year. The second quintile made between $15,500 and $32,000, the third quintile made between $32,000 and $55,000, the fourth quintile made between $55,000 and $90,000, and the fifth quintile made over $90,000.

7. The Congressional Budget Office, "Housing Wealth and Consumer Spending," CBO Background Paper, 2007, https://www.cbo.gov/sites/default/files/110th -congress-2007-2008/reports/01-05-housing.pdf, provides a useful survey of this literature with an emphasis on the U.S. experience.

8. Federal government revenue as a share of GDP has averaged just over 17.5 percent since World War II. It is currently more than 19 percent, not far from the record high set in the technology boom.

9. See Olivier Coibion, Yuriy Gorodnichenko, Marianna Kudlyak, and John Mondragon, "Does Greater Inequality Lead to More Household Borrowing?," Federal Reserve Bank of Richmond Working Paper No. 14-01, January 2014, https://www .richmondfed.org/publications/research/working_papers/2014/wp_14-01.

10. This analysis is presented in Mark Zandi, Brian Poi, and Scott Hoyt, "Wealth Matters (A Lot)," Moody's Analytics white paper, October 2015, https://www .economy.com/mark-zandi/documents/2015-10-10-Wealth-Matters-A-Lot.pdf.

17. Rising Inequality and Economic Stability

This chapter draws from parts of the author's DPhil thesis at University of Oxford, "The Long Run Evolution of Economic Inequality and Macroeconomic Shocks" (2013). It also draws on of earlier joint research with Anthony B. Atkinson and Paolo Lucchino, whose contributions are greatly acknowledged. I thank Heather Boushey, Giulio Fella, Ian Malcolm and Stefan Thewissen for very helpful comments and discussion on the first draft of this chapter. Finally, special thanks go to Joe Hasell, whose comments and contribution greatly improved the chapter.

1. Thomas Piketty, *Capital in the Twenty-First Century,* trans. Arthur Goldhammer (Cambridge, MA: Belknap Press of Harvard University Press, 2014). In relation to this point Piketty writes, "In a sense, it sums up the overall logic of my conclusions" (25).

2. In general, I will not address political instability or social instability, though clearly these are linked (see discussion elsewhere within this volume).

3. J. E. Stiglitz, "Macroeconomic Fluctuations, Inequality, and Human Development," *Journal of Human Development and Capabilities* 13, no. 1 (2012): 31–58.
4. Piketty, *Capital,* 471, 515.
5. Ibid., 515. A series of other measures were proposed in the recent book by Anthony Atkinson, ranging from the institution of a participation basic income to what governments can do to influence the direction of technological process and market competition policies to address distributional concerns. A. B. Atkinson, *Inequality: What Can Be Done?* (Cambridge, MA: Harvard University Press, 2015).
6. Atkinson, *Inequality,* 11.
7. A. Demirgüç-Kunt and E. Detragiache, "Cross-Country Empirical Studies of Systemic Bank Distress: A Survey," *National Institute Economic Review* 192, no. 1 (2005): 68–83.
8. P. Aghion, A. Banerjee, and T. Piketty, "Dualism and Macroeconomic Volatility," *Quarterly Journal of Economics* 114, no. 4 (1999): 1359–1397.
9. The model replicates in a more conventional macroeconomic framework the work by R. M. Goodwin, *A Growth Cycle* (Cambridge: Cambridge University Press, 1967), in which functional income distribution (not personal income distribution) has a crucial role in generating endogenous growth cycles. Higher profits share fosters higher investments, which in turn generate employment. However, the latter increases the wage share, reducing in turn the investment and growth in the economy.
10. John Kenneth Galbraith, *The Great Crash, 1929* (Boston: Houghton Mifflin, 1954).
11. For post-1970 trends in economic inequality, see S. Morelli, T. Smeeding, and J. Thompson, "Post-1970 Trends in Within-Country Inequality and Poverty," in *Handbook of Income Distribution,* vol. 2, ed. A. B. Atkinson and François Bourguignon (Amsterdam: Elsevier North Holland, 2015). For a more detailed analysis for the United States, see J. A. Parker and A. Vissing-Jorgensen, "Who Bears Aggregate Fluctuations and How?," *American Economic Review* 99, no. 2 (2009): 399–405; S. Morelli, "Banking Crises in the US: The Response of Top Income Shares in a Historical Perspective," CSEF Working Paper No. 359 (April 2014); F. Guvenen, G. Kaplan, and J. Song, "How Risky Are Recessions for Top Earners?," *American Economic Review* 104, no. 5 (2014): 148–153; and F. Guvenen, S. Ozkan, and J. Song, "The Nature of Countercyclical Income Risk," *Journal of Political Economy* 122, no. 3 (2014): 621–660.
12. R. Frank, *The High-Beta Rich: How the Manic Wealthy Will Take Us to the Next Boom, Bubble, and Bust* (New York: Random House, 2011), 157.
13. B. B. Bakker and J. Felman, "The Rich and the Great Recession," IMF Working Paper WP / 14/225 (December 2014).
14. A. Mian and A. Sufi, *House of Debt: How They (and You) Caused the Great Recession, and How We Can Prevent It from Happening Again* (Chicago: University of Chicago Press, 2014).

15. This issue will be further discussed below.
16. A. Berg, J. D. Ostry, and J. Zettelmeyer, "What Makes Growth Sustained?," *Journal of Development Economics* 98, no. 2 (2012): 149–166.
17. B. Z. Cynamon and S. M. Fazzari, "Inequality, the Great Recession and Slow Recovery," *Cambridge Journal of Economics,* no. 5 (2015); T. Neal, "Essays on Panel Econometrics and the Distribution of Income" (PhD thesis, University of New South Wales, 2016).
18. D. Rodrik, "Where Did All the Growth Go? External Shocks, Social Conflict, and Growth Collapses," *Journal of Economic Growth* 4, no. 4 (1999): 385–412.
19. Ibid.
20. Stiglitz, "Macroeconomic Fluctuations."
21. Piketty, *Capital.*
22. In the case of perfect competition and constant returns of the aggregate production function, for instance, "distribution of income and wealth is irrelevant for the determination of aggregate variables." G. Bertola, R. Foellmi, and J. Zweimüller, *Income Distribution in Macroeconomic Models* (Princeton, NJ: Princeton University Press, 2006), 15. It is indeed the linear saving function (independent from wealth or income) that reproduces, in neoclassical models of economic growth, a law of aggregate accumulation of capital that is independent from income and wealth distribution. J. E. Stiglitz, "Distribution of Income and Wealth Among Individuals," *Econometrica* 37, no. 3 (1969): 382–397. This result also led to a pervasive use of the representative agent hypothesis, which rules out the heterogeneity of agents by construction.
23. For detailed descriptions, see, e.g., P. Aghion, E. Caroli, and C. Garcia-Penalosa, "Inequality and Economic Growth: The Perspective of the New Growth Theories," *Journal of Economic Literature* 37, no. 4 (1999): 1615–1660; and G. Bertola, "Macroeconomics of Distribution and Growth," in Atkinson and Bourguignon, *Handbook of Income Distribution,* 1:477–540.
24. The theoretical work by Benhabib highlights this idea. J. Benhabib, "The Tradeoff between Inequality and Growth," *Annals of Economics and Finance* 4 (2003): 491–507.
25. On the role of inequality of opportunity, see F. Bourguignon, F. Ferreira, and M. Menendez, "Inequality of Opportunity in Brazil," *Review of Income and Wealth* 53, no. 4 (2007): 585–618.
26. O. Galor and O. Moav, "From Physical to Human Capital Accumulation: Inequality and the Process of Development," *Review of Economic Studies* 71, no. 4 (2004): 1001–1026.
27. Indeed, under the assumption that the marginal propensity to save of workers (living off their wages) is lower than that of capitalists (living off the returns to their capital), a higher profit-to-wage ratio implies higher accumulation of physical capital and therefore higher economic activity in the long run. This topic will be also discussed in detail within the next section. N. Kaldor, "A Model of Economic Growth," *Economic Journal* 67 (1957): 591–624; L. L.

Pasinetti, "Rate of Profit and Income Distribution in Relation to the Rate of Economic Growth," *Review of Economic Studies* 29, no. 4 (1962): 267–279.

28. F. H. Ferreira, C. Lakner, M. A. Lugo, and B. Ozler, "Inequality of Opportunity and Economic Growth: A Cross-Country Analysis," IZA Discussion Paper No. 8243 (June 2014).

29. The first works to establish a negative correlation between inequality and growth made use of a cross-country regression approach linking the level of inequality in income at the beginning of the period to subsequent average growth. These findings were soon scrutinized and deemed unrobust in the face of better data and a panel structure that could reduce measurement errors as well as estimation bias from omitted consideration of time-invariant variables.

30. A. V. Banerjee and E. Duflo, "Inequality and Growth: What Can the Data Say?," *Journal of Economic Growth* 8, no. 3 (2003): 267–299; and D. J. Henderson, J. Qian, and L. Wang, "The Inequality Growth Plateau," *Economics Letters* 128 (2015): 17–20, deploy a nonparametric regression to estimate a nonlinear relationship between inequality and growth partly in line with the theoretical prediction of Benhabib, "The Tradeoff."

31. S. Voitchovsky, "Does the Profile of Income Inequality Matter for Economic Growth?," *Journal of Economic Growth* 10, no. 3 (2005): 273–296.

32. F. Cingano, "Trends in Income Inequality and Its Impact on Economic Growth," OECD Social, Employment and Migration Working Paper No. 163 (2014).

33. M. Ravallion, "Why Don't We See Poverty Convergence?," *American Economic Review* 102, no. 1 (2012): 504–523.

34. G. A. Marrero and J. G. Rodríguez, "Inequality of Opportunity and Growth," *Journal of Development Economics* 104 (2013): 107–122.

35. F. H. Ferreira et al., "Inequality of Opportunity."

36. Piketty, *Capital,* 39.

37. T. Persson and G. Tabellini, "Is Inequality Harmful for Growth?," *American Economic Review* 84, no. 3 (1994): 600–621; and A. Alesina and D. Rodrik, "Distributive Politics and Economic Growth," *Quarterly Journal of Economics* 109, no. 2 (1994): 465–490.

38. In essence these are complementary arguments at the heart of the classic dichotomy between efficiency and equity postulated by Okun's book using the famous metaphor of transferring resources with a "leaky bucket." In particular, Okun argued that a redistribution from rich to poor would have wasted resources and could even be counterproductive to the extent that poorer households, receiving more government transfers, exerted less effort and that richer individuals, facing higher marginal tax rates, had lower incentive to work hard. A. M. Okun, *Equality and Efficiency: The Big Tradeoff* (Washington, DC: Brookings Institution, 1975).

39. Piketty, *Capital,* 499.

40. J. Benhabib and A. Rustichini, "Social Conflict and Growth," *Journal of Economic Growth* 1, no. 1 (1996): 125–142.

41. A. Jayadev and S. Bowles, "Guard Labor," *Journal of Development Economics* 79, no. 2 (2006): 328–348.

42. E. Glaeser, J. Scheinkman, and A. Shleifer, "The Injustice of Inequality," *Journal of Monetary Economics* 50, no. 1 (2003): 199–222, at 200.

43. See also J. A. Robinson and D. Acemoglu, *Why Nations Fail: The Origins of Power, Prosperity, and Poverty* (New York: Crown, 2012).

44. A. Bonica and H. Rosenthal, "The Wealth Elasticity of Political Contributions by the Forbes 400" (2015), https://papers.ssrn.com/sol3/papers.cfm?abstract _id=2668780.

45. B. I. Page, L. M. Bartels, and J. Seawright, "Democracy and the Policy Preferences of Wealthy Americans," *Perspectives on Politics* 11, no. 1 (2013): 51–73.

46. S. Bagchi and J. Svejnar, "Does Wealth Inequality Matter for Growth? The Effect of Billionaire Wealth, Income Distribution, and Poverty," *Journal of Comparative Economics* 43, no. 3 (2015): 505–530.

47. J. E. Stiglitz, "New Theoretical Perspectives on the Distribution of Income and Wealth among Individuals," in *Inequality and Growth: Patterns and Policy,* vol. 1, *Concepts and Analysis,* ed. K. Basu and J. E. Stiglitz (Houndsmill, Basingstoke: Palgrave Macmillan, 2016).

48. J. Stiglitz, "Inequality and Economic Growth," in *Rethinking Capitalism,* ed. M. Mazzucato and M. Jacobs (Hoboken, NJ: Wiley-Blackwell, 2016), 9.

49. O. Galor and J. Zeira, in "Income Distribution and Macroeconomics," *Review of Economic Studies* 60, no. 1 (1993): 35–52, assume that there are enforcement and supervision costs for borrowers so that borrowing rate differs from the lending one. In other words, credit is available exclusively to those who inherit a sufficiently high wealth endowment. Therefore the market would not fund a great deal of profitable investments, resulting in a misallocation of resources and thereby reducing aggregate productivity and growth.

50. A. V. Banerjee and A. F. Newman, in "Occupational Choice and the Process of Development," *Journal of Political Economy* 101, no. 2 (1993): 274–298, assume a different structure of credit market imperfection than O. Galor and J. Zeira in "Income Distribution and Macroeconomics," *Review of Economic Studies* 60, no. 1 (1993): 35–52. Briefly stated, the presence of limited liability (the borrower's repayment to his lender is bounded above by the value of personal wealth) creates a source of moral hazard reducing the amount of optimal effort (costly and unobservable) the borrower is willing to exert. This in turn reduces the success probability of investments in risky projects.

51. J. Furman and J. E. Stiglitz, "Economic Consequences of Income Inequality," in *Income Inequality: Issues and Policy Options—A Symposium* (Kansas City, MO: Federal Reserve Bank of Kansas City, 1998), 255.

52. A. S. Blinder, "Distribution Effects and the Aggregate Consumption Function," *Journal of Political Economy* 83, no. 3 (1975): 447–475. This principle is also clearly stated in Keynes's work: "Since I regard the propensity to consume as being (normally) such as to have a wider gap between income and consumption

as income increases, it naturally follows that the collective propensity for the community as a whole may depend on the distribution of incomes within it." J. M. Keynes, "Mr. Keynes on the Distribution of Incomes and 'Propensity to Consume': A Reply," *Review of Economics and Statistics* 21, no. 3 (1939): 129.

53. Recent crisis has re-presented us with the problem that central banks face when the economy is experiencing a liquidity trap problem at the "zero lower bound" (nominal interest rate reaches or nears zero). At the "zero lower bound," it is argued, one needs either a huge fiscal stimulus or unconventional monetary policy (e.g., buying government bonds or transferring money directly to households) in order to stabilize the economy.

54. The Friedman-Modigliani-Blumberg type of permanent income hypothesis generally predicts a constant MPC. The consumption function remains concave at the cross sectional level if differences in income depend on transitory deviation from the permanent level of income. (An individual whose income is temporarily below its permanent level consumes much more than the individual whose income is temporarily above its permanent level.) The optimal consumption function returns to a strict concave form as soon as uncertainty is introduced back into the optimization problem (C. D. Carroll and M. S. Kimball, "On the Concavity of the Consumption Function," *Econometrica: Journal of the Econometric Society* 64, no. 4 [1996]: 981–992). Moreover, existing and future uncertainty create the need for precautionary savings, which substantially reduce the level of consumption with regard to baseline "perfect foresight" model (the precautionary saving motive is stronger at lower levels of cash-on-hand, implying a higher MPC). Models including liquidity constraints also replicate the concavity feature of the consumption function, as shown in C. D. Carroll and M. S. Kimball, "Liquidity Constraints and Precautionary Saving," NBER Working Paper No. 8496 (2001).

55. Data are based on FES data between 1984 and 2000–2001, the Expenditure and Food Survey (EFS) data between 2000–2001 and 2007, and Living Costs and Food Survey (LCF) thereafter.

56. E. Saez and G. Zucman, "Wealth Inequality in the United States since 1913: Evidence from Capitalized Income Tax Data," NBER Working Paper No. 20625 (2014); T. Jappelli and L. Pistaferri, "Fiscal Policy and MPC Heterogeneity," *American Economic Journal: Macroeconomics* 6, no. 4 (2014): 107–136.

57. J. E. Stiglitz, *The Price of Inequality* (London: Penguin, 2012), 85.

58. The effect is much stronger for the bottom decile, with a reduction in the saving rate of 15 percentage points from 1993 to 2006. This change is three times the size of the decline in saving rate for the highest decile over the same period. Thus, the differences between the saving rates of different deciles tend to broaden in the latest decades.

59. K. Schmidt-Hebbel and L. Serven, "Does Income Inequality Raise Aggregate Saving?," *Journal of Development Economics* 61, no. 2 (2000): 417–446; J. C.

Cuaresma, J. Kubala, and K. Petrikova, "Does Income Inequality Affect Aggregate Consumption? Revisiting the Evidence," Vienna University Department of Economics Working Paper No. 210 (2016).

60. As is discussed, in the context of the 2007 / 2008 U.S. crisis, in B. Milanovic, "Two Views on the Cause of the Global Crisis?," YaleGlobal Online (2009), http://yaleglobal.yale. edu/content/two-views-global-crisis; J. Fitoussi and F. Saraceno, "Inequality and Macroeconomic Performance," *Documents de Travail de lOFCE,* (2010), 13; and R. G. Rajan, *Fault Lines: How Hidden Fractures Still Threaten the Global Economy* (Princeton, NJ: Princeton University Press, 2010).

61. See, for instance, O. P. Attanasio and G. Weber, "Is Consumption Growth Consistent with Intertemporal Optimization? Evidence from the Consumer Expenditure Survey," NBER Working Paper No. 4795 (1994).

62. On the asset value increase (both housing and financial wealth) see, for example, A. Mian and A. Sufi, *House of Debt: How They (and You) Caused the Great Recession, and How We Can Prevent It from Happening Again* (Chicago: University of Chicago Press, 2014). On the availability of credit, see, for example, Mian and Sufi, "House Prices, Home Equity-Based Borrowing, and the U.S. Household Leverage Crisis," NBER Working Paper No. 15283 (2009); and K. E. Dynan and D. L. Kohn, "The Rise in US Household Indebtedness: Causes and Consequences," Divisions of Research & Statistics and Monetary Affairs, Federal Reserve Board (2007).

63. M. Bertrand and A. Morse, "Trickle-Down Consumption," NBER Working Paper No. 18883 (2013).

64. The authors merged data from the U.S. Consumer Expenditure survey (CEX) with data from the Panel Study of Income Dynamics (PSID), March Current Population Survey (CPS) and the University of Michigan's Survey of Consumers.

65. Blinder, "Distribution Effects," 472.

66. This is recalled in K. Arrow et al., "Are We Consuming Too Much?," *Journal of Economic Perspectives* 18, no. 3 (2004): 147–172, at 158.

67. For further discussion of the theoretical conditions under which the presence of relative concerns at the individual level leads to aggregate suboptimal consumption level, see K. J. Arrow and P. S. Dasgupta, "Conspicuous Consumption, Inconspicuous Leisure," *Economic Journal* 119 (2009): F497–F516; and C. Quintana-Domeque and F. Turino, "Relative Concerns on Visible Consumption: A Source of Economic Distortions," *B.E. Journal of Theoretical Economics* 16, no. 1 (2016): 33–45. See also the "expenditure cascades" model in R. Frank, A. Levine, and O. Dijk, "Expenditure Cascades" (September 2010), doi: 10.2139/ssrn.1690612, for a more complete characterization of consumption responses to changes in distribution of income.

68. A. B. Atkinson and S. Morelli, "Inequality and Banking Crises: A First Look," report for the International Labour Organisation (2010), https://www.nuffield

.ox.ac.uk/Users/Atkinson/Paper-Inequality%20and%20Banking%20Crises
-A%20First%20Look.pdf; Atkinson and Morelli, "Economic Crises and Inequality," UN Development Programme Human Development Research Paper
2011.06 (2011), http://hdr.undp.org/en/content/economic-crises-and-in
equality; and M. D. Bordo and C. M. Meissner, "Does Inequality Lead to a Financial Crisis?," *Journal of International Money and Finance* 31, no. 8 (2012):
2147–2161.

69. S. Morelli, and A. B. Atkinson, "Inequality and Crises Revisited," *Economia Po-
litica* 32, no. 1 (2015): 31–51.

70. The source of the data is A. B. Atkinson and S. Morelli, "Chartbook of Economic Inequality," ECINEQ Working Paper 324 (2014).

71. S. Morelli, and A. B. Atkinson, *Inequality and Crises Revisited,* 48.

72. A detailed account is found in O. J. Blanchard, D. Romer, M. Spence, and J. E.
Stiglitz, *In the Wake of the Crisis: Leading Economists Reassess Economic Policy*
(Cambridge, MA: MIT Press, 2012).

73. Stiglitz, "Macroeconomic Fluctuations."

74. This theory may appear in contrast with the credit constraint hypothesis discussed in previous section, but it is not necessarily inconsistent with it.

75. J. Zinman, "Household Debt: Facts, Puzzles, Theories, and Policies," *Annual
Review of Economics* 7 (2015): 251–276, provides a thorough and lucid account
of household indebtedness determinants.

76. The model underlines how a very high inequality between factor incomes (i.e.,
a growing share of capital), together with a substantial degree of separation between investors and savers, determines the condition for the realization of
lengthier economic cycles with a "debt-buildup phase." Aghion, Banerjee, and
Piketty, "Dualism."

77. M. Iacoviello, "Household Debt and Income Inequality, 1963–2003," *Journal of
Money, Credit and Banking* 40, no. 5 (2008): 929–965; M. Kumhof and R.
Rancière, "Inequality, Leverage and Crises," IMF Working Paper WP / 10/268
(November 2010); and M. Kumhof, R. Rancière, and P. Winant, "Inequality,
Leverage, and Crises," *American Economic Review* 105, no. 3 (2015): 1217–1245.

78. W. Kopczuk and E. Saez, "Top Wealth Shares in the United States: 1916–2000:
Evidence from Estate Tax Returns," NBER Working Paper No. 10399 (2004).

79. S. P. Jenkins, "Has the Instability of Personal Incomes Been Increasing?," *National Institute Economic Review* 218, no. 1 (2011): R33–R43.

80. The correlations between debt and inequality measures are substantially above
.8 and are significant at the 1 percent significance level.

81. C. Perugini, J. Hölscher, and S. Collie, "Inequality, Credit Expansion and Financial Crises," MPRA Paper No. 51336 (2013), https://mpra.ub.uni-muenchen
.de/51336/. This work is at odds with study mentioned above by Bordo and
Meissner, *Does Inequality,* that used the same data for a panel of fourteen developed countries from 1920 to 2000. In this latter case, the rise in top income
shares does not lead to a credit boom.

82. A. Scognamillo et al., "Inequality Indebtedness and Financial Crises," technical report, Università degli Studi di Firenze, Dipartimento di Scienze per l'Economia e l'Impresa (2015).

83. O. Coibion, Y. Gorodnichenko, M. Kudlyak, and J. Mondragon, "Does Greater Inequality Lead to More Household Borrowing? New Evidence from Household Data," IZA Discussion Paper No. 7910 (2014), http://ftp.iza.org/dp7910.pdf.

84. M. Carr, and A. Jayadev, "Relative Income and Indebtedness: Evidence from Panel Data," Department of Economics, University of Massachusetts Boston, Working Paper No. 2013-02 (2013), http://repec.umb.edu/RePEc/files/2013_02.pdf.

85. D. Georgarakos, M. Haliassos, and G. Pasini, "Household Debt and Social Interactions," Netspar Discussion Paper No. 11/2012-042 (2012), http://arno.uvt.nl/show.cgi?fid=127996.

86. One exception to this is the Dutch household survey, which, for instance, asks every individual about the perceived average income of their group of reference.

87. For instance, G. De Giorgi, A. Frederiksen, and L. Pistaferri, "Consumption Network Effects," CEPR Discussion Paper, No. DP11332, (2016), do exactly this using Danish administrative micro data.

88. D. Rodrik, "Good and Bad Inequality," Project Syndicate, December 11, 2014, http://www.project-syndicate.org/commentary/equality-economic-growth-tradeoff-by-dani-rodrik-2014-12.

18. Inequality and the Rise of Social Democracy

I thank Branko Milanovic, Arthur Goldhammer, John Schmitt, Steven Durlauf, and my coeditors Heather Boushey and Brad DeLong for their helpful comments, as well as John Taylor Hebden for the reference to *The Persistence of the Old Regime*.

Bibliographic note: This chapter draws heavily on secondary sources and narrative accounts of national politics: Eric Foner, *America's Unfinished Revolution, 1863–1877* (New York: Harper and Row, 1988); Arno Mayer, *The Persistence of the Old Regime: Europe to the Great War*, 2nd ed. (London: Verso, 2010); George Dangerfield, *The Strange Death of Liberal England* (1935; Stanford, CA: Stanford University Press, 1997); Eric Weitz, *Weimar Germany: Promise and Tragedy* (Princeton, NJ: Princeton University Press, 2007).

1. For a formal treatment of the idea that mass enfranchisement limits the extent of post-tax-and-transfer income inequality, see A. H. Meltzer and S. F. Richard, "A Rational Theory of the Size of Government," *Journal of Political* Economy 89, no. 5 (1981): 914–927. A more nuanced view, explicitly relating democracy to public education as the channel by which inequality might be reduced by politics, is offered by John E. Roemer, *Democracy, Education, and Equality*, Graz-Schumpeter Lectures, Econometric Society Monographs (2006).

2. For the argument that income and wealth tax policy was a crucial determinant of inequality dynamics, see Thomas Piketty, *Capital in the Twenty-First Century*, trans. Arthur Goldhammer (Cambridge, MA: Belknap Press of Harvard University Press, 2014); and T. Piketty and G. Zucman, "Capital Is Back: Wealth-Income Ratios in Rich Countries 1700–2010," *Quarterly Journal of Economics* 129, no. 3 (2013): 1255–1310.

3. For the role that unionization and regulation of the labor market played in declining inequality, see G. E. Gilmore and T. J. Sugrue, *These United States: A Nation in the Making, 1890 to the Present* (New York: W. W. Norton, 2015).

4. For the contribution of improvements to health, education, and infrastructure to reductions in inequality, see R. Fogel, *The Escape from Hunger and Premature Death, 1700–2100* (Cambridge: Cambridge University Press, 2004); D. L. Cosa, "Health and the Economy in the United States from 1750 to the Present," *Journal of Economic Literature* 53, no. 3 (2015): 503–570; and J. Ferrie and W. Troesken, "Water and Chicago's Mortality Transition," *Explorations in Economic History* 45, no. 1 (2008): 1–16.

5. The gold standard was the primary reason the economic crises of the late nineteenth and early twentieth centuries were so disastrous and why labor market recoveries were long and painful. See M. Friedman and A. J. Schwartz, *A Monetary History of the United States, 1867–1960*. National Bureau of Economic Research Publications (1963).

6. In the case of Germany, that process failed when the Spartacists split from the Social Democrats and eventually formed the Communist Party, and the two never unified, a necessary condition for the Nazi takeover. In the United States, it was ultimately the older political group, the Democratic Party, that survived and the younger left-wing movements that merged into it, leaving a coalition that was radically different from what the Democratic Party had been at the start of the period. In France, the Popular Front never effected a full merger of its constituents, and politics was hopelessly divided in the face of Nazi aggression. See below.

7. A large body of research argues that, on the contrary, it was precisely democratization that brought about the triumph of capitalist ideology in France over the corporatism of the *ancien régime*. See Chapter 19 in this volume, as well as Pierre Rosanvallon, *The Demands of Liberty: Civil Society in France since the Revolution* (Cambridge, MA: Harvard University Press, 2007). Mayer, *Persistence of the Old Regime*, argues that it was precisely the unification of capitalist ideology and its political support among the bourgeoisie that sustained the political power dynamic of the *ancien régime* into the era of mass enfranchisement.

8. See E. Foner, *America's Unfinished Revolution, 1863–1877*, updated ed. (New York: Harper Perennial Modern Classics, 2014); and I. Katzelson, *Fear Itself: The New Deal and the Origins of Our Time* (New York: Liveright, 2013).

9. The controversy over Henry George and the single tax is covered in Mary O. Furner, *Advocacy and Objectivity: A Crisis in the Professionalization of American Social Science, 1865–1905* (Lexington: University Press of Kentucky, 1975).

10. S. C. Walker, "The Movement in the Northern States," *Publications of the American Economic Association* 8 (1893): 62–74. Thanks to Professor Jenny Bourne for this reference.

11. Piketty writes, "Becker never explicitly states the idea that the rise of human capital should eclipse the importance of inherited wealth, but it is often implicit in his work. In particular, he notes frequently that society has become 'more meritocratic' owing to the increasing importance of education (without further detail)." Piketty, *Capital,* 616.

12. P. Temin and B. A. Wigmore, "The End of One Big Deflation," *Explorations in Economic History* 27 (1990): 483–502.

13. Even following the Third Reform Act, many men and all women remained without the franchise. Those remaining disenfranchised were disproportionately in Ireland.

14. Pierre Rosanvallon and, in Chapter 19 in this volume, David Grewal both argue that democratic politics was in fact a critical element in establishing capitalist ideology by creating a constituency, the bourgeoisie, that favored limiting the power of the state over the economy. Arno Mayer argues that it was exactly this synthesis of two political interests (bourgeoisie and aristocracy) behind one ideology that sustained right-wing politics throughout the nineteenth century. See Mayer, *Persistence of the Old Regime,* and Rosanvallon, *The Demands of Liberty.*

15. Mayer, *Persistence of the Old Regime.*

16. F. Scheuer and A. Wolitzky, "Capital Taxation under Political Constraints," working paper (2015), http://web.stanford.edu/~scheuer/capital_tax_reforms .pdf.

17. In that sense, his posture was similar to that of successive recent Greek governments in seeking to renegotiate the terms of Greece's debts to the Eurozone, and not surprisingly, it failed for the same reason: it's unwise to put the gun to your own head if you're not willing to pull the trigger (and arguably unwise if you are).

18. There are (at least) two different, wrong strands to the historiography of Weimar hyperinflation. Among economists, the foundational citation is Thomas J. Sargent, "The Ends of Four Big Inflations," in *Inflation: Causes and Effects,* ed. R. E. Hall (Chicago: University of Chicago Press, 1982), which anachronistically interprets the four contemporaneous hyperinflations in Germany, Austria, Hungary, and Poland as independent phenomena, and the concurrent nonhyperinflation in Czechoslovakia as a meaningful control. According to Sargent, the blame rests on a captive central bank suffering under the thumb of a fiscally irresponsible treasury, and the solution in each case was found when the domestic political authorities permitted independent central banking to exist alongside fiscal austerity. In fact, the hyperinflations, which were all caused by a reparations schedule so onerous as to be unsupportable at any tax rate, ended when the Allies decided to moderate their claims and allow the postwar governments, and in particular Weimar, to exist. Sargent's retrospective interpretation is

heavily informed by the stagflation of the 1970s, but it has important predicates in contemporaneous right-wing arguments about the causes of hyperinflation. The government's domestic opponents, in addition to blaming Versailles and Germany's defeat and stab in the back, also blamed spending on left-wing social policy. The other false historiographical thread sees the hyperinflation as a calculated attempt to evade rightful reparations by a nationalistic, expansionistic German political system that was not sufficiently tamed by losing the war. This reading sees the Allies' eventual moderate policy vis-à-vis reparations as the first act in the Long Appeasement that resulted in the Nazi takeover thanks to Allied spinelessness. For more on the historiography of Weimar hyperinflation, see M. Steinbaum, "The End of One Big Inflation and the Beginning of One Big Myth" (2015), The Steinblog, http://steinbaum.blogspot.com/2015/01/the -end-of-one-big-inflation-and.html.

19. Weitz, *Weimar Germany,* 145.
20. Like the Fair Labor Standards Act that followed in the United States ten years later, the German legislated exempted agricultural workers and the sporadically employed. It is thus an interesting counterexample to Katzelson's argument that such provisions in the U.S. legislation were the result of the political peculiarities of white supremacy.
21. George Orwell, *The Road to Wigan Pier* (New York: Harcourt, 1958), first published in the U.K. by the Left Book Club, 1937.

19. The Legal Constitution of Capitalism

I thank Heather Boushey, Ian Malcolm, Marshall Steinbaum, and especially Brad DeLong for comments on this chapter, which draws on my previously published review of *C21,* "The Laws of Capitalism," *Harvard Law Review* 128 (December 2014): 626–667, and on my forthcoming book, *The Invention of the Economy: A History of Economic Thought* (Harvard University Press).

1. Thomas Piketty, *Capital in the Twenty-First Century,* trans. Arthur Goldhammer (Cambridge, MA: Belknap Press of Harvard University Press, 2014).
2. As depicted in fig. 10.9 in Piketty, *Capital,* 354.
3. Ibid., 571.
4. Keynes, *The General Theory of Employment, Interest, and Money* (London: Harcourt, 1964): 217–221, 372–384.
5. Marx, *Capital,* vol. 3, pt. 3, esp. chap. 13. Marx derives a falling rate of profit as a logical consequence of the continual increase of "constant" capital to "variable" capital (i.e., capital as opposed to labor) in capitalist production. Because he argues that profit is generated through the extraction of surplus labor, this increasing ratio progressively reduces the rate of profit by squeezing "living" capital out of the system.
6. In explaining his data, Piketty proposes a "first law of capitalism": that the share of national income going to capital, α, is equal to the rate of return on capital,

r, multiplied by the ratio of capital to income, β (Piketty, *Capital,* 50–55.) This is an accounting identity that allows Piketty to relate the ratio of the value of capital assets to the value of annual production—(the ratio β)—to the share of total income going to capital owners, via the rate of return on their assets (as depicted in fig. 6.5 in ibid., 222).

7. Piketty's second law is that the ratio of capital to income reflects the ratio of the savings rate to the overall growth rate (ibid., 166–170). This second law is not actuarial but asymptotic: over the long run, given various assumptions, the relationship of the value of national assets to national income will be determined by the ratio of savings to annual growth.

8. Compare Piketty's claim, "When the rate of return on capital exceeds the rate of growth ... capitalism *automatically* generates ... inequalities" (ibid., 1, emphasis added), with his later statement, "If ... the rate of return on capital remains significantly above the growth rate ... then the *risk* of divergence in the distribution of wealth is very high" (25, emphasis added), which suggests a tendency rather than an automatic process. More generally, note his statement that "the inequality $r > g$ should be analyzed as a historical reality dependent on a variety of mechanisms and not as an absolute logical necessity" (361).

9. See ibid., 25, 350, 353, 358, 571, 572, respectively.

10. Ibid., 361–366, 372–375.

11. Ibid., 30–33, 573–575.

12. Adam Smith, *The Wealth of Nations,* I.I.

13. On this point, see Istvan Hont and Michael Ignatieff, "Needs and Justice in *The Wealth of Nations,*" in *Wealth and Virtue: The Shaping of Political Economy in the Scottish Enlightenment,* ed. Hont and Ignatieff (Cambridge: Cambridge University Press, 1983), 3–6, 23–25.

14. For an account of Smith's renown as a social radical during his lifetime, and the posthumous change in his reputation, see Emma Rothschild, "Adam Smith and Conservative Economics," *Economic History Review* 45 (1992): 74–96.

15. Henry Maine, *Ancient Law* (1861), chap. 5.

16. See, for example, John Stuart Mill, *Chapters on Socialism* (1879). For a key transformation in his thought (which dovetailed with his late-life support for unionism), see Mill, "Thornton on Labour and Its Claims," pt. 1, *Fortnightly Review,* May 1869, 505–518; and Mill, "Thornton on Labor and Its Claims," pt. 2, *Fortnightly Review,* June 1869, 680–700. Marx's comments on these matters are scattered across different works. For a careful study of the emancipatory and egalitarian aspirations in Marx's thought, see Allen Wood, *The Free Development of Each* (Oxford: Oxford University Press, 2014), 252–273.

17. Kuznets won a Nobel Prize in 1971 for his study of U.S. economic growth and national income between 1913 and 1948; see Simon Kuznets, *Shares of Upper Income Groups in Income and Savings* (New York: National Bureau of Economic Research, 1953).

18. Hans Ritter, *Dictionary of Concepts in History* (Westport, CT: Greenwood Press, 1986), 26–27; note that the terms "capital" and "capitalist" were well established in the eighteenth century.

19. Istvan Hont, Bela Kapossy, and Michael Sonenscher, *Politics in Commercial Society* (Cambridge, MA: Harvard University Press, 2015); C. J. Berry, *The Idea of Commercial Society in the Scottish Enlightenment* (Edinburgh: Edinburgh University Press, 2013).

20. Smith, *Wealth of Nations,* 1.4.

21. For introductions to these debates, see Jean-Claude Perrot, *L'histoire intellectuelle de l'économie politique, 17e–18e siècles* (Paris: Éditions de L'EHESS, 1992); and Peter Groenewegen, *Eighteenth Century Economics* (New York: Routledge, 2002).

22. Johan Heilbron, "French Moralists and the Anthropology of the Modern Era: On the Genesis of the Notions of 'Interest' and 'Commercial Society,'" in *The Rise of the Social Sciences and the Formation of Modernity: Conceptual Change in Context, 1750–1850,* ed. Johan Heilbron, Lars Magnusson, and Bjorn Wittrock (Dordrecht: Kluwer Academic, 1998), 77–106.

23. For Pufendorf's admission that he takes the natural law and the Roman law to be roughly equivalent (in setting out the commercial attributes of pre-political society), see his *De Jure naturae et gentium, libri octo,* trans. and ed. C. H. Oldfather and W. A. Oldfather (Oxford: Clarendon Press, 1934), 226–227. For an important discussion of Pufendorf's place in the history of economic thought, see Istvan Hont, "The Language of Sociability and Commerce: Samuel Pufendorf and the Theoretical Foundations of the 'Four Stages Theory,'" in *The Languages of Political Theory in Early-Modern Europe,* ed. Anthony Pagden (Cambridge: Cambridge University Press, 1987), 253–276.

24. This is not to deny the important differences between later seventeenth-century contract theory and eighteenth-century political economy; on which see John Dunn, "From Applied Theology to Social Analysis: The Break between John Locke and the Scottish Enlightenment," in Hont and Ignatieff, *Wealth and Virtue.*

25. See James Gordley, *The Jurists: A Critical History* (Oxford: Oxford University Press, 2013); Peter Stein, *Roman Law in European History* (Cambridge: Cambridge University Press, 1999).

26. More precisely, "economy" came into its modern usage from the ancient term *oikonomia* or household-management, used even in antiquity to describe the government of the universe (with God sometimes described as an economist of the cosmos), later transposed to describe the social universe of commercial exchange governed by divine providence; on this point, see my forthcoming book, *Invention of the Economy.* Pufendorf was pivotal in the transformation of the category of the "oeconomic," adapting the *status oeconomicus* of the Lutheran *Dreiständelehre* theory (the "economic state") to describe not the domain of the familial household but a "private" status based on individual will and aiming at

commercial advantage. See Pufendorf, *Elementorum jurisprudentiae universalis libri II* (Cambridge: John Hayes (for the university), 1672), 16.

27. On the political-theoretic and theological underpinnings of laissez-faire theory, see my "The Political Theology of Laissez-Faire: From *Philia* to Self-Love in Commercial Society," *Political Theology* 17 (September 2016): 417–433.

28. Pierre Nicole, *Œuvres philosophiques et morales de Nicole: Comprenant un choix de ses essais,* ed. Charles Jourdain (Paris: L. Hachette, 1845); see also Grewal, "Political Theology of Laissez-Faire." For a collection of Boisguilbert's writings as well as secondary sources on his work, see *Pierre de Boisguilbert ou la naissance de l'économie politique,* 2 vols., ed. Alfred Sauvy (Paris: Institut National d'Études Démographiques, 1966); see also Gilbert Faccarello, *The Foundations of Laissez-Faire: The Economics of Pierre de Boisguilbert* (New York: Routledge, 1999).

29. Vincent de Gournay is traditionally credited with originating the slogan "Laissez faire, laissez passer," which may have adapted the retort that a seventeenth-century merchant named Le Gendre (probably the wealthy converted Huguenot, Thomas) gave to Louis XIV's great minister of finance, Jean-Baptiste Colbert, when Colbert asked how the state could advance commerce: "Laissez nous faire." See Gustav Schelle, *Vincent de Gournay* (Paris: Guillaumin, 1897), 214–221.

30. Michel Foucault, *Security, Territory, Population: Lectures at the Collège de France, 1977–78* (London: Palgrave Macmillan, 2009), 346–357.

31. On Gournay, see Loïc Charles, Frédéric Lefebvre, and Christine Théré, eds., *Le cercle de Vincent de Gournay: Savoirs économiques et pratiques administratives en France au milieu du XVIIIᵉ siècle* (Paris: Institute National d'Études Démographiques, 2011); on Physiocracy, see Liana Vardi, *The Physiocrats and the World of the Enlightenment* (Cambridge: Cambridge University Press, 2012).

32. Smith, *Wealth of Nations,* 4.9.

33. Soon after the Jansenist theologian Pierre Nicole first put forward his arguments about the beneficial effects of the exchange of sinful self-love, we see the first recognizably economic analysis of the market in the work of Pierre de Boisguilbert, a Norman noble and administrator, who had studied with Nicole in the Jansenist school of Port-Royal des Champs. Boisguilbert used his analysis of the unintended benefits of market interaction to criticize the overreaching governmental bureaucracy of Louis XIV. For a collection of Boisguilbert's writings as well as secondary sources on his work, see *Pierre de Boisguilbert.* See also Faccarello, *Foundations of Laissez-Faire.* Marx later identified Boisguilbert as the founder of the French branch of political economy. Marx, *Grundrisse* (1973 ed.), 883.

34. See Adam Smith, *Lectures on Jurisprudence,* ed. R. L. Meek et al. (Oxford: Clarendon Press, 1978). For a canonical statement of Physiocratic theory, see Pierre-Paul Le Mercier de la Rivière, *L'Ordre naturel et essentiel des sociétés*

politiques (1767); for a discussion of grain policy, see Steven Kaplan, *Provisioning Paris* (Ithaca, NY: Cornell University Press, 1984), 420–440. For Marx's discussion of the length of the working day, see Marx, *Capital,* Vol. 1, III.10.

35. Hilary Putnam, *The Collapse of the Fact/Value Dichotomy* (Cambridge, MA: Harvard University Press, 2002), 7–45.

36. This is a theme I explore in my forthcoming *Invention of the Economy.* It is also a prominent theme in Michel Foucault, *The Birth of Biopolitics,* ed. Michel Senellart (Basingstoke: Palgrave Macmillan, 2008); and in Karl Polanyi's work—see, e.g., "The Economy as an Instituted Process," in *Trade and Market in the Early Empires,* ed. Polanyi et al. (Boston: Beacon Press, 1957), 243–270.

37. Edward P. Thompson, "The Moral Economy of the English Crowd in the Eighteenth Century," *Past & Present* (February 1971): 76–136. On antifeudal regulations, see John Markoff, *The Abolition of Feudalism* (University Park: Pennsylvania State University, 1996), 554–556.

38. See Hont and Ignatieff, "Needs and Justice," 13–26; Emma Rothschild, *Economic Sentiments* (Cambridge, MA: Harvard University Press, 2001), 72–86.

39. See the lucid discussion of these issues in the introduction to Steven L. Kaplan, ed., *Bagarre: Galiani's "Lost" Parody* (Boston: M. Nijhoff, 1979); see also Hont and Ignatieff, "Needs and Justice," 17–19.

40. Boisguilbert, *Dissertation sur la nature des richesses* (1704); Smith, *Wealth of Nations,* eds. Andrew S. Skinner and R. H. Campbell (Oxford: Clarendon Press, 1979), 135–159, 469–471, 524–543.

41. Peter Groenewegen, "Boisguilbert and Eighteenth-Century Economics," in *Eighteenth Century Economics* (New York: Routledge, 2002).

42. A similar theme is elaborated in Foucault, *The Birth of Biopolitics,* in the description of how laissez-faire ideology was justified as an internal limitation on *raison d'état,* recommended for use by states in their own interest.

43. Jedediah Purdy, *The Meaning of Property* (New Haven, CT: Yale University Press, 2010), 9–43; Foucault, *Security, Territory, Population,* 311–357.

44. For a genealogy of the modern conception of the "private," see Raymond Geuss, *Public Goods, Private Goods* (Princeton, NJ: Princeton University Press, 2001).

45. On Britain, see P. J. Cain, "British Capitalism and the State: An Historical Perspective," *Political Quarterly* 68 (1997): 95–98; David McNally, *Political Economy and the Rise of Capitalism* (Berkeley: University of California Press, 1988); John Shovlin, *The Political Economy of Virtue* (Ithaca, NY: Cornell University Press, 2006); David Laven and Lucy Riall, eds., *Napoleon's Legacy* (Oxford: Berg, 2000).

46. For background on Domat, see James Gordley, *The Jurists: A Critical History* (Oxford: Oxford University Press, 2013), 141–155.

47. On Portalis, see Jean-Luc Chartier, *Portalis: Pere du Code Civil* (Paris: Fayard, 2004); A. A. Levasseur, "Code Napoleon or Code Portalis?," *Tulane Law Review* 43 (1969): 762–774.

48. Jean-Louis Halpérin, *L'Impossible Code Civil* (Paris: Presses Universitaires de France, 1992).

49. On "legal despotism" as a feature of Physiocratic thought, see Shovlin, *Political Economy of Virtue,* 107–109. The economic orientation of the Directory is well established in the secondary literature; see, e.g., Judith Miller, "The Aftermath of the *Assignat,*" in *Taking Liberties: Problems of a New Order From the French Revolution to Napoleon,* ed. Howard G. Brown and Judith A. Miller (Manchester: Manchester University Press, 2002), 1–72.

50. For an English translation of these decrees, see J. M. Roberts, *French Revolution Documents,* vol. 1 (Oxford: Basil Blackwell, 1966), 151–153.

51. McNally, *Political Economy,* 122–129.

52. For a history of the debate over capital theory, see Avi Cohen and Geoffrey Harcourt, "Retrospectives: Whatever Happened to the Cambridge Capital Theory Controversies?," *Journal of Economic Perspectives* 17, no. 1 (Winter, 2003): 199–214.

53. Compare the stock-flow conception (Piketty, *Capital,* 47–50) with Piketty's frequent discussions of the political determinants of the return to capital (e.g., ibid., 20, 47, 55, 372–375).

54. See Cohen and Harcourt, "Retrospectives," 202–206; Piero Sraffa, *Production of Commodities by Means of Commodities* (Cambridge: Cambridge University Press, 1960), 33–44.

55. Piketty, *Capital,* 372–75.

56. The extent to which the French revolution was a "bourgeois" revolution within the familiar Marxist scheme remains much debated, but the intent of the August Decrees, for example, was straightforwardly to abolish feudal forms of property and privilege along with the traditional labor obligations of the peasantry (which was finally accomplished through the Code Civil). For a defense of its characterization as bourgeois, see Colin Mooers, *The Making of Bourgeois Europe* (London: Verso, 1991); for a critical examination of the concept of bourgeois state form, see Heide Gerstenberger, "The Bourgeois State Form Revisited," in *Open Marxism,* ed. Werner Bonefeld et al. (London: Pluto Press, 1995): 151–176.

57. One route to such a political analysis of capitalism is via an interrogation of the Marxist concept of the "bourgeois state," particularly if understood in its legal dimension and without a necessary dependence on the classical Marxist theory of revolution. For an account of nineteenth-century German history along these lines, see David Blackbourn and Geoff Eley, *The Peculiarities of German History* (New York: Oxford University Press, 1984), 190–210; and for a similar ambition with respect to earlier French and British history, see Heide Gerstenberger, *Impersonal Power,* trans. David Fernbach (Leiden: Brill, 2007), 662–687. See also many of the contributions to the first volume of *Open Marxism* (Pluto Press, 1992), particularly Werner Bonefeld, "Social Constitution and the Form of the Capitalist State," 93–132.

58. For a discussion of public and private goods, see Geuss, *Public Goods, Private Goods;* for an articulation of a variety of spheres of human action, each with its own normative orderings and purpose, see Michael Walzer, *Spheres of Justice* (New York: Basic Books, 1983).

59. For a history of the origin of this distinction in Bodin and its subsequent adaptation by Hobbes, Rousseau, and the theorists of the French and American revolutionary orders, see Richard Tuck, *The Sleeping Sovereign* (Cambridge, MA: Harvard University Press, 2016); for an application of these ideas to modern constitutional theory, see Daniel E. Herz-Roiphe and David Singh Grewal, "Make Me Democratic but Not Yet: Sunrise Lawmaking and Democratic Constitutionalism," *New York University Law Review* 90, no. 6 (December 2015), 1975–2028.

60. See Tuck, *The Sleeping Sovereign,* 8–16, 26–27.

61. Questions about the appropriate institutionalization of the sovereignty / government distinction began to be debated in the eighteenth century. Written constitutions of the familiar modern kind—enactments of a separate, foundational legislator—first began to be drafted and ratified in the individual states of the United States (the first being Massachusetts in 1778), followed about a decade later by the U.S. federal constitution and the various constitutions of revolutionary France. The sovereignty / government distinction was central to these political projects, although realized differently across them. Ibid., 117–119, 154–155, 159–160.

62. See Hobbes, *On the Citizen,* ed. Richard Tuck (New York: Cambridge University Press, 1998) 99–100; this is the metaphor that Tuck takes for his title, *The Sleeping Sovereign.*

63. The result, as Hirschl describes it, is a new form of "juristocracy." See Ran Hirschl, *Towards Juristocracy: The Origins and Consequences of the New Constitutionalism* (Cambridge, MA: Harvard University Press, 2004), 97–99, 146–148.

64. Ralph Miliband, "Reform and Revolution," in *Marxism and Politics* (Oxford: Oxford University Press, 1977), 154–190, esp. 183–189.

65. Martin Gilens, *Affluence and Influence* (Princeton, NJ: Princeton University Press, 2012); Martin Gilens and Benjamin Page, "Testing Theories of American Politics: Elites, Interest Groups, and Average Citizens," *Perspectives on Politics* 12, no. 3 (2014): 564–581.

66. See David Singh Grewal and Jedediah Purdy, "Law and Inequality after the Golden Age of Capitalism," *Theoretical Inquiries in Law* (forthcoming, 2017).

67. See the collection of essays in John Holloway and Sol Picciotto, eds., *State and Capital: A Marxist Debate* (Austin: University of Texas Press, 1978).

68. For an analysis that supposes "struggle" and "structure" to be ultimately reconciled via a theory of class antagonism in the capitalist state, see Bonefeld, "Social Constitution." The theoretical requirement, broadly, is a reconciliation of a

synchronic analytics of exploitation within the diachronic evolution of the system, including any countersystemic tendencies.

69. For a discussion (and exemplification) of institutional political economy, see Charles Maier, *In Search of Stability* (Cambridge: Cambridge University Press, 1987), 6.

70. Wolfgang Streeck, "Taking Capitalism Seriously: Towards an Institutionalist Approach to Contemporary Political Economy," *Socio-Economic Review* 96 (2011): 137–167, See 140, 137–138.

71. See ibid., 147, 150, 143–146, 147–148.

72. C. A. R. Crosland, *The Future of Socialism* (London: Jonathan Cape, 1956), 56–76.

73. John Commons, *Legal Foundations of Capitalism* (Madison: University of Wisconsin Press, 1924); Robert Hale, *Freedom through Law* (New York: Columbia University Press, 1952); Barbara Fried, *The Progressive Assault on Laissez Faire* (Cambridge, MA: Harvard University Press, 1998), 10–15.

74. Samuel Bowles and Herbert Gintis, "Contested Exchange: Political Economy and Modern Economic Theory," *American Economic Review* 78, no. 2 (2003): 145–150.

75. For further consideration of the legal scholarship on these and related topics, see Grewal, "The Laws of Capitalism," *Harvard Law Review* 128, no. 2 (2014): 658–659.

76. Piketty, *Capital,* 83–84.

77. John Stuart Mill, "The Remedies for Low Wages Further Considered," *Principles of Political Economy* (1848), Book II.13. Mill's group of philosophical radicals "took up in the contrary sense" Malthus's thought (as described in his *Autobiography* [1873], ed. John Robson, London: Penguin, 1989), 94.

78. Piketty, *Capital,* 397 (on "reconstruction capitalism").

79. Andrajit Dube and Sanjay Reddy, "Threat Effects and Trade: Wage Discipline through Product Market Competition," *Journal of Globalization and Development* 4, no. 2 (2014).

80. Along these lines, Dean Baker points to the curious lack of discussion of low-cost Chinese labor in Piketty's analysis of recent economic trends; see Dean Baker, "Capital in the Twenty-First Century: Still Mired in the Nineteenth," Huffington Post, May 9, 2014.

81. On this point, see my "The Demographic Contradiction of Capitalism, or, What *Will* Bosses Do?," Rethinking Development Conference, Southern New Hampshire University, April 8, 2007 (on file with author).

82. Karl Marx, "The Civil War in France," reprinted in Karl Marx and Friedrich Engels, *On the Paris Commune* (1871; Moscow: Progress, 1971), 68.

83. Gilens, *Affluence and Influence;* Martin Gilens and Benjamin Page, "Testing Theories of American Politics: Elites, Interest Groups, and Average Citizens," *Perspectives on Politics* 12, no. 3 (2014): 564–581.

20. The Historical Origins of Global Inequality

1. According to the institutional school of thought, inclusive political and economic institutions, which feature constraints on the executive branch, enforcement of private property rights, centralized state power, and well-functioning markets, lay the foundation for economic growth. These are contrasted with extractive institutions, where labor coercion, a limited distribution of political rights, and a high risk of expropriation often act in confluence to undermine development. Douglass C. North, *Institutions, Institutional Change and Economic Performance* (Cambridge: Cambridge University Press, 1990); Daron Acemoglu, Simon Johnson, and James Robinson, "Institutions as a Fundamental Cause of Long-Run Growth," in *Handbook of Economic Growth,* vol. 1 (Amsterdam: Elsevier, 2005), 385–472.

2. Mamdani's schematic for individuals living under institutionally segregated late-colonial Africa, foreshadowing the apartheid state of South Africa, extends easily to the context of wealth under extraction over the much longer time scale that I describe here. Mamdani uses these terms to describe the separate societies of the white urban colonial elite and the black native rural poor. The former enjoy the rights of citizens and live in a world "bounded by the rule of law and an associated regime of rights" while the latter languished as subjects at the mercy of customary law and discretion of local elites. Mahmood Mamdani, *Citizen and Subject: Contemporary Africa and the Legacy of Late Colonialism* (Princeton, NJ: Princeton University Press, 1996), 19.

3. Thomas Piketty, *Capital in the Twenty-First Century,* trans. Arthur Goldhammer (Cambridge, MA: Belknap Press of Harvard University Press, 2014).

4. Daron Acemoglu, Simon Johnson, and James A Robinson, "The Colonial Origins of Comparative Development: An Empirical Investigation," *American Economic Review* 91 (2001): 1369–1401. This is not without controversy. See David Albouy, "The Colonial Origins of Comparative Development: An Empirical Investigation: Comment," *American Economic Review* 102, no. 6 (2012): 3059–3076. See also Alexandre Belloni, Victor Chernozhukov, and Christian Hansen, "High-Dimensional Methods and Inference on Structural and Treatment Effects," *Journal of Economic Perspectives* 28, no. 2 (2014): 29–50. Belloni et al. show that the settler mortality instrument is robust to a wide variety of geographic controls selected via a LASSO-penalized regression.

5. Monique B. Mulder et al., "Intergenerational Wealth Transmission and the Dynamics of Inequality in Small-Scale Societies," *Science,* October 30, 2009, 682–688.

6. See R. P. Thomas and D. N. McCloskey, "Overseas Trade and Empire 1700–1860," in *The Economic History of Britain since 1700* (Cambridge: Cambridge University Press, 1981), 87–102. See also Barbara L. Solow and Stanley Engerman, *British Capitalism and Caribbean Slavery: The Legacy of Eric Williams* (Cambridge: Cambridge University Press, 2000); and Kenneth Morgan, *Slavery,*

Atlantic Trade and the British Economy, 1660–1800 (Cambridge: Cambridge University Press, 2000).

7. Joseph E. Inikori, *Africans and the Industrial Revolution in England: A Study in International Trade and Economic Development* (Cambridge: Cambridge University Press, 2002).

8. Richard D. Wolff, *The Economics of Colonialism: Britain and Kenya, 1870–1930* (New Haven, CT: Yale University Press, 1974).

9. Morgan, *Slavery*, 4.

10. Walker W. Hanlon, "Necessity Is the Mother of Invention: Input Supplies and Directed Technical Change," *Econometrica* 83 (2015): 67–100.

11. Gregory Clark, "Why Isn't the Whole World Developed? Lessons from the Cotton Mills," *Journal of Economic History* 47, no. 1 (1987): 141–173, at 143. See discussion of the dissolution of the British cotton textile industry in the interwar years in Sven Beckert, *Empire of Cotton: A New History of Global Capitalism* (New York: Knopf, 2014), 381–382.

12. Felipe Gonzalez, Guillermo Marshall, and Suresh Naidu, "Start-up Nation? Slave Wealth and Entrepreneurship in Civil War Maryland," *Journal of Economic History,* forthcoming.

13. Caitlin C. Rosenthal, "Slavery's Scientific Management: Accounting for Mastery," in *Slavery's Capitalism,* ed. Seth Rockman, Sven Beckert, and David Waldstreicher (University of Pennsylvania Press, forthcoming).

14. Greg Grandin, *The Empire of Necessity: Slavery, Freedom, and Deception in the New World* (New York : Metropolitan Books, 2014); Stephanie Gonzalez, "The Double-Edged Sword: Smallpox Vaccination and the Politics of Public Health in Cuba" (PhD diss., City University of New York, 2014); José Tuells and José Luis Duro-Torrijos, "The Journey of the Vaccine against Smallpox: One Expedition, Two Oceans, Three Continents, and Thousands of Children," *Gaceta Médica De México* 151, no. 3 (2015): 416–425; Cristóbal S. Berry-Cabán, "Cuba's First Smallpox Vaccination Campaign," *International Journal of History and Philosophy of Medicine* 5 (2015): 1–4.

15. William Darity Jr., "A Model of 'Original Sin': Rise of the West and Lag of the Rest," *American Economic Review* 182 (1992): 162–167. See also Ronald Findlay, "The 'Triangular Trade' and the Atlantic Economy of the Eighteenth Century: A Simple General-Equilibrium Model," *Essays in International Finance* 177 (1990): 1–33.

16. Brandon Dupont and Joshua Rosenbloom, "The Impact of the Civil War on Southern Wealth Holders," NBER Working Paper No. 22184 (April 2016).

17. Ibid.

18. Philipp Ager, Leah Boustan, and Katherine Eriksson, "Intergenerational Mobility in the 19th Century: Evidence from the Civil War" (manuscript, 2016).

19. Ellora Derenoncourt, "Testing for Persistent Slaveholder Dynastic Advantage, 1860–1940," working paper, 2016.

20. Gregory Clark, *The Son Also Rises: Surnames and the History of Social Mobility* (Princeton, NJ: Princeton University Press, 2014).

21. Derenoncourt, "Testing."

22. Avidit Acharya, Matthew Blackwell, and Maya Sen, "The Political Legacy of American Slavery," *Journal of Politics* 78, no. 3 (May 2016).

23. These nonlinear effects further suggest institutional dynamics not currently captured by the model described earlier in this chapter. Historically determined institutions are static in the model, making it difficult to make contemporary claims on the descendants of citizen and subject. Instead, perhaps, institutions tend to remake themselves in the image of past institutions with similar distributional effects. Writer and journalist Ta-Nehisi Coates makes a case for reparations for African Americans that draws heavily on the experience of twentieth-century policies that excluded African Americans from the most popular form of asset building in the United States—home ownership. He traces the line of continuity from slavery to Jim Crow to federal redlining in Chicago. His is an argument that relies on institutional path dependence: even when one extractive institution comes to an end, a new one may emerge to maintain the line between "citizens" and "subjects." The Coates version of institutions is one in which institutions have a dynamic component and share the distributional consequences of past institutions. The evidence from the U.S. case supports rethinking the mechanisms by which historical institutions affect contemporary outcomes. See Coates, "The Case for Reparations," *Atlantic Monthly,* June 2014, 54.

24. Douglass C. North, "Institutions," *Journal of Economic Perspectives* 5 (1991): 97–112; Daron Acemoglu, Simon Johnson, and James Robinson, "Institutions," in *Handbook of Economic Growth*, vol. 1 (2005): 385–472.

25. See Melissa Dell, "The Persistent Effects of Peru's Mining *Mita,*" *Econometrica* 78 (2010): 1863–1903; Acemoglu, Johnson, and Robinson, "Colonial Origins."

26. Acemoglu, Johnson, and Robinson, "Colonial Origins."

27. Daron Acemoglu, Simon Johnson, and James Robinson, "The Rise of Europe: Atlantic Trade, Institutional Change, and Economic Growth," *American Economic Review* 95 (2005): 546–579.

28. Camilo García-Jimeno and James Robinson, "The Myth of the Frontier," in *Understanding Long-Run Economic Growth: Geography, Institutions, and the Knowledge Economy,* ed. Dora L. Costa and Naomi R. Lamoreaux (Chicago: University of Chicago Press, 2011), 49–88.

29. Acemoglu, Johnson, and Robinson, "Colonial Origins"; Anthony B. Atkinson, "The Colonial Legacy: Income Inequality in Former British African Colonies," WIDER Working Paper 45/2014 (2014).

30. I located the first year of income taxation for the following countries: Venezuela, South Africa, Indonesia, Uruguay, Colombia, Mexico, Nigeria, Uganda, Tanzania, Singapore, Malaysia, Australia, Canada, United States, Jamaica, New Zealand, Bangladesh, Pakistan, Chile, Argentina, Kenya, Egypt, Trinidad and

Tobago, Gambia, Hong Kong, Ghana, Ethiopia, Sierra Leone, Haiti, Brazil, Vietnam, Costa Rica. I cross-referenced with the World Wealth and Income Database for several countries. For former British colonies in Africa, I use Atkinson, "The Colonial Legacy." For a complete list of sources used, please contact me at elloraderenoncourt@fas.harvard.edu.

31. www.wid.world/.

32. Gabriel Zucman, *The Hidden Wealth of Nations: The Scourge of Tax Havens,* trans. Teresa Fagan (Chicago: University of Chicago Press, 2014).

21. Everywhere and Nowhere

1. Thomas Piketty, *Capital in the Twenty-First Century,* trans. Arthur Goldhammer (Cambridge, MA: Belknap Press of Harvard University Press 2014), 20.

2. Ibid., 25.

3. Ibid., 26.

4. Stephen Marche, "The Most Important Book of the Twenty-First Century," *Esquire,* April 24, 2014.

5. Claudia Goldin and Lawrence Katz, "Long Run Changes in the Wage Structure: Narrowing, Widening, Polarizing," *Brookings Papers on Economic Activity* 2 (2007).

6. Piketty, *Capital,* 350.

7. Marche, "The Most Important Book."

8. Piketty, *Capital,* 1.

9. Daron Acemoglu and James Robinson. "The Rise and Decline of General Laws of Capitalism." *Journal of Economic Perspectives* 29 (2005): 3–28, at 3.

10. Ibid., 4.

11. Daron Acemoglu and James Robinson. *Why Nations Fail: The Origins of Power, Prosperity, and Poverty* (New York: Crown, 2012).

12. Peter Hall and David Soskice, eds., *Varieties of Capitalism: The Institutional Foundations of Comparative Advantage* (Oxford: Oxford University Press, 2001).

13. Piketty, *Capital,* 32.

14. Ibid., 474–475.

15. Margaret Levi, "A New Agenda for the Social Sciences," paper presented at the Crooked Timber Seminar on Thomas Piketty's *Capital in the Twenty-First Century,* January 2016, http://crookedtimber.org/wp-content/uploads/2016/01/piketty-final.pdf, 13.

16. Piketty, *Capital,* 474.

17. Ibid.

18. Ibid., 480.

19. Amy Gutman and Dennis Thompson, *Why Deliberative Democracy?* (Princeton, NJ: Princeton University Press, 2004), 3.

20. Jürgen Habermas, *Between Facts and Norms: Contributions to a Discourse Theory of Law and Democracy,* trans. W. Reng (Cambridge, MA: MIT Press, 1996).

21. Miriam Ronzoni, "Where Are the Power Relations in Piketty's *Capital?*," paper presented at the Crooked Timber Seminar on Thomas Piketty's *Capital in the Twenty-First Century,* January 2016, http://crookedtimber.org/wp-content/uploads/2016/01/piketty-final.pdf, 34.

22. Ibid., 35.

23. Piketty, *Capital,* 2–3.

24. Werner Sombart, *Why Is There No Socialism in the United States?,* trans. Patricia M. Hocking and C. T. Husbands (New York: M. E. Sharpe, 1979), originally published in German in 1906.

25. Consider the inflammatory rhetoric from Republican presidential candidate Donald Trump in the 2016 U.S. presidential contest. One textual analysis of Trump's campaign speeches identified a strong "Us versus Them" pattern that capitalized on Americans' high levels of economic insecurities and anger in a style reminiscent of historical demagogues. See Patrick Healy and Maggie Haberman, "95,000 Words, Many of Them Ominous, from Donald Trump's Tongue," *New York Times,* December 5, 2015.

26. Albert Hirschman, *Exit, Voice, and Loyalty* (Cambridge, MA: Harvard University Press, 1970).

27. Robert Dahl, *Who Governs? Democracy and Power in an American City* (New Haven, CT: Yale University Press, 1961).

28. E. E. Schattschneider, *The Semisovereign People: A Realist's View of Democracy in America* (New York: Holt, Rinehart and Winston, 1960).

29. Kay Lehman Schlozman, Sidney Verba, and Henry E. Brady, *The Unheavenly Chorus: Unequal Political Voice and the Broken Promise of American Democracy* (Princeton, NJ: Princeton University Press, 2012).

30. Benjamin Page, Larry Bartels, and Jason Seawright, "Democracy and the Policy Preferences of Wealthy Americans," *Perspectives on Politics* 11 (2013): 51–73.

31. Martin Gilens and Benjamin Page, "Testing Theories of American Politics: Elites, Interest Groups, and Average Citizens," *Perspectives on Politics* 12 (2014): 564–581, quotation at 564.

32. Larry Bartels, *Unequal Democracy: The Political Economy of the New Gilded Age* (Princeton, NJ: Princeton University Press, 2008).

33. Page, Bartels, and Seawright, "Democracy."

34. Ibid.

35. See the homepage for the Survey of Economically Successful Americans at the National Opinion Research Center, University of Chicago, http://www.norc.org/Research/Projects/Pages/survey-of-economically-successful-americans.aspx. See also Page, Bartels, and Seawright, "Democracy," for more detail on how they constructed the SESA.

36. Jacob Hacker and Paul Pierson, *Winner-Take-All Politics: How Washington Made the Rich Richer—and Turned Its Back on the Middle Class* (New York: Simon and Schuster, 2011).

37. David Card and John DiNardo, "Skill Biased Technological Change and Rising Wage Inequality: Some Problems and Puzzles," *Journal of Labor Economics* 20, no. 4 (2002): 733–783.

38. Henry Farrell, "Review: Jacob Hacker and Paul Pierson—Winner Take All Politics," Crooked Timber (blog), September 15, 2010, http://crookedtimber .org/2010/09/15/review-jacob-hacker-and-paul-pierson-winner-take-all -politics/.

39. Kathleen Thelen, *How Institutions Evolve: The Political Economy of Skills in Germany, Britain, the United States, and Japan* (Cambridge: Cambridge University Press, 2004).

40. Theda Skocpol, "Unravelling from Above," *American Prospect,* March–April 1996, 20–25.

41. Ibid.

42. Lee Drutman, *The Business of America Is Lobbying: How Corporations Became Politicized and Politics Became More Corporate* (Oxford: Oxford University Press, 2015); Drutman, "How Corporate Lobbyists Conquered American Democracy," *The Atlantic,* April 20, 2015.

43. Peter Hall, "Historical Institutionalism in Rationalist and Sociological Perspective," in *Explaining Institutional Change: Ambiguity, Agency, and Power,* ed. James Mahoney and Kathleen Thelen (New York: Cambridge University Press, 2009).

44. Bo Rothstein and Sven Steinmo, *Restructuring the Welfare State: Political Institutions and Policy Change* (London: Palgrave MacMillan, 2002), 2.

45. Francis G. Castles, *The Impact of Parties: Politics and Parties in Democratic Capitalist States* (Beverly Hills, CA: Sage, 1982); Walter Korpi, *The Democratic Class Struggle* (London: Routledge, 1980).

46. Sven Steinmo, "Political Institutions and Tax Policy in the United States, Sweden, and Britain," *World Politics* 41 (1989): 500–535, at 504.

47. Hacker and Pierson, *Winner-Take-All Politics;* Drutman, *The Business of America.*

48. Steinmo, "Political Institutions and Tax Policy," 523.

49. Margaret Weir and Theda Skocpol, "State Structure and the Possibilities for Keynesian Response to the Great Depression in Sweden, Britain and the United States," in *Bringing the State Back In,* ed. Peter Evans, Dietrich Rueschmeyer, and Theda Skocpol (Cambridge: Cambridge University Press, 1985).

50. Steinmo, "Political Institutions and Tax Policy," 512.

51. See Madison's discussion of the dangers of "faction" in *The Federalist Papers: Alexander Hamilton, James Madison, John Jay,* ed. Ian Shapiro (New Haven, CT: Yale University Press, 2009).

52. Steinmo, "Political Institutions and Tax Policy," 512.

53. See, for example, Pablo Baramendi et al., eds., *Democracy, Inequality, and Representation* (New York: Russell Sage Foundation, 2011).

54. Stephen Lukes, *Power: A Radical View* (New York: Macmillan, 1974).

55. Nolan McCarty, Keith Poole, and Howard Rosenthal, *Polarized America: The Dance of Ideology and Unequal Riches* (Cambridge, MA: MIT Press, 2006).

56. John V. Duca and Jason L. Saving, "Income Inequality and Political Polarization: Time Series Evidence over Nine Decades," Federal Reserve Bank of Dallas Working Paper No. 1408 (2014).

57. Hirschman, *Exit, Voice, and Loyalty,* 272, 274.

58. Richard Florida and Charlotte Mellander, "Segregated City: The Geography of Economic Segregation in America's Metros," Martin Prosperity Institute at the University of Toronto's Rotman School of Management (2015), http://martinprosperity.org/media/Segregatedpercent20City.pdf.

59. Kendra Bischoff and Sean Reardon, "Residential Segregation by Income: 1970–2009," in *The Lost Decade? Social Change in the U.S. after 2000,* ed. John Logan (New York: Russell Sage Foundation, 2013).

60. Ta-Nahesi Coates, "The Case for Reparations," *The Atlantic,* June 2014.

61. Mel Oliver and Thomas Shapiro, *Black Wealth / White Wealth: A New Perspective on Racial Inequality* (New York: Routledge, 1995).

62. Thomas Shapiro, Tatjana Meschede, and Sam Osoro, "The Roots of the Widening Racial Wealth Gap: Explaining the Black-White Economic Divide," Brandeis University Institute on Assets and Social Policy Research Brief (2015), http://iasp.brandeis.edu/pdfs/Author/shapiro-thomas-m/racialwealthgapbrief.pdf.

63. Raj Chetty, Nathan Hendren, Patrick Kline, and Emmanuel Saez, "Where Is the Land of Opportunity? The Geography of Intergenerational Mobility in the United States," *Quarterly Journal of Economics* 128 (2014): 1553–1623.

64. Alberto Alesina, Reza Baqir, and William Easterly, "Public Goods and Ethnic Divisions," *Quarterly Journal of Economics* 114 (1999): 1243–1284.

65. Daniel Hopkins, "The Diversity Discount: When Increasing Ethnic and Racial Diversity Prevents Tax Increases," *Journal of Politics* 71 (2009): 160–177.

66. David Cutler, Douglas Elmendorf, and Richard Zeckhauser, "Demographic Characteristics and the Public Bundle," *Public Finance / Finance Publique* 48 (1993): 178–198.

67. Leah Platt Boustan, Fernando Ferreira, Hernan Winkler, and Eric M. Zolt, "The Effects of Rising Income Inequality on Taxation and Public Expenditures: Evidence from U.S. Municipalities and School Districts, 1970–2000," *Review of Economics and Statistics* 95 (2013): 1291–1302.

68. Hirschman, *Exit, Voice, and Loyalty,* 76.

69. Ibid., 81.

70. Ibid., 85.

71. See Gabriel Zucman, *The Hidden Wealth of Nations*, trans. Therese Lavender Fagan (Chicago: University of Chicago Press, 2015).

72. Mark Schmitt, "Political Opportunity: A New Framework for Democratic Reform," Brennan Center for Justice Working Paper (2015).

73. Ibid.
74. Mark Schmitt. "The Wrong Way to Fix Citizens United," *New Republic,* January 20, 2012.

22. Toward a Reconciliation between Economics and the Social Sciences

1. I am grateful to Brad DeLong, Heather Boushey, and Marshall Steinbaum for having assembled these essays and to the authors for the attention and time they were willing to devote to my work.
2. In particular, see the following two foundational works: Simon Kuznets, *Shares of Upper Income Groups in Income and Savings* (New York: National Bureau of Economic Research, 1953); Anthony Atkinson and Alan Harrison, *Distribution of Personal Wealth in Britain* (Cambridge: Cambridge University Press, 1978). The different stages in the construction of the data assembled in my book are summarized in *Capital in the Twenty-First Century,* trans. Arthur Goldhammer (Cambridge, MA: Belknap Press of Harvard University Press, 2014), 16–20.
3. In particular, see François Simiand, *Le salaire, l'évolution sociale et la monnaie: Essai de théorie expérimentale du salaire, introduction et étude globale* (Paris: Alcan, 1932); Ernest Labrousse, *Esquisse du mouvement des prix et des revenus en France au XVIIIᵉ siècle* (Paris: Dalloz, 1933); Jean Bouvier, François Furet, and Marcel Gillet, *Le mouvement du profit en France au XIXᵉ siècle: Matériaux et études* (Paris: Mouton, 1965); and Adeline Daumard, ed., *Les fortunes françaises au XIXᵉ siècle: Enquête sur la répartition et la composition des capitaux privés à Paris, Lyon, Lille, Bordeaux et Toulouse d'après l'enregistrement des déclarations de successions* (Paris: Mouton, 1973).
4. See *Capital,* 575–577.
5. In particular, see Pierre Bourdieu and Jean-Claude Passeron, *The Inheritors: French Students and Their Relation to Culture* (Chicago: University of Chicago Press, 1979); Bourdieu and Passeron, *Reproduction in Education, Society and Culture* (London: Sage, 1990); and Christian Baudelot and Anne Lebeaupin, "Les salaires de 1950 à 1975 dans l'industrie, le commerce et les services" (Paris: INSEE, 1979).
6. In different registers, see, for example, Michèle Lamont, *Money, Morals and Manners: The Culture of the French and American Upper-Middle Class* (Chicago: University of Chicago Press, 1992); Jens Beckert, *Inherited Wealth,* trans. Thomas Dunlap (Princeton, NJ: Princeton University Press, 2004; repr. 2008); Pierre Rosanvallon, *The Society of Equals,* trans. Arthur Goldhammer (Cambridge, MA: Harvard University Press, 2013); and Jules Naudet, *Entrer dans l'élite: Parcours de réussite en France, aux États-Unis et en Inde* (Paris: Puf, 2012).
7. Piketty, *Capital,* 20.

657

8. In particular, see the case of the conservative revolutions that took place in America and the United Kingdom, notably analyzed in ibid., chaps. 2 and 14.

9. Karl Polanyi, *The Great Transformation* (New York: Farrar and Rinehart, 1944).

10. Ibid., chaps. 8 and 13.

11. Ibid., chaps. 14 and 15.

12. Ibid., chap. 13.

13. Ibid., 47.

14. Ibid., chap. 4.

15. Note also that these computations are based upon total numbers of slaves recorded in censuses, whether they are owned by private individuals, corporations, or municipal governments, so I am not sure they are as strongly underestimated as suggested by Daina Ramey Barry (they are already quite large). In any case, these are clearly issues that deserve a lot more attention and research.

16. Ibid., chap. 5.

17. Ibid., chaps. 3–6.

18. Ibid., chaps. 12.

19. Ibid., chaps. 1, 5, 12, 15, and 16.

20. Ibid., chaps. 3 and 4.

21. Ibid., chap. 16.

22. Ibid., chaps. 3–6.

23. The fact that rising housing values explain a large fraction of rising capital / income ratios in recent decades (with large variations across countries) is not particularly good news for inequality dynamics. In particular, high housing values make it difficult for new generations with limited family wealth to access property. Also, note that booming top billionaire wealth (or booming top financial endowments) has little to do with housing values.

24. Ibid., chaps. 11, 12, and 13.

25. Giacomo Todeschini, "Servitude and Labor at the Dawn of the Early Modern Era: The Devaluation of Salaried Workers and the 'Undeserving Poor,'" *Annales HSS* (English ed.) 70, no. 1 (2015).

26. Cited in Piketty, *Capital*, 487.

27. Ibid., 485–486.

28. See ibid., chaps. 8 and 14, esp. 508–512.

29. http://www.equality-of-opportunity.org/.

30. Generally speaking, I fully agree with Eric Nielsen that the diffusion of knowledge, skills, and human capital is the most powerful force to reduce inequality in the long run (as I frequently mention in my book). However, I am not sure that it is particularly useful to capitalize human capital into monetary values and add it to other asset values; both dimensions of capital (human and nonhuman) are very important, but they raise different issues that ought to be analyzed separately.

31. www.wid.world.

32. Ibid., 558–562.

33. On this topic, see Julia Cagé, *Saving the Media: Capitalism, Crowdfunding and Democracy* (Cambridge, MA: Harvard University Press, 2016).

34. Piketty, *Capital,* 570.

Acknowledgments

The editors thank Ian Malcolm and the team at Harvard University Press for all their help with this entire volume. We also want to thank the volume's contributors, many of whom gave generously of their time and ideas at a three-day conference in December 2015, where we worked through our ideas. Two contributors made essays available which were previously published elsewhere. Robert M. Solow's "Thomas Piketty Is Right: Everything you need to know about Capital in the Twenty-First Century" (Chapter 2) first appeared in *The New Republic*, April 22, 2014. (© 2014 The New Republic. All rights reserved. Used by permission and protected by the Copyright Laws of the United States. The printing, copying, redistribution, or retransmission of this Content without express written permission is prohibited.) And Paul Krugman's "Why We're in a New Gilded Age" appeared in *The New York Review of Books*, Volume 61, Number 8 (May 8, 2014). It is reprinted by permission of the author.

Finally, we thank the staff at the Washington Center for Equitable Growth, who supported our work in the volume.

Index

Aaronson, Daniel, 584–585n19

Abraham, Katherine, 594n26

Acemoglu, Daron, 8, 23; on cheap labor, 96–97; on economic effect of institutions, 496, 503; on laws of capitalism, 101, 515–516; Piketty on, 368; on U.S. job losses, 93

Additive manufacturing (3D printing), 201–202

Adkins v. Children's Hospital (U.S., 1923), 448

Adopted children, 166, 585n22

Affirmataive-action policies, 561

Africa, 269, 602–603n32; British colonialism in, 498, 504; colonial societies in, 650n2

African Americans. *See* Blacks

Agenda-setting, 525

Ager, Philipp, 501

Aghion, P., 416, 430

Airline industry, 111

Alesina, Alberto, 421, 534–535

Altgeld, John Peter, 446

Alvaredo, Facundo, 308

Amalgamated Railway Union (UK), 451–452

American Economic Association, 29, 445

American Federation of Labor (AFL), 445, 447, 448

American Railway Union, 445

Anand, S., 262

Andrews (judge), 139

Antras, Pol, 86–87, 573n11

Aoki, Shuhei, 332, 333

Appelbaum, Eileen, 361

Apple Operations International (firm), 293

Arrow, Kenneth, 360

Artificial intelligence (AI), 172, 200–201

Ashford, J. P., 142

Asquith, H. H., 451

Atkinson, Anthony B., 261, 571n46, 598n7; on banking crises, 429; on capital as substitute for low-skilled labor, 272; on effects of institutions on inequality, 504; on inequality and social spending, 274; on inequality of outcomes, 414; on London, 296; Piketty on, 544; Piketty's work with, 49, 60; policy proposals of, 318, 632n5; on redistribution of tax revenues, 275

Atkinson, Tony, 241

Austen, Jane, 294, 312, 372, 375

Auto industry, 209–210

Automated teller machines (ATMs), 95

Automation, 95–98

Autor, David H., 93, 95–96, 177, 205

Baby-boom generation, 402–403

Bach, J., 286

Bagchi, S., 422

Baker, Dean, 41, 649n80

Bakija, Jon, 315–316

Ballard, J. G., 284

Baltimore (Maryland), 532

Balzac, Honoré de, 65, 312, 372, 373

Banerjee, A. V., 423, 635n50

Banking crises, 429

Baptist, Edward, 135–137

Bartels, Larry, 522

Barth, Erling, 226

Bartmanski, Dominik, 45

Basker, Emek, 95

Basu, K., 272

Baudelot, Christian, 545

Beaudry, Paul, 96

Becker, Gary, 164–165, 446, 591n12, 641n11

Beckert, Sven, 42–43, 135

Beckles, Sir Hilary, 149

Belle Époque, 5, 6, 65; poverty during, 13; second, 60

Bengtsson, Erik, 237

Benhabib, Jess, 332, 333

Bequests, 338–339; current patterns of, 376–377; gender and, 379; marriage patterns and, 375–376

Berlinski, Samuel, 224